PARTNERS IN WONDER

PARTNERS IN WONDER
Women and the Birth of Science Fiction 1926–1965

Eric Leif Davin

LEXINGTON BOOKS

A division of
ROWMAN & LITTLEFIELD PUBLISHERS, INC.
Lanham • Boulder • New York • Toronto • Oxford

LEXINGTON BOOKS

A division of Rowman & Littlefield Publishers, Inc.
A wholly owned subsidary of The Rowman & Littlefield Publishing Group, Inc.
4501 Forbes Boulevard, Suite 200
Lanham, MD 20706

PO Box 317
Oxford
OX2 9RU, UK

British Library Cataloguing in Publication Information Available

Library of Congress Cataloging-in-Publication Data

Davin, Eric Leif.
  Partners in wonder : women and the birth of science fiction, 1926–1965 / Eric Leif
Davin.
    p.   cm.
  Includes bibliographical references and index.
  ISBN 0–7391–1266-X (cloth : alk. paper)—ISBN 0–7391–1267–8 (pbk. : alk. paper)
    1. Science fiction, American—History and criticism.   2. Women and literature—
United States—History—20th century.   3. American fiction—Women authors—History
and criticism.   4. American fiction—20th century—History and criticism.   I. Title.
PS374.A35D38   2005
823′.087209928705—dc22
                                                                          2005021913

Printed in the United States of America

⊗ ™ The paper used in this publication meets the minimum requirements of American
National Standard for Information Sciences—Permanence of Paper for Printed Library
Materials, ANSI/NISO Z39.48–1992.

For the 203 Known "Women" Who Published in U.S. Science Fiction Magazines, 1926–1960

1. Mrs. Agate
2. Lillian M. Ainsworth
3. "Thaedra Alden" (Elizabeth Hansen)
4. Karen Anderson
5. Mary Armock
6. Charlotte Armstrong (Lewi)
7. "Pauline Ashwell" (Pauline Whitby)
8. Myrle Benedict
9. Margot Bennett
10. Pansy E. Black
11. Elizabeth Mann Borgese
12. Lila Borison
13. "Elizabeth Bowen" (Dorothea Cole)
14. M. Bower
15. Leigh Brackett
16. Marion Zimmer Bradley
17. Rhoda Broughton
18. Florence V. (Verbell) Brown
19. Rosel George Brown
20. Doris P. (Pitkin) Buck
21. Alice Bullock
22. Dorothy Donnell Calhoun
23. "Esther Carlson" (Joanna Collier)
24. Clara E. Chestnutt
25. Agatha Christie
26. Mollie Claire
27. Pauline Clarke
28. Helen (Worrell) Clarkson (McCloy)
29. Mildred Clingerman
30. Adrien Coblentz
31. Barbara Constant
32. Lucy Cores
33. Mary Elizabeth Counselman
34. Virginia Cross
35. M. (Monette) A. Cummings
36. (Elizabeth M.) "Betsy" Curtis
37. "Clemence Dane" (Winifred Ashton)
38. Dorothy Salisbury Davis
39. Lavinia R. Davis
40. Catherine C. de Camp
41. Dorothy de Courcy
42. Frances M. Deegan
43. Miriam Allen deFord
44. Diane Detzer (de Reyna)
45. Leah Bodine Drake
46. Garen Drussai (Mrs. Kirk Drussai)
47. Theodora Du Bois
48. Norma Lazell Easton
49. Merab Eberle
50. Phyllis H. Economou
51. Dorothy H. Edgerly
52. "Beth Elliott"
53. Sophie Wenzel Ellis
54. Carol Emshwiller
55. "Mona Farnsworth" (Muriel Newhall)
56. Harriet Frank, Jr.
57. Betty Fuller
58. Lee Hawkins Garby
59. Frances Garfield
60. Doris Gilbert
61. Inez Haynes Gillmore (Irwin)
62. Ellen Glasgow
63. (Margaret) Rumer Godden
64. Laura Goforth
65. Ruth Goldsmith
66. Evelyn Goldstein
67. Phyllis Gotlieb
68. Doris Greenberg
69. Ann (Warren) Griffith
70. Barbara J. Griffith
71. Augusta Groner
72. Marion Gross
73. Joy Hall
74. T. (Thelma) D. Hamm (Evans)
75. L. (Lucile) Taylor Hansen
76. Clare Winger Harris
77. Genevieve Haugen
78. Dorothy K. Haynes
79. Hazel Heald
80. Zenna Henderson
81. "Charles Henneberg" (C. & Nathalie Henneberg)
82. Alma Hill
83. Louise Hodgson
84. Elizabeth Sanxay Holding
85. Millicent Holmberg
86. Helen Huber
87. E. (Edna) Mayne Hull
88. Margaret S. Hunt
89. "Minna Irving" (Minna Odell)
90. Margaret Irwin
91. Shirley Jackson

92. Sylvia Jacobs
93. Garda Jamieson
94. Jean M. Janis
95. F. (Friniwyd) Tennyson Jesse
96. Alice Eleanor Jones
97. Leslie Jones
98. Marcia Kamien
99. D. (Doris) E. Kaye
100. Phyllis L. Kaye
101. Jessie Douglas Kerruish
102. Zelda Kessler
103. Emilie H. Knarr
104. Karen Kuykendall
105. Joy Leache
106. Madeleine L'Engle
107. Dorothy LesTina
108. Elisabeth R. Lewis
109. Ethel G. Lewis
110. A. (Alice) M. (Martha) Lightner (Hopf)
111. Victoria (Endicott) Lincoln
112. Amelia Reynolds Long
113. (Mildred) "Mindret" Lord (Loeb)
114. "Lilith Lorraine" (Mary Maude Dunn Wright)
115. Kathleen Ludwick
116. (Mabel) Dana Lyon
117. Anne McCaffrey
118. Winona McClintic
119. Helen McCloy
120. Mildred McCune
121. Katherine MacLean
122. Rachel Maddux
123. Dorothy (Haynes) Madle
124. "Rory Magill" (Dorothea M. Faulkner)
125. Evelyn Martin
126. J. (Julian) C. May
127. "Judith Merril" (Josephine Juliet Grossman)
128. C. (Catherine) L. (Lucille) Moore
129. Maria Moravsky
130. "Andre Norton" (Alice Mary Norton)
131. M. (Mary) J. (Jane) Nuttall
132. "Marian O'Hearn" (Anita Allen)
133. Louise Lee Outlaw
134. Avis Pabel
135. "Leslie Perri" (Doris Baumgardt Pohl Wilson)
136. Phyllis Lee Peterson
137. Nina Pettis
138. Dorothy Quick
139. "Ayn Rand" (Alyssa "Alice" Rosenbaum)
140. Kaye Raymond
141. Margaretta W. Rea
142. Amabel Redman
143. "Kit" (Lillian Craig) Reed
144. "L. Major Reynolds" (Louise Leipiar)
145. Gerda Rhoads
146. "Craig Rice" (Georgiana Ann Randolph)
147. Jane Rice
148. Louise Rice
149. Jane Roberts
150. Mary-Carter Roberts
151. Kay Rogers
152. Margaret Rogers
153. Margaret Ronan
154. Babette Rosmond
155. M. (Margaret) F. Rupert
156. Joanna Russ
157. Margaret St. Clair
158. G. (Gladys) St. John-Loe
159. Mabel Seeley
160. Elizabeth Shafer
161. Wilmar H. (House) Shiras
162. Vivian Shirley
163. Barbara Silverberg
164. Anna Sinclare
165. April Smith
166. Evelyn E. Smith
167. Phyllis Sterling Smith
168. Dorothy Stapleton
169. I. (Inga) M. (Marie) Stephens
170. Ruth Sterling
171. G. (Gladys) B. (Bronwyn) Stern
172. "Francis Stevens" (Gertrude Barrows Bennett)
173. Leslie F. Stone
174. "Jan Struther" (Joyce Anstruther Placzek)
175. "Doris Thomas" (Doris Vancel)
176. Judith Trevelyan
177. Helen M. Urban
178. Rena M. Vale
179. Emma Vanne
180. Joan Vatsek
181. (Marilyn) "Lyn" Venable
182. Ruth Laura Wainwright
183. Anne Walker
184. Ruth Washburn
185. Helen Weinbaum (Kasson)
186. Elma Wentz
187. Elaine Wilber
188. Kate (Meredith) Wilhelm
189. Jeanne Williams
190. "Gabriel Wilson" (Gabrielle Wilson Cummings)

Contents

Bibliographic Tables

The Tales of Scheherazade

Acknowledgments

FOR READING EARLY DRAFTS and offering their thoughtful suggestions and advice, I thank Anita Alverio, Nick Coles, Paul Dellinger, Timons Esaias, George Goverman, William B. Hall, Richard Oestreicher, and Joanna Russ. While these readers offered many helpful improvements to my work, they are in no way responsible for my errors or interpretations.

In addition, Mike Ashley confirmed the gender identity of two women for me, Anita Alverio contributed material on C. L. Moore, and Richard and Everett F. Bleiler added two women authors to my total and uncovered the true first name of L. Taylor Hansen. Ann Cecil found information on Connie Willis, Paul Dellinger produced information on Mary Shelley and Connie Willis, and Monte Herridge provided useful information on Frances M. Deegan. Englishman John Howard provided information on British authors, Robert Lichtman provided additional research, and Graham Stone provided long-distance assistance from Australia. Steve Hines made available his extensive magazine collection. Steven E. Ericson, owner of Books From the Crypt, also sold me many pulps in good condition, at good prices, carefully and promptly delivered. He can be found on the Web and I recommend him as a good source for these rare old magazines, should a research library not be accessible. The final product owes much to them all.

Two people I am particularly indebted to are Julius Schwartz and A. Langley Searles. Despite his health problems, Julius Schwartz vetted the chapter "Haven in a Heartless World," returning the corrected manuscript to me in early December, 2003, only two months before his death on February 8, 2004, at age 88. It may have been the last editorial job of this long-time comic book editor.

A. Langley Searles patiently copy edited the manuscript, making it far more readable. In the process he showed me how to look at my writing for useless verbiage. If such remains in my text, it is my own fault. He then published much shorter and much different versions of some sections in his journal, *Fantasy Commentator*. Thus, table 1 and a shorter and different version of part 1 appeared in *Fantasy Commentator*, Volume X, Nos. 1 and 2, winter, 2001–2002. A shorter and different version of "Haven in a Heartless World" also appeared in that same issue. Tables 2–5 and a shorter and different version of part 2, under the title "Hidden from History," appeared in *Fantasy Commentator*, Volume X, Nos. 3 and 4, spring, 2003.

Finally, I am greatly indebted to Norm Metcalf and his encyclopedic knowledge of the genre. The idea for this book originated in conversations we had concerning what we both believed were universal, but mistaken, interpretations of early science fiction. Despite poor health, Norm read several drafts of the manuscript, answered many research questions, and corrected innumerable errors on my part. No doubt others slipped through. For those I take full responsibility.

Introduction

Science Fiction and the Contested Terrain of Popular Culture

"The trouble with people is not that they don't know, but that they know so much that ain't so."

"Josh Billings"
(Henry Wheeler Shaw, 1818–1885)

ONCE UPON A TIME, "Back in the old, old days (gosh fifteen or twenty years ago or so), there *were* no women in science-fiction. They didn't read it, they didn't write it, and they certainly didn't star in it. . . . For some reason (no one *really* knows why . . .), in the mid-to-late 1960s, this situation began to change. Suddenly women were turning up at science-fiction conventions; names like Joanna [Russ], Ursula [Le Guin], and Joan [Vinge] began appearing on the tables of contents of science-fiction magazines; and real, honest-to-God female characters were showing themselves in stories. . . . To be certain, this sudden influx of women into the onetime hallowed halls of SF did not go unchallenged. . . . But despite all this *sturm und drang* (or maybe even because of it) female writers, readers, and fans hung on. . . . And so it stands. Women have joined the club."[1]

So said Shawna McCarthy in 1983, editor, at the time, of *Isaac Asimov's Science Fiction Magazine*. The reason for this history and struggle was because, as pulp magazine era scholar Peter Haining reminds us, "both Science Fiction and fantasy are predominantly *a man's literature*."[2] McCarthy's synopsis is thus accepted as the thumbnail history of women in science fiction.

In 1992, almost a decade after McCarthy limned this history, noted science fiction writer Connie Willis was hearing the same story. In a guest editorial in the same magazine that McCarthy had edited, Willis wrote that, "The current version of women in science fiction before the 1960s (which I've heard several times lately), goes like this: There weren't any. Only men wrote science fiction because the field was completely closed to women. Then, in the late '60s and early '70s, a group of feminist writers led by Joanna Russ and Ursula Le Guin stormed the barricades, and women began writing (and sometimes even editing) science fiction. Before that, nada.

"If there were any women in the field before that (which there weren't)," Willis continues, "they had to slink around using male pseudonyms and hoping they wouldn't get caught. And if they did write under their own names (which they didn't), it doesn't count anyway because they only wrote sweet little domestic stories. Babies. They wrote mostly stories about babies.

"There's only one problem with this version of women in SF—it's not true."

Willis went on to enumerate some of the women science fiction writers she had read and loved as a teenager in the 1950s. "People are always asking me how *I* stormed the barricades," she concluded, "and my answer is always that I didn't know there *were* any barricades. It never occurred to me that SF was a man's field that had to be broken into. How could it be with all those women writers? How could it be when Judith Merril was the one editing all those *Year's Best SF*'s? I thought all I had to do was write good stories, and they'd let me in. And they did."[3]

So compelling has been the "current version of women in science fiction before the 1960s" that no one seems to have paid much attention to Connie Willis's attempt to set the record straight. For example, one anonymous academic reader of this manuscript complained, after finishing it, that I had failed to examine "the dynamics of how [women] came to be excluded." Thus, for the most part, the science fiction community has continued to believe, as an article of faith, that the science fiction field was irremediably hostile to women and deliberately "excluded" them. Because of this "exclusion," there were only a handful of early women science fiction writers, all of whom disguised their female identity. And it has accepted—on faith—that this handful of women writers produced stories exactly like those written by men (further concealing their gender) or trivial little domestic stories not worth reading. So the genre had few redeeming qualities, at least as far as women were concerned. Science fiction was just as conservative and sexist—perhaps even more so—as the rest of society.

However, as Willis tried to point out, this traditional exclusion narrative is nothing but mythology which has simply been accepted, unquestioned, in both the academic and non-academic worlds. This faith-based mythology has a long pedigree, and solidified its hold over the science fiction community in the early 1970s with the coming of the women's movement. In 1976, Mary Kenny Badami articulated a "Feminist Critique of Science Fiction" which contained many of the elements which still dominate popular awareness. She declared that women neither produced, consumed, nor were represented in science fiction before the 1970s. Thus, she said, "There is little to discuss about 'the role of

women in science fiction' because . . . until very recently women have had
almost no role in science fiction. . . . I propose to illustrate three theses about
the non-role of women in science fiction: Women have *not* been important as
characters in sf; Women have *not* been important as fans of sf; Women have *not*
been important as writers of sf."[4]

Over the course of this book I intend to demonstrate that a close look at the
record presents problems with this traditional exclusion narrative. For example,
in the accounts given by both McCarthy and Willis, Joanna Russ and Ursula Le
Guin figure prominently as women who "suddenly" appeared in the late Sixties
and early Seventies to lead an assault on the genre's barricades, forcing a female
presence upon the field. But *both* women's genre debuts predated the modern
women's movement. Ursula Le Guin first published in 1962 and Joanna Russ
debuted in the 1950s. Their presence in the field before popular perception
places them there should at the very least cast a doubt on the field's reputed
early hostility to women writers. It should also raise questions about the role of
the early Seventies women's liberation movement in "changing" the field.

Thus, at the risk of seeming hyperbolic, I am prepared to defend the proposition that early science fiction was not a hide-bound stronghold of political and
cultural conservatism. Rather, from its very genesis science fiction was a battleground where representatives of dominant groups and traditional values were
jostled by "outsider" groups contending on a basis of relative equality for recognition. Because it offered an open door for the participation of these outsiders
and a forum for their concerns, science fiction culture between 1926–1965 was
more liberal, tolerant, and progressive than is commonly portrayed.

I will provide empirical support for this thesis by looking primarily at the
field's orientation toward a particular "outsider" group, women, supposedly
shunned by the field. I will argue that, compared to many other cultural arenas
in American society at that time, such as higher education and professional
fields like science, early science *fiction* was a haven in a heartless world, especially
open to participation by women. For example, the letters published in these
magazines reveal that the predominantly male readership, as a body, was much
more welcoming to women writers than has been commonly portrayed. For the
most part, male readers overwhelmingly *praised* stories by women. Thus, in a
letter he quickly wrote to *Astounding* ("Brass Tacks," January, 1935, p. 153),
E. E. "Doc" Smith enthusiastically lauded C. L. Moore's debut in that magazine
("Bright Illusion," October, 1934) and referred to her as female. Similar letters
praising Moore and referring to her as female can be found in the *Astounding*
issues of February, April, and December, 1935; February, 1936; and February,
1937.

This is not to say that letters hostile to women did not sometimes appear.
Such hostility, however, was not directed against women writers, per se. Rather,
irate males usually condemned "mush" and "slop" in stories written by either

men or women which introduced what was usually referred to as a "love inter-est." Such "feminine" elements were felt to be inappropriate in a proper science fiction story, which should deal strictly with hardware and scientific fact. But men expressing such views were a minority, often criticized by other male read-ers for their troglodyte attitudes.

One notable example of this phenomenon was the vitriolic series of emo-tional and combative anti-"mush" letters Isaac Asimov wrote to *Astounding* in 1938–1939 (first analyzed by A. Langley Searles in 2001 and later by Justine Larbalestier in 2002).[5] Asimov eventually established a great reputation as a lib-eral in gender relations, but for most of his life he was quite sexist in his per-sonal relations and dismissive of women in science fiction. For instance, Asimov was notorious for his roving hands, which roamed freely over the bodies of women he encountered at science fiction conventions. Edward L. Ferman, for example, long-time editor of *The Magazine of Fantasy and Science Fiction*, recalled first meeting Asimov at a science fiction convention *in the late 1960s*, after the modern women's movement had already begun. He introduced his date to Asimov, who, the appalled Ferman said, "instead of shaking my date's hand, shook her *left breast.*"[6] Cele Goldsmith, who edited *Amazing* and *Fantastic* until mid-1965, told author Paul Dellinger (whose debut, "Rat Race," she pub-lished in the January, 1962 *Fantastic*), a similar story about Asimov. It seems Asimov chased Goldsmith around her desk a few times during his visits to her office.[7]

Asimov also displayed sexist attitudes toward women in his letters to *Astounding* thirty years earlier. In these letters Asimov denounced as "mush" and "slop" the appearance of romance or other female-identified interests in science fiction, a literature he claimed was just for men. But, besides shedding light on Asimov's early hostility toward women in science fiction, the most sig-nificant thing about his series of hostile letters is that he was *not* able to stir other male writers to similar resentment. In their respective discussions of these letters, Searles recognized Asimov's isolation and commented on it, but Lar-balestier neither commented on it nor seemed to notice it. Instead, she focused on the fact that Asimov objected to these themes and took his views to be typi-cal. In fact, the case was just the reverse. Letters poured in from both women *and* men criticizing Asimov for his benighted attitudes. One male writer observed that Asimov was "creating an issue where one doesn't exist."[8] Even Asimov, in his patronizing manner, lamented that no men rallied to his crusade. "It must be a conspiracy," he complained to the editor, John W. Campbell, Jr. "Do you mean to say you have received no letters upholding my courageous stand against slop? . . . Are all the males married and afraid to breathe a word lest the little wife lift the rolling pin? . . . They're henpecked! All of them!"[9]

In sum, it is clear that, despite an occasional Neanderthal like Asimov, the mostly male readers were a receptive audience for stories by women writers, of which there were many.

In addition, male science fiction authors also welcomed female authors. For example, in the summer of 1959, the novice Kate Wilhelm was invited to attend the prestigious Milford Conference for professional science fiction writers. It was there, she said, that she and her work were taken seriously for the first time. While such respect and acceptance was unknown to Wilhelm outside the science fiction world, it was the norm inside the science fiction world.

In passing, and as further support for my thesis, I will also argue that early science fiction was receptive to the participation of two other "outsider" groups: Jews and blacks. Perhaps this receptivity to "outsider" groups was because early science fiction was, itself, a new and disdained "outsider" in the literary world. The field was a ghetto of poorly paid scribes with little prestige attached to their efforts. It could be that, for this reason, the gates were a bit more ajar than in other literary fields.

I realize my claims are at odds with the common perception of early science fiction. Certainly I do not wish to portray the genre as completely immune from the passions and prejudices of the age. I am speaking, after all, of a literature which flourished in a society which had not yet learned the horrors of the Holocaust; which had not yet experienced the civil rights movement; which had not yet undergone the social upheaval caused by the "Second Wave" of the women's movement. Under those circumstances, any type of popular culture *had* to reflect at least *some* of the stereotypes and worldviews of a largely anti-Semitic, racist, and sexist society.

And science fiction did. For example, Justine Larbalestier recently highlighted a long tradition of magazine science fiction "battle of the sexes" stories dating back to 1926. And, she tells us, "Most of these sexbattle stories attempt to teach that the rule of men is natural."[10] How could it be otherwise?

Nevertheless, the operative word here is "most." In its treatment of women and gender issues, early science fiction was *not completely* a medium of the dominant gender, nor were women and their concerns completely absent from the field. Instead, *203 different women authors—identifiable as women—published almost 1,000 stories in the science fiction magazines* between April, 1926 (when Hugo Gernsback published the first such), and 1960, a date usually thought of as being *before* women "stormed the barricades" and "invaded" the field.

Without a doubt, these women remained a distinct minority, both in percentages and in absolute numbers. Even so, the secular trend of female participation in the field was steadily upward over the decades. Each decade witnessed a doubling, tripling, or quadrupling over the previous decade of female science fiction authors and stories by them. For example, six female authors appeared in the science fiction magazines during the last three years of the 1920s. In the 1930s, the number quadrupled to twenty-five. In the 1940s, the number again climbed, virtually doubling to forty-seven. (See summary figures for table 1.) And in the

1950s, the number of known female authors again more than tripled, to 154 for that decade. (See summary figures appearing after table 3.)

We see the same steady and regular increase over the decades in the number of stories women contributed. Between 1926–1960, there were 922 known female-authored stories in the science fiction magazines. For the earliest period, the abbreviated 1920s, there were seventeen stories. This figure more than tripled in the 1930s to sixty-two stories. In the 1940s, the figure again more than tripled to 209 stories. And this pattern was repeated in the 1950s when the number again tripled, with 634 stories by female authors in that decade.

This secular trend tells us much about the nature of sociocultural change. The traditional exclusion narrative is rather ahistorical. Shawna McCarthy tells us that, "For some reason (no one *really* knows why . . .), in the mid-to-late 1960s" women "suddenly" began appearing at SF cons and in the pages of the magazines, like thunderbolts from a clear sky. However, things do not "suddenly" come out of nowhere. All things have a past, even if the observers are unaware of that past. The women's movement of the Seventies, for instance, was preceded by the civil rights movement, which provided a moral inspiration. And even before that there was the woman suffrage movement. But even the woman suffrage movement was preceded by the activity of women in the antebellum abolitionist movement—many of whom went on to become active in the suffrage movement. And so it goes.

So, we *do* know why women were present in science fiction in the mid-to-late 1960s . . . and it wasn't so "sudden." To begin with, women had *always* been there, invisible though they were to observers such as McCarthy. Second, the increasing participation of women in science fiction, decade after decade, reflected the increasing participation of women in other aspects of American culture. It was the predictable unfolding of a secular trend due to ongoing changes in American society.

The raw numbers of female authors and this secular trend of quantum leaps from decade to decade are important beyond the mere historiographical fact that "women were there." Their presence also tells us much about the nature of gender relations in early science fiction culture between 1926–1965. For instance, the steadily increasing female presence demonstrates that gender relations in the field were far more cordial than usually portrayed and that early science fiction editors, publishers, and most readers and fans were exceedingly welcoming to female writers.

And, because women were not only accepted, but *welcomed*, our view of the early science fiction field must change quite radically. The presumed absence or marginal appearance of women gives us a distorted view of early science fiction. It encourages us to think of it as reactionary when it was, instead, quite progressive in its orientation toward "outsider" groups like women. Instead of a closed and hostile society, it was in fact a relatively open and receptive society. Instead of being a field in which "outsiders" faced almost insurmountable barricades and locked doors, we now know it was a field in which they found open doors and no barricades. The traditional exclusion narrative, then, must be replaced with a narrative of acceptance.

Beyond that, enough of the stories written by women at this time were different enough from the stories written by male authors so that *we can speak of there existing an entirely separate school of female science fiction*, with its own themes and concerns. Further, these themes and concerns introduced some of the very qualities that critics have long claimed were absent from early science fiction.

Finally, this archaeological dig into the archives and the dismantling of a pervasive mythology helps clarify the nature of popular culture as a whole. Pulp science fiction is revealed to have been yet another cultural arena receptive to "outsider" participation. It reminds us that positive, as well as the more commonly accepted negative, tendencies and practices can be found in popular culture.

The Theory of Cultural Hegemony

Pulp science fiction's popular image as a patriarchal and sexist genre is partly due to that image being still mired in an early 1970s' feminist time warp. As cultural historian Michael Denning noted, "Like many insurgent movements, the women's movement emerged with an intransigent hostility to mass culture, denouncing, satirizing, and criticizing the popular paraphernalia of the feminine—beauty pageants, fashion, Hollywood cinema, and advertising."[11] In science fiction, this "intransigent hostility to mass culture" took the form of denouncing the field as a bastion of sexist patriarchs who perpetuated reactionary stereotypes of women and gender relations and who resisted—*and had always resisted*—the equal participation of women.

Feminist cultural critics as a whole moved on from this initial monochromatic condemnation of popular culture. By the 1980s, they had reassessed the impact of popular culture on women and female participation in it and had come to more ambiguous conclusions about the nature of mass commercial culture. Some of the earliest feminist reassessments of popular culture were in the areas of romance novels and Hollywood "chick flicks" aimed at women.

For instance, in Janice Radway's now-classic 1984 *Reading the Romance*, she used reader responses, anthropology, and feminist psychology to reveal how women readers subversively used romance novels to temporarily escape the social roles imposed upon them by patriarchy. Thus, these novels were not simply "sexist trash," reinforcing stereotypical social norms. The act of reading expressed a dissatisfaction with and small protest against traditional social roles. By reading romances, women participated in a "ritual of hope" that men and traditional relationships might meet their emotional needs. Even so, this act of defiance was bounded by a basic acceptance of gender roles. Romance novels, then, do not mean just one thing. They are ambiguous, expressing dual, even conflicting, messages.[12]

Radway's reinterpretation of romance literature helped lead feminist cultural critics to completely revamp their interpretations of many other forms of popular culture. For example, Christine Gledhill edited an influential feminist reevaluation of the role of Hollywood films in *Home Is Where the Heart Is,* which similarly revolutionized the way feminist cultural critics looked at female-targeted melodramas.[13]

Feminist science fiction critics, however, have for the most part remained outside the mainstream of such now-standard feminist studies of popular culture. Thus, their studies of pulp science fiction remain divorced not only from the record, but also from the intellectual currents of the larger world of cultural and feminist studies. This lingering influence of a superseded (by other feminists) early Seventies feminist worldview has helped give us a distorted image of the genre's past. It also means that the common critical views of the field reflect a more simplistic state of cultural theorizing than any real sophisticated thought on the subject. To understand how this is so, let us briefly review the evolution of cultural studies.

Modern cultural studies really began with Karl Marx and Frederich Engels and their interest in power relations. Marx and Engels were "materialists" who felt that economics (material conditions) was the foundation of all societies. Everything else, including culture, was mere "superstructure," the foam on the vast material ocean's surface. Ideas—and culture—were created by material conditions and only had importance as reflections of those conditions. As Marx said in his 1846 essay, *The German Ideology,* "Men's ideas are the most direct emanations of their material state."

And, as an expression of their material state, their economic status, capitalists used their ideas to reinforce their rule over society and over the great mass of people, the workers. Thus, "ideology" (a set of ideas) was a powerful means of social control. What these ideas primarily did was justify the status quo by arguing that the status quo, which only benefitted capitalists, was the "natural" and "proper" order of things. Thus, the ruling class imposed its worldview on subordinate classes. If workers accepted this worldview as a truthful description of the experience of all humankind, then workers were exhibiting "false consciousness," because they were not really "conscious" of their own economic interests and, instead, identified with the economic interests of their oppressors.

However, Marx and Engels were not greatly interested in questions of culture and ideas, in what they called "ideology." They were more interested in questions of power and, for them, power came down to economic relations, with ideology seen simply as a side issue. Indeed, much of what became the modern Marxist interpretation of culture was elaborated later by others. For instance, Marx himself seems never to have used the phrase "false consciousness" at all.

Neither did Engels until shortly before his death in 1895 and, when he did, he was never clear on what he meant by this elusive term.[14] Thus, it was left for their followers to clarify the issue, although their elaborations retained the basic outlines described by Marx and Engels.

The most important revisions of the concept of "ideology" and "false consciousness" were attempted in the 1920s with the work of Italian Marxist Antonio Gramsci and the German Marxist "critical theorists" who came to be known as the Frankfurt School. These Frankfurt School theorists included people such as Theodor Adorno, Max Horkheimer, and, later, Herbert Marcuse. Although they were unknown to each other at the time, both Gramsci and the Frankfurt School felt there was a major problem with the old-time view of "ideology" expressed (or not expressed) by Marx and Engels.

Like Marx and Engels, Gramsci and the Frankfurt School were also preoccupied with how a ruling class ruled. However, they felt that the emphasis on economics by Marx and Engels had slighted the role of culture. They acknowledged that ruling classes had great economic and military power. But they argued that ruling classes also had more overwhelming cultural power than Marx and Engels truly realized. And this cultural power was, they felt, far more important in guaranteeing the rule of the capitalist class (especially in a nominally "democratic" society) than Marx and Engels, with their economic reductionism, had understood. It was primarily through their cultural power that ruling classes justified themselves, gained mass acquiescence, and reproduced their rule over time. Admittedly, ruling classes used force as a last recourse to preserve their power. But such use of force was an indication that their cultural power had failed. In his prison notebooks Gramsci termed this cultural power "cultural hegemony."

Just as Engels was never very clear about what he meant when he discussed "false consciousness" (and Marx even less so), likewise Gramsci never gave us—at least in his translated writings—any clear definition of "cultural hegemony." The closest he came was when he defined it as, "the 'spontaneous' consent given by the great masses of the population to the general direction imposed on social life by the dominant fundamental group."[15]

Even so, Gramsci and the Frankfurt School argued that the mass consumer-oriented culture of an advanced capitalist society was primarily a cultural hegemony designed to inculcate the values of the ruling class. But, it wasn't about naked ideological "domination," the forcing of ideas upon people against their wills. It was more about bringing "the great masses" of people to willingly accept the ruling class worldview as the only "natural" or "common sense" view of things. These views thus became so deeply held by the masses that they were never questioned, never subjected to critical analysis, because they were what "everybody knows" to be true.

Thus, for example, it might be commonly accepted by "the great masses" that "one's betters" (however that is defined) "obviously" ought to run things. Or, "the great masses" of people—women as well as the male "ruling class"—might come to believe that men were "naturally" superior to women and it was "obvious" that this was the way God and Nature intended it to be. In both cases, the ruling classes would not have to resort to force to impose their rule. The subservient groups "spontaneously" accepted their rule as the natural order of things and did not question it.

The experience of Italian and German fascism (which imprisoned Gramsci in the 1920s and exiled the Frankfurt School theorists in the 1930s) reinforced these interpretations. Fascism was seen as a powerful political system which effectively used mass media to bring people into compliance and consent with the ruling party. Indeed, so important was mass media in establishing and maintaining the Nazi rule that the regime created a ubiquitous Ministry of Propaganda headed by Joseph Goebbels. It was in large part due to the work of this Propaganda Minister that there was no German homefront collapse in World War II, as there had been in 1918. German civilians resisted to the bitter end, despite overwhelming military disasters on every front.

Mass culture, then, was a means to manipulate the masses in order to inculcate "false consciousness" among the masses and subservience to the ruling class. Because of such false consciousness, the masses basically "consented" to the rule of their oppressors, as they accepted it as natural. Of course, being Marxists, the cultural hegemony theorists also argued that such mass media induced false consciousness occurred not only under fascism, but also in capitalist societies.

So far, so good. Many later theorists, however, stop right there. They believe that Gramsci and the Frankfurt School felt mass culture was unambiguously fascist, even under capitalism. However, like Marx and Engels before them, Gramsci and the Frankfurt School were deeply influenced by Hegelian dialectics. In other words, for them nothing was ever just one way. No hegemony was ever total and complete. There was a constant back-and-forth struggle between forces, trends, developments, and ideologies. Thus, while the ruling class used culture as a means of creating "false consciousness" among the masses and gaining mass acceptance of the ruling class worldview, its hegemony was never either absolute or permanent. Creating and maintaining cultural hegemony was always a struggle. There was always resistance. Some, always a minority, might not agree that capitalists, say, were "one's betters" and ought to run things. Some might not agree that men were "naturally" superior to women.

Thus, minorities advocating competing interpretations and worldviews were also and forever expressing themselves through the same cultural forms used by the ruling class. Such advocates were always a minority because, were they to become a majority, then it would be *their* worldviews which possessed social legitimacy and cultural hegemony. Culture was therefore an eternal arena of "contested terrain," although Gramsci did not use that exact phrase.

For example, the invention of the printing press around 1450 by Johannes

Gutenberg radically transformed the nature of power and culture in Europe. For the first time it was possible to mass produce the written word. The Catholic Church quickly began using the new medium to strengthen its hold over the imagination of the common people, as well as to create an incredibly more effective bureaucracy.

But dissidents like Martin Luther also had access to the printing press and simultaneously began using it to spread their ideas. Luther translated the Bible from Latin, the knowledge of which was a monopoly of the clerics and academics, into the vernacular of the common people, in his case German. Then this vernacular version, as well as myriad pamphlets arguing Luther's interpretations of it, were mass produced and disseminated. The result was a mass protest movement to reform the Church—a Protestant Reformation. And, in countries such as England or Holland, or in northern Germany or Scandanavia, this minority protest movement eventually gained enough power to exercise religious cultural hegemony in those regions. The Catholic Church was not destroyed and continued to exercise cultural hegemony in other areas, such as Ireland, Spain, Italy, and Poland. But its monopoly over Christian interpretations was destroyed, as alternative worldviews challenged Catholic cultural hegemony at large. And these competing religious worldviews continue to vie for dominance today, because the creation and maintenance of cultural hegemony not static. It is a constant process.

This nuance, however, was often lost in later iterations of the theory of cultural hegemony. The realization that hegemony was never complete, never absolute, was overlooked. Instead, simplistic interpretations of Gramsci's famous aphorism, "The ruling ideas of an age are the ideas of the ruling class," became widespread. Thus, in the years immediately after World War II, cultural critics such as Harvard sociologist David Riesman, Hannah Arendt, and Dwight MacDonald popularized a one-sided version of cultural hegemony theory. They, and their disciples, decried capitalist "mass culture" as a uniform threat to individuality, democracy, and creativity. By its very nature, they argued, the mass culture of advanced capitalism promoted hierarchy, domination, and the oppression of subaltern groups, such as workers, racial minorities, and women.

Reflecting such critiques of mass culture, these themes also became prominent in the male-authored science fiction of the 1950s, which I will discuss in part 2. In that case, however, the male authors were not criticizing mass culture because it supposedly oppressed subaltern or outsider groups. Rather, they criticized it from an elitist vantage point. They saw themselves as "intellectuals" and, as such, victims oppressed by a mass culture which stifled individualism and creativity.

Such one-dimensional interpretations of mass culture did not cease with the 1950s, however. They lingered on and some later cultural critics in diverse areas continued to espouse versions of misunderstood hegemony theory. One of these popular culture areas was film. Movies were born as a form of working class entertainment in the immigrant ghettos of America's large cities around the turn of the twentieth century. Despite this origin, prolific cultural critics Stuart and Elizabeth Ewen saw the movies, not as a genuine form of working class culture, but as merely another form of bourgeois cultural hegemony.[16]

In the beginning, the Ewens acknowledge, movies addressed working class tastes and were especially attractive to immigrant women. From 1903 to 1915, "Movies showed the difficult and ambiguous realities of urban tenement life in an idiom that spoke directly to immigrant women . . . everyday situations were depicted, the causes of poverty were held to be environmental, and economic injustice was deplored."[17] But this, they said, was only a brief stage in film development. Because "movies were primarily an institution of the larger society, subject to its shifts and pulls . . . [they] spoke increasingly to the social and sexual dynamics, the ideological superstructure of an evolving consumer culture."[18]

The role of movies was thus an integrative one, assimilating working class immigrants into the larger bourgeois Anglo culture. They introduced immigrants to the mores of American society and told them how to look and how to act. Again, this impact was felt most keenly by young immigrant girls. The movies provided these girls with the opportunity to live like "Americans." They offered a rare secluded rendezvous away from parents for girls and their beaus. The movies also encouraged immigrant girls to spend some of their hard-won pay upon themselves (as the price of admission), rather than contributing all of it to the family. "While the old family ways of understanding seemed inadequate as a guide to industrial culture, the movies seemed more shaped to the tempo of urban life. Increasingly, the social authority of the media of mass culture replaced older forms of family authority and behavior. . . . [They] symbolized a cultural environment that assumed greater individual freedom and less formal relations with the opposite sex."[19]

Superficially, the Ewens claimed, this may have appeared to have validated Gramsci's idea of the contested nature of mass culture. For example, in a patriarchal Old World family structure, such female independence was inherently subversive. But this greater individual freedom was actually only the freedom to become like the dominant "Americans." This, in turn, meant buying clothes like the Americans, wearing one's hair like the Americans, consuming like the Americans. The movies thus became "manuals of desire, wishes, and dreams. . . . In this sense, the imagery of the films . . . made possible the liquidation of traditional culture."[20]

Such monochromatic interpretations of the role of popular culture came under intensifying attack in the turbulent 1960s. An oppositional counterculture emerged among the young centering around rock and roll and disquieting fashion trends, such as long hair on men. Meanwhile, iconoclastic Hollywood films like *Bonnie and Clyde* and *Easy Rider* celebrated outlaws and outsiders.[21] Such developments, in both America and Europe, suggested that popular culture could be a source of resistance and rebellion to ruling elites and their values, an antihierarchical democratic political force.

One theoretical support for such views came from Frankfurt School theorist Herbert Marcuse, whose 1964 book, *One-Dimensional Man: Studies in the Ideology of Advanced Industrial Societies*, influenced the emerging New Left of the young radicals.[22] His book initiated a new round of debate over the nature of popular culture. On the one hand, the young rebels recognized the sterility and conformity of suburbanized middle class life in an advanced capitalist society like America. At the same time, however, their own heroes—Bob Dylan, John Lennon, Mick Jagger, Jimi Hendrix, Janis Joplin, Jim Morrison—defied the values of mass culture and used the mass media to project an oppositional stance toward bourgeois society.

In the mid-1960s other cultural critics, such as Marshall McLuhan and Susan Sontag, offered more intellectual support to the counter-cultural interpretation. McLuhan embraced the mass media technology denounced by simplistic interpreters of the Frankfurt School. Instead of seeing it solely as a means of inculcating ruling class values, he saw it as leading to a liberated and democratic "global village." Meanwhile, in a series of influential essays, Sontag celebrated rock and roll, impromptu hippie "happenings," and the pop art of Andy Warhol as liberating influences.

By the 1970s, the women's movement was still applying a simplistic understanding of the cultural hegemony critique to science fiction and many other cultural arenas. They saw science fiction and other such forms of popular culture simply as bastions of ruling class values. Even so, a more sophisticated interpretation of popular culture was already taking shape in the field of cultural studies. This interpretation represented a more nuanced understanding of the Gramsci-Frankfurt School's thesis of cultural hegemony and came to be known as the theory of "contested terrain."

One academic work which helped introduce this more nuanced version of hegemony theory to the study of popular culture was historian Herbert Gutman's influential essay, "Work, Culture, and Society in Industrializing America," published in the *American Historical Review* in 1973. Gutman agreed that corporate capitalism certainly came to dominate America by the end of the nineteenth century. However, previously unstudied aspects of working class culture, such as the prevalence of secular holidays like "Holy Monday," where workers slept in and just didn't come to work on Monday, were evidence of enduring resistance to that corporate dominance. Thus, he argued, instead of being a manifestation of a monolithic hierarchical force or an entirely rebellious counter-culture, popular culture was actually multi-faceted, it was "contested terrain."

At the same time, the work of other observers, such as sociologist Warren Susman, reinforced the belief that popular culture was contested political terrain. Echoing Gramsci and the Frankfurt School, Susman agreed that there are repressive possibilities within mass culture. However, he said, also echoing Gramsci and the Frankfurt School, there are also real possibilities of liberation. Thus, he claimed, it was a potential source of democratic and egalitarian values, as well as hierarchical oppression. The task of the good cultural historian, then, is to understand the nuances and ambiguities of mass culture. Only such a clear-eyed approach holds out the "hope for a radical rebuilding of the world on the ideological vision of a culture of abundance."[23]

Other cultural studies theorists elaborated upon these interpretations, the most influential being Fredric Jameson and Stuart Hall, both in 1979. In Jameson's "Reification and Utopia in Mass Culture" and Hall's "Notes on Deconstructing 'the Popular'," they also argued that popular culture was neither just a form of hierarchical social control for the replication of ruling class values, nor simply a form of lower class resistance and rebellion. It was indeed "contested terrain."[24]

Which brings us to today.

At present, works on cultural theory and history commonly start with the acknowledgement that much historical work in many cultural arenas has revealed the "contested terrain" synthesis to be the most accurate depiction of popular culture in its various manifestations. Thus, for example, Roy Rosenzweig explicitly challenged the monolithic interpretation of the films of the Twenties offered by Stuart and Elizabeth Ewen. Given the inability to discern how working class or immigrant audiences actually responded to the films, he felt it was "more fruitful to focus on the movie-going experience, rather than the movie content. Whatever the degree of control of the middle and upper classes over movie content, the working class was likely to determine the nature of behavior and interaction within the movie theater."[25]

And this behavior, he contended in his study of working class leisure in Worcester, Massachusetts, was raucous, smelly, informal, and intensely gregarious, especially in the early days of the nickelodeons. As such, the new movie theaters became central arenas of conflict between the working class audiences and middle class reformers who felt the uninhibited and independent experience of working class moviegoing had to be brought under control. Over time, this was what the reformers managed to do, with regularized schedules for the films, a military-style usher corps designed to bring the unruly behavior of the masses into line, opulent picture palaces intended to lure in middle class audiences, and sanitized bourgeois movie content.

Yet, even so, far from being an unambiguous vehicle for the transmission of middle class and consumerist views, the moviegoing experience served to transform middle class audiences just as it altered working class audiences. "With its mixing of sexes and classes, its lack of formality, and its intimacy, [movies] represented a radically new experience for the native middle class . . . it was a shift toward working class norms."[26]

Perhaps more importantly, the gravitational tug of movies, which pulled immigrant girls out of patriarchal families, also helped pull all young immigrants out of their separate ethnic spheres into a larger pan-ethnic working class community. Because the movies helped create a mass culture by being "an arena for the mixing of ethnic groups, classes, age groups, and sexes," they could indeed be transmission belts of the dominant consumer ethos to the immigrant young.[27] But at the same time, "young workers were likely to meet members of other ethnic groups . . . [and] these recreational associations could begin to facilitate some of the workplace organizing that had proven so difficult in earlier decades" of intense ethnic rivalries. Additionally, "The workers' new perception of themselves as 'Americans' could lead them to expect a good deal more than their parents had ever received from the larger society. . . . Having already made the transition from the rum shop to the Rialto, at least some workers now made the more important and more difficult shift from the cinema to the CIO."[28]

Likewise, in the introduction to his study of nineteenth-century dime novels, Michael Denning began by stating that, "These popular stories . . . can be understood neither as forms of deception, manipulation, and social control nor as expressions of a genuine people's culture, opposing and resisting the dominant culture. Rather they are best seen as a contested terrain, a field of cultural conflict where signs with wide appeal and resonance take on contradictory disguises and are spoken with contrary accents."[29] And, in the same fashion, in a 2002 study of the 1890–1940 origins of celebrity journalism in America, the author opened by describing mass-produced popular culture as "Janus-faced, a repository of utopian hopes as well as a vehicle encouraging acceptance of the status quo."[30]

Indeed, so accepted is the "contested terrain" thesis in cultural studies that now textbooks in the field usually begin with a statement about the validity of this interpretation. Thus, in a typical 2003 text on mass media, the authors say at the outset, "Media are, without doubt, not simple agents of the powerful, and . . . the ideas of the powerful are not simply imposed on readers or viewers. Media are cultural sites where the ideas of the powerful are circulated and where they can be contested."[31]

But, such sophisticated analyses are as scarce as hens' teeth in the study of pulp science fiction. For the most part, the academic analysis of early science fiction is still enmeshed in a simplistic misunderstanding of the Gramsci-Frankfurt School thesis of mass culture. This misinterpretation sees popular culture solely as a form of monolithic dominance, oppression, hierarchy, and social control. Thus, as an aspect of popular culture, pulp science fiction was the province of a white, male, Protestant "ruling class" which was racist, sexist, and anti-

Semitic to the core, expressing all the hierarchical values of the reactionary society in which it flourished.

There are exceptions to this biblical version, such as Robin Roberts's studies of the "female alien," the work of Jean Pfaelzer, Jane Donawerth, and Carol Kolmerten on early feminist utopias, and Justine Larbalestier's examination of the enduring battle of the sexes motif in early science fiction. These are among the bare handful of academic investigations which genuinely explore the nuances and ambiguities of, for instance, gender relations in pulp science fiction.[32] But they are exceptions. Further, while the studies of these writers offer implicit support to the Gramscian "contested terrain" thesis, not one of even these authors makes a single reference to it. Their work might well have gained more theoretical coherence had it been expressed in a Gramscian framework.

Thus, the dominant interpretation of early science fiction remains out of step with current mainstream feminist and cultural studies theory. Moreover, the dominant paradigm doesn't even fit the facts. And it is *because* most academic criticism of pulp science fiction is frozen in a "one-dimensional" theory of popular culture that its interpretation of pulp science fiction doesn't fit the facts. The interpretation *prevents* the close examination of the record which would *refute* the interpretation. Pulp science fiction is *assumed* to have been a manifestation of patriarchal cultural hegemony; therefore, there is no investment in uncovering countervailing evidence. The theory says we don't need to actually *investigate* the past, as everyone already *knows* what pulp science fiction was like. And, because "of course" pulp science fiction was as described, countervailing evidence doesn't exist, in any case—and one does not look for what one believes does not exist.

This one-dimensional understanding of science fiction has, itself, come to exercise "cultural hegemony" over the field. It is accepted as the "obvious" story of the genre's past, and people accept it without question, without subjecting it to critical analysis. This state of affairs is the very definition of cultural hegemony.

Because of this hegemonic version of the genre's past, relatively little has been written about gender relations in pulp science fiction. What would there be to write about? What evidence could there possibly be? Thus, the expanding body of work on women in science fiction has focused on the late 1960s and thereafter, the years when feminist women, supposedly, finally "crashed" the bachelor party. In 2002 Justine Larbalestier made this very point in one of the few other book-length studies of early women's science fiction. "The period from 1926 to 1973 is absolutely critical to the formation of contemporary feminist science fiction," she said, "and yet very little critical work has been undertaken on that period. For example, almost all feminist accounts of the field concentrate on the period from the 1970s onward."[33]

Were we to actually look at gender relations in the period *before* the 1970s, we might dispel some of the "false consciousness" which currently dominates our views of women and science fiction history. But in order to conduct such an investigation we would have to look at where early science fiction was actually located—in the science fiction magazines and in fandom. Unfortunately, as Larbalestier also noted, the prolific academic commentators are almost entirely ignorant of these areas. "The majority of academic work on science fiction," she said, "either ignores or says very little about the importance of the science fiction magazines and of science fiction fandom."[34] It is as if historians ignored the actual records and simply fabricated events and interpretations out of their own nebulous musings. The subsequent academic pontificating would be the very epitome of professional irresponsibility.

My own investigation of the record reveals a history of pulp science fiction very different from the biblical version. I do not deny that the majority of those involved in pulp science fiction were men. Nor do I deny that the stories *usually* portrayed gender relations in very stereotypical fashions.

But I do assert that the relations between the majority males and the women in their midst were very different from what is commonly believed. And I do assert that female fans were an accepted and important part of science fiction fandom. And I do assert that female authors were an accepted and important part of the science fiction magazines. And I do assert that these female authors presented stories dramatically at odds with the dominant male paradigm.

Thus, rather than a monolithic bastion of gender oppression and female exclusion, early science fiction was, in fact, largely democratic, egalitarian, and accepting of outsider groups, such as women. In short, pulp science fiction was contested terrain.

And, unlike the champions of the culturally hegemonic version, who merely assert without proof, I will present the evidence to support my thesis.

Further, by demonstrating that the contested terrain thesis best explains the nature of early science fiction, I also hope to further validate this thesis as the best explanation of the nature of popular culture at large.

When Does Science Fiction Begin?

Some have argued that the beginning of science fiction lies in the ancient past. Perhaps it can be found in the fog-shrouded mists of legendary Atlantis, which Plato invented c. 350 B.C. in two of his dialogues, the "Critias" and the "Timaeus." Or perhaps it can be found in Homer's older tales of brave Ulysses facing Circe, the Cyclops, and the Sirens. Or perhaps it can be found even earlier in the Epic of Gilgamesh, c. 2400 B.C., wherein our hero descended into Hell and returned to tell the tale. Indeed, when noted science fiction author Jack Williamson taught courses on science fiction at the University of Eastern New

Mexico, this is exactly where he began, as did Philip Klass ("William Tenn") in his Penn State science fiction courses.

But Isaac Asimov dismissed all this as "nonsense." He argued that science fiction "cannot predate popular awareness of the connection between advancing science and technology and social change, and that brings us up to the Industrial Revolution." He also discounted stories by Hawthorne, Poe, and even Mary Shelley's *Frankenstein* (1818), as examples of "Gothic tales" rather than true science fiction. Even dating the beginning with stories from the 1860s by Jules Verne or the 1890s Victorian era "scientific romances" of H. G. Wells is problematic, he said. While Verne and Wells (both of whom wrote many other types of stories) were *themselves* popular, it could not be said that they were part of a popular literary genre known as "science fiction." Rather, the *true* beginning of science fiction, Asimov argued, should be situated at that point where stories of this type became a "mass phenomenon."

And when, he asked, did science fiction "begin to be turned out in quantity, by first dozens, then scores, and then hundreds of writers? What set it on the road to where it is today, an extraordinarily popular literary phenomenon that has many first-rate luminaries? . . . Clearly [Asimov answered himself], what is responsible for this is *magazine* science fiction, which began with the first issue (April, 1926) of *Amazing Stories* published by Hugo Gernsback."[35] It was Gernsback who gave the genre a place and, eventually, a name: "Science Fiction." And for this he is rightly called, "The Father of Science Fiction."

Thus, my own study begins where Isaac Asimov placed the beginning of science fiction: with Gernsback and his magazine and the birth of science fiction as a popular and identifiably separate literary genre. My study basically ends in 1960, the end of the Fifties decade, although part 3, "Hidden from History," looks at the first half of the Sixties in an attempt to understand why early women's science fiction has been so forgotten. But, there is a good reason for essentially ending my story with the end of the Fifties. That decade is now "a far-off and almost forgotten era of science fiction," says SF author Robert Silverberg, "when the core of the s-f industry was made up of magazines, not books."[36] Thus, taking the story, for the most part, from 1926–1960 makes sense because throughout this period the "core of the s-f industry" was to be found primarily in a single monolithic venue, the magazines. This makes it relatively easy to study, make comparisons, and come to conclusions.

However, there is another reason to end this present study with the end of the 1950s. I wish to examine in explicit isolation what I see as a "First Wave" of women's science fiction before the coming of "Second Wave" feminism in the late 1960s and early 1970s. In many ways, I believe, it was this pre-1960 "First Wave" women's science fiction that made possible the better-known feminist science fiction of the latter era. By isolating the earlier period and looking only at it, we can get a better idea of its nature and how it made possible later female progress in the field.

Organization

My book is divided into three parts, each of which has several mini-chapters. Part 1, "Presumption of Prejudice," deals with the period from 1926, when the first science fiction magazine appeared, to 1949, the date after which it is commonly agreed there were "some" female science fiction authors. I investigate (and dismiss) the almost universal presumption that there were no women science fiction authors during this period. I also discuss the nature of gender relations in the field among male and female fans and between editors and female writers. And, in passing, I look at the relationship between early science fiction and two other "outsider" groups, Jews and blacks.

I then turn to the contributions of early women authors and briefly survey and describe their stories and identify two themes they brought to the genre at this time: 1) Political speculation of a sometimes "socialist" and explicitly "feminist" persuasion; and 2) An empathetic treatment of aliens not usually found in the fictions of contemporary male authors. Also presented is the most comprehensive bibliography of women's magazine science fiction ever compiled for the period.

The subject of part 2 is "Science Fiction's Female Counter-Culture, 1950–1960." Contemporary participants recognized that there was an explosion of female participation in the genre at that time. As with earlier science fiction, this was because 1950s' science fiction was also an "open door" for female participation. At the same time, the gender differences between male and female science fiction, which I earlier discerned, became clearly noticeable in that decade, as a distinct female counter-culture developed in the literature. That counter-culture manifested a heavy emphasis upon empathy with "others" and the creation of community, themes largely missing from the alienated stories of male science fiction authors in this crucial decade.

Part 3 is a short section on the period 1961–1965 and is an attempt to explain why the "First Wave" of women's science fiction was forgotten. It examines the roles played by both the collapse of the science fiction magazine market, which was the previous heartland of science fiction, and the ideology of second wave feminism.

Complete bibliographies of women's magazine science fiction from 1926–1965 are then presented. (A complete bibliography of women's science fiction for the 1950s in *British* magazines is also presented, although my findings are not based upon the British figures.) Also included are tables detailing the female publication record in *Weird Tales*, the premier fantasy magazine of the age, women's publication in other contemporary "weird fiction" magazines, a list of early female science fiction and fantasy magazine editors and a filmography of women fantasy and science fiction screenwriters, 1916–1949. This is followed by brief biographies of 133 of the 203 women who published in the science fiction magazines from 1926–1960.

For this investigation, the primary sources—the science fiction magazines themselves—were used. This means *every* issue of *every* science fiction magazine published in the United States during these years was physically examined. Stories written under both female names and pseudonyms of known women were sought.[37] Pertinent editorial comments and readers' letters were also examined. As previously noted, one of the results of this research has been the assembly of the most complete bibliography of female authors in the science fiction magazines.[38]

This bibliography reveals a fascinating form of "invisibility"—scores of female authors and hundreds of their stories "hiding in plain sight." In the twenty-three years between 1926–1949, for example, there were sixty-five authors identifiable as women who produced a total of 288 stories.[39] Further, female contributions were widely distributed among the magazines, rather than concentrated in any one or type of them. This alone suggests that the long-accepted claim that either science fiction publishers or their editors were blatantly prejudiced against women writers must be questioned. Instead, it is clear that early science fiction editors were much more welcoming to female participation than routinely described.

By discovering that women were accepted on a basis of equality in pulp science fiction, we are also forced to confront the true nature of prejudice which women face in the field. The real prejudice these women experienced was not prejudice by the editors or fans of the pulp era, who welcomed them. Rather, the real prejudice is at the hands of *current* science fiction fans, readers, historians, and critics who continue to deny their existence and their true relationship to early science fiction.

Caveat Emptor

Some clarifications before we begin:

I am discussing only women who published in the science fiction magazines and presenting bibliographies only for the stories they published in these magazines. Women also published science fiction in general interest magazines during our period. For example, Minna Fiebleman Bardon (1900–1974) was a well-known writer for the mystery and romance pulps in the 1920s and 1930s. However, writing as "Minna Fiebleman," she published a science fiction story, "Ambassador to Mars," which was the cover story of the October 1st, 1930 issue of *Top-Notch*. This was unusual for *Top-Notch*, as most of its stories fell into the Western, detective, sports, or men's adventure genres. Thus, one would not expect a science fiction story, much less one by a woman, to appear there. But, it did.

However, I do not include such women or their stories appearing outside the explicit science fiction magazines. Were I to do so, the number of women science fiction authors and their stories during our period would, obviously, be higher than the totals I present.[40]

Next, I have heretofore been using the phrase "pulp science fiction," as this early period is sometimes referred to as "the pulp era." That era, however, was not perfectly aligned with the years 1926–1960 that I will primarily discuss. Technically, the first science fiction pulp was the January, 1930, *Astounding Stories*, which went on sale during December, 1929. Not only was it printed on pulp paper, but it was of pulp size (7" x 10"). Earlier issues of Gernsback's magazines which superficially appear to have been published on pulp paper were actually published on what he called "bulk-weave," a quality somewhere between pulp and "slick" paper. The reason he gave for this decision was to increase the thickness of issues, thus making it seem the buyer was getting more for his or her money. In addition, his magazines were of the larger, bedsheet size (8.5" x 11"), instead of pulp size. Finally, the last regular science fiction pulp was the February, 1958 *Science Fiction Quarterly*, although most of the revived issues of *Wonder Stories* were pulps for years afterward.

Thus, my study of women in the early science fiction magazines actually begins three years earlier (in April, 1926) and extends two years beyond (1960) the technically exact science fiction "pulp era." I acknowledge this objection to the phrase I use to describe early magazine science fiction. Having agreed that we all know the correct parameters of the science fiction "pulp era," I hope, for the sake of convenience, that purists will forgive me these few years when I refer to "pulp."

Also, the science fiction magazine was invented in America and, although there were a handful of early and small British magazines, magazine science fiction remained primarily an American literary phenomenon until after World War II. Hence, from now on when I speak of "early science fiction" or "magazine science fiction" or "pulp science fiction," I am speaking only of American magazines and the literature as it evolved in America. I acknowledge that the handful of British science fiction magazines published between 1926–1949, the first period I investigate, might show different patterns from what I discern in American magazines at that time.

For example, in addition to the foreign editions of many American science fiction magazines that circulated in England during this period, only five domestic titles were issued there: *Scoops* (1934), *Tales of Wonder* (1937–1942), *New Worlds* (1946–1953, and thereafter under various names), *Fantasy* (1938–

1939, 1946–1947), and *Yankee Science Fiction* (three issues, all in 1942). I have checked the contents of these for entries written by women using Graham Stone's comprehensive *Index to British Science Fiction Magazines, 1934–1953* (three volumes, Australian Science Fiction Association, 1977). I found only three such stories for the period under discussion: a reprint of the 1929 American story, "A Baby on Neptune" (here "Child of Neptune") by Miles J. Breuer and Clare Winger Harris (*Tales of Wonder,* #14, spring, 1941), "Beast of the Crater" by British writer Marion F. Eadie (Mrs. Harry E. Turner) (*Tales of Wonder,* #16, spring, 1942), and "Invasion From Venus" by British writer "Paul Ashwell" (Pauline Whitby) (*Yankee Science Fiction,* July, 1942). I therefore infer that the circumstances, reasoning and conclusions set forth in my study cannot be applied to the development of the field in Great Britain.

Let me now offer a final caveat: Despite my previous discussion of cultural studies theory, this book is not primarily a work of literary criticism in which I "deconstruct" either "hegemonic" or "subaltern" texts and "theorize" about their rival "discourses." I am trying to do something very different. I am investigating the lived culture of gender relations in early science fiction, as I believe how men and women actually related to each other will tell us the most about the genre at that time. Thus, I explore the real-world relations of female authors, fans, and readers with editors and the field as a whole from 1926–1960. I do this in order to shed light on the actual status and condition of outsider groups in science fiction at this time and, thereby, the nature of science fiction culture itself.

Further, because this is a study of real-world relations, my approach has been to situate the literature in real-world developments. Histories of science fiction have not always done so. For example, in their influential study of the field's development, Brian Aldiss and David Wingrove explicitly stated that, "Our concern is to present SF as a literature"[41] Therefore, Aldiss and Wingrove focused solely on texts and completely ignored the social context which produced them.

I do not believe that such a hermetically insulated approach is truly revealing about the genre's evolution. Instead, I agree with Andrew Ross that the literature cannot be completely separated from the social environment which produced it. Thus, he argued that the "Gernsback Continuum" of early pulp science fiction could not be divorced from "the national cults of science, engineering, and invention" which obsessed early twentieth-century America and out of which the science fiction genre coalesced.[42]

Likewise, I believe that outsider groups and science fiction during this same period cannot be understood in isolation from the socioeconomic, cultural, and political developments which shaped early twentieth-century America. For this reason, I will briefly discuss such changes, especially in part 2. I will also explore how the changing nature of mid-twentieth-century America brought about a change in the focus of both men's and women's science fiction published at that time.

Let us begin.

Notes

1. Shawna McCarthy, Ed., "Editor's Note," *Isaac Asimov's Space of Her Own, Science Fiction Anthology #8,* 1983, p. 9. "15 or 20 years ago," before 1983, would have been 1968 or 1963. She admits this is "a bit of an overstatement." "However," she continues, "the fact remains . . ." that, in outline, this is the history of women in science fiction.

2. Peter Haining, Ed., *The Fantastic Pulps,* Vintage Books: N.Y., 1975, p. 315. Emphasis added.

3. Connie Willis, "The Women SF Doesn't See," guest editorial in *Asimov's Science Fiction Magazine,* October, 1992, p. 4.

4. Mary Kenny Badami, "Feminist Critique of Science Fiction," *Extrapolation,* 18, No. 1, (December) 1976, p. 6.

5. For an extended discussion and photo-reproduction of all the letters involved, see A. Langley Searles, "'Mush and Slop': Isaac Asimov's Early Attitudes Towards Women," *Fantasy Commentator,* X, Nos. 1 & 2, 2001–2002, p. 75 ff. Also, see Justine Larbalestier's much less insightful discussion of them in *The Battle of the Sexes in Science Fiction,* p. 117 ff.

6. Charles Platt, *Dream Makers, Volume II: The Uncommon Men & Women Who Write Science Fiction,* Berkley Books: N.Y., 1983, p. 246. Emphasis in original.

7. Paul Dellinger letter to Eric Leif Davin, January 11, 2005.

8. Charles M. Jarvis, "Brass Tacks," *Astounding Science-Fiction,* April, 1939, p. 161.

9. Isaac Asimov, "Brass Tacks," *Astounding Science-Fiction,* July, 1939, p. 107.

10. Justine Larbalestier, *The Battle of the Sexes in Science Fiction,* Wesleyan University Press: Middletown, Conn., 2002, p. 229.

11. Michael Denning, "The End of Mass Culture," *International Labor and Working-Class History,* No. 37, spring, 1990, p. 7.

12. Janice Radway, *Reading the Romance: Women, Patriarchy, and Popular Literature,* University of North Carolina Press: Chapel Hill, 1984.

13. Christine Gledhill, Ed., *Home Is Where the Heart Is,* University of Illinois Press: Urbana, 1987.

14. See Martin Seliger, *The Marxist Conception of Ideology: A Critical Essay,* Cambridge University Press: Cambridge, 1977, pp. 30–31, notes 20, 21, and Raymond Williams, *Keywords: A Vocabulary of Culture and Society,* Oxford University Press: N.Y., 1976, pp. 126–130.

15. Antonio Gramsci, *Selections From the Prison Notebooks,* translated and edited by Quintin Hoare and Geoffrey Nowell Smith, International Publishers: N.Y., 1971, p. 12. Also, see p. 366. Gramsci began writing his prison notebooks in 1929.

16. Stuart Ewen and Elizabeth Ewen, *Channels of Desire: Mass Images and the Shaping of American Consciousness,* McGraw-Hill: New York, 1982.

17. Ewen and Ewen, pp. 88–89.

18. Ewen and Ewen, p. 92.

19. Ewen and Ewen, pp. 95, 93.

20. Ewen and Ewen, p. 102.

21. Peter Coyote placed the genesis of *Easy Rider* in an informal discussion he was party to with Peter Fonda and Dennis Hopper, the film's stars. Also present was Emmett Grogan, who was, like Coyote, a member of the counter-cultural San Francisco Diggers, and "Sweet William," a fellow-traveling Hell's Angel. They were discussing how best to translate "what was happening" onto film when "Sweet William" said, "You know what I'd do? I'd make a movie about me and a buddy just riding around. Just going around the country doing what we do, seeing what we see, you know.

Showing the people what things are like." And this, essentially, was exactly what the movie did. See Peter Coyote, *Sleeping Where I Fall: A Chronicle,* Counterpoint: Washington, D.C., 1998, pp. 100–101.

22. See, e.g., Carl Oglesby, Ed., *The New Left Reader,* Grove Press: NY, 1969, which republished a selection from Marcuse's book, *One-Dimensional Man.* This anthology was perhaps the first comprehensive collection of the seminal writings which shaped New Left thought.

23. See Warren I. Susman, *Culture as History: The Transformation of American Society in the Twentieth Century,* Pantheon: N.Y., 1973, p. xxx.

24. See Fredric Jameson, "Reification and Utopia in Mass Culture," *Social Text,* I, 1979; and Stuart Hall, "Notes on Deconstructing 'The Popular'," in Raphael Samuel, Ed., *People's History and Socialist Theory,* Routledge and Keegan Paul: London, 1981, originally delivered as a paper in 1979. Also, see Stuart Hall, "The Rediscovery of 'Ideology': Return of the Repressed in Media Studies," in M. Gurevitch, T. Bennett, J. Curran, and S. Woollacott, Eds., *Culture, Society, and the Media,* Routledge Kegan Paul: London, 1982, pp. 56–90.

25. Roy Rosenzweig, *Eight Hours For What We Will,* Cambridge University Press: Cambridge, England, 1983, p. 199.

26. Rosenzweig, p. 212.

27. Rosenzweig, p. 220.

28. Rosenzweig, p. 228.

29. Michael Denning, *Mechanic Accents: Dime Novels and Working-Class Culture in America,* Verso: London, 1987, p. 3.

30. Charles L. Ponce de Leon, *Self-Exposure: Human-Interest Journalism and the Emergence of Celebrity in America, 1890–1940,* University of North Carolina Press: Chapel Hill, 2002, p. 4.

31. David Croteau and William Hoynes, *Media Society: Industries, Images, and Audiences,* Pine Forge Press—Sage Publications: London, Third Edition, 2003, p. 168.

32. Robin Roberts, "The Female Alien: Pulp Science Fiction's Legacy to Feminists," in *Journal of Popular Culture,* fall, 1987, pp. 33–52, and *A New Species: Gender and Science in Science Fiction,* University of Illinois Press: Urbana, 1993; Jean Pfaelzer, "A State of One's Own: Feminism as Ideology in American Utopias, 1880–1915," *Extrapolation,* winter, 1983, V. 24, No. 4; Jane L. Donawerth and Carol A. Kolmerten, Eds., *Utopian and Science Fiction by Women: Worlds of Difference,* Syracuse University Press: Syracuse, 1994, and *Frankenstein's Daughters: Women Writing Science Fiction,* Syracuse University Press: Syracuse, 1997.

33. Larbalestier, p. 2.

34. Justine Larbalestier, "Researching *The Battle of the Sexes in Science Fiction,*" a talk given to the Friends of the University of Sydney Library, August 19, 2002. This can be found at: www.justinelarbalestier.com/Musings/Musings2003/research.htm.

35. Isaac Asimov, "Introduction: Science Fiction Finds Its Voice," in Isaac Asimov, Charles G. Waugh, and Martin H. Greenberg, Eds., *The Mammoth Book of Classic Science Fiction Short Novels of the 1930s,* Carroll & Graf Publishers, Inc.: N.Y., 1988, pp. ix-x.

36. Robert Silverberg, "Introduction," in Robert Silverberg, *World of a Thousand Colors,* Arbor House: NY, 1982, p. 11.

37. My consultant on pseudonyms was Norm Metcalf. He is the author of *(The) Index (of)/(to) (the) Science(-)Fiction Magazines 1951–1965,* J. Ben Stark, Publisher: El Cerrito, CA, 1968. In their encyclopedia entry on him, John Clute and Peter Nicholls term this book "essential to the serious sf researcher." Perhaps few have done as much research on the pseudonyms of science fiction authors as Metcalf.

38. Some of this is based on the checklist produced by Norm Metcalf in *The Devil's Work,* 2, #38, January, 1995, a fanzine distributed in mailing #230, February, 1995, of the Fantasy Amateur Press Association (FAPA).

39. Of these, five stories were written by four men writing *as women* (see Table 1). Other women, such as Susie M. Best, Clio Harper, Pauline E. Thomas, and especially Julia Boynton Green, published much poetry in these SF magazines, which I have not tabulated. Their additional

presence also belies the myth of exclusion. (I did, however, tabulate the number of female poets who appeared in *Weird Tales* during its first incarnation and discovered that 40% of the gender-identifiable poets published by the magazine were women. I will refer to this later.)

40. I thank John Locke for drawing my attention to this phenomenon.

41. Brian Aldiss and David Wingrove, *Trillion Year Spree: The History of Science Fiction*, Paladin Books: London, 1988, p. 346.

42. Andrew Ross, *Strange Weather*, London: Verso, 1991, p. 103.

Part I

Presumption of Prejudice

Science Fiction's Contested Terrain, 1926–1949

1

The Genesis of the Mythology

I T WAS 1927. A young mother finished her tale of disaster in outer space by typing "Mrs." on her byline and sending it off as an entry in a new magazine's short story contest. First prize was $500. The odds were against her. Attracted by the huge prize, 359 other aspiring authors had also sent in stories. Also, she was a novice and had only published one previous story, in the fantasy magazine *Weird Tales* ("A Runaway World," July, 1926).

And she did not win the top prize. . . .

But she did win Third Place, with a cash award and quick publication. Her story, "The Fate of the Poseidonia," appeared in the June, 1927 issue of Hugo Gernsback's *Amazing Stories*. With this, only a year after the medium was invented, Clare Winger Harris became the first woman to appear in a science fiction magazine. It was the beginning of a popular and rewarding science fiction career for Harris (see table 1), a field still so young that it was composed of only a single magazine. Nevertheless, she was there, almost from the beginning, with her name splashed on future covers to attract readers.

But, she should not have been there. As Shawna McCarthy informed us, there *were* no women in science fiction before the 1960s. McCarthy's version of women in science fiction, with which I opened this book, might well have been learned at the knee of Isaac Asimov himself. Asimov enunciated his version at St. Vincent College in Latrobe, Pennsylvania on April 14, 1983. In the 1930s and 1940s, he asserted, any woman who wanted to write for the science fiction magazines had to obscure her gender. This was because, he said, "science fiction was a male chauvinist field of unimaginable intensity. For one thing, it was 'understood' by everyone that science was not for women. Science was exclusively male. Furthermore, adventure stories were not for women. They were exclusively male, too. . . . Therefore science fiction, which was essentially adventure stories involving science, was *doubly* not for women!

"Besides," Asimov continued, perhaps thinking of himself, "most of the readership of science fiction magazines in their first decade or two of existence consisted of male adolescents who were . . . afraid of girls—I remember that very well! Therefore they didn't *want* girls in science fiction stories, and they didn't want women writing them."

Further, while science fiction editors in the 1930s might not have automatically rejected stories written by women, "some would've insisted on a male pseudonym." So pervasive was this supposed hostility that it was something female writers knew instinctively. They just sensed it and automatically hid their sex.[1]

Not, of course, that the practices Asimov describes would have applied to many women. According to science fiction writer Charles Platt, "women writers first invaded the field in large numbers during the 1960s," so there were virtually none before that date.[2] Baird Searles agreed that, "The female writers of science-fiction could be counted on the fingers of one hand in the days of the pulp magazines . . . science-fiction, until the last decade [the 1970s], had only a handful of women writers."[3]

But even this handful is too many for Janrae Frank, Jean Stine, and Forrest J. Ackerman. In their version of science fiction history, while some women wrote in the late 1920s, there was only a single one in the 1930s: Helen Weinbaum. And even her work, they assert, would never have been published had she not been the sister of the well-known Stanley G. Weinbaum. "Men of the 1930s," they asserted, "were unwilling to believe that a female writer could capture convincingly the reactions of a brawny, two-fisted masculine hero."[4]

Yet another SF writer, Thomas M. Disch, set forth similar views in his acclaimed 1999 Hugo Award-winning survey of science fiction. Very few women, he wrote, were "tempted to fight for rooms of their own" during the pulp era, and Judith Merril, along with C. L. Moore, were "The first women who did crash the party."[5] He alleged that the handful of women writing before 1956 got involved mainly because they were spouses of genre writers and "Often, like both Moore and Merril, they published under male pseudonyms."[6]

Many scholarly historians promulgate similar views. For example, Dr. William Sims Bainbridge flatly states (without ever producing any evidence) that there was a "prejudice against women authors" in early pulp science fiction. This "complex pattern of discrimination against women," he says, was "aggravated by factors like the targeted group of readers, the author's style and message, and the personalities of writer and editor."[7]

That sounds impressively authoritative, as do comparable assertions from other genre historians and commentators. "George Sand and George Eliot [neither of whom wrote for science fiction magazines] were not alone in having to assume male pseudonyms in self-defense," claimed Harlan Ellison in 1972. "For . . . almost fifty years in speculative fiction, we have denied ourselves perhaps *half* the great writers who might have been . . . we have disenfranchised and even blotted out an infinitude of views of our world as seen through eyes different and wonderful."[8] Almost 20 years later, editor Susanna J. Sturgis, in introducing her 1989 anthology of feminist science fiction stories, declared that the years before "the late 1970s" were "decades in which the few women in the field were often camouflaged by initials or androgynous first names."[9] Indeed, I could fill this page with a list of similar claims.[10]

Some critics have attempted to refute these charges. Science fiction author Pamela Sargent's pioneering 1970s anthologies performed invaluable work in making available stories by women writers from the 1940s and 1950s. In the 1980s Robin Roberts discussed "pulp science fiction's legacy to feminists," while in the 1990s Jane Donawerth revealed the utopian yearnings of the earliest women science fiction writers. In 2002 Justine Larbalestier explored the "battle of the sexes" as an enduring motif of 1926–1973 science fiction, and throughout these years Marleen S. Barr has investigated "feminist fabulation."[11]

Even so, their findings have not percolated out beyond their small audiences into the larger science fiction world and the world of most feminist academics who study science fiction. Instead, mythology continues to characterize the accepted wisdom of the field. However, as Connie Willis noted, the problem with the conventional wisdom—whether asserted by magazine editors, amateur historians, ostensibly scholarly academics, popular commentators, award-winning authors, presumably knowledgeable fans or even some feminists—*is that it simply isn't true*. The emperor has no clothes. These charges are part of a pervasive but entirely imaginary history concocted out of preconceptions and prejudice which, however plausible and compelling, is not grounded on evidence.

And that is the crucial point: *No evidence has ever been produced to substantiate these allegations.* Apparently none of these writers and critics have done what was necessary to establish their opinions and biases as facts: look at the record. Instead of going to the primary sources to discover the truth—the pulp magazines themselves—they have assumed what never was, and then invented elaborate reasons to rationalize their assumptions. If getting the facts right is what scholarship is all about, then there is as yet very little scholarship on women and early science fiction. What we have been presented with is simply theory without facts. Not only have *explanations* for the phenomenon been at fault, the historians and commentators cited have *not even demonstrated that the phenomenon itself existed.* The ruling worldview is never subjected to critical investigation and verification. It is so "obvious" that it needs no proof. This is a hallmark characteristic of cultural hegemony.

For example, was there was an active bias against women in the early science fiction magazines, as alleged? Ideally, this would require proof of sexual discrimination against women writers. Legally, one proves sex discrimination by finding disparate treatment of those similarly situated. In this case, that would be done by comparing rejection rates for stories *of equal quality*, and showing that those by women were disproportionately rejected. But, even if it were possible to agree on standards (always subjective in artistic situations) that would allow stories to be compared, the evidence—submitted manuscripts and rejection letters—has, of course, long since been lost. A lesser alternative would be to document examples of particular editors rejecting manuscripts from women out-of-hand simply because they were women. And that no one has done, either.

I acknowledge that historical research can be difficult. One must dig deeply to unearth the truth. This is especially the case with old magazines. While the pulps and their successors were a principal form of entertainment for millions of Americans for decades, relatively few survive. By their very nature, they were ephemeral, designed to appear on the newsstands for a month or two and then be tossed aside. Which most readers did. Few saved their copies.

Nor did the fragile survivors from this flood of magazines fare well. They were called "pulps" for a reason, being cheaply produced on cheap paper. Thus, the remnants from this tidal wave of print are hard to locate.

This makes it difficult to speak with any authority about what (and who) these magazines published, especially when it comes to women writers. As one group of presumed experts on these old writers admits, "With the exception of a rare anthologization, the works of all the women (and men) who wrote science-fiction before the mid-1960s are out of print, and considering the current structure of the publishing industry, likely to remain so. Their books can only be found by lucky browsers in used bookstores; whereas stories by women who wrote before 1950 are simply unobtainable except to the wealthy, who can afford to pay premium prices for the moldering pulps that alone contain their work."[12]

But getting one's hands dirty with the data—literally, when dealing with old magazines—is what scholarship is all about. And there are comprehensive archives of pulp magazines (or microfilms of them) in university libraries scattered all across America and places as far afield as Australia. Academic historians, in particular, should know this—and they have the least excuse for shoddy scholarship. It is their *job* to dig in the archives before presenting us with their interpretations. But the very basis of the scientific method—verification—is too often ignored by those who presume to write science fiction history.

A. Langley Searles pointed out this exact problem more than twenty years ago. In a survey of thirty-six books on the history and criticism of science fiction published before 1973, he said there was "a tendency to write books whose contents are open admissions that necessary backgrounds have not been researched properly."[13] Little seems to have changed in the two decades since he wrote those words.

I contend that the writing of science fiction history should be held to the same rigorous standards that govern every other type of historical writing. This means that conclusions must be grounded on the best available evidence, rather than presumptions and speculations. Conclusions must be based not on what one thinks *might* have happened or what *should* have happened or what *ought* to have happened—but, so far as it is possible to verify, on what *did* happen. Otherwise, as has often been the case, writing about speculative fiction simply becomes more speculative fiction.

Why is the mythology so hegemonic if there is no factual basis for it? One could simply dismiss it as an instance of Parson Weems's Law: "Historical fancy is more persistent than historical fact."[14] However, as psychologist Abraham Maslow once observed, if the only tool one has is a hammer—then all problems tend to look like nails to be hammered. Thus, it is true that science fiction, as it developed over the course of the 20th century, was predominantly a male cultural phenomenon. And if one's only tool for explaining gender disparity is gender *prejudice,* then it seems obvious that this is a salient example of prejudice at work, an obvious nail to hammer. But, in truly understanding why early science fiction was primarily a male activity, we should look beyond the simplistic charges of gender prejudice in science fiction.

For the most part, those who have attempted to explain why there have been fewer women than men in the science fiction field have failed to comprehend the social pervasiveness of *sexism* and have seen the problem simply as *bigotry.* Bigotry is essentially that of which early science fiction stands falsely accused. It is relatively straight forward, overt, and describes the alleged cases of someone refusing to print a story with a female byline simply and only because of the author's sex.

Since time immemorial women have indeed faced such open male bigotry and discrimination—in all societies and in all realms. Over 2,400 years ago in the fifth century B.C. the heroine of the Athenian playwright Aristophanes' *Thesmophoriazousae* was already lamenting, "Of course, everyone vies in condemning the tribe of women. That we are a scourge upon humanity and that everything is our fault: quarrels, discord, ominous civil war, sorrow."[15] Thus, it is easy and natural to believe that bigotry was the problem in pulp SF.

But the real hurdle early women SF writers faced was not alleged bigotry in the science fiction community, but the buried bias of sexism in society at large. Perhaps the reason critics have failed to understand this is because a cultural force like sexism (or racism) is more pervasive, more subtle, harder to see and harder to comprehend than bigoted actions resulting in blatant discrimination.

Critics have also failed to fully understand the nature of creativity and how sexism can exploit that nature in order to reinforce male dominance in a patriarchal society. The question is often asked, why haven't women "accomplished" more things and produced more "outstanding" individuals, at least according to the dominant society's standards? Obviously, women have been a majority in some activities, such as needle work or quilting. But these are considered "minor" activities, primarily *because* they are seen as "female." Recently, two peripheral art forms gaining more respect in the larger society are Navajo rug-weaving and Southwestern Pueblo Indian pottery. In both areas, women are the majority, and the most renowned, of the artists. (Interestingly, both began as purely private, domestic, utilitarian activities pursued daily by women and evolved into "public" art forms as they lost their primarily utilitarian aspect.)

Even so, there is a *perceived* lack of female "creativity" throughout human history and "creative" women have always been a minority in most fields, certainly the fields society most highly values.

To properly understand this phenomenon we must go beyond our usual naive understanding of creativity and of creative individuals. Almost universally we have adopted an inheritance from the Romantic era which sees creativity as a heroic solitary activity and the creative individual as a lone Byronic genius who will prevail in "his" vision no matter what the odds.

However, this Romantic myth distorts the nature of creativity and misinterprets the roles of both the individual and society. The work of University of Chicago psychologist Mihaly Csikszentmihalyi and Harvard University psychologist Howard Gardner, in particular, has transformed our understanding of the nature of creativity. Csikszentmihalyi significantly altered our conception of creativity by asking not, "What is creativity?," but, rather, "Where is creativity?" As he pointed out, creativity is not primarily an isolated individual activity, but the result of a social system at work. "Therefore, creativity does not happen inside people's heads, but in the interaction between a person's thoughts and a sociocultural context. It is a systemic rather than an individual phenomenon."[16]

Gardner elaborated upon this insight when he asserted that, "creative activities are only known as such when they have been *accepted in a particular culture* . . . nothing is, or is not, creative *in and of itself.* Creativity is inherently a communal or cultural judgment." Both Gardner and Csikszentmihalyi see the "creative system" as a dynamically interactive "creativity triangle" involving the individual, the domain or discipline within which that individual is working, and the field (judges and/or institutions acting as "gatekeepers") which renders the verdict as to whether or not the domain work of the individual is creative. "No matter how talented the individual is, in some abstract sense," says Gardner, "unless he or she can connect with a domain and produce works that are valued by the relevant field, it is not possible to ascertain whether that person in fact merits the epithet 'creative.'"[17]

Creativity, then, results from the dialectic of these three elements working to change an existing domain or to transform it into a new domain. In other words, creativity operates in a reciprocal rather than unidirectional fashion. It is born out of the *interaction* between the individual and society, rather than from the individual alone. And the workings of this system begin when the individual is exposed (often at a young age) to a domain ("connects with a domain," in Gardner's words) absorbing its symbolic rules and procedures. Only through such initial (leading to long-term) exposure to a domain will the individual acquire the knowledge and skills necessary to propose something "new" to the expert gatekeepers who then weigh the proposal against the standards of the field.

Thus, because creativity is a systemic phenomenon, the crucial factor that determines "success" for the "creative" individual is whether or not the system will encourage, support, and nurture the individual's talents, that is, allow that individual to "connect." When that social validation and support happens, the individual is deemed "creative."

In our present discussion, in addition to failing to distinguish between bigotry and sexism, critics have also universally failed to discern how the creative system works. They have presumed a prejudice (bigotry) against women would-be science fiction writers on the part of the field—the publishers, editors, and readers who made up the gatekeepers of the domain. In fact, however, the problem was (like sexism itself) in another part of the creativity system. *Because of the buried bias of sexism, society denied women exposure to pertinent domains of activity, the most basic level of the creative system.* Entire realms of cultural activity therefore became "hidden knowledge" because they were closed to women. The system did not provide the social support and validation needed for women to become "creative" (at least in the fields that the dominant society valued). Historically, women have not been allowed to "connect" to socially valued domains of artistic activity.

Indeed, the system actively worked *against* women, *withholding* the crucial social support and resources, the exposure to the knowledge, and the validation of effort needed to be "creative." It was akin to placing a potted plant in a darkened closet and starving it of water and nutrients—and then deriding the stunted plant for not producing a bountiful harvest. Motivated by a virtually universal patriarchal ideology of female subordination, a male ruling class manipulated the nature of the creativity system to maintain male dominance and prevent women from being "creative."

For example, throughout history and in all societies, there have been formal prohibitions against educating women, against women becoming writers, actors, painters, or artists of many other kinds. There has been a gendered separation of spheres of activity. The "proper" and "moral" male sphere was the public world stage, where war and politics and history happened. Meanwhile, the "proper" and "moral" female sphere was seen as that of the private domestic world: home and hearth.

Today, in many fundamentalist Islamic (and some Hindu) societies, women still enter purdah at puberty, a secluded existence in which they literally vanish from the public eye. They don the burka, the chador, or the veil, walling themselves off from the world and from the eyes of all men save their husbands, and that only in the privacy of the home.

But, this is only an extreme version of how the West once treated women, as well. Almost 2,500 years ago, in his essay *Oeconomicus,* the Greek historian Xenophon argued that women should—literally—be kept indoors and out of public sight at all times and he praised the unnamed bride of his character, Ischomachus, as the model of a virtuous "kept" woman. The great Athenian leader Pericles also pronounced that the most admirable and "virtuous" woman was she whose name was never spoken in public—the more absent and invisible the woman, the more unheard and unmentioned, the more honorable she was deemed. Thus, for example, we don't know the name of the aristocratic mother of Alcibiades, one of the most important and charismatic figures in Athenian history.

Not surprisingly, therefore, Athens, the reputed wellspring of Western civilization, passed laws restricting women from appearing in public or participating in any civic activities. The only "public" women were women without virtue, the *hetairai,* prostitutes and concubines. Hence, almost by definition, for a woman to be seen in public was to be seen as a prostitute, a situation very similar to that in modern fundamentalist Islamic cultures.[18]

Nor was there public education of any kind for ancient Greek women. They had no need of it in their domestic married lives. Nor was there much time for any such education before they were married off. Citizen-class women could be married as young as age eleven and were very frequently married by thirteen or fourteen. Their youth, therefore, was cut short and their adult lives as wives and mothers began early. Nor, once they became widows, could they inherit property.[19]

Likewise, the women of Rome, that other fount of Western civilization, could not vote, serve on juries, or partake in political life. Indeed, their very names were virtually generic, signifying their family lineage. "Julia" was of the Julian clan, "Claudia" was of the Claudian clan, and so on. It therefore came as a shock to Romans when they encountered women in other societies—such as Cleopatra of Egypt, Boudicca of Britain, or Zenobia of Palmyra—who not only partook of public life, but ruled. It seemed unnatural to them, indeed, a perverse aberration. And in all three of these examples, Rome conquered these queens and destroyed their countries. Of the three, only Zenobia lived to be paraded in chains through the streets of Rome in the triumphal procession of her conqueror, reduced, at last, to the private sphere where she belonged.

This private sphere to which Pericles and the Romans and their comrades around the world relegated women was a world essentially outside of history, timeless and unchanging throughout the ages. Therefore, from the dominant male viewpoint, there was no real "female past" to human history, as nothing "happened" in the domestic world. "A woman's work was never done," as it was simply an endless round of the same domestic chores, repeated daily, for all time. History was past politics—and women did not take part in politics. History was literally "his story," the story of "Great Men" and what they did on the public stage. Basically, women, did not have a past.

And for their eternal domestic lives, women could be instructed by their mothers. Education was at best pointless, at worst dangerous, as it might raise women above their "natural" station. But for the male public sphere, education was essential. Thus, for long eons (and even still in some parts of the world), education and training in public activities of all kinds (such as the arts) were properly seen as a male monopoly. And not only was education and the arts properly "male," but education and the arts themselves taught that this exclusion of women from the public sphere was "morally correct" and "in accordance with the whole tradition of western civilization."[20] Therefore, as Jane Austen noted in her 1818 novel, *Persuasion,* "Men have had every advantage of us in telling their own story. Education has been theirs in so much higher a degree; the pen has been in their hands."

In her essay, "A Room of One's Own," Virginia Woolf famously highlighted a few of the obstacles which might have kept the pen out of the hands of a hypothetical sister of William Shakespeare, who began his interaction with the theater as an actor. His "sister" could not have begun acquiring her knowledge of the theater in like fashion because the Elizabethan Age was one in which Lady Macbeth and Juliet had to be played by men and boys, as women were forbidden to appear on the (public) stage. Indeed, women had no exposure to the domain at any level except that of passive audience. Hence, the "sister" would never have had a chance to absorb its symbolic rules and procedures. The bigoted gatekeepers of the field would therefore never even have been presented with the products of Shakespeare's "sister" to accept or reject because she would not have been able to master step one: produce a play. The necessary knowledge had been hidden from her. She thus would not have become a "creative" person, at least in this public realm.[21]

Likewise, how difficult it must have been for the few European female painters of the 1500s and 1600s to learn their skills in an age which judged talent above all by the ability to portray the nude—and yet the age prohibited women from viewing the nude body. Again, the necessary knowledge was, literally, hidden from them. Indeed, since history began much "public" cultural knowledge has been similarly hidden from women by their exclusion from all but domestic activities. Even the "privileged" women of the Ottoman seraglio were kept illiterate.

Because of such exclusion, all "creative" women of the past had to struggle initially just for simple exposure to and knowledge of the pertinent domain of cultural activity, struggle for access to the hidden knowledge, struggle just to learn to read and write. Without such exposure and knowledge, they were largely unable to proceed to the next stage and produce something for the field's gatekeepers to judge—which is the only stage most critics are able to discern. Thus, it is because societies have routinely failed to nurture (indeed, have stifled) the creative "public sphere" talents of women at the most basic level—and shunted them off into a purdah of "private, domestic sphere" activities instead—which has accounted for the dearth of female artists in most fields, rather than any lack of intellectual or artistic potential.

But, time marches on and barriers fall. And sometimes they *don't*. History is not necessarily linear and sometimes "progress" conceals regressive aspects. As Joanna Russ reminds us, "it's important to realize that the absence of formal prohibitions against committing art does not preclude the presence of powerful, informal ones."[22] Social forces continued to discourage female participation in the (public) arts and the world of ideas. They continued in myriad subtle (and not-so-subtle) ways to withhold cultural knowledge to the advantage of men and disadvantage of women. For example, "In 1873, when less than 15 percent of college students [in America] were female, Harvard's Edward Clarke explained scientifically how expanding a woman's brain would make her uterus shrink. In 1889, when women still made up less than 20 percent of the college students, the eminent scientist R. R. Coleman warned college women, 'You are on the brink of destruction. . . . Beware! Science pronounces that the woman who studies is lost.' "[23] Here we see how the buried bias of sexism works informally to deny women exposure to and a working knowledge of various (public) cultural domains, even in the absence of formal prohibitions.

A pertinent example of this phenomenon for our purposes might be found in Isaac Asimov's contention that the prevailing social attitude of the 1930s was that science itself was not for women.[24] What an anomaly, then, for someone like two-time Nobel Prize-winner Marie Curie to have emerged. Even her "best friend" and husband, French scientist Pierre Curie, dismissed and discouraged her when she first contacted him seeking technical assistance on her own research. He felt women were a distraction from scientific work. And even after winning Pierre over, she was still alone in scientific circles. At the famous 1911 Solvay Conference of outstanding scientists, for example, Marie Curie was the only female among the 24 scientists in attendance.

Science fiction writer Charles Platt argued that this was still the objection made against women science fiction writers decades later, when they supposedly "first invaded the field" in the 1960s. "Could they really write the hard stuff [science-oriented SF]? Could they handle drive tubes and tractor beams and hyperspace? Shouldn't they leave high-tech to the men, and concentrate instead on more, er, appropriate material?"[25]

Indeed, the culture has in the past seen and continues in the present to see science as "male" and, therefore, an inappropriate area of interest and activity for women. In fact, some continue to argue that women are simply not as "biologically" suited for science and the related field of mathematics as are men. This was what Dr. Lawrence H. Summers, the president of Harvard University, raised as a possibility at an academic conference of scientists and engineers in 2005, thereby igniting a firestorm of criticism. Summers cited research documenting that more high school boys than girls tended to score at very high levels on standardized math tests and suggested this may be due to biological differences between the sexes. "I certainly believe that there's been some move in the research away from believing that all these things are shaped only by socialization," he said.[26]

It is true that there are great differences between American males and females when it comes to test scores in math and science, as in other areas. Indeed, "Researchers who have explored the subject of sex differences from every conceivable angle and organ say that yes, there are a host of discrepancies between men and women—in their average scores on tests of quantitative skills, in their attitudes toward math and science, in the architecture of their brains, in the way they metabolize medications, including those that affect the brain."[27] And these "sex differences" have long been clear when it comes to math, where American boys have outscored American girls on the standardized SAT exam by 30 to 35 points for decades.

But, it still remains unclear which roles nature and nurture play in these gender differences. For example, "In an international standardized test administered in 2003 by the international research group Organization for Economic Cooperation and Development to 250,000 15-year-olds in 41 countries, boys did moderately better on the math portion in just over half the nations. For nearly all the other countries, there were no significant sex differences." Further, "Japanese girls . . . were on a par with Japanese boys on every math section save that of 'uncertainty,' which measures probabilistic skills, and Japanese girls scored higher over all than did the boys of many other nations, *including the United States.* In Iceland, girls broke the mold completely and outshone Icelandic boys by a significant margin on all parts of the test, as they habitually do on their national math exams. . . . The modest size and regional variability of the sex differences in math scores . . . convince many researchers that neither sex has a monopoly on basic math ability, and that culture rather than chromosomes explains findings like the gap in math SAT scores."[28]

Thus, we cannot so quickly dismiss socialization as the cause for this phenomenon, as Harvard President Summers later admitted.[29] This is because it is unarguable fact that women have traditionally been *discouraged* from investigating science. Science fiction writer Chelsea Quinn Yarbro (b. 1942), for instance, recalls that, "When I was in grammar school the librarian would not allow me to read books on paleontology because that wasn't for girls. So I had to content myself with the encyclopedia at home."[30] Likewise, science fiction writer Joan D. Vinge (b. 1948) tells us that, "When I was young I swallowed the line that girls don't really need to know about math . . . [and] I never got a strong background in technology."[31]

Donna Shirley also shared this experience of discouragement. At the age of 12 she read science fiction writer Arthur C. Clarke's 1951 book, *The Sands of Mars*, and became enthralled with the idea of space travel. "I remember thinking, 'I can do this. I can build spaceships and go to Mars,'" she said. But when she entered college and told her adviser at the University of Oklahoma that she wanted to be an engineer, he told her that, "girls do not become engineers." Against the opposition of her advisor, Shirley persisted in her science and science fiction dreams. She went on to lead the NASA team that built the Mars Pathfinder spacecraft which deposited the robot rover Sojourner on Mars in 1997. She also managed NASA's entire Mars exploration program from 1994–1998. In her 32 years as an engineer at NASA's Jet Propulsion Laboratory she helped build and send spaceships to every planet in the Solar System except Pluto.[32]

Yarbro was in elementary school in the late 1940s and early 1950s, Vinge was there in the late 1950s and early 1960s, and Shirley entered college in 1960, but such social discouragement of young girls and women from expressing an interest in science, math, and engineering seems to have persisted for decades thereafter. For instance, genre historian Jane Donawerth's research reveals that, "In the United States in 1984, women composed 20 percent of the scientific staff in medical research, 9 percent of the academic appointments (but only 1.5 percent of the faculty) in chemistry, and held less than 5 percent of engineering doctorates. . . . Although women made up 45 percent of the workforce in the United States in 1983, they represented only 13 percent of the science and engineering jobs. College training for women in the sciences decreased from the 1920s to the 1960s, and the increases from 1970 to 1985 seem to have stopped. In Great Britain in 1986–1987, only 11 percent of the students in engineering at universities were women and only 9 percent of the students at polytechnics. In computer studies, the percentage of women students in higher education decreased from 24 percent in 1980 to 10 percent in 1987. . . . In 1992, women constituted only 18 percent of engineers and scientists in the United States; only 14 percent of the bachelor's degrees in engineering, 31 percent of the bachelor's degrees in the physical sciences, and 34 percent of master's degrees and 28 percent of doctoral degrees in science and engineering went to women."[33] Meanwhile, a June, 2000 survey of its membership by the American Astronomical Society discovered that only 18.7 percent of its 6,000-plus members were female and that only 5 percent of full professors of astronomy were female.[34]

And there are many reasons to believe that such gender socialization continues to this day, at least in America, as math and science are still seen as "inappropriate" fields for women. For instance, Dr. C. Megan Urry, a Yale professor of physics and astronomy, cites a 1983 study in which 360 people, half men and half women, rated math papers on a five-point scale. "On average, the men rated them a full point higher when the author was 'John T. McKay' than when the author was 'Joan T. McKay.' There was a similar, but smaller, disparity in the scores the women gave." Again, in a recent Princeton experiment, "when students were asked to evaluate two highly qualified candidates for an engineering job—one with more education, the other with more work experience—they picked the more educated candidate 75 percent of the time. But, when the candidates were designated as male or female, and the educated candidate bore a female name, suddenly she was preferred only 48 percent of the time."[35]

Such biased attitudes toward women in science were also revealed by the research of Harvard-Radcliffe social psychologist Mahzarin Banaji. Dr. Banaji developed an "Implicit Association Test" of our unconscious "prejudices, stereotypes, racial profiles, and ingrained biases." Making it available online, she collected data from one and a half *million* web site visitors between 1998–2001. "It demonstrates that nearly all of us have unconscious, preformed attitudes about race, sex, ethnicity, sexual preference, and obesity," she said. "Yet when we ask people about their attitudes, that's not what we hear. . . . What people say *explicitly* is quite different from what the tool shows about their *implicit* attitudes." Thus, we find that "unconscious stereotypes are deeply embedded in both individuals and cultures. Common associations, like male = science or female = liberal arts, are stubbornly fixed in the unconscious, even when they run counter to consciously held beliefs."[36]

Bear in mind, these are not just attitudes held by males. Females also hold attitudes toward science and math which see these fields as inappropriate areas in which women should excel. Thus, for example, "Women's math scores are also known to fall when the proportion of men in the room increases," suggesting that the "maleness" of the subject is being made more salient to the participating females.[37]

These ingrained gender attitudes seem to be in place at a very young age, as research by the American Association of University Women has revealed.[38] They found that girls begin to lose interest in math, computers, and related topics at the elementary school level. These implicit social biases then have a continuing impact upon the later gender makeup of the sciences. For example, although more women than men now graduate from American colleges and 56 percent of all college students in the year 2000 were women (accounting for 1.6 million more female than male students), women were a *minority* of majors in subjects such as computer science.

On July 12, 2000, the American Association of University Women released the results of a two-year study of American girls and computer use. The study found that, despite anecdotal evidence to the contrary, "girls are . . . turned off by America's computer culture." Department of Education statistics reported that only 17 percent of high school computer science advanced placement tests were taken by girls. At the college level, "just 28 percent of computer science undergraduate degrees" were earned by women. (This seemed to reflect an upward trend from 10 percent of college computer science students being female in 1987, but female interest in computer science has tended to fluctuate instead of following a steadily upward pattern.)

But this minority participation by women in the computer revolution was not found to be due to any active anti-female bias by a male establishment. Rather, the study concluded, girls just "find computer programming boring, electronic games too redundant and violent, and computer careers too solitary and anti-social." Put simply, girls, beginning at a very young age, just aren't as interested in computers as are boys.[39] Thus, because "Getting girls interested in computers and mathematics and encouraging them to stick with it is a tall order for schools," many colleges, such as the University of Pittsburgh, are developing intervention programs to provide elementary and middle-school girls with computer and math skills.[40]

Nevertheless, what seems to be true of computer science and math appears to be also true in other scientific areas. For instance, of the 21 million subscribers to *Discover, Scientific American,* and seven other popular science magazines in 2002–2003 dealing with such areas as engineering, astronomy, and physics, more than 80 percent were male. *Popular Mechanics,* the most popular of the magazines, had virtually no female subscribers.[41]

This female aversion to science is at odds with other trends in female education. Throughout the industrial world, according to the previously cited 2003 report released by the Paris-based Organization for Economic Cooperation and Development, girls are better readers than boys and more women than men graduate from college (except in Switzerland, Japan, and Turkey). This corresponds with various American surveys which reveal that girls comprise 60 percent of high school National Honor Society memberships and high school girls greatly outnumber boys in advanced placement courses.

Obviously, women everywhere have the ability to excel intellectually. Why, then, do American girls continue to score lower than boys in math and science? Simply, "A lot [of this] has to do with the way women are reared and socialized," explains microbiologist Alice Reinarz, Associate Dean for Undergraduate Studies at Texas A&M in College Station. "If they get the message from families and teachers that they can do well in science, they will. If they get several messages that they can't do math or science, then they won't."[42]

For a variety of social reasons, then, women are peripheral to science (which is seen as a "male" domain) and seem to be (have been conditioned to be?) less interested in it than men. The pervasive sexism of a patriarchal society, which divided (and still divides) men and women into gendered spheres of "proper" and "appropriate" activity, subtly denied or discouraged female exposure to and knowledge of the pertinent domains, which were seen as "inappropriate" for them.

Hence, few women would even *read* science fiction (and gain exposure to it as a domain of creativity) if society at large saw it as "the literature of science" and actively discouraged women from reading this "gender-inappropriate" literature. For example, Marilyn vos Savant, a member of Mensa and the author of a popular syndicated newspaper column which purports to answer all questions of logic, tells us that, when she was a girl, "My parents strongly encouraged reading, but not science fiction, which both thought would be harmful."[43]

This cultural division into separate public (male) and private (female) spheres—and not the commonly (and simplistically) alleged bigotry and discrimination of the field's gatekeepers—was the primary reason why women made up a minority of science fiction writers (and readers) in the 1920s and beyond—as, indeed, they still do today. If society at large said science was not for women, and if science fiction was seen to be *the literature of science,* then, obviously, both men *and women* would believe that women were unwelcome (or did not exist) in the science fiction community. (Or could not contribute anything worthwhile to the field.)

However, this perception never had anything to do with reality. In reality, the fields of science and science fiction were completely at odds with each other—at least when it came to participation by outsider groups, such as women. Where elitist and patriarchical science shunned women and tolerated their presence only reluctantly—democratic and egalitarian science fiction welcomed them enthusiastically. Thus, in the question of who could participate, the *reality* of science fiction was one of *opposition* to science. The reason for this difference in the realm of actual practice is that, *science fiction is a form of popular culture.* Hence, the actual *practice* of science fiction partakes more of the nature of popular culture than of the professionalized nature of science. And, because of the contested terrain nature of popular culture, it is much more democratic and open to participation by outsider groups than institutionalized professional fields, like science.

In addition, Joanna Russ has argued that the very nature of science fiction, *as a literature,* is different from other forms of literature, making it especially receptive to female participation. Other types of literature are inherently limited because they are tied to depictions of traditionally gendered societies. But, "The myths of science fiction (the plots, the basic stories) are without gender. They can happen to either sex. The problems-conflicts-plots of science fiction are about the adventures of the human mind or spirit, so it is perfectly possible to imagine a world with seven sexes or perfect equality, though I do not think we do this very well, as writers are only human, and most SF writers subscribe to the good old cliches. But still, SF is committed to exploring new worlds, not only physically but conceptually; finding out what the rules of a society are; making machines; assessing social and ecological consequences. It is its science-fictional-ness that keeps it free from gender stereotypes . . . SF is open-ended *per se*."[44]

Unfortunately, because this particular form of popular culture, this literature, is so closely linked to a particular professional field, science, it has often been perceived as merely the popular expression of that professional field. Because the image has been so blinding, few have been able to see past it to the reality. The science fiction field, as a realm of *popular culture,* may have been holding the door open for increased participation by women—but if the larger society was doing all it could to discourage women from being interested in and partici-pating in the "male" sphere of science, few women would walk through the open door.

And perhaps such pervasive sexism and gendered expectations also goes far in explaining why some male *authors* from that era had difficulty in remember-ing their female counterparts: These women could not be contributing anything of consequence to a field which was, obviously, "not for them." If some of those males who were also "present at the creation" believed there were few or no women writers, it may have been because their own expectations (created by sexist presumptions of the field) made it difficult (or impossible) for them to see, or to remember, female colleagues. For example, perhaps they simply didn't take any story written by a woman (in a field which was "not for them") *seri-ously* and so didn't *read* stories by their fellow (female) authors—and so would not remember what they had ignored.

This *perception* of the field as "male" (because it was the literature of "male" science) may also have contributed to viewers, both male and female, overlook-ing the women who were actually there in early science fiction. One sees what one expects to see and *everyone's* worldview in the period under discussion was seen through the distorting lens of sexism. Hence, if society believed women weren't *interested* in (reading about) science or adventure stories, it therefore followed that women obviously weren't *writing* about science and adventure. Perhaps preconceptions so colored perceptions that people didn't register aber-rant observations which didn't fit the expected pattern, so these discrepancies were forgotten. Thus, women authors in these early science fiction magazines literally became "the women men didn't see." Likewise, their stories became "the stories men didn't read." The dominant cultural paradigm said such women and such stories could not exist—therefore they did not.

Maybe this explains well-known SF writer Frederik Pohl's statement that no one *knew* there were any female writers before the mid-1940s. He agreed there were *some* female writers, but "Until the mid-40s at the earliest, and maybe later than that," he said, "they either wrote under initials like C. L. Moore, for Catherine Moore, or with a pen name like Andre Norton, for Mary Alice Norton [sic], or with an androgynous name like Leslie F. Stone."[45] This is an extraordinary statement coming from someone who was *married* to *three* early female science fiction writers: "Leslie Perri" (published in 1941), Dorothy LesTina (published in 1943), and "Judith Merril" (first published in 1948).[46]

Pohl's attitude sounds suspiciously like a husband's standard sexist dismissal of the "little lady's" artistic efforts, which are not to be taken seriously, even though published, and therefore not to be read, not to be remembered. Thus, Pohl's amnesia about the work of his own wives (two of whom had published SF before they married him and the third published *while* they were married) may also help explain the amnesia of some other male authors from our period. If these men didn't see women authors or read them because they felt their work was trivial or irrelevant or because women writers and their work could not possibly exist—the men had no memory of them.

This discounting of female contributions would also explain why *later* editors of anthologies, seeking "the best" to republish for new readers, would so seldom select stories by female authors. For example, although they were not literally the first, perhaps the two most important early SF anthologies, which set the tone for many that were to follow, were the now-classic *Adventures in Time and Space* (Random House, 1946), edited by Raymond J. Healy and Francis McComas, and *The Best of Science Fiction* (Crown, 1946), edited by Groff Conklin. These anthologies reprinted stories from the almost impossible to find old pulps which the editors claimed were "representative" of the field. It is significant, however, that *none* of these three men had ever edited a science fiction magazine.

The two books had a pervasive and influential impact on the post-World War II perception of early science fiction because they were issued by major publishers and were large hardcover overviews of the literature announcing, in effect, that this genre was now worth consideration. Nothing of their like had previously appeared. They were widely-distributed and became major reference sources on pulp science fiction for decades thereafter. Frequent publication of new editions also made them newly-available to subsequent generations of readers. Random House, for example, published a new edition of the Healy and McComas book in 1957 and Conklin's was republished by Bonanza in 1963 and by Del Rey in 1979. Thus, they essentially established the canon of early science fiction—a canon in which women writers were glaringly absent.

Of the forty stories in Conklin's book, only one might have been perceived as being by a woman: Leslie F. Stone's "The Conquest of Gola." Another story, "The Piper's Son," was by "Lewis Padgett," one of the pseudonyms of Henry Kuttner and C. L. Moore. Of the thirty-three stories (there were two additional articles) in the Healy and McComas book, there was *not one* female byline (although there were three stories by "Lewis Padgett"). Thus, only one out of the seventy-three stories in these seminal anthologies was perhaps identifiable as being by a woman—and then only if new readers were already aware that pulp author Leslie F. Stone was female, a doubtful proposition. The female presence may as well have been non-existent. No wonder new readers being introduced to "pulp science fiction" for the first time via these popular reprint anthologies believed there were no women in early science fiction!

There were also other, more mundane, obstacles to female participation in science fiction which illustrated how gendered social roles kept women from "connecting" with the domain. Not only did sexism exclude them from the public sphere, but the private domestic sphere to which they were relegated tended to consume all of their time and energy. For example, women have always—even in today's more "enlightened" times—shouldered the major burdens of childcare and housework. These are full-time jobs, leaving little time for "creative" endeavors like writing stories. To do so would be like rowing against the wind and tide, as Harriet Beecher Stowe once put it. Stowe, the author of the classic *Uncle Tom's Cabin*, described a typical day for her as beginning with the teaching for an hour in the local school and ending with two hours of reading in the evening to her children. Since starting the writing of a note describing her daily routine she was called off a dozen times: Once to buy codfish from a fisherman selling door-to-door, once to see a man who brought a barrel of apples, then to nurse the baby, then into the kitchen to make a chowder for dinner. Nothing but deadly determination ever enabled her to write, she said, and she wrote more than she ever thought she could.

But, said Nobel laureate James Watson, decoder of DNA mysteries, one must be slightly underemployed if one is going to do something significant. Few women throughout history have been privileged enough to be slightly underemployed. Nor have they been without duties, almost without external communication, which the great German poet Rainer Maria Rilke said was necessary for creativity. Nor have they shared Joseph Conrad's great isolation from the world, "in a room of one's own," in which he supposed that he slept and ate the food put before him, but he was never aware of the even flow of daily life, made easy and noiseless for him by a silent, watchful, tireless affection from his wife—who is remembered today only by Conrad scholars.[47]

How might such domestic responsibilities, restrictions from domain knowledge, and dismissal of one's work as trivial have worked on female science fiction writers? Naomi Mitchison (1897–1998), author of the science fiction classics *Memoirs of a Space Woman* and *Solution Three*, touched on a few of the social and psychological barriers. For her, they were primarily a lack of education (even though born in a wealthy family) and the responsibilities of motherhood. She was related to two noted British scientists. Her father was the biologist J. S. Haldane and her brother the geneticist J. B. S. Haldane. As a child she worked in her father's lab as his assistant, performed scientific experiments with her brother and Aldous Huxley when they were children, and "Hoped to be a scientist."

But, this early exposure to a domain of knowledge was shortly curtailed and, while her brother was sent to the best schools, she was educated at home by a governess. She insightfully realized that, because of what we would today term sexism, "certain avenues of understanding were closed to me by what was considered suitable or unsuitable for a little girl." Therefore, "owing to incomplete education and no degree—[I] had to write . . . largely while pushing prams. . . . Had four boys and two girls."[48]

Carol Emshwiller (b. 1921) and Kate Wilhelm (b. 1928) represent a later generation of women science fiction writers. Emshwiller began writing in the 1950s when childcare was still expected to be a mother's full and only job. "Sometimes she would pick up her typewriter and sit with it inside the children's playpen while her children played and raged around her. She sat and wrote, ignoring them as best she could."[49] Hardly an environment conducive to great writing—or writing at all!

Kate Wilhelm also encountered many social deterrents to artistic expression, not least being the disproportionate responsibilities of motherhood and the nearly universal trivialization to which women's artistic efforts have been consigned. "The family . . . [will] think it's cute or precocious, or at least, not dangerous, when a woman starts to write stories," she said. "What I got from my in-laws was that line that it didn't hurt anything, kept me home nights, and didn't cost anyone anything . . . no one . . . thought it was anything but a passing fancy. . . . It's the condescension that's hardest to take. . . . My first husband never read a word I wrote until after I left him. He knew it was all trivial."[50]

Even after Wilhelm divorced her first husband and married fellow science fiction author Damon Knight, "There were so many pressures to force me into giving up writing again, to become mother, housewife, etc. . . . My husband was sympathetic and wanted me to write, but seemed powerless. . . . I realized the world, everyone in it practically, will give more and more responsibilities to any woman who will continue to accept it [sic]. And when the other responsibilities are too great, her responsibility to herself must go. Or she has to take a thoroughly selfish position and refuse the world, and then accept whatever guilt there is. Unless a woman knows she is another Virginia Woolf or Jane Austen, how can she say no . . . ? It is generally expected that the children, the house, school functions, husband's needs, yard, etc. all come first . . . to reverse that order . . . is hard. Nothing in our background has prepared us for this role."[51] Unfortunately, unlike men, wives don't have wives to take the daily burdens of life from them so that they may become creative geniuses.

Finally, the "standard operating procedure" of the magazine world (the social system of pulp magazine creativity, if you will), centered in New York City, also

worked against female participation, against connecting to that particular cultural domain.

First of all, pulp authors made very little money, even as late as the 1950s.
One had to be exceedingly prolific (difficult for a woman, for the reasons noted
above) to make any substantial material returns on the time investment. Robert
Silverberg recalled that, in the Fifties, the SF magazines "were cheap—35 cents
was the universal cover price—and they were cheaply printed, most of them, by
nonunion houses in odd corners of the country, and they paid their writers
pretty cheaply, too. The best that a writer could hope for, generally, was three
cents a word; some paid as little as a cent a word. (The average magazine short
story was about six thousand words. At a fee of three cents a word, the writer
would have received $180 for a story that might have taken him a week or two
[of splendid isolation] to write. At one cent a word, the same story would have
brought $60. Out of this . . . came a share for the IRS and very often a 10 percent
commission for the writer's agent.) Nobody got rich writing for those magazines, and I doubt that anybody got rich publishing them."[52]

Such lack of financial reward for so much time investment would alone have
discouraged many wives and mothers from becoming pulp writers. How were
they to justify such trivial and irrelevant activity in a realm which was, in any
case, inappropriate for a woman—especially when their husbands knew there
were far more important domestic duties they should be attending to?

And then there was the way one managed to break out of the slushpile. Silverberg, who lived in New York City in the Fifties, made a point of visiting the
various SF magazine publishers and getting to know them. "In their offices," he
recalled, "I saw the stacks of manuscripts, five and six feet high, that hopeful
writers sent to them every day. Some of the editors read everything that came
in that way, some of them read hardly any of it, but all of them agreed that 99
percent of it was unpublishable. They preferred to deal with reliable pros who
visited their New York offices, talked with them about the art of writing science
fiction, and brought stories in person. Very quickly they sized me up, promoted
me to that little group of pros and by the time I was twenty-one I was earning
a living, and quite a nice living, writing for their magazines.

"Every morning," Silverberg continued, describing a bachelor routine seemingly devoid of all domestic chores, "I went to my desk and watched stories
come flowing from my typewriter. In a really hot week I might write one a day,
Tuesday through Friday. On the weekend I rested and on Monday I made the
rounds of the editorial offices, dropping off last week's output and picking up
any that might have been rejected. (Not too many were rejected, thank God,
but when it did happen I smiled bravely and carried the story over to someone
else's office, where it usually sold.)"[53]

For women writers who might not have lived in New York City, who might
not have been free to go directly to their typewriters in the morning and spend

the entire day isolated at the keyboard, and who might not have been able to visit editors in their offices every Monday to schmooze about the art of science fiction—the odds of publication were against them, even if they were outstanding writers. The social system of creativity itself worked against them as it did not encourage, support, and nurture their participation. Instead, it served to confine them to their domestic spheres and discourage and disable their participation in the public sphere of magazines.

Thus, most likely, they would have remained in that six foot high pile of unread manuscripts. This was not because the editors were biased against publishing women writers, but because, due to social pressures and strictures, they simply were not able to live the lifestyle a successful pulp writer needed to live in order to publish and survive. Even Silverberg, who said he was possessed by a "demonic energy" at the time, admitted that no one could continue to live that way for a protracted period. Most women could not live that way for even a short period. It was simply the way the world was. It wasn't organized in a way that would support and encourage a woman who wanted to engage in this type of life.

And this was why there were so few women writers in the pulp science fiction magazines. It wasn't because of alleged bigotry on the part of science fiction editors who refused to publish anything from a woman. It was because of the nature of a creative system designed by a sexist society to connect men to the wider world, while simultaneously disconnecting women to that same world.

Nevertheless, not only did women writers—against all the odds the world could deal them—appear in the science fiction magazines, but women were present from the very beginning of the literature.

Notes

1. Eric Leif Davin, "The Good Doctor at St. Vincent," *Fantasy Commentator,* VII, No. 4, 1992, p. 248.

2. Charles Platt, *Dream Makers, Volume II,* p. 192.

3. Baird Searles, with Martin Last, Beth Meacham, and Michael Franklin, *A Reader's Guide to Science Fiction,* Avon Books: N.Y., 1979, pp. 23, 264.

4. Janrae Frank, Jean Stine, and Forrest J. Ackerman, Eds., "Introduction," *New Eves: Science Fiction About the Extraordinary Women of Today and Tomorrow,* Long Meadow Press: Stamford, Conn., 1994, p. ix.

5. Thomas M. Disch, *The Dreams Our Stuff Is Made Of: How Science Fiction Conquered the World,* The Free Press: N.Y., 1998, p. 115.

6. Disch, p. 115. As with so many other of these statements, this Hugo Award-winning claim is false. Both Merril and Moore published *before* they married genre authors and neither ever published solo under a male pseudonym. They *later* adopted male pseudonyms, but only for their *collaborations* with male authors. Moore married Henry Kuttner in 1940 and they sometimes published their collaborations afterward under male pseudonyms. But Moore debuted *years* before Kuttner published his first story ("The Graveyard Rats," *Weird Tales,* March, 1936, while Moore

debuted with "Shambleau," *Weird Tales,* November, 1933) and before the two even knew each other.

Meanwhile, Judith Merril later published under the amalgamated name "Cyril Judd" when she collaborated with fellow Futurian fan club member Cyril Kornbluth. Even then, however, "Cyril Judd's" first novel, *Outpost Mars* (Abelard Press: N.Y., 1951) featured a photo of *both* Merril and Kornbluth taking up half the book's back cover. Thus, the fact that this "male author" was half female was obvious to any oblivious fan who looked at the cover to see Merril's smiling face. The other half of the back cover was devoted to brief bios of the duo which told us that the name, "Cyril Judd," represents a "well-known compound personality," that of Kornbluth and Judith Merril, "a brilliant young writer."

Thus, Merril obviously made no effort to conceal her identity when she collaborated with Kornbluth under a "male" pseudonym which was a "well-known compound personality" of male and female authors. Further, the publisher evidently had no problem in publishing or reservations about touting this "brilliant young [female] writer."

Finally, these "Cyril Judd" collaborations were after our period (and after Merril had already established herself under her own female name). As will be seen later, *there is only one case* of any woman, "Francis Stevens," using a male pseudonym in the science fiction magazines before 1950—*and none at all before Moore married Kuttner in 1940*, the period of the allegedly most intense discrimination against women. Disch's unsubstantiated claims merely perpetuate the erroneous belief that early science fiction was a bachelor party and the "few" women who crashed it did so mainly as cross-dressers, concealing their identity lest the hostile boys turn on them.

7. William Sims Bainbridge, *Dimensions of Science Fiction,* Harvard University Press: Cambridge, 1986, p. 181.

8. Harlan Ellison, Editor, *Again, Dangerous Visions I,* New American Library: N.Y., 1973, 1972, p. 268.

9. Susanna J. Sturgis, Ed., *Memories and Visions: Women's Fantasy & Science Fiction,* The Crossing Press: Freedom, Calif., 1989, p. 1.

10. See, e.g., Curtis C. Smith, Ed., *Twentieth-Century Science-Fiction Writers,* St. James: Chicago, 2nd Ed., 1986, pp. vii-ix. For another feminist version of the same claims, see Pamela Sargent, Ed., *Women of Wonder: Science Fiction Stories by Women about Women,* Vintage Books: N.Y., 1974, pp. xvi-xx.

11. See Sargent, Ed., *Women of Wonder,* 1974, and *More Women of Wonder: Science Fiction Novelettes by Women About Women,* Vintage Books: N.Y., 1976; Robin Roberts, "The Female Alien: Pulp Science Fiction's Legacy to Feminists," in *Journal of Popular Culture,* fall, 1987, pp. 33–52, and *A New Species: Gender and Science in Science Fiction,* University of Illinois Press: Urbana, 1993; Jane L. Donawerth and Carol A. Kolmerten, Eds., *Utopian and Science Fiction by Women: Worlds of Difference,* Syracuse University Press: Syracuse, 1994, and *Frankenstein's Daughters: Women Writing Science Fiction,* Syracuse University Press: Syracuse, 1997.

On Marleen S. Barr, see her edited volume, *Future Females: A Critical Anthology,* Bowling Green State University Popular Press: Bowling Green, Ohio, 1981, *Alien to Femininity: Speculative Fiction and Feminist Theory,* Greenwood Press: Westport, Conn., 1987, *Feminist Fabulation: Space/Postmodern Fiction,* University of Iowa Press: Iowa City, 1992, and editor, *Future Females, The Next Generation: New Voices and Velocities in Feminist Science Fiction Criticism,* Rowman and Littlefield: Lanham, Md., 2000.

12. Frank, Stine, and Ackerman, *New Eves,* p. xvi.

13. A. Langley Searles, "A Critical Evaluation of Books on SF," *Essays in Arts and Sciences, IX,* 1980, p. 193.

14. This maxim was formulated by the editors of *American Heritage* to "honor" Parson Weems, the early hagiographer of George Washington. Weems invented many myths about his hero, including that of the cherry tree. Concerning the chopping down of this tree, Parson Weems put the words, "I cannot tell a lie," into young George's mouth. Unlike his hero, Parson Weems *could* tell lies.

15. Quoted in Nicole Loraux, *The Experience of Tiresias: The Feminine and the Greek Man,* Princeton University Press: Princeton, N.J., 1995, p. 236.

16. Mihaly Csikszentmihalyi, *Creativity: Flow and the Psychology of Discovery and Invention,* HarperCollins: N.Y., 1996, p. 23.

17. Howard Gardner, *Creating Minds: An Anatomy of Creativity Seen Through the Lives of Freud, Einstein, Picasso, Stravinsky, Eliot, Graham, and Gandhi,* Basic Books: N.Y., 1993, pp. 36, 380. Emphases in the original.

18. See Pierre Brule, *Women of Ancient Greece,* Edinburgh University Press: Edinburgh, 2003.

19. The single exception seems to have been Spartan women. They were the only women of ancient Greece publicly schooled in music, poetry, and dance, as well as public speaking. They could inherit property, engage in sports, and were famous both for their assertiveness and, even in ancient times, for their beauty. Helen of Troy, for example, was a Spartan queen. For more, see the only scholarly monograph so far on Spartan women, Sarah B. Pomeroy's *Spartan Women,* Oxford University Press: N.Y., 2002.

20. Barbara Caine, *Victorian Feminists,* Oxford University Press: Oxford, England, 1992, p. 39.

21. Yes, and then there was Aphra Behn (1640–1689), not exactly Shakespeare's "sister," as he died in 1616, but close enough to be his "granddaughter." The wife of a wealthy merchant, Behn became England's first professional female dramatist, producing a number of vivacious comedies. The English Civil War (1640–1644), which overthrew and executed King Charles I, and the subsequent Puritan Commonwealth (1644–1660) seems to have made it possible for English women (even royalist supporters such as Behn) to publish for the first time. Thus, because of revolution and regicide, civil war and counter-revolution, Behn's situation (and that of her literary sisters) was greatly different from that of would-be female authors in Shakespeare's time.

It might also be noted that upon the Restoration of the monarchy in 1660, the new king, Charles II, banned the practice common during Shakespeare's time of males performing female roles. From 1660 onward, then, we have the appearance of actresses on the English stage, another manifestation of expanded possibilities for female artists. This also made it more possible for a woman to follow in Shakespeare's footsteps of learning about the drama world by being involved in it directly.

22. Joanna Russ, *How to Suppress Women's Writing,* University of Texas Press: Austin, 1983, p. 6.

23. Ellen Goodman, "Danger Ahead! Educated Women!," *Boston Globe* syndicated column reprinted in *The Pittsburgh Post-Gazette,* September 4, 2002.

24. Eric Leif Davin, "The Good Doctor at St. Vincent," p. 248.

25. Platt, *Dream Makers, Volume II,* p. 192.

26. Sam Dillon, "Harvard Chief Defends His Talk on Women," *The New York Times,* January 18, 2005.

27. Natalie Angier and Kenneth Chang, "Gray Matter and Sexes: A Gray Area Scientifically," *The New York Times,* January 24, 2005.

28. Angier and Chang, "Gray Matter and Sexes." Emphasis added.

29. In a "Letter from President Summers on Women and Science," dated January 19, 2005, and addressed to "Members of the Harvard Community," the Harvard president seemingly retracted his statements, writing, "I did not say, and I do not believe, that girls are intellectually less able than boys, or that women lack the ability to succeed at the highest levels of science. As the careers of a great many distinguished women scientists make plain, the human potential to excel in science is not somehow the province of one gender or another. It is a capacity shared by boys and girls, by women and men, and we must do all we can to nurture, develop, and recognize it, along with other vital talents. That includes carefully avoiding stereotypes, being alert to forms of subtle discrimination, and doing everything we can to remove obstacles to success."

30. Chelsea Quinn Yarbro, "Symposium: Women in Science Fiction," *Khatru,* Nos. 3 & 4, November 1975, 2nd Printing, May, 1993, p. 14.

31. Platt, *Dream Makers, Volume II,* p. 212.

32. Kenneth Chang, "Making Science Fact, Now Chronicling Science Fiction," *The New York Times,* June 15, 2004, and Tomas Alex Tizon, "Where Science, Fiction Meet," *The Los Angeles Times,* December 10, 2004.

33. Jane Donawerth, *Frankenstein's Daughters,* pp. 3–4.

34. Survey cited in "Prime Numbers," *The Chronicle of Higher Education,* July 11, 2003, p. A9.

35. Angier and Chang, "Gray Matter and Sexes."

36. Craig Lambert, "Stealthy Attitudes: Buried Bias and Bigotry," *Harvard Magazine,* July-August, 2002, p. 18. For those interested in testing themselves, the test is available, as of this writing, at www.i-a-t.com.

37. Carolyn Y. Johnson, "Culture a Crucial Factor in Science Gender Gap," *Boston Globe* story reprinted in *The Pittsburgh Post-Gazette,* January 31, 2005.

38. Donald I. Hammonds, "Pitt program seeks to give girls extra push into tech, math fields," *The Pittsburgh Post-Gazette,* March 27, 2003, p. E-1.

39. Lisa Hoffman, "Computer culture appears to be leaving women behind," Scripps Howard News Service story appearing in *The Pittsburgh Post-Gazette,* July 12, 2000.

40. Hammonds, "Pitt program seeks to give girls extra push into tech, math fields."

41. "Science: Women on the Periphery," *The Week,* February 14, 2003, p. 12.

42. Alaina Sue Potrikus, "Girls Making Great Strides Academically in the World," Knight Ridder Newspapers syndicated story in *The Pittsburgh Post-Gazette,* September 20, 2003, p. A-12.

43. Marilyn vos Savant, "Ask Marilyn," *Parade,* March 28, 2004, p. 20.

44. Joanna Russ interview in Paul Walker, ed., *Speaking of Science Fiction: The Paul Walker Interviews,* Luna Publications: Oradell, N.J., 1978, p. 251. Originally in *Moebius Trip 14,* 1972.

45. Frederik Pohl, interview in the fanzine *Pig Iron Science Fiction,* Youngstown, Ohio, 1982. The correct sequence for Norton's name is "Alice Mary Norton." This is a common error. The Science Fiction Book Club also erroneously labeled her as originally being named "Mary Alice," claiming that she legally changed her name to "Andre Alice" in 1934 (see their monthly catalog for July, 2002, p. 9). It is chronologically inaccurate for Pohl to use Norton to establish his claim pertaining to these years. Except for two obscure fanzine contributions in 1947 and 1948, Norton did not begin her professional science fiction career until the 1950s.

46. Pohl's first wife, Doris Baumgardt, published "Space Episode" in the December, 1941, *Future combined with Science Fiction* under the pseudonym "Leslie Perri." She and Pohl were married at the time, so he obviously knew that, at least in this case, "Leslie" was the name of a woman. She was also, along with Pohl, an active member of the Futurians.

His second wife, Dorothy LesTina, whom he married in 1945, published "When You Think That . . . Smile!" in the February, 1943, *Future Fantasy and Science Fiction.*

And in 1948 Pohl began living with a third SF writer, Josephine Juliet Grossman Zissman (aka "Judith Merril"), who made her debut in the science fiction magazines the same year. They formally married in 1950.

47. For a powerful overview of how circumstances such as these help or hinder creativity see Tillie Olsen, *Silences,* Dell Publishing Co.: N.Y., 1965, 1979.

48. Naomi Mitchison, autobiographical entry in *Twentieth Century Authors,* Oxford University Press: N.Y., 1942 edition, p. 969, and interview in Leonie Caldecott, *Women of Our Century,* Ariel and BBC: London, 1984, pp. 14–15.

49. Justine Larbalestier, "Carol Emshwiller, Guest of Honor," *Thrilling Wiscon Stories,* Progress Report #2, announcing upcoming Wiscon 27, May, 2003, p. 3. The annual Wiscon is billed as the "world's only feminist science fiction convention."

50. Kate Wilhelm, "Women Writers: A Letter from Kate Wilhelm," in *The Witch and the Chameleon,* No. 3, April, 1975, p. 21. Wilhelm won the Nebula Award for best novel in 1977.

51. Wilhelm, "Women Writers," p. 21.

52. Robert Silverberg, "Introduction," in Robert Silverberg, *World of a Thousand Colors,* Arbor House: N.Y., 1982, p. 11.

53. Robert Silverberg, *World of a Thousand Colors,* p. 12.

2

Present at the Creation

In Olden Days, as everybody knows, it was common for immigration officials at New York's Ellis Island (and other points of entry to the United
States) to change the names of the ragged millions pouring in from obscure
provinces of Southern and Eastern Europe. Names that impatient American
authorities found difficult to spell or pronounce were routinely anglicized.
Numerous family histories confirm this practice. Take the case of Isaac Asimov.
Asimov claimed that when his family arrived at Ellis Island in 1923, his father
"managed to misspell our name, making it 'Asimov' instead of 'Azimov'
through a misunderstanding as to the nature of the sound of the letter *s*."[1] Such
name changes are part of the common knowledge.

There's just one problem with this common knowledge. It isn't true. It is
simply mythology which has, over time, solidified into "fact." According to
Vincent DiPietro, the U.S. National Park Service's Education Specialist at the
Statue of Liberty National Monument and Ellis Island Immigration Museum, it
is "completely false folklore." Barry Moreno, Librarian of the Ellis Island Immigration Museum and the editor of an encyclopedia on the Statue of Liberty,
agreed. "It's romantic nonsense," he said. "It never happened at any time,
period. It's mythology."[2] "U.S. immigration officials did not—as popular American myth persistently claims—change arbitrarily and cavalierly any immigrant's name," says John Philip Colletta, of the Institute of Genealogy and
Historical Research at Samford University (Birmingham, Alabama) and the Salt
Lake Institute of Genealogy. Nevertheless, he continued, it "is one of the most
widespread and oft-repeated myths" concerning Ellis Island.[3]

The Curator of the Ellis Island Immigration Museum and the official historian of the U.S. Immigration and Naturalization Service assured me that there
was no "name-changing room" at Ellis Island, no "name-changing book," no

name-changing routine. The vast archives of the U.S. government do not document a single instance of immigration officials anglicizing anyone's name, at any time, for any reason. They did not (and do not) have the legal authority to change names, and have never done so. Indeed, stated Moreno, an immigration official "could be severely disciplined or even dismissed for altering a name, due to suspicion of helping an undesirable alien enter."

In fact, the officials never even wrote names down. There was no need to. In 1893, the year after Ellis Island opened as an immigrant receiving station, Congress legislated expanded passenger lists. Thus, Colletta tells us, "The inspector had in his hands a written record of the immigrant he was inspecting." All the inspector did was check the immigrants against the passenger list and ask various questions. Nor did any immigrant ever leave Ellis Island with any document—a "green card," an entry permit, etc.—which might have had a "new" name written on it.

The belief that names were changed at Ellis Island seems to be based on a presumption of prejudice among "arrogant" English-speaking immigration officials who couldn't (or wouldn't try to) understand what the disdained foreigners were trying so desperately to say. In fact, however, Colletta tells us that, "even if [the officials] had trouble understanding the name the immigrant pronounced, or could not pronounce the name themselves, they had at their service a large staff of translators who worked alongside them in the Great Hall of the Ellis Island facility."[4] DiPietro verifies this, saying there were three dozen translators available at Ellis Island who spoke every variety and dialect of the Southern and Eastern European languages—and even languages uncommon in this country, such as Arabic.

Indeed, the many well-known photographs of Ellis Island immigrants taken by Lewis Hine in 1904–1905 confirm that officials there attempted to communicate with immigrants in their own languages. One such, entitled "Immigrants waiting at Ellis Island," portrays a man and woman dancing while a seated man plays an accordion. On the wall behind them is a sign in six languages, including Italian, Slovak, and Hebrew, proclaiming that there was "No charge for meals here."[5] (After Boston Brahmins led the successful crusade to stem the tide of Southern and Eastern European immigration by passing legislation forbidding entrance to illiterates it was discovered, to the great surprise of many, that most of these immigrants were, in fact, literate! They were thus able to read signs such as this.)

But what of all those thousands of ethnic family names which were, in fact, anglicized in America? Colletta acknowledges that, "Certainly, the surnames of many immigrants were indeed changed around the time of their arrival in America or shortly thereafter. But that change was effected—often by the immigrant himself—due to a variety of causes other than callous U.S. officials."[6] DiPietro agrees, saying such names had to have been anglicized *after* leaving

Ellis Island. Perhaps the immigrant, or relatives, felt a more "American" name might make it easier to get a job or assimilate into the new country. "Changing one's name," said Moreno, seems to have been "part of this thing about coming to America and starting a new life." Or perhaps, unlike immigration officials, an employer could not comprehend a new employee's name and gave him a new one.

All of this can be verified by researching the record. But try telling it to someone of Southern or Eastern European descent. They won't believe you. They're sure they already know what happened at Ellis Island. Everybody knows names were changed there, regardless of what National Park Service officials at the Immigration Museum might say. Don't countless family anecdotes, such as that told by Isaac Asimov, attest to the fact? Authors like Asimov don't just repeat their fathers' myths without checking them out, do they?

Unfortunately, they do. And because of this, as DiPietro told me, "folklore and common knowledge are often wrong."

The commonly-accepted history of women in science fiction is another egregious example of just such unverified folklore and common myths passing for history. For instance, as recently as 2004 Gary Hoppenstand, an academic who has written introductions to a number of pulp fiction reprints from the University of Nebraska Press, repeats the creaky cliche that, "With *the single exception* of Francis Stevens, female authors were not publishing speculative fiction in the early twentieth century."[7] Likewise, British feminist academic Sarah Lefanu tells us that, "early twentieth- and mid-twentieth-century science fiction does lack women-identified women as writers and readers."[8]

The reason for this, as everybody knows, is that before the "mid-to-late 1960s" (as Shawna McCarthy told us) the male-dominated science fiction community—readers, editors, and publishers—was irrevocably hostile to women and did not tolerate the female presence in its midst. Hence, said Asimov, the very few women science fiction writers who existed before 1960 "used initials, or pseudonyms, or first names of ambiguous gender in order to hide the fact."[9]

Historians of the genre have disagreed over "When It Changed" and women finally became equal participants in the all-male science fiction world. Some, writing like Lefanu for prestigious university presses, have pinpointed the entrance of women writers into the genre as being anywhere from the 1970s, which brought a "recent influx of female science fiction writers,"[10] to the 1980s because, "until recently women authors had reason to believe that science fiction did not welcome them."[11] British science fiction author Brian Aldiss is among those who nominate the 1970s for what he calls, "the revolution." "In the seventies," he tells us in his acclaimed history of the field, "there was a great influx of women writers. . . . By the end of the seventies it had become clear that SF was no longer a kind of juvenile men's club. Women were to be seen at the bar. SF's unexpressed half was *beginning* to speak out."[12]

Some, more daring, have pushed the entrance of women writers into science fiction further back into the past. Even the latter, however, perpetuate the myth of male hostility as the reason women did not appear in any numbers earlier in the genre. Thus, prolific anthologizer Martin H. Greenberg writes, "The fifties witnessed the emergence of a small number of woman science fiction writers who added immeasurably to the field. They included Zenna Henderson, Margaret St. Clair, Mildred Clingerman, Andre Norton, and Katherine MacLean. Like Judith Merril, Catherine L. Moore, and Leigh Brackett before them, they sometimes encountered publishing difficulties because of their sex."[13]

Science fiction historian, writer, and college professor James Gunn agrees there were a *handful* of women writers in the Fifties, while "Before 1948 few women wrote science fiction." The reason, as everybody knows, was the aforementioned male hostility. Therefore those intrepid few "usually concealed their sex behind male pseudonyms or neutral initials," and he names the usual suspects: Leigh Brackett, C. L. Moore, etc. But now, he wrote, "Times have changed. The old male preserve has been invaded by women readers . . . and women writers are challenging men for an equal place in the literature of ideas." What changed things, he claimed, was John W. Campbell's publication of Judith Merril's "That Only a Mother," in the June 1948, *Astounding*. Somehow this one story had a ripple effect and emboldened women everywhere; timorously and gradually they then "began to come out of the science fiction closet."[14]

People seem to cherish such ahistorical bolts from the blue as the supposed impact of Merril's story. Hence, writer "William Tenn" (Philip Klass) recounted this same myth to the members of PARSEC, the Pittsburgh science fiction club. He embellished the myth, however, in two ways. First, he stated there were absolutely no women writers at all before Judith Merril. Further, he claimed Merril's story was his idea. Thus, even the supposed entry of women writers into science fiction, springing like Athena from the brow of Zeus, is the story of a patronizing male triumph.[15]

Of course, neither Gunn nor "Tenn" cited any evidence, such as interviews with contemporary female authors concerning the impact of Merril's story upon their decisions to enter the field. So, I did what Gunn and "Tenn" *should* have done. I asked contemporary women writers about Merril's impact. None could verify the legend.

One I queried was Julian May, who debuted only three years after Campbell published Merril's piece. In fact, her debut, "Dune Roller," was in *Astounding* (December, 1951), the same magazine where Merril's story appeared. Julian May denied any knowledge, *at the time*, of *either* the story *or* Judith Merril.[16] So Merril's story seems to have had no influence upon Julian May entering the field shortly after its publication. Nor am I aware of any evidence that it influenced any other contemporary female author.[17] This is merely fiction about fiction.

Just as there were supposedly no women science fiction writers before Judith

Merril, the traditional exclusion narrative also has it that something called "women's science fiction" did not emerge until the mid- or late 1960s or early 1970s when some women authors began writing a form of "feminist" science fiction. In fact, however, the self-consciously politicized feminist science fiction of the late Sixties and early Seventies was merely a "Second Wave" of women's science fiction. The First Wave came into existence with the birth of the genre itself in magazine form in the late 1920s. This First Wave grew throughout the 1930s and 1940s and matured in the crucial decade of the 1950s when it evolved into a recognizable "female counter-culture" to the dominant male culture.

This First Wave of women's science fiction was able to grow and flourish because it did not face the pervasive male hostility from the science fiction "establishment" which features so prominently in the field's cherished mythology. Women—as writers, fans, and readers—had not been shut away in some dark closet from which they began to emerge, timorously and tentatively, only in the Eighties, Seventies, Sixties, or Fifties (depending on which claim about "When It Changed" you believe). As with name-changing at Ellis Island, such ostracism is merely mythology. However, as with immigration history, it is difficult to disabuse people of what "everybody knows." People *want* to believe in the Emperor's fine new clothes. Hence, historians of the genre have exerted their energies in chasing after the chimera of "When It Changed."

But the genre never "changed" to allow the entrance of women. The door had always been open and women had always been active participants ever since the dim and obscure origins of the literature which eventually came to be called science fiction. In fact, it seems that Lady Margaret Cavendish, the woman described by her biographer, Katie Whitaker, as "the first woman to live by her pen" was also the first female "science fiction" writer.[18] In 1666 Lady Margaret Cavendish, the Duchess of Newcastle, published the first utopian novel written by a woman, *The Description of a New World, Called the Blazing World.*

Born Margaret Lucas in 1623, Lady Cavendish was the daughter of a little-known country gentleman. She became a lady-in-waiting to Queen Henrietta Maria and, with the Queen, was driven into exile by the triumphant Puritan forces at the end of the English Civil War. While sojourning in Paris as a member of the royalist expatriate circle she met and married William Cavendish, a duke who had commanded King Charles I's army in the north of England. In Paris, and then Antwerp, she took up writing, although she and her husband actually seem to have lived largely on loans during their exile. She debuted in 1653 with *Poems and Fancies,* a book of well-received poetry. She followed this with two dozen plays, many stories in both prose and verse, six philosophical treatises, her autobiography, and a biography of her husband. By the age of 40 this utopianist (among many other things) was a literary celebrity.

Not all critics, however, have taken note of the nature of her work. Margaret Drabble, for example, in her definitive work on English literature, says not one word about the Duchess of Newcastle's pioneering utopian novel. Instead, Drabble dwells on Lady Cavendish's "singularity in dress and manners."[19]

Nevertheless, Lady Cavendish was soon followed by other women utopianists. Roger C. Schlobin (while including a handful of obvious males and overlooking some important females) has listed an additional 375 female authors who wrote 830 book-length English-language science fiction novels, collections and anthologies over a course of almost 300 years from 1692 to 1982.[20] And, according to no less than Brian Aldiss, James Gunn, and Isaac Asimov himself, science fiction was launched by a woman in 1818 with Mary Shelley's *Frankenstein*.[21] This was followed in 1826 with her science fiction novel, *The Last Man*.

Other women soon joined Shelley, such as Jane Webb Loudon who, in 1827, published *The Mummy! A Tale of the Twenty-Second Century*. Around a melodramatic plot, Loudon presciently speculated about future inventions, including movable housing, mechanical farming, and weather control, possibly the first time this last concept appeared in the literature. In 1836 Mary Griffith published *Three Hundred Years Hence*, believed to be the first utopian novel written by an American—male or female.

Other American women also soon engaged in the genre of utopian speculation, sometimes with clearly feminist agendas. For example, in 1848 women's rights advocates launched the woman suffrage movement at a convention in Seneca Falls, New York. That same year Jane Sophia Appleton published a 22-page description of a utopia which emphasized women's rights. It was, "Sequel to the Vision of Bangor in the Twentieth Century," in *Voices from the Kenduskeag* and was intended as a reply to a utopian novel also written in 1848 by one Edward Kent, which had highlighted traditional sex roles. Charlotte Perkins Gilman also championed women's rights in her explicitly feminist utopia *Herland* (1915).

Such proto-science fiction novels were an aspect of the larger world of increasingly accepted female book publishing in the nineteenth century and later. "Women are here to stay," said Agnes Rogers, writing in 1949. "Granted that some women formerly thought it advisable to use a masculine nom de plume for purposes of modesty or whatever, there is no real discrimination in training, wages, or working conditions in the writing of books. It may be significant that the best-selling books in the United States between 1852 and 1861 were equally divided between the sexes, twelve authors were women, twelve were men."[22]

As general interest and adventure magazines began being published in the mid-nineteenth and early twentieth centuries, many of what Nathaniel Hawthorne derided as "scribbling women" also appeared regularly in these new venues. What is more, the stories in these popular magazines often presented much more unconventional roles for both women and African Americans than the "distinguished" fiction of the times which has made its way into the academic canon. Thus, to study only the accepted literary canon for such mid-nineteenth century periods as the Civil War Era gives us a skewed view of the contemporary literary presentation and popular perception of these "outsider" groups. Reinforcing the "contested terrain" thesis of popular culture, what the common people of such times actually read in the early equivalent of "pulp fiction" was much less stereotypical in its treatment of women and blacks than usually presumed.[23]

Science fiction writer Jessica Amanda Salmonson reinforced these points, noting both the prominence of female authors during these periods and their often unconventional attitudes toward gender relations. "From the 1830s through the 1920s," she said, "women were the dominant presence in British and U.S. magazines as poets, essayists, story writers, readers, and often enough as editors; hence, women dominated the fashions in literature. . . . [Further,] a sizable percentage were consciously feminist and, depending on the degree of radicalism decade by decade, at certain historical moments feminists were the majority."[24]

Women writers also stepped outside customary social bounds when they wrote ghost stories, which became a popular fad in the Victorian Era. Although well-known male writers participated in the phenomenon, such as J. Sheridan Le Fanu and M. R. James (not to mention Charles Dickens and his "Christmas Carol"), they were not alone. They had their equals among notable women writers such as Mrs. J. H. Riddell, Amelia B. Edwards, Elizabeth Gaskell, Mary Wilkins Freeman, Sarah Orne Jewett, Harriet Prescott Spofford, and even Edith Wharton.

In the associated spiritualist movement of the age, women also figured prominently as some of the leading spiritualist mediums. For later researchers, it is sometimes difficult to categorize such efforts, as from time to time spiritualism shaded off into what we would now call "science fiction." For example, in 1906 Sara Weiss published, *Decimon Huydas: A Romance of Mars,* described in the subtitle as, "A Story of actual experiences in Ento [Mars] many centuries ago given to the Psychic."

Additionally, intrepid women writers often chose to write less traditional stories for the general interest magazines, which published tales of adventure appealing to a mostly male audience. Even so, from the beginning these women found a welcome reception in such media. Their numbers grew steadily, suggesting a sizeable number of women might also have been among the audiences for these magazines. Such authors ranged from the well remembered, such as Agatha Christie, Dorothy Sayers, and Mary Roberts Rinehart, to those who published prolifically, but who have now been largely forgotten, such as Katherine Pinkerton and Inez Haynes Gillmore Irwin. Indeed, science fiction historian Everett F. Bleiler informed me that, "Several years ago, when I first got on the Internet, I started to tabulate female authors' names in cover positions in the early pulps, mostly *Argosy* and *All-Story*. There were so many, and so many covers obviously oriented toward females, that I gave it up as something too obvious to bother with."[25]

As with the adventure pulps, women writers also figured prominently in another aspect of popular culture, detective fiction. Although appearing in *Beadle's Monthly* earlier, in 1866 Metta Victoria Fuller Victor, under the name "Seeley Regester," published *The Dead Letter*, the first American detective novel that we know of written by a woman. "However," says Michele Slung, "since so many now-lost stories were pouring out from the presses of the cheap-edition publishers, in addition to the fiction that appeared in so many magazines, it is likely that there were other women writing mysteries as well."[26]

Anna Katharine Green's *The Leavenworth Case*, which featured a female detective and which also preceded Sir Arthur Conan Doyle's first contributions to the genre by nine years, followed this in 1878. It proved extremely popular, making a name for the author and remaining in print almost continuously until 1937. Then, between the two world wars, detective fiction flourished and women writers dominated the novels of the period. Not only were writers such as Agatha Christie, Dorothy L. Sayers, Josephine Tey, Ngaio Marsh, and Margery Allingham critically acclaimed and widely read—much of their work remains popular to this day.

As in the world of books, women were also present in the world of pulp crime fiction. Although presumed to be entirely a "man's world," detective pulps regularly featured female authors writing under their own names, including such well-known authors as Dorothy L. Sayers, Carolyn Wells, and Agatha Christie. Two of Christie's novels, for instance, *The Murder of Roger Ackroyd* and *The Tuesday Club Murders,* first appeared in America in the pulps. In addition, 20 of Christie's short stories made their American debuts in pulp detective magazines such as *Detective Fiction Weekly, Mystery Magazine, Flynn's Weekly,* and *Street & Smith's Detective Story.* (Christie also published in other types of magazines, such as *Ghost Stories* and *Blue Book.*)

Typical of such detective pulps was *Black Mask.* From its inception in 1920 it regularly published female authors writing under their own names. Although they are now forgotten, the contents pages of *Black Mask* were sprinkled throughout the Twenties with names such as Florence M. Pettee, Elizabeth Dudley, Sally Dixon Wright, Eliza Mae Harvey, Helen Holley, Wyona Dashwood, and Marjorie Stoneman Douglas. In the 1930s, these women were joined by others, such as Marian O'Hearn, Kay Krausse, Frances Beck, Tiah Devitt, and, most prolific female detective pulpster of all, Dorothy Dunn, a St. Louis elementary school teacher.[27]

Some of these women detective story authors, such as Miriam Allen deFord and Leigh Brackett, also made a name for themselves in science fiction. Brackett specialized in hard-boiled detective fiction and authored seven such stories in the pulps between 1943 and 1945, as well as three such novels. Typical of her stories was "I Feel Bad Killing You," a Chandleresque novelette (*New Detective*, November, 1944). Such was her reputation in this genre that Hollywood hired her in 1946 to co-author, with William Faulkner, the screenplay of Chandler's classic novel, *The Big Sleep*, which became the film of the same name starring Humphrey Bogart and Lauren Bacall.

But even among the myriad stories by earlier women in the general interest magazines, many could be classed without question as "science fiction." For instance, "My Invisible Friend," by Katherine Kip (*The Black Cat*, February, 1897), preceded H. G. Wells' "The Invisible Man" into print by four months. Indeed, the very first issue of the popular pulp, *The All-Story Magazine* (January, 1905), carried a science fiction story by Margaret P. Montague entitled, "The Great Sleep Tanks," which supposed that sleep was a tangible thing which could be captured and stored in huge tanks.

Meanwhile, "A Rule That Worked Both Ways," by Octavia Zollicoffer Bond (*The Black Cat*, December, 1904) was about a machine which materialized spirits from the ether or, with a reversal of polarization, could cause a person to disappear. Another marvelous invention was "The Ray of Displacement" (*The Metropolitan Magazine*, October, 1903), by the popular nineteenth-century writer of ghost stories Harriet Prescott Spofford (mentioned above), which described a means for humans to pass through solid matter.

Irish-British writers L. T. Meade (Elizabeth Thomasina Meade Smith) and Robert Eustace (Dr. Eustace Robert Barton) collaborated on several proto-science fiction stories, the best perhaps being "Where The Air Quivered" (*The Strand Magazine*, December, 1898). This concerned the use of a new scientific invention for the purpose of committing a crime. Meade also wrote 230 books for girls and was a prolific mystery writer. Indeed, she is credited with being the first writer to feature a female villain in a series of stories, beginning with *The Brotherhood of the Seven Kings* (1899). Her collection *The Sorceress of the Strand* (1903) featured yet another female villain.

Then there was "Francis Stevens" (Gertrude Barrows Bennett), a well-known female writer of the early pulp magazines who pioneered with several influential stories, some of which were reprinted in *Famous Fantastic Mysteries* and *Fantastic Novels* as late as the 1940s. Many rank her as the most important female science fiction writer since Mary Shelley. Her "Friend Island" (*All-Story Weekly*, September 7, 1918) depicted, among other things, a parallel-universe or near-future Earth where millennia-old gender roles had been abolished. The concept of a parallel universe is unmistakably clear in her novel "The Heads of Cerberus" (*The Thrill Book*, August 15-October 15, 1919). This idea would not be taken up again until "Murray Leinster" (William F. Jenkins) used it for his "Sidewise in Time," (*Astounding Stories*, June, 1934). Today the science fiction world gives an annual award for this type of story. It is not known as the "Cerberus Award." It is called the "Sidewise Award," yet another example of how the contributions of early women science fiction writers have been forgotten.

The appearance of women writers in the later pulp science fiction magazines, then, was a logical continuation of this tradition of female magazine authorship, both within the genre and in the larger world of publishing. Indeed, surveying the literary scene in 1936, Margaret Lawrence declared that, "For the present we are in the middle of a period of commercial feminism [sic] which would have astonished Plato, who in the memory of the race was the first man to take up the cause of women to mind. And what it would do to John Stuart Mill, who in the nineteenth century championed women, is an idea for idle cogitation."[28]

Women authors, then, appeared more often than credited in the pulps—and especially so in the magazines in which science fiction first began to take shape as a genre.

Notes

1. Isaac Asimov, "Ellis Island and I," in *The Tyrannosaurus Prescription and 100 Other Essays,* Prometheus Books: Buffalo, N.Y., 1989, p. 311.

2. Telephone interviews by Eric Leif Davin, July 17, 2001.

3. John Philip Colletta, "Ellis Island: What's Myth, What's Reality?," *Family Chronicle,* July-August, 2003, p. 12.

4. Colletta, "Ellis Island: What's Myth, What's Reality?," p. 12.

5. Richard Lacayo and George Russell, *Eyewitness: 150 Years of Photojournalism,* Time Books: N.Y., 1995, p. 65.

6. Colletta, "Ellis Island: What's Myth, What's Reality?," p. 12.

7. Gary Hoppenstand, "Francis Stevens: The Woman Who Invented Dark Fantasy," in Francis Stevens, *The Nightmare and Other Tales of Dark Fantasy,* University of Nebraska Press: Lincoln, Neb., 2004, p. ix. Emphasis added.

8. Sarah Lefanu, *Feminism and Science Fiction,* Indiana University Press: Bloomington, 1989, p. 2.

9. Isaac Asimov, "The Feminization of Science Fiction," in *The Tyrannosaurus Prescription and 100 Other Essays,* Prometheus Books: Buffalo, N.Y., 1989, p. 294. Originally published as "The Feminization of Sci-Fi," *Vogue,* October, 1982.

10. Robert Scholes and Eric S. Rabkin, *Science Fiction: History, Science, Vision,* Oxford University Press: Oxford and New York, 1977, p. 186.

11. Bainbridge, *Dimensions of Science Fiction,* p. 180.

12. Aldiss and Wingrove, *Trillion Year Spree,* p. 465. Emphasis added.

13. Martin Harry Greenberg and Joseph Olander, Eds., *Science Fiction of the Fifties,* Avon Books: N.Y., 1979, p. 9. It's unclear what Greenberg and Olander mean by "emergence," but for the record St. Clair and MacLean debuted in the Forties, although they became better known in the Fifties.

14. James Gunn, Ed., *The Road to Science Fiction, Volume 3: From Heinlein to Here,* White Wolf Publishing: Clarkston, Calif., 1979, pp. 108, 109.

15. See Eric Leif Davin, "Women Didn't Write Science-Fiction!," *Fantasy Commentator* IX, 1998, p. 229. Judith Merril doesn't mention Klass as having any input at all in her story. In *her* version, she wrote it independently and told John W. Campbell about it in August, 1947, when Ted Sturgeon introduced her to him in Philadelphia at her first SF con. "It was friendship—forever

at first sight," she said of Campbell. (Both were drunk at the time.) After it had been rejected by all the slicks, she sent it to Campbell, who immediately accepted it. Letter to Justine Larbalestier, November 16, 1996, in Larbalestier, *The Battle of the Sexes in Science Fiction*, pp. 176–77.

16. Phone interview with Julian May by Eric Leif Davin, August 1, 2003. At least this is the official version May tells about her career. However, there may be reason to doubt her ignorance of the Merril story. See my later discussion of May submitting her debut story to Campbell under initials.

17. Philip Klass seems to be completely ignorant of any female science fiction writer before Judith Merril. At the same meeting of PARSEC noted above I mentioned to him the names of various pre-Merril women science fiction authors (beginning with Clare Winger Harris). He waved his hands in exasperation and spluttered that *he* never heard of *any of* them! The implication, since he taught the history of science fiction at Pennsylvania State University, was that if *he* didn't know about them—they probably didn't exist!

18. See Katie Whitaker, *Mad Madge: The Extraordinary Life of Margaret Cavendish, Duchess of Newcastle, the First Woman to Live by Her Pen*, Basic Books: N.Y., 2002.

19. See the entry on Lady Margaret Cavendish in Margaret Drabble, Ed., *The Oxford Companion to English Literature*, Fifth Edition, Oxford University Press: Oxford and New York, 1985, pp. 692–93.

20. Roger C. Schlobin, *Urania's Daughters: A Checklist of Women Science Fiction Writers, 1692–1982*, Starmont House: Mercer Is., Wash., 1983, Starmont Reference Guide No. 1. Schlobin's date of 1692 cannot be accepted, as the date refers to a novel by Gabriel Daniel, a prominent French historian and Jesuit priest whom Schlobin mistakenly believed to be a woman. The earliest female author to actually appear in his guide is Eliza F. Haywood, writing in 1755. However, he omits the well-known Lady Margaret Cavendish, Duchess of Newcastle, who I mentioned as publishing the first utopian novel by a woman in 1666. So, we can still correctly speak of women utopian and science fiction writers publishing over a span of more than 300 years. See the review of Schlobin's guide by Eric Leif Davin, *Fantasy Commentator*, VI, 1987, p. 32.

21. See the chapter, "The Origins of the Species: Mary Shelley," in Brian Aldiss, *Billion Year Spree: The True History of Science Fiction*, Schoken Books: N.Y., 1974, and his entry on her in E. F. Bleiler, Ed., *Science Fiction Writers: Critical Studies of the Major Authors from the Early Nineteenth Century to the Present Day*, Charles Scribner's Sons: N.Y., 1982; James Gunn, *Alternate Worlds: The Illustrated History of Science Fiction*, Prentice-Hall, Inc.: N.Y., 1975, pp. 45–46; and Isaac Asimov, *Asimov on Science Fiction*, Avon Books: N.Y., 1982, chapter entitled, "The First Science Fiction Novel." However, in the courses he taught on the history of science fiction at Eastern New Mexico State University, Jack Williamson argued that science fiction began with the Greek myths.

I had an exchange concerning this novel with a female student of mine (who also wrote much unpublished fan fiction) at the University of Pittsburgh. It was a sad commentary on both youthful ignorance and the pervasiveness of the presumption of prejudice. In response to my statement that many consider Mary Shelley's novel to be the first true SF novel, the student asked, in all seriousness, "Under what male name did she write *Frankenstein*?"

22. Agnes Rogers, *Women Are Here To Stay*, Harper: N.Y., 1949, p. 39.

23. c.f., Alice Fahs, "A Thrilling Northern War: Gender, Race, and Sensational Popular War Literature," in Paul A. Cimbala and Randall M. Miller, Eds., *An Uncommon Time: The Civil War and the Northern Home Front*, Fordham University Press: N.Y., 2002.

24. Jessica Amanda Salmonson, Editor's Preface, *What Did Miss Darrington See?—An Anthology of Feminist Supernatural Fiction*, The Feminist Press: N.Y., 1989, pp. x-xi.

25. Letter, Everett F. Bleiler to Eric Leif Davin, February 11, 2003.

26. Michele Slung, "Introduction," Anna Katharine Green, *The Leavenworth Case*, Dover Publications, Inc.: N.Y., 1981, p. iii.

27. See Bill Pronzini, "Women in the Pulps," in Jan Grape, Dean James, and Ellen Nehr, Eds., *Deadly Women: The Woman Mystery Reader's Indispensable Companion*, Carroll & Graf Publishers, Inc.: N.Y., 1998, pp. 17–19.

28. Margaret Lawrence, *The School of Femininity*, Stokes: N.Y., 1936, p. 11.

3

Weird Sisters

WHICH BRINGS US to the matter of actual *numbers* of women writers in the pulp science fiction magazines, a major reason women were presumed to have been discriminated against in the past by a hostile male science fiction "establishment." It is true that women *were* a minority in the pulp era. This minority status has contributed to the field's image problem, as the very fact of their minority status is pointed to as proof of the hostility of the field toward them. There must have been an institutional bias—bigotry—by the gatekeepers, it is argued, limiting the otherwise equal participation to be naturally expected of women.

Two items to consider: First, a closer examination reveals that, while women were a minority, they were actually present in far larger numbers than commonly credited. Second, women continue to be a comparable minority in the field currently—yet there are no claims that the field is currently biased against women. Clearly, the different eras are not being held to the same standards of evidence.

Let us first look at the actual numbers and percentages of women in the pulp era, which no one else has done. And, once we look closely at the numbers, we are forced to revise some of the most cherished myths of the genre.

For instance, it is commonly asserted (I will give examples of such assertions later when dealing with the issue of initials) that important writer Catherine L. Moore was forced to conceal her gender from the alleged monolithically male (and, being male, presumably hostile) readership of *Weird Tales* by using the initials C. L. Moore on her 1933 debut in that magazine ("Shambleau," November, 1933).

However, the personnel and culture of *Weird Tales* was very far from being monolithically male and might better be described as ambisexual. After all, for almost half of the magazine's existence, from May, 1940, until the demise of the first incarnation of *Weird Tales* in September, 1954, it was edited by a woman, Dorothy McIlwraith (who had actually begun as an editorial assistant in 1938). Further, the much-praised (and beloved-by-readers) artist who painted 66 monthly covers for the magazine in the 1930s, and who is most-closely associated with that era of *Weird Tales*, was also a woman, Margaret Brundage. At one point, Brundage painted thirty-nine consecutive covers for the magazine, including nine for Robert E. Howard's Conan stories. Indeed, it was Brundage who gave us our first visual depiction of Conan, as well as our first glimpse of C. L. Moore's warrior princess, Jirel of Joiry. And she continued painting *Weird Tales* covers into World War II.

And, judging from the letters this magazine published, a sizeable portion of the readership was also female. By tabulating the gender of those who wrote letters to the magazine we can use this as a proxy for the elusive question of readership gender, a question perhaps impossible to definitively answer (though many have presumed to do so). Once we do this, we discover that all of the pulp fantasy and science fiction magazines had a likely female readership of a size (and assertiveness) which wise editors dared not ignore—especially in the economically perilous times of the 1930s' Great Depression.

Thus, during the span of its first existence (1923–1954) *Weird Tales* printed letters from 1,817 readers, of whom I was able to identify the gender of 1,429. Of these, 382 were clearly female, *more than a quarter (26.6 percent) of the identifiable letter writers.* (But, even if we counted all the letters of those with ambiguous or unknowable gender as if they were male-authored, which is unlikely, the clearly female writers would still account for almost 21 percent of the total.)[1] In fact, the most prolific letter writer to *Weird Tales* in its entire history was a woman.

Nor did these letter writers hesitate to touch on "female" topics. For example, Everil Worrell, an author who also wrote for the magazine, discussed how she and her husband humorously used Lovecraft's purple prose to describe mundane household events. "If something particularly smelly boiled over in the kitchen," she said, "we might refer to it as a 'foul mephitic vapor,' and when the baby howled, we might invite one another to do something about the 'horrific ululations.'"[2]

There is also another way of getting a clue as to the gender breakdown of *Weird Tales* readers. In the 1940s the magazine launched the "Weird Tales Club." If readers submitted a stamped self-addressed envelope, along with their names and addresses, they would be sent an official membership card and their names and addresses would be printed in the magazine as new club members. I chose six issues of the magazine at random—one from 1943, two from 1947, two from 1949, and one from 1952—and did a gender analysis of the listed club members.

Of the 448 club members I could gender-identify from these six lists, 118 were female. *Thus, 26.33 percent of the listed and gender identifiable Weird Tales Club members were female,* almost exactly the same gender breakdown as revealed by an analysis of all the letter writers to the magazine. Nor were the female club members skewed toward any one period. The percentage of female club members hovered around this level for the entire decade I examined, 1943–1952, although the percentage was 26.8 percent in 1943 and 31.3 percent in 1952. Three of the six issues revealed female club memberships of over 30 percent with only the September 1949 female club membership falling below 26 percent.[3] As the club membership lists and the letters reveal, women, although a minority, were nevertheless a major, vocal, and crucial part of the *Weird Tales* readership.

Perhaps in order to appeal to this relatively large female readership (among whom we must obviously count Catherine L. Moore, who sent her first story to the magazine), *all* of the editors of *Weird Tales,* including the male editors who preceded Dorothy McIlwraith, regularly published female authors. Indeed, stories with female bylines began appearing in *Weird Tales* with *its very first issue,* March 1923 (Meredith Davis, "The Accusing Voice"). Its second issue, April 1923, had stories by two women. And so it went. In addition, as early as that first year of publication the covers themselves were sometimes devoted to stories by authors such as Effie W. Fifield, Greye La Spina, Sophie Wenzel Ellis, and Katherine Metcalf Roof.[4]

What is more, according to legendary SF editor Donald A. Wollheim, women authors such as these were crucial to this magazine in its early years. *Weird Tales* was a novel experiment in magazine publishing. Instead of running a variety of stories to appeal to all tastes, which was the norm, it was an all-fantasy magazine—the world's first such. No one was sure it would work. Thus, early female authors like Greye La Spina (1880–1969), who already had a track record in earlier pulp magazines like 1919's *The Thrill Book,* brought needed cachet to the venture. "Greye La Spina," he said, "is one of the original group of *Weird Tales* writers whose stories helped a good deal to establish that oldest existing fantasy magazine in its formative days of 1923 and 1924."[5] La Spina's stories were so popular that one of her *Weird Tales* serials was published in book form as *Invaders From the Dark* as late as 1960 when she was 80 years old.

In fact, *at least* 114 such female authors appeared in the pages of *Weird Tales* in a total of 107 of the 117 issues which were published *before* Moore's debut in 1933. Nor were these token appearances, as there were often four, five, or six female authors in a single issue. The female authors who *preceded* Moore in the pages of *Weird Tales*—many of whom made multiple appearances—included Vida Taylor Adams, Marguerite Lynch Addis, Edith M. Almedingen, Leona May Ames, Frances Arthur, Meredith Beyers, Anne M. Bilbro, Muriel Cameron Bodkin, Lady Anne Bonny, Edna Goit Brintnall, Mary S. Brown, Loretta G. Burro-

ugh, Grace M. Campbell, Hanna Baird Campbell, Lenore E. Chaney, Valma
Clark, Martha May Cockrill, Mary Elizabeth Counselman, Marjorie Darter,
Meredith Davis, Edith de Garis, Frances Elliott, Elsie Ellis, Mollie Frank Ellis,
Sophie Wenzel Ellis, Mary McEnnery Erhard, Effie W. Fifield, Alice T. Fuller,
Louise Garwood, Elizabeth Cleghorn Gaskell, Myrtle Levy Gaylord, Nellie C.
Gilmore, Sonia H. Greene, Anne H. Hadley, Clare Winger Harris, Lyllian Hunt-
ley Harris, Margaret M. Hass, Cristel Hastings, Marietta Hawley, Sarah Hender-
son Hay, Hazel Heald, Helen Rowe Henze, Marjorie Holmes, Terva Gaston
Hubbard, Edith Hurley, Alice I'Anson, Thelma E. Johnson, Theda Kenyon,
Minnie Faegre Knox, Binny Koras, Lois Lane, Genevieve Larsson, Greye La
Spina, Nadia Lavrova, Helen Liello, Amelia Reynolds Long, Josie McNamara
Lydon, Isa-Belle Manzer, Maybelle McCalment, Laurie McClintock, Rachael
Marshall, Kadra Maysi, Violet M. Methley, Maria Moravsky, Sarah Newmeyer,
Dorothy Norwich, Stella G. S. Perry, Dorothy M. Peterkin, Alice Pickard, Lilla
P. Price (Savino), Mearle Prout, Edith Lyle Ragsdale, Ellen M. Ramsay, Alicia
Ramsey, Sybla Ramus, Zealia Brown Reed (Zealia B. Bishop), Helen M. Reid,
Susan A. Rice, Eudora Ramsay Richardson, "Flavia Richardson" (Christine
Campbell Thomson), Jean Richepin, Katharine Metcalf Roof, Mrs. Edgar Saltus,
Sylvia B. Saltzberg, Jane Scales, Mary Scharon, Edna Bell Seward, Mary Sharon,
Elizabeth Sheldon, Mary Wollstonecraft Shelley, Mrs. Chetwood Smith, Lady
Eleanor Smith, Mrs. Harry Pugh Smith, Emma-Lindsay Squier, "Francis Ste-
vens" (Gertrude Bennett), Edith Lichty Stewart, Gertrude Macaulay Sutton,
Pearl Norton Swet, Tessida Swinges, Jewel Bothwell Tull, Lida Wilson Turner,
Maud E. Uschold, Louise van de Verg, Isobel Walker, Elizabeth Adt Wenzler,
Everil Worrell, Gertrude M. Wright, Stella Wynne, and Katherine Yates. *All* of
these women appeared in *Weird Tales* before C. L. Moore made her debut in
that magazine and the gender of *none* of them was hidden behind initials or
ambiguous names—and three even publicized their status as married women.

Many of these female authors were favorites of the readership (which, in turn,
may have been over 26 percent female). Some of the highest reader-voted stories
in the entire existence of *Weird Tales* were by female authors Greye La Spina
("Invaders From the Dark," three-part serial beginning in April, 1925, published as a book in 1960) and Everil Worrell ("The Bird of Space," September,
1926, subject of that issue's cover). Mary Elizabeth Counselman's "Three
Marked Pennies" (August, 1934) generated such a popular response that readers
fondly mentioned it in letters for years to come and voted it "one of the most
popular stories the magazine ever published."[6] Counselman was introduced to
the magazine while a member of a Tallahassee fan club and eventually published
30 stories and six poems in *Weird Tales* over a period of two decades, from
1933–1953.

Nor was Counselman the most prolific female *Weird Tales* author. Allison V.
Harding, for example, published thirty-six stories in the magazine, many of

which were heralded on the cover with her full name. Meanwhile, Dorothy Quick also published well-received poetry and prose for two decades, from 1934–1954, the year the magazine folded.

Further, the very November, 1933 issue which carried Moore's debut *also* featured *three other women authors:* Mary Elizabeth Counselman, Cristel Hastings, and Brooke Byrne. The last was a debut and therefore the 115th known female author *accepted* before Moore's debut. Thus, C. L. Moore was the 116th *known* female fiction author to appear in *Weird Tales* since it was founded a decade before. Indeed, a total of at least 127 women published 365 stories in *Weird Tales* over the course of its lifetime from 1923–1954 (see table 7 for a complete bibliography of them and their stories). These women represented over 17 percent of all the gender-identifiable fiction authors to appear in the magazine.[7]

Finally, *two-fifths of all the gender-identifiable poets published in the magazine—over 40 percent, amounting to 63 in number—were female, and these female poets published 30 percent of all the poetry to appear in the magazine.*[8] (See table 8 for a complete bibliography of these women and their poems.)

So, what we have here is a magazine which published women from the very beginning of its existence, in which all editors published women writers during their tenures, a magazine with a long-time female editor, with a female artist sometimes called "The First Lady of pulp magazine illustration" as the most famous of its cover artists, with a readership which may have been over a quarter female, with a membership in the magazine's fan club which may have been between a quarter and almost a third female, with over 17 percent of its fiction authors female, and with over 40 percent of its poets female. Obviously, there was no need for Moore to conceal her gender from anyone at *Weird Tales.* "Weird sisters" were highly visible at all levels of *Weird Tales* during its existence, from editor to primary cover artist to writers to the readership.

Such high visibility makes one wonder why, decades later, Alice Sheldon felt compelled to send her first story to a science fiction editor under the gender-concealing pseudonym of "James Tiptree, Jr." She said she did so because she presumed the field was biased against women and she didn't want to be rejected because of her gender. Yet she *also* told us that her introduction to the field was at the age of nine, in 1924, when her uncle gave her a copy of *Weird Tales.* She claimed she devoured all subsequent issues of *Weird Tales.*[9] How, then, could she have failed to see all those female names in that very magazine—emblazoned in full on the cover, in the table of contents, on the stories and poems themselves, in the letter column, and in the club membership lists?

Of course, *Weird Tales* was a *fantasy* magazine, which perhaps attracted more female readers and writers than the explicitly science fictional magazines. This may also have been a factor in the two Munsey magazines, *Famous Fantastic Mysteries* (1939–1953) and *Fantastic Novels Magazine* (1940–1951), both edited for their entire duration by Mary Gnaedinger. Although both published science fiction, they also published fantasy. And here, female authors accounted for 11.58 percent of the gender-identifiable authors in these two magazines.[10] Meanwhile, a gender analysis *of the number of stories* published in two other "weird fiction" magazines reveals similar percentages of female authorship. For example, at least 15.8 percent of the stories in *The Thrill Book* (published only in 1919) were by identifiable female authors, while at least 16.3 percent of the stories in *Oriental Stories* (1930–1932) were by identifiable female contributors (see bottom of table 8 for both magazines).[11]

But even among the most "male-oriented" of the science fiction magazines, female authors could be found. *Planet Stories* (1939–1955), for instance, had a reputation for publishing the most juvenile "space opera" adventure stories of its age. Its appeal was entirely to teenage boys who wanted action above all else—but even here five percent of all *Planet Stories* authors were female.[12] And things improved in the 1950s. For example, 10.15 percent of all the authors published in *Galaxy* between 1950–1960 were female, while 16.12 percent of the authors published in *The Magazine of Fantasy and Science Fiction* between 1949–1960 were female, a figure comparable with the 17 percent in *Weird Tales*.[13]

Yet the invisibility of these early women writers (not to mention female letter writers and club members), even to other women, seems to be a continuing problem. We are routinely told, without being given any numbers, that women were an insignificantly small minority in the early fantasy and science fiction magazines—if they existed at all. By actually looking at the numbers, however, we find that their minority status has been grossly misrepresented.

Even so, despite possible female readership being 26 percent or more in magazines like *Weird Tales*; despite female authors numbering 127 in *Weird Tales* alone and accounting for over 40 percent of *Weird Tales* poets and 16 to 17 percent of the *Weird Tales* and *Magazine of Fantasy and Science Fiction* fiction authors—women *were* a minority. And, *because* they were a minority, this is used as evidence, per se, of the field's hostility toward them.

But, is minority status, in and of itself, evidence of active discrimination—bigotry—by a male establishment? I contend it is not. Rather, this seems to me a highly selective, indeed, prejudicial view of minority status. If the genre at that time was not already *presumed* to be bigoted, female minority status would not be so quickly trotted out as proof of prejudice. Let me illustrate.

The minority status of women genre writers before 1950 did not make the period all that different from later, presumably more "enlightened" times, such as the 1970s, when the women's movement began to make itself felt in the field. According to Pamela Sargent, as late as 1974 only 10–15 percent of all science fiction writers were female, meaning that even in the mid-Seventies women were outnumbered perhaps nine to one by men.[14] This ratio is even worse than the gender ratio in *The Magazine of Fantasy and Science Fiction* twenty years before. Joanna Russ calculated the female membership of the Science Fiction

Writers of America (SFWA) for that same year at 18 percent (about the same as the percentage, 17 percent, of female fiction authors in *Weird Tales* from 1923– 1954).[15] And, in fact, women were a minority of *all* American writers in the Seventies. The 1970 U.S. Census, for instance, found that only 30.5 percent of 26,004 professional authors were women.[16]

Nevertheless, in 1970, Ursula K. Le Guin won the Hugo Award for Best Novel with *The Left Hand of Darkness* and, between 1969 and 1973, 14 percent of the 87 works nominated for Hugos were by women, a percentage proportionate to their membership in the profession. Between 1974 and 1978, this percentage climbed to women writing 18 percent of the ninety-nine works nominated for Hugos. At the same time, Le Guin again won the Hugo for Best Novel in 1975 with *The Dispossessed* and Kate Wilhelm winning for Best Novel in 1977 with *Where Late The Sweet Birds Sang*. In 1979, women were honored all out of proportion to their numbers when 34 percent of the twenty-five works nominated for Hugos were by women—including four of the five nominees for Best Novel, which Vonda McIntyre won for *Dreamsnake*.[17]

So, while women were *always* in a minority almost exactly comparable to that of earlier periods throughout the Seventies they *were* being nominated for the field's highest award—and they were winning! Hence, it is difficult to believe there was a biased male establishment operating against women in the Seventies, despite their minority status. Indeed, Marion Zimmer Bradley stated as much in 1977. "If any woman believes that science fiction and fantasy publishers are closed to women," Bradley said, "she is either gravely misinformed, or she is making excuses for her own incompetence by attributing her failure to editorial prejudice."[18]

And women *continued* to be a minority. Let us advance a quarter of a century to 1999, on the cusp of the twenty-first century. In that year we find that identifiably female authors accounted for only 36 percent of the professional members of the Science Fiction and Fantasy Writers of America, Inc. (SFFWA), worse than the percentage of female poets in *Weird Tales* decades before.[19]

But, unlike accusations against the field in the twenties, thirties, forties, and fifties, to our knowledge no one in 1999 was claiming that a pervasive bias against women authors limited them to just over a third of the membership. This was because in 1999 the field was not *presumed* to be prejudiced against them—so minority status was not seen as evidence of exclusion and discrimination. Indeed, as science fiction writer Charles Platt stated in 1983, "Today, although women are still a minority in science fiction, they are not in any sense oppressed."[20]

Minority status alone, then, is not necessarily a sign of "oppression." Unless, that is, we are speaking of science fiction before the coming of the women's liberation movement. *Then* minority status is seen as an obvious sign of "oppression." It is an article of faith. Thus, continued Platt, "Twenty years ago

[1963], when there were hardly any women at all writing science fiction, we had an obligation to . . . speak out against any prejudices that existed."[21]

And yet, as we have seen, the figures for women writers for the Seventies and for earlier periods for some magazines are almost exactly the same! Yet women appearing in virtually the same percentages in the earlier periods are deemed to have been non-existent, "excluded" due to sexism. Meanwhile, women authors totaling almost the very same percentages appearing in the Seventies are deemed to have "at last" won entrance into the field and their very existence is offered as proof of the absence of gender barricades.

The reason minority status *alone* is accepted as proof of "oppression" before 1963 is because the field before 1963 was *presumed* to have been prejudiced against women—so minority status is accepted as all the proof one needs of the field's active bias against them. The reasoning is a closed loop. First we presume prejudice, then we point to minority status, which is then seen as proof of prejudice, even if that minority status is virtually identical to later periods praised for their lack of prejudice. The eras discussed are thus subjected to a double standard of evidence and logic.

We should realize that minority status, of *whatever* percentage, by itself proves nothing. It doesn't tell us anything at all about the relationship *between* the minority and the majority. For example, we know that women represented 36 percent of the professional science fiction writers in the 1990s. But, in *Isaac Asimov's Science Fiction Magazine*, October 1992, a sample 1990s magazine chosen at random (a friend simply mailed it to me), we find women disproportionately *over*-represented at 50 percent. There were six stories in this issue. Three stories were by men and three by women: Pamela Sargent, Maureen F. McHugh, and Sharon N. Farber. Women can easily be a minority, then, and yet still be treated as equals if there is an egalitarian ethos permeating the environment.

Hence, in order to honestly answer the question of possible discrimination, we have to look beyond the simplistic numbers game to examine the culture in which men and women actually operated, we have to look at real-world gender relations. Only by doing this can we determine if the glass was half empty—or half full. In an attempt to get at real-world gender relations, let us look at the world of science fiction fandom, beginning with the actual readership of the magazines.

Notes

1. See T. G. Cockcroft, "An Index to 'The Eyrie' and Other Readers' Departments," *Fantasy Commentator*, VIII, Nos. 3 & 4, 1995, pp. 217–229. "The Eyrie" was the *Weird Tales* letters column. Cockcroft lists the names of letter writers and gives a total count of letters to the magazine, but he does not give a total count of letter writers, nor does he break them down by sex. Based upon his listing, I performed these calculations myself.

2. Everil Worrell, Letter to the Editor, *Weird Tales*, May, 1953, p. 94.

3. The six issues and their specifics were: The January, 1943 issue, of which eighteen of the sixty-seven gender-identifiable new members were female, for a female percentage of 26.8 percent; the May, 1947 issue, of which twenty-one of the sixty-two gender-identifiable new members were female, for a female percentage of 33.8 percent; the September, 1947 issue, of which twenty-three of the seventy-five gender-identifiable new members were female, for a female percentage of 30.6 percent; the September, 1949 issue, of which fourteen of the 102 gender-identifiable new members were female, for a female percentage of 13.72 percent; the November, 1949 issue, of which twenty-six of the ninety-one gender-identifiable new members were female, for a female percentage of 28.57 percent; and the May, 1952 issue, of which sixteen of the fifty-one gender-identifiable new members were female, for a female percentage of 31.37 percent. The January, 1943 membership roster listed sixteen-year-old Hugh Hefner, of Chicago, the future *Playboy* magazine publisher, as a new member.

4. See Effie W. Fifield, "The Amazing Adventure of Joe Scranton," October, 1923; Greye La Spina, "A Suitor From the Shadows," June, 1927; Sophie Wenzel Ellis, "The White Wizard," September, 1929; and Katherine Metcalf Roof, "A Million Years After," November, 1930.

5. Donald A. Wollheim, *Avon Fantasy Reader No. 16*, 1951, p. 59, introducing Greye La Spina's story, "The Wax Doll," reprinted from *The Thrill Book*, August 1, 1919.

6. Mike Ashley, *The Illustrated Book of Science Fiction Lists*, Cornerstone Library/Simon & Schuster: N.Y., 1982, p. 88.

7. This is my gender analysis of the complete listing of authors in Thomas G. Cockcroft, *Index to the Weird Fiction Magazines*, Cockcroft: Lower Hutt, New Zealand, 1964. *Weird Tales* published 843 authors between 1923–1954. Of these, I was able to identify 127 as female, representing 15 percent of the total. However, I was unable to identify the gender of 112 authors due to ambiguous first names, the use of initials, or because four stories were published by anonymous authors. This left 725 gender-identifiable authors, of whom 606 were male. The 127 identifiable female authors represented 17.44 percent of the 728.

8. This is my gender analysis of the complete listing of authors in Thomas G. Cockcroft, *Index to the Verse in Weird Tales, Including Oriental Stories and The Magic Carpet Magazine and The Thrill Book*, Cockcroft: Melling, New Zealand, 1960. (This was cross-referenced with the list of poets in *The Collector's Index to Weird Tales*, by Sheldon R. Jaffery and Fred Cook, Bowling Green State University Popular Press: Bowling Green, OH, 1985.) Cockcroft listed a total of 161 poets, of whom I could identify the gender of 156. Of these, 63 were female, or 40.38 percent of the 156.

9. Alice Sheldon, "A Woman Writing Science Fiction and Fantasy," in Denise Du Pont, Ed., *Women of Vision*, St. Martin's Press: N.Y., 1988, p., 46.

10. This is my gender analysis of the complete listing of authors in Ray F. Bowman, *An Index to Famous Fantastic Mysteries and Fantastic Novels Magazine*, Bowman: Carmel, Indiana, 1991. These two magazines published a total of 180 poets and fiction authors over their life spans. Of these, sixteen could not be gender-identified due to ambiguous first names or the use of initials. Of the remaining 164, I identified nineteen as female. These nineteen represented 10.55 percent of the 180 grand total and 11.58 percent of the 164 gender-identifiable total.

11. These are percentages derived from an analysis of *all stories* published in these two magazines. Had I eliminated stories by authors who could not be gender-identified because of the use of initials or ambiguous names, no doubt the percentages of stories by female authors would have been higher.

12. This is my gender analysis of the complete listing of authors in Ray F. Bowman, *An Index to Planet Stories*, Bowman: Carmel, Indiana, 1989. *Planet Stories* published 209 authors over the course of its existence. Of these, I was unable to identify the gender of fourteen, due to the use of initials or ambiguous first names. Of the 195 gender-identifiable authors, ten were female. These ten represented 4.7 percent of the 209 grand total and 5.1 percent of the 195 gender-identifiable total.

13. This is my gender analysis of the complete listing of authors in Ray F. Bowman, *An Index*

to Galaxy Science Fiction, Bowman, Toledo: Ohio, 1987 and Ray F. Bowman, *Index to The Magazine of Fantasy and Science Fiction*, Bowman, Carmel: Indiana, 1988. From 1950–1960, *Galaxy* published 203 authors, of which I was unable to gender-identify six due to ambiguous first names or the use of initials. Of the remaining 197 gender-identifiable authors, 20 were female. These 20 represented 9.85 percent of the 203 grand total and 10.15 percent of the 197 gender-identifiable total.

From 1949–1960 *The Magazine of Fantasy and Science Fiction* published 424 poets and fiction authors. Of these, I was unable to identify the gender of 27 due to ambiguous first names or the use of initials. Of the remaining 397 gender-identifiable authors, 64 were female. These 64 represented 15.10 percent of the 424 grand total and 16.12 percent of the 397 gender-identifiable total.

14. Pamela Sargent, Ed., *Women of Wonder*, 1974, p. xiv.

15. Russ, *How To Suppress Women's Writing*, p. 97.

16. Bureau of the Census, *Census: 1970 Occupational Characteristics*, U.S. Government Printing Office: Wash., D.C.

17. See Donald Franson and Howard DeVore, *A History of the Hugo, Nebula, and International Fantasy Awards*, Misfit Press: Dearborn, MI, 1978, and *Science Fiction Chronicle* and *Locus* for 1979.

18. Marion Zimmer Bradley, "An Evolution of Consciousness," *Science Fiction Review*, August, 1977, p. 45.

19. This percentage is my own computation. Based upon their names, I tabulated all identifiable male and female authors in the 1999 SFFWA Directory, as well as those unidentifiable due to the use of initials or ambiguous names. There were 1,023 active members. Of these, 574 (56 percent) were male; 366 (36 percent) were female; and 83 (8 percent) were unidentifiable by me as to their sex, either because of ambiguous names or the use of initials. Were we to look only at the 940 gender-identifiable authors, then the female percentage would increase to 38.9 percent, still less than the percentage of female *Weird Tales* poets.

20. Platt, *Dream Makers, Volume II*, p. xii.

21. Platt, *Dream Makers, Volume II*, p. xii.

4

Female Fandom

P ULP SCIENCE FICTION editors invariably encouraged female readers and their
participation. As Managing Editor Charles D. Hornig said to two women
who published letters in the June, 1934 *Wonder Stories*, "As we have repeatedly
stated, we are particularly pleased to receive letters from our female readers,"
(pp. 115, 120). Samuel Merwin, Jr., editor of *Thrilling Wonder Stories*, said much
the same when he lamented in the December, 1946 issue (p. 100) that he didn't
have a letter from a "femme fan" to publish that month and encouraged his
female readers to send in letters.

This welcoming stance toward women readers was reciprocated. Even
Astounding (later *Analog*), usually considered the hardest of the hard science
fiction magazines, had more female readers than generally acknowledged. A
gender analysis of all those who wrote letters to it between its founding in 1930
and 1960 (a date after which it is presumed women were more welcome) reveals
that during these three decades, 1,947 readers wrote to the magazine. I was able
to identify the gender of 1,634 writers (eliminating those who published under
initials or androgynous names, as well as those with missing first names or written anonymously). Of these, 111 were women, representing just under 7 percent
(6.8 percent) of the identifiable writers. (This percentage climbed to 9 percent
for 1961–1979.)[1] Meanwhile, a gender analysis of all the letter-writers to John
W. Campbell's *Unknown* (later *Unknown Worlds*) tells us that 9.5 percent of all
writers were female.[2]

But women were almost 17 percent of all the gender-identifiable letter writers
to the family of "new Munsey" magazines which included *Famous Fantastic
Mysteries, Fantastic Novels*, and *A. Merritt's Fantasy*.[3] And a sampling of two
issues of *Fantastic Adventures* chosen at random (April, 1948 and April, 1949)
reveals that women were 40 percent of the gender-identifiable letter writers.

To highlight the importance of these numbers, recall that most of these genre magazines perpetually balanced on the knife edge of insolvency. This financial fragility was an enduring problem. Sam Moskowitz, for instance, tells us that *Science Fiction Plus*, the magazine he edited for Hugo Gernsback in 1953, never earned a profit. Even so, if, at the end, he could have increased circulation by only 3 percent, it would have at least broken even. If he could have increased circulation by only 4 percent, he said, it would have been a profitable magazine and survived.[4] Given this harsh economic reality, every reader counted and editors could not afford to ignore a segment of their readership which might number anywhere from 7 to 40 percent. Economics alone, then, would have induced editors to encourage female readership and letter writing.

Both of which, we are discovering, were significant. And the letters in these science fiction magazines from female readers give us perhaps our best insight into what the average female reader of the magazines felt about her participation in the genre.

Typical of such readers was Joyce Kuhn, of Grand Rapids, who wrote to the editor of *Thrilling Wonder Stories* (February, 1949, p. 149) saying, "I like science fiction and fantasy very much and you have one of the best magazines on the market. Oh, mine editor friend, orchids to you." In that same issue of *Thrilling Wonder Stories*, Grace Mosher, of Binghamton, NY, said (p. 148), "I started reading science fiction from books. . . . The first magazine in this category I ever bought was *Startling Stories* and I've never missed an issue. . . . Today I have three or four years of magazines. Some day my son and my daughters will read them too—and until they do you have one staunch friend in our house and she is a woman." And Evangeline Brunson, of Beaumont, TX, even sent in a poem praising *Thrilling Wonder Stories* (April, 1947, p. 98):

> I turn each page from age to age,
> I read the livelong night.
> My eyes grow wide, my ways grow wild,
> My hair is turning white!
>
> Yet still I seek . . . yet still I buy . . .
> Yet still I read the stuff!
> And, though my reason's tottering,
> I cannot get enough!

In like manner, Winifred Beisiegel, of Sparrowbush, New York, wrote to *Startling Stories* in May, 1952 (p. 132) that she'd been reading SF magazines since at least 1932—and her mother had read the literature when she, in turn, had been a young girl, particularly enjoying H. Rider Haggard's *The Return of She*. Indeed, it seems a lot of female fans began reading the magazines as girls. For example, Susan Powell, of Rumson, NJ, wrote in the March, 1957 issue of *Imag-*

inative Tales (p. 128) that, "Although I am only 12 years of age, I have been reading your magazine for some time, and I already am a confirmed science fiction fan. The same goes for my best girl friend, Carole Cushman. In fact, we're both so interested in science fiction we're writing a book! Please keep us happy with your great magazines." In that same issue of *Imaginative Tales,* eighteen-year-old Dorothy Silva, of Providence, RI, wrote (p. 123), "I have been reading science fiction for five years now [i.e., since age 13], and love it."

Zillah Kendall, of San Bernardino, California, wrote to *Thrilling Wonder Stories* in February, 1953 (p. 133), saying that she'd been reading SF magazines since she "was about 14 years old—(back in the Hugo Gernsback days)." Likewise, Miss Ona Mills, of Statesville, NC, wrote in the August, 1956 issue of *Science Fiction Quarterly* (p. 94) that, "I've been reading SF since I was 14—I'm an old lady of 27."[5] In the October, 1952 issue of *Imagination: Stories of Science and Fantasy* (p. 155), eighteen-year-old Sherry Payne Kohler wrote that she'd been reading science fiction since age nine. And in that same issue science fiction author Mari Wolf wrote in her column on fanzines (p. 145) that she began reading the literature in 1939 when she was not yet a teenager.

Other female science fiction authors recalled similar beginnings. For example, Zenna Henderson, later to become a prolific SF writer in the 1950s, remembered that "I started reading SF when I was about twelve [which would be c.1929, as she was born in 1917], with the old *Astounding Stories* and *Amazing Stories,* and fantasy with the old *Weird Tales.*"[6] Madeleine L'Engle, who was also to publish magazine SF in the Fifties, but who became better known for juvenile SF novels such as *A Wrinkle in Time,* also began reading SF around then. She was born in 1918 and said, "I discovered science fiction early, as a lonely only child growing up, for my first 12 years, in New York City. . . . For me, the real world was clearer in the books of E. Nesbit and H. G. Wells than in the world of school. So, I started writing science fiction when I was eight or nine [which would have been c. 1926–1928]."[7]

In 1940 at the age of fourteen, Anne McCaffrey, today one of the field's most popular writers, read and re-read Austin Tappan Wright's classic utopian novel, *Islandia.* She has been, of course, reading (and writing) SF ever since.[8] Meanwhile, well-known SF writer Joanna Russ, born in 1937, seems to have begun reading SF around 1948 or 1949 at the age of twelve. She recalled that, "my mother brought home huge Groff Conklin anthologies to put her to sleep. I stole them. . . . SF and fantasy seemed to me a revelation, a tremendous widening of horizons. . . . I would look at the stars and thrill at the idea that there might be life on other planets . . . those stories are transfigured by memory . . . they were magic."[9]

NASA engineer Donna Shirley also began reading science fiction at age twelve, in 1954. There was only one science fiction book in the library of the small Oklahoma town where she lived, Ray Bradbury's *The Martian Chronicles.*

"I checked the book out over and over again," she recalled. Later, Arthur C. Clarke's *The Sands of Mars* also fascinated her. "It was the first time I realized that people could go and live on another planet." So she decided to become a space explorer and go to Mars.[10]

And she did. She led the NASA team that built the Mars Pathfinder spacecraft which deposited the rover Sojourner on Mars in 1997. Indeed, from 1994–1998 she was the manager of the entire NASA Mars exploration program. And in 2004, half a century after picking up Bradbury's book at age twelve, she became director of the Science Fiction Museum and Hall of Fame in Seattle.

Thus, there is reason to believe some of these female readers remained interested in the genre over many years and decades, just as did male readers. Henrietta McGee, of Woodhaven, Long Island, wrote to *Fantastic Adventures*, July 1950 (p. 155), to say she'd been reading that particular magazine since 1940. On the same page, Mary Bitters wrote from Chicago to say she'd been reading the magazine since 1947. In the June, 1946 *Famous Fantastic Mysteries*, Mrs. M. Dominick, of New Brunswick, NJ, wrote (p. 8) saying she'd been reading that magazine since 1940. Likewise, in the April, 1948 *Famous Fantastic Mysteries*, Lois Turner, of Wichita, Kansas, wrote (p. 123) saying she'd been reading the magazine since 1940. And in 2004, more than half a century after being introduced to SF, Science Fiction Book Club member Verna Skogland remembered that, "The pulps were great in their day. . . . I read my first science fiction in the old *Planet Stories* in 1948, a little epic called 'The Rocketeers Have Shaggy Ears,' and was hooked."[11]

Molly Acreman, of Austin, TX, wrote to the March, 1941 *Science Fiction* (p. 88) to not only say she'd been reading science fiction since 1931, but that she was also a member of the nationwide fan club, the Science Fiction League. But Wanita Norris, of Fort Wayne, Indiana, wasn't so lucky as to be involved with fellow fans. Writing to the summer, 1954 issue of *Startling Stories* (p. 125) she said that, "if there are any males who don't think a girl is nuts because she likes SF and parapsychology (there don't seem to be any around here), I wish they'd drop me a line. Gals are welcome too, of course."

In fact, many female fans wrote similar letters saying that they had to endure the hostility or ridicule of family or friends in order to enjoy their favorite literature. In response to a female fan who had written to *Planet Stories* saying her friends and husband thought she was "foolish" to read science fiction, Mrs. Richard Leek, of Oak Ridge, NJ wrote to *Planet Stories* (fall, 1954, p. 95) saying, "She and I are in the same boat only MY friends and husband don't think I am *foolish* for reading SF; they think I'm *nuts!*"

Such hostile attitudes from the friends and relatives of female fans were in stark contrast to the warm welcome female science fiction fans normally received from male fans. In those days the magazines routinely published a letter writer's entire address along with the letter. Because of this, female fans often wrote about the many friendships with male fans which resulted. Thus, in the February, 1949 issue of *Thrilling Wonder Stories,* Gwen Cunningham, of Oakland, CA, wrote (p. 143) thanking the many male fans who had helped her find back issues of the magazine. "I'd like, first of all," she said, "to thank you for publishing a letter of mine and the many fans who answered it so kindly. . . . I am grateful for so many kind friends, all of whom I tried to thank at once. If I missed anybody, please let me thank him [sic] now. It was wonderful to realize how many helpful and generous people there are after all. And to the others who sent cards with hints on how to get magazines I want in the future, I extend thanks also. I am proud to belong to such a swell bunch of folks—the fans of stf [science fiction] and fantasy!"

But, while male fans generally welcomed them, these female readers felt equal enough to take issue with male fans, if need be. Writing to *Thrilling Wonder Stories* (February, 1949, p. 148), Grace Mosher of Binghamton, NY, objected to some ungentlemanly comments from a male reader saying, "May a mere woman reader of fifteen years standing say something to that big lug Rodney 'Rodway' Palmer? You know he is really asking to be put in his place. . . . My dear Rod, where would you be if it weren't for a woman? Don't belittle us. I read these magazines when I had to hide them from my mother or see them burned and I liked them. I'll admit that some of the dry scientific data went over my head, but for years I have returned again and again to the same magazine. I've made a great many others read them by lending or giving mine and have helped fandom to grow. I know how I feel and, after fifteen years, I don't feel like changing my style of reading just to please a man!"[12]

Marian Cox, of Hilton Village, Virginia, also took issue in a letter to *Startling Stories* (July, 1951, p. 134) with stereotypical male attitudes toward intelligent women. "Why, oh, why," she asked, "do you poor misguided males seem to think that any female fan, or even any intelligent girl, has to be first cousin to Lena the Hyena? [That is, ugly.] Won't your male vanity let you admit that a girl can have brains and beauty too?"

Likewise, Vieve Masterson wrote to *Startling Stories* (Spring, 1954, pp. 119–120) to chastise male letter-writers for troglodyte attitudes. "Ah, the male ego," she wrote, "'tis, indeed, a wondrous thing to behold! . . . Especially if it's a little bit irked. I have a few answers for [a male letter-writer], too, but I won't put them all down here, wouldn't be very ladylike. . . . The whole thing stems from the time when the men were the 'lord and master' and women were 'chattels.' Oh well, the battle of the sexes always has been, is, and most likely will be around until men realize and quit resenting the fact that women can do most anything as well, and sometimes better, than they can. I can't speak for the rest of the Fanettes, but I, for one, am not afraid I couldn't hold my own in a mixed group."

Nor were male SF authors immune from female criticism in the pages of the magazines. Writing in the fall, 1955 issue of *Startling Stories* (p. 8, 108), Diane Tenglin, of Burlington, Iowa, said, "Being a woman, I don't believe the lead story [by Bryce Walton] in the Spring *Startling Stories* is possible, realistic, intelligent, well-thought-out, or even worth reading. Not because I am defending myself, but because I have had, I think, considerably more contact with women than the author, and that type of woman does not predominate. Also, women do not live longer just because they don't work as hard, as most men seem to think. Many women work just as hard as many men. Women, and this may or may not surprise you, are built differently than men, physically and emotionally. Society allows them a greater expression of emotion. So less ulcers, fewer repressions, etc. Also, and more significantly, more male infants die, and male children suffer more from the common childhood illnesses."

Nor were female readers shy about describing what they wanted the editors to publish in the SF magazines. In a letter to the fall, 1955 issue of *Startling Stories* (p. 8), female fan Rory Magill Faulkner (a long-time member of the Los Angeles Science Fantasy Society and a sometime writer of science fiction verse and prose under the name "Rory Magill") complained about the demise of *Thrilling Wonder Stories* and *Fantastic Story* and the fact that *Startling* had fallen to quarterly publication. "Is this a sign of the decline and fall of science fiction?," she asked. "I hope not, for what am I going to read then? I don't like slick magazines, love stories, and am fed to the teeth with murder mysteries. In sheer self defense I have gone back to the beginning of my SF collection and have been reading the old ones over again." She objected to "The Snows of Ganymede," by Poul Anderson, because there was, "Too much sociological stuff in this story for me. I like'em more human—and I don't mean love stories, either."

Likewise, in the second issue of Louis Silberkleit's *Science Fiction*, June, 1939, editor Charles D. Hornig prominently featured (pp. 118–121) a letter from Kansas nurse Naomi D. Slimmer, a reader of the first issue, who said that she and her sisters were enthusiastic readers of science fiction pulps. We are "two housewives, an office worker, a high school girl, and a trained nurse among us five sisters and we all read *Science Fiction* (when we can snag it from brother and two husbands) . . . ," she wrote. "You'd be surprised how many women read magazines of this type. Even the pussy-cats who go for sticky romances make a grab for a copy when I'm dealing out magazines to the patients at our hospital. The nurses read them too . . . to keep awake and think of something besides a cranky patient. So how about giving us females a thought when you are picking tales for future issues? Phooey on the hussies who are always getting their clothes torn off and walling an amorous eye at the poor overworked hero."

Hornig replied sympathetically, "I have received so many letters from women who read science-fiction, just lately. . . . Their group has grown to such proportions that they must certainly be taken into consideration by the male adherents."

But, if such female readers and their concerns were *not* taken into consideration, they let their displeasure be known. For example, Gwen Cunningham, who thought male science fiction fans were a "swell bunch of folks," nevertheless commented sarcastically on the absurd attire of so many science fiction magazine cover girls. Writing in the summer 1946 issue of *Thrilling Wonder Stories* (p. 100) she asked, "What I'd like to know is *how* (really, now) do the various bras of your various pictured heroines stay put? For such scientific atmosphere as your mag exudes, I'm afraid the laws of gravity, triangulation, the point of strain, etc., are entirely overlooked. Also, please tell me where I can get a few of those—er, intimate articles for myself. Maybe with a little liquid cement."

Ethel M. David, of Schenectady, NY, also wrote to *Amazing Stories* (September, 1951, p. 150) ridiculing the proliferation of scientifically impossible scantily clad outer space females on the magazine's covers. "Why clad the males from head to foot in space suits and helmets," she asked, "and have the women practically naked? Is it because the women are superior in resisting the elements, space, or the atmosphere of a planet than the males—or is it because you think so little of your magazine? If you have to have sex on the covers, why not also include naked men, as well?"

Marian Cox, of Hilton Village, Virginia, complained to *Startling Stories* (July, 1951, p. 134) about the same problem. "Apparently," she wrote, the cover artist of the March issue "never heard of the law of gravity. . . . If that gal leans over or even takes a deep breath, oh brother! My uncle's reaction when he saw it—'It's startling, all right.' Someday, gravity will triumph over modesty, and then where will the poor girl be? Probably in jail. Holy Suffering Catfish! My family disapproves of science fiction enough as it is. Must you prejudice them more? It's getting to the place where I have to sneak my mags in."

Indeed, such covers were sometimes one of the main reasons female fans had to endure even more disdain than male fans did in order to buy and read pulp science fiction. Perhaps Josephine Bishop, of San Leandro, CA, was typical in facing this hurdle when she wrote to *Thrilling Wonder Stories* (February, 1949, p. 146) saying, "Being a female of the species and one who has had her share of the wolf whistles, I still don't like that knowing leer that comes over the faces of the idle loungers and the characters in attendance every time I pick up this mag. They do leer in a most crude and moronic manner. Why, oh why, must I be subjected to this when I L-O-V-E you the way that I do?"

As can be seen from these letters, female readers weren't reticent in asserting their right to inclusion or in taking editors to task over provocative depictions of semi-nude women on the covers. And, eventually, it seems they were at least partially successful concerning this latter controversy. Writing in the July, 1956 issue of *Amazing* (p. 120), Lethalu Ray, a female reader from Burlington, Washington, noted that women finally "got the cover question settled" to their satisfaction.

Indeed, tenacious lobbying by the female readership seemed to slowly change the content of the stories, as well as the covers. Writing in the July, 1963 issue of *Amazing's* sister magazine, *Fantastic Stories of Imagination* (p. 4), Anna Livia Plurabelle reminisced, "The first copy of *Weird Tales* I have saved (O what we throw away!) is 1936. My uncle, who was then the proper dean of a very proper law school, used to slip them to me. . . . In those days the great thrill was when the green octopus chased the heroine thru the swamps of Venus and she lost her brassiere. Now it's vice versa, but just as thrilling."

The very next letter in that same issue was from an angry male reader who complained to female editor Cele Goldsmith that, "You also give the impression that sex is a taboo factor in modern s/f artwork. Give me the good old days of Seabury Quinn and heaving bosoms. More Gray Mouser tales are in order, at least."

To which Goldsmith replied, "Sex is not taboo. Heaving bosoms are. There is not necessarily an equivalence between the two. The Gray Mouser, due again in our August [1963] issue ["Bazaar of the Bizarre"], reports the heaving bosoms are becoming passe in Lankhmar, as well." And the cover of the issue in which this discussion took place was a surrealistic painting of aliens by Jacquelyn Blair, one of the female cover artists Goldsmith used.

Women, therefore, were a larger share of the science fiction readership than realized. In addition, the comments they made in the letter columns of all the science fiction (and fantasy) magazines indicate that the female readership of these magazines was a dedicated, enthusiastic, and influential cohort of readers. And it seems these female fans valued highly their freedom to write to the science fiction magazines and to sometimes engage in heated discussions on a basis of equality with male fans. Thus, when the editor of *Planet Stories* raised the possibility of abolishing letters to the editor in 1949, prolific letter writer Virginia L. Shawl, of Freeport, Illinois, protested. "Where else can a lady enjoy a good literary brawl and still remain a lady?," she asked in the fall, 1949 issue, p. 107. "Where else can she indulge in the wildest flights of fancy? Take down her hair, kick off her shoes, and really dish it out to all and sundry? Not to mention, getting dished, too. . . . Abolish the ads. Abolish the stories. Abolish the covers. But keep the Vizigraph [the letters column]. . . . Here is one fevered and fervent vote for keeping it!"

Thus, we have seen that letters from women readers were common in the early science fiction and fantasy magazines. We have also seen that these letters suggest an egalitarian gender culture existed in those letters columns. Now let us turn our attention to the participation of female fans in fan clubs and similar early fan activities.

As with the readership of early science fiction magazines, women were also a much larger proportion of active early science fiction fandom than has usually been acknowledged. As Leigh Brackett always insisted, "There always were a certain number of women fans and women readers."[13] The long-lived National Fantasy Fan Federation, for example, which is still in existence, had a large number of female fans as both ordinary members and as officers. In 1954, for instance, Janie Lamb was the Treasurer and Honey Wood and Nan Gerding co-edited the group's fanzine, while Susan Magnus reviewed other fanzines for that publication.[14] And it is in looking at these first "fem fans" (as they sometimes called themselves) and their relations with the majority male fans that we can begin to really unveil the nature of gender relations in early science fiction.

Despite the fact that female fans were also "present at the creation," their presence, like that of women writers, has usually been either denied or dismissed. For example, in the 1980s another myth began to develop about "When It Changed": Supposedly, it was the TV show *Star Trek* (1966–1969) that made all the difference in female science fiction participation. British science fiction writer Lisa Tuttle, for one, argued that the influence of *Star Trek* "should not be underestimated" in bringing women into science fiction.[15]

Isaac Asimov, again, also contributed to this mythologizing. He erroneously believed the program began airing in 1965, that it was immediately popular, and was especially so with women. "When the television moguls tried to end it after its first year," he said in 1982, "the outpouring of protest was one of the phenomena of the age. For once (and perhaps only that once), the front office was frightened by the sheer weight and force of popular anger into continuing a program they thought unprofitable. . . . More important than that mere fact was this: For the first time, a piece of science fiction not only gained a mass following, but gained one in which women made up a large percentage. . . . The result is that from 1965 on we have seen the gradual feminization of the audience for printed science-fiction. At the very least, 25 percent of the readers of science-fiction magazines and novels are now women. I suspect that the percentage is now nearer the 40 percent mark."[16] (Since Asimov gets everything else wrong in this statement, one should also be skeptical about his claim for 25–40 percent of science fiction readership being female in 1982. This could be true, but since he gives no basis for his figures, which is typical when discussing female participation, it could also be completely imaginary.)

Both Tuttle and Asimov, however, took their cues from Los Angeles fan and female author Bjo Trimble who, if she did not originate this myth, certainly continues to be a major promulgator of it. Trimble, too, claims *Star Trek* changed the gender composition of fandom by radically increasing the number of female fans. "Back in ancient fannish times," she said in 1980, "before *Star Trek*, the ratio of women to men in active science-fiction fandom was about one female for every 22 males," that is, about 4.5 percent.[17]

Twenty-five (and more) years later, this claim has now become part of the accepted wisdom. For example, when Bjo and her husband were the Fan Guests of Honor at the 2002 ConJose, the Worldcon in San Jose, CA, the con's web page repeated this myth. "Most people know about Bjo's campaign to save 'Star Trek' and the concomitant influx of female fans," it tells us. "That was a major influence on fandom as we know it now."[18]

As this accolade suggests about what "most people know" concerning her, Trimble has a vested interest in promoting the perceived impact of *Star Trek* and touting her relationship to it. She, of course, organized the letter-writing campaign to save it following its dismal first season. But, there is a further reason for her to promote this myth. Following the letter campaign, she was hired by Paramount Pictures as a PR flack for the show. She has also published several books about both the TV series and the movies. Hence, she has a financial stake (as well as her ego) invested in sustaining the myth of *Star Trek*.

Perhaps this myth developed because *Star Trek* later became closely identified with the 1960s. It would therefore be a convenient "cause" to explain the perceived "effect" of increased female participation in that decade. There is, however, a major chronological problem with this myth-making by Asimov, Trimble, and their followers. If one accepts the claim (which I do not) that *Star Trek* was the seminal catalyst for increased female readership and fan involvement in science fiction, we cannot at the same time accept the claim for increased female participation in the 1960s. This is because *Star Trek* "was actually not very successful in its original run. It was regularly beaten in its time period by all sorts of competition, and it placed number 52 among all series in 1966–1967, its [first and] peak season, behind such programs as *Iron Horse* and *Mr. Terrific. Star Trek* was finally cancelled by NBC in 1969 due to gradually declining audiences."[19]

So, contrary to Asimov's claim, *Star Trek* did *not* develop what he called a "mass following" during its first season. One should not confuse the obsessive enthusiasm of its small coterie of fans (which has typified science fiction from its very beginning) with widespread popularity. Very few people, male *or* female, watched the original Sixties presentation—that's why *Star Trek* was almost cancelled after its first season, and viewership went quickly downhill thereafter. Only in its syndicated afterlife, *in the 1970s*, did it begin to develop a significant fan following. And in the 1980s the myth began to develop that it *also* had a large fan base in the 1960s. Therefore, if one accepts the impact of *Star Trek*, then one must argue that female readership and fan involvement only began to increase a full decade later than Asimov and Co. claim, in the Seventies. Conversely, if female participation suddenly increased in the 1960s—then it cannot be attributed to *Star Trek*.

Truth be told, however, although women were always outnumbered, the numbers probably weren't quite as lopsided as the mythology makes them out to be. For example, in 1947, decades before *Star Trek*, prominent fan Wilson "Bob" Tucker distributed an elaborate questionnaire to active fans throughout the country and reported his findings in the form of a paper presented at the 1948 World Science Fiction Convention. According to Tucker's survey, 11 percent of active fandom at the time was female, almost 150 percent greater than Trimble would have it.[20] In 1955 an active Canadian fan, Gerald A. Steward, surveyed 1,800 active fans in the United States and Canada with a questionnaire similar to Tucker's of 1947 and discovered that 20 percent of active fandom in 1955 was female, a near doubling over the 1947 figure.[21] Likewise, according to *The Directory of 1960 Science Fiction Fandom* compiled by Ron Bennett, over 20 percent of active fans in 1960 were women.[22] Further, of the 462 paid memberships (attendees) to the 1960 Worldcon in Pittsburgh (the Pittcon), a minimum of 112 were identifiably female, coming to 24.24 percent of the attendees.[23]

Thus, instead of Bjo Trimble's claim that, before *Star Trek*, there was only one female for every 22 males in active SF fandom, it is probably safe to say that throughout the Fifties there was actually at least one female for every four males, and perhaps even one female for every three males if the 1960 Worldcon is the measure. This is a ratio more than 400 percent *higher* than Trimble and mythology would have us believe.

And Bjo Trimble is very well aware of such active and welcome female fandom in the Fifties. She chaired the most popular panel at the 1959 Detroit Worldcon, that on fanzines. She was selected as the panel's moderator because she was thought to be intimately familiar with contemporary fanzines—almost all of which published fiction, columns, or letters by female fans.

It was this great involvement with fandom which explains Trimble's listing in the aforementioned 1960 fan directory. And, not only is she listed in the 1960 fan directory, but Ron Bennett sent a directory to every fellow member of the Fantasy Amateur Press Association (FAPA) in the regular February, 1961, mailing of fanzines to members. Bjo was at that time a FAPA member, having joined in May, 1960. Thus, she was mailed a copy of the fan directory. Active fan that she was, as soon as the postman delivered it to her door she no doubt ran down the list of fans to see who she knew. As she did so, perhaps Bjo noted the listing for G. (Gertrude) M. Carr, who published fanzines continuously from the early 1950s to the late 1990s, when she finally ran out of energy at age 94.

Or perhaps Bjo noted the listing for fellow female fan and activist Dirce ("Dir-say") Archer. Archer was the Chair of Pittcon, the 1960 World Science Fiction Convention in Pittsburgh, where 24.24 percent of the paid attendees were female. Bjo worked closely with Archer for the year leading up to that Worldcon. This was because she was the main organizer of that Worldcon's art show. Pittcon was the first Worldcon to feature a fan art show and it was a task which consumed much of Bjo's energy in 1959–1960. Indeed, Archer thanked her good friend Bjo, as well as Alma Hill (fan and published SF author), for their organizing efforts in the first paragraph of thanks on the first page of the 1960 Worldcon program.

Not only was Trimble a major force in SF fandom by 1960, but she had been active in various fan clubs since at least 1952, when she was known as Bjo Wells. In 1958 she joined the influential Los Angeles Science Fantasy Society (LASFS) and the members quickly recognized her leadership. John Trimble, who became her husband, remembered that, "Early '50s meetings [of LASFS] had an average of maybe 12 people. By 1959, Bjo spark-plugged a club revival with an average attendance of 35–40. She, Al Lewis, [fem fan] Djinn Faine [Dickson] [also listed in the 1960 fan directory] and Ernie Wheatly revived the clubzine *Shangri-L'Affaires* and LASFS was once again a center of fanac [fan activity]."[24]

Robert Lichtman, who, like Bjo, joined LASFS in 1958, corroborates this. He recalled that, "At that time Bjo had gotten the club energized to the point of bringing back the clubzine title, *Shangri-L'Affaires,* that had been abandoned in the late '40s. . . . When I first began attending meetings, she was part of the group that was organized to sell shares in the club's first Gestetner [mimeograph machine]."

In addition, Lichtman tells us that, "I remember quite a few other women of various ages attending the club meetings at that time with varying levels of frequency: Djinn Faine (who coedited the first couple issues of the revived *Shangri-L'Affaires* with [Charles] Burbee), Anna Moffatt . . . Eleanor Turner . . . Miriam Dyches . . . Edith Ogutsch, Julie Jardine, Virginia Mill (and her 12-year-old daughter, Terry), Helen Urban [a published SF author], Dorothy (Rory) Faulkner [listed in the 1960 fan directory and also a published SF author], Barbara Gratz . . . Ann Chamberlain (N3F [National Federation of Fantasy Fans] stalwart and seller of rubber stamps), Jill Vuerhard, Ingrid Fritsch, Lil Neville (wife of Kris), and even now and then Wendayne Ackerman [wife of Forrest J.]. . . . I don't remember more than just a few women at any given meeting; but the ranks of the possible distaff attendees were larger than I thought before I went looking in *The LASFS Album,* 'published on the occasion of the 1500th meeting, May 12, 1966,' [*Star Trek*'s TV debut was not until September 8, 1966] to refresh my memory. It provided an interesting view of LASFS' feminine past. Organized by eras, one notes that there were women attending the club in *every* one of them."[25]

Indeed, there *were* female fans in every era of the Los Angeles club, and not everyone has forgotten their names. In 1946, a dozen years before Bjo joined LASFS, Jack Speer visited L. A. fandom and remembered that, "There were a number of females in LASFS. . . . Es gab Morojo, of course, Pogo out on the edge, Beverly Bronson, Tigrina, Abby Lu Ashley, Lora Crozetti, a Helen Finn and daughter, another Helen [perhaps Helen Urban]."[26] Given the smaller membership of LASFS in the Forties, these female fans were perhaps a significant percentage of the overall membership.

Thus, it is obvious that women were active members and leaders of science fiction fan clubs in greater numbers and at earlier dates than later commentators of both sexes have generally been willing to concede. Indeed, women were members of the very first fan clubs and attended the first World Science Fiction Conventions. For instance, The Science Fiction League, a fan club launched by Hugo Gernsback in the early 1930s, claimed many female members. One such was Molly Acreman, of Austin, Texas, who started reading the science fiction magazines in 1931.[27] Another was Millie Taurasi, a member of the Queens (NY) chapter of the League and sister of well-known fan James V. Taurasi. Under the heading, "Another Girl Fan," she wrote a short piece to the January, 1941 issue of *Science Fiction* (p. 59) saying, "I hope this shows you that girls join this wacky field called 'science fiction.'"

Meanwhile, the Futurians, the famous and influential New York fan club of the late Thirties and early Forties, also had a significant female contingent, eventually more than a third of the total. According to Damon Knight, also a member, the Futurians had a core membership of fourteen, five of whom were women: Doris Baumgardt ("Leslie Perri," who married Futurians Frederik Pohl and, later, Richard Wilson), Rosalind Cohen (who later married Futurian "Dirk Wylie"), Jessica Gould, (who married Richard Wilson before Baumgardt), Virginia Kidd (who became a literary agent in the field and married James Blish), and Elsie Balter (who later married fellow Futurian Donald Wollheim and helped him launch DAW Books). Judith Merril and Mary Byers later became active members—and later Merril also married Pohl, while Byers married Futurian Cyril Kornbluth. The extended Futurian membership included Sylvia Rubin and Gertrude Lee Winters.

Also, non-member women often attended Futurian meetings, fans such as "stf artist" Barbara Hall. Other frequent visitors included Vida Jameson (daughter of science fiction writer Malcolm Jameson and later wife of writer Cleve Cartmill) and Mary Gnaedinger, both present for the meeting of August 21, 1940. Gnaedinger was the editor, at that time, of *Famous Fantastic Mysteries* (1939–1953), as well as the sister magazine, *Fantastic Novels* (1940–1951). Her presence suggests a close relationship between science fiction professionals and science fiction fans at the time.[28]

Other well-known female fans included Myrtle R. Jones ("Morojo") Douglas and Mary ("Pogo") Gray, both active in LASFS in the late 1930s and mentioned above by Jack Speer. "Morojo," dressed in supposed twenty-fifth century fashion, made a big impression on New York fans at the First World Science Fiction Convention in 1939. Both "Morojo" and "Pogo," as well as prominent fan Gertrude Kuslan, were also highly visible and celebrated at the Second World Science Fiction Convention in Chicago in 1940.[29] "Morojo" was famous enough to be asked to write about "The Woman in Science-Fiction" for the June, 1940 issue of *Science Fiction* (p. 55). She explained why she liked science fiction and said "undoubtedly" other women would soon be writing in to give their own reasons.

Futurian "Leslie Perri" (who, like "Morojo," attended the 1939 First World Science Fiction Convention) was also a founding member of the Fantasy Amateur Press Association (FAPA). This was the famous (and still active) fan group begun in 1937 by Donald A. Wollheim to facilitate distribution of members' fanzines. Indeed, "Perri" signed on with FAPA a full year before Fred Pohl, her future husband, joined. "Morojo" was another 1937 founder of FAPA, in which she remained active until 1947, while "Pogo" joined in 1940. Gertrude Kuslan was active in FAPA from 1940–1945 and in 1946 Futurians "Judith Merril" (as Judy Zissman) and Virginia Kidd (as Virginia K. Emden) became FAPAns. Meanwhile, Marion Zimmer Bradley (as Marion E. Zimmer) joined FAPA in 1948 and remained an off-and-on member until 1974. While these were the most well-known female FAPA members, Helen V. Wesson has been the longest-active. She joined in 1946, and remains a member today with a lapse of only a few months due to illness.[30]

There were also female fans outside of FAPA who were actively involved in producing some of the major fanzines of the time. A short list of just the most important would have to include *Cry [of the Nameless]*. This famous fanzine was begun as a report on the activities of the Seattle fan club, The Nameless Ones, and co-edited from 1950–1964 by G. (Gertrude) M. Carr, a long-time member of the club. As mentioned above, Gertrude Carr would continue producing fanzines until age 94.

And, of course, there was *Yandro*, begun in 1953 under the editorship of Beverly J. Amers and Juanita Wellons. Originally titled *EISFA* (because it began life as the clubzine of the Eastern Indiana Science Fiction Association), it took on great importance in fan circles in the mid-Fifties and early Sixties. After Wellons married Robert ("Buck") Coulson (to become Juanita Coulson and famous as a genre author under that name), he joined the fanzine as a regular book reviewer. Illustrative of how popular this fanzine was in fan circles, *Yandro* was Hugo-nominated as Best Fanzine every year between 1959–1968. It won the Hugo in 1965. After 1968 it began to appear irregularly as the professional writing careers of Buck and Juanita Coulson began to prosper.

Meanwhile, Orma McCormick produced the mid-Fifties fanzine *Star Lanes*, devoted entirely to SF poetry. Even the comments of readers, such as long-time SF poet Lilith Lorraine, were written entirely in verse. Lorraine also published her own SF poetry fanzines, *Different* and *Challenge*, which carried much poetry by female fans. Rog Phillips, long-time fanzine reviewer for *Amazing*, praised and reprinted a poem by Edith Ogutsch from *Challenge* in his August, 1951 column (p. 136), saying it should have been turned into a story. Ogutsch was a stalwart of the Los Angeles Science Fantasy Society and her letters appeared frequently in the magazines of the day.

Another prominent female fan known for her fanzine work was Lee Hoffman, a Savannah, Georgia fan who wrote and published *Quandary*. She was known as a "BNF" (Big Name Fan) for many years and was a major presence at the 1951 World Science Fiction Convention in New Orleans. She was also a prominent presence at the 1955 Worldcon in Cleveland and later married *Infinity* magazine editor Larry T. Shaw.

Young girls were also putting out fanzines. One of the best, according to Rog Phillips in his *Other Worlds* (November, 1955, p. 90) review of fanzines, was published by Jan Sadler, of Jackson, Mississippi. Jan was fifteen, attending regional SF cons, and contributing to other fanzines (such as *Hark,* out of Dallas) in addition to producing *Slander*, her own fanzine.

As Jan Sadler's experience illustrates, when not producing their own fanzines, female fans also appeared regularly in other top-ranked fanzines of the day. One of these was Joel Nydahl's mid-Fifties *Vega,* coming out of Marquette, Michigan. It featured columns by Marian Ellison in each issue, as well an numerous articles by active female fans such as Marion Zimmer Bradley. Of course, female fans were also publishing fan fiction in many of these fanzines published by male fans, with no evident prejudice against them by the fan publishers. For example, five years before she made her professional debut in 1953, Marion Zimmer Bradley's novice effort, "Outpost," was published in a 1948 issue of the fanzine *Spacewarp,* produced by fan Arthur H. Rapp, in Saginaw, Michigan. Meanwhile, Alice Bullock, who would break into the professional ranks in 1954, had a 1951 novice effort published in the fanzine *Fan-Fare,* produced by fan W. Paul Ganley out of Tonawanda, N.Y.

Many other female fans attempted to launch fanzines, but were stymied by a lack of resources. For example, in 1948 Rog Phillips published a letter in his fanzine column from Margaret Ann Rose, of Hutchinson, Kansas. She wrote, "I can't seem to drown the fanzine urge," and asked for assistance from any others who also wanted to launch a fanzine. "I have a pretty good share of addresses," she said, "places where wholesale paper, etc., are available, the best ways of getting photos done, etc. I've been through the mill with my own mag. Now if anybody has access to a press and type and would be willing to put in some work, we could get up a pretty good mag. . . . I edit, think up advertising schemes, and any odd job such a venture requires. How about it, anyone game to try?"[31]

Many fanzines which managed to make it into print were sent to Belle C. Dietz, a mover and shaker in New York fandom. For example, she was one of the founders of that city's Lunarian fan club. More importantly, in the late Fifties she was the president of the Eastern Science Fiction Association, the major East Coast fan organization. For this reason, in 1959 she was asked by the professional SF magazine *Fantastic Universe* to write a regular fanzine review column entitled "Fannotations."

Female fans also worked to organize early Worldcons, the World Science Fiction Conventions. For example, a third of the 1950 Eighth Worldcon organizing committee were women (two out of six members, Judith Merril and Evelyn Harrison, wife of writer Harry Harrison).[32] But, female fans were also taking leadership roles at various other levels in the organization of conventions. For example, Juanita Sharp, as convention secretary, was a driving force behind the 1950 Norwescon in Portland, Oregon. In its first post-con issue, *Incinerations*, a Portland fanzine, complimented-insulted her on her work to make the con happen by congratulating her for staying in office, "under conditions which would have caused any intelligent person to resign."[33]

Meanwhile, female fan and later author Julian May chaired ChiCon II, the 1952 Worldcon in Chicago, becoming the first woman to chair a Worldcon. Not only that, but this 1952 Worldcon was also the largest Worldcon ever held before the 1960s, with a paid membership of 1,000. It was further notable in that Hugo Gernsback, "The Father of Science Fiction," was Julian May's Guest of Honor at the convention.

Such leadership roles for female fans suggest that male fans made a point of promoting female fans to important leadership positions in early fan organizations. As another example, Fifties California fan Len Moffatt, active in both the Los Angeles Science Fantasy Society (LASFS) and the affiliated Outlander Society, remembers when Alan Hershey and his wife Freddie joined these clubs in the early 1950s. Both quickly became central members of the clubs, with Alan being elected as Director of LASFS and Freddie being especially crucial to keeping alive the LASFS fanzine, *Shangri-LA*. He remembers that, "When the Outlanders sponsored the third Westercon [a major regional SF convention in 1950], we decided that Freddie should chair it. We may have been wrong, but we assumed this would be the first science fiction convention to be chaired by a woman, at least on the West Coast. [It may well have been—and only eleven years after the first Worldcon, in 1939.]

"So, naturally, the precedent was established that if we did win the bid for the 1958 Worldcon, it would be chaired by a woman, presumably Freddie. But Freddie dropped out of fandom before then. We then assumed it would be Mari Wolf, who had joined the Outlander Society after attending the third Westercon [in 1950]. But that wasn't to be, either, as the fannish fates would have it."[34]

By the middle and end of the Fifties, however, women chairing Worldcons was no longer pathbreaking. For example, three years after Julian May Chaired ChiCon II, Noreen Falasca (now Noreen Shaw) co-chaired (with then-husband Nick Falasca) the 1955 Cleveland Worldcon, at which Isaac Asimov was the Guest of Honor. Thus, when well-known female fan Dirce Archer was chosen to Chair Pittcon, the 1960 Worldcon in Pittsburgh (at which James Blish was Guest of Honor), it was accepted as routine. What was unusual, then, about Pittcon wasn't that a woman was chairing a Worldcon, as Noreen Falasca and

Julian May had already done so. What was unusual was that Archer had used her power in fandom to bring the Worldcon to the unlikely and smoky steel town of Pittsburgh at all, hardly a tourist mecca. Indeed, the locating of the 1960 Worldcon in Pittsburgh was an illustration of the extraordinary power which some female fans, such as Archer, had achieved in the science fiction world by the end of the Fifties.

Ted White recalled that Archer had "Vast Power in those days." White later became an assistant editor at *The Magazine of Fantasy and Science Fiction* (1963–1968) and the editor of *Fantastic* and *Amazing Stories* (1969–1978), as well as *Heavy Metal* (1979–1980). He also had an extensive genre writing career. But, in 1960, when he attended Pittcon, he was still "just" a fan, although an active one. He remembered that Dirce Archer wanted desperately to bring a Worldcon to Pittsburgh, where she lived, and she wanted to Chair it, so she used her "Vast Power" in fandom to move heaven and earth to bring this about.

"A number of prominent people in the field, like P. Schulyer Miller [book reviewer for *Astounding*, who also lived in Pittsburgh] strove in her behalf," remembered White. "The bid mounted for Pittsburgh in 1959 was a steamroller of BNFs [Big Name Fans], which included fake bids [by fans in other cities] placed so that they could be strategically withdrawn 'in favor of Pittsburgh,' as well as bid parties fueled by the Pittsburgh hotel" where the convention would be held.[35]

And so it came to pass.

By existing accounts, Archer handled her duties as 1960 Worldcon Chair responsibly and competently, although, writing soon after Pittcon, attendee Jay Kay Klein recalled that she "had some of the countenance of a somnambulist," as she dealt with one crisis after another. Meanwhile, Bjo Trimble was in charge of Pittcon's art show and "concentrated the work of nearly a year in the well-conceived and carried-out science fantasy art show. . . . The show was one of the hits of the Pittcon." Thus, women were the top organizers of the convention, the art show and the chairing of many panels. Women were also active in the hallways and in the masquerade costume ball, the traditional highlight of Worldcons for generations. Klein recalled that, "The masquerade ball really deserves a couple of pages in color. The costume most commented on was Sylvia White's, which was prominently displayed to the satisfaction of all. Bjo Trimble's costume achieved comparable results but with more cloth and less gooseflesh."

Women also organized and led many of the raucous Worldcon parties in Pittsburgh. Published author, FAPA member, and well-known Midwestern fan Phyllis Economou was there, "of course," commented Klein, "with her inimitable flair for partying. One of the sublime moments of the convention came at 4 a.m. when I found her at the head of several dozen fans pouring forth from a much-too-small room like bees from a hive. A very grim-faced representative of the management was standing by. Phyllis muttered something about 'singing too loud' and swept on to another party."

But, remembered Klein, "Probably the bestest with the mostest [of the parties] was held in the [Dirce] Archer suite the night of the masquerade ball. Starting sometime after midnight, the party soon became the prime gathering spot of all conventioneers. Literally, everyone was there, at one time or another. At one party, when it started dying down about 4:30 a.m. . . . I left. Several floors down, in Jim Blish's room, were gathered Dirce Archer, Fred Pohl, Gordon Dickson, and Lester del Rey, lolling at ease on the floor, quaffments at hand, discussing literature and writers, ranging from science fiction and Harlan Ellison to medieval poetry and Geoffrey Chaucer."

And at the end of this last Worldcon of the Fifties, female fan Dirce Archer, who had used her "Vast Power" to "steamroll" it into existence, formally handed the convention gavel over to female fan Elinor Busby, a principal organizer of the first Worldcon of the Sixties, to be held the next year, 1961, in Seattle. Thus, not only were female fans accepted on a basis of equality as an integral part of SF fandom, but this passing of the gavel from one female Worldcon organizer to another, from the Fifties to the Sixties, tells us that SF fandom also acknowledged female fans as leaders of the sub-culture.[36]

But female fans had also long been organized as an entirely separate branch of science fiction fandom. Like Belle Dietz, Mari Wolf (a professional science fiction writer herself, with seven stories in *If* and *Fantastic Story Magazine* in the Fifties) published a magazine column on fandom. Wolf's was entitled "Fandora's Box" and appeared in *Imagination: Stories of Science and Fiction.* In the May, 1953 issue her column carried a notice for *The Femzine,* a fanzine filled with stories written by female fans and published by Marion Cox out of Sioux City, Iowa. *The Femzine* was just for "fanettes, meaning us girls," said Mari Wolf. It was "Written only for the female fan, [but] Marion has decided to let any mere male who is curious subscribe to it too."

Some of the "fanette" fiction mentioned as appearing in *The Femzine* included "Wild Talent," by Jean Leighton Moore, "The Hyperspace Hot Rod," by Juanita Wellons (Coulson), and Marion Cox's own "The Lonely Robot." Evidently, female fans were writing many science fiction stories which never showed up in the professional magazines. Appearing only in their own fan publications, this particular parallel world of female science fiction has long since been lost beyond recovery.

Knowledge of (and participation in) *The Femzine* seems to have spread quickly. In the August, 1953 issue of *Thrilling Wonder Stories,* reader Lula B. Stewart, of Harmony, PA (a suburb of Pittsburgh), wrote to say (pp. 133–34) that she was a contributor to "that great, new, all-female *Femzine,*" where she had a "formidable phalange of femfans" who were "backing her up."[37] In that same issue of *Thrilling,* Stewart published a poem, "To Fandom's BNFs" (Big

Name Fans), which revealed that she was well-acquainted with the current movers and shakers of science fiction fandom.

But, *The Femzine* was certainly not the first such all-female science fiction publication. In January, 1946 female fan Jim-E. Daugherty published a feminist science fiction fanzine entitled *Black Flames,* in honor of Stanley G. Weinbaum's Amazon queen, "Margaret of Urbs." "All stories and articles," she said, "will be by Wo-fans only." However, even *Black Flames* was not the earliest fanzine published by and for female fans. That seems to have been *STF-ETTE,* launched by "Pogo" in September, 1940, in which only women were supposed to be published and which Sam Moskowitz thought was the "first feminist fanzine" in the field.[38]

Fanzines are, by their very nature, ephemeral and few survive. These feminist fanzines dating back to at least 1940 (and perhaps earlier?) have proven even more ephemeral. As we have seen, women were demonstrably active and welcome in SF fandom from the very beginning, a fact usually ignored. However, with the loss of *The Femzine, Black Flames,* and *STF-ETTE,* including even the memory of them among current feminist science fiction writers, historians, and fans, we have also lost an entire alternate history of explicitly female science fiction fandom.[39]

Notes

1. This is based upon the letter index in Mike Ashley, *The Complete Index to Astounding/Analog,* Robert Weinberg Publications: Oak Forest, IL, 1981. Ashley simply listed the letter writers. The gender analysis is my own. Surprisingly, the gender of letter writers did not significantly change in the 1960s and 1970s. From 1961–1979 there were 953 writers whose gender I was able to identify out of a total of 1,064. Of these 953, female writers numbered 86, representing 9 percent of the total. This is an increase over the previous decades, but not as much as I expected. One way of interpreting this is that women were, essentially, as interested (and as welcome) in the earliest decades as they were in the more "enlightened" Sixties and Seventies.

2. This is based upon a gender analysis I performed of the letters index published by Stefan R. Dziemianowicz, *The Annotated Guide to Unknown & Unknown Worlds,* Starmont House: WA, 1991, Appendix VI. According to this index, 124 readers wrote letters to the magazine during its existence. Of these, I could not gender-identify 19 due to initials or androgynous first names or because of no name (other than "The Neophyte"). There remained 95 I identified as male, ten as female, for a total of 105 gender-identifiable writers.

3. See T. G. Cockcroft, "Famous Fantastic Mysteries Letter Index," *Fantasy Commentator,* X, Nos. 3 & 4, 2003. There were 1,207 letter writers, of whom 157 could not be identified as to gender. There remained 874 male and 176 female writers, for a total of 1,050 gender-identifiable writers. The 176 female writers thus represented 16.7 percent of the identifiable writers. Again, I performed the gender analysis myself.

4. Sam Moskowitz, "The Return of Hugo Gernsback, Part IV," *Fantasy Commentator,* Vol. X, Numbers 3 & 4, spring, 2003, p. 235.

5. Interestingly, the entire back cover of the issue of *Science Fiction Quarterly,* in which Miss Ona Mills's letter appeared, was devoted to an ad for a women's fingernail lengthening product. Interior ads touted products designed to increase women's bustlines and advice books on how to

"win and hold a husband." Evidently, some businesses thought ads in an SF magazine was a good way to reach potential female customers.

6. Zenna Henderson interview in Paul Walker, ed., *Speaking of Science Fiction: The Paul Walker Interviews,* Luna Publications: Oradell, N.J., 1978, pp. 278–279. Originally in *LUNA Monthly 52,* 1974.

7. Madeleine L'Engle in Curtis C. Smith, Ed., *Twentieth-Century Science-Fiction Writers,* St. Martin's Press: N.Y., 1981, p. 327.

8. See Anne McCaffrey's comments in Curtis C. Smith, Ed., *Twentieth-Century Science-Fiction Writers,* St. Martin's Press: N.Y., 1981, p. 364.

9. Joanna Russ interview in Paul Walker, ed., *Speaking of Science Fiction,* p. 246.

10. Kenneth Chang, "Making Science Fact, Now Chronicling Science Fiction," *The New York Times,* June 15, 2004.

11. Verna Skogland, letter to the editor of the Science Fiction Book Club newsletter, May, 2004. The story to which Skogland refers was by Keith Bennett and appeared in the spring, 1950 *Planet Stories*—close enough!

12. Perhaps this is an appropriate place to mention that I was introduced to written science fiction in the late 1950s by women readers. As a boy in Phoenix, Arizona, I spent many an afternoon with an elderly neighbor, a widow who had pioneered the territory in the days before 1912. It was she who introduced me to Edgar Rice Burroughs and his Barsoom novels when she loaned me her first edition copies.

Then, in 1956, the wife of one of my father's friends, to entertain me during a boring visit to her house, gave me her copy of Judith Merril's *S-F: The Year's Greatest Science-Fiction and Fantasy,* which completed my seduction. And, not only was that anthology (which I still own) edited by a woman, it contained stories by Mildred Clingerman, Zenna Henderson, Shirley Jackson, and C. L. Moore.

Later, when I discovered the magazines, the housewife next door routinely borrowed them. Thus, from the beginning of my contact with the literature, I knew women not only wrote and edited, but also read science fiction—and this did not strike me as odd. I simply accepted it.

13. Leigh Brackett, interview in *Science Fiction Voices, #5: Interviews with American Science Fiction Writers of the Golden Age,* Darrell Schweitzer, Borgo Press: San Bernardino, Calif., 1981, p. 40.

14. See Mari Wolf's column on fanzines, *Imagination: Stories of Science and Fantasy,* November, 1954, pp. 112–113.

15. Lisa Tuttle, "Women As Portrayed in Science Fiction," in John Clute and Peter Nicholls, *The Encyclopedia of Science Fiction,* St. Martin's Griffin: N.Y., 1993, update 1995, p. 1343.

16. Asimov, "The Feminization of Science Fiction," pp. 295–296.

17. Bjo Trimble, "Ideas about Ideas," *Starlog,* No. 40, November, 1980, p. 21.

18. This July 19, 2001 posting can be reached at www.conjose.org/Guests/fans.html.

19. Tim Brooks and Earle Marsh, *The Complete Directory to Prime Time and Cable TV Shows, 1946-Present,* Ballantine Books: N.Y., 1999, 7th ed., p. 960.

20. See Wilson Tucker, *The Neo-Fan's Guide,* Mafia Press: Fond du Lac, 1955; Harry Warner, Jr., *All Our Yesterdays,* Advent: Chicago, 1969, p. 26; and Robert Bloch, "Some of My Best Fans Are Friends," *The Magazine of Fantasy and Science Fiction,* September, 1955, p. 53.

21. Gerald A. Stewart, *The Second Tucker Fan Survey,* in *Canfan,* Toronto, 1956.

22. Ron Bennett, *The Directory of 1960 Science Fiction Fandom,* compiled and produced for the Fantasy Amateur Press Association (FAPA) and included in FAPA mailing #94, February, 1961. The directory listed 494 fans active in the large English-speaking nations, including the USA, England, Scotland, Ireland, Canada, Australia, New Zealand, and even Hong Kong. It also listed fans tied into the English network in Germany, France, and Sweden.

I isolated all fans with USA addresses, which came to 357. I was unable to identify the gender of three fans because of ambiguous first names or, in one case, a missing first name. Of the remaining 354, I identified 72 as female and 282 as male.

Seventy-two female fans out of the 354 gender-identifiable total comes to 20.34 percent of the total. If we took the entire USA listing of 357 fans, then 72 known female fans would be 20.16 percent of the total, both figures of over 20 percent being a much higher percentage of female fans than anyone else has acknowledged. (My thanks to Robert Lichtman, listed in the 1960 Directory and someone who knew virtually everyone listed, for helping me identify the gender of these fans.)

Of course, those who insist there were no women in early fandom always have a fall-back position. First, they say there were no women, period. When it is pointed out that there *were* women in fandom, their new position becomes, "Oh, but they were 'Just Wives' of the *real* fans. They may have been in the fan directories, but they weren't *really* fans." For this reason, I divided the 72 female fans into solo women and women listed as part of a couple. The solo female fans were a solid majority of the total, amounting to 40. Therefore, *most* of the female fans were *not* "Just Wives." They were there by themselves!

But, we should not then dismiss the remaining 32 female fans as mere hangers-on. They included, for instance, Bjo Trimble, who was just as (or perhaps more) active as her husband. Others listed along with their husbands included Karen Anderson, Dorothy de Courcy, and Barbara Silverberg, all of whom published stories in the professional science fiction magazines in the Forties and Fifties (in the case of de Courcy it was nineteen stories!). True, in all three cases, these stories were in collaboration with their husbands. Still, this would suggest a sincere interest in the genre and a higher degree of involvement in the professional aspects of the field than a mere hanger-on would exhibit.

The next fall-back position of the objectors then becomes, "Oh, but *they were exceptions!*" And, of course, the original objection that there were no women *at all* (much less ones as active as Bjo Trimble, Dirch Archer, Gertrude Carr, and LASFS stalwarts Djinn Faine and Rory Faulkner) is completely forgotten as the new fall-back trench lines are dug. As Rosanne Rosannadanna on the old *Saturday Night Live* used to say, "It's always *something!*"

23. Pittcon paid memberships are listed on pp. 44–48 of the 18th World Science Fiction Convention program. I performed the gender analysis of listed attendees.

24. John Trimble, "Bjo Trimble—My Friend Freckles," ConJose Program, 2002, p. 23.

25. Robert Lichtman, *King Biscuit Time,* No. 42, no page number, personal fanzine mailed to members of the Fantasy Amateur Press Association (FAPA), February, 2004, mailing number 266.

A note about *Shangri-L'Affaires,* the club fanzine. It had been founded in 1936 simply as *Shangri-LA* and seems *not* to have been abandoned in the late 1940s. More likely it went comatose in the early 1950s. For example, in the February, 1952 issue of *Startling Stories,* Jerome Bixby noted in his column on fanzines (p. 146), that he'd received a letter from club member Al Lewis, who identified himself as the Chairman of the Associate Member Committee. Based on Lewis' information, Bixby wrote that the fanzine was now, ". . . sweet sixteen and never been missed [meaning it had never missed an issue] but this singular record in fanzine publication now threatens to be terminated by a dearth of dollars." It seems that dearth was not rectified and the fanzine ceased publication in 1952 or soon thereafter, to be revived by Lewis and Trimble in 1958.

26. Jack Speer, *Synapse,* p. 6, May, 2004, personal fanzine mailed to members of the Fantasy Amateur Press Association (FAPA), May, 2004, mailing number 267.

27. See her letter in *Science Fiction,* March, 1941, p. 88.

28. Rubin and Winters, along with "Leslie Perri," were reported to be in attendance at the December 26, 1938 Futurian meeting at Fred Pohl's apartment. Rosalind Cohen was probably also there. See *Futurian News,* V. 1, No. 5, January 4, 1939, p. 1. Except for the information on Rubin and Winters, the source for this paragraph is Damon Knight, *The Futurians: The Story of the Science Fiction "Family" of the 30's That Produced Today's Top SF Writers and Editors,* John Day: N.Y., 1977, pp. 36, 53. For artist Barbara Hall, see p. 86. Also, see Damon Knight, "Knight Piece," in Brian W. Aldiss and Harry Harrison, Eds., *Hell's Cartographers,* Futura Publications Ltd.: London, 1976, 1975, p. 117ff.

29. See Frederik Pohl, *The Way the Future Was: A Memoir,* Del Rey-Ballantine Books: N.Y., 1978, p. 90.

30. "FAPA Memberships, Numeric Listing—Mailings 1–260," compiled by Ron Ellik and Milt Stevens and distributed to FAPA members in 2003, in the author's possession.

31. See "The Club House," the SF club and fanzine column written by Rog Phillips, *Amazing Stories,* May, 1949, p. 135.

32. Pohl, *The Way the Future Was,* p. 193. Evelyn was the wife of SF writer Harry Harrison. She later married SF writer Lester del Rey.

33. Quoted by Rog Phillips in "The Club House," the column he wrote about SF clubs and their fanzines in *Amazing Stories,* January, 1951, p. 156.

34. This account comes from "The Outlander's Tale: Part Three," in Len Moffatt's fanzine, *Califania Tales.*

35. Ted White's comments were made in a posting to the PulpMags online discussion group, August 5, 2004, in response to a query I made about Pittcon and Dirce Archer.

36. This account of the 1960 Pittcon is taken from Jay Kay Klein, "Convention Annual No. 1, Pittcon Edition 1960, Section Two," written in 1961. The full account can be found online at: http://members.tripod.com/stromata/id268_m.htm.

37. Meanwhile, pioneering science fiction writer "Lilith Lorraine" was publishing *Different,* her own fanzine, in the early 1950s, which presented much poetry and fiction by herself and others, including the fiction debut of Robert Silverberg in 1953. See Robert Silverberg, "Sounding Brass, Tinkling Cymbal," in Aldiss and Harrison, *Hell's Cartographers,* p. 15.

38. Sam Moskowitz, "The Immortal Storm II: A History of Science-Fiction Fandom," *Fantasy Commentator,* IX, No. 2, fall, 1997, p. 132.

39. "Pogo" joined FAPA in September of 1940. As the purpose of the organization is to exchange members' fanzines, it is very likely her fellow members received copies of *STF-ETTE,* which she began that same month. Perhaps copies are still to be found in the archives of remaining long-time members. If so, a perusal of their contents might reveal a wealth of information about science fiction's female past during this period. I have queried some still-surviving members from that period, but so far no copies have been forthcoming.

5

Women Without Names

B UT, IF WOMEN WERE such a large percentage of female readership and active
fandom, if women were welcomed and, indeed, powerful leaders in the
early science fiction world—why did women writers supposedly have to hide
their gender behind male names or initials?

The proclaimers of prejudice commonly assert, again without substantiation,
that to be published at all, women writers of the pulp era were forced to use
male or androgynous names,[1] or to deliberately conceal their sexual identity
through the use of obscuring initials. Indeed, so wedded are they to this thesis
that sometimes their views have driven them to absurd extremes. Responding
to the statement that C. L. Moore published under her real name, Big Name
Fan Laurie Mann (who, among many other things, helped organized the 2001
Worldcon and runs the heavily-visited website, "AwardWeb: Collection of Literary Information and Photos") denied this, claiming that "C. L. Moore" was not
actually a name. Rather, it was "just initials."[2]

This is akin to asserting that some names aren't names, they're just letters! It
defies both common sense and the accepted English language conventions on
names. As noted scholar Jacques Barzun tells us in his classic manual on all
aspects of research and writing, "In seeking identities, it is well to remember
that persons' names follow certain conventions. Knowing the conventions may
shorten the search, and observing them in narrative will mark off the trained
writer from the amateur. To begin with, names should be given as the bearers
themselves used them. It is H. L. Mencken, A. P. Herbert, Calvin Coolidge,
H. G. Wells—not Henry L., Alan Patrick, John Calvin, or Herbert George."[3]
This same convention of identity and name usage tells us that Moore's proper
and accepted name is "C. L. Moore," not "Catherine L. Moore." As Barzun
remarks, "All this is common knowledge."[4]

Except, that is, among some feminist ideologues, who stubbornly defy both common knowledge and English language conventions in order to pursue their agenda. Such fans, however, are merely parroting the statements of presumed "experts." Again, Isaac Asimov is one such. Introducing Moore's "Greater Than Gods" (1939) in one of his many anthologies, Asimov (perhaps remembering his own views from that time) claimed that, while women were not welcome in the science fiction magazines of the 1930s, "even in the depth of the male-chauvinist Thirties there were women who dared, successfully, to compete. C. L. Moore was perhaps the best of these, but Leslie F. Stone and A. R. Long [Amelia Reynolds Long] were two others. Notice the use of initials and epicene [gender neutral] given names to hide the fatal feminism [sic] of the writers. . . . [the use of initials] is dramatic evidence of the then status of women in the field."[5]

Evidently, for Asimov and those of similar belief, nothing but a complete full name is actually a "name." In which case, it would seem that the names of many male authors are not actually "names," including J. G. Ballard, J. M. Barrie, E. F. Benson, E. F. Bleiler, G. K. Chesterton, C. S. Forester, H. L. Gold, O. Henry, E. T. A. Hoffmann, M. R. James, C. M. Kornbluth, C. S. Lewis, D. H. Lawrence, T. E. Lawrence, H. P. Lovecraft, H. L. Mencken, A. Merritt, S. J. Perelman, J. D. Salinger, M. P. Shiel, E. E. Smith, C. P. Snow, J. R. R. Tolkien, A. E. van Vogt, H. G. Wells, E. B. White, and P. G. Wodehouse (not to mention myriad men in other fields of endeavor, such as P. T. Barnum and W. C. Fields). What are we to deduce about the status of such *male* writers in their fields from their much greater use of initials? Were they discriminated against and had to hide their male gender?

Perhaps, might be the reply, their choice was simply a stylistic convention which said nothing at all about their status within their fields. Indeed, this might be the case with current female writers, such as J. K. Rowling and P. D. James, who use initials. But if the male use of initials is entirely acceptable as "names," while the female use of initials is not, then proponents of the prejudice thesis are promoting a sexual double standard for women. This, itself, reflects prejudice and preconceived notions, not logical thinking. Surely feminist ideologues are not claiming that P. D. James and J. K. Rowling are today using initials to escape any female bias? Thus, despite Asimov's contention to the contrary, the use of initials obviously tells us nothing in isolation. As with the numbers of female authors, then, we have to examine the context of initial usage to make any sense of things.

This insistence upon prejudice forcing women writers to conceal their gender in early science fiction is found even in the most respected encyclopedias of the field. John Clute and Peter Nicholls, for example, echoing Asimov, claim that in 1950 the field was "notoriously male-chauvinist" and suggest that women writers needed male pseudonyms at that time if they wished to be published.[6] Nicholls was more explicit in the first edition of his encyclopedia, saying,

"Because it was felt that a predominantly male readership might not accept women writers generally, in the early days especially, *many women* used pseudonyms, or forms of their name which did not clearly reveal their sex."[7] These, British academic Sarah Lefanu tells us, are the "hidden women," forced to disguise their appearances like chameleons.[8]

Another enduring myth promulgated by Janrae Frank, Jean Stine, and Forrest J. Ackerman even persists that Street & Smith publishers (who put out *Astounding*) banned all female names from the pages of their magazines![9] This trio's entirely fictitious history of Street & Smith reveals an abysmal ignorance of Street & Smith policies throughout all the many magazines this huge publisher produced. It is instructive, for example, to look at this publisher's policies toward women in the detective genre where their pulp, *Street & Smith's Detective Story,* was not only a dominant magazine, but was the very first crime fiction pulp. And female authors, Bill Pronzini tells us, figured prominently in its pages from the beginning:

> 'Born' in 1915, when S&S converted its dime-novel weekly, *Nick Carter,* to the pulp format, *Street & Smith's Detective Story* throughout its 34 year life [i.e., to 1949] regularly showcased stories by and of interest to women. A number of its contributors enjoyed successful careers as mystery novelists: Agatha Christie, Dorothy L. Sayers, Carolyn Wells, Helen Reilly, Elizabeth Sanxay Holding, Ethel Lina White, Margaret Millar . . . Sue McVeigh . . . Zola Helen Ross, Mary Collins . . . and Muriel Bradley. Above average *Street & Smith Detective Story* mainstays who confined their output to short stories, and are therefore known today only to pulp collectors and aficionados, include Margaret Manners, Marion Scott, Madeleine Sharps Buchanan, Agatha Gandy, and Inez Sabastian.[10]

And, just as female bylines were to be easily found in the pages of Street & Smith's detective magazines, the same was true in their science fiction. Thus, for instance, we find the well-known byline of Amelia Reynolds Long (using her *full* name) in the pages of Street & Smith's *Astounding.* We also find the bylines of many women in Street & Smith's *Unknown.*

And which Street & Smith editors would have been enforcing this ban on female authors? Would it, perhaps, be Babette Rosmond, herself a genre author, but also a Street & Smith editor from 1941–1948? Indeed, Rosmond simultaneously edited two of the most legendary pulp magazines, Street & Smith's *Doc Savage* (from 1944–1948) and Street & Smith's *The Shadow* (from 1946–1948). She was followed in these positions by Daisy Bacon, who edited *Doc Savage* in 1949 and *The Shadow* from 1948–1949. Would these two female Street & Smith editors have looked askance at female bylines? Indeed, would they even have been hired to edit two of the most famous pulps in history if Street & Smith was biased against women?

But, we are told, nevertheless "many women" had to hide behind male names. If these allegations *were* true, *where are all those mandated male pseud-*

onyms? If there was an anti-female prejudice, then this would have been a widespread practice and we should expect to quickly and easily find clear evidence of this phenomenon when we look at women writers attempting to publish in the early science fiction magazines. *But, it is impossible to find any evidence of the practice—anywhere.* This widespread allegation is a complete fiction! We have 288 stories under consideration for the 1926–1949 period (see table 1)— and *not one* was originally published by a woman deliberately attempting to hide her sexual identity by using a male pseudonym.

Hence, early science fiction was *not* like mainstream literature, where female authors often hid behind male bylines. Mary Ann Evans may have had to write as "George Eliot" to publish her novels and later Pearl Buck may have had to write as "John Sedges"—but *no woman* in early science fiction had to write under a male byline to see her story in print. By this criteria, then, early science fiction comes across as the most egalitarian and sexually "liberated" literary genre in existence.

Indeed, what we have is just the opposite. We find well-known writers such as Malcolm Jameson appearing in Street & Smith's *Unknown Worlds* under the name of "Mary MacGregor" and Robert W. "Doc" Lowndes publishing stories under the name of "Carol Grey." (See end of table 1). This makes absolutely no sense if Street & Smith, for instance, or other pulp publishers, had a bias against female authors.

Out of a total of 65 female authors published during our 1926–1949 period, the record reveals only three instances, once in the Thirties, and twice in the Forties, of a female writer using a male pseudonym at all, and none were deliberate attempts to conceal gender identities from the science fiction community.

In two of these three cases, this happened because wives collaborated on stories with their husbands—and the resulting co-authored stories by spouses appeared under a single male pseudonym. In 1936 Mrs. Raymond K. Cummings published one collaboration with her husband under a male pseudonym. Likewise, in 1940 the already well-established C. L. Moore married fellow science fiction writer Henry Kuttner. Thereafter, she published collaborations with her husband under male pseudonyms (*vide infra*)—while still continuing to publish under her own name. (See table 1.)

In the third case, Mary Gnaedinger, editor of *Famous Fantastic Mysteries* and *Fantastic Novels*, reprinted five stories in the 1940s by "Francis Stevens" (Gertrude Barrows Bennett) which had originally appeared in the Frank Munsey magazines between 1918–1920 (see table 1). Stevens' first published story, "The Nightmare," had appeared in the April 14, 1917 of Munsey's *All-Story Weekly*. She had sent the story to the editor, Bob Davis, under her own name, Gertrude Bennett. She felt no need to conceal her gender, as *All-Story* frequently published women writers. Indeed, an earlier issue of that magazine, August 19, 1916, was an almost all-female issue, as all the stories, except two serials carried over from the previous issue, were by women. These included eight of the ten stories and all of the seven poems. However, Bennett requested that her story appear under another female name, the pseudonym of "Jean Vail."[11]

For unknown reasons, Davis seems to have decided otherwise and the story appeared under the by-line of "Francis Stevens." Reader response was positive and Davis encouraged Bennett to write more. Having been established, though not of her choosing, under the "Francis Stevens" by-line, she thereafter continued to publish under that name.

However, by the time Bennett's stories were republished, not only were they considered classics, *but it was well known in the science fiction community that "Francis Stevens" was a woman.* Indeed, the editor who reprinted *all* of Bennett's stories in the Forties was also female, and so not likely to be biased against female authors. Indeed, it is conceivable that Mary Gnaedinger resurrected Gertrude Bennett's stories precisely *because* Bennett was a woman.

Further, according to P. Schuyler Miller, long-time book reviewer for *Astounding,* Stevens was exceedingly popular with Mary Gnaedinger's readers. And, on the occasion of the 1952 re-publication of her novel *The Heads of Cerberus,* by Lloyd Arthur Eshbach's Polaris Press, Miller hailed it as a "legendary novel by a legendary author. The story [originally] appeared in Street & Smith's *Thrill Book* in 1919 under a pen name which shortly became famous."[12] Likewise, the reviewer in *Other Worlds* raved about the book and told his readers, in case they'd forgotten, that "'Francis Stevens,' whose real name was Gertrude Bennett, was one of the best of the old-time writers of fantasy. Her work was on a par with the best writing of A. Merritt, Charles B. Stilson, J. U. Giesy, Garrett Smith, George Allan England, Victor Rousseau, and others."[13]

Damon Knight, who admitted that he panned about 80 percent of the books he reviewed, also lavishly praised this novel in a 1954 column in *Future Science Fiction* and repeatedly referred to Stevens as female. Quoting the three opening paragraphs of chapter 5, he said, "Now that, I submit, is not dated writing and never is likely to be; it's lucid, didactic, analytical and above all, zestful: an adjective which describes nearly the whole of the book. 'Francis Stevens,' we are given to understand, wrote only out of need and stopped at once when the need ended; but she [sic] wrote in the only way good writing is ever done: with joy. There is no plot-necessity for the interlude in the half-world of Ulithia; it's pure fantasy for the love of it; and there are lines in that chapter that are feather touches along the cheek."[14]

Thus, far from there being "many women" who engaged in this practice, there is not a single instance, anytime, anywhere, of a solo woman publishing an original story under a male pseudonym in the early science fiction magazines. This universally accepted claim is a total fabrication.

The record further reveals that *only four women,* Lee Hawkins Garby, Leigh Brackett, Leslie F. Stone, and well-known Futurian fan activist "Leslie Perri"

(Doris Baumgardt), published under what could be considered androgynous names between 1926–1949.[15] In addition, there were *only eight* who used initials. This handful of authors has been magnified in the public consciousness into amorphous, yet presumably large, numbers. And these, in turn, have then been used as evidence of prejudice. Again, let us look at the record.

As I noted, there were only four female authors who published under what might be considered androgynous names: Lee Hawkins Garby (the collaborator with E. E. "Doc" Smith on "The Skylark of Space," of whom not even the feminist historians take notice), "Leslie Perri," Leslie F. Stone, and Leigh Brackett. The latter two are the ones most often cited.

Let us begin with Lee Hawkins Garby.

There was never any effort made by either publishers, Smith, or Garby herself to conceal her sex. Indeed, in the August, 1930 issue of *Amazing Stories* (p. 389), "Doc" Smith explicitly referred to his collaborator as "Mrs. Garby" in the "Author's Note" accompanying "Skylark Three." He again referred to her as "Mrs. Garby" in *Astonishing Stories* (June, 1942, p. 6) when he explained that he had sought "Mrs. Garby" as a collaborator because he did not feel competent to handle the love interest and compose conversations by female characters.

Later, in 1946, when *The Skylark of Space* was first published in book form, the title page explicitly identified her as "Mrs. Lee Hawkins Garby." Evidently, no one feared that knowledge of either the co-author's sex or marital status would alienate readers—and no one tried to conceal it in connection with the sole story she published.

"Leslie Perri" was the fan name of Doris Baumgardt, a core member of the Futurian science fiction club during the 1930s. And, as "Leslie Perri," she wrote prolifically for the Futurian fanzines. Her single professional story in this 1926–1949 period (she published two more in the 1950s) was "Space Episode," in the December, 1941 issue of *Future combined with Science Fiction*.

As we have seen from her fan activities, previously discussed, she was well known in the field. Fellow Futurian Damon Knight described her as, "a tall, cool brunette who looked a little like the Dragon Lady in 'Terry and the Pirates.'"[16] She was the high school sweetheart of Futurian Frederik Pohl, who later married her. Pohl said she was, "strikingly beautiful, and strikingly intelligent, too, in a sulky, humorous, deprecatory way."[17] Pohl's marriage to her didn't last long. After their divorce, she married another Futurian, science fiction writer Richard Wilson. In one of Futurian Robert W. "Doc" Lowndes's fanzines, she published what Knight termed "remarkably perceptive" character sketches of many of her fellow Futurians, including Lowndes, Frederik Pohl, Donald A. Wollheim, and Cyril Kornbluth.[18]

When such by-lined essays, or her many illustrations, were not being published in the *Futurian News*, it was frequently carrying stories about her activities. One such activity was an elaborate costume ball she threw at her apartment on Valentine's Day, 1939, at which she was described as wearing "black patent leather panties, tulle skirt and bodice and hat to match." The May, 1939 *Science Fiction News Letter* reported the sad plight of Futurian Harry Dockweiler, who "has on his dressing table a large photograph of Mrs. Doris (Leslie Perri) Pohl, to which he has attached a plate swiped from a public telephone, reading 'Temporarily Out of Service.'"[19] Note that the passage identifies "Leslie Perri" as "Mrs. Doris Pohl"—which, however, was premature, as she and Fred Pohl did not marry until August, 1940.

Leslie Perri was one of only five Futurians Sam Moskowitz actually allowed inside the hall at the 1939 First World Science Fiction Convention. (Isaac Asimov, Richard Wilson, David Kyle, and Jack Rubinson were the others). She was also, at the time, a member of the Fantasy Amateur Press Association (FAPA), a nationwide group of fantasy and science fiction fans who exchanged their fanzines with each other. In fact, she was a founding member of that organization. Leslie Perri was, therefore, a prominent actor on the New York science fiction scene and was well known to science fiction fans nationally.

Finally, the editor of the magazine which published her sole story during our period was her good friend (and fellow Futurian) Robert W. Lowndes, who obviously knew her identity. Lowndes, in fact, had solicited the story from her. Hence, there is no possibility that Leslie Perri was attempting to conceal her gender identity from editors or anyone else—or that the "gender-neutral" first name of "Leslie" confused anyone. Everyone in science fiction knew "Leslie Perri" and everyone knew she was very much a woman.

The other Leslie on our list is Leslie F. Stone, who published eighteen stories between 1929 and 1940. Echoing Asimov, Frederik Pohl claimed that Stone, along with C. L. Moore, "felt a need to tinker with or change their names to deceive an overwhelmingly male audience."[20] First, Stone never "tinkered with" her name. She was born "Leslie." Next, Stone was frequently identified as female. Near the very beginning of her career, for example, a Frank Paul drawing of her accompanied her story about a race of powerful alien females, "Women with Wings" (*Air Wonder Stories*, May, 1930). Further, the blurb for the story three times referred to "Miss Stone." That same month, May, 1930, *Amazing Stories* editor T. O'Conor Sloane published Stone's, "Through The Veil," and, in his blurb, also referred to her as "Miss Stone."

Her picture also accompanied three more of her stories in the early Thirties ("The Conquest of Gola," *Wonder Stories*, April, 1931; "The Hell Planet," *Wonder Stories*, June, 1932; and "Gulliver, 3000 A. D.," *Wonder Stories*, May, 1933). When her story, "The Rape of the Solar System," appeared in the December, 1934 *Amazing Stories*, after a two-year hiatus from that magazine, eighty-one-year-old editor Sloane welcomed her back in an introductory blurb which said, "For some time we have hoped to have one of Miss Leslie Stone's quite charming stories appear in our magazine." She was also explicitly identified as female when she published "The Man with the Four-Dimensional Eyes" (*Wonder Stories*, August, 1935, p. 287). She is again referred to as female when her "The Fall of Mercury" appeared in the December 1935 *Amazing Stories* (p. 27).

Finally, the editors who enthusiastically published Stone made a point of correcting some letter-writers who mistakenly referred to her as male. Stone is "Miss, by the way, and not Mr.," Charles D. Hornig corrected a fan commenting on "The Man with the Four-Dimensional Eyes." Hornig then refers to her as "Miss Stone" twice more in his reply (*Wonder Stories*, November-December, 1935, p. 756). Later, in that same issue, a letter from Leslie F. Stone herself explains how her three-month-old son was the inspiration for her story "Cosmic Joke," which is answered by Hornig again explicitly referring to the "well-liked author" as female (p. 759).

There was no secret, then, to Stone's sexual identity (or even her motherhood) among either editors or their magazines' readership. Indeed, when T. O'Conor Sloane published her story, "The Human Pets of Mars," in the October, 1936 *Amazing Stories*, he not only put Stone's name on the cover as a "draw," but also introduced her story with a blurb in which he described her as a "much admired authoress" (p. 83). From Sloane's accolade and the fact that he advertised her on the cover, it would appear that not only was her gender well known, but Leslie F. Stone was popular with the mostly-male readers, as well as with the oldest editor in the business.

It is, then, an error to use Leslie F. Stone, as Pohl did, as example of a woman author who either attempted to conceal her gender, or whose gender was unknown to her editors and readers. There was no attempt by anyone to deceive anyone else about Stone's gender. The allegation is a complete fabrication.

The most famous and most often cited case of name ambiguity is that of Leigh Brackett. She had what Frederik Pohl termed, "a perfectly ambiguous name for a female writer in the forties."[21] She is also cited as one who "assumed a . . . non-gender specific name[s] to avoid prejudice on the part of editors and readers alike."[22] Another source states that, after Street & Smith allegedly banned all female names from its pages, she alone was allowed to continue publishing under her own name because her "moniker sounded masculine enough to allow her safe passage . . . no one suspected her gender for many years."[23] And as recently as 1995 she was singled out, along with Moore, Wilmar Shiras, and Judith Merril, as a lonely trail blazer who struggled against vast anti-female prejudice in order to publish. "When assessing the work of these early writers," wrote Pamela Sargent, "we should keep in mind that they were in a real sense pioneers, with few examples and female mentors to inspire and guide them. . . . To be a woman writing science fiction, and to succeed, was to overcome great odds."[24]

First of all, "Leigh" was not a pseudonym that Brackett "assumed." It was her given name. Nor did she use it to conceal her sexual identity from either editors or readers. As Marion Zimmer Bradley (who described Brackett as "a close and much-loved friend") pointed out, "Leigh never made any secret of her sex. . . . Everyone in science fiction knew her gender by 1946, when I came into the field [as a fan]."[25]

Such had been the case, however, from the very beginning of Brackett's career. And at no time did editors or other writers exhibit any hostility toward her because of her gender. Indeed, it was a male SF author, Henry Kuttner, who was her entree to the science fiction community. While struggling to learn to write, she told us, "I gambled on Laurence D'Orsay and his agency-cum-writing-course, and it was the most fortunate thing I ever did. Henry Kuttner was reading for Laurence then, and he took a special interest in my limping efforts at SF and fantasy, writing me long and detailed criticisms on his own time. If it hadn't been for Hank, I might never have made it; it would certainly have taken me much longer. . . .

"Hank did more. He introduced me to LASFS [the Los Angeles Science Fantasy Society], where I met the science-fiction world, both fan and professional, and made friendships that have lasted ever since, with Ray Bradbury, Jack Williamson . . . Heinlein, Willy Ley, Cleve Cartmill . . . all invaluable in sparking my own imagination and ambition. And, of course, Ed Hamilton [who became her husband]."[26]

One of the Los Angeles fans who immediately took a liking to the novice Brackett was Ray Bradbury, also struggling to become a writer at that time. "He and I became close friends," said Brackett, "and spent many a Sunday at the beach going over each other's manuscripts, talking writing and science fiction . . . a couple of thirsty castaways in a cultural desert."

However, even the "Big Names" welcomed her. "Heinlein was urbane, courteous, a great raconteur," she recalled. "I had the pleasure of attending a few of the 'evenings' on Lookout Mountain [Heinlein's mountain home in Laurel Canyon], which were immensely stimulating. Willy Ley . . . [was] quite charming . . . Jack [Williamson] was tall and shy and Jimmy-Stewartish, Ed [Hamilton] was breezy and articulate, both of them great to talk to. . . . Ed and I both came to love [Doc Smith]; there was never a finer man."[27]

Jack Williamson, who also attended those same soirees of "The Manana Literary Society" at Heinlein's home in the Hollywood hills, fondly remembered socializing with Brackett at those SF social gatherings, along with C. L. Moore, Phyllis Boucher, Annette McComas, and "a fetching redhead named Marda Brown." All the fans and writers in attendance accepted, encouraged, and "enjoyed" (Williamson's word) Leigh Brackett. The only resistance to her desire to be a science fiction writer, it seems, came from her own family, as Williamson recalled that, "I got a sense of quietly stubborn conflict with her mundane family environment."[28]

It was editor John W. Campbell, Jr. who "officially" discovered Brackett, buying and publishing her first story, "Martian Quest," for the February, 1940 *Astounding Science Fiction.* The story proved popular with readers, as did Brackett's second story in the April issue, "The Treasures of Ptakuth." Campbell knew he was discovering and publishing a woman. He had purchased both stories in late 1939 in the same week *directly from the novice Brackett,* instead of from her agent, Julius Schwartz.[29]

Enthusiastic letters praising the novice followed. Shortly thereafter, in the July, 1940 issue and in response to a reader who referred to Brackett as "he," Campbell corrected the mistaken reader. He announced at the beginning of *Astounding*'s letter column in a bold headline for the entire readership of *Astounding* to see: "The 'Leigh' in 'Leigh Brackett' Is Feminine." Thus, only months after her initial appearance in his magazine (then the most widely-read in the field), John W. Campbell proudly broadcast to the entire science fiction world what the Los Angeles fans already knew—that this new writer he'd discovered, Leigh Brackett, was a woman. Obviously, Campbell had no reservations about either publishing her or announcing Brackett's gender to his mostly-male readership.

It was likewise made clear from her very first appearances in other magazines that Leigh Brackett was female. For example, when she debuted in *Amazing Stories* with her tale, "No Man's Land in Space" (July, 1941), the editor, Ray Palmer, introduced the new author to *his* readers by featuring her in the ongoing author biography column of the magazine, *where her photograph was also printed.*[30] Hence, everyone who read *Amazing* also knew from the outset of her career in that magazine that she was a woman.

Similarly, when Oscar J. Friend purchased her "Shadow Over Mars" for *Startling Stories* (fall, 1944), he gushed in the preceding issue (summer, 1944) over the upcoming story saying, "Not since Marie Corelli have we had a woman writer who could unleash her imagination so vividly and set the pictures down in such strong, graphic style," (p. 6). When the heralded story appeared, it was accompanied by a short autobiographical essay by Brackett, *as well as her photograph* (see pp. 112–113).

And, of course, we also know from her own account, previously cited, that not only were the various editors who published her stories (and her photographs) repeatedly stating that Leigh Brackett was a woman, but that *fans* also knew she was a woman—and were aware of her gender identity from the very beginning of her career. In September, 1940 Mary ("Pogo") Gray, a popular fellow-member of the Los Angeles Science Fantasy Society (LASFS) launched *STF-ETTE,* which Sam Moskowitz, as I noted, believed was the "first feminist fanzine" in the field. "Pogo" intended that everything published in her 'zine was to be produced *by female writers alone.* In its second issue, May, 1941, this "feminist" showcase for the genre's female writers featured Leigh Brackett with an article entitled "Earth's Renaissance."

As such participation in fan activities made clear, Brackett did not isolate herself from the fans and readers. Indeed, in a sense Brackett emerged from the Los Angeles fan community. Fellow member Ray Bradbury remembers her frequent attendance at LASFS's weekly meetings, which Bradbury began attending in 1937 at age seventeen. "My God, how beautiful," was how he described her.[31]

In the early 1940s Bradbury, eager to become a science fiction writer, began hanging out with her at Muscle Beach, comparing stories, an experience Brackett, as we saw, remembered fondly. No doubt this explains why Bradbury collaborated with Brackett on an early story in his oeuvre, "Lorelei of the Red Mist," *Planet Stories,* summer, 1946. When Leigh Brackett married science fiction writer Edmond Hamilton in 1946, Bradbury served as Hamilton's best man at the well-publicized wedding, being best friends with both of them.

Obviously, then, from the very beginning of Brackett's career, the knowledge that she was a female writer was widespread in the science fiction world, not only among professional editors and their readers, but also in fandom itself.

And, knowing she was female from her very first stories, were the mostly-male readers hostile toward her? According to Lester Del Rey, "She quickly became the favorite writer of [*Planet Stories*]."[32] While implying (with no evidence) that it *did* matter to readers that *other* writers were female, Pamela Sargent concedes that "It did not seem to matter to Brackett's readers that she was female; her colorful stories . . . were well-liked."[33]

Indeed, the summer, 1950 issue of *Planet Stories* carried *two* letters from male readers pleading for more stories by her. "BRING BACK BRACKETT!," demanded one from Waterloo, Iowa, in capital letters (p. 112). The other (p. 102), from Jamaica, Long Island, plaintively asked, "When do we see Brackett again? It's been six months since her fair name has graced the table of contents. Something must be done about this sad state of affairs."

When Brackett's "Black Amazon of Mars" finally appeared in the March 1951 *Planet Stories,* subsequent letters lavished praise on it. Writing in the September 1951 issue of *Planet Stories* (p. 105), Canadian reader Mavis Hartman said it was the best story in the issue. "Miss Brackett is an author (ess) to beat all authors. . . . That adventure style of hers is captivating." In the same issue (p. 106), Lin Carter, who later became an influential writer and editor in the field, lauded the story, calling it "poetry." Leigh Brackett, he said, was, "a talented and imaginative authoress. . . . She knows the secret of fusing poignant emotion, rich description, convincing action, and above all, a tremendous sense of atmosphere and lavish, excellent use of the English language . . . 'Black Amazon' was a good story, colorful, poetic, and exciting. Let's have more from Brackett." The letter columns of the issues following her "Shadow Over Mars" in *Startling Stories* were also typical in being filled with similar praise.

Nor, clearly, did her popularity have anything to do with making it acceptable for her and subsequent writers to be women, as some have claimed. She was known to be female first. She became popular later. In one of the most famous instances cited to "prove" prejudice against women, then, we discover that it is completely impossible to find any prejudice at all from editors, fans, or readers. Nor can we find any evidence that there was ever any attempt at gender-concealment on Leigh Brackett's part or on the part of the editors who published her. Indeed, the latter went out of their way to proudly publicize her gender with photographs, profiles, and announcements, and it was fellow writers, such as Henry Kuttner, who brought her into the science fiction world.

Thus, as with Leslie F. Stone, it is a complete fiction to use Leigh Brackett as example of a woman author who either attempted to conceal her gender, or whose gender was unknown to her editors and readers, or who was discriminated against because of her gender.

Now let us turn to the issue of initials. Of the eight authors published under initials in our period, I believe three did not choose this option. Rather, it appears to have been the idiosyncrasy of *Astounding* editor F. Orlin Tremaine— who even abbreviated his own name! (Tremaine is known to have used a female pseudonym himself, "Anne Beal," and so obviously had no objection to female by-lines.) Two of them, Kaye Raymond and Amelia Reynolds Long, first published under their full names, seemingly their preference. Raymond, for instance, first appeared in print under the name "Kaye Raymond" when Hugo Gernsback published her "Into the Infinitesimal" (*Wonder Stories*, June, 1934, which devoted the Frank Paul cover to her story). However, when *Astounding* editor F. Orlin Tremaine later published three more of her stories, they appeared as by "K. Raymond."

Likewise, when Gernsback and T. O'Conor Sloane (was his use of an initial an attempt at gender concealment?) published Long's first stories in their separate magazines, they did so under her full name (see table 1). Additionally, Long published all of her stories in *Weird Tales* under her full name, debuting with "The Twin Soul," March, 1928, more than five and a half years before F. Orlin Tremaine at *Astounding* began to abbreviate her name. She published three more stories in *Weird Tales* under her full name ("The Thought-Monster," March 1930; "The Magic-Maker," June, 1930; and "The Undead," August, 1931) before Tremaine took the reins as editor of *Astounding*. She then published two more *Weird Tales* stories under her full name *at the very same time Tremaine was abbreviating her name*. ("Flapping Wings of Death," June, 1935 and "The Album," December, 1936.) She also published "The Box From the Stars" in *Strange Stories* (April, 1939) under her full name. And when she wrote to "The Eyrie," the readers' letters department of *Weird Tales*, she wrote under her full name. (See, e.g., her letter of November 1931). Hence, Amelia Reynolds Long had become well known in both the fantasy and science fiction fields under her full female name before (and even during) the time of Tremain's editorship of *Astounding*.

But, when she began to appear in Tremaine's *Astounding* in 1934, he abbreviated her as "A. R. Long." And, despite Asimov's use of her as a sterling example of the need of women writers at the time to conceal their names behind initials if they wanted to be published—this is the *only* instance in which her initials were ever used! I believe this was simply because Tremaine, who edited the magazine from 1933–1937 and was the *only* editor who abbreviated Long's name, simply liked to abbreviate author's names—and did so regardless of sex. Thus, Gladys St. John-Loe (the third initialled author I believe did not choose her initialed by-line) became simply "G. St. John-Loe" when he published her story, "Where Four Roads Meet" (October, 1933).

However, Tremaine's successor at *Astounding*, John W. Campbell (1937–1972), restored or expanded initialed by-lines of both male and female authors. Therefore, under Campbell's aegis, L. A. Eshbach became Lloyd Arthur Eshbach, C. C. Campbell became Clyde Crane Campbell, R. R. Winterbotham became Russell R. Winterbotham, E. E. Smith became Edward E. Smith—*and A. R. Long once more became Amelia Reynolds Long, which she remained for the rest of her stories.* Indeed, the majority of her stories were published under her full name and six of the seven fantasy and science fiction editors who published her did so under her full name. Tremaine, again, was the sole exception. However, even during Tremaine's tenure it is clear from numerous letters in *Astounding*'s readers' department in 1936–1937 that readers not only loved her stories but were well aware of her sex and her full name.

The record therefore makes it quite clear that Amelia Reynolds Long preferred her full female name—and had no difficulty finding editors willing to publish her under her full female name. Thus, it is also a complete fiction to use Amelia Reynolds Long as example of a woman author who either attempted to conceal her gender, or whose gender was unknown to her editors and readers.

Who, then, were the five women who actually *chose* to publish using initials during our period and what was the truth behind their usage? They include M. F. Rupert and I. M. Stephens, who today seem virtually forgotten, as well as the almost equally forgotten E. Mayne Hull. There is C. L. Moore, who has *not* been forgotten. And finally we have L. Taylor Hansen, who seems to be the *sole* case I have been able to discover of a female author who actually *did* attempt to conceal her gender identity through the use of initials.

Of these five, the most important is Moore, whose very existence is part of the basis for British feminist Sarah Lefanu declaring that, in the 1930s and 1940s, "there were women writers, like C. L. Moore and Leigh Brackett, who may have assumed a male voice and non-gender specific names to avoid prejudice on the part of editors and readers alike."[34] As we shall see, neither the "male voice" nor any other part of this statement is true.

Let us begin with M. F. Rupert, as she published only a single story and can be quickly dispensed with. M. (Margaret) F. Rupert's only appearance was an impressive account of a feminist (she uses that very word!) utopia, "Via the Hewitt Ray," in the spring, 1930, *Science Wonder Quarterly*.[35] If the subject matter did not clue in readers, they could scarcely miss the Frank Paul drawing of her accompanying the author's biographical profile published along with the story. Readers thus had her photograph, her profile, and a story about a feminist utopia before them. In her case, there can be no doubt that initials were not meant to conceal her sexual identity.

I. M. Stephens (Inga Marie Pratt, *nee* Stephens) co-authored two stories with her husband, the well-known science fiction author Fletcher Pratt. She may even have been responsible for others. Sam Moskowitz claimed that Pratt "was never a good story teller," and that Inga "collaborated with him for years on his early science fiction."[36] In any case, when Frederik Pohl once dined with the Pratts at their home, "The Ipsy-Wipsy Institute," Fletcher introduced his wife to Pohl as co-author of the stories which Pohl admired.[37] (Odd, then, that Pohl would claim, as I noted earlier, that no one knew there were any female authors until the mid-Forties or even later.)

The "Ipsy-Wipsy Institute" was an immense 200-year-old, 23-room mansion on many acres in New York's Monmouth County overlooking the Shrewsbury River. Pohl described it as the "summer home" of the New York science fiction community, and, in his autobiography, named some of the "regulars." These included Lester del Rey and his wife; L. Sprague de Camp and his wife; Cyril Kornbluth and his wife Mary, both members of the Futurians; Willy Ley and his wife; Katherine MacLean and Charles Dye, her writer husband; as well as Fritz Leiber and Theodore Sturgeon. After Dona Campbell divorced John W. Campbell, she married SF writer George O. Smith and they moved into the Pratts' home.

Laurence Manning, a popular *Wonder Stories* writer from the 1930s, bought property from the Pratts and built a home next door. Poet John Ciardi, who was also an SF editor for Twayne publishers, was another regular. So was Basil Davenport, a Book-of-the-Month Club editor (and later editor of many SF anthologies) who boasted to the group at the Institute that he'd persuaded BMOC to accept an Arthur C. Clarke novel as an alternate selection.[38]

And so it went.

It was thus very well known in the influential and well-connected New York science fiction world that I. M. Stephens was Pratt's wife. Additionally, Inga illustrated Fletcher's book, *Tales From Gavagan's Bar*, in which she was explicitly identified on the dust jacket as Pratt's wife. Her use of initials, then, was not an attempt to conceal her sexual identity from either editors or readers. Inga was embedded in the small world of science fiction publishing. Everyone knew who she was—and no one cared that the was a woman.

How about E. (Edna) Mayne Hull, the 1946 Worldcon co-Guest of Honor? Was her use of an initial done to conceal her gender? This hardly seems believable, as the fans and editors at the 1946 Worldcon were obviously quite aware that their co-Guest of Honor was female and were not biased against the woman they'd chosen to honor at their festivities. In addition, when she and her husband, A. E. van Vogt (who also used initials) published their co-authored Fantasy Press book, *Out of the Unknown* in 1948, the rear flap of the dust jacket carried her photo, identified her as "Mrs. van Vogt," and specified that, while her first name was "Edna," she preferred to be called "Mayne."

Further, in the course of a visit with her just before Christmas of 1954, she told Norm Metcalf that the reason she didn't use her first name in print was simply because she just didn't like it. "Please call me 'Mayne,'" she asked of him. Independent verification of this can also be found in the autobiographical writings of her husband. Throughout these he uniformly refers to her as "my wife, Mayne."[39]

E. Mayne Hull's use of an initial, then, was obviously not done to escape some presumed anti-female bias, nor to deliberately conceal her gender.

Then we have C. (Catherine) L. Moore, the person upon whom this particular mythology mostly rests. I have already cited Frederik Pohl's claim that C. L. Moore, along with Leslie Stone, "felt a need to tinker with or change their names to deceive an overwhelmingly male audience."[40] Based upon no cited evidence whatsoever, Baird Searles also states flatly about Moore that, "the initials were adopted to disguise her sex in the mainly masculine world of science fiction in the '30s."[41]

Virtually every commentator has repeated this myth. "Moore was long thought to be a man," Dr. Frederick Shroyer tells us in an important reference work on science fiction authors.[42] Indeed, feminist theorist Hilary Rose explicitly refers to Moore as a "female man," typical of "all those women writers of SF from C. L. Moore to James Tiptree who wrote as female men," presumably a large (though unknown) number.[43]

Meanwhile, feminist historian Sharon Yntema says that, "Catherine Lucille Moore used only her first two initials in order to disguise her gender in the male-dominated science-fiction world of the 1930s."[44] "When 22-year-old Catherine Moore began writing professionally in 1933," says Robert Silverberg, "she chose to conceal her sex behind those impersonal initials, perhaps because she thought she stood a better chance of getting published that way. . . . Moore's work was surprisingly popular with the science-fiction audience, which seems to have had little or no inkling of her true sex."[45]

Dr. William Bainbridge asserts that "A few early women authors actually kept their gender secret from readers." His only evidence for this risky extrapolation from the particular to the general is a citation of Sam Moskowitz, who once said, "The fact that C. L. Moore was a woman was carefully kept from the readers of *Weird Tales*."[46]

Absolutely *none* of this is true and *none* of these authors produced any evidence to substantiate their allegations. There simply was no prejudice against women writers at *Weird Tales*, where Moore debuted. All of these statements are based upon yet another ubiquitous presumption of prejudice which colors every commentary on this era: an alleged unremitting hostility toward women writers on the part of the majority male readership, thus offering yet another reason for a female writer, such as Moore, to conceal her gender. This assumption about the nature of pulp science fiction is seldom ever stated. All one has to do is say, "mainly male," and the subsequent words, "and hostile," are automatically presumed without being spoken. But again, no evidence supports this presumption. A culturally hegemonic idea *needs* no evidence.

But the available evidence suggests that the fact that Moore was a woman caused no problems for either her fellow male authors or the readers of *Weird Tales*. For example, Robert E. Howard, one of the reigning giants of *Weird Tales* and the creator of "Conan the Barbarian," numbered himself among Moore's fans and friends. In their biography of Howard, L. Sprague and Catherine Crook de Camp tell us that, "Late in 1934 [Howard] finished, but did not sell, a novelette, 'Sword Woman,' laid in Renaissance France. Perhaps he was influenced by the work of a beautiful young writer who had just entered the heroic fantasy field, Catherine Lucille Moore. . . . In the October, 1934 issue of *Weird Tales* appeared [Moore's] 'Black God's Kiss,' the first of five novelettes about a red-haired medieval warrior-woman, Jirel of Joiry. . . . When a second Jirel story was published ['The Black God's Shadow,' *Weird Tales*, December, 1934], Howard sent Miss Moore a letter of congratulation and a manuscript of his 'Sword Woman.'"[47]

"Sword Woman" featured the adventures of "Dark Agnes," who proclaimed, "You deny me a place among men? By God, I'll live as I please and die as God wills, but if I'm not fit to be a man's comrade, at least I'll be no man's mistress." She was one of many warrior women created by Howard, even before the appearance of Jirel of Joiry. Howard's other warrior women included Conan's lover-companion Belit, Red Sonya of Rogatino ("The Shadow of the Vulture," *The Magic Carpet Magazine*, January, 1934), Valeria of the Red Brotherhood ("Red Nails," *Weird Tales*, July–October, 1936), and Helen Tavrel ("The Isle of Pirate's Doom," like "Sword Woman," unpublished at Howard's death). The mere existence of such female characters in the heroic pulp fiction of the Thirties (and coming from the typewriter of perhaps the most macho of pulp authors) suggests the contested terrain of the literature, wherein it was not unknown for women to match blades with men.

It was unusual for Howard to share an unpublished manuscript with a fellow author and indicates that he knew and trusted Moore and accepted her as an equal, even at this early stage in her career, and regardless of her gender. His trust was rewarded in January 1935, when Moore wrote back praising "Dark Agnes" and discussing Howard's work in a familiar manner. "My blessings!," she wrote. "I can't tell you how much I enjoyed *Sword Woman*. It seemed such a pity to leave her just at the threshold of higher adventures. Your favorite trick of slamming the door on a burst of bugles! And leaving one to wonder what happened next and wanting so badly to know. Aren't there any more stories about Agnes?"[48]

The readers of *Weird Tales* were just as receptive of Moore and her work. As Moskowitz points out, she quickly became known as "Catherine the Great, toast of *Weird Tales*,"[49] and issue after issue carried letters of praise from male readers, such as H. P. Lovecraft. These readers voted "Shambleau," along with its sequels "Black Thirst" (April, 1934) and "Scarlet Dream" (May, 1934), the best stories in their respective issues, beating out contributions by E. Hoffmann Price, Robert E. Howard, Jack Williamson, Edmond Hamilton, Frank Belknap Long, and Clark Ashton Smith.[50]

Moore followed up these triumphs in October 1934, with "The Black God's Kiss," the debut of her famous warrior princess Jirel of Joiry. Editor Farnsworth Wright hailed this story of a powerful female protagonist as being on a par with H. P. Lovecraft, Arthur Machen, and Algernon Blackwood. Reader response to this emotionally wrenching love story was so positive that it was quickly followed by sequel adventures of the warrior princess. Later, when Donald A. Wollheim began editing the *Avon Fantasy Reader*, he acknowledged as early as volume three in 1947 that "most of you readers included requests" for her work and he eventually reprinted three of her stories from *Weird Tales*.

Nor were these readers unaware of Moore's gender. Her gender became publicly known to fandom only a few months after her debut, "Shambleau," appeared. Julius Schwartz and Mort Weisinger revealed it in the May 1934 issue of their fan magazine, *The Fantasy Fan*. *Weird Tales* itself explicitly referred to her as female in its September 1935 issue. And, when Moore herself published a letter in its readers' column, she made no attempt at concealment, signing herself, "Miss Catherine Moore."[51]

Meanwhile, at the supposedly anti-female Street & Smith, F. Orlin Tremaine had been assiduously wooing Moore for his *Astounding Stories*. He was eventually successful and, the same month that Moore debuted Jirel of Joiry in *Weird Tales*, October, 1934, she made her first appearance in a science fiction magazine. Her science fiction debut was a fascinating love story about a human male and an alien female entitled "The Bright Illusion."

Reader reaction to Moore's debut in *Astounding* was warmly receptive. Among those writing letters to praise her first story were Robert W. Lowndes (later an editor himself) and E. E. Smith, both explicitly referring to Moore as a woman.[52] Indeed, the Lowndes letter appeared in the November *Astounding*, the *very next issue* after her debut. Such instantaneous response and knowledge of her gender meant that readers had to be familiar with her from *Weird Tales* and the fact that they knew she was female suggests her gender was not a problem for them.

Typical of the letters praising Moore's science fiction debut was that from E. E. "Doc" Smith (January, 1935, p. 153), where he said, "I read five of her stories without being impelled to rave. [These would have been her prior stories in *Weird Tales.*] Good jobs they all were, and done in workmanlike fashion. . . . Then 'Bright Illusion'! Man, there is a job of work—adult fare, that, no fooling! I have read it three times so far, and haven't got it all yet . . . a truly remarkable and really masterly piece of writing. I have no idea whether Miss (or Mrs.) Moore is a young girl with an unusually powerful mind and a full store of unsullied idealism, or whether she is a woman whose long and eventful life has shown her that real love is man's supreme dower. But whoever or whatever she may be, I perceive in her 'Bright Illusion' a flame of sublimity."

Similar letters praising Moore and referring to her as female can be found in the *Astounding* issues of February, April, and December, 1935; February, 1936; and February, 1937. Such, then, was the immediate reaction to C. L. Moore's professional debut in the science fiction field.

Several of Moore's subsequent appearances in Street & Smith's magazines were similar love stories or had strong female protagonists—both alleged to be anathema to their largely male readership. Among others, these stories include "Tryst in Time," "Fruit of Knowledge" (published by Campbell and in the Fantasy Hall of Fame), and the classic "No Woman Born" (also published by Campbell). Their existence and their popularity clearly challenge the prevailing wisdom that readers were uniformly hostile to such themes—or even that readers, even to *Astounding*, were universally male. Thus, wrote reader Ruby Wylie McDonald, of Flint, MI, in *Astounding* ("Brass Tacks," October, 1936, p. 153), "Romance should *not* be taken from science fiction stories. It puts human interest into what would otherwise be a mechanical story."

None of these love stories, or the Jirel of Joiry stories, reflect the "male voice" feminist academic Sarah Lefanu claimed Moore was forced to assume in her stories. The presumption of feminist critics like Lefanu is that of a simplistic "cultural hegemony," that a hostile patriarchy dominated everything and all were forced to conform. The type of stories actually published in the magazines, however, as well as reader reaction to them, does not support this interpretation. Rather, the actual publication record is a powerful vindication of the "contested terrain" thesis.

Moore also had extensive dealings with fans and published in their fanzines. (See, e.g., her Northwest Smith story, "Werewoman," which she gave to H. P. Lovecraft's good friend R. H. Barlow sometime in 1937 and which he published in the 1938 issue of his mimeographed fanzine, *Leaves.*) And, like Leigh Brackett, she made regular appearances at the weekly meetings of the Los Angeles Science Fantasy Society once she and her husband, Henry Kuttner, moved to

Southern California (which is where young fan Ray Bradbury first met her).[53] Obviously, it was quickly and widely known in both the fantasy and science fiction communities that the popular "C. L. Moore" was a woman—and it mattered not in the least.

Why, then, did C. L. Moore use initials? Most knowledgeable fans have known the true reason for many years. Far from any desire to conceal her gender from the fantasy or science fiction worlds, where absolutely no one cared, the reason was purely mundane: to protect her job. Moore worked at a bank, said Marion Zimmer Bradley, and "C. L. Moore told me once that she had adopted initials because had she published her first story . . . under her own name, she might have lost her job as a bank teller. In 1933, the depths of the Depression, Ms. Moore was the only working member of her family and the sole support of her aging parents; she did not wish to risk her livelihood on the uncertain business of fiction writing."[54]

Thus, Moore simply did not want her employer to know that she wrote fantastic fiction for disreputable pulp magazines, lest they fire her. We tend to forget this prejudice against pulp literature which *all* pulp authors, regardless of gender, labored under at the time—and for decades thereafter. Every "old timer" can tell stories about the disdain and ridicule they endured as kids for reading science fiction. Others were forbidden, outright, to read the disreputable literature. For instance, *Parade* magazine columnist Marilyn vos Savant recalls that when she was young, "My parents strongly encouraged reading, but not science fiction, which both thought would be harmful."[55]

And, as adults, the writers suffered similar disdain. For example, between 1931 and 1935 Frank K. Kelly published a number of tales in *Wonder Stories* and *Astounding* and seemed to have a promising future in the field. Then, in 1935, the stories abruptly ceased and nothing more was heard from him. When I asked him in 1988 why he stopped writing, Kelly said he entered college in 1935 and his respected English professor ridiculed his stories. "He said I was wasting myself on trash, and I ought to write serious literature," Kelly said. "He convinced me that what I was doing wasn't worthwhile."[56]

Meanwhile, prolific slick magazine writer Will F. Jenkins felt compelled to make his debut in a science fiction magazine ("The Runaway Skyscraper," *Amazing Stories*, June, 1926, originally in *Argosy*, 1919) under the pseudonym of "Murray Leinster." As his friend Julius Schwartz explained, "He had a talent and a passion for science fiction, but felt he couldn't afford for his more reputable clients—the editors of those slick magazines—to know about it."[57]

Likewise, Harry Clement Stubbs, a Harvard undergraduate, feared incurring the disapproval of his Ivy League professors if they knew he published in a science fiction magazine. So, when he sold his first story in 1941, to *Astounding Science-Fiction*, he hid his name from his professors under the pen name of "Hal Clement."[58]

As a kid, Isaac Asimov could only read his beloved science fiction magazines after he convinced his disapproving father that the stories were "educational" because they dealt with *science*. But, even as late as November, 1949, Dr. Asimov offered his resignation in shame and humiliation to the dean of the Boston University School of Medicine when he learned that his publisher had, much to his chagrin, listed his university affiliation on the back cover of his first novel, *Pebble in the Sky*. Asimov wanted to spare Boston University the disgrace of association with a despicable science fiction writer. The dean was less embarrassed about Asimov's novel than Asimov seemed to be, however, and he refused to accept Asimov's resignation.[59]

Gender, then, had nothing to do with the desire of such early science fiction writers to conceal their "extracurricular activities" from their employers or professors—and many of both genders did so by using initials or pseudonyms or by simply keeping their work as hidden from the "mundane world" as possible.

In summation, the record documents that it is a myth that C. L. Moore used initials to conceal her gender from the fantasy or science fiction community; or that this was necessary for publication; or that her readers did not know she was a woman; or, knowing this, that the mostly male readership was either hostile to her presence or failed to credit the quality of her work. It is therefore also a complete fiction to use C. L. Moore as example of a woman author who either attempted to conceal her gender, or whose gender was unknown to her editors and readers.

Finally, there is L. Taylor Hansen, the only early woman author who seems to have deliberately concealed her gender. Over a period of almost twenty years (1929–1948) L. (Lucile) Taylor Hansen published eight stories, mostly in *Amazing Stories*. In addition, she also had a long-term business relationship with *Amazing*. From 1941–1949 Hansen wrote fifty-seven articles on science and history for the magazine, then edited by Raymond A. Palmer. She also intermittently attended the University of California at Los Angeles (UCLA) in the 1920s, although she never graduated. And she may also have been the sister of chemist Louis Ingvald Hansen, who received his Ph.D. from the University of Minnesota.

There is no evidence that Palmer was unaware of Hansen's gender. Certainly she would have had no reason to conceal it from a man who also regularly published articles by such women writers as Gale Stevens, June Lurie, Frances Yerxa, Fran Ferris, Lynn Standish, Mildred Murdoch, Letty Liebert, and many others. (See articles by these women, which I am citing just at random, in the September, 1947 and November, 1949 issues of *Amazing Stories*, as well as the January, 1945, April, 1948, and April, 1949 issues of *Fantastic Adventures*, which Palmer also edited. Virtually every issue of one of Palmer's magazines had articles by such women writers.)

Indeed, Palmer had so little trouble working with women that in 1949, while attending Cinvention, that year's Worldcon, he recruited twenty-two-year-old Cincinnati fan Beatrice "Bea" Mahaffey (1926–1987) to be his managing editor at *Other Worlds*. Later, for long periods, he turned most editorial tasks over to her (helped briefly by Assistant Editor Marge Sanders Budwig). Hence, it seems reasonable to believe Palmer knew exactly with whom he was dealing.

Nevertheless, Palmer does seem to have conspired with Hansen to deliberately conceal her gender from readers, the only case I've been able to find of this happening. Thus, when Hansen published a letter rebutting attacks on one of her articles, Palmer headlined the letter, "L. Taylor Hansen Defends Himself" (*Amazing Stories*, June, 1943). Hansen also submitted a photo of a man purporting to be her which accompanied her story "The City on the Cloud" (*Wonder Stories*, October, 1930) and even (if we can believe Forrest J. Ackerman) invented an imaginary brother (or perhaps it was Louis Ingvald Hansen) to whom she attributed her stories.

There seems to be some confusion on Ackerman's part (and he is our only source concerning this claim) about the imaginary brother. For instance, Ackerman was presumably the source of Donald Tuck's information on Hansen in his encyclopedia entry on her when he said, "she once appeared at a meeting of the Los Angeles Science Fantasy Society in 1939 and told F. J. Ackerman that she had placed [her] stories for her brother, a world traveller, who had written them."[60]

However, in "Paging Louise [sic] Taylor Hansen!" Ackerman specifically denies that Hansen attended that meeting and goes on to say, publicly addressing Hansen, "I'd like to meet you. I've never laid eyes on you."[61] Even so, Ackerman does say he spoke, once, with Hansen on the phone and she *then* told him her (imaginary or not) brother wrote her stories and she merely published them under her own name.

But, while we have to take this latter assertion with a grain of salt (as, again, Ackerman's contradictory memory is the only source), it is not inconsistent with Hansen's actions. Indeed, she seems to have been such an exceedingly secretive person that it appears she even misled people about her true full first name. Virtually every authoritative source gives her first name as "Louise." This is how she is referred to, for instance, by Ackerman (who is currently acting as Hansen's literary agent and collecting royalties for her stories, although he does not have a signed contract to represent her), Sam Moskowitz, and Tuck in the work cited above. Additionally, according to a letter to Norm Metcalf from bibliographer Donald B. Day, it is also the name Hansen herself supplied when she answered Day's query as to her full first name.

However, E. F. Bleiler and his son, Richard, and have expended much effort in tracking down the elusive Ms. Hansen and seem to have confirmed that her first name was actually "Lucile" (neither "Louise" nor even "Lucille"). "I got her books on interlibrary loan and worked through them for matters of biographical information," Ev Bleiler said. "I phoned her publisher, a vanity house. Richard managed to track down a correspondent of hers, a fairly well known authority on American archaeology. The British Museum (now Library) Catalogue carries her books as by Lucile, which is completely authoritative. . . . Richard also got information about her University of California attendance, where records carried her as Lucile. And the Social Security Death Index carries her properly. Everywhere that her first name is given it is Lucile. . . . There can be no doubt but that her name was really Lucile."[62]

So, with Hansen it seems we are dealing with someone unwilling to be forthcoming about her true first name, even when she was dealing with people who *knew* she was a woman.

Furthermore, Hansen also published one story, "The Fire Trail" (*Amazing Stories* and *Fantastic Adventures,* January, 1948), under the bizarre asexual pseudonym of "Oge-Make"! Thus, Hansen appears to have deliberately tried to baffle her reading public about who she really was. At this late date, however, it is quite impossible to definitively ascertain why this odd person wanted to bury her true identity to such an extent.

But that hasn't stopped at least one widely respected academic from authoritatively pronouncing on the issue, despite the complete lack of evidence. Further, this academic authority uses the sole case of Hansen's deception to construct an entirely fictitious literary history. Professor Jane Donawerth teaches a course on women's science fiction at the University of Maryland and has written about Hansen and other early women writers. When she discusses early feminist utopias, Dr. Donawerth seems quite perceptive. But, when discussing the psychology of Hansen, her preconceptions seem to have blinded her to the salient point.

In dealing with L. Taylor Hansen, Jane Donawerth constructed an elaborate and absolutely unsubstantiated psychological scenario. This post-hoc and long-distance psychoanalysis is based upon Donawerth's presumption of prejudice in the early science fiction community. Supposedly, the rampant male hostility toward women writers in the science fiction world would have stripped Hansen of her "writerly authority" had her gender been known to her editors and readers. Hence, Donawerth asserts that, "owing to social norms and generic convention, [Hansen] felt it unacceptable for a woman to author a science fiction, and so published under initials. . . . Hansen was undergoing a crisis of writerly authority . . . and she did not want to lose her authority as a science fiction writer by revealing her feminine gender."[63] Dr. Donawerth then uses the sole example of Hansen (as if it were typical of many other, unnamed, cases) as the linchpin to an entire chapter on "Cross-Dressing as a Male Narrator."

Donawerth's only source of all information on Hansen (whom she also calls "Louise") is Donald Tuck's one-paragraph entry in his encyclopedia, which recounts Ackerman's contradictory story of the brother. And, of course,

Donawerth did not present any other case of such deliberate gender concealment among women science fiction writers. She could not, because it does not
exist. Thus, her entire theory of gender relations in early science fiction is concocted out of pure speculation about a single individual based upon a few sen-
tences of doubtful data. Extrapolating an entire sociology of gender relations
from such sparse facts on a single peculiar person is dubious at best and cannot
be accepted as responsible research, even if produced by a respected academic.

It is conceivable that Hansen might have been suffering from some kind of
psychological crisis concerning her "writerly authority." As Bleiler points out,
"she invoked an imaginary brother, sent in a photo of a man to accompany her
stories in *Amazing* [sic], and for her first story claimed as co-author a non-
existent Ph.D."[64] Jane Donawerth sees this as somehow typical of early women
science fiction writers. However, her presumptions of prejudice blind her to the
significant point: L. Taylor Hansen is the *only* early female science fiction author
who seems to have *deliberately* concealed her gender identity. The real problem
we have to deal with, then, is not how Hansen was *like* other women writers, but
how Hansen was *different* from every other early science fiction woman writer!

Once we frame the question this way, the salient information is immediately
evident: Hansen is the *only* female author who wrote mostly science *fact*. She
wrote only eight stories, five of them quickly in 1929–1930, and a later one
seemingly as a joke ("The Fire Trail" written by "Oge-Make"). Her primary
emotional and intellectual energies seem to have been invested in the fifty-seven
history and science fact articles she published in *Amazing Stories* during the bulk
of the 1940s. Indeed, in the instance quoted above where editor Ray Palmer said
Hansen was defending "himself," Hansen was defending "his" reputation for
something "he" wrote in one of these fifty-seven articles, not for anything said
in a story.

Hansen, then, staked her reputation on her work as a scholar and saw herself
mainly as an author of science *fact*, not as a writer of science *fiction*. As I discussed earlier in my chapter on the genesis of the mythology, the field of professional science is seen as predominantly male. And for *science fact* this college
drop-out and (perhaps) sister of a chemist Ph.D. brother needed to invoke non-
existent credentials and assume the credibility of the male gender. At that time,
maleness alone had acceptable authority in her major field of endeavor. Her
crisis of "writerly authority," then, had absolutely *nothing* to do with her
peripheral commitment to science fiction and *everything* to do with her heavy
investment in science fact. Thus, it is precisely because she did *not* see herself
primarily as a science fiction writer that Hansen, alone of all her sex, attempted
to conceal her gender from her readers.

L. Taylor Hansen, then, along with the other women writers discussed in this
chapter, cannot legitimately be used to support the never-substantiated accusa-

tion that pulp science fiction was dominated by a hostile patriarchy, from which women writers had to hide by hiding their gender.

As it happens, *some* early women science fiction writers actually *did* adopt pseudonyms. However, in every case they were clearly *female* pseudonyms. Minnie Odell wrote as "Minna Irving." Mary Maude Dunn (later Mrs. Mary M. Wright) wrote as "Lilith Lorraine." Doris Vancel wrote as "Doris Thomas." Elizabeth Hansen wrote as "Thaedra Allen." Winifred Ashton wrote as "Clemence Dane." Margaret St. Clair wrote as "Idris Seabright." And Josephine Juliet Grossman used as a pseudonym (and later legally became) "Judith Merril."[65]

Why would "Judith Merril," or any other woman writer, go to all the bother of assuming a different name if she thereby also assumed an additional obstacle to publication and reader acceptance? If there was a *disadvantage* to writing under a female name, deliberately *choosing* to do so makes no sense at all. The only thing which *does* make sense is that "Judith Merril" and these other women did *not* perceive submitting stories under a female name to be any kind of a handicap.

However, there were three significant women science fiction writers who *did* publish either briefly at a later time, or in a fantasy (as opposed to science fiction) magazine, or in a special circumstance, under male pseudonyms. In none of these instances, however, was there a deliberate effort to conceal their gender identities.

Let us examine these three cases.

Katherine MacLean, who'd already published critically acclaimed stories under her own name, wrote "Syndrome Johnny" (*Galaxy*, July, 1951) and "The Man Who Staked the Stars" (*Planet Stories*, July, 1952) as "Charles Dye," the real name of her husband. According to Damon Knight, the purpose was to boost her husband's budding career as a science fiction writer.[66] MacLean, however, told me the reason was merely because she was too prolific (!) at a time when editors wanted to publish as many different authors as possible. In the case of "Syndrome Johnny," for example, she finished two stories in the same month, so she simply put her husband's name on the second story, "Syndrome Johnny."[67]

She also published "The Carnivore" (*Galaxy SF*, October, 1953) as by "G. A. Morris," but the reason she did so highlights the fact that she had no difficulty in dealing with an editor because of her sex. MacLean told me the reason she used this pseudonym was because she was embarrassed by the story and wanted to disclaim ownership. H. L. Gold had called and specifically asked her to write a story for his magazine, *Galaxy*, with a female character. So, she tossed off a quick story, sent it to him, and he published it.

But, she told me, "It introduced no technology or biotech, just the obvious prediction that if aliens [were] observing us [they] would consider us a dangerous race. . . . Since it was not an original concept I was ashamed of it," and so, she concealed her authorship from the readers. Obviously, however, she did not conceal her identity from the editor who commissioned it because he wanted a story with a female protagonist.[68]

Finally, she published "Collision Orbit" (*Science Fiction Adventures,* May, 1954) as by "K. MacLean," but it is highly unlikely it was to conceal her gender identity from either readers or the editor. By this time she had already published sixteen stories in a variety of magazines under her full name and readers knew who "MacLean" was. Additionally, the editor was Harry Harrison, who tells us, "I love female writers, I always try to anthologize women who write."[69]

Harrison also knew MacLean very well. Not only had he previously co-authored a story with her ("Web of the Worlds," *Fantasy Fiction,* November, 1953), but they were both members of the Hydra Club, the famous New York City social club for science fiction writers. Harrison (who became president of the club) lists both MacLean and Judith Merril among those he socialized with at Hydra Club meetings at the home of Fletcher and Inga Pratt and describes "Judy" Merril as "one of the pillars of the club." He also lists editors H. L. Gold, Sam Merwin, Groff Conklin, Hans Santesson, and Larry Shaw as club members and says Anthony Boucher came to club meetings when visiting from out of town. These editors were therefore also on an almost incestuous first-name basis with MacLean and "Judy" Merril, as well as "I. M. Stephens" (Inga Pratt).[70]

Amelia Reynolds Long also used a male name during her career, once, but it was not, as Forrest Ackerman tells it, "in *Astounding* in the '30s."[71] (She never published in *Astounding* under anything but her own name.) Her story, "Bride of the Antarctic," appeared under the pseudonym "Mordred Weir" (a name chosen for its Arthurian connection) in the fantasy magazine *Strange Stories* (June, 1939).

Chet Williamson asked Long why she used a pen name on this story and she replied, "It was because there was a shortage of s. f. writers at the time, and several writers were using pen names in order that two or three of their stories could appear in the same magazine. I joined the trend and sent [in] two sto-ries—one under my own name and the other under . . . Mordred Weir. . . . But the fool editor crossed me up by publishing the story under my own name in one issue and 'B. of A.' in the next, and listing my authorship of the first under my pen name. I gave up the pen name in disgust."[72]

Meanwhile, in 1940, well after she had established herself as a major and well-known female name in the field, C. L. Moore married fellow author Henry Kut-tner. Thereafter, much of their writing was produced via the "hot typewriter" method, where one would leave off writing with a story unfinished, and the other would take over without missing a beat. Their style of collaboration was well known to fans and editors at the time, as many visitors to their home wit-nessed and reported on it.[73] In this way they became a fiction factory, earning enough in one month for the down payment on their first home. In fact, they wrote in such a blur of intense collaboration that they themselves had difficulty in later teasing out who wrote what.[74]

Such collaborations were published under male pseudonyms, such as "Lewis Padgett" or "Lawrence O'Donnell," but these were not chosen to obscure Moore's sexual identity. It was done because they wrote so much they were flooding the market with their output. They needed multiple identities in order to place all their work in various venues. Even so, magazine editors knew exactly who was behind these pseudonyms and welcomed their stories. For example, in 1945 John W. Campbell complained to L. Ron Hubbard that, "the Kuttner-Padgett-Moore-O'Donell [sic] corporation has moved west for a rest" and he wasn't getting any stories out of them. Because of this (and because other authors, such as Asimov, were in the army), "*Astounding* is in a mell of a hess [sic]."[75]

Obviously, science fiction editors like Campbell (and fellow authors like Hubbard) knew who "Padgett" and "O'Donnell" were and, further, any editor in the 1940s would have been pleased to receive a manuscript by-lined simply "C. L. Moore." Indeed, she did continue to publish simultaneously under her own name.

So, the few peripheral instances we can find of women using male names (or deliberately obscuring initials) serve only to highlight the fact that they found no difficulties in using their own names in the field during the period under discussion. Indeed, the *only* unambiguous examples we have of gender-switching in the science fiction magazines during the first quarter century of their existence are by *men* who wrote as *women*. In a field supposedly hostile to female bylines, this is certainly a curious phenomenon. Let's look at these male authors writing with a "female voice."

We have four *male* authors who, at both the beginning and end of our period (1934 and 1940s), published under *female* names.[76] With Roger Phillips Graham (best known as "Rog Phillips"), we have a *fifth* male author who published under *two* female pseudonyms, "Melva Rogers" and "Inez McGowan," theoretically doubling his likelihood of rejection, if the mythology were true. His Rogers story, "To Give Them Welcome," appeared in the January, 1950 issue of Raymond A. Palmer's *Other Worlds*. This is technically a month too late to include in my discussion, but noted because it was purchased and the issue of the magazine distributed during 1949. And, speaking of Ray Palmer, with him we also have an *editor* who used the female pseudonym "Miss Rae Winters" on stories he wrote in 1930s fanzines. Curious, indeed.

Some academic reviewers have jumped to criticize me for not adding an additional author to my count by including "Aladra Septama," the pseudonym of Judson W. Reeves. However, one must go by more than a seemingly "female" name, which appears to be all that these critics have done. A careful scrutiny of contemporary readers' letters and editorial comments (see, e.g., the blurb for his "Tanni of Ekkis," *Amazing Stories Quarterly,* winter, 1930, p. 104) reveals that this author was commonly referred to, by both editors and readers, as a man. Hence, it would be a mistake to include him as a man attempting to "pass" as a woman.

This use of female pen names by male writers defies all logic if there were, indeed, a *disadvantage* to being a female author. There is a well-known sociological concept known as *status contamination.* The advantaged in any social situation have a vested interest in insuring that their high status is not confused with that of the disadvantaged, that they are not "contaminated" by being associated with them. Hence, honored Vietnam vets jealously "out" fakers who claim to have fought in 'Nam. Unless they're writing books on the subject or composing rap songs, whites don't attempt to pass as blacks.

And privileged male writers would not attempt to pass as disadvantaged women writers if that made it harder to get published. And yet, these "privileged" male writers *did* pass themselves off as women! There is no way to explain this crazy topsy-turvy situation if there were, indeed, a bias against women writers. It makes as much sense as a Vietnam vet posing as a draft dodger on Veterans' Day. The only logical explanation is that male writers in the field perceived no disadvantage in submitting manuscripts under female names.

And, for the same reason, female writers felt absolutely no need to conceal themselves behind male or ambiguous names, or use initials.

And so they did not.

Notes

1. E.g., Bainbridge, *Dimensions of Science Fiction,* p. 180.
2. Laurie Mann to Eric Leif Davin, PARSEC (Pittsburgh science fiction club) meeting, October 13, 2001.
3. Jacques Barzun and Henry F. Graff, *The Modern Researcher,* Harcourt Brace Jovanovich, Inc.: N.Y., Third Edition, 1977, p. 71.
4. Barzun and Graff, p. 72.
5. Isaac Asimov and Martin H. Greenberg, Eds., *Isaac Asimov Presents: Great Science Fiction Stories of 1939,* DAW Books: N.Y., 1979, Dorset Press: N.Y., 2001, p. 194. Instead of "feminism" Asimov surely means "femininity," as neither author wrote politically "feminist" fiction.
6. John Clute and Peter Nicholls, Eds., *The Encyclopedia of Science Fiction,* St. Martin's Griffin: N.Y., 1993, 1995, p. 760, entry on Katherine MacLean. In the face of reputed male prejudice, they claim that MacLean still managed to compete "on equal terms."
7. Peter Nicholls, "Women," in Peter Nicholls, General Editor, *The Science Fiction Encyclopedia,* Doubleday & Co.: N.Y., 1979, p. 661. Emphasis added.
8. Lefanu, *Feminism and Science Fiction,* p. 2.
9. Janrae Frank, Jean Stine, and Forrest J. Ackerman, Eds., Introduction, *New Eves: Science Fiction About the Extraordinary Women of Today and Tomorrow,* Long Meadow Press: Stamford, Conn., 1999, p. x.
10. Bill Pronzini, "Women in the Pulps," p. 18.
11. See Sam Moskowitz, Editor, *Under the Moons of Mars: A History and Anthology of 'The Sci-*

entific Romance' in the Munsey Magazines, 1912–1920, Holt, Rinehart and Winston: N.Y., 1970, p. 407.

12. P. Schuyler Miller, "The Reference Library," *Astounding Science Fiction,* Sept., 1952, p. 170.

13. Darrell C. Richardson, "Book Reviews," *Other Worlds,* November, 1952, p. 159.

14. Damon Knight, "Readin' And Writhin'," *Future Science Fiction,* June, 1954, pp. 87–88.

15. It is conceivable that someone might think of Wilmar H. Shiras as having an androgynous first name. Her editors, however, were not confused. John W. Campbell discovered her ("In Hiding," *Astounding,* November, 1948, was her debut) and addressed her as "Mrs. Shiras" in his letters to her. (See his letter in Perry A. Chapdelaine, Sr., Tony Chapdelaine, and George Hay, Eds., *The John W. Campbell Letters, Vol. 1,* AC Projects, Inc.: Franklin, Tenn., 1985, pp. 504–505.) Additionally, other editors publicly referred to her as female, thus not only informing readers she was female, but showing that they were well aware of her gender. See, for example, Anthony Boucher and J. Francis McComas, Eds., *The Best From Fantasy and Science Fiction,* Little, Brown & Co.: Boston, 1952, p. 82.

16. Knight, *The Futurians,* p. 22.

17. Pohl, *The Way the Future Was,* p. 74.

18. Knight, *The Futurians,* p. 23.

19. Knight, *The Futurians,* pp. 21–24.

20. Frederik Pohl, introduction to Moore's story, "Doorway into Time," in Frederik Pohl, ed., *Science Fiction of the 40's,* Avon Books: N.Y., 1978, p. 143.

21. Frederik Pohl, introduction to Brackett's story, "The Halfling," in Frederik Pohl, ed., *Science Fiction of the 40's,* Avon Books: N.Y., 1978, p. 121.

22. Lefanu, p. 2.

23. Frank, Stine, and Ackerman, pp. x, 70.

24. Pamela Sargent, Ed., *Women of Wonder: The Classic Years, Science Fiction by Women from the 1940s to the 1970s,* Harcourt Brace & Co.: N.Y., 1995, p. 6.

25. Marion Zimmer Bradley, "One Woman's Experience in Science Fiction," in Denise Du Pont, Ed., *Women of Vision,* p. 88.

26. Leigh Brackett interview in Paul Walker, ed., *Speaking of Science Fiction,* p. 377. Originally in *LUNA Monthly 61,* 1976.

27. Brackett interview in Paul Walker, p. 378.

28. Jack Williamson, *Wonder's Child: My Life in Science Fiction,* Bluejay Books: N.Y., 1984, pp. 129, 127.

29. According to Julius Schwartz' records he did not sell his first story for Brackett, "The Demons of Darkside," until June 21, 1940. It later appeared in *Startling Stories,* January, 1941. Thus, Brackett sold to Campbell on her own, with no intervention from an agent. See John L. Carr, *Leigh Brackett: American Writer,* Chris Drumm Booklet 22: Polk City, Iowa, 1986, pp. 33–34.

30. See Leigh Brackett, "Meet the Authors," *Amazing Stories,* July, 1941, p. 136.

31. Ray Bradbury interview in Charles Platt, *Dream Makers: The Uncommon People Who Write Science Fiction,* Berkley Books: N.Y., 1980, p. 175.

32. Lester Del Rey, *The World of Science Fiction: 1926–1976, The History of a Subculture,* Ballantine Books: N.Y., 1979, p. 125.

33. Pamela Sargent, Ed., *More Women of Wonder: Science Fiction Novelettes By Women About Women,* Vintage Books: N.Y., 1976, p. xix.

34. Lefanu, p. 2.

35. Reprinted in the summer, 1951, *Fantastic Story Magazine.*

36. Letter, Sam Moskowitz to Eric Leif Davin, October 19, 1986.

37. Frederik Pohl, "Wipsy Institute," *Fantasy Newsletter,* August, 1983, p. 13 (an essay prepared for the Conference on the Fantastic in the Arts, 1983).

38. See Pohl, *The Way the Future Was,* pp. 201–203.

39. C.f., A. E. van Vogt, "My Life Was My Best Science Fiction Story," in Martin H. Greenberg, Ed., *Fantastic Lives: Autobiographical Essays by Notable Science Fiction Writers,* p. 179. Also, see the

eulogy he delivered at "my darling Mayne-a's" funeral, January 25, 1975, published in *Locus*, #169, Feb. 16, 1975, pp. 1–2.

40. Frederik Pohl, introduction to Moore's story, "Doorway into Time," in Frederik Pohl, ed., *Science Fiction of the 40's*, Avon Books: N.Y., 1978, p. 143.

41. Baird Searles, et al., *A Reader's Guide to Science Fiction*, p. 127.

42. Frederick Shroyer, entry on C. L. Moore and Henry Kuttner, in E. F. Bleiler, Ed., *Science Fiction Writers: Critical Studies of the Major Authors from the Early Nineteenth Century to the Present Day*, Charles Scribner's Sons: N.Y., 1982, p. 161.

43. Hilary Rose, *Love, Power, and Knowledge: Towards a Feminist Transformation of the Sciences*, Indiana University Press: Bloomington, 1994, p. 224.

44. Sharon Yntema, Ed., *More Than 100 Women Science Fiction Writers: An Annotated Bibliography*, The Crossing Press: Freedom, Calif., Updated Edition, 1988, p. 91.

45. Robert Silverberg, Ed., Introduction, *Robert Silverberg's Worlds of Wonder*, Warner Books: N.Y., 1987, pp. 126–127.

46. Bainbridge, *Dimensions of Science Fiction*, p. 180. His source is Sam Moskowitz, *Seekers of Tomorrow: Masters of Modern Science Fiction*, The World Publishing Co.: Cleveland and N.Y., 1966, p. 305.

47. L. Sprague de Camp, Catherine Crook de Camp, and Jane Whittington Griffin, *Dark Valley Destiny: The Life of Robert E. Howard*, Bluejay Books, Inc.: N.Y., 1983, p. 330.

48. Quoted in Michael J. Venables, Editor, *The Illustrated World of Robert E. Howard*, Wandering Star Books, 2004, entry on "Dark Agnes, Sword-Woman."

49. Quoted in Sam Moskowitz, *Seekers of Tomorrow*, p. 307.

50. Moskowitz, *Seekers of Tomorrow*, p. 309.

51. See her letter in "The Eyrie," *Weird Tales*, October, 1935.

52. Robert W. Lowndes, "Brass Tacks," *Astounding*, November, 1934; Edward E. Smith, Hillsdale, Mich., "Brass Tacks," *Astounding*, January, 1935.

53. Ray Bradbury interview in Charles Platt, *Dream Makers*, p. 175.

54. Bradley, "One Woman's Experience in Science Fiction," in Denise Du Pont, *Women of Vision*, p. 86.

55. Marilyn vos Savant, *Parade*, March 28, 2004, p. 20.

56. Eric Leif Davin, *Pioneers of Wonder: Conversations With the Founders of Science Fiction*, Prometheus Books: Amherst, N.Y., 1999, p. 237.

57. Julius Schwartz, "Memoirs of a Time Traveller, Part 1: My Amazing Stories," *Amazing Stories*, May, 1993, p. 49.

58. Recounted in his obituary by Gerald Jonas, "Harry Clement Stubbs, Writer of Classic Science Fiction, Dies at 81," *The New York Times*, October 31, 2003.

59. Isaac Asimov, *In Memory Yet Green*, New York: Doubleday, 1979, p. 573. Asimov's publisher, Doubleday, brought out the novel in January, 1950. Asimov had received an advance copy of the dust jacket and had decided to discuss the matter with his dean before the book appeared.

60. Donald H. Tuck, *The Encyclopedia of Science Fiction and Fantasy Through 1968, Vol. 1: Who's Who, A-L*, Advent Publishers: Chicago, 1974, p. 205. Ackerman's story of Hansen attending this meeting is also repeated by Sam Moskowitz in his introduction to Hansen's "The Undersea Tube" in *Science Fiction Classics Annual, 1970*, p. 4.

61. Forrest J. Ackerman, Ed., *Gosh! Wow! (Sense of Wonder) Science Fiction*, Bantam Books: N.Y., 1981, p. 209, introducing her story, "The Prince of Liars."

62. Letter, E. F. Bleiler to A. Langley Searles, July, 2002.

63. Donawerth, *Frankenstein's Daughters*, p. 114.

64. Letter, E. F. Bleiler to A. Langley Searles, July, 2002. Bleiler slipped in claiming Hansen sent multiple photos to accompany her stories in *Amazing*. It was Bleiler who drew my attention to the single instance of her doing this in *Wonder Stories*. Additionally, Bleiler noted that forthcoming notices for Hansen's debut ("What the Sodium Lines Revealed," *Amazing Stories Quarterly*, Winter, 1929) announced the story as a collaboration with "L. H. Edwards, Ph.D.," although the story

was credited solely to Hansen on publication. Bleiler searched the *Comprehensive Dissertation Index, 1861–1972* and could not discover any Ph.D. being awarded to an "L. H. Edwards."

65. About which, referring to her maiden and married names, Damon Knight had this to say: "Juliet Grossman Zissman Pohl/ Hated her name from the bottom of her soul;/ Went to court in imminent peril;/ Changed her name to Judith Merril." See Damon Knight, "Knight Piece," in Brian W. Aldiss and Harry Harrison, Eds., *Hell's Cartographers,* Futura Publications Ltd.: London, 1976, 1975, p. 125.

66. See Knight, *The Futurians,* p. 32. It's unfortunate MacLean gave her husband the credit for her genetic engineering story, "Syndrome Johnny," as it is perhaps the earliest story of gene splicing in which a virus transfers alien genetic material into human cells. Off hand, I can't think of any counter examples of men putting their wives' names on their own work. However, MacLean's name appears on the story in recent anthologies.

67. Letter, Katherine MacLean to Eric Leif Davin, March 28, 2001.

68. Letter, Katherine MacLean to Eric Leif Davin, May 26, 2002.

69. Charles Platt, *Dream Makers, Volume II,* p. 224.

70. Harry Harrison, "The Beginning of the Affair," in Aldiss and Harrison, *Hell's Cartographers,* p. 80.

71. Forrest J. Ackerman, introducing a reprinting of Long's "The Box from the Stars," *Fantasy Book,* August, 1983, V. 2, #3, p. 71.

72. Amelia Reynolds Long to Chet Williamson, Feb. 16, 1978, quoted in "Yours, Amelia," *Etchings & Odysseys,* #10, 1987, p. 66. The first story was "The Box from the Stars" (*Strange Stories,* April, 1939).

73. One was Julius Schwartz, who, in an August 27, 2002 discussion, told me about witnessing Moore and Kuttner at work in this fashion while visiting their home at Hastings-on-the-Hudson, N.Y.

74. The Moore stories in table 1 published under the name "Lawrence O'Donnell" are the ones both Moore and the science fiction field have subsequently considered to have been principally authored by Moore.

75. John W. Campbell, Jr., to L. Ron Hubbard, November 21, 1945, in Perry A. Chapdelaine, Sr., Tony Chapdelaine, and George Hay, Editors, *The John W. Campbell Letters, Volume 1,* p. 55.

76. See these authors listed at the end of table 1. "Florence" Matheson, who published "The Molecule Trapper" in *Amazing Stories,* September, 1934, is listed on the title page as "Florence." However, on the table of contents the author is listed as "Donald." Did the editor slip up and reveal that "Florence" was really "Donald"? It's unlikely that the situation would be the reverse (Florence publishing as "Donald"), as more care would be given to the title page.

Then there is the curious case of Don Wilcox, a prolific writer of the Forties who published many stories in Ray Palmer's *Amazing Stories* and *Fantastic Adventures.* He used several pseudonyms, including "Max Overton," "Miles Shelton," and the "house name" "Alexander Blade." For his story "Sapphire Enchantress," which Palmer published in the December, 1945 *Fantastic Adventures,* he even used a female name, "Cleo Eldon." It was later claimed that Don Wilcox actually *was* "Cleo Eldon," his birth name being Cleo Eldon Knox (although Mike Ashley tells me Wilcox told Ashley he was born "Cleo Eldon Wilcox"). Such, at least, is how he is listed in the most recent edition of *The Encyclopedia of Science Fiction,* John Clute and Peter Nicholls, Eds., St. Martin's Griffin: N.Y., 1995. He died on March 9, 2000, at age 94. Afterward, his obituaries also gave "Don Wilcox" as the pseudonym of the person who was *really* Cleo Eldon Knox. (See, cf., Andrew I. Porter's obituary, *Science Fiction Chronicle,* August-September, 2000, p. 50.)

However, I am inclined to doubt this story for two reasons. First, in reply to a specific query about his real name, Don Wilcox assured Donald B. Day that "Don Wilcox" was his *real* name. Second, following his death Norm Metcalf searched the Social Security Death Index for information on him. He discovered that, according to the records of the U.S. government, "Don Wilcox" really *was* his name. He may have told the science fiction world at large that he was really "Cleo

Eldon Knox" or Mike Ashley that he was really "Cleo Eldon Wilcox," but it's a lot harder to lie to the U.S. government, especially when claiming benefits. The Social Security Administration believed "Don Wilcox" to be his true name—and I stand by that documentation. Further, I am not aware of any female SF writer being thought by the SF world to have *really* been born with a different "man's" name.

6

The Usual Suspects

S PEAKING OF SCIENCE FICTION in the 1930s, Donald A. Wollheim recalled that, "In those days science fiction was a very, very small field. Anybody who read science fiction was pretty hard up to find anybody else who did, unless you joined a club, and a club in those days would be ten or twelve people, no more. So there was always that embattled feeling: we were this little group of crackpots that ran around and believed that people were going to fly to the moon."[1] The science fiction community, then, felt it was an embattled minority surrounded by a hostile larger world.

And how did women fit into this embattled community? Were science fiction women an embattled minority within an embattled minority? Or were they welcomed as comrades in a common cause?

Previously we saw that female fans were, in fact, accepted as equals and, in some cases, even leaders in early science fiction fandom. But what about the *professional* circles of the science fiction world? And, most especially, what was the relationship between women writers and the editors? Bigoted editors loom large in the legend as the biased gatekeepers past whom potential female authors had to sneak. Isaac Asimov, for one, claimed that "some editors would've insisted on a male pseudonym" before publishing a female writer. Hence, perhaps more than anything else, my claim for the openness of pulp science fiction stands or falls on the nature of the relationship between genre editors and their female authors—whether women were accepted or rejected, encouraged or discouraged, by the primary gatekeepers of the science fiction world.

Let us examine the evidence.

Writing in the November, 1958 issue of *Science Fiction Stories* (p. 104), editor Robert A. W. Lowndes said, "There is no deep, dark conspiracy among editors to exclude the upstart newcomer. . . . The majority [of editors]—and it has always been close to 100 percent—are delighted to find a new writer who can deliver what the editor wants." While Lowndes was affirming that there was no editorial conspiracy against *novice* writers, he could just as well have affirming that there was no editorial conspiracy against *female* writers.

Nevertheless, from the very beginning of magazine science fiction, perhaps because the larger society has always seen science as a male preserve, *some* would-be female authors and those completely unconnected with the field, have thought of the editors as potentially prejudiced against women. Such was the case in 1929 when the unpublished Leslie F. Stone thought about submitting her very first offering to Hugo Gernsback at *Amazing Stories.* "A friend [with no connection to the field, and who therefore confused science fiction with the field of science] advised me that a woman writer . . . would probably be unacceptable, not only to an editor or two, but also to some readers."

Instead, "On his discovery of my gender, Hugo Gernsback accepted [that first story] quite amiably." Indeed, Stone believed that Gernsback enjoyed having women writers for his magazine. "Nor did T. O'Conor Sloane, dear man, have any qualms about women writers in his stable when he took over the *Amazing Stories* editorship, never turning down any story I submitted." In fact, she said, at all the magazines where she appeared, "For the most part, my own relationships with editors were congenial and not very demanding."[2]

As it was in the beginning, so it continued to be. For example, the bibliographic tables at the end of this book reveal that a number of the 922 stories published by the 203 known women authors in the science fiction magazines between 1926–1960 were reprints from mainstream sources. This tells us that the editors *themselves* were doing one of two things. The first possibility is that they were deliberately seeking out these *women* in order to republish them in their own magazines. The second possibility is that the editors were merely doing what editors are supposed to do: Find and publish good *stories,* no matter what the gender of the author.

Many of the early women writers themselves affirm this latter belief—that editors of this era were just looking for good stories, didn't care about the gender of the authors, and warmly welcomed any who could provide what they sought. Certainly this was the feeling of Leigh Brackett. Writing in 1944 Brackett declared that, "The editors of the science-fiction mags are a swell bunch—my special and personal thanks to Alden Norton, Malcolm Reiss, W. Scott Peacock, Leo Margulies, and Oscar Friend."[3]

Flogging the feminist fiction that these SF editors and their readers did not welcome women writers, in 1981 Rosemary Herbert synopsized Margaret St. Clair's career by writing that she, "is an example of a woman writer who did not have to disguise her sex in order to be successful as a writer in a male-dominated field."[4] But, one might more accurately say that *every* woman SF writer was an example of someone who did not have to "disguise her sex" to succeed. That was, in fact, St. Clair's own opinion, who was on friendly terms with the editors and never reported problems with any of them.

For example, in 1947 the fledgling Margaret St. Clair (who debuted in the SF magazines in November, 1946 and published almost 100 SF stories between then and 1960) termed science fiction editors in general, "a darned nice bunch," singling out for special praise Sam Merwin, Jr., at *Startling Stories* and *Thrilling Wonder Stories*, and L. Jerome Stanton, associate editor of Street & Smith's *Astounding*. The editors are one of the "chief advantages" of writing science fiction, she said, because, "If one shows some promise, he gets a letter from the editor. The people who edit these magazines . . . take a real interest in writers and are ready to encourage them all they can. Those unpleasant printed rejection slips are few and far between. . . . Sam Merwin . . . writes the most tactful letters of rejection I have ever seen. He caresses the vanity so tenderly, touches with such delicate understanding on the flaws of the yarn you presented him with, that he makes being rejected very nearly pleasurable.

"L. Jerome Stanton . . . is another friendly editor. One of the most amusing letters I have ever had (it began, 'OOOh! What a bad girl you are, Mrs. St. Clair, cozening a poor, moss-grown old editor with such a story . . .') came from him. Unfortunately, after that initial outburst, he became lamentably businesslike and devoted the rest of his two pages to advising me how to plug up the holes in the story I'd sent him. It was good advice, too."

St. Clair also praised *Astounding* editor John W. Campbell, Jr., "noted for his hospitality to newcomers," with both Campbell and Stanton being "broadminded in the extreme" with "a minimum of taboos." Then, "Last, but not least, there is Ziff-Davis' Wm. L. Hamling, who took the first story I sent to him."

As for the fans, while noting that there "are some devoted feminine ones," St. Clair acknowledged that most were male, but that she never met any objection from them because, "In my belief, the science fiction fan is a definitely superior type—but I may be prejudiced." Contrary to later feminists who have projected their own biases onto her and her sisters, the only drawback to writing for the science fiction magazines that St. Clair herself could think of was that there weren't enough magazines![5]

St. Clair might also have included as supportive of female talent editor Samuel Mines at *Startling Stories,* who replaced Merwin in 1952. In the February 1952 issue of that magazine (p. 137), Mines praised St. Clair's Oona and Jiks series. And the superior Earle K. Bergey cover of that issue (with typically compelling interior illustrations by the legendary Virgil Finley) was devoted to St. Clair's story, "Vulcan's Dolls." Mines described the story (p. 13) as, "a work of rare beauty, a many-faceted, glittering gem, full of paradoxes and surprises. It is a delight to read, a privilege to present to you." And in that same issue Mines also lavished praise (p. 137) on the "wonderful" Leigh Brackett stories,

"Shadow Over Mars" and "The Sea Kings of Mars," while also highlighting her name on the cover just below that of St. Clair's.

Miriam Allen deFord also claimed she had good working relations with science fiction editors. She was a self-described "born feminist" who had been active in the woman suffrage movement before 1920 and labor and radical causes thereafter. She debuted in *The Magazine of Fantasy and Science Fiction* in 1950 and published thirty-one science fiction stories in the decade of the 1950s (and many more in the 1960s). "Some of my science fiction is more oriented towards feminism," she noted, "for instance, my collection *Xenogenesis* is all about matrimony, reproduction and sex on other planets and in the future." Despite this, deFord said she never had a problem publishing any of these science fiction stories because, "I was in one of the few professions where there is no sexual discrimination. I have never heard an editor say, for instance, that he didn't want a story because it was by a woman. . . . No, I should say there's less prejudice. For instance, it's almost impossible for a woman to get a good job as the conductor of an orchestra, but there's no trouble at all about becoming a successful writer if you can produce."[6]

Thus, unlike later feminist academics who purport to champion them, the pioneering science fiction women writers themselves tell us, not of prejudice, but of editorial support at every turn. Leigh Brackett is typical. John W. Campbell discovered her, published her first two stories, and was a consistently enthusiastic supporter. She went on to publish thirty-four stories in nine different science fiction magazines just in the 1940s alone. Were any of her editors biased against her? Certainly not *Startling Stories* editor Samuel Mines, who advertised her name and story, "Runaway" on the cover of his Spring, 1954 issue, while saying, "it embodies the wonderful color and imagery which is the hallmark of her talent" (p. 63).

Leigh Brackett herself tells us that, "I have never been discriminated against because of my sex." And, refuting the charge that she adopted her first name to escape sexist editorial prejudice, Brackett continued, "Editors aren't buying sex [i.e., a writer's gender], they're buying stories. . . . I am not a woman writer. I am a writer, period. That I also happen to be a woman is beside the point."[7]

This denial of editorial discrimination was echoed by Judith Merril (who also had a story, "Peeping Tom," in the same issue of *Startling Stories*, above, wherein Mines praised Brackett). "I grew up in the radical 'thirties," Merril said. "My mother had been a suffragette. It never occurred to me that the Bad Old Days of Double Standard had anything to do with *me*. The first strong intimation, actually, was when the editors of the mystery, western, and sports 'pulp' magazines, where I did my apprentice writing, demanded masculine pen names. But, of course, they were pulps, oriented to a masculine readership, and the whole thing was only an irritation: as soon as I turned to SF, the problem disappeared."[8] (Interestingly, this suggests that Merril did not see the science fiction magazines as "oriented to a masculine readership.")

Even in the mystery pulps, however, Merril was eventually able to publish under her own name—at least when a "science fiction editor" was doing the editing. See, for instance, her story, "I Could Kill You," in *Smashing Detective Stories,* March 1952, edited by her old Futurian comrade, Robert W. "Doc" Lowndes.

Amelia Reynolds Long is another case in point. She began her genre career in 1928 when she sold her story, "The Twin Soul," to editor Farnsworth Wright at *Weird Tales.* She then went on to sell five more stories to Wright, and two to the fantasy magazine *Strange Stories.* She also sold an additional eleven to the science fiction magazines, including *Astounding, Amazing, Science Fiction,* and Gernsback's Science Fiction Series of paperbacks. In response to a question from interviewer Chet Williamson, Long flatly stated, "I don't think being a woman held me back with any of the science fiction magazines. . . . I don't think it ever did make much difference. I know it never did in my case, and I don't think it did with any of the others [other women SF writers]."[9]

Williamson, perhaps because this did not fit his preconceptions, found this hard to believe, so he asked Long the question again, to make sure he heard her right. She reiterated her previous statement: "I'm sure that my sex made no difference to *Weird Tales* and I doubt that it did with *Amazing Stories* or *Astounding Stories.*" She then went on to praise *Weird Tales* editor Farnsworth Wright as, "a really fine editor." As for her own career, she believed that, "The best I can say for myself is that I had more stories accepted than I had rejected."[10] Long stopped writing science fiction at the end of the Thirties, not because of any hardship due to being female, but because "Science fiction had hit the comic strips and I felt that it was sort of degrading to compete with a comic strip."[11]

This friendly and supportive relationship with editors is reiterated by women science fiction writers during the entire time span of magazine science fiction. In more recent times, feminist writer Ursula K. Le Guin (who debuted in 1962 and is often cited as one who stormed the sexist barricades of the genre) said that she never experienced any resistance toward her as a female writer, at any time, from any editor in the science fiction field. Indeed, "the first (and . . . only) time I met with anything I understood as sexual prejudice, prejudice against me as a woman writer, from any editor or publisher," came in 1968 from the men's magazine *Playboy.* When it bought her science fiction story, "Nine Lives," the editors asked if they could publish it using only her first initial, so it appeared as by "U. K. Le Guin." And this non-genre appearance was the only time "Ursula" did not appear in her by-line on any story.[12]

So, it seems that early female authors themselves discerned a welcoming hand held out to them by science fiction editors. Indeed, Oscar J. Friend (praised by

Brackett) spoke for all such editors in 1944 when he said, "we are happy to note the constantly increasing number of women readers—and contributors—in this field."[13]

The willingness of these editors to publish female authors *as* female authors suggests a lack of bias on their parts. Indeed, not only did the field as a whole attempt to recruit female readers and fans, but science fiction editors also actively tried to recruit female *writers* and welcomed them whenever they appeared. For this reason, female authors were published *as* female authors in all but five short-lived and mostly obscure magazines and by *every* science fiction editor from 1926 to 1949. Let me repeat that: *All* of the early science fiction editors published female authors *as* female authors. *There was not a single exception.*[14]

Who, then, were the supposed culprits of feminist legend? Surely we cannot be talking about Dorothy McIlwraith, who edited *Weird Tales* from 1940 until its first demise in 1954 and who published many female science fiction authors. McIlwraith also edited the adventure magazine *Short Stories* and made it clear in her articles on writing that she'd accept a story from *anyone* who could write well.[15]

Among the science fiction magazines we cannot be talking about Mary Gnaedinger, the only editor of *Famous Fantastic Mysteries* and *Fantastic Novels*. Certainly it does not appear that she discriminated against her own sex from all the space she devoted to the early pulp female writer Francis Stevens. Stevens, we are told, "was one of the best fantasy writers to emerge from the pages of the Munsey magazines. . . . Between them, *Famous Fantastic Mysteries* and *Fantastic Novels* reprinted six of the eleven fantasies Stevens is known to have authored."[16] Gnaedinger also published Lillian M. Ainsworth, Dorothy D. Calhoun, Clemence Dane, Theodora DuBois, Inez Haynes Gillmore, Augusta Groner, Jessie Douglas Kerruish, C. L. Moore, Amabel Redman, Margaret St. Clair, and Laura Withrow and featured these writers on her covers (see table 1).

Likewise, we cannot be thinking of Miriam Bourne, associate editor and then managing editor of *Amazing Stories* and *Amazing Stories Quarterly* from October, 1928 to November, 1932. Nor can we be thinking of Lila E. Shaffer, who served as associate editor and then managing editor of both *Amazing Stories* and *Fantastic Adventures* from October, 1948 to March, 1953. Nor can we be thinking of Beatrice "Bea" Mahaffey and Marge Saunders Budwig, who began editing *Other Worlds* and *Universe* in 1949 and 1950, nor Catherine "Kay" Tarrant, assistant editor at *Astounding* from at least 1949 (and perhaps an unlisted editor from 1942).[17]

Indeed, if we expanded the period under investigation to the 1950s, we would also have to exclude such female science fiction magazine editors as Katherine Daffron at *Two Complete Science-Adventure Books*, Frances Hamling (who had herself been a genre author, under the name of Frances Yerxa) at *Imagination*, Cylvia Kleinman at *Satellite Science Fiction*, and Eve P. Wulff at *If*.

And, of course, we would have to dismiss from consideration as a biased editor the influential Cele Goldsmith at *Amazing Stories* and *Fantastic Stories*. It was she who discovered and published the debut stories of Keith Laumer, Roger Zelazny, and Thomas M. Disch, as well as the debuts of Kate Wilhelm in 1956, Phyllis Gotlieb in 1959, and Ursula K. Le Guin in 1962. Goldsmith also encouraged and published female artists, such as Jacquelyn Blair and Paula McLane, both for interior illustrations and for the covers of her magazines.[18] And it was also under her stewardship that, in 1960, *Amazing* received its first Hugo nomination for Best Magazine and Goldsmith's work on both magazines was honored in 1962 with a Worldcon Special Convention Award.

These female editors all had the professional respect and admiration of their male cohorts, as the 1962 Worldcon Special Convention Award to Cele Goldsmith indicates. Howard Browne's judgment of Lila Shaffer was also typical. Browne, who had preceded Shaffer in her editorial positions at *Amazing* and *Fantastic Adventures* termed her, "a very bright young woman and an excellent editor."[19] And surely none of these female science fiction magazine editors had any particular animus against female bylines which happened to cross their desks. Indeed, they published many women writers. Further, the very existence of twenty-six such genre magazine editors between 1928–1960 gives the lie to the image of the field before 1960, or even 1950, as comprising an all-male (and, thus, presumably hostile) editorial establishment. (See table 6 for a complete list of these female editors, their positions, and terms of office.)

What other editorial villains might there have been? Could it have been Farnsworth Wright, editor in the 1930s of the fantasy magazine *Weird Tales*, where Clare Winger Harris, C. L. Moore, and so many of the other early women science fiction writers actually debuted before moving on? But one of his female authors, Greye La Spina, who published 18 stories in *Weird Tales*, recalled that he was "One of the finest editors I ever met. . . . His letters to me were enthusiastic and inspiring . . . he bought practically all the weird or occult material I submitted . . . it never occurred to me that writers could have trouble selling their yarns!"[20]

And, according to an anecdote by fantasy writer E. Hoffmann Price, the most enthusiasm Wright ever showed for a story was prompted by receiving the manuscript for Moore's "Shambleau." Wright closed the office and declared a "C. L. Moore Day" in her honor. After reading the manuscript, Hoffmann also claimed that, "This, of all times, was when my enthusiasm equaled Farnsworth's."[21] Further, Wright triumphantly advertised and unreservedly lauded all of Moore's further contributions.

Was the villain Hugo Gernsback, the founder of the world's first science fiction magazine and the revered "Father of Science Fiction"? But, as we've seen,

Leslie F. Stone testified that in 1929 he welcomed her presence in *Amazing Stories*. As noted, it was Gernsback who discovered her, publishing the first science fiction stories she ever wrote.[22] Two of these stories were "Men With Wings" (*Air Wonder Stories*, July 1929) and its sequel, "Women With Wings" (*Air Wonder Stories*, May, 1930." Readers particularly liked them. As genre historian Sam Moskowitz reported in 1963, these novice tales by Stone (whom he also identified as Mrs. William Silberberg in writing about them) were, "The most popular stories of winged humans in the early science fiction magazines."[23]

It was also Hugo Gernsback who published Clare Winger Harris ("The Fate of the Poseidonia," *Amazing Stories*, June, 1927), the first woman to appear in a science fiction magazine. And not only did he publish her, he awarded Harris a prize for her tale, an entry in a contest which attracted 360 stories. (When Gernsback announced her prize in the May, 1927 issue, he referred to her as "Mrs. F. C. Harris," although the story was bylined "Clare Winger Harris.")

Gernsback then welcomed her subsequent stories. These included "The Miracle of the Lily," *Amazing Stories*, April, 1928; "The Menace of Mars," *Amazing Stories*, Oct., 1928; "The Fifth Dimension," *Amazing Stories*, Dec., 1928; and "The Diabolical Drug," *Amazing Stories*, May, 1929. Her "The Evolutionary Monstrosity," *Amazing Stories Quarterly*, winter, 1929, one of the very earliest stories featuring the artificial evolution of a human into a monster, was also published by Gernsback. Harris soon became popular enough to begin appearing on the cover as a "draw" for readers.[24] Indeed, future "Superman" co-creator Jerome Siegel, then a Cleveland teenager and an avid reader of *Amazing Stories*, included Harris in his list of the magazine's top writers.[25]

Sam Moskowitz and Mike Ashley have pointed to correspondence between Gernsback and his authors while he was publishing *Amazing*, which indicates that he took an active editorial role in that magazine. In this capacity he not only regularly published women in *Amazing Stories* (and hired a woman—Miriam Bourne—as his associate editor) and *Amazing Stories Quarterly* (where he published the debut of another of his discoveries, L. (Lucile) Taylor Hansen), but also published them in his Stellar Science Fiction Series of paperbound booklets. These included *When the Sun Went Out* by Leslie F. Stone, the feminist utopia *The Brain of the Planet* by Lilith Lorraine, *The Mechanical Man* by Amelia Reynolds Long, and two stories by Pansy E. Black, *The Valley of the Great Ray* and *The Men from the Meteor*. Of the eighteen booklets in this series—five (more than 25 percent) were by women. What is significant about all of these is that, in each case, these were debuts, women writers discovered for the science fiction world by Hugo Gernsback.

Even with his last magazine, *Science-Fiction Plus* (March–December, 1953), Gernsback was still discovering and publishing women writers, such as Anne McCaffrey and her first science fiction story, "Freedom of the Race" (*Science-Fiction Plus*, October, 1953).

Further, Gernsback had already established this pattern of encouraging female authors much earlier in *The Electrical Experimenter,* which he edited from 1913 to 1920. In 1918 he invited Isabel M. Lewis of the U.S. Naval Observatory to begin a series of articles on astronomy for this magazine. And, in 1918–1919, he published articles by Grace T. Hadley, Pauline Ginsberg, Dorothy Kant, Pauline Bergins, Esther Lindner, and Nelly F. Gardner. Indeed, his magazine seemed to try to attract a female audience, for there were articles on women engineers and inventors and women who operated radios or the wireless as careers. All of these were efforts by Gernsback to combat the image of science as being purely for men.

Gernsback also seemed to welcome women as readers to *Amazing Stories.* And, judging by readers' letters, he had some success. The issue which carried Harris' "The Fate of the Poseidonia" (*Amazing Stories,* June, 1927) also published a letter (p. 308) from "Miss I. K.," of Brooklyn, NY, commenting on the stories in the magazine. Miss E. M. C. Poppe, of W. Brownsville, PA, one of two women letter writers in the April, 1934, *Amazing,* noted that she'd begun reading the magazine in late 1927 or early 1928 (p. 136). Miss Jeanne Du Rand, of Chicago, one of two women letter writers in the February 1930 issue (and a self-described aviatrix who held several parachute records) said she'd been reading *Amazing Stories* "for years" (p. 1104). The May, 1929 issue (assembled before he left the magazine) published five letters from women, including one from Alice K. Crout, of Parkersburg, West Virginia, who wrote to Gernsback, "You always seem glad to get letters of comment on *Amazing Stories* from girls, so here goes." (p. 189).

Mrs. L. Silberberg, of Augusta, Georgia, writing in the October, 1928 issue, said, "It seems as if, as early as I can recall, I was reading stories such as the tales of Edgar Rice Burroughs, Jules Verne and H. G. Wells. The *Argosy All-Story* with its 'different stories' came to my notice, and I was greatly elated when you reprinted *The Moon Pool* of Mr. Merritt's from that magazine. . . . I am a constant reader of scientifiction," and, when she traveled with her husband, she always made a point of buying *Amazing Stories* in whichever city they found themselves. To which Gernsback replied, "We are glad to hear from one of the fair sex and would be glad if more . . . were contributors to our Discussions Column" (p. 667).[26]

Gernsback carried this policy of welcome toward female fans and readers over to his new magazine, *Science Wonder Stories.* In the January, 1930 issue, Mrs. Verna Pullen, of Lincoln, Nebraska, wrote to say she enjoyed his new magazine—but supposed he wouldn't publish her letter, it being from a woman. Under the bold-type headline, "No Discrimination Against Women," Gernsback replied (p. 765), "We have no discrimination against women. Perish the thought—we want them! As a matter of fact, there are almost as many women among our readers as there are men. . . . We are always glad to hear from our feminine readers."

Gernsback, then, not only welcomed women to the first science fiction magazines ever to be published, but seems, from the beginning, to have had success in attracting them both as readers and writers of the new genre.

Then there were the editors who worked under Gernsback. As publisher of *Science Wonder Stories* and *Wonder Stories* from 1929–1936, Gernsback seemingly left much of the editorial work to David Lasser and, later, Charles D. Hornig.[27] How did these two editors regard women writers?

It was Lasser who chose and wrote the introductory blurb for one of the most extreme feminist stories to appear in the early science fiction magazines, Lilith Lorraine's "Into the 28th Century" (*Science Wonder Quarterly,* winter, 1930). Indeed, he was particularly enthusiastic in his praise for the socialist revolution that produced her sexually egalitarian society. (And why not? He was a member of the Socialist Party at the time.[28])

Nor was Lorraine's the only feminist utopia Lasser promoted. In the *Wonder Stories Quarterly* for spring, 1930, Lasser simultaneously published "Via the Hewitt Ray" by M. (Margaret) F. Rupert, in which women rule in a parallel universe, and Clare Winger Harris's "The Ape Cycle," which featured a supremely competent female protagonist who operated on a par with the male characters. In Harris's story, Sylvia Danforth helps her fiance to destroy the rule of intelligent apes. She flies his plane (and can repair it too) while discussing the fact that, earlier, "women finally came into professions that had been hitherto considered solely man's field, and they found they could do just as well as their brothers." Lasser also discovered Hazel Heald ("The Man of Stone," *Wonder Stories,* October, 1932), another woman writer who featured strong female characters. Lasser, it seems, had a certain enthusiasm for stories of this nature, as the critic Susan Wood noted.[29]

So did Charles D. Hornig, who replaced Lasser at the magazine. Hornig was another Socialist Party member and a religious pacifist who would serve time in prison during World War II for being a conscientious objector.[30] He left *Wonder Stories* in 1936 when it was sold, but later bounced back as editor of Louis Silberkleit's *Science Fiction,* where he published such female authors as Amelia Reynolds Long, Helen Weinbaum, and Leigh Brackett.

Other male editors were similarly welcoming to female writers. Such was the case of those at *Planet Stories,* whom Leigh Brackett praised in glowing terms. "For fifteen years," she said, "from 1940 [when she debuted] to 1955, when the magazine ceased publication, I had the happiest relationship possible for a writer with the editors of *Planet Stories.* They gave me, in the beginning, a proving ground where I could gain strength and confidence in the exercise of my fledgling skills, a thing of incalculable value for a young writer. They sent me checks, which enabled me to keep on eating. In later years, they provided a steady market for the kind of stories I liked best to write. In short, I owe them much. To Malcolm Reiss, and to Wilbur Peacock, Chester Whitehorn, Paul L. Payne, Jack O'Sullivan, and Jerome Bixby, my fondest salutations."[31]

Nor, it would seem, can the villains be editors Anthony Boucher, J. Francis McComas, and Robert P. Mills, and publisher Lawrence E. Spivak, who together produced what was soon to become a major magazine in the field, *The Magazine of Fantasy & Science Fiction*.[32] They were enthusiastic about publishing women, feeling they brought elements to the genre which men did not. Indeed, at a 1956 meeting of a Berkeley, California fan club to which Norm Metcalf belonged, Boucher explicitly told the members that he was going out of his way to publish women writers because he felt the field would benefit greatly from their presence.

Thus, in their fall, 1949 inaugural issue Boucher and his fellow editors printed Winona McClintic's "In the Days of Our Fathers," and hailed her with the blurb, "a distinctive new fantasy writer." They later included her story in the very first of the magazine's "best of" anthologies, saying "with the subtlety of a poet and the precision of a philologist, Miss McClintic has managed to compress into one very short story the theme of an entire [Aldous] Huxley novel. . . . [her story is] one of the most strikingly effective of the many 'first stories' which *Fantasy & Science Fiction* has published."[33]

In that same collection they published "The Listening Child" by a new writer, "Idris Seabright" (Margaret St. Clair), of whom they claimed they knew virtually nothing. Nevertheless, they compared her to the best of the writers from the period I am discussing. "One of the most pleasant—and certainly most stimulating—aspects of current science-fiction and fantasy writing is the growing importance of women in these twin forms," they said. "The best of them, from such old hands as C. L. Moore and Margaret St. Clair, to such recent discoveries as Judith Merril, Betsy Curtis, and Wilmar Shiras, bring to the field a welcome warmth and sensitivity and immediacy of impact. Women writers especially seem to realize that *every* type of fiction must essentially deal with people. (Not for them the 'gadget story' or 'space opera'!) Miss Seabright . . . has written a truly distinguished story of mood and emotion—one that will stay in your mind (and heart) long after you have forgotten the most sensational transgalactic epics."[34]

Who, then, were the editors who might have been biased against women? One of the few commentaries I've found which actually names names indicts Harry Bates, Mortimer Weisinger, and Raymond Palmer.[35] But, when we look at the record (table 1), we find, in instance after instance, that all three of these maligned editors actually welcomed, championed, promoted and published female writers. Unfortunately, this commentary, perhaps because of the long-standing reputation of one of its three authors, may have an undue influence in shaping our perception of women in early science fiction.[36] For this reason, it deserves careful scrutiny.

Janrae Frank, Jean Stine, and Forrest J. Ackerman have concocted an amazingly confused account of the 1930s. In it, they refer to the Thirties (indeed, the entire 20 years between 1930 and 1950) as the era "When Women Were Frozen Out" and "exiled" from science fiction by the nefarious triumvirate of Bates, Weisinger, and Palmer. First, let me present their account of the Thirties.[37]

According to these authors, "In 1930 an event occurred which was to have a devastating impact on the women who wrote science fiction, an event from which neither they nor the field would recover for more than two full decades: Hugo Gernsback lost control of *Amazing Stories.* . . . [which] fell under the editorship of the notorious Ray Palmer." (Actually, Gernsback's last *Amazing* was the April, 1929 issue. Far more serious is their elision of the entire nine years after that loss, when the magazine was edited by T. O'Conor Sloane, who regularly used contributions by women. Palmer did not become managing editor of *Amazing* until June, 1938.)

"At the same time, Gernsback's second set of futuristic publications, *Wonder Stories,* etc. ended in the hands of the Standard Magazine group, where Mort Weisinger quickly transformed it into *Thrilling Wonder Stories.*" (Gernsback founded *Science Wonder Stories,* later simply *Wonder Stories,* in 1929 after he lost *Amazing.* He sold it to Standard in 1936. Thus, two of the reputed villains who supposedly banned women at the beginning of the Thirties didn't even appear on the scene until most of the Thirties had passed.)

"While, over at Clayton Publications, a new science fiction pulp, *Astounding Stories of Super Science,* had risen under the editorship of Harry Bates." (At last we really do get to the beginning of the Thirties. Bates edited *Astounding* from January, 1930 to March, 1933. We're still missing the mid-Thirties, however.)

"Bates, Weisinger, and Palmer saw that if science fiction was to sell for their publishers, it could only be marketed as a subcategory of pulp magazine men's adventure fiction. To a certain degree, considering . . . that 90-plus percent of *Amazing* and *Wonder Stories'* readership had been male [How did this trio determine these particular figures? As is always the case in such matters, we are never told.], these three editors were probably right."

No evidence is given for the claim that these editors simultaneously adopted this identical outlook. In fact, since they actually adopted markedly different editorial policies from each other, and came into the field at different times, they *cannot* be lumped together as adopting any such joint stance.

Further, the claim that science fiction could be profitably marketed only as "men's adventure fiction" is dubious on the face of it. During the years (1926–1929) when Gernsback owned *Amazing* and which, as far as women were concerned, these authors praise as more enlightened times, science fiction was exceedingly profitable. Indeed, before it was six months old *Amazing* had a monthly circulation of 100,000, and reached 150,000 within its first year. At the same time, Gernsback commented, "a great many women are already reading the new magazine."[38] So, the genre was profitable *and* it appealed to women. It is true that circulation for any particular magazine shrank once the Depression hit and there was more than one magazine to share the genre market. But even if the evidence did not contradict it, there is no reason to believe that an editorial consensus thought Gernsback's original formula was no longer a recipe for continued success.

"The immediate consequence of the realignment of magazine science fiction," our commentators continue, "was a radical diminution in the number of women writers. . . . *Thus, women writers were to disappear almost overnight from the pages of science fiction magazines and remain in exile for the next twenty years.* [Emphasis added.] Talents such as Lilith Lorraine and Leslie Francis [sic] Stone simply had no reason to go on writing, and no place to publish their work if they had. . . . The only woman writer whose work received any welcome at all during this period [the 1930s] was Helen Weinbaum."

If we were to accept this pseudo-history as true, it would have to mean that only a *single* story by a woman was published in the 1930s, as that was all that Helen Weinbaum published ("Tidal Moon," *Thrilling Wonder Stories*, December, 1938). But these authors contradict themselves by including stories from the 1930s by Hazel Heald ("The Man of Stone," *Wonder Stories*, October, 1932) and Leslie F. Stone ("The Conquest of Gola," *Wonder Stories*, April, 1931) in the anthology where they make these statements!

Obviously, these claims simply aren't true. Stone, for example, had every reason to go on writing and plenty of places in which to publish. And she did. She enjoyed a prolific career during the entire decade of the Thirties, placing stories in *Astounding, Amazing, Wonder,* and *Future Fiction.* (See table 1.) Indeed, as we have seen, Stone herself flatly denied she ever experienced any bias against her as a woman writer from *any* editor before an alleged encounter with John W. Campbell in 1938, which I will discuss later.[39]

As for Lilith Lorraine, she drifted in other directions, becoming more and more immersed in poetry. But, while she established a reputation in "mainstream" literature as a reputable poet, her more genre-related poetry continued to appear under her name in the science fiction magazines throughout the Thirties and beyond. Indeed, the end of the Forties finds her as the poetry editor for William Crawford's *Fantasy Book*, where she presided over a column entitled, "Songs of the Spaceways." By the early Fifties she was publishing poetry (her own and that of others) and science fiction stories in her fanzines, *Challenge* and *Different.* In this capacity she discovered a teenager named Robert Silverberg in 1953, purchasing and publishing his first short story.[40]

Then there is the claim that, after 1930, there "was a radical diminution in the number of women writers . . . [as] women writers were to disappear almost overnight from the pages of science fiction magazines and remain in exile for the next twenty years." A look at the record (summary, end of table 1) reveals just the opposite. Instead of "disappearing," there was a steady increase in the female presence over the entire course of the next twenty years. Both the number of women science fiction writers and the number of stories published by them *more than tripled* in the 1930s over the 1920s. Further, in the 1940s, the number of women science fiction writers almost *doubled* over their number in the 1930s, while the number of stories published by them again *more than tripled* over the number published in the 1930s.

And what of these three supposedly anti-female editors themselves? As the record demonstrates, all three published female writers in the pages of the magazines they edited. In *Startling Stories,* which he edited for Standard Magazines, Mort Weisinger published Leigh Brackett at the very beginning of her career. Meanwhile, Ray Palmer not only published articles by Gale Stevens, June Lurie, Frances Yerxa, Lynn Standish, Fran Ferris, and many others, he also published stories by Leigh Brackett (along with her photo for her debut in his magazine), L. Taylor Hansen, Dorothy Quick, and even "Cleo Eldon." Meanwhile, he also published the work of female artists, such as Eileen Hayes.[41]

Further, Ray Palmer was the editor who discovered writers Mollie Claire, Dorothy de Courcy, Frances M. Deegan, Norma Lazell Easton, Frances Garfield, Millicent Holmberg, Margaret Rogers, Doris Thomas, Frances Yerxa, and Margaret St. Clair (see Table 1). And, he not only displayed commendable zeal in finding new female talent, he then gave the newcomers considerable publicity. For example, when he published St. Clair's debut, "Rocket to Limbo," *Fantastic Adventures,* November 1946, he devoted the entire inside cover to an autobiographical sketch, accompanied by a large photograph of the novice author. Later, in his editorial comments, Palmer said he found St. Clair's story in the slush pile and immediately wrote her a check. "If this first story of hers is any indication," he said, "you'll be seeing her name again. . . . The lady knows how to write."

And, if "the notorious Ray Palmer" wouldn't publish women, why is it that, when Doris Vancel decided to publish under a pseudonym, she didn't choose a male name for Palmer's magazine? Instead, she chose another female name, "Doris Thomas." Even more problematic is the case of well-known author Don Wilcox. He chose to publish in Palmer's magazine under the name "Cleo Eldon." Likewise, Rog Phillips sold to Palmer as "Melva Rogers" when Palmer edited *Other Worlds* in 1950. Where is the logic in a male author choosing a woman's byline if the editor he wants to sell to is known to be biased against women?

Additionally, we have the testimony of one of Palmer's female writers that refutes these charges against him. For example, Frances M. Deegan, one of Palmer's discoveries, recalled how she came to be a writer. "I had been reading

Ziff-Davis fiction mags for some time," she said. "I suddenly remembered that I had always intended to write, so I went down to see Mr. [Ray] Palmer [editor of both detective magazines as well as *Amazing Stories* and *Fantastic Adventures* for Ziff-Davis]. The reception room was elegant, but it was very informal inside. I simply walked in and said, 'Do you mind if I write something for you?' And Mr. Palmer said, 'No, go right ahead.' I went home and wrote a story, and he bought it."[42] Deegan went on to a long career as a writer of detective stories and 17 SF stories for *Fantastic Adventures* and *Amazing Stories*, the last appearing in 1952.

Finally, between 1936–1938 Ray Palmer himself wrote five stories featuring the strong and independent female protagonists "Carla Romaunt" and "Fay Langdon," which appeared in the female-oriented pulp *Scarlet Adventuress*. This magazine advertised for "Stories concerning the adventures of women in pitting their wiles and wits against the world," and this is the type of woman Palmer celebrated in his work. This would be strange, indeed, if Palmer disapproved of women appearing in the pulp world. (The very existence of this female-oriented adventure pulp, with a third of the authors appearing within its pages being female, is also evidence of the contested nature of pulp fiction.)[43]

Perhaps most difficult to reconcile with the alleged anti-female bias is Harry Bates, the editor who presumably inaugurated the ban on women (at least he was the only one of the three who was actually an editor at the beginning of the Thirties). First, Bates published the socialist-feminist Lilith Lorraine ("Jovian Jest," *Astounding*, May, 1930), who supposedly had no place to publish after Bates appeared on the scene. Even harder to explain is Bates' publication of two powerful feminist utopian stories by Sophie Wenzel Ellis ("Creatures of the Light," February, 1930—in only the second issue of *Astounding*—and "Slaves of the Dust," December, 1930).

Further, Ackerman knew very well that Bates published these two stories, as he has served as Ellis' literary agent for many decades, even unto the present. Indeed, in early 1953 he tore the pages of these two stories out of the *Astounding* issues in which Bates had published them and sent them to Sam Moskowitz in an attempt to get Moskowitz to reprint them in Gernsback's *Science Fiction Plus*, which Moskowitz was then editing.[44]

The only possible explanation for these contradictions is that what is claimed about Harry Bates is false. In short, the "history" of male editorial discrimination against women written by this trio is a tale from the Twilight Zone, bearing no relation to reality.

Perhaps, then, the villain was John W. Campbell, Jr., thought by many to rival (or overshadow) Gernsback as the most influential editor in the history of science fiction. In the 1970s Joanna Russ (who never published in Campbell's magazine) wrote that, "within the memory of living adolescents, John Campbell Jr. proposed that 'nice girls' be sent on spaceships as prostitutes because married women would only clutter everything up with washing and babies."[45] And, while in 1947 Margaret St. Clair had praised Campbell as being extremely broadminded and welcoming to newcomers, by 1981 she was repeating gossip to the effect that he "was reputed never to accept a story by a woman if he were aware of her sex."[46]

Because of allegations such as these, Campbell certainly developed an unfortunate reputation for being anti-female. But, was there any truth to the charges? Given Campbell's towering stature and the long shadow he cast over the field, it behooves us to examine these assertions closely. As it happens, in doing so we will glean perhaps our best idea yet about the relationship between male editors and their female authors during the years under discussion.

To start with, Campbell never made the comments Russ attributed to him. The person who *actually* made the inflammatory suggestion was astronomer and science fiction author "Philip Latham," who published non-fiction under his real name of Robert S. Richardson. Dr. Richardson advocated "nice girl" prostitutes for tired spacemen in his article "The Day After We Land on Mars" in the December, 1955 issue of *The Magazine of Fantasy and Science Fiction.* There he proposed that "nice girls" would be needed on Mars "to relieve the sexual tensions that develop among healthy normal males (p. 52)."

Richardson's proposal brought two rebuttals in the May, 1956 issue. The first was from author Poul Anderson, who simply felt the idea was technically unfeasible because the cost of getting the "nice girls" to Mars would be "astronomical." Besides, the "nice girls" would just "generate tension and discord (p. 49)." The other was from author Miriam Allen deFord, who said, "I am going to tell Dr. Robert S. Richardson a secret. Women are not walking sex organs. They are human beings. They are people, just like men (p. 53)."

So, at the time, the science fiction community obviously knew that Richardson was the author of this notorious proposal. But, Campbell seems to have been a lightening rod for false allegations concerning his attitudes and statements, perhaps because of his macho personal style. Thus, by the early 1970s people had forgotten the true author of these sentiments and attributed them to Campbell.

But Campbell published stories which gave the lie to such attributed views. In 1966–1967, for example, years before Russ attacked Campbell for statements he never made, he published "Amazon Planet" by "Mack Reynolds" (Dallas McCord Reynolds), a Socialist Labor Party activist whose father had repeatedly been the SLP's presidential candidate. In the story, Reynolds posited a peaceful gender role-reversal society. Interestingly, Joanna Russ praised this story in 1980 as an enlightened look at gender relations.[47]

However, perhaps Campbell's actual relations with and support for female authors is a better indicator of his attitudes toward women in science fiction. For example, Campbell was the one who discovered and published Judith Merril's science fiction debut ("That Only a Mother," *Astounding*, June, 1948). Merril told Justine Larbalestier that Campbell first learned of the story when they were partying drunkenly together in a Philadelphia hotel room in August, 1947. Merril, an unpublished would-be author, was attending her first science fiction convention and Theodore Sturgeon had introduced her to "the great editor."

"It was friendship—forever at first sight," Merril said of her and Campbell. She then told Campbell she'd written a story that was too good for him, as he couldn't pay what it was worth. In the sober light of the next morning, Merril was "horrified" at what she'd said to Campbell, fearing she'd offended him. But, six months later, after all the higher paying slicks had rejected the story, she sent it to Campbell—who quickly accepted and published it.[48]

However, female author Julian May, whose debut Campbell would also soon publish, claims she had no knowledge of Merril's debut and had to sneak into the pages of *Astounding* using initials because Campbell refused to publish women.[49]

By 1951 Julian May was already a leading light of the Chicago science fiction community. Indeed, her reputation was such that she would be chosen as co-chair of the 1952 Worldcon Committee. Thus, everyone who was anyone (including Campbell) already knew who she was by 1951. That was when she sent her first story ("Dune Roller," *Astounding*, December, 1951) to Campbell under the initials of "J. C. May" (for "Julian Chain May"). She told me that she did this because Campbell was "known to be a piggie who wouldn't publish women" and she was afraid that her given name, "Julian," which she claimed was once common among women, would betray her gender.[50]

But her reputed fear of rejection if Campbell saw the supposedly betraying female name of "Julian" on her manuscript was obviously unwarranted. This was because, just a few months before Campbell published her December debut, he had, in a sense, already published her! In a bizarre development which would bedevil future bibliographers, an unknown author had already used her actual first and middle names, "Julian Chain," as a pseudonym under which to publish two stories with Campbell ("Success Story," *Astounding*, May, 1951 and "Prometheus," *Astounding*, August, 1951). If Campbell was prejudiced against manuscripts bearing obvious female names, as May says she felt "Julian" was, then he would not have published those two prior stories by "Julian Chain"— nor two subsequent ones soon thereafter ("Cosmophyte," *Astounding*, April, 1952 and "The Captives," *Astounding*, January, 1953).

Further, as already noted, Campbell had recently discovered and published, under their full female names, the debut stories of several women writers, including that of Judith Merril, who Campbell proudly hailed in a blurb accompanying her story as "a new feminine science fiction author" (*Astounding*, June, 1948, p. 88). He soon thereafter published her story, "Death Is the Penalty"

(*Astounding*, January, 1949). He also discovered Katherine MacLean and published her debut, "Defense Mechanism" (*Astounding*, October, 1949), as well as her "And Be Merry" (*Astounding*, February, 1950), "Incommunicado" (*Astounding*, June, 1950), and "Feedback" (*Astounding*, July, 1951).

I mentioned these obviously-female authors to May, all of whom appeared in the magazine she submitted her story to prior to her submittal. She replied that she was just a college student at that time and had only begun reading SF in 1947 (and yet was co-chairing a Worldcon five years later!), and so didn't know what Campbell may have published *before* 1947. I then pointed out the post–1947 dates of all these publications. May claimed she was completely unaware of these authors and their stories—just as she was unaware at the time that "Julian Chain" was publishing in the same magazine both *before* and *after* her own debut.

These claims of ignorance, however, seem very unlikely. First, May was extremely active in the science fiction world at that time. Second, the very June, 1948 issue of *Astounding* which carried Judith Merril's debut story, "That Only a Mother," *also* published a letter (p. 156) from "J. C. May," the pseudonym May admits using in relation to *Astounding*, and giving Julian May's home address in Illinois! The letter commented with intimate familiarity on earlier stories published in the magazine and suggested she was also knowledgeable about Campbell's 1930s' stories under the pseudonym of "Don A. Stuart." And she no doubt also read every story—including Judith Merril's—in the very issue in which she was, herself, published.

So it turns out that Julian May, despite her copious reading of the contemporary literature and her fan activity, either knew absolutely nothing of Campbell's actual publication record concerning women (or even what was published in his magazine)—or, for reasons unknown, she is rewriting her personal history to correspond with the biblical version of women in science fiction. Given the circumstances of her intense early involvement in the field and given her own publication in the same issue which carried Merril's debut story, the deliberate rewriting of her own past seems easier to believe. Thus, although she could not cite a single example of bias on Campbell's part (and despite evidence, in May's case, that she knew the contrary was true), Julian May still claims to this day that the man who launched her career by accepting and publishing her first story was "a piggie" who wouldn't publish anyone suspected of being female. Such is the power of a hegemonic idea.

More than a decade earlier Leslie F. Stone had claimed much the same about Campbell in the only specific example of alleged sexual discrimination I have been able to find for our period. According to Stone, she visited Campbell in early 1938 to discuss her story, "Death Dallies Awhile" (*Weird Tales*, June, 1938). Supposedly, Campbell rejected her story out-of-hand, saying acidly, "I do not believe that women are capable of writing science-fiction—nor do I approve of it!"[51]

Perhaps Campbell *did* reject Stone's story, as *all* editors reject *many* stories. However, it's unclear. Campbell began as an assistant editor at the magazine in September 1937 and officially took over the top editorial reins from F. Orlin Tremaine with the December, 1937 issue. Even so, he seems not to have been fully in charge until the May, 1938 issue, just a month before *Weird Tales* published Stone's short story.[52] Obviously, then, *Weird Tales* had to have accepted the story even before Campbell was completely in command at *Astounding*, so we don't know if Campbell was the one who rejected Stone's story, if rejected it was.

But, if he did, perhaps he did so because it was more fantasy than science fiction—which was why it soon appeared in a fantasy magazine rather than any *other* science fiction magazine. I say this because Campbell's own actions as an editor belie the sentiments attributed to him.

It was Campbell, for instance, who discovered and published the debuts of several new female science fiction/fantasy authors during this time, including "Mona Farnsworth" (Muriel Newhall) (1939), Leigh Brackett (1940), "Marian O'Hearn" (Anita Allen) (1940), Jane Rice (1940), Margaret Ronan (1941), E. Mayne Hull (1942), Babette Rosmond (1942), Judith Merril (1948), Wilmar H. Shiras (1948), and future Nebula Award-winner Katherine MacLean (1949). (And, soon, even "Julian Chain," if that unknown author is considered to be a woman.) Indeed, shortly before Stone's visit, he published Amelia Reynolds Long ("The Mind Master," *Astounding*, December, 1937) in the first official issue of his tenure. Shortly after the visit, in 1939, he also published "Mona Farnsworth" (three times), C. L. Moore, Dorothy Quick, and, again, Amelia Reynolds Long (see table 1).

Isaac Asimov pointed out that after Campbell took over there was a period of editorial experimentation at *Astounding* as he felt his way into his position and that he didn't really put his stamp on the magazine until the summer of 1939. "The July, 1939 issue," said Asimov, "was the first issue that was truly marked by Campbell's thinking and Campbell's new authors, and it is usually considered as the first issue of 'the Golden Age of science fiction.' "[53] And in this issue we find "Greater Than Gods" by C. L. Moore—present at the creation as part of Campbell's "Golden Age of science fiction." Campbell soon thereafter published Moore's "Fruit of Knowledge" (*Unknown*, October, 1940), a love story to which he devoted the cover of his magazine and which was later chosen by the field for inclusion in the Fantasy Hall of Fame. He also published Moore's classic "No Woman Born" (*Astounding*, December, 1944), which featured a strong female protagonist.

Campbell, in short, would publish anyone who wrote a good story. And this included complete novices. Perhaps sensing this, Ursula Kroeber sent him her first science fiction story in 1942. Campbell rejected it—but no doubt this was only because Ursula K. Le Guin was just twelve years old at the time and the story needed a lot of work.[54] "Pauline Ashwell" (Pauline Whitby) had better luck. In 1958 Campbell discovered her and published her first story ("Unwillingly to School," *Astounding*, January, 1958). It was later Hugo-nominated for best short story of the year, a promising debut for any writer. He also published her second and third stories. The latter ("The Lost Kafoozalum," *Astounding/ Analog*, October, 1960) was also Hugo-nominated for best short story. Quality, not gender, was what Campbell wanted in a writer.

Campbell also championed women in venues other than his magazines. For example, in 1954 Sam Moskowitz edited his first professional science fiction anthology, *Editor's Choice in Science Fiction*. In it, a number of editors who'd published science fiction and fantasy were asked to choose one exceptional story from their magazines for inclusion. When given the chance to choose the one story he felt should represent *Unknown*, Campbell selected Mona Farnsworth's "All Roads," from the August, 1940 issue. "It had a refreshing flavor when it was published," recalled Campbell, and "Its incorporation into hard covers has been long overdue."[55] He also chose Jane Rice's "The Refugee" and Babette Rosmond's "One Man's Harp" for his "best of" anthology, *From Unknown Worlds* (1948). These choices belie the accusations about his refusal to publish women.

But, once they get into the cultural mind, myths die hard, even when an editor walks the extra mile to kill them. A salient example of this is Campbell's initial relations with Katherine MacLean, an unpublished writer he nurtured and cajoled into print for the first time. As does Julian May, MacLean still claims that Campbell was prejudiced against women writers, despite the fact that he published the debuts of both authors. Her own experience with Campbell, however, dramatically reveals just the opposite.[56]

When the novice Katherine MacLean prepared to send her first fiction attempt, "Incommunicado" (*Astounding*, June, 1950), to Campbell in 1947, her father and brothers (none of them connected with the science fiction world in any way) made the common mistake of confusing image and reality. Because pervasive cultural sexism proclaimed that science (and, thus, science fiction) was "not for women," her male relatives convinced her that neither Campbell nor any other science fiction editor ever would accept a story written by a woman. Imbued with the sexism of the times, MacLean saw no reason to doubt them. After all, she confessed, "at the time I thought most women were dumb and cowardly and devious." Any responsible editor *would* reject a story written by such a creature.

Therefore, with much fear and trembling, she timorously submitted her story as by "K. MacLean." Campbell enthusiastically accepted that first effort, soon discovered she was female, and began telling his associates about a wonderful new writer he'd found.

Campbell also felt her story would have the greatest impact if published entire in one issue. However, the manuscript was around 155 pages, "tightly typed," much too long for him to do this. Therefore, Campbell called MacLean into his office to discuss revising her story. At that face-to-face meeting Campbell shook her hand and told her the story was "A real blockbuster." Then he asked her to cut it down to 60 pages or so. Not only would this make it possible for him to publish it in one issue and do so before the end of the year, but he also felt a tighter story would be a stronger story.

Campbell was legendary for requesting extensive revisions from authors, both male and female, and this request to MacLean was his standard operating procedure with authors he deemed promising. As he told Frederik Pohl, "When [a story] just doesn't come across, there's nothing I can say," and therefore he just rejected such a story with no comment. But, if he thought a story had potential, "I can tell you how to fix it."[57] It is reported, for example, that Campbell made Tom Godwin rewrite his classic "The Cold Equations" (*Astounding*, August, 1954) *seven times* before he produced something of which Campbell approved, a story in which the "heroine" dies at the end. Notably, this is also the only story for which Godwin is now remembered.[58]

Not all authors, of course, appreciated Campbell's suggestions about how to "fix" their stories. Philip K. Dick complained to Norm Metcalf that Campbell made him rewrite his story, "Imposter" (*Astounding*, June, 1953), several times. He said he'd rather write several first-draft stories for one cent a word than spend time revising a single story for Campbell, despite the higher pay.

Obviously, however, gender had nothing to do with Campbell's insistence upon revisions. Campbell required them because, as A. Bertram Chandler noted, he "was a perfectionist. If he wanted a story, and if it fell short of his standards, he would say, take it away and do so-and-so and such-and-such; this is your story, your idea and I want it from you!"[59] And he told MacLean much the same at their meeting. He also told her, as they parted, "I will want more stories from you!"

Nevertheless, so powerful was the presumption of prejudice in her own mind and "so frightened of rejection that I couldn't think clearly," that MacLean left Campbell's office feeling that he had actually *rejected* her and her story, simply because he'd asked for revisions. And, not only did she believe he had rejected her, she believed he had rejected her *because she was a woman*.

Still, clinging to some glimmer of hope, MacLean worked with increasing frustration for months thereafter to tighten what she felt was already a tight story. She didn't want to eliminate a single episode, as "each one had a different new idea. So I set about the painful task of retyping each page and cutting out extra words and shortening descriptions. Like trying to boil down a bullion cube." And the more she worked, the more she became convinced that the men in her family were right. Despite the fact that Campbell had actually *accepted* her story and told her he wanted more from her, she felt that he had set her the task of revision *merely as an excuse to reject a story written by a woman.*

MacLean voiced her fears to Campbell's associate editor, L. Jerome Stanton, who was in constant telephone contact with her to monitor her progress and to encourage her. He repeatedly assured her that her presumption was unfounded. If Campbell wanted to reject her, Stanton told her, he'd have rejected her out-of-hand instead of wasting valuable editorial time on her. Stanton also cited Judith Merril as another woman Campbell was publishing. This should have reassured MacLean, as she knew Merril, having met her in the fall of 1947 at a party of science fiction writers. At that party Merril had told MacLean that, "the word was out that Campbell had bought a story from me" and she gave MacLean the manuscript of "That Only a Mother" to read. It had just been rejected by *Colliers* and Merril said she was thinking of sending it to Campbell. Now Stanton was telling MacLean that Campbell had accepted the story. But MacLean remained unconvinced and prepared to abandon the revision effort as a waste of time.

To assure MacLean that her suspicions of Campbell were completely unfounded, Stanton suggested that she dash off a quick short story, which he guaranteed Campbell would accept (such was his faith in her) and publish *under her full name.* She did so, and "Defense Mechanism," her official debut, soon appeared in the October, 1949 *Astounding* as by "Katherine MacLean." Shortly thereafter, to further encourage her, Campbell also accepted "And Be Merry . . ." (February, 1950), which featured a central female character, *and published it also under her full name.* Groff Conklin, a prolific anthologist of the time, quickly reprinted it as one of the foremost stories in the field.[60]

Finally persuaded that her task of revision was legitimate, the fearful novice finished "Incommunicado" and Campbell soon published it *under her full name.* She was the only novice in the issue in which her story appeared. Every other author in that issue—Isaac Asimov, A. E. van Vogt, L. Sprague de Camp, Cleve Cartmill, and Frank M. Robinson—was already well known. But Campbell chose *her* story as the one for which he commissioned a cover painting. He also gave her pride of place, running her story as the very first one in the issue. In addition, in the May issue prior to its June, 1950 publication, Campbell alerted his readers (p. 42) to "Katherine MacLean's" (full name) forthcoming story and told them they were going to like it. And, indeed, they did. Shortly after its publication, MacLean attended an engineering convention at which the male engineers crowded around her in adulation, shaking her hand and showering her with praise when they discovered she was the author of the story.[61]

Following these initial stories, which Campbell coaxed and cajoled out of her, MacLean quickly published thirteen more, *under her full name,* in *Astounding, Galaxy, Thrilling Wonder Stories,* and six other magazines before using a pseudonym for "The Carnivore" (*Galaxy SF,* October, 1953) and her initial in the

Harry Harrison-edited *Science Fiction Adventures*, May, 1954, both of which I have already discussed. Indeed, such was her cachet that H. L. Gold called the still-new MacLean in early 1950 and, in her words, "begged" her to send him a story to help launch a new magazine he was starting with Vera Cerutti as his editor-in-chief. Hence, her outstanding "Contagion" appeared in the debut issue of *Galaxy*, October 1950.[62]

In July, 1951, she even had stories simultaneously in Gold's *Galaxy* and Campbell's *Astounding*. She also became one of the very few American women to publish in British SF magazines during the 1950s. In addition, her well-known story, "Pictures Don't Lie," was chosen for broadcast on *Out of This World*, August 11, 1962. Hosted by Boris Karloff, this was Britain's first SF anthology television series.

Thus, within a very short period of time, Katherine MacLean catapulted into the upper ranks of science fiction's professional circles and, as we have seen earlier, was welcomed into such fabled professional social gatherings as New York's Hydra Club. Even her visits to fan clubs around the nation were cause for celebration and reportage. For example, when she visited the Los Angeles Science Fantasy Society (LASFS) in December 1953, she was warmly received by such luminaries as Chad Oliver, James Schmitz, Kris Neville, and Forrest J. Ackerman and his wife. The occasion was duly noted by Robert A. Madle in his "Inside Science Fiction" column in the June 1954 issue of *Future Science Fiction* (p. 107).

However, such outstanding publication and social success from the very out-set of MacLean's career, and her exceptional experience of nothing but strong editorial support and encouragement from editors like Campbell and Gold, have been universally discounted. Instead, historians have cited MacLean's mere existence as illustrative of a reputed editorial bias against women writers. For instance, Frederik Pohl tells us how MacLean supposedly bullied and forced "And Be Merry . . ." and subsequent stories into print over the obstinate resistance of Campbell, Gold, and other editors. Introducing "And Be Merry . . ." in one of his anthologies, Pohl asserted that, "For many years [women] hid under cryptic initials, like C. L. Moore, or ambiguous names like Leslie F. Stone. Not Kay MacLean. She came into science fiction on her own terms—as a person who happened to be female, *but asked no favors* and accepted no penalties because of that—and won over editors and readers to that point of view simply by writing stories as good as this one."[63]

Of course, Pohl could not have communicated with MacLean (as I did) about how and why this story was written or how Campbell came to accept it, or he could not have written such tosh. He just made it up out of whole cloth. As we have seen, MacLean *did* come into the field hiding fearfully behind a "cryptic initial," but Campbell would have none of it. Further, Campbell performed many extraordinary favors for her in order to encourage her to continue.

But it is through such repeated (and presumably authoritative) assertions as Pohl's that the mythology has become embedded in the field's collective memory. One wonders how many female writers, experiencing the more typical initial rejection rates of novices, quickly gave up because "experts" like Pohl had convinced them that science fiction editors were "of course" biased against women writers. If any at all were thus disheartened, then commentators like Pohl have done more to discourage female participation in the field than any magazine editor he criticized.

But so ingrained is this mythology that, to this day, MacLean continues to believe that Campbell and his fellow editors were prejudiced against female participation in the field. She also told me that Campbell deliberately published her first submission, "Incommunicado," *as by "K. MacLean"* in order to conceal her female identity. This is despite the fact that *the actual magazine lists her as "Katherine MacLean" in three separate places:* on the cover devoted to her story, the table of contents, and the story itself. It is also despite the fact that Campbell additionally used her full name in the preceding issue to announce her upcoming story. Such is the power of a hegemonic myth that it even distorts the memory of personal experience, regardless of extensive documentation to the contrary. Such concrete evidence can do little when up against "what everybody knows to be true."

Nevertheless, the personal relations between John W. Campbell and early female authors such as Judith Merril, Julian May, and Katherine MacLean reveal a truth which is the complete opposite of the mythology. As with every other science fiction editor, even this most reputedly hostile male editor's record shows him to have been exceptionally welcoming and helpful toward women writers. Indeed, it is quite impossible to find any evidence at all to document the universally accepted charge of editorial hostility toward female writers in early science fiction. It is simply part of a hegemonic idea that has no need of proof, as "it is obvious."

Notes

1. Platt, *Dream Makers, Volume II*, p. 237.
2. Leslie F. Stone, "Day of the Pulps," *Fantasy Commentator*, IX, 1997, pp. 101, 103. This was originally presented as a speech at Balticon, 1974.
3. Leigh Brackett, "The Science-Fiction Field," *Writer's Digest*, July, 1944, pp. 26–27.
4. Rosemary Herbert, entry on Margaret St. Clair in Curtis C. Smith, Ed., *Twentieth-Century Science-Fiction Writers*, St. Martin's Press: N.Y., 1981, p. 465.
5. Margaret St. Clair, "Twenty-Seven Captured Suns," *Writer's Digest*, July, 1947, pp. 12–15. Hamling was managing editor of both *Amazing Stories* and *Fantastic Adventures* January, 1948-February, 1951. He was editor of *Imagination* February, 1951-October, 1958, *Imaginative Tales*, September, 1954-May, 1958, and *Space Travel*, July-November, 1958. As St. Clair published this comment before Hamling was officially credited with editing either *Amazing Stories* or *Fantastic*

Adventures, it's unclear to which story she is referring. Could it be "Whenever the Sun Shines," *Fantastic Adventures,* October, 1947?

6. Miriam Allen deFord, "On the Soapbox," in Sherna Gluck, Ed., *From Parlor to Prison: Five American Suffragists Talk About Their Lives,* Vintage Books: N.Y., 1976, pp. 177, 173.

7. Leigh Brackett, interview in Paul Walker, *Speaking of Science Fiction,* pp. 382–383. Originally in *LUNA Monthly 61,* 1976.

8. Judith Merril, *Survival Ship and Other Stories,* Kakabeka Publishing Co.: Toronto, 1973, p. 32.

9. Amelia Reynolds Long in Chet Williamson, "A Visit With Amelia Reynolds Long," *Etchings & Odysseys,* #10, 1987, p. 61.

10. Amelia Reynolds Long to Chet Williamson, April 30, 1976, June 20, 1977, and August 11, 1976, quoted in "Yours, Amelia," *Etchings & Odysseys,* #10, 1987, pp. 63, 65.

11. Long in Williamson, "A Visit With Amelia Reynolds Long," p. 61.

12. Ursula K. LeGuin, *The Wind's Twelve Quarters,* Bantam Books: N.Y., 1975, pp. 23, 119.

13. . *Startling Stories,* fall, 1944, p. 112.

14. The magazines were: *Amazing Stories Annual,* whose editor Hugo Gernsback published women in all of his other science-fiction magazines; *Miracle Science and Fantasy Stories,* which existed for only two issues in 1931, published a total of five authors, and whose editor, Harold Hersey, had published women in *The Thrill Book*; *Marvel Science Stories,* with variant titles, which flickered in and out of existence over nine issues between 1938–1941; two issues of *Dynamic Stories,* both edited by Robert O. Erisman, who published women in *Marvel* after 1950; and *Captain Future* (whose pages were chiefly devoted to the exploits of a single eponymous character, written on contract by Edmond Hamilton and Joseph Samachson), edited by Oscar J. Friend (who published women in *Startling Stories* and *Thrilling Wonder Stories)* and by Mortimer Weisinger (who also published women in *Startling Stories).* Thus, I feel I am justified in saying *all* SF editors published women.

15. C.f., Dorothy McIlwraith, "Every Good Pulp Loves a Hero," *The Writer,* May, 1949.

16. Stefan R. Dziemianowicz, Robert Weinberg, & Martin H. Greenberg, *Famous Fantastic Mysteries: 30 Great Tales of Fantasy and Horror from the Classic Pulp Magazine,* Gramercy Books: N.Y., 1991, p. 1. Stevens actually published at least twelve stories, and possibly more.

17. Catherine Tarrant, assistant editor of *Astounding Science-Fiction* (later *Analog),* began her decades-long service in January, 1942, and served until February, 1972. However, Tarrant seems to have had only administrative duties, as Campbell claimed he made the decision on every story which came into his magazine.

18. C.f., *Fantastic Stories of the Imagination,* July, 1963, which has a surrealist cover by Jacquelyn Blair for Jack Sharkey's, "The Trouble with Tweenity." Two nice covers by Paula McLane are *Amazing Stories,* April, 1965, illustrating Edmond Hamilton's "The Shores of Infinity" and *Fantastic Stories of the Imagination,* September, 1963, illustrating Robert F. Young's "The House That Time Forgot."

19. Letter, Howard Browne to Mike Ashley, February, 1982.

20. Greye La Spina, "Recollections of *Weird Tales,*" in Robert Weinberg, *The Weird Tales Story,* Wildside Press: Berkeley Hgts., N.J., 1999, p. 50.

21. Sam Moskowitz, *Seekers of Tomorrow: Masters of Modern Science Fiction,* The World Publishing Co.: Cleveland and N.Y., 1966, p. 303.

22. . *When the Sun Went Out* and "Men with Wings," as well as "Women with Wings" (see table 1). Her story, "Out of the Void," was also accepted by Gernsback, but published by Sloane after Gernsback left *Amazing.* See Stone, "Day of the Pulps," p. 100.

23. Sam Moskowitz, introduction to Edmond Hamilton's reprinted 1938 *Weird Tales* story, "He That Hath Wings," *Fantastic Stories of Imagination,* July, 1963, p. 22.

24. See, e.g., "The Menace of Mars," *Amazing Stories,* Oct., 1928, and "The Diabolical Drug," *Amazing Stories,* May, 1929.

25. See his letter, *Amazing Stories,* August, 1929, p. 474. Siegel noted that Harris also wrote for

Weird Tales, of which he was also a devoted reader. Actually, Harris had appeared in *Weird Tales* even before she appeared in *Amazing Stories*. Her story, "A Runaway World," was in the July, 1926 issue.

26. Could this letter writer be Mrs. Leslie Frances (Stone) Silberberg (Mrs. William Silberberg)? This is the only letter under this by-line in *Amazing*.

27. For elaboration on this point, see Eric Leif Davin, *Pioneers of Wonder: Conversations With the Founders of Science Fiction,* Prometheus Books: Amherst: N.Y., 1999, especially the chapters on David Lasser, Charles Hornig, and Raymond Z. Gallun. However, Norm Metcalf feels Gernsback had a more active role in editorial decisions at this time, citing the fact that, according to the Weinbaum correspondence, Gernsback had to approve payments to Stanley G. Weinbaum.

28. See the chapter on David Lasser in Davin, *Pioneers of Wonder.*

29. Susan Wood, "Women and Science Fiction," *Algol, The Magazine About Science Fiction,* winter, 1978–1979, p. 11.

30. See the chapter on Charles D. Hornig in Davin, *Pioneers of Wonder.*

31. Leigh Brackett, Ed., "Introduction: Beyond Our Narrow Skies," *The Best of Planet Stories, #1: Strange Adventures on Other Worlds,* Ballantine Books: N.Y., 1975, p. 1.

32. For its first issue, it was known simply as, *The Magazine of Fantasy.* "Anthony Boucher" was the pseudonym of William Anthony Parker White, who used his birth name in *Weird Tales.*

33. Anthony Boucher and J. Francis McComas, Eds., *The Best From Fantasy and Science Fiction,* Little, Brown & Co.: Boston, 1952, p. 170.

34. Boucher and McComas, p. 82. St. Clair, of course, was not all that much of an "old hand," having launched her career only in 1946.

35. Frank, Stine and Ackerman, pp. viii-ix.

36. E.g., See Garyn Roberts, Ed., *The Prentice Hall Anthology of Science Fiction,* Prentice-Hall, Inc.: N.Y., 2001. Included is Hazel Heald's "The Man of Stone" and Leslie F. Stone's "The Conquest of Gola." These stories were reprinted not from the original magazine publications, but from this trio's *New Eves,* as the most accessible source of stories and information on early women SF writers. Letter, Frederick T. Courtright to Forrest J. Ackerman, August 28, 1999. And so error is perpetuated.

37. The following account and quotes are from Frank, Stine, and Ackerman, pp. viii-ix.

38. Gernsback's comments about the "great many women" readers, along with the circulation figure of 100,000 copies per month, come from his editorial in the September, 1926 *Amazing* (issue number six). The 150,000 figure comes from his editorial in the March, 1927 *Amazing* (issue number 12). Gernsback again quotes the 150,000 figure in his editorial in the August, 1927 issue.

39. Stone, "Day of the Pulps," p. 101.

40. See the letter in *The Writer's Digest,* July, 1947, which described a writers' conference organized in Salt Lake City by the League of Utah Writers. One of the featured speakers was Lilith Lorraine, described as a "well-known poet."

Anyone who presumes to discuss Lorraine's career should first read the pertinent literature, as these writers obviously have not. One of the most important essays on Lorraine is Steve Sneyd, "Empress of the Stars: A Reassessment of Lilith Lorraine, Pioneering Fantasy Poetess," *Fantasy Commentator,* VII, No. 3, Spring, 1992. This reprints eleven samples of Lorraine's science fictional poetry from the pulps. Also, see Jane L. Donawerth, "Lilith Lorraine: Feminist Socialist Writer in the Pulps," *Science Fiction Studies,* No. 17, 1990.

41. See, for example, the interior illustrations of Eileen Hayes in *Other Worlds Science Stories,* March, 1950. That issue also carried a story by Alma Hill.

42. Frances M. Deegan, "Presenting the Author," *Mammoth Detective,* January, 1946. Deegan went on to write both detective and science fiction stories for the magazines Palmer edited.

43. *Scarlet Adventuress* was published by Associated Authors, Inc., owned by George Shade, from July, 1935 to either February or July, 1938. The title was changed to *Modern Adventuress* for four issues from March, 1937 to September, 1937, returning to *Scarlet Adventuress* with the December, 1937 issue (interior dated November). Unknown number of issues. Palmer's stories

were "Hot Lipstick," March, 1936 (featuring Fay Langdon), "Crimson Heart," September, 1936 (featuring Carla Romaunt), "The Cobra Strikes," November, 1936 (Carla Romaunt), "A Rose In Her Hair," January, 1937, (Carla Romaunt), and "Love and Politics," March, 1937, (Carla Romaunt).

Of the fifty-three gender-identifiable authors we know appeared in this magazine, seventeen were women. This is just under a third, approximately the same ratio of female members in the Science Fiction and Fantasy Writers of America in 1999. By far the most prolific contributor to the magazine was Thelma Ellis, with ten stories. Obviously, pulp adventure magazines were not entirely a male domain. Thanks to Doug Ellis, who compiled the index from which I derived this information.

44. Sam Moskowitz, "The Return of Hugo Gernsback, Part Three," *Fantasy Commentator*, X, Nos. 1 & 2, 2001–2002, pp. 119–20. Ackerman is hereby maligning his own client, since, according to his listing in the 1999 directory for the Science Fiction and Fantasy Writers of America, he is also the representative for the estate of Harry Bates. He should be expected to know that one of his clients published the other. The SFFWA Directory also lists him as the agent for the estates of L. Taylor Hanson, E. Mayne Hull, Amelia Reynolds Long, and Leslie F. Stone, so he should also be familiar with their publication records for the entire period under discussion.

45. Joanna Russ, "The Image of Women in Science Fiction," *Vertex*, 1, No. 6, (1971), (February) 1974, p. 55.

46. Margaret St. Clair, "Wight in Space: An Autobiographical Sketch," in Martin H. Greenberg, Ed., *Fantastic Lives: Autobiographical Essays by Notable Science Fiction Writers*, Southern Illinois University Press: Carbondale, Ill., 1981, p. 151.

47. Campbell published "Amazon Planet" serially in the December, 1966, January, 1967, and February, 1967 issues of *Analog*. Ace published it as a paperback under the same name in 1975. Russ praised the story in her classic feminist critique of the genre, *"Amor Vincit Foeminam:* The Battle of the Sexes Story in SF," *Science-Fiction Studies*, V. 7, #1, March, 1980, pp. 2–15.

48. Judith Merril, letter to Justine Larbalestier, November 16, 1996, quoted in Larbalestier, *The Battle of the Sexes in Science Fiction*, pp. 176–77.

49. The following information comes from a phone interview with Julian May by Eric Leif Davin, August 1, 2003.

50. When questioned, the only other female "Julian" that Julian May could think of was the medieval anchorite Dame Julian of Norwich, of whom Julian May only learned in a college English literature course. Other than Dame Julian (who is referred to as "Dame Julian" by scholars to indicate her gender) and Julian May, I know of no other females named "Julian."

51. Leslie F. Stone, "Day of the Pulps," p. 101.

52. C.f., the entry on *Analog* in Marshall B. Tymn and Mike Ashley, *Science Fiction, Fantasy, and Weird Fiction Magazines*, Greenwood Press: Westport, Conn., 1985, pp. 65, 71.

53. Isaac Asimov, "Introduction," in Isaac Asimov, Charles G. Waugh, & Martin Greenberg, Eds., *Science Fiction: Classic Stories from the Golden Age of Science Fiction*, Galahad Books: N.Y., 1989, p. 5.

54. See Ursula K. Le Guin, *The Wind's Twelve Quarters*, Bantam Books: N.Y., 1976, p. 23.

55. Sam Moskowitz, Ed., *Editor's Choice in Science Fiction*, The McBride Co.: N.Y., 1954, p. 129.

56. The following account comes from letters, Katherine MacLean to Eric Leif Davin, March 31, and April 10, 2001 and May 3, 2002.

57. Pohl, *The Way the Future Was*, p. 82.

58. See Tom Shippey, Ed., *The Oxford Book of Science Fiction Stories*, Oxford University Press: N.Y., 1992, p. xxiii, footnote 17.

59. A. Bertram Chandler in Perry A. Chapdelaine, Sr., Tony Chapdelaine, and George Hay, Eds., *The John W. Campbell Letters, Vol. 1*, AC Projects, Inc.: Franklin, Tenn., 1985, p. 25.

60. See Groff Conklin, Ed., *The Omnibus of Science Fiction*, Crown Publishers, Inc.: N.Y., 1952.

61. Letters, Katherine MacLean to Eric Leif Davin, March 31 and April 10, 2001.

62. Letter, MacLean to Davin, June 21, 2002.

63. Carol and Frederik Pohl, Eds., *Science Fiction: The Great Years, Volume II*, Ace Books: N.Y., 1976, p. 49. Emphasis added.

7

Anecdotes and Antidotes

A ND SUCH MYTHS DIE HARD. Even though science fiction editors were, as I have shown, clearly welcoming and supportive of women writers, a presumption of editorial prejudice lingered. Thus, when Alice Sheldon entered the field in 1968 with "Birth of a Salesman" in *Analog,* she did so as "James Tiptree, Jr." This was despite the fact that the editor she sent it to, John W. Campbell, had, by then, compiled a thirty-year track record of discovering and publishing female authors.

Sheldon kept up this subterfuge until her gender was accidentally revealed in 1977. Given the number of women who were being nominated for and winning Hugos by that time, it is difficult to believe there was any real need for such secrecy. Indeed, Andre Norton, another woman who published under a male pen name (which has also been frequently cited as another example of discrimination), explicitly said as much. Speaking in the 1970s she stated that, while there might have been a need for male pseudonyms earlier in the field, "This is not true today, of course."[1]

Nevertheless, some have pointed to Sheldon's subterfuge as evidence of science fiction's anti-female bias even into the 1970s.[2] And Sheldon believed the same. This was even though she said she was a constant reader of science fiction and fantasy magazines since 1924 when, at the age of nine, her uncle gave her a copy of *Weird Tales,* a magazine in which she had to have seen many female bylines. Although she claimed there were other reasons she chose a male pseudonym, nevertheless, "I stood ashamed before the women writers who had used their own female names in cracking the predominantly male world of science fiction. I had taken the easy path."

But was this "easy path" really necessary to "crack" into science fiction's "male world," something, presumably, no earlier women had done? Sheldon herself admitted that, "I can't honestly tell," because not only did all the first stories she submitted to Campbell sell—but "so did the next, and the next," and so on.[3] Indeed, her second story submission ("Fault," *Fantastic,* August, 1968) was to Harry Harrison, who also immediately accepted it, his acceptance letter arriving just one day before Campbell's first check. As Harrison had already publicly put his name on co-authored fiction with Katherine MacLean (see table 1), there was no more reason to use a male pseudonym in order to sell to Harrison than there was to sell to Campbell, who'd been publishing women since he took over the editorial reins at *Astounding.*

Here we come to another reason otherwise knowledgeable authorities have presumed the existence of a prejudice against early women science fiction writers: The unexamined assertions of a few prominent women writers (who, in the cases of Tiptree and Norton, made their professional debuts *after* our period), that they faced anti-female bias. These have been eagerly accepted at face value, without examination, because they seemed to prove the stereotypes people already wanted to believe. They simply reinforced preconceptions, thus embedding myth as "official" history.

It should be emphasized that *all* writers, regardless of gender, usually have a difficult time breaking into print. It's the nature of the game. The immediate success of MacLean and Tiptree is *not* the norm. When I spoke with Isaac Asimov about this he said, "The life of a writer in 99 percent of the cases for 99 percent of the time is nothing but the cruelest disappointment. If you can't take disappointment, then you'll never be a writer."[4]

And disappointment is exactly what Asimov endured at the beginning of his own, eventually prolific, career. "I submitted my first eight stories to Campbell and got rejected," he said. "[Campbell] took my ninth story, 'Trends.' He then rejected my next nine stories and took my nineteenth, 'Homo Sol.' After one or two more rejections (here I lose count), he took my first two positronic robots stories, 'Reason' and 'Liar!', and immediately afterward took 'Nightfall'; and after that, I sold everything I wrote, though not always to the first market to which it was submitted."[5]

Rejection, then, is at least the initial lot of virtually *every* writer. Having said that, did female writers face more than their fair share of rejection *because* they were women? For the first time, let us investigate some of the personal anecdotes which have been so influential in shaping the accepted mythology and see if they are indeed myth—or reality.

Andre Norton claimed that, "When I entered the [science fiction] field I was writing for boys, and since women were not welcomed, I chose a pen name which could be either masculine or feminine."[6] "I was a woman in a man's field," she continued. "There were only about four of us women and we either wrote under men's names or under our initials. We had to! This didn't make me resentful; I accepted it as part of the customs of the times. There was no women's liberation movement then."[7]

This claim has carried much weight and been widely cited. Dr. William Bainbridge, for example, repeated and relied upon the first quote to build his history of discrimination in early science fiction.[8] The Science Fiction Book Club told their many members the same thing, saying Norton "changed her name legally from 'Mary Alice' [sic] to 'Andre Alice' in 1934 to improve her chances in a male-dominated market."[9]

Marion Zimmer Bradley also echoed Norton when she stated that the reason Norton chose the name "Andre" was because when Norton entered the field, "the climate of writing science fiction in those days [was such that] female names were just, as the British say, 'not on' since the publishers of pulp science fiction, and the conventional wisdom thereof, held that women didn't read science fiction—women, in the conventional wisdom, being limited to the love pulps and the confession magazines."[10]

Likewise, Pamela Sargent asserted that, "Women . . . were . . . suffering some form of discrimination in science fiction."[11] Citing this same unsubstantiated Norton statement Sargent goes on to say, with no further evidence, "Andre Norton was restricted by publishers who wanted a male byline (or at least an androgynous one) on books which had male protagonists; in other words, she was limited by commercial considerations as well as by prevailing attitudes toward women."[12]

But was the assertion that "publishers wanted a male byline" really true when Norton entered the science fiction field? Interestingly, Norton's most recent account of her genre debut, published in 2003, makes no mention of any anti-female discrimination in the field at all. The only discrimination, if one could call it that, was against her specialty—novels. (Indeed, Norton only published *two* stories in the magazines before 1960, both in the early 1950s.) "In that era," she recalled, "the only market for speculative tales was short stories. Unfortunately, my pattern of thought has always made it difficult for me to compose brief tales; my efforts generally read like outlines for novels. So for the time being I kept to my familiar field of adventure, spy, or historical books."[13]

It seems we can rely on this being Norton's real reason for adopting a male pseudonym, as she told Charles Platt the same thing twenty years earlier, in 1983. "I've been writing since 1934," she told Platt. "But when I began writing, there was no market in America for book-length science fiction. It was strictly a short-story form, and I find it very hard to write short stories. I've only done about twelve in my whole career. So I started out writing in other fields. I had always preferred, myself, adventure stories. Talbot Mundy, Haggard, and that type of thing, so that is what I wrote, into the early 1950s."[14]

Likewise, she told Paul Walker in 1972 that she quit working as a librarian in the late 1940s due to her poor health. Then, "I was asked by World Publishing to edit some SF anthologies and so worked into the field. I had wanted to do this earlier but, since I found the writing of short stories almost impossible, I could not. There was very little market for books then."[15]

Thus, contrary to the impression the Science Fiction Book Club gave its members in 2002, the "male-dominated market" Norton entered in 1934 was not the science fiction market at all, but the "adventure, spy, [and] historical" book market. That year, at age 22, she published her debut novel, *The Prince Commands.* However, like her 1944–1954 World War II espionage trilogy, it was a mainstream adventure novel having absolutely nothing to do with science fiction. Her second book, *Ralestone Luck,* was actually the first she wrote, while still in high school. "These were mystery and adventure stories," she recalled. In 1944 she published a book on the Dutch anti-Nazi underground which was picked up by the Junior Literary Guild and did very well. "Thereafter," she said, "I brought out a book a year: historical or spy stories."[16] We can therefore say that Roger Schlobin got it right in his synopsis of Norton's career when he said, "Andre Norton's early intention was to write fiction for boys, and she changed her name to enter this male-dominated market."[17]

Thus, if Norton changed her name to deal with anti-female bias, it had absolutely nothing to do with the science fiction field, where she wasn't even writing stories for submission. It had to do with bias in those other literary fields, boys' historical and spy stories, where she first established her name and reputation. Andre Norton would not enter the science fiction field for almost another 20 years, long after she'd established herself as "Andre Norton." She entered science fiction *professionally* only in 1952 with her novel *Star Man's Son.* She did not publish in a professional science fiction magazine until the next year, 1953.

The 1950s, then, would be the period when Norton erroneously claimed, "There were only about four of us women and we either wrote under men's names or under our initials." This is complete fiction. In fact, there were 154 published women science fiction writers at that very time. Further, Norton was unique because she was the *only* one of those 154 women writers in the 1950s who published under a man's name!

There was even less reason for Andre Norton to use a male name when she made her *amateur* debut in the field in 1947. She did so under the name of "Andrew North," when *Fantasy Book* published her short story, "The People of the Crater," in its premiere issue. It later published her "The Gifts of Asti" in issue #3, 1948, also under the North byline. Norton later confessed that she didn't believe the story was good enough to actually be "marketable" and had never tried submitting it to a professional magazine, so her debut tells us nothing about professional science fiction publishing in the late 1940s.[18]

Even then, however, she did not really need a male byline to break into print. *Fantasy Book* was a well-produced fanzine self-published by Los Angeles fan William Crawford and his wife in the basement of their home. No sales were involved. Norton donated her stories to the couple, who were her friends. Crawford was excited to get the "Andrew North" story and trumpeted its publication. Indeed, he had been promoting it as "forthcoming" ever since he acquired it a dozen years before in 1935.[19]

Of course, being her friend, Crawford knew "North's" sexual identity. In addition, Crawford and his wife prided themselves on the fact that theirs was "a liberal magazine—with no 'thought police' guiding its destiny. Our main requirement for stories is that they should be different—capable of stimulating a new line of thought."[20] And, we are told, "*Fantasy Book*'s stories are conspicuously lacking in . . . sexual exploitation."[21]

That very first issue of *Fantasy Book* also carried a notice from Clare Winger Harris, from "one fan to another," announcing the publication of *Away From the Here and Now,* an anthology of eleven of her stories. She noted (p. 18), "The fan press has been very complimentary to my collection." A little further in the issue (p. 28) we find that Crawford himself was selling copies of Harris' anthology. Further, well-known science fiction author "Lilith Lorraine" edited a bylined poetry column, "Songs of the Spaceways," beginning in issue #3, 1948—the same issue which carried Norton's "Gifts of Asti" under her male byline. Finally, Crawford had already published Amelia Reynolds Long, under her own name, in the fourth issue of his earlier fanzine, *Marvel Tales,* in 1934.

There was no need, therefore, for Norton to conceal her gender identity in order to make even her amateur debut in the field. She would have been published regardless of what name she used—but she chose a male pseudonym because she had already been writing under a male name in the "adventure, spy [and] historical" fields. Likewise, Norton had to know of the other female science fiction writers whose names appeared in the fanzine carrying her science fiction debut—neither of whom, Clare Winger Harris or Lilith Lorraine, published under either male names or initials.

Just as we can give no credence to the distorted accounts of when and how Norton entered the science fiction field, neither can we give any credence to Norton's self-aggrandizing account of her influence on the field. Reinforcing the traditional exclusion narrative of the genre's bigoted past, in 2002 Norton claimed that her 1964 Witch World novel, *Ordeal in Otherwhere,* was responsible for "the opening of a gateway to the stars that had been closed to half the human race for far too long." This was because that novel featured a female protagonist and, "At the time [1964], it elicited dubious head-shakes from my editor, who held that 'space stories' had no appeal for female readers, and that male readers wanted any fictional woman to merely stand in the background and admire the hero as he wielded his laser against the bug-eyed monster that had been pursuing her." But her book sold well and, "it was good to be able to say 'I told you so' to the critics."[22]

Be that as it may, Andre Norton, in the mid-1960s, was not the first author to feature a female protagonist, even in the "hard" SF sub-field (although this Witch World novel is as much fantasy as it is science fiction). Nor did her novel open any "gateway to the stars" which had been "closed" to women heretofore. The gateway had never been closed! Norton's claims for both herself and the date for "When It Changed" are simply more spurious anecdotes which reinforce the accepted mythology of the field.

Another writer who contributed greatly to the creation and perpetuation of this myth was Marion Zimmer Bradley. "When I came into the field," she claimed, "it was expected that women would have to be about twice as good as men. . . . Most of us reveled in the thought that we'd made it against terrific odds, and took it as proof that we were at least twice as good as the men."[23]

What, exactly, were those "terrific odds" that Marion Zimmer Bradley "reveled" in beating when she came into the field?

To begin with, Bradley was immediately accepted by male fans when she discovered fandom in 1946. Indeed, it was a male fan who introduced her to her first fan gathering. "I took the train to New York City [she then lived in Albany], all by myself on the spur of the moment," she remembered, "called up a [male] fan I'd exchanged letters with, and he took me to a conference where a hundred fans . . . listened to a group of scientists talk about the possibility of man on the Moon before the year 2000 A.D."[24] Soon thereafter she became perhaps the age's most prolific writer of letters to the magazines under her then name of "Marion Zimmer." In fact, in 1948 Rog Phillips, in his fan column for *Amazing Stories*, termed her "undoubtedly [the] No. 1 feminine fan" in the nation.[25]

As the nation's "No. 1 feminine fan," Bradley had much support from male fans, who were eager to publish her novice fictional efforts in their own fanzines. One example was her story, "Outpost," which Arthur H. Rapp, of Saginaw, Michigan, published in the December, 1948 issue of his fanzine, *Spacewarp*—and which Rog Phillips, in the *Amazing Stories* column cited above, praised as a "very entertaining story."

Then, when she began publishing professionally, Bradley (like MacLean, Tiptree, and several other women writers) was luckier than most debuting science fiction writers, as her first two sales were published simultaneously. Both appeared in the second issue of *Vortex Science Fiction*, winter, 1953. *Vortex* was edited and published by Chester Whitehorn, a former editor at *Planet Stories*, where female author Leigh Brackett was the reigning writer. His stated goal was, as he said in the premier issue, to publish "more stories than any magazine of its kind." This meant 160 pages worth in each issue—even though skeptics claimed he'd never find enough good stories to fill 160 pages per issue on a regular basis. The first issue carried twenty stories. The second had twenty-five, including Bradley's. As a novice she had plenty of company, for in that issue nine of the authors were, like her, seeing their first publication. Given the context, it's hard to believe Bradley faced "terrific odds" in finding her way into print.

Nor did she fare poorly the next year, when she broke into *The Magazine of Fantasy & Science Fiction*. In the March issue, touting her upcoming story the next month, editor Anthony Boucher, known for favoring women writers, hailed Bradley as an "Outstanding Writer" that the magazine was "lucky" to get. This "novice," he said, "is Marion Zimmer Bradley, whose long novelet [sic], 'Centaurus Changeling,' is one of the solidest pieces of detailed true science fiction that we've seen in some time—a study in biological problems of the interstellar future which should establish Mrs. Bradley as a major new contender."[26]

In his editorial introduction to that story in the April issue, Boucher heaped even more glowing praise upon the new author. "Here, by a young writer, is a remarkably perceptive and detailed study," he said. It is a "moving story" with "fascinating details," all "sketched in with a sure hand." He ended by saying, "Perhaps the warmest recommendation we can make to you of Marion Bradley's first (and not last!) appearance in this magazine is to say that her story is, from beginning to end, completely and inarguably *science* fiction."[27]

The stories that would become Bradley's first books appeared in magazine form in 1957. These were "Falcons of Narabedla," in the May issue of *Other Worlds*, and "Bird of Prey" in *Venture*, published in book form in 1961 as *The Door Through Space*.

Other Worlds was owned and edited by Raymond A. Palmer, former editor at *Amazing Stories*, where he'd published the work of many women. Palmer claimed he was paying for everything out of his own pocket, saying he once dumped $40,000 into the magazine. Hence, as Mike Ashley points out, he "could not match [larger science fiction magazine] rates."[28] Even this might be too generous a statement, as Roger P. Graham told Norm Metcalf that he donated his stories to Palmer out of gratitude for affording him a good living in the 1940s, and with a promise of later payment if Palmer's cash flow improved. Meanwhile, in James V. Taurasi's fanzine, Palmer admitted that his circulation dropped from over 50,000 to around 12,000, meaning he had even less money to pay for stories.

Palmer therefore had difficulty finding writers. In an editorial response to a letter from reader George W. Earley in the September 1955, issue Palmer said, "we are begging stories from authors." So, he began publishing stories by novice writers, such as Marion Zimmer Bradley's "Falcons of Narabedla." As early as 1956 he accepted "The Sword of Aldones," Bradley's Hugo-nominated first novel in her famous Darkover series, but the magazine ceased using science fiction before he got it into print.

Meanwhile, *Venture* was founded as a companion to *The Magazine of Fantasy & Science Fiction*. It was edited by *Fantasy & Science Fiction* editor Robert

P. Mills and, as advisory editor, Anthony Boucher. In the new magazine they regularly published women writers, such as Judith Merril (as "Rose Sharon") and Leigh Brackett—as well as Bradley.

Thus, despite what Bradley claimed, she herself found very receptive editors in the 1950s and faced no "terrific odds" against women writers at all. In fact, though few choose to take notice of it, Bradley contradicted herself by admitting as much. "When the time came for me to start writing," she said, "I never met an editor who cared whether I was a man, a woman, a little girl, or a chimpanzee—as long as I could write the kind of story they wanted to read."[29] Indeed, "Everybody was very nice to me when I was starting out," she later confessed.[30]

And, as we have seen, others of these pioneering female science fiction authors experienced much the same receptivity throughout their careers. Therefore, in privileging individual testimony we must look at the record. We cannot uncritically accept personal anecdotes at face value, even from famous authors like Norton and Bradley, without checking their authenticity. Doing so has helped give us an "official history" of science fiction which is completely fictional. It has been readily accepted only because it reinforces the traditional exclusion narrative. However, the reality of Andre Norton's and Marion Zimmer Bradley's entrance into the science fiction field is one of inclusion, rather than exclusion. Once more, the neglected evidence contradicts the accepted myth.

Notes

1. Andre Norton interview in Paul Walker, *Speaking of Science Fiction*, p. 269. Originally in *LUNA Monthly 40,* 1972.
2. E.g., William H. Keith, Jr., a prolific author of military science-fiction paperbacks, speaking at Carnegie-Mellon University, Pittsburgh, March 28, 2001.
3. Alice Sheldon, "A Woman Writing Science Fiction and Fantasy," in Du Pont, Ed., *Women of Vision*, pp. 46, 51, 52.
4. Davin, "The Good Doctor at St. Vincent," p. 247.
5. Isaac Asimov, letter to the editor, *Future Science Fiction,* No. 31, winter, 1956–1957, p. 125. He seemed to have forgotten that his first positronic robot story was "Strange Playfellow" (*Super Science Stories,* September, 1940).
6. Norton, in Walker, p. 269.
7. Platt, *Dream Makers, Volume II,* p. 98.
8. See Bainbridge, p. 180.
9. Science Fiction Book Club monthly catalog, July, 2002, p. 9. Again, her name was "Alice Mary," not "Mary Alice." This mythology by the Science Fiction Book Club is a prime example of how the genre's mythological past is being continually presented, even now, to a great many novice readers as the "true bigoted history" of the field.
10. Marion Zimmer Bradley, "A Rather Prolific Hobbyist," *Andre Norton: Fables & Futures: Niekas, Science Fiction and Fantasy,* #40, 1989, p. 37.
11. Sargent, *More Women of Wonder,* p. xxxii.
12. Sargent, *More Women of Wonder.* fn 24, p. xlviii.

13. Andre Norton, Introduction to "People of the Crater," in Steven H. Silver and Martin H. Greenberg, Eds., *Magical Beginnings,* DAW Books: N.Y., 2003, p. 18.

14. Platt, *Dream Makers, Volume II,* p. 96.

15. Norton interview in Paul Walker, *Speaking of Science Fiction* pp. 266–267. The interview was conducted in January-February, 1972.

16. Norton interview in Paul Walker, *Speaking of Science Fiction* p. 266.

17. Roger C. Schlobin in Curtis C. Smith, Ed., *Twentieth-Century Science-Fiction Writers,* St. Martin's Press: N.Y., 1981, p. 402.

18. Norton, Introduction to "People of the Crater," p. 18.

19. As early as 1935 Crawford had planned to publish "People of the Crater" as a chapbook, although this never happened. See Sam Moskowitz, *The Immortal Storm: A History of Science Fiction Fandom,* Hyperion Press: Conn., 1974, 1988, p. 23.

20. "Introduction," *Fantasy Book,* Vol. 1, No. 1, July, 1947.

21. Marshall B. Tymn and Mike Ashley, *Science Fiction, Fantasy, and Weird Fiction Magazines,* Greenwood Press: Westport, Conn., 1985, p. 263.

22. Science Fiction Book Club monthly catalog, July, 2002, p. 9.

23. Bradley, "One Woman's Experience in Science Fiction," in Du Pont, *Women of Vision,* pp. 92–93.

24. Marion Zimmer Bradley, "My Trip Through Science Fiction," *Algol,* V. 5, No. 1 [winter], 1977–1978, p. 13.

25. Rog Phillips in "The Club House," *Amazing Stories,* May, 1949, p. 136. In that column, Phillips noted that he was writing the entries on December 31, 1948, so his comment about Bradley pertained to her status in 1948.

26. Anthony Boucher, "Two More Outstanding Writers!," *The Magazine of Fantasy & Science Fiction,* March, 1954, p. 127.

27. Anthony Boucher, editorial introduction to "Centaurus Changeling," *The Magazine of Fantasy & Science Fiction,* April, 1954, p. 85.

28. Mike Ashley, entry on *Other Worlds* in Tymn and Ashley, *Science Fiction, Fantasy, and Weird Fiction Magazines,* p. 461.

29. Bradley, "One Woman's Experience in Science Fiction," in Du Pont, p. 86.

30. Darrell Schweitzer, "Interview With Marion Zimmer Bradley," *Science Fiction Review,* February, 1992, p. 10.

8

Haven in a Heartless World

I T WAS 1926. A New York Jewish businessman with a passion for science was looking around for new entrepreneurial possibilities. He was already publishing a science magazine that discussed new inventions in the realm of radio and electronics. But he thought there might be a way to make science more popular with young people. One way to make it more interesting might be to combine science with fiction.

And so, in April of that year, he published the world's first magazine devoted to "science fiction," a phrase he later coined to describe the new genre of literature he was publishing. The magazine was *Amazing Stories* and the Jewish businessman was Hugo Gernsback. Because of these things, Gernsback would become known as "The Father of Science Fiction" and the person after whom the Hugo Awards, the "Oscars" of the science fiction field, are named.[1]

As Julius Schwartz later noted, "Most of the material in . . . [early issues of] *Amazing Stories* was reprinted from classic stories or from other less specialized magazines. Hardly anyone was writing science fiction at the time; the field was not lucrative enough."[2] Another reason "hardly anyone was writing science fiction at the time" was because it was a medium in the process of being invented, so there were very few practitioners of this new art form. It was also disdained as a vulgar and debased type of literature (if it could even be called that) by the reigning cultural arbiters. For all these reasons, this beleaguered literature did not attract the top magazine writers of the day. But for these same reasons it was wide open to anyone who wanted to participate. And many of those who did so were, like Hugo Gernsback himself, New York Jews.

It has commonly been asserted that pulp science fiction was a world characterized by rampant anti-Semitism. For instance, science fiction critic Janrae Frank, author Jean Stine, and long-time fan and genre legend Forrest J. Ackerman leveled this charge against the gigantic magazine publisher, Street and Smith, which owned *Astounding*, the leading science fiction magazine after 1933. Speaking of Street and Smith in the Thirties they said, "These conservative East Coast establishment gentlemen dictated that writers whose names were ethnic (*especially Jewish*) adopt Anglo-Saxon pseudonyms."³

This supposed anti-Semitism, in turn, bolstered the contention that pulp science fiction was *also* prejudiced against other "outsider" groups at the time, such as women. Proof of one prejudice is seen as automatic proof of others, as well, with no further evidence required. This, in fact, is the argument Pamela Sargent makes when she recounts the charge of anti-Semitism as illustrative of the kind of bias supposedly operating against women authors at the same time. "Women, *of course*," she tells us, "were not the only ones suffering some form of discrimination in science fiction." Sargent then repeats Jewish science fiction writer H. L. Gold's claim that, because of deep anti-Semitism at *Astounding* (owned by Street and Smith publishers) he was forced to use an Anglo-Saxon pseudonym in order to publish his first science fiction story, "Inflexure," in the October, 1934 issue of that magazine. "Nazism's anti-Semitism had spread all through the world," Sargent quoted Gold as saying, "and it permeated Street and Smith, so I knew better than to write under my own name." Having used Gold's unexamined allegation to tar science fiction publishers with the taint of anti-Semitism, Sargent then used this alleged institutional bias as evidence of a similar anti-female bias.⁴

Frederik Pohl went even further, putting three such areas of prejudice—race, gender, and religion—together into one all-purpose charge against John W. Campbell, Jr., the legendary editor of *Astounding*. Pohl termed Campbell a roaring and reactionary "bull dinosaur," saying of him, "I have no doubt that he was always a little embarrassed by people who didn't have the sense to be born white, male, and Protestant."⁵

Thus, as with women in early science fiction, the traditional exclusion narrative has also been applied to Jews. In this way it has been used to bolster the contention that pulp science fiction was a bastion of reaction and prejudice.

But, once more, a look at the evidence proves just the opposite. As with women, early science fiction's stance in regard to Jews was one of openness and receptivity. Therefore, also as with women, the field's acceptance of Jewish participation is further evidence of the validity of the contested terrain thesis regarding popular culture.

Let us examine both the allegations of anti-Semitism in pulp science fiction—and the evidence. As with the study of women in early science fiction, this examination will give us a better idea of the true nature of pulp science fiction. And, as the proponents of prejudice also believe, insight into the field's stance toward one "outsider" group will indeed also give us a better understanding of the field's stance toward some *other* "outsider" group, such as women.

As in so many other periods, America was not immune from anti-Semitism in the pulp era. While not as virulent as Europe's at the same time, it nevertheless found expression in many forms and places. Yale University, for just one example, had a "Jewish quota" on student admissions that existed up to the 1960s. It seemed natural, therefore, to assume that science fiction publishing also exhibited the same anti-Semitic bias found in so many other institutions. Because this was so easy to believe—it *has* been believed. But the charge, like that of prejudice against women, has never actually been investigated. Both were assumed to be too self-evident to need either investigation or proof.

For example, at a gathering of PARSEC, the Pittsburgh science fiction club, Jewish science fiction author Philip Klass (who writes science fiction under the name of "William Tenn") also pointed to Gold's claim of Street and Smith's opposition to "Jewish" names as evidence of anti-Semitism in the science fiction world of the 1930s. The members at this April 14, 2001 meeting readily accepted Klass' charge. When I questioned Klass for evidence, other than Gold's story, I encountered disdain and hoots of derision from the audience. The allegation was "obvious" and needed no proof.

Nevertheless, I asked for other examples. Klass then described his own mundane-world job-hunting difficulties because of his religion and an anti-Jewish hiring policy someone had told him about at Simon & Schuster. I noted to Klass and the meeting that neither of these pertained to the science fiction world and again asked for science fiction examples. My observation and request were met with further hostility by the members. The charge was too apparent to need such investigation—and the discussion moved on to other matters.

However, investigation, once initiated, shows that the reality of pulp science fiction was exactly the opposite of the accusations. For example, recall that Ackerman and his collaborators charged that the publisher of *Astounding* banned Jewish and other "ethnic" names from its pages. But upon examination we find that the contents pages of *Astounding* during the 1930s listed many stories by well-known Jewish writers under their "Jewish" names. These authors included Isaac Asimov, Stanley G. Weinbaum, Nathaniel Schachner, and H. L. Gold by the end of the Thirties—under his actual name, not the pseudonym he adopted earlier in the decade.

Also, while the names of other Jewish authors, such as Raymond Z. Gallun and Arthur Leo Zagat, may not have been obviously "Jewish," they were obviously "ethnic"—but that didn't stop Street and Smith from featuring them in *Astounding*. Meanwhile, also in the early 1930s, Jewish authors Allen Glasser and Mortimer Weisinger were appearing in *Amazing Stories*, while Weisinger also sold to Gernsback's *Wonder Stories*.

Likewise, an examination of the other allegations reveals that, far from being a stronghold of anti-Semitism, early science fiction was a haven for Jewish editors, publishers, and writers. Indeed, it was a field they essentially created and, in the early years, dominated. Thus, a close examination of the record reveals that pulp science fiction offered an open door for Jewish participation. Further, this participation also reinforces the interpretation of the field as another arena of popular culture's "contested terrain."

Let us begin such an investigation.

Certainly a diligent search can reveal anti-Semitic stereotypes in early proto-science fiction (especially the science fiction of Jules Verne and even H. G. Wells). However, early *magazine* science fiction was *not* an arena of widespread anti-Semitism or exclusion.

In this regard, science fiction was much like other forms of early twentieth-century American mass entertainment that were heavily influenced by Jewish artists and entrepreneurs. Much research by historians has revealed that American popular culture, in its myriad forms, was especially receptive to Jewish participation. Indeed, argues Dr. Stephen J. Whitfield, a professor of American Studies at Brandeis University, Jews and popular culture were heavily intertwined. "What's odd is that Jews and mass culture come to the United States at about the same time," he says. "Mass culture offered economic and cultural opportunities that were basically unavailable in the Old World. You can say the ethos of popular culture is democratic with a small 'd' in that you're judged on the basis of talent and not ancestry. It's more about what you can do . . . rather than who you are or your parents were or how far back your ancestors came to the United States."[6]

Thus, because of this "democratic ethos," Jews played major roles in shaping such new forms of American popular culture as films, radio, and television. In fact, the very first feature-length talking movie, *The Jazz Singer* (1927), centered on a Jewish family and its story derived from the life of its Jewish star, Al Jolson. Cultural historian Neal Gabler has extensively documented "How the Jews Invented Hollywood," in the process creating "An Empire of Their Own."[7] Since the nickelodeon era, the film industry had a strong Jewish presence, and most of the famous Hollywood moguls were at least cultural, if not religious, Jews. His account of the Jewish studio executives and producers, writers, actors, and talent agents who dominated the American film industry until shortly after World War II makes it clear that Jews were the moving forces behind the creation of this cultural industry. Many others have elaborated upon the same theme, detailing how Jews were "entertaining America" from the beginning of broadcast media.[8]

Of course, just because there were large numbers of Jews in pre-World War II Hollywood does not mean there was no anti-Semitism there. Negative stereotypes were often still portrayed in movies and it was almost a given that Jewish actors had to "Anglicize" their names for popular acceptance. Indeed, the Eastern European Jewish immigrants who created the American film industry and dominated it by the 1920s faced a cultural backlash due to that very dominance.[9] The story of Jews and the film industry is, therefore, an ambiguous one, a primary illustration of the "contested terrain" of popular culture.

The story appears to have been a bit more positive in the new print variants of popular culture. For instance, Arie Kaplan has illustrated how Jews were crucial to the creation of the comic book industry in the 1930s, at the same time Jews were coming to prominence in other areas of popular culture.[10]

Comic strips had been a feature of newspapers ever since Richard Felton Outcault launched the genre in the 1895 with "Down in Hogan's Alley." This comic was a series of single-frame color tableaus of city life appearing in Joseph Pulitzer's *New York World*. The central, unnamed, character wore a yellow nightshirt and so came to be known as "The Yellow Kid." Outcault later created Buster Brown, an even more popular character.

From the beginning, women, another outsider group, were a part of this phenomenon. For example, "In 1895, Rose O'Neill won a drawing contest in Nebraska which brought her to New York as America's first woman illustrator and soon to be creator of the famous, cute, innocent Kewpie. Other women followed and for years the pages of magazines like *Harper's Magazine* hired women artists. . . . By 1901, comic strips by women appeared in the Sunday newspapers and popular magazines of the day, mostly catering to other women."[11]

Also by 1901, the first proto-comic books were being published by the newspapers in which the original comics could be found. These books were reprints of Sunday color newspaper strips, usually published with cardboard covers and often as big as 11 × 16.5″, and looked nothing like later comic books. One of the first was a 1902 Hearst reissue of Rudolph Dirks's popular *The Katzenjammer Kids*.

Perhaps the next major step in this new genre's evolution was Winsor McCay's "Little Nemo in Slumberland" for the Hearst papers, which contained many fantastical elements as early as 1906. Hearst also reissued the "Little Nemo" Sunday strips as "hardcover" books, one in 1906, another in 1909. Also by 1906, however, the newspapers were facing competition from book publishers in the republication of newspaper comic strips in book form. For example, publisher Cupples & Leon produced more than a hundred different proto-comic books between 1906 and 1934, including such popular titles as "Buster Brown," "Little Nemo," "Smitty," and "Bringing Up Father."

By the second decade of the twentieth century, daily black and white strips were supplementing the Sunday color strips. One of the most popular was Bud Fisher's "Mutt & Jeff," which was first republished in book form in 1910. Two other popular strips were "Blondie," by Chic Young, and "Little Orphan Annie," by Harold Gray, which first appeared in 1924. (Although by the 1930s,

"Little Orphan Annie" was being drawn by Edwina Dumm, a pioneering female political cartoonist.) In January, 1929, "Tarzan of the Apes" began appearing as a daily strip drawn by Hal Foster, who also drew "Prince Valiant." Later in 1929 Grosset & Dunlap published *The Illustrated Tarzan Book*, the first Tarzan comic book, reprinting the first seventy-eight daily strips.

Women comic strip artists were a part of this growth in newspaper comics. "However," we are told, "many [female] comic strip artists were not housewives presenting a view of home and family. Being single, working for a living and looking for a husband added a new dimension to their work. In Colorado, a young illustrator, Nel Brinkley, was working for the *Denver Post* for $7 a week before coming to New York to work for the *Hearst Journal* where she created "The Brinkley Girls," a flapper fad which set the tone for the new independence influenced by Hollywood glamour and elegance. The Roaring Twenties ushered in images of beautiful women with fun loving spirits like "Flapper Fanny" and "Mopsey," who were designed by Gladys Parker. Independent Flapper female heroines touched the hearts of women across the country and these strips caught on enough to allow women artists to explore wit and humor in a new graphic context."[12]

Meanwhile, all of the proto-comic books produced heretofore simply featured reprints of newspaper comics. This included a reprint magazine, *Comic Monthly*, which appeared briefly in 1922 and sold for a dime. It was printed with a soft-paper cover, was 8.5 × 10", and appeared monthly. It therefore came closer to resembling a modern comic book than anything previously published. Each issue of *Comic Monthly* was devoted to reprinting a single comic strip and perhaps this limited its appeal, as it did not last long.

Then, in January, 1929, George Delacorte, owner of Dell Publishing Company, conceived the idea of producing a stand-alone magazine of original comics. The result was *The Funnies on Parade* #1, which actually looked more like a tabloid newspaper than a comic book. It sold on the newsstands every Sunday for a dime, where it competed with the popular and free Sunday comic supplements in the newspapers, so sales were poor. Delacorte reduced the price to a nickle with #25, but his "comic book" failed after issue #36.

It is unclear if Max Gaines (born Max Ginzberg) a Jewish salesman for Eastern Color Printing Company, ever knew of Delacorte's brief *The Funnies on Parade* or the existence of *Comic Monthly*. In any case, Gaines and Harry Wildenberg, a friend and an advertising salesman at the same company, had been experimenting with comics as advertising premiums. Eastern routinely printed the Sunday comics sections for many regional newspapers. Having the resources available, Wildenberg had printed a tabloid-sized reprint of comics and convinced Gulf Oil to give it away to customers at its gas stations. After producing a number of such premiums for other companies, Wildenberg eventually worked out a method for using his company's presses to print two reduced Sunday comic strip pages on a single standard-sized tabloid sheet. This was a crucial technical break through.

In 1933 Gaines suggested to Wildenberg that they publish a comic book of reprinted newspaper comics in a "new" book format, cheaper than the earlier "hardcover" and cardboard cover formats. It would be on cheap paper, have a soft-paper cover, and be smaller than tabloids as it would use the reduction method Wildenberg had worked out. Together they persuaded their employer, the Eastern Color Printing Company, to take a chance on the project. In February, 1934, under Gaines' supervision, Eastern printed 35,000 copies of *Famous Funnies* #1, Series 1, the first successful modern format comic book. Unlike *Comic Monthly*, which featured just one comic strip per issue, *Famous Funnies* reprinted several of the most popular newspaper comic strips of the day, such as "Joe Palooka" "Mutt & Jeff," and "Tailspin Tommy." Gaines convinced Eastern customers Procter & Gamble, Kinney Shoes, Canada Dry, and similar customers to give the comic book away as a free premium. The books disappeared quickly.

Encouraged, Gaines and Eastern Color Printing followed up in May, 1934, with *Famous Funnies* #1, Series 2. This issue also proved popular with the public, so the experiment continued. Subsequent issues had print runs of anywhere from 100,000 to a million copies. Realizing they had discovered a lucrative new market, Gaines and Wildenberg decided to stop producing it as a free premium and sell the book directly to kids. They approached magazine distributor American News Company to put it on newsstands across America at a dime a copy. The first dime issue sold over 180,000 copies. Eastern lost money on that initial issue, but was soon bringing in a profit of $30,000 a month—and a new popular culture industry was under way. By 1939 *Famous Funnies* was selling 400,000 copies a month.

Science fiction first appeared in this new format in October, 1934, when the third issue of *Famous Funnies* began reprinting the popular Sunday "Buck Rogers" strips from 1933. "Buck Rogers" had originally appeared in Philip Francis Nowlan's "Armageddon 2419 A. D.," a story in Hugo Gernsback's *Amazing Stories*, August, 1928. Thus, the two popular culture genres were closely entwined almost from the beginning.

In late 1934 Max Gaines parted company with Eastern Color Printing. Instead, he negotiated a deal with the McClure Newspaper Syndicate to use a pair of idle two-color presses to print rival comic books, using Wildenberg's method. George Delacorte soon approached him to publish a new comic book, to be called *Popular Comics*, technically owned by Dell Publishing, but splitting the profits 50–50 with Gaines. Like *Famous Funnies*, it consisted of reprinted newspaper strips.

It proved successful and Gaines brought aboard a teenage Jewish cartoonist, Sheldon Mayer, in January, 1936, as his assistant. In the summer of 1936, Gaines and Mayer began producing a second comic book for Dell, called simply *The*

Funnies. In March, 1937, the Gaines and Mayer team began publishing yet a third comic book for Dell, also with a simple title: *The Comics*. It was a mixed bag of newspaper reprints and original comics, which Mayer had already begun including in *The Funnies* with his own comic strip, "Scribbly." Again, science fiction was part of the mix, with Paul Jepson's "Rod Rian of the Sky Police" being one of the comics.

Imitators were already appearing, such as 1934's *Comic Cuts* (which featured new material). In 1936 United Feature Syndicate, owned by Scripps-Howard, introduced *Tip Top Comics* and the King Features Syndicate brought out *King Comics*. The latter was edited by Ruth Plumly Thompson, who, from 1921 to 1939, also wrote a book a year in the Wizard of Oz series. In addition to editing the comic book, Thompson also wrote short filler stories and poems about the adventures of a teenage girl. Both stories and poems were illustrated by Marge Buell, who later created "Little Lulu."

Comic books soon became the fastest growing periodical medium in the country. By 1941, "thirty comic book publishers were producing 150 different titles monthly, with combined sales of 15 million copies and a youth readership of 60 million, making the emerging comic book industry one of the few commercial bright spots of the Great Depression."[13] By 1947 over 60 million comic books were being sold each month.

Nor were these comic books composed of merely superficial stories. They covered a wider literary spectrum than commonly assumed. For example, in 1941 Russian Jewish immigrant Albert Kanter launched the long-lived and influential *Classics Illustrated* line of comic books. Kanter's comics successfully introduced millions of American kids to the masterpieces of classic literature up until 1971. Originally entitled *Classic Comics,* Kanter changed its name to the more well-known title in 1947 and sold more than 200 million copies of 169 titles in the United States alone.

Meanwhile, in February, 1935, National Allied Publications (soon to become National Periodicals, then Detective Comics, Inc., then DC Comics) had launched *New Fun Comics*. In a departure from the reprint pattern, it tested the waters with original strips featuring original characters. And, in addition to original characters, it supplemented the routine comedy strips with something else new, adventure strips like "Sandra of the Secret Service." Issue number one also featured Adolphe Barreaux's "The Magic Crystal of History," in which the fore-named crystal transported two boys back through time to participate in historic events. The strip was a regular feature which, by issue #12, changed the crystal from a time machine used to visit the past to a time viewer used only to view the past.

The first three issues also carried the adventures of "Don Drake on the Planet Saro," a blatant imitation of the popular "Flash Gordon" strip which had debuted in the newspapers the previous year (which, in turn, was an imitation of "Buck Rogers"). Later in the year, *New Fun* featured another science fiction series, "2023/Super Police." Both these strips were drawn by Clemens Gretter.

In October, 1935, *New Fun* #6 witnessed the appearance of "Doctor Occult," a "ghost detective" who fought ghosts, vampires, and wizards on a monthly basis. He was the creation of two Jewish teenagers from Cleveland, Jerome ("Jerry") Siegel, the writer, and Joseph ("Joe") Shuster, the artist. Siegel and Shuster were avid readers of the new science fiction magazines and in October, 1932, while still in high school, had launched *Science Fiction*, perhaps the second SF fanzine ever to be created. In a 1933 issue of their fanzine, which appeared as Adolf Hitler was coming to power in Germany, Siegel said he "was at present working upon a scientific fiction cartoon strip with an artist of great renown." That artist was J. Allen St. John, a famous pulp illustrator, and the strip would eventually become the legendary comic "Superman."[14]

First, however, Siegel and Shuster tried out their "scientific fiction" creation with "Doctor Occult." For three issues, beginning in October, 1936, with issue #14 of *New Fun* (now called *More Fun Comics*), Siegel and Shuster dressed Doctor Occult (who usually wore a trenchcoat and a fedora) in blue tights and a red cape and temporarily endowed him with such powers as flight and super strength. It was the first professional appearance of "Superman," though he wasn't called that just yet.

Jewish comic book historian and pioneer cartoonist Will Eisner (1917–2005) (creator of *The Spirit*, as well as the first modern graphic novel) saw Siegel and Shuster's "Superman" as a direct "mythic descendant of the Golem and thus a link in the chain of Jewish tradition." The Golem was the artificial human of inhuman strength which, according to legend, was created to protect the Jews of medieval Prague from persecution. In the 1930s, said Eisner (after whom the comic industry's prestigious Eisner Award has been named), "[Jews needed] a hero who could protect us against an almost invincible force. So [Siegel and Shuster] created an invincible hero," a child survivor sent to Earth, like Moses in the bullrushes, from his about-to-be destroyed homeland, Krypton, where his birth name had been "Kal-El," Hebrew for "All that is God."[15]

In 1937 Sheldon Mayer told his boss Max Gaines (who was now also the DC Comics print broker), about the "Superman" character that Siegel and Shuster were developing. Mayer assured Gaines it would be "the next big thing" in comic books. Gaines was convinced and the four of them—Mayer, Gaines, Siegel, and Shuster—quickly cut and pasted "Superman" strips into a dummy comic book. Gaines then took the dummy book to his friend Harry Donenfeld, a printer who, with his accountant and partner Jack Liebowitz, now owned DC Comics. Gaines convinced Donenfeld to take a chance on "Superman." Donenfeld decided to make the character the hero of *Action Comics* #1, a new comic book he launched in June, 1938. That first issue also introduced Superman's alter ego, Clark Kent, and would-be love interest Lois Lane—the name of an actual *Weird Tales* author Siegel and Shuster appropriated. Superman was an immediate hit and in May 1939, the new superhero took off on his own in *Superman Quarterly Magazine.* The next year, in 1940, the Superman comic book sold 1,250,000 copies and grossed almost one million dollars.

The rest, as they say, is history. The "Golden Age" of comic books was thus launched and new comic books and new superheroes with names like "The Batman," "The Blue Beetle," "The Human Torch," "The Green Arrow," and "Sub-Mariner" proliferated. In *More Fun* #52, February, 1940, DC introduced the Spectre, written by Jerry Siegel. Sheldon Mayer and Max Gaines, meanwhile, produced a number of different comics for DC, including those featuring "The Flash" and, in 1942, "Wonder Woman." Mayer also created *All Star Comics* for DC, which introduced the Justice Society of America, a teaming of The Flash, the Green Lantern, Hawkman, the Spectre, Sandman, the Atom, and Hour-Man. In addition, Mayer oversaw *The Green Lantern,* where he hired famed science fiction author Alfred Bester as one of his writers. One of the most famous of the new superheroes would eventually be "The Spider-man," co-created by Jewish Marvel Comics editor Stan Lee (born Stanley Lieber).

In the early 1940s Jewish pulp publisher Aaron A. Wyn joined the fray with such comics as *Super Mystery Comics, Lightning Comics, Secret Agent X, Ace Sports, Flying Aces,* and *Ten Detective Aces.* Even more successful, however, were Jewish pulp publishers John Goldwater and Louis Silberkleit (publisher of a string of low-budget science fiction magazines). Near the end of 1939 they launched MLJ Magazines, which produced such titles as *Pep Comics, Top-Notch Comics, Zip Comics,* and *Blue Ribbon Comics,* for which female cartoonist Ramone Patenaude drew "The Green Falcon." Their *Pep Comics* #1, January, 1940, featured "The Shield," the first of what Ron Goulart termed the war-time "superpatriotic" heroes.[16] His American flag motif costume became the prototype of costumes later made more famous by characters like "Captain America," created by "The King of Comics," Jewish cartoonist Jack Kirby (born Jacob Kurtzberg). The Shield routinely either smashed Nazi villains or rescued innocents from Nazi terror.

By 1944 these partners were selling over two million copies a month of their combined titles. However, they became even more successful with their creation of "Archie," who made his first appearance in *Pep Comics* #22. By 1942 Archie and his whole gang of blonde girlfriend Betty, dark-haired Veronica, and pal Jughead had their own comic book. This gang of friends went on to become the archetypal 1950s teenagers.

Publishers who could not afford in-house staffs often contracted with the Eisner-Iger Studio for packaged comics. Nineteen-year-old Will Eisner had published his first comic strip in 1936 in an obscure publication called, *Wow, What a Magazine!* It was edited by another Jewish cartoonist, Samuel ("Jerry") Iger. In 1937, after the demise of *Wow,* Eisner and Iger founded their studio where they employed a crew of mostly Jewish artists who could do everything needed to create a comic book to order—write, draw, letter, color, edit, and design the overall book. Thus, for example, the Eisner-Iger Studio created *Wings Comics, Jungle Comics,* and *Planet Comics* for Fiction House.

In 1938 Eisner and Iger created *Jumbo Comics* for themselves, which introduced "Sheena, Queen of the Jungle," a blonde female Tarzan. Meanwhile, their employees comprised a Who's Who of soon-to-be-famous comic book creators and artists. Among the young Jewish artists they employed were future "Captain America," "Fantastic Four," "Thor," "The Hulk," and "X-Men" creator and/ or co-creator Jack Kirby and "Batman" co-creator Bob Kane (born Robert Kahn). Two other Jewish employees were Al Jaffee and Dave Berg, who went on to comic book fame at *MAD* magazine, where they joined renowned Jewish cartoonist Harvey Kurtzman.

In 1962 Harvey Kurtzman co-created and then drew the long-running "Little Annie Fannie" comic character for *Playboy,* but he was best-known for his work in *MAD.* That magazine was owned by Jewish publisher Bill Gaines, the son of Max Gaines, one of the original creators of the comic book genre. Indeed, *MAD* had begun life as one of Max Gaines's EC Comics in 1952. EC Comics was the last line of comics published by Max Gaines and they gained notoriety in the 1950s for such gory publications as *Tales from the Crypt, The Vault of Horror* and *The Haunt of Fear,* as well as the legendary science fiction titles *Weird Science* and *Weird Fantasy.*

None of these developments had been lost on the science fiction community, which was also populated by many Jewish fans and writers, such as Mort Weisinger. Thus, when Weisinger took over as editor at *Thrilling Wonder Stories* with the August, 1936 issue, he introduced a science fiction comic strip to the magazine called "Zarnak." It lasted for eight issues, a little more than a year. The Jewish artist for "Zarnak" was Max Plaisted, who also drew for the new *Startling Comics* and who helped launch the "The Space Rovers" series in *Exciting Comics* (May, 1940). Both of these comics, as well as *Thrilling Comics,* were owned by Weisinger's Jewish publisher, Ned Pines.

Ned Pines had gotten into comic books by way of pulp magazines. In 1931 a distributor had asked Pines to publish a line of dime pulps in all genres. So, with the aid of his Jewish editorial director, Leo Margulies, he founded Better Publications. These featured magazines with "Thrilling" in the title: *Thrilling Mystery, Thrilling Love Stories, Thrilling Detective, Thrilling Western.* When Pines purchased *Wonder Stories* from Hugo Gernsback, it joined the line-up as *Thrilling Wonder Stories.* And when Pines branched out into the new field of comic books, they carried similar titles: *Thrilling Comics, Exciting Comics,* and *Startling Comics.*

In 1941 Mort Weisinger left the editorship of *Thrilling Wonder Stories, Startling Stories,* and *Captain Future,* all owned by Ned Pines, to work at *Superman,* published by DC Comics. In 1944 he was joined by his Jewish boyhood friend and fanzine partner Julius Schwartz, who was interviewed and hired by Max Gaines's former partner, Sheldon Mayer.[17] At DC Comics Schwartz helped create the *Batman* villain, "The Riddler." He was also responsible for premiering and editing many new comic books, including the August-September, 1950 *Strange Adventures*, the field's third all-science fiction comic. In August-September, 1951, he launched *Mystery in Space*, the fourth all-science fiction comic.

Meanwhile, comics continued to appear in the science fiction magazines. Such was the case with the 1950 pulp, *Out of This World Adventures*, overseen by Jewish editor Donald Wollheim. The thirty-two-page folio of comics in this short-lived magazine was actually conceived as a separate magazine inserted in every issue. In the first issue of the magazine, July, 1950, Wollheim claimed that the comic folio was "an innovation in the realm of science-fiction. It combines the modern techniques of the full-color pictorial story with the best of the established fiction-magazine presentation, to achieve a new effect in fantasy." Wollheim had been a leader of the Futurians fan club in the Thirties. No surprise, therefore, that he turned to his old Futurian comrade John Michel for contributions. Thus, Michel wrote the lead comic story in each issue.

This was all part of a huge crossover between writers, artists, and publishers in the comic book world and science fiction magazines. For example, noted science fiction magazine cover artist Alex Schomburg not only painted many covers for the Pines-Margulies magazine group, but was also a prolific comic book artist. From the late 1930s to the late 1940s he painted over 500 comic book covers. He didn't entirely leave comics until the 1950s, after which he continued painting covers for such leading SF magazines as *Fantastic Universe*, *Amazing Stories*, and *Isaac Asimov's*. As another example, *Marvel Comics*, which continues to be a major player in the comic book field to this day as a publisher, was launched in October, 1939, by Martin Goodman, publisher of the science fiction magazine, *Marvel Science Stories*. The first issue of the comic book featured a cover by famed science fiction magazine artist Frank R. Paul.

This crossover could also be seen in the activities of the publisher with whom Frank Paul was most closely associated, Jewish science fiction magazine pioneer Hugo Gernsback. Even in late 1939, despite the dozens of science fiction strips in the comic books, there was not yet a comic book devoted entirely to science fiction. Sensing an entrepreneurial possibility, Gernsback decided to enter the new field. He commissioned Paul to do the artwork for *Superworld Comics,* his projected comic book, and recruited Charles D. Hornig, who had been his editor at *Wonder Stories*, as editor.

Gernsback planned to launch this first all-science fiction comic book in April, 1940. Unfortunately, Fiction House beat him out of the gate with *Planet Comics*, produced by the Eisner-Iger Studio, which appeared in January, 1940. The first two science fiction comic books, therefore (like the third and fourth), were both

Jewish creations. However, Gernsback's *Superworld Comics* lasted only three issues. Although Gernsback scheduled issues four and five for publication, poor sales forced him to cease publication with his August, 1940 issue. Meanwhile, *Planet Stories* continued until the winter of 1953.

The career of Jewish businessman Sol Cohen also illustrates the close intersection of comics and science fiction magazines. Sol Cohen began working at DC Comics in 1938, becoming the company's business manager. He followed Max Gaines to EC Comics to also become business manager and circulation director there. Following Max Gaines's death in a boating accident, Cohen managed EC Comics until the reins could be handed over to Max's son, Bill Gaines. Cohen then moved on to Avon Books which, during his tenure, briefly experimented with the idea of comics inserted inside a pulp SF magazine. This was the Donald Wollheim-edited *Out of This World Adventures* in 1950, previously discussed, published by Avon. While at Avon Cohen was also the credited editor of *Avon Science Fiction and Fantasy Reader,* a short-lived quarterly launched in 1953.

Cohen left Avon to become the publisher of both *Galaxy* and *If,* two of the most notable science fiction magazines of the Fifties. In 1963 he conceived the idea of launching the Fred Pohl-edited *Worlds of Tomorrow,* the first new SF magazine since 1958. Finally, in 1965, he purchased Gernsback's venerated *Amazing Stories,* along with its companion, *Fantastic Stories.* He published both until 1979. Then Sol Cohen, who had begun his career forty years before in 1938 at DC Comics, sold them and retired from the science fiction world to Florida.

What was it about the world of comic books that attracted so many Jewish artists, writers, and even businessmen, such as Sol Cohen, Ned Pines, Leo Margulies, and Hugo Gernsback? Primarily, it was the fact that this new popular culture medium actually welcomed them. "We couldn't get into newspaper strips or advertising," explained Al Jaffee, who worked at the Eisner-Iger Studio. "Ad agencies wouldn't hire a Jew. One of the reasons we Jews drifted into the comic book business is that most of the comic book publishers were Jewish. So, there was no discrimination there." "Also," added Will Eisner, "this business was brand new. It was the bottom of the social ladder, and it was wide open to anybody. Consequently, the Jewish boys who were trying to get into the field of illustration found it very easy to come aboard."[18]

Both of these aspects were also true of the closely associated and also new popular culture medium of science fiction magazines. As with the comic book industry, science fiction in the 1930s was a popular culture field at "the bottom of the social ladder." Thus, by its very nature, it was also "wide open to anybody." Just as most comic book publishers, such as Albert Kanter and Max Gaines, Ned Pines and Leo Margulies, were Jewish, and just as Jewish artists and writers dominated the comic book field, one could also argue that Jews likewise created and dominated early magazine science fiction, as well as early science fiction fandom. This Jewish dominance of pulp science fiction helped to create a prevailing ethos in the field of tolerance and acceptance for all mainstream outsiders.

Let us now look more closely at this other new world of popular culture and Jewish participation in it.

Early science fiction fandom was overwhelmingly Jewish. Indeed, observed Frederik Pohl, "most of the science-fiction fans and writers I grew up with were Jews."[19] For example, the world's very first science fiction fan club, the Scienceers, launched in New York City in either 1929 or 1930, was composed mostly of Jewish teenagers like Mort Weisinger, Allen (Aaron) Glasser, and (joining in 1931) Julius Schwartz, all of whom would later become professionals in the field.[20] Some of the thirteen members who did not go on to professional status included Jewish fans Isidore Manson, Arthur J. Berkowitz, Lester Blum, Leo Schubert, and Philip Rosenblatt.[21]

Two members of this club, Mort Weisinger and Julius Schwartz, soon launched the world's first science fiction fanzine, *The Time Traveller* (January, 1932), edited by Allen Glasser. The first issue, comprised of only six mimeographed pages, carried the first installment of a history of science fiction. "What we did not realize at the time," Schwartz later recalled, "was that its history was actually about to begin."[22]

In fact, the history of science fiction *was* beginning with Jewish kids such as these. In October, 1932, two Jewish high school kids in Cleveland, Jerry Siegel and Joe Shuster, the creators of "Superman," produced perhaps the world's second SF fanzine, *Science Fiction.* Two years later, in 1934, Schwartz and Weisinger, still in their teens, founded Solar Sales Service, the world's first literary agency specializing in science fiction. Within a short time they were representing many of the established professionals in the field, including Stanley G. Weinbaum, Henry Kuttner, Robert Bloch, Alfred Bester, Eric Frank Russell, Leigh Brackett, H. P. Lovecraft, Edmond Hamilton, Otto Binder, Manley Wade Wellman, John Russell Fearn, and Dr. David H. Keller, as well as a new writer they discovered, Ray Bradbury.

Later fan clubs, largely of New York City provenance like the Scienceers, were also heavily Jewish. Damon Knight, for instance, claimed that he and Robert "Doc" Lowndes were the only two non-Jewish "core members" of The Futurians, the most famous New York fan club, founded in 1937.[23] (At the very least he should have also included founding member and lapsed Protestant Frederik Pohl among the "goyim." However, he was no doubt right in principle.) Many of the Jewish Futurians (like Isaac Asimov, Donald Wollheim, and Cyril Kornbluth) went on to become writers, editors, or publishers in the field.

Sam Moskowitz, a leader of New Fandom, another major science fiction club and rival to the Futurians, was also Jewish. And it was primarily Moskowitz, helped by other Jewish fans like Julius Schwartz, who organized the First World Science Fiction Convention in 1939.

And, what was true of early fandom was also true of early science fiction publishing, beginning with the very first Jewish science fiction magazine editor and publisher, Hugo Gernsback. In 1929, when Gernsback lost control of *Amazing,* the world's first science fiction magazine, he rebounded that same year by founding the world's *second* science fiction magazine, *Science Wonder Stories.* As his managing editor he hired a recent Jewish M.I.T. graduate, David Lasser, making Lasser the world's second Jewish science fiction magazine editor.

After twelve issues, the magazine became simply *Wonder Stories* and, in 1936, Gernsback sold it to *another* Jewish publisher, Ned Pines. Pines changed the name of the magazine to *Thrilling Wonder Stories* and hired Mort Weisinger as *his* editor, making Weisinger the world's *third* Jewish magazine editor. And so it went.

Indeed, a list of Jewish science fiction and fantasy magazine publishers of the Twenties, Thirties, and Forties would include Jacob Hennenberger, who launched *Weird Tales,* the world's first all-fantasy magazine, in 1923; Hugo Gernsback, who launched *Amazing Stories,* the world's first science fiction magazine in 1926 and, in 1929, *Wonder Stories* and who dominated science fiction publishing between 1926–1933; Ned Pines, publisher of *Thrilling Wonder Stories, Startling Stories, Captain Future, Fantastic Story Magazine,* and *Strange Stories;* Louis Silberkleit, publisher of *Science Fiction, Future Fiction, Dynamic Science Fiction,* and *Science Fiction Quarterly;* and Bernard Ziff, publisher of *Amazing Stories* from 1938 and *Fantastic Adventures* from 1939.[24]

It is for reasons such as this that science fiction author Robert Silverberg (Jewish himself) asserts that, "A better case could be made for Jewish *domination* of American s-f publishing than for any sort of anti-Semitism in it. . . . By the time I came along [in the mid-1950s], the three most important magazine editors were Horace Gold (Jewish), John Campbell (who began buying my work immediately) and Anthony Boucher (a Catholic of ultra-liberal social ideals). The stories they rejected I sold to magazines published by [Jewish publishers and editors] Irwin Stein (*Infinity*), Louis Silberkleit (*Science Fiction Stories*) and Leo Margulies (*Fantastic Universe*). Most of my early novels were bought by Ace Books' Donald Wollheim [Jewish]. And so on."[25]

How is it, then, that history has come to condemn early science fiction—like comics, almost a Jewish invention—for being dominated by a reputed anti-Semitic bias?

Some of the blame can be attributed to the claims of a few Jewish science fiction writers who have proven themselves largely ignorant of their Jewish predecessors. One of these is Jewish author Philip Klass, who made his science fiction debut in 1946 under the pseudonym "William Tenn." Klass was the featured speaker at the April 14, 2001 meeting of PARSEC, the Pittsburgh science fiction club. There he claimed that, because of anti-Semitism in the field, there was no Jewish science fiction magazine editor until Horace L. Gold was hired at *Galaxy* in 1950.

Logically, of course, this doesn't make sense, as absence alone does not prove bias. One has to actually produce evidence (not the lack of evidence) to prove a charge. But, there is a more important reason Klass is completely wrong in his allegation. This is because, as I have already pointed out, *the first Jewish science fiction editor was Hugo Gernsback, the "Father of Science Fiction."* Gernsback became the first Jewish science fiction magazine editor when he launched *Amazing*, the world's first science fiction magazine, in April, 1926.

And, in June, 1929, Gernsback hired Jewish M.I.T. graduate David Lasser to edit his next major venture in science fiction magazines, *Science Wonder Stories*. Lasser edited *Wonder Stories* until October, 1933, and it was arguably the major SF magazine of the early Thirties. Thus, from its inception through the early 1930s, *magazine science fiction was completely dominated by Jewish editors and publishers.* In 1936 Gernsback sold *Wonder Stories* to Jewish publisher Ned Pines. Pines renamed it *Thrilling Wonder Stories* and installed a Jewish editor, Mort Weisinger. In turn, Weisinger hired a Jewish assistant, Horace L. Gold.

However, it seems that Gold, like Klass, knew very little about his Jewish predecessors. In a conversation, he told me that he'd never heard of David Lasser, who, merely three years before, edited the very magazine that employed him.[26]

But, while Gold claimed to be ignorant of David Lasser, he could not have forgotten his boss, Mort Weisinger, who preceded him among Jewish SF editors. Besides becoming the first editor of Ned Pines's *Thrilling Wonder Stories* in 1936, Weisinger was also Pines's founding editor of *Startling Stories* in 1938, as well as Pines's editor of *Captain Future*. And on all of these magazines he was assisted by Horace L. Gold.

Philip Klass, of course, also forgot about Gernsback, Lasser, and Weisinger (unfortunate in someone who taught science fiction history for decades at Pennsylvania State University). He also overlooked Weisinger's Jewish supervisor at Ned Pines's Standard Magazines, Leo Margulies, who later became publisher of *Fantastic Universe*, *Satellite Science Fiction*, and *Weird Tales*. As editorial director of more than a dozen magazines for Ned Pines, Margulies sometimes made the editorial decisions on what was purchased. For example, it was Margulies who wrote literary agent Julius Schwartz on February 28, 1936, accepting client Stanley G. Weinbaum's "The Circle of Zero" for *Thrilling Wonder Stories*. Everyone involved in this transaction—publisher, editor, agent, and author—was Jewish.

But, perhaps most interesting of all, Philip Klass forgot about Donald A. Wollheim, one of the Jewish kids who founded the Futurians and who went on to become one of the most influential editors in the field.

In 1941 Wollheim became editor of not one, but two science fiction magazines, *Cosmic Stories* and *Stirring Science Stories*. In 1943 he edited *The Pocket*

Book of Science Fiction, the first reprint anthology to offer science fiction to a mass book market. In 1945 he followed up with another important reprint anthology, this time from Viking, *Portable Novels of Science*.

Then, from 1947–1952 he edited eighteen paperback installments of the *Avon Fantasy Reader*, as well as three volumes of the *Avon Science Fiction Reader*, both of which are treated as magazines by John Clute and Peter Nicholls in their encyclopedia. Marshall B. Tymn and Mike Ashley, in their comprehensive survey of the field, also considered both to be magazines, with contributor Thomas D. Clareson giving the rationale: "At the time," he explained, speaking of the *Avon Fantasy Reader*, "paperback anthologies, let alone regular series, were rarities, and by reader reaction the series came to be regarded as a magazine."[27]

In 1950 Joseph Meyers, the publisher of Avon Books (the first competitor of Pocket Book) asked Wollheim, his executive editor, to edit the short-lived (only two issues) interplanetary adventure magazine, *Out of This World Adventures*. The first issue came out in July, 1950, preceding Gold's *Galaxy*, which appeared three months later with its October debut issue. One of the stories in Wollheim's magazine issue was "The Puzzle of Priipiirii" by none other than "William Tenn," aka Philip Klass. Since it was his first issue, no doubt Wollheim had solicited the story from Klass.

But, the previous year, Meyers had asked Wollheim to edit an earlier science fiction magazine he intended to launch. Wollheim purchased six stories for the magazine's debut—which failed to materialize for financial reasons. Wollheim was reluctant to waste good original material. Therefore, he persuaded Meyers to release the stories that year in what some claim to be the first science fiction anthology of original stories. This was 1949's *The Girl with the Hungry Eyes*, the title taken from the lead story by Fritz Leiber.

One of the other stories Wollheim published in that would-be magazine and pathbreaking anthology was "Venus and the Seven Sexes"—by none other than "William Tenn," aka Philip Klass. Indeed, Wollheim even splashed the title of Klass's story on the cover of the book. Wollheim, it seems, liked stories by Klass, a novice writer at the time, and made an effort to promote his early career in multiple venues. How unfortunate that Klass seems to have forgotten his patron.

Now let us turn to Horace Gold's allegation, cited by Pamela Sargent, that he was forced to conceal his Jewish identity—or at least his name—because of anti-Semitism in the field. This is part of the larger charge of anti-Semitism leveled not only at *Astounding*, but at that magazine's editor, John W. Campbell, Jr. Campbell, in turn, is used as but the foremost example of the anti-Semitism which supposedly permeated early science fiction. These charges against *Astounding* and, especially, Campbell deserve close evaluation because of Campbell's decisive influence as perhaps the greatest science fiction editor the field ever produced. For many years his magazine was the field's foremost venue, the trend setter for all lesser magazines. If such a magazine was edited by an anti-Semite, it would have had a disproportionate influence on early science fiction. Let us look closer, then, at John W. Campbell and his relationship with his Jewish writers, such as Horace Gold and others.

"Nazism's anti-Semitism had spread all through the world," Sargent quoted Gold as saying, "and it permeated Street and Smith, so I knew better than to write under my own name." This pervasive anti-Semitism at *Astounding* was "somewhat altered," Sargent simplistically explained, when Jewish publisher Hugo Gernsback published Jewish writer Stanley G. Weinbaum's first story, "A Martian Odyssey," at the rival *Wonder Stories* in July, 1934. "Weinbaum used his own name as a byline, readers loved the story, and anti-Semitism vanished at Street and Smith. [Despite this alleged anti-Semitism abruptly vanishing at *Astounding* after July, Gold was supposedly still compelled to conceal his Jewish identity in the October issue.] When John Campbell took over *Astounding* in 1938 [sic], he encouraged writers like Gold and, later, Isaac Asimov, to use their own names."[28]

Interestingly, Pamela Sargent's claim that Campbell encouraged his Jewish writers (such as Asimov, Gold, Morton Klass, and Robert Silverberg) to use their own names contrasts greatly with Frederik Pohl's explicit and baseless allegation that John W. Campbell was an anti-Semite who did not want his writers using such names. (This contradiction, alone, calls into question both claims.) Citing no proof, Pohl said (as I noted earlier), "I have no doubt that he was always a little embarrassed by people who didn't have the sense to be born . . . Protestant. Like most WASPs of his generation, he was brought up to believe that . . . Jews [were] kind of comical. . . . So he invited his Jewish writers to conceal that blemish. When I sold him Milt Rothman's first story ["Heavy Planet," *Astounding*, August, 1939], he laid it on the line. 'The best names,' John declared, 'are Scottish or English. That's true for characters and for bylines. It has nothing to do with prejudice. They *sound* better.' It was not just for Milt that he insisted on that. It is only because Isaac Asimov and Stanley G. Weinbaum were first published elsewhere that we don't know them now as, maybe, Tam MacIsaacs and S. G. Macbeth. John was not, *of course*, the only editor who thought that."[29]

In this same passage Pohl did confess that, "My feelings about John Campbell have to be colored by the fact that throughout my later career as a science-fiction magazine editor I was competing with him." And, *of course*, Pohl doesn't name any of those other editors who would have insisted on Scottish or English names. Nor does he reveal any of the *other* Jewish authors besides Rothman whom he claims Campbell "invited" to conceal their "Jewish" names. (He could not because they simply do not exist). But there are other problems with these allegations. True, Milt Rothman did publish under the pseudonym "Lee Gregor." For example, he published "Formula for Murder" under this name in the November, 1957 issue of Jewish publisher Irwin Stein's *Infinity*. But the purpose in *that* case could not have been to escape an anti-Semitic publisher's prejudice. But John W. Campbell published *all* of his articles and book reviews in *Astounding* under his "Jewish" name of "Milton A. Rothman."[30]

Further, if Campbell supposedly insisted on a non-Jewish pseudonym for Rothman in order to publish his debut in August, 1939, then how does Pohl explain Campbell publishing Horace L. Gold's debut under his *"Jewish"* name the *previous* year ("A Matter of Form," *Astounding*, December, 1938)? The *only* stories Gold had published prior to this (all in *Astounding* in 1934 and 1935) were under the non-Semitic pseudonym of "Clyde Crane Campbell." Pohl claims John W. Campbell accepted names used in prior publication. Gold had already established a track record of an Anglicized pseudonym in Campbell's very magazine. Given Campbell's supposed antipathy to "Jewish" names, it thus makes sense that Campbell would have insisted that Gold continue to publish under his established non-Semitic pseudonym.

But that's not what happened. Instead, Campbell not only published Gold under his "Jewish" name for the very first time *anywhere*—he also put Gold's "Jewish" name on the magazine's cover. Campbell, therefore, was responsible for "outing" Gold as a Jewish author many months before Pohl presented him with Rothman's story. Odd behavior for an editor who supposedly resisted the use of "Jewish" names and "invited" his Jewish writers to conceal their "blemish."

Pohl's description of Campbell's hypothetical attitude toward Weinbaum is also inappropriate. Weinbaum died in 1935, two years and several months before Campbell became editor of *Astounding*. Thus, Campbell was never presented with the question of changing Weinbaum's name.

And what of Isaac Asimov, whose name Pohl says Campbell would also liked to have changed? As Asimov himself pointed out, "with the possible exception of Moses," his first name was "the most clearly Jewish" name one could possibly imagine. In addition, his last name was Slavic. For this reason, people who had absolutely *nothing* to do with science fiction warned him "that [science fiction] editors would probably want to call me John Jones." However, he said, the issue of his name never came up with *any* editor, including John W. Campbell.[31]

And why should it? Asimov was not the first "Isaac" to be published under that name in a science fiction magazine, and no one had indicated any problem with the previous appearance of the name. Almost a decade before Isaac Asimov made *his* debut, Isaac R. Nathanson made simultaneous debuts in Hugo Gernsback and David Lasser's *Science Wonder Stories* ("The Falling Planetoid," April, 1930) and *Amazing Stories* ("The Conquest of the Earth," April, 1930). *Amazing*'s editor at the time, the Protestant T. O'Conor Sloane, liked "Conquest" so much he put Isaac Nathanson's full name on the cover, which also featured a Leo Morey painting devoted to the story. In the accompanying blurb, either

Sloane or Managing Editor Miriam Bourne said, "We know you will be glad to know there are more stories by Mr. Nathanson coming soon," as indeed there were. Isaac Nathanson published nine more popular stories in *Amazing Stories, Amazing Stories Quarterly,* and *Wonder Stories Quarterly,* all before Isaac Asimov made his debut.

And, appearing in the very same April, 1930 *Amazing* which carried Isaac Nathanson's debut was the "The Metal Horde," by a young science fiction writer named John W. Campbell, Jr. Thus, if nothing else, Campbell knew Asimov was not the first science fiction writer named "Isaac" Further, he knew there was no readership problem with a Jewish name like "Isaac."

Of course, Pohl claimed that Campbell didn't make Isaac Asimov change his name only because Asimov had already established a publication record under his own name. Let's examine the likelihood of this further allegation.

On June 21, 1938, *before he'd published anything but letters,* Asimov began meeting on a regular basis with Campbell to cordially discuss and dissect stories he'd submitted to Campbell for publication. One searches in vain through Asimov's autobiography, *In Memory Yet Green,* in which he discusses these meetings, for any mention of Campbell expressing any opinion whatsoever about Asimov's "Jewish" name, which would appear on any accepted stories (and such acceptance Campbell later told Asimov was inevitable). And, when Campbell finally *did* accept a story from Asimov ("Trends," July, 1939, originally entitled "Ad Astra" in manuscript), Asimov mentions no discussion with Campbell about the name under which it would appear. *It was assumed* by all concerned that "Isaac Asimov" would be the by-line.

In addition, Campbell implicitly accepted this first story from Asimov, pending revisions, at a meeting on January 5, 1939, *before* Asimov's first publication ("Marooned Off Vesta," *Amazing Stories,* March, 1939) appeared on the newsstands on January 10. Thus, Campbell knew *nothing* of Asimov's "prior" publication record (there wasn't any) when he accepted the story. Therefore, he could not have been forced to "accept" Asimov's "Jewish" name because of a publication track record. When Asimov visited Campbell on January 24, to submit his revision of "Trends," all Asimov records Campbell as saying was that a correspondent had informed him that "Marooned Off Vesta" was the best story in its issue. And that was the extent of any discussion of Asimov's "prior" publication record between Asimov and Campbell.

Hence, according to Asimov's encyclopedic autobiography, based upon his comprehensive daily diary entries, his religion and his name simply never came up as a topic of conversation with Campbell. Indeed, in conversation I explicitly asked Asimov about this very issue and Asimov firmly told me that Campbell never, at any time, said a word to him about his name.[32]

Thus, Asimov himself never knew Campbell's feelings about his name, if he had any at all. How, then, could Pohl assert any knowledge about Campbell's alleged hostile attitude toward Asimov's name? Indeed, from the fact that Campbell never brought the subject up with Asimov, one can only honestly assume the opposite, that he had no problem at all with Asimov's "Jewish" name.

Nevertheless, the charge of Campbell's alleged anti-Semitism lingered. Pohl recounted, for example, one California banquet at which "the principal speaker denounced John for anti-Semitism. John took it imperturbably enough."[33] Perhaps Campbell took the allegation "imperturbably enough" because he knew it wasn't true. Rather, it seems Campbell felt just the opposite about Jews.

At his April 14, 2001 presentation to PARSEC, mentioned earlier, Philip Klass recounted a meeting he had with John W. Campbell in 1945 shortly after Klass returned from military service in Europe. Klass had seen the Nazi concentration camps soon after they were liberated and Campbell wanted to hear a full account. After Klass related the ghastly sights he'd seen, Campbell was silent for a moment. Then he said to Klass, "Phil, I'm very sorry and I want you to know that I have always considered Jews to be *Homo Superior.*"

Klass, who said he believes there are no superior or inferior humans, responded by telling Campbell this was racist. Campbell was confused by this response and, thinking Klass had misheard him, said, "No, Phil, I said Homo *Superior!*"

Thus, according to Klass' interpretation, Campbell should be condemned because, rather than being anti-Semitic, he was *pro-*Semitic. And it is here, perhaps, that one can level the only possible "anti-Semitic" charge against Campbell, that of *stereotyping.* However, it seems his stereotype of Jews was a positive, rather than a negative one.

Commenting on this attitude, Jewish writer Robert Silverberg states that, "John Campbell is often, and wrongly, called an anti-Semite. . . . Campbell— who had no hesitation about publishing a dozen or more Silverberg stories under that name—once told me the same thing [that he considered Jews to be superior people] . . . John saw it as praise, and I was willing enough to take it at that. . . . And, when I needed a pseudonym to use for some of my stories in *Astounding,* I chose 'Calvin M. Knox,' which was the most Presbyterian name I could think of. Many years later, chatting with John late one night in his suite at some Worldcon, I admitted to him that the middle initial in that name stood for 'Moses,' and he broke into wild guffaws of Campbellian laughter. And then he said, 'Have you ever heard the name of Isaac Asimov?' [whom Campbell had by then often published]"[34]

Silverberg believes that Klass was perhaps reflexively seeing anti-Semitism where none existed. He points out that, "Philip Klass, when he began writing SF for Campbell [in the late 1940s], adopted the byline of 'William Tenn' in the belief that he needed an Anglo-Saxon monicker, but I doubt that John really had let him know that he would not be permitted to sully the contents page of

Astounding with the vile Semitic name of Klass. (Just five years after 'William Tenn's' debut, his brother published a story in John's magazine under his own name, Morton Klass.) [Further,] Campbell . . . had no hesitation about publishing a dozen or more Silverberg stories under that name."[35]

Obviously, then, Campbell had no problem publishing Silverberg or Asimov (or Gold or Rothman) under their own names. Indeed, in 1959 he told E. E. "Doc" Smith that he liked both of them. "Bob Silverberg is a kid: a nice kid, whom I like," he said, "just as I did Ike Asimov some 20 years ago [i.e., around 1939]." He then went on to say Silverberg had his "highest respect."[36] So, there are problems and contradictions in the charges of anti-Semitism against John W. Campbell.

There are also reasons to doubt the validity of the entire fabricated history of Street and Smith anti-Semitism, the publisher for whom Campbell worked. Not the least of these reasons is that the origin of the allegations seems to be Horace Gold who, like Frederik Pohl later, was the editor of a rival science fiction magazine, *Galaxy*. Indeed, Gold made his charges of anti-Semitism against Street and Smith's *Astounding* in the pages of that rival magazine. At the time he made the statement Gold was no longer editor of *Galaxy*, but his antagonism toward rival Street and Smith was of long duration. When *Galaxy* was launched in 1950, with Gold as editor, *Astounding*, edited by Campbell, was the foremost magazine of the day. Street and Smith's magazine was the horse to beat. And this Gold worked hard to do, beginning with paying writers more money for magazine publication to woo them from Street and Smith.

Additionally, Gold was frustrated by Campbell's initial refusal to allow him to reprint stories from *Astounding* as part of Gold's series of *Galaxy* paperback novels. In fact, this issue generated much bad blood between Gold and Campbell, which lingered interminably. The reason for Campbell's refusal was that he felt Gold was cheating authors. According to Campbell, Gold was paying a flat rate of $500 for these novels when the then-going rate in paperback royalties to authors was between $1,500 and $2,500 (and the $500 was also much less than Street and Smith paid for a serialized novel).

Also, "what H. L. God [sic] calls a 'pocket book'," complained Campbell, "is a magazine, and he's been using Second Serial Rights, in effect, without our permission by calling it a 'pocket book,' which it isn't. . . . I don't mind competition; it helps the field. But I have a very deep resentment when some guy starts a magazine and tries to make his reputation not by using stories *like* those I helped build up, but by using the stories I worked on. That I consider with an extremely jaundiced eye. . . . [and] I intend to take all possible measures to stop a bird who starts using Second Serial Rights by calling his magazine a book. . . . It's a nice deal from his view; he's beating the magazine competition by saving nearly $1,000 on manuscript costs by using in effect Second Serial Rights. And he's beating the pocket books by saving $1,000 to $2,000 by not paying royalties.

I'm not accustomed to dealing that way, and I'm going to block his tendency to do so in any way I can." Even so, Gold finally overcame this resistance and the first of his *Galaxy* novels was Eric Frank Russell's "Sinister Barrier," which had appeared in Street and Smith's *Unknown*, also edited by Campbell. And, about this sale, Campbell said, "Eric was boiling mad; he got only a pared down cut of $500."[37]

Gold had yet another reason for his enduring hostility toward Campbell. He seems to have mistakenly blamed Campbell for sabotaging the financial success of *Galaxy* in the mid-Fifties. While *Galaxy* had been launched in a blaze of glory in 1950, by 1953 it entered a lingering sales slump. At a 1955 picnic of the Little Men, the Berkeley, California, science fiction club, Gold's wife, Evelyn, told Norm Metcalf the slump was due to Campbell. American News, the distributor for *Galaxy*, was, she said, deliberately restricting the magazine from many of the nation's outlets, no doubt having been told this by her husband. When Metcalf asked why they would do this, Mrs. Gold said it was because American News was owned by the Street and Smith syndicate, which, of course, owned *Astounding*. Street and Smith wanted to sabotage *Galaxy* so that Campbell's magazine could thrive.

Metcalf pointed out that this could hardly be the case, as Street and Smith had sold American News in 1951. Besides, the mid-Fifties was when the early Fifties boom for science fiction magazines had collapsed. Over a dozen science fiction magazines folded just in 1954–1955. Every magazine in the field was facing hard times. Nevertheless, her (and, presumably, her husband's) animosity against Campbell was unabated.

Horace L. Gold also had an intensely personal resentment of Campbell, which he readily expressed. As late as 1986 (fifteen years after Campbell's death) Gold told me that he resented Campbell because Gold was going to be the editor of *Astounding* before the job was given to Campbell. In addition, Gold said he disliked Campbell because Campbell "made" him "H. L. Gold." This happened when Campbell couldn't fit Gold's full name onto the cover of the 1938 issue of *Astounding* which carried "A Matter of Form," Gold's debut under his "Jewish" name. Therefore, Campbell abbreviated Gold's name. "I'm *Horace* L. Gold," he told me, "not 'H. L. Gold.' *Campbell* made me 'H. L. Gold.' You don't *do* that to a writer!"[38]

So Campbell gets credit for being the first to publish Gold under his "Jewish" name, but demerits for using an abbreviation. It seems Campbell couldn't win no matter *what* he did.

Horace L. Gold appears to have retaliated for this perceived slight, for the belief that Street and Smith was sabotaging *Galaxy* distribution, and for Campbell's opposition to Gold using stories Campbell had previously bought and edited, by spreading lies about Campbell's editorship. For example, he told Damon Knight that, "Campbell had told him on the phone that he [Campbell]

threw away readers' letters and made up the percentages in his 'AnLab' department," wherein readers rated each issue's stories, with the winner getting a
bonus above the going pay rate.[39]

Given the animosity between these two men, it is hard to believe Campbell
would have confessed this to Gold, if it were true. And there is much to refute
it. For example, Campbell sometimes paid the bonus ahead of time to an author
he thought would be most popular. If the readers' votes proved him wrong,
however, he allowed the first author to keep the bonus, while paying the second
author, as well. Given his always tight budget, it would have made no sense for
him to pay duplicate bonuses if he just faked the whole contest month after
month, year after year. He would have simply rigged the votes to support his
initial guess and saved his publisher the scarce money.

Thus, given this bitter and frequently-expressed animosity between Street and
Smith's Campbell and the man he repeatedly and disparagingly called, "H. L.
God," anything Horace L. Gold said about Campbell or his publisher in the
pages of his *own* magazine should have been investigated by subsequent histori-
ans for veracity before endorsing. But, there is a further reason for doubting
Gold's charges of anti-Semitism at Street and Smith. The record itself refutes it.

Street and Smith purchased *Astounding* in mid-1933 from the bankrupt Clayton Publishing Company. F. Orlin Tremaine, who had been an executive at
Clayton, but was now working for Street and Smith, was named editor. However, he handed most of the editorial chores over to Australian-born Desmond
Hall, who had been assistant editor of *Astounding* at Clayton for about nine
months.

Thus, both of the editors in charge of Street and Smith's *Astounding* had been
Clayton employees and were new to Street and Smith. They were therefore
unlikely to have been acculturated by any anti-Semitism which may have swiftly
"permeated" Street and Smith due to Hitler's rise to power in Germany a few
months before, in January, 1933. And these two were the ones who dealt with
the authors at that time, buying and rejecting stories. Indeed, according to Gold
himself, most of his dealings with the magazine under the new ownership were
with ex-Clayton employee Desmond Hall.

In *the very first* Street and Smith issue of *Astounding*, October, 1933, new editors F. Orlin Tremaine and Desmond Hall published not one, but *two* stories
by Jewish author Nat Schachner, under his "Jewish" name. The next month,
November, Street and Smith's *Astounding* trumpeted an upcoming story by
Schachner with this blurb: "The next issue of *Astounding Stories* will contain a
story that will awaken *more controversy* than any story ever published in a
science-fiction magazine. ANCESTRAL VOICES by Nat Schachner slices dar-
ingly through the most precious myths, legends, and folklore of mankind, and
attacks boldly a present-day wave of race-hysteria."

That story, published in the December, 1933 issue, was a devastating critique of Nazi-inspired race hatred. In it, a time traveler from 1935 went back to ancient Rome. There, in self-defense, he killed a Hun who attacked him. The time traveler disappeared. So did tens of thousands of others in the present of the 1930s, including blacks, whites, Asians, and those of all classes and occupations. The reason was that the Hun never lived to sire children. The time traveler, and all the others who disappeared, were descendents of these children. Among the "disappeared" was the Aryan superman Adolf Hitler, described in a wild caricature. The gist of the story was to mock the absurdity of Nazism's concept of "racial purity"—a bold anti-Nazi statement that would have been impossible for a Jewish author to have published in *Astounding* if anti-Semitism had indeed "permeated" the magazine. Indeed, in a long letter in the same issue, Schachner drove home the point that he *meant* it to be an attack on the entire idea of "racial purity."

Thus, it seems there was no need for Gold to have concealed his Jewish identity in order for Desmond Hall to publish him in Street and Smith's *Astounding* the very next year, 1934. Indeed, at a time when mainstream American media was largely non-critical of Hitler, *Astounding* had proven itself to be more receptive than any to critiques of Nazi anti-Semitism.

The decline of the alleged anti-Semitism at Street and Smith's *Astounding* is similarly difficult to credit. Gold published his first story in *Astounding* in October 1934. This was less than a year after Schachner's furious attack on Hitler in the same magazine. It was also three months after Weinbaum's July publication of "A Martian Odyssey," which Sargent tells us had supposedly already cracked the reputed anti-Semitic barrier in the field. Gold did so under an Anglo-Saxon pseudonym, "Clyde Crane Campbell." This was reputedly in order to conceal his Jewish identity from Desmond Hall, who, presumably, had been quickly saturated with the anti-Semitism which "permeated" the magazine.

Yet, well before this and long before reader reaction to Weinbaum's debut could be known, Desmond Hall was asking Jewish literary agents Julius Schwartz and Mort Weisinger to obtain a story from the Jewish Stanley G. Weinbaum. This they were eager to do. Having obtained his address, Schwartz and Weisinger wrote Weinbaum on June 18, 1934, soliciting his business and telling him a top editor had commissioned them to get a story from him.[40] The July issue of *Wonder Stories* containing Weinbaum's "A Martian Odyssey" was on the stands by June, when this correspondence began. But, evidently, Hall was seeking stories by Weinbaum because he liked his writing and before reader reaction to "A Martian Odyssey" was known. Weinbaum immediately agreed to send a story to Schwartz and Weisinger, which he did in late June. This was "The Circle of Zero," which Hall read and rejected due to weak science in August.[41] However, Leo Margulies soon purchased it from Schwartz and Weisinger for his publisher, Ned Pines.

However, Weisinger wrote Weinbaum on September 23, 1934, to say that

Desmond Hall had purchased "Flight on Titan" for *Astounding*. (This was the same month the October *Astounding* appeared on the stands with Gold's story published under a WASP pen name in order to sneak past the supposedly anti-Semitic Desmond Hall.) On October 22, 1934, Weisinger wrote that Hall had also liked and purchased "Parasite Planet," and enclosed payment for both stories.[42] Four months later, in February, 1935, *Astounding* enthusiastically published Stanley G. Weinbaum's "Parasite Planet" under Weinbaum's name—and then the supposed deeply rooted racial hatred at *Astounding* immediately vanished.

It is highly dubious that such an elemental ideology could have been dispelled so quickly and easily—if it had existed. But there is no reason to believe it ever existed at all. At the very time Gold claimed he had to conceal his Jewish identity in order to sell to Desmond Hall, that same editor (in his dealings with the Jewish agents Schwartz and Weisinger) was pursuing, purchasing, and publishing stories from the Jewish Weinbaum. At the same time, he was allowing Jewish author Nat Schachner to use the magazine as a forum to attack Nazi race hatred.

However, from such a thin strand of suspect testimony an entire web of supposed anti-Jewish discrimination and exclusion at *Astounding* has been woven. And historians and critics have been easily, almost willingly, ensnared in it. No doubt Gold in the Thirties and Klass in the late-Forties felt worried about the acceptability of their "Jewish" names, else they would not have, at least initially, chosen to Anglicize them. At issue here, however, are their charges that they were *forced* to do so because of deliberate and overt discrimination and exclusion from the science fiction magazines (and particularly *Astounding*) due to their Jewish identity. But a close reading of the record does not bear out their allegations. Instead, the examination reveals that the science fiction field (including *Astounding*) was, for a variety of reasons, actually quite receptive to Jewish participation.

By accepting the charge that science fiction magazine editors and publishers in general, and those at *Astounding* in particular, shared in the general anti-Semitism of the times, the fact that a genuine refuge for Jewish writers and, even, their attacks on Nazi race hatred has gone unrecognized. There is much that America and its institutions should apologize for during the Holocaust era. Rampant anti-Semitism in science fiction publishing, however, is not among them. Rather, we should be proud that science fiction magazines had many Jewish publishers and editors from the very beginning, *starting in 1926 with Hugo Gernsback*. We should also be proud that, in the 1930s, science fiction offered a forum for Jewish authors not only to publish, but also to speak out against the gathering storm.

And there is a final benefit from closely investigating the validity of the charges of anti-Semitism levelled at pulp science fiction publishers and editors. By doing so, we discover that the genre, like other new forms of popular culture emerging in America in the early twentieth century, was at the very least an arena of "contested terrain"—but more plausibly an open door welcoming Jews (as well as women) inside.

Notes

1. The identification of Hugo Gernsback as Jewish comes from two sources. The first is Sam Moskowitz, "The Jew in Science Fiction," *Worlds of Tomorrow,* November, 1966, p. 119. Moskowitz again, and more explicitly, states that Gernsback was Jewish in his revision of that essay for his book, *Strange Horizons: The Spectrum of Science Fiction,* Charles Scribner's Sons: N.Y., 1976, p. 44. Moskowitz, who was Jewish himself, knew Gernsback personally and in 1953 worked as Gernsback's editor at *Science Fiction Plus.*

The second source is Mike Ashley in his definitive biography of Gernsback, in which he tells us that Gernsback, though born in Luxembourg, came from a family of German Jews originally from the town of Gernsback near Baden-Baden in southern Germany. See Mike Ashley and Robert A. W. Lowndes, *The Gernsback Days: A Study of the Evolution of Modern Science Fiction from 1911 to 1936,* Wildside Press: Holicong, Penn., 2004, p. 16.

2. Julius Schwartz, "Memoirs of a Time Traveller, Part 1: My Amazing Stories," *Amazing Stories,* May, 1993, p. 49.

3. Janrae Frank, Jean Stine, and Forrest J. Ackerman, Eds., Introduction, *New Eves: Science Fiction About the Extraordinary Women of Today and Tomorrow,* Long Meadow Press: Stamford, Conn., 1994, p. x. Emphasis added.

4. Pamela Sargent, Ed., *More Women of Wonder: Science Fiction Novelettes by Women About Women,* Vintage Books: N.Y., 1976, pp. xxxii-xxxiii. (Emphasis added.) The Gold quote was originally in *Galaxy,* October, 1975, p. 22.

5. Frederik Pohl, *The Way the Future Was: A Memoir,* Del Rey-Ballantine Books: N.Y., 1978, p. 83.

6. Michael Ollove, "In and Out of Character," *The Baltimore Sun,* October 26, 2003.

7. Neal Gabler, *An Empire of Their Own: How the Jews Invented Hollywood,* Bantam Doubleday Dell Publishing Group: N.Y., 1988, 1989.

8. See, e.g., Jim Hoberman and Jeffrey Shandler, Eds., *Entertaining America: Jews, Movies, and Broadcasting,* Princeton University Press: Princeton, N.J., 2003, as well as David Desser and Lester D. Friedman, *American-Jewish Filmmakers: Traditions and Trends,* University of Illinois Press: Urbana, 1993, and Michael P. Rogin, *Blackface, White Noise: Jewish Immigrants in the Hollywood Melting Pot,* University of California Press: Berkeley, 1996.

9. See, e.g., Steven Alan Carr, *Hollywood and Anti-Semitism: A Cultural History, 1880–1941,* Cambridge University Press: N.Y., 2001.

10. The following account is drawn from Arie Kaplan, "Kings of Comics," *Reform Judaism,* fall, 2003, pp. 14–22; Eric Leif Davin, *Pioneers of Wonder: Conversations with the Founders of Science Fiction,* Prometheus Books: Amherst, N.Y., 1999, pp. 104–107; and Ron Goulart, *Comic Book Culture: An Illustrated History,* Collectors Press: Portland, Oregon, 2000.

11. Jackie Leger, "Dale Messick: A Comic Strip Life," *Animation World Magazine,* July, 2000.

12. Leger, "Dale Messick: A Comic Strip Life."

13. Kaplan, p. 14.

14. The identification of the artist as St. John comes from Julius Schwartz, letter to Eric Leif Davin, December 4, 2003. This entire chapter was sent to Julius Schwartz for his vetting in November, 2003. He returned it to me on December 4, 2003, with his corrections and additions. The editing of this chapter was perhaps the last editing job Schwartz ever did. He died on February 8, 2004, at age 88.

15. Kaplan, p. 16.

16. Ron Goulart, *Comic Book Culture: An Illustrated History,* Collectors Press: Portland, Oregon, 2000, p. 173.

17. Julius Schwartz, "Memoirs of a Time Traveller, Part 2: The Bester Years of My Life," *Amazing Stories,* July, 1993, p. 57.

18. Al Jaffee and Will Eisner quoted in Kaplan, p. 17.

19. Frederik Pohl, in Robert Silverberg and Grania Davis, Eds., *The Avram Davidson Treasury: A Tribute Collection,* Tor: N.Y., 1998, 1999, p. 205.

20. The 1930 date comes from Sam Moskowitz, *The Immortal Storm: A History of Science Fiction Fandom,* Hyperion Press: Westport, Conn., 1974, 1988, pp. 9–10. First serialized in A. Langley Searles's journal, *Fantasy Commentator,* 1945–1952. Allen Glasser, one of the Scienceer founders, claimed the club began in 1929. His account appeared in the fanzine *Sphere* #12, 1959, published by Joe Christoff and Larry Thorndyke out of Atlanta, Georgia.

21. The entire 1931 membership of the club, comprising thirteen members, can be found in Julius Schwartz, "Memoirs of a Time Traveller, Part 1: My Amazing Stories," *Amazing Stories,* May, 1993, p. 50.

22. Julius Schwartz, "Memoirs of a Time Traveller, Part 1: My Amazing Stories," *Amazing Stories,* May, 1993, p. 51.

23. Damon Knight, "Knight Piece," in Brian W. Aldiss and Harry Harrison, Eds., *Hell's Cartographers,* Futura Publications Ltd.: London, 1976, 1975, p. 111.

24. Sam Moskowitz, "The Jew in Science Fiction," *Worlds of Tomorrow,* November, 1966, p. 119.

25. Bob [sic] Silverberg, *Snickersnee,* Vol. Oy, Number Goy, pp. 3–4, fanzine included in Fantasy Amateur Press Association (FAPA) mailing #260, August, 2002.

26. H. L. Gold, in telephone conversation with Eric Leif Davin, August 21, 1986.

27. Thomas D. Clareson, "Avon Fantasy Reader," in Marshall B. Tymn and Mike Ashley, Eds., *Science Fiction, Fantasy, and Weird Fiction Magazines,* Greenwood Press: Westport, Conn., 1985, p. 128.

28. Sargent, *More Women of Wonder,* pp. xxxii-xxxiii. Campbell did not become editor of *Astounding* in 1938. Rather, it was December, 1937.

29. Pohl, *The Way the Future Was,* pp. 85, 83–84. Emphasis added.

30. E.g., see Rothman's book reviews and articles in the *Astounding* issues of September, 1948, February, 1950, April, 1951, and January and September, 1957. Additionally, all of his 18 letters to *Astounding* were published under the Rothman name, beginning in 1934 and ending in 1978. Six of Rothman's letters were published under Campbell's editorship.

31. Isaac Asimov, *I. Asimov: A Memoir,* Doubleday: N.Y., 1994, pp. 15, 17.

32. Eric Leif Davin, "The Good Doctor at St. Vincent," *Fantasy Commentator VII,* No. 4, 1992, p. 248.

33. Pohl, *The Way the Future Was,* p. 83.

34. Silverberg, *Snickersnee,* pp. 2–3.

35. Silverberg, *Snickersnee,* p. 3.

36. John W. Campbell to E. E. Smith, May 26, 1959, in Perry A. Chapdelaine, Sr., Tony Chapdelaine, and George Hay, Eds., *The John W. Campbell Letters, Vol. 1,* AC Projects, Inc.: Franklin, Tenn., 1985, p. 367.

37. Both Campbell quotes in John W. Campbell to L. Sprague de Camp, February 28, 1951, in Perry A. Chapdelaine, Sr., Tony Chapdelaine, and George Hay, Eds., *The John W. Campbell Letters, Vol. 1,* AC Projects, Inc.: Franklin, Tenn., 1985, pp. 62–63.

38. H. L. Gold, in telephone conversation with Eric Leif Davin, August 21, 1986. Gold continued to publish using his initials and also listed himself as editor of *Galaxy* under his initials. Odd behavior for a man who claimed to hate the use of his initials. Even though Gold never forgave Campbell for using his initials instead of his full name, he credited (in his conversation with me) Campbell for "making" "A Matter of Form." Campbell told Gold that the story, about a man

trapped in a dog's body, was "a problem in communication." Thus, Gold said, "Campbell made it clear for me."

39. Damon Knight, "Knight Piece," in Aldiss and Harrison, *Hell's Cartographers,* p. 133.

40. Sam Moskowitz, "The Marketing of Stanley G. Weinbaum," *Fantasy Commentator VII,* 1991, p. 107. They did not tell Weinbaum at the time that the editor was Hall, perhaps fearing he would sell directly to Hall instead of through them. Only after Weinbaum agreed to become their client did they reveal the identify of the editor who had sent them after Weinbaum. Weinbaum's correspondence is located in the Special Collections Dept. at Temple University, but see the synopsis of the Schwartz-Weinbaum-Weisinger correspondence in the Moskowitz article.

41. Moskowitz, "The Marketing of Stanley G. Weinbaum," p. 108.

42. Moskowitz, "The Marketing of Stanley G. Weinbaum," p. 109.

9

Ebony and Ivory

IT WAS 1930. It was Harlem and James Fitzgerald, a "Negro" resident of New York City's black ghetto, was welcoming his friends into his living room. They had taken the subway from other parts of the city to meet in his apartment because they all belonged to the same club. It had been recently formed and Fitzgerald had been unanimously elected its first president.

The main item on the agenda was planning a club bulletin, *The Planet*. The club, composed mostly of Jewish kids like Mort Weisinger and Allen (Aaron) Glasser, was the Scienceers, the world's first science fiction fan club. The fan magazine which these kids later launched, produced by Julius Schwartz and Weisinger and edited by Glasser, was *The Time Traveller*, the world's first science fiction "fanzine." What these Jewish kids and their black president launched was science fiction "fandom," a way of fan participation in the new world of science fiction which would soon become common throughout the science fiction community, right up to the present.[1]

Perhaps the most salient example of pulp science fiction's open door was the fact that blacks, like Jews, were welcome to participate as equals in the science fiction community from the very beginning. In 1930, America was still a quarter of a century away from the 1954 *Brown vs. The Board of Education* Supreme Court decision striking down racial segregation in public facilities. In the South by law and in the North by custom, blacks were routinely segregated from whites in theaters, hotels, restaurants, swimming pools, schools, and other facilities.

But not in science fiction fandom. There (and almost *only* there), blacks and whites could and did interact on a basis of equality. Consciously or not, this egalitarian practice made the science fiction world oppositional to and subversive of the larger society's norms of racial exclusion and discrimination. Therefore, as with the field's stance toward women and Jews, pulp science fiction's stance toward race relations reveals that it was indeed culturally contested terrain.

The practice, from the beginning, of racial equality in the science fiction world makes it impossible to accept the charge of endemic racism often levelled against the field. Science fiction is, after all, the medium which presented the first interracial kiss in television history, despite the opposition of network executives. (It was between Kirk and Uhura—the feminization of "uhuru," the Swahili word for "freedom"—in 1968 on the *Star Trek* episode, "Plato's Stepchildren.")

Therefore, such generic accusations of racism serve only to blind us to the important reality, which was two-fold. First, the black presence in science fiction, although a minority presence, was there from the beginning. Second, this black presence was accepted and treated sympathetically more often than not. These two realities highlight the difference between early science fiction and the larger culture, in which blacks were excluded and, when acknowledged at all, were noticed only to be treated in a hostile and discriminatory fashion. Thus, pulp science fiction's open door reveals a popular culture which was dramatically more democratic, egalitarian, and accepting of blacks than the dominant culture of white America, especially in the 1930s.

Typical of the erroneous allegations of racism in early science fiction are those made by *Philadelphia Inquirer* reporter Annette John-Hall. Although speaking primarily about movies, she claimed that, "From Buck Rogers on through the '70s, blacks didn't figure into the sci-fi equation. . . . Futuristic science fiction [was] a genre once so white that blacks wondered if filmmakers assumed their race was headed for extinction."[2]

Others, speaking specifically of written science fiction, have gone further than just accusing the genre of ignoring blacks. They have alleged that from the beginning science fiction was actually *prejudiced* against blacks and deliberately excluded them as characters and as writers. One of these accusers is black *Pittsburgh Post-Gazette* journalist Tony Norman. In his discussion of visits to a Pittsburgh writers' conference by black science fiction authors Octavia Butler and Samuel R. Delany, Norman claimed that these two authors, "are revered as pathbreakers in a genre that was once about as accommodating to blacks as an afternoon romp on Main Street with Bull Connor's police dogs. . . . There was . . . a time when even the future had a large neon 'Whites Only' sign tacked above it."[3]

The truth of the matter is just the opposite. The science fiction community was *very* accommodating to Delany and Butler. For example, in 1966, only four years after he entered the field at the age of twenty, his peers awarded Delany the Nebula, the top prize they could award, for his novel, *Babel-17.* The next year, 1967, his peers again awarded him the Nebula, this time for *The Einstein Intersection*, a novel featuring a black hero.

As for Octavia Butler, science fiction author Harlan Ellison financially supported her out of his own pocket in her early years and paid her way to and tuition for the famous Clarion science fiction workshop in 1970, even though she'd sold nothing at the time. And, not only did the SF community at Clarion embrace her, but that crucial support was her breakthrough, as she was able to sell her very first story the next year, 1971.[4] The field's warm and supportive treatment of these two authors is typical of the field's attitudes toward blacks from the very beginning.

Despite this, Samuel Delany has leveled charges of racism against the genre in an influential recent book. Unlike Tony Norman, however, Delany names names—or at least one name. Again, it is that of John W. Campbell, Jr. Delany has no direct knowledge of Campbell's alleged racism. Rather, according to Delany's hearsay testimony, Campbell revealed his racism to Delany's agent, who in turn relayed it to the author. Because Campbell's alleged racism is presented as typical of the genre, let us investigate the charge.

Delany claims that in June 1967, he submitted *Nova*, his forthcoming Doubleday novel, to Campbell for possible prior serialization in *Analog*. "Campbell rejected it," Delany says, "with a note and phone call to my agent explaining that, while he liked pretty much everything else about it, he didn't feel his readership would be able to relate to a black main character. That was one of my first direct encounters, as a professional writer, with the slippery and always commercialized form of liberal American prejudice: Campbell had nothing against *my* being black, you understand. . . . No, perish the thought! Surely there was not a prejudiced bone in his body! It's just that I had, by pure happenstance, chosen to write about someone whose mother was from Senegal (and whose father was from Norway), and it was the poor benighted readers, out there in America's heartland, who, in 1967, would be too upset. . . . It was all handled as though I'd just happened to have dressed my main character in a purple brocade dinner jacket. (In the phone call, Campbell made it fairly clear that this was his only reason for rejecting the book. Otherwise, he rather liked it. . . .) Purple brocade just wasn't big with the buyers that season. Sorry."[5]

Frederik Pohl joined in the condemnation of Campbell's supposed racism, although he offered no examples. Instead, he took us, somehow, inside the mind of John W. Campbell and said, (as noted earlier), "I have no doubt that he was always a little embarrassed by people who didn't have the sense to be born white. . . . Like most WASPs of his generation, he was brought up to believe that blacks were shiftless."[6] (This is the same passage where Pohl also claimed Campbell was embarrassed by people who weren't Protestant and that he thought Jews were "comical.")

Pohl doesn't tell us how he knew of Campbell's upbringing and thinking.

And, of course, unlike Pohl and Delany, Campbell is no longer with us. There-fore, we can't ask him about either his attitudes nor the Delany incident. How-ever, circumstantial evidence at least casts doubt upon the alleged reason for Campbell's rejection of the proposed 1967 *Nova* serialization as well as Pohl's characterization of Campbell's racial attitudes.

To begin with, there is Delany's unwarranted presumption that in 1967 Campbell had an all-white (and presumably racist) "poor benighted" reader-ship, to which he catered. But, as early as 1955, just as the civil rights movement was beginning, Campbell proudly boasted of his magazine's substantial black readership and the reasons for it (and at the same time giving us a glimpse of his attitudes toward race and color). "As our circulation records show," he told a private correspondent, "we have sales peaks near . . . the Negro districts of large cities. Seemingly, many Negro readers appreciate our attitude that it is important to be human; they seem to like our attitude that Man is important beyond the narrow limits of race or creed or color."[7]

Perhaps it was this disdain for racism (and the knowledge of his substantial black readership) which prompted Campbell to publish several stories by "Mack" Reynolds featuring black heroes before Delany even began writing sci-ence fiction. These stories started with the incendiary "Summit" (*Astounding Science Fact and Fiction*, February, 1960). This story portrayed a kind of "Black Power" revolt by American blacks seven years before the purported conversa-tion between Campbell and Delany's agent.

Campbell subsequently printed Reynolds' 1961–1962 series of "Black Man's Burden" stories, beginning with "Black Man's Burden," *Analog*, December, 1961–January, 1962. These featured a team of highly educated and charismatic American black protagonists attempting to unite an Africa still ruled by Euro-pean powers (which it still was in the early 1960s) in an anti-imperialist war of liberation. In early August, 1967, only weeks after Campbell's June rejection of Delany's novel, Reynolds thanked Norm Metcalf for a letter of praise about sto-ries such as these, saying, in part, "I could use the ego-boo. I've just got several letters [seemingly in July], through Campbell, beefing about the very things in my stories that you like. I think about half the readers figure I'm a commie, and the other half think I'm a fascist."[8] Such objections to the stories did not seem to bother Campbell. Perhaps this was because, as Reynolds later stated, "these stories *were written at a suggestion of John Campbell's, and whole chunks of them were based on his ideas.*"[9]

Thus, despite *some* strong reader opposition to Reynolds's racially and politi-cally provocative stories featuring black heroes (unlike anything else then being published in the field), Campbell continued to publish them. Indeed, claimed Reynolds, Campbell did not always agree with what Reynolds (a supporter of the Socialist Labor Party) said, "but would defend to the death the right to say it." In this case, however, that may not have been necessary, as, according to Reynolds, "The serial was so successful that *John Campbell ordered a sequel.*"[10]

"Border, Breed, Nor Birth," the immediate sequel to "Black Man's Burden," appeared in two installments (*Analog*, July-August, 1962) and was just as popular with Campbell's readers as the first tale. In this story (written, according to Reynolds, per Campbell's order and containing Campbell's ideas), one of the leaders of the black anti-imperialist fighters emerges as the mythic hero of a united African revolution against European white rule—and Campbell's readers rated them the best and second best stories in their respective issues in subsequent An Lab voting! Obviously, Campbell was giving his readers the kind of stories they (and he) wanted.

The popularity of these stories with the readers gives us an opportunity to see just how absurd some of the charges against Campbell are. Recall from the previous section the charge which Damon Knight claimed H. L. Gold made against Campbell—that Campbell threw away readers' votes for stories and made up the percentages in the An Lab balloting. Let us assume this was true. Then it would be *Campbell* who was responsible for rating these stories featuring a black hero as the best and most popular in the magazine. This would make Campbell a major champion of black science fiction and Delany's allegations would have to be completely false.

In fact, however, there are other reasons to doubt *both* Gold and Delany, but at least these rival allegations reveal some of the untenable contradictions of the charges against Campbell. There is a good reason to trust that the An Lab voting was honest and accurate, as Reynolds, the era's third most-often published author in *Astounding/Analog*, was genuinely popular with readers in the field.[11] For example, in 1969 Fred Pohl and Lester del Rey, as editors of *Galaxy*, conducted a mail survey of their subscribers to discover their readers' most popular writers, to whom they distributed prizes worth several thousand dollars. Pohl was surprised by the great popularity of Mack Reynolds, "with every story rated high by the readers—and we had published a lot of his stories that year. . . . What was he doing beating out so many of the Big Names?"[12]

Thus, circumstantial evidence casts doubt upon Delany's charge of Campbell's latent racism. Campbell had already chosen and published (in fact, even ordered and contributed ideas to) stories with politically-charged racial themes and black protagonists, even though some of his readers violently objected to them. It is also unlikely that Campbell would have claimed that his readers might have objected to Delany's story, as the majority reader response to Reynolds' "Black Man's Burden" stories in the An Lab (to which Campbell paid close attention) reveals that *Analog* readers, even years before Delany's agent submitted the novel in question, had no problem with black protagonists.

Further, Campbell himself believed as early as the mid-Fifties that he had a substantial black readership, which he had gained by the implicitly anti-racist stories he published. Indeed, perhaps it was *because* he knew he had a substantial black audience that Campbell asked Reynolds to write stories with black heroes.

Therefore, while we simply do not have enough evidence to know *why* Campbell rejected serialization of Delany's novel, we *do* have enough evidence to reject Delany's widely accepted charge of personal racism on Campbell's part. The contemporary record simply does not support such an allegation. Indeed, the record strongly refutes it.[13]

Nor does the record support Tony Norman's charges of the genre's generic racism. Of course, Norman gives no evidence for his claims of prejudice. Hence, we can only guess at what he might be referring. Perhaps it is simply the fact that there have been (and are) few black SF writers and Delany and Butler really are path breakers in that respect. But, was (and is) the lack of black SF writers due to prejudice against black writers by SF editors or readers, or were there more subtle reasons? Paper is, after all, color-neutral and does not betray the race of the writer submitting it. Further, as Campbell's comments reveal, editors seemed to be aware that they had black readers and, if they were good editors like Campbell, they would have wanted to give those readers stories which appealed to them. Racism, therefore, remains not only unproven but unconvincing as the reason for the dearth of black authors.

Nor has science fiction fandom, as we have seen, excluded blacks, although there have been and still are few active black fans. For example, PARSEC, the Pittsburgh science fiction fan club, has among its more than 100 members only one black fan. But PARSEC (like all other SF fan clubs) discriminates against no one for any reason and welcomes all to its membership.

Such low membership levels of black fans have been the case since the beginning of science fiction fandom. However, as I noted earlier, far from excluding or discouraging blacks from participation, the earliest SF fans honored black participation. Sam Moskowitz, in *The Immortal Storm*, his late-1940s history of science fiction fandom in the Thirties, tells us that in 1930 a group of mostly Jewish New York City fans formed, "the first true science fiction club and published the first true science fiction fan magazine." This group, which included such fans as Allen (Aaron) Glasser, Mort Weisinger and Julius Schwartz, was called the Scienceers. *And the first president of this first SF fan club was a black fan, James Fitzgerald.* And the black ghetto of Harlem, where Fitzgerald lived, was where the first SF fan club met—in Fitzgerald's living room.

Nevertheless, Moskowitz tells us, "The willingness of the other members to accede to his leadership, regardless of racial difference, *has never had an opportunity for duplication,* for James Fitzgerald was the first and last colored man ever actively to engage in the activities of science fiction fandom. [Moskowitz is speaking of SF fandom from 1930–1940.] It is an established fact," he continues, "that colored science fiction readers number in the thousands, but with the exception of Fitzgerald, the lone Negro who attended the first national science fiction convention in 1938, and the single Negro members of the later groups, the Eastern Science Fiction Association and the Philadelphia Science Fantasy Society, they play no part in this history."[14]

So, James Fitzgerald, the first president of the first SF fan club, was a lonely representative of his race. Blacks simply did not become fans, despite the willingness of white fans to welcome them. In fact, so eager were white fans to welcome blacks that, in the 1950s, they even created them—or at least one. In the mid-Fifties a certain prolific Midwest fan wrote numerous racist letters to the professional magazines. In response, Terry Carr and other Berkeley fans created "Carl Joshua Brandon," a literate, erudite, jazz-loving black fan who became a "Big Name Fan" in the mid-Fifties. His learned letters of comment discussing myriad aspects of science fiction and general culture (authored by Carr and his circle) filled the magazines. In the process, they refuted the racism expressed by a small minority of rustic fans. Indeed, "Carl Brandon" finally even published a story in a professional magazine ("Stanley Toothbrush," *The Magazine of Fantasy and Science Fiction*, July, 1962). Only when the white fan community was on the verge of electing black fan "Carl Brandon" an officer of a major fan organization was the ruse finally exposed.

Thus, much as many white fans wanted so desperately to believe that Fifties fandom had become multi-racial, it was not so. But, not for lack of trying on the part of whites. Hence, racist exclusion cannot be accepted as an explanation for sparse black participation in SF fandom, either in the present or in the past. In the end, Moskowitz offered no explanation for this phenomenon.

Nor can I explain why, even today, there is sparse black participation in various other cultural activities, such as attendance at art films, art galleries, natural history museums, operas, symphonies, chamber music concerts, ballets, and plays. By now a sizeable black middle class has developed which can afford such activities if it wished. But blacks rarely attend such cultural offerings, even when they are free. For example, Pittsburgh's Frick Art Museum has *always* offered free admission to all. But the Museum, like most of Pittsburgh's other "highbrow" cultural venues and events, has few black patrons.

This lack of black interest in such cultural activities has publicly troubled the Pittsburgh arts community and the city's cultural mavens have puzzled over black non-participation, no doubt replicated in other cities. However, they have come to no consensus on the black absence at such cultural events. Among black male teenagers, academic achievement is often discouraged and disparaged as "acting white." In like manner, perhaps many black adults perceive the cultural activities mentioned as "white" activities and so avoid participating in them because that would be "acting white."[15]

So, too, perhaps certain scholarly areas, such as archaeology, are avoided because they are perceived to be "white" fields of interest. For instance, the study of American slave sites is a booming archaeological field—but, overwhelmingly, it is white archaeologists who are studying this black past. In a 1994 survey of 1,644 members of the Society of American Archaeology, historical archaeologist Anna Agbe-Davies discovered only two members who identified themselves as being of African American descent. Obviously, this was not due to a racist exclusion by the archaeological field. Rather, Agbe-Davies says that, "The 'common sense' answer is that talented people from financially marginal backgrounds, which includes many members of racial minorities, choose fields that offer better financial rewards than academia. But I suspect the truth is more complicated. When you look at professional and graduate degree recipients by race, you see that black men and women are *not* flocking to traditionally high-paying fields at the expense of other pursuits."[16]

Perhaps there is a socioeconomic explanation for this phenomenon that is not readily apparent. Perhaps there is a cultural explanation, such as the fields being perceived by blacks as "white" fields of endeavor, and therefore to be avoided. But to properly understand this black absence, in a myriad of fields and areas, we need more tools in our intellectual toolbox than just the hammer of racial accusation and the simplistic charge that blacks are being deliberately barred from participation.

Likewise, if black authors had submitted science fiction stories with black protagonists, there is every reason to believe that sympathetic literary gatekeepers in the early science fiction world (such as ex-Scienceers Mort Weisinger, who became an editor, and Julius Schwartz, who became an agent) would have welcomed such submissions. But, despite the fact that no one was forbidding them entrance into the Promised Land, there were no black authors knocking at the door and submitting black-themed stories to such sympathetic recipients. Perhaps this was because blacks at that time perceived science fiction to be a "white" field of endeavor, and therefore declined to enter it.

If so, this would be despite the fact that science fiction was sympathetic to blacks and their concerns long before America as a whole became so, and long before Samuel Delany (who entered the field in 1962) and Octavia Butler (who entered in 1971) began publishing. Indeed, once one actually begins looking, a sympathetic black *presence* is more extensive in the genre than one might at first suspect, especially given the dearth of black fans and authors.

In fact, as Sam Moskowitz noted in 1967 (at almost exactly the same time Campbell was rejecting Delany's novel, for *whatever* reason), "The subject of racial intolerance has been a common one in science fiction," although this theme was often sublimated in a discussion of either tolerance or intolerance of extraterrestrials. As one example of this, Moskowitz pointed to Eric Frank Russell's "Dear Devil" (*Other Worlds Science Stories,* May, 1950), "which told how Earthmen overcame their repugnance to a blue, tentacled, bug-eyed Martian who gradually guided a shattered world back to the path of progress." Another example was a story by John Beynon Harris (better known as "John Wynd-

ham"), "The Living Lies" (*Other Worlds Science Stories*, November, 1950, as by
"John Beynon"), which explored racial tensions among red, green, black, and
white Venusians.[17]

In their examination of the field's history, Robert Scholes and Eric S. Rabkin
echo Moskowitz in this evaluation of the genre. Science fiction, they say, "has
been . . . advanced in its treatment of race and race relations. The xenophobia
that created alien races in the image of Bug-Eyed Monsters had already begun
to yield in the Thirties to more hospitable notions of foreignness. On the popular fringes of the form, of course, when it was fashionable to think of the 'Yellow
Peril,' the villains in series like *Flash Gordon* could be expected to have a Mon-
golian appearance. But because of their orientation toward the future, science
fiction writers frequently assumed that America's major problem in this area—
black/white relations—would improve or even wither away. . . . The presence
of unhuman races, aliens, and robots, certainly makes the differences between
human races seem appropriately trivial, and one of the achievements of science
fiction has been its emphasis on just this feature of human existence. . . . Post-
World War II science fiction, when it does make race a conscious issue, takes a
firm stand along the political lines that have popularly been called 'liberal.' [For
example, in Robert A. Heinlein's *Starship Troopers*, about midway in the 1959
novel] the hero looks into a mirror and his black face looks back at him. In the
book, this is not remarkable in any way, and many readers are probably not
even clearly aware that the hero is black."[18]

Likewise, most people have probably missed the fact that the protagonist of
Harlan Ellison's award-winning short story, "I Have No Mouth and I Must
Scream" is black. Understandable, as there is only a fleeting mention of his black
skin. And perhaps this is one of the points Ellison wants to make, that this is a
universal story, and the color of the protagonist is irrelevant.

However, as Moskowitz also made clear, the genre's respectful treatment of
blacks and their concerns actually predated World War II—and even predated
the appearance of science fiction magazines. In fact, the black presence began in
the early proto-science fiction novels of the late nineteenth century. Perhaps
the first SF novel to sympathetically portray a black character was published in
1864—before the Civil War had ended and before the 13th Amendment abolished American slavery. This was *A Voyage to the Moon* by the Rev. Crysostum
Trueman, which began with a search in the Rocky Mountains for an anti-gravity
metal (similar to H. G. Wells' Cavorite, which he used in his 1901 novel, *The
First Men in the Moon*). A former slave named Rodolph figures prominently in
this portion of the story and, said Moskowitz, "Rodolph is very clearly etched
as an extremely intelligent and able man, with high moral and ethical standards,
capable of admirable resourcefulness and possessing distinct managerial
skills."[19]

A positive treatment of blacks is also to be found in the popular and long-running (almost twenty years, from 1879–1898) Frank Reade and Frank Reade, Jr. stories by the Jewish writer "Harry Enton" (born Harry Cohen) and, later, Luis P. Senarens.[20] This influential series featured Frank Reade (and later his son) as teenage inventors of fantastic machines and became the prototype of the later and perhaps more famous Tom Swift stories. In all the stories, Reade had as his sidekicks representatives of the two most maligned groups of the age, Irishmen and blacks.

Pomp, the black character, appeared in the second in the series, "Frank Reade and His Steam Horse," serialized in the weekly *Boys of New York*, July 21, 1879-October 20, 1879. Although both the Irishman, Barney Shea, and Pomp had episodes of comic relief and spoke in the stereotyped vernacular of their groups, the hero treated them as complete equals. Further, both proved to be courageous fighters, expert marksmen, and the greatest horsemen of the age. Because of this, concludes Moskowitz, "a positive view of these minorities occurs when the reader is shown by *action* that those very Negroes and Irishmen, whom he may have regarded with condescension, the same ones he was likely to meet during his daily business, could perform deeds that were marked by considerable fortitude and great physical prowess, and that these deeds could be inspired by the highest concepts of fair play and patriotism. Furthermore, Pomp and Barney are not merely saddled with menial tasks, but operate at the pioneering end of scientific advancement in feats of adventure involving submarines, aircraft, space travel and tanks."[21]

This positive portrayal of black characters was continued by Edward Stratemeyer in 1906 when he began his *Great Marvel Series* with the dime novel *Through the Air to the North Pole* and, in 1907, *Under the Ocean to the South Pole*. A major character was Washington Jackson Alexander White, the black aide of the principal scientist, who not only displayed physical courage, but was also the engineer of the dirigible that flew to the North Pole and the submarine that made it to the South Pole.

Stratemeyer was also the creator of the popular and well-known Tom Swift series of boys' books, beginning in 1910 with *Tom Swift and His Motor Cycle*. In that very first Tom Swift novel we find Eradicate Sampson, an older black character who will become, over the course of the later novels, a good and useful friend to the teenage Swift. Thus, notes Moskowitz, "in teenage science fiction from 1879, when the Frank Reade series was begun, through to 1940, when the first Tom Swift series petered out, millions upon millions of white youngsters who read these books were given a very friendly and positive view of the Negro."[22]

These novels for young boys appeared at a time (1880–1920) when racism was becoming ever stronger in America. The 1896 Supreme Court decision of *Plessy vs. Ferguson* made racial segregation the law of the land. An average of 200 blacks a year were lynched for each and every year of the 1890s. The year

1900 was a "good" one. "Only" 115 blacks were lynched. By the 1920s a "new" Ku Klux Klan had emerged. It dominated the state politics of Indiana, Ohio had the nation's largest Klan membership, and Pennsylvania alone had 300,000 KKK members. Although the treatment of blacks in the proto-science fiction novels just mentioned resisted this trend, America's endemic racism could not help but be reflected in the popular fiction of the age, thus reflecting the "contested terrain" nature of popular culture.

For the most part, the racism in late nineteenth-century popular fiction was usually directed toward "The Yellow Peril," and several future war novels described savage warfare between civilized Anglo-Saxons and insidiously evil Orientals. But blacks did not escape such treatment, even by otherwise admirable authors. Jack London is a notable example.

Although known mainly for his "dog stories," London was also a member of the Socialist Party (and had been their mayoralty candidate in Berkeley, California) and his Leftist political concerns found expression in some of his fiction. London wrote several proto-science fiction short stories and one powerful future war novel, *The Iron Heel* (1907), describing the rise of a fascist state in America. George Orwell praised this novel for correctly (and virtually alone) predicting the appearance of fascism well in advance of the political reality. "Most Socialists," Orwell said, "did not foresee the rise of Fascism," but London knew that "when the working-class movements took on formidable dimensions and looked like dominating the world, the capitalist class *would hit back*. They wouldn't simply lie down and let themselves be expropriated, as so many Socialists had imagined."[23] Unfortunately, the triumph of fascism in London's novel is precipitated by a race war and blacks are on the wrong side, fighting for fascism against "democratic" whites.

Likewise, the British socialist and Fabian Society member H. G. Wells portrayed blacks as the "obedient muscle" of dictators in his 1899 novel, *When the Sleeper Awakes*. In the year 2200 a third of humanity lives in slavery and, when these white slaves rise in revolt, "Massa Boss" flies in black troops from Africa to crush them, first in Paris, then in London.

Blacks were also cast as villains by lesser lights. One of these was the well-known early SF writer Dr. David H. Keller in his series of four stories in *Amazing Stories Quarterly*, Summer, 1928. These stories—"The Menace," "The Gold Ship," "The Tainted Flood," and "The Insane Avalanche"—acknowledge the shoddy treatment of blacks at the hands of white America. But the main thrust of the action is to thwart the attempts of black scientists and leaders to destroy the United States in revenge. In addition to a racist tone, there is also a large element of sexism in these stories. Keller's anti-black bias resurfaced in "The Metal Doom" (*Amazing Stories*, May-July, 1932). Here, civilization collapses when, for some unexplained reason, all metal dissolves into dust. The South, however, fares the worst, because the subjugated blacks murder all whites before themselves descending into savagery. At the least, however, these stories acknowledged America's long racist barbarity directed against blacks.

A reanimated black king from the Stone Age and his black warriors figure as the villains in Charles W. Diffin's "When the Mountain Came to Miramar" (*Astounding Stories*, March, 1931). Likewise, blacks were the antagonists in Henry J. Kostkos's "Men Created for Death" (*Amazing Stories*, December, 1934). In the latter story, a brilliant black scientist unites all of Africa and then launches a genocidal race war against America as a prelude to world conquest. Only hordes of test tube babies saves "white" America from destruction.

At the same time, however, more sympathetic treatment of blacks can be found in such novels as *The White Man's Burden* (1915) by T. Shirby Hodge and *Black No More* (1931) by George Samuel Schuyler, who was himself black.[24] In Edgar Rice Burroughs's popular Barsoom novels, readers were presented with noble colored (red and green) men and Dejah Thoris, the love interest of the hero, John Carter, is colored. In the second novel, *The Gods of Mars* (*All-Story*, January–May, 1913, novel 1918) the big villains on Mars were revealed to be white. It wasn't until "The Black Pirates of Barsoom" (*Amazing Stories*, June, 1941) that Burroughs introduced black villains.

In the science fiction magazines proper, perhaps the earliest positive presentation of blacks was in J. (Joseph) Schlossel's "The Second Swarm" (*Amazing Stories Quarterly*, spring, 1928), immediately preceding David Keller's anti-black series in the same magazine. Interestingly, the story also featured a favorable portrayal of female spaceship commanders. After a huge space opera battle, an enormous Earth invasion fleet conquered and exterminated the intelligent but hostile arachnid inhabitants of a planet circling Sirius. The Earth fleet was divided by both race and gender, with white, black, and Asian contingents, which were further divided into male and female contingents. Even so, the various cohorts cooperated as equals and the female leaders (especially the black female leader) were highlighted more than the male leaders.

Next we find "The Moon Conquerors," by R. H. Romans (*Wonder Stories Quarterly*, winter, 1930), and its sequel, "War of the Planets" (*Wonder Stories Quarterly*, summer, 1930). Both stories posited modern blacks as the descendants of an advanced ancient civilization (with whites as their slaves) that once existed on the fifth planet from the sun in the Solar System. As that planet broke up to form the present asteroid belt between Mars and Jupiter, they migrated to Earth, where they recreated their civilization in Africa. That summer 1930, issue of *Wonder Stories Quarterly* also carried "Electropolis" by Otfrid von Hanstein, which featured, in passing, an Australian aborigine saving the life of a white pilot through delicate brain surgery. The same year, Louise Rice and Tonjoroff-Roberts portrayed black scientists as equals with white scientists in "The Astounding Enemy," (*Amazing Stories Quarterly*, winter, 1930).

From 1931–1932 Harry Bates and Desmond Hall, both editors at *Astounding*, published the "Hawk Carse" space opera series in the pages of their magazine. All these stories featured the heroic exploits of "Hawk" and "Friday," his black companion. Blacks were also sympathetically treated in Stanton A. Coblentz's "The Planet of Youth" (*Wonder Stories*, October, 1932), where they were kidnapped by powerful white-controlled corporations and transported to Venus as slaves. In Clifton B. Kruse's "The Drums" (*Astounding Stories*, March, 1936), millions of blacks from Earth colonized Saturn, only to be enslaved by the natives of Saturn. A slave revolt ensued in which the blacks massacred their masters.

Frank K. Kelly's "Red April, 1965" (*Wonder Stories*, March, 1932), about a war between America and the Soviet Union which began in 1961, was told almost entirely from the viewpoint of two black soldiers. Meanwhile, Leslie F. Stone's "The Fall of Mercury" (*Amazing Stories*, December, 1935) featured a black hero who used super-science to destroy an entire white race bent on conquering the solar system. As Stone described the two races, "The white race counted itself superior to the black race. They were arrogant and quarrelsome. The black race was more good-humored, peaceable, but they did not take well to the airs of their neighbors. They were both evolved from the same lowly species; they occupied equal ground and they were both highly intelligent. They were equals, mentally and physically" (p. 52). Three letters from readers discussing this story appeared in the April, 1936 issue of *Amazing*. Not one objected to the presence of the black hero.

Mort Weisinger (a 1930 Jewish member of the Scienceers, which black fan James Fitzgerald headed) highlighted the undesirable state of being black in white America in his story, "Pigments is Pigments" (*Wonder Stories*, March, 1935), the title being a reference to Ellis Parker Butler's well-known story, "Pigs Is Pigs." A ruthless white businessman was turned black by a scientist he wronged. He willingly paid everything he had to escape his condition and regain his white skin privilege. At about the same time, Olaf Stapledon, in his classic 1930 novel, *Last and First Men*, made the final humans a non-white race. Arthur C. Clarke returned to this device in his 1953 novel, *Childhood's End*, in which the narrator and final observer of the human race was a highly evolved black man. Then genre veteran Robert Bloch, in "The Funnel of God" (*Fantastic Science Fiction Stories*, January, 1960), portrayed an immortal black African shaman who became God and destroyed Earth with a great gob of spit.

In the early 1950s, even *before* the Civil Rights Movement erupted on the scene, many stories were published addressing the issue of equality for oppressed groups. Often these dealt with aliens or robots and an entire essay could be written about the sympathetic treatment of the two in Fifties SF. For example, in Richard Wilson's "Love" (*The Magazine of Fantasy and Science Fiction*, June, 1952), a blind Earth girl's entire family and community is adamantly opposed to her marrying a Martian. As Bill Pronzini later said of it, "This sensitive story is, of course, as much about racial prejudice in contemporary society as it is about a union between an alien and an Earthwoman. . . . that it found *a ready market and was well-received in 1952* is testimony not only to the then-budding maturation of science fiction, but to the then-budding maturation of the American outlook on civil rights."[25] (Perhaps there is some truth in the second part of this statement—but the story was published in a *science fiction magazine,* not in a "slick," and so is perhaps testimony more to science fiction's open door than to the maturation of American society.)

The same month "Love" was published, Daniel Keyes, in "Robot Unwanted" (*Other Worlds,* June, 1952), treated the issue of racial equality in a story about prejudice against a "free robot" which had no master. Mari Wolf called for "Robots of the World! Arise!" (*If,* July, 1952) and Harry Harrison's "The Velvet Glove" (*Fantastic Universe,* November, 1956) spoke of "robot slaves" and a "Robot Equality Act" which did not actually bring equality.

Meanwhile, William C. Gault's "Title Fight" (*Fantastic Universe,* December, 1956) explicitly linked robot and racial oppression in a story about an android boxer fighting a human in a championship bout. If the android won this "Man vs. Machine" contest, it would be the signal, not only for a world-wide robot revolution, but also a revolution of blacks and Asians, united with robots to exterminate the ruling white man. "Win this one, and blood will run in the streets," the android's robot trainer told the boxer, "White man's blood. We've got the Negro, and the Jap and the Chinamen and all the rest of them who got their rights so recently. And what kind of rights have they got? Civil, not in the people's hearts. You think those races don't know it? . . . We've got the combined venom of a billion non-whites." (This, in a story published in 1956!)

The issue of alien or robot equality was (as Bill Pronzini noted) usually a metaphor for the greatest domestic political conflict of the times, the conflict over civil rights for black Americans. Some writers, like Gault, either combined or stepped beyond the trope of alien or robot equality to directly address the issue of race relations and black equality in various venues. For example, in Al Feldstein's story, "Judgment Day," in the comic book *Weird Fantasy* (#18, March/April, 1953) from the Jewish-owned EC Comics, an Earth astronaut was sent to Cybrinia, a robot populated planet, to determine if the intelligent robots there were ready to join the Earth's Galactic Republic. He found that Cybrinia was a color-segregated society, with the dominant orange robots subjecting blue robots to ghettos and economic discrimination. The astronaut decided that Cybrinia could not join the Republic until its robots learned, like the people of Earth, to live together without prejudice and discrimination. After the astronaut returned to his ship, he removed his helmet to reveal himself as a handsome black man with "the beads of perspiration on his dark skin twinkling like distant stars."

A few years before this Ray Bradbury wrote a bitter and explicit tale of race relations, "Way in the Middle of the Air" (*Other Worlds Science Stories,* July, 1950), later included in *The Martian Chronicles,* published by Doubleday the same year. In the story, Southern blacks migrated *en masse* to Mars to escape white America's racism. The next year, in a new and small literary magazine, Bradbury published a sequel, "The Other Foot" (*New-Story,* March, 1951), later included in his 1951 collection, *The Illustrated Man.* In the sequel, the prospering black Martian settlers awaited the first rocket from Earth since a nuclear holocaust twenty years before. They planned to invert the racism they suffered at the hands of whites and lynch the white astronauts as they emerged from their ship. After the ship landed, one lone and haggard white man emerged to tell them of Earth's devastation. The blacks realized there was no place for their reverse racism and looked forward to a "new start for everyone."

Bradbury said he had problems finding a publisher for the first story. By the late Forties he'd graduated to the slick magazines and regularly published in such high-paying markets as *The Saturday Evening Post, Collier's, Mademoiselle, The New Yorker,* and *Harper's.* But, all these slicks rejected the story when Bradbury submitted it to them. "In 1948," he said, "I wrote a story titled 'Way in the Middle of the Air,' concerning a group of southern blacks who, tired of repression, built their own rockets and went off to Mars. The story was rejected by about every magazine in the country, and I finally sold it, late in the day, to a small s-f magazine for $80. [*Other Worlds Science Stories,* July, 1950, edited by Ray Palmer.] Not long after, I wrote another story about a group of priests who, arriving on Mars, try to decide whether a creature that they encounter, a fiery spirit which drifts on the air, is or is not 'human.' That story, 'The Fire Balloons,' suffered a similar history. Rejected everywhere, it was published many years later in a small s-f magazine in Chicago [*Imagination,* April, 1951, as "In This Sign"].

"On a political level, in early 1950, I wrote a story titled, 'And the Rock Cried Out.' It told the tale of a white man and his wife, trapped in South America, in an Indian village, shortly after an atomic holocaust. The man and his wife were forced to shine shoes and wait on tables for an existence. The shoe was indeed suddenly on the other foot, for the story questioned whether the couple could make do, accept being a white minority in a dark culture. This story, like the other two, was rejected by editors afraid to tell a tale that, with all its simplicity, might be considered anti-American and therefore pro-Communist."[26]

However, Bradbury's experiences with these stories reveal that some SF authors were attempting to overtly address racial issues in the immediate post-World War II period—and that some SF editors were ready to publish them, even if mainstream editors were not. Seemingly, at that time science fiction magazines were the only popular magazines where questions of racial justice could be addressed.

One reason for this is that their readers were writing them letters requesting (even demanding) such stories. For example, in the summer, 1949, issue of *Planet Stories,* reader David Hitchcock Green asked the magazine to run stories with black protagonists. In the fall, 1949, issue of the magazine, reader Radell Faraday Nelson, of Cadillac, Michigan, repeated Green's request. "You would do well to heed this call for unbiased tales," he said. "Set a precedent and run a tale with a Negro hero. Hmmm?" Another reader, Ray Ramsay, had previously also complained about the lack of non-white heroes in science fiction. In the same issue of *Planet Stories* cited above, reader Roy R. Wood, of Boon, North Carolina (!), said, "Ray Ramsay, you have a point there; I've never thought much about it before but most heroes are American or at least Anglo-Saxon. Why doesn't dear old *Planet Stories* run a story with a Chinese hero or something?"[27]

Likewise, Hattie Chesney, of Columbus, Ohio, wrote to *Startling Stories* editor Sam Merwin, Jr. (July, 1951, p. 137), demanding the same thing. "As a female who hates dithering and demands action," she said, "I now expect to see, in a coming issue, a story . . . in which the hero is as black as basalt (and twice as hard and slick) and in which the villain is a sinister lily-livered Albino. You may think that I am kidding but I am not. The integrity of your magazine rests on whether or not you publish such a story. . . . And don't give me any malarkey about not getting such a story—just whistle at that stable of well groomed writers and command one to hang upside down by his tail and type the tale."

Merwin responded by saying, "As for the story you want, take a skim through the lead in the September [1951] SS. The black man in question is not the hero but he comes closer than anyone else. Alack, no albinos, however."

And, as the Fifties continued, more such stories appeared. One of these was "Dark Interlude" (*Galaxy Science Fiction,* January, 1951), by Fredric Brown and Mack Reynolds, about a time traveller from the future stranded in a rural Southern backwater. One thing the stranger had trouble understanding about the past was the concept of "race." It seems that in the distant future, there *were* no races. All of humanity had been put through the genetic blenderizer. Indeed, in answer to a question, the stranger revealed that, because of this, his own great-great-great (and so on) grandfather was black. By then, the stranded time traveller had been so assimilated into the community that he had married into a local family. But, once his redneck brother-in-law learned of the attenuated black bloodline, he murdered the time traveller in what the local sheriff agreed was a case of "justifiable homicide."

"Dark Interlude" reflected the popular sentiment in Fifties science fiction that race would become irrelevant in the future. Speaking of this and, more particularly, *If* magazine in the Fifties, Algis Budrys wrote, "I remember . . . a short story in which a returning white astronaut finds the U.S. firmly in the hands of blacks. The blacks were depicted as rather middle-class types, given to three-piece suits and lip-service liberalism, which made their ineradicable basic antiwhite racial bias all the more poignant. The whites were called 'sharkies'—this was long before the common use of 'honky,' or of 'black' for 'Negro'—and the story was altogether—uncomfortably altogether—out of place in the early 1950s. At the time, it was clear to (almost) everyone that the Negroes were being swiftly and easily assimilated into the only culture that counted—the urban, enlightened civilization of the future which had already come into being in the North. Many SF stories, such as Fredric Brown's and Mack Reynolds's contemporaneous *Galaxy* piece, 'Dark Interlude,' casually assumed that the Earthman of the future would be slightly, attractively, cocoa-and-milk in color, rather like Lena Horne in MGM makeup. The indignant and effective liberalism of 'Interlude' did directly attack Southern rural anti-Negro bias, by showing its protagonist [the redneck brother-in-law] murderously opposed to the romanticized miscegenation which I think we all believed would, over the generations, solve that sociopolitical problem in the nicest possible way."[28]

Science fiction's majority belief in casual integration, so that race becomes irrelevant, was reflected in Theodore Sturgeon's "Baby Is Three" (*Galaxy Science Fiction*, October, 1952), later incorporated into his 1953 novel, *More Than Human*, winner of the 1954 International Fantasy Award. The story was about several castoff pieces of human debris who learned to coalesce into "Homo Gestalt," a superior species of humanity. This group was composed of a telepath, a Mongoloid idiot who could solve any mental problem . . . *and twin black girls with the ability to teleport.*

We find the same attitude toward race relations in Miriam Allen deFord's "The Last Generation?" (*The Magazine of Fantasy and Science Fiction*, winter-spring, 1950). Due to a nuclear accident, all mammals on Earth were rendered sterile. As humanity faceed the prospect of extinction, all resources were poured into an international research effort headed up by four eminent scientists. These four numbered *an American black*, a Chinese, a German-Jewish Irishman, and an English-Russian woman. And in deFord's "Operation Cassandra" (*Fantastic Universe*, November, 1958), four volunteers, comprising *a black Harvard philosopher and poet*, two white men, and a woman, awoke from suspended animation after a nuclear holocaust and confronted the necessity of rebuilding civilization from the four of them. Meanwhile, in Naomi Mitchison's 1962 novel, *Memoirs of a Spacewoman*, a number of black female scientists were integrated into her story.

In the June, 1960 issue of *Fantastic Science Fiction Stories*, p. 128, a reader from Eugene, Oregon, wrote praising the use of a black protagonist in Steven S. Gray's "When He Awakens" (*Fantastic Science Fiction Stories*, March, 1960). In response, editor Cele Goldsmith echoed Campbell's comments of 1955 and no doubt reflected the majority sentiment among SF editors when she said, "There should be no segregation in space, either."

By the mid-1960s and early 1970s, black characters and even protagonists had become so numerous in science fiction that they were no longer unusual. Indeed, as noted earlier, the professional organization of science fiction writers, the Science Fiction Writers of America, gave Samuel Delany's *The Einstein Intersection* the Nebula Award for best novel of 1967. The hero of the novel was a black musician. The fact that he was black raised no eyebrows at the time.

Nor was it particularly shocking to have a 1973 story about a black astronaut begin with, "Up from the Ghetto to the Stars. No shit, that was one of the headlines when I was picked for the mission by NASA. The first spade on Mars, from rats in the cradle to my black ass lighting up the firmaments."[29] Also in 1973, the science fiction community voted the novice author Christopher Priest Third Place in competition for the John W. Campbell Memorial Award for *Fugue for a Darkening Island*, a bold examination of race relations in a near-future England.

It is clear, then, that for many white SF fans, writers, and editors, blacks were not "invisible men" excluded from the future. Indeed, as Ray Bradbury's experience in the late Forties and early Fifties suggests, SF writers and editors were addressing issues of racial discrimination and intolerance—and suggesting a desirable solution—long before mainstream American magazines were willing to discuss the same issues. And, judging by reader response, such attempts were welcomed by the fans, as the top-ranking of the "Black Man's Burden" stories by Reynolds indicates.

This survey is not a comprehensive compendium of the black presence in early science fiction. Nevertheless, it should make it clear that there was an open door in science fiction for this particular outsider group. While there may well have been present an echo of the racism of the larger society, there were far more voices raised in opposition to that racism. As Scholes and Rabkin argue, long before Delany and Butler entered the field as "pathbreakers," science fiction had attempted, "to get beyond even 'liberal' attitudes, to make stereotyping itself an obsolete device and the matter of race comparatively unimportant. Science fiction, in fact, has taken the question so spiritedly debated by the Founding Fathers of the United States—of whether the rights of man included black slaves as well as white slave owners—and raised it to a higher power by asking whether the rights of being end at the boundaries of the human race. The answers have ranged from the most xenophobic human racism to the most transcendent worship of being itself—but the important thing is that the questions have been raised and are continuing to be raised by works of science fiction."[30]

Indeed, that is the important thing. In the realm of race relations, early science fiction (unlike the larger society) was not a monolithic field of racism and exclusion. Rather, it was "contested terrain," in which racial justice was more often championed than not and the black presence was usually welcomed, even as it was shunned in America as a whole.

Notes

1. Moskowitz, *The Immortal Storm:*, pp. 9–10. By June, 1931, when Julius Schwartz joined the Scienceers at age 16, Fitzgerald had dropped out of the club, which was then meeting in the basement of Mort Weisinger's parents' home in The Bronx. Comments made by Schwartz in vetting this chapter, December 4, 2003.

While Moskowitz gives the date of 1930 for the founding of The Scienceers, Allen Glasser, one of the founders, claimed the club was started in 1929. Glasser's account appeared in the fanzine *Sphere* #12, 1959, published by Joe Christoff and Larry Thorndyke our of Atlanta, Georgia. Either the 1929 or 1930 dates would still make The Scienceers the first SF fan club.

2. Annette John-Hall, "'Matrix' Diversity at Odds With Sci-Fi's White History," *The Philadelphia Inquirer,* reprinted in *The Pittsburgh Post-Gazette,* June 7, 2003, p. B-6.

3. Tony Norman, "Strangers in a Strange Land No More," *The Pittsburgh Post-Gazette,* January 16, 2001.

4. See the Harlan Ellison interview in Charles Platt, *Dream Makers: The Uncommon People Who Write Science Fiction,* Berkley Books: N.Y., 1980, p. 167.

5. Samuel R. Delany, "Racism and Science Fiction," in Sheree R. Thomas, Ed., *Dark Matter: A Century of Speculative Fiction from the African Diaspora,* Warner Books: N.Y., 2000, pp. 387–388. Delany also relays the rumor that author Dean Koontz has a letter from Campbell reflecting racist views. However, Delany does not claim to have read this letter and until Koontz produces it, this must remain, like Delany's report of what Campbell supposedly told his agent, merely hearsay.

6. Pohl, *The Way the Future Was,* pp. 83–84.

7. Letter, John W. Campbell to Forrest J. Ackerman, June 19, 1955. Reprinted in Chapdelaine, Sr., Chapdelaine, and Hay, *The John W. Campbell Letters, Vol. 1,* pp. 288–289. Circulation of *Astounding-Analog* in black neighborhoods can also be attested to by the experience of Norm Metcalf. Norm told me that from 1963–1966 he worked for a distributor stocking San Francisco Bay area newsstands with British SF magazines. Not only did such magazines sell in the mostly-black neighborhood of north Oakland, but he noticed that Campbell's magazine was also always to be found on local newsstands. Indeed, the drugstore right around the corner from the north Oakland headquarters of the Black Panther Party regularly sold *Analog.*

8. Letter, Reynolds to Norm Metcalf, August 2, 1967.

9. Dallas McCord ("Mack") Reynolds, introduction to "Black Sheep Astray," the third in his series, in Harry Harrison, Ed., *Astounding: John W. Campbell Memorial Anthology,* Ballantine Books: N.Y., 1973, 1974, p. 219. Emphasis added. This is a collection of original stories by *Astounding* authors in which each chose a theme he thought would honor Campbell the most. Reynolds chose to write a new installment of the "Black Man's Burden" stories.

10. Reynolds, introduction to "Black Sheep Astray," p. 219. Emphasis added.

11. For Reynolds' ranking as third most-published author, see Mike Ashley, *The Complete Index to Astounding/Analog,* Robert Weinberg Publications: Oak Forest, Ill., 1981, p. 246.

12. Pohl, *The Way the Future Was,* p. 275.

13. It is also possible Campbell rejected Delany's novel simply because he didn't have room. Campbell rejected a number of excellent novels he'd have liked to have published, solely for space considerations. His magazine had room for only four genuine novels per year. The two-part serials were actually of only novelette length.

Delany's ignorance of Campbell's editorial policies—and Campbell's track record in publishing racially-themed stories—might be because Delany wasn't actually reading Campbell's magazine, or perhaps any *other* SF magazine. Delany began his career with novels and didn't publish a short story until the very year in question ("The Star Pit," *Worlds of Tomorrow,* February, 1967). Thus, he wasn't looking at the magazines as a potential market.

14. Moskowitz, *The Immortal Storm:*, pp. 9–10.

15. See L. A. Johnson, "Crossing the Culture Line: Why Do So Few African Americans Attend the City's Highbrow Cultural Events?," *The Pittsburgh Post-Gazette,* June 19, 2003, p. D-1.

16. Anna Agbe-Davies interview in anonymous column, "Archaeology and the Black Experience," *Archaeology,* published by the Archaeological Institute of America, January–February, 2003, p. 22.

17. Sam Moskowitz, "The Negro in Science Fiction," *Worlds of Tomorrow,* May, 1967, p. 41. Reprinted in Moskowitz, *Strange Horizons.*

18. Robert Scholes and Eric S. Rabkin, *Science Fiction: History, Science, Vision,* Oxford University Press: Oxford and New York, 1977, pp. 187–188.

19. Moskowitz, "The Negro in Science Fiction," p. 43.

20. Moskowitz identifies "Enton" as Jewish in *Strange Horizons,* p. 45.

21. Moskowitz, "The Negro in Science Fiction," p. 45.

22. Moskowitz, "The Negro in Science Fiction," pp. 47–48.

23. George Orwell, "Jack London," BBC radio lecture delivered March 5, 1943, reprinted in *Orwell: The Lost Writings,* Arbor House: N.Y., 1985, p. 124. Emphasis in the original.

24. See the obituary of Schuyler by George Goodman, Jr., "George S. Schuyler, Black Author," *The New York Times,* September 8, 1977, p. 40.

25. Bill Pronzini in Barry N. Malzberg and Bill Pronzini, Eds., *The End of Summer: Science Fiction of the Fifties,* Ace Books: N.Y., 1979, p. 61.

26. Ray Bradbury, "Science Fiction: Before Christ and After 2001," Introduction to Edmund J. Farrel, et al., Eds., *Science Fact/Fiction,* Scott, Foresman, & Co.: Glenview, Ill., 1974, pp. ix–x.

27. Radell Faraday Nelson and Roy R. Wood, letters to the editor, *Planet Stories,* fall, 1949, p. 104 and p. 109.

28. Algis Budrys, "Memoir," in Frederik Pohl, Martin Harry Greenberg, and Joseph D. Olander, *Worlds of If,* Bluejay Books, Inc.: N.Y., 1986, p. 96.

29. Joe Gores, "Faulty Register," in Thomas N. Scortia and Chelsea Quinn Yarbro, Eds., *Two Views of Wonder,* Ballantine Books: N.Y., 1973.

30. Robert Scholes and Eric S. Rabkin, *Science Fiction: History, Science, Vision,* p. 189.

10

Femalien Empathy

L ET US NOW PRAISE Pamela Sargent. True, her work has helped perpetuate the myth of discrimination against women (and others) in the early science fiction magazines. But, at least she is not one of those who denies the female presence altogether. Instead, she asserts that "we should not lose sight of the fact that, however outnumbered women science-fiction writers have been, they have also been a part of the genre since its beginnings."[1]

Indeed they have—but what did they contribute? Disparagers of female artistic accomplishment maintain, "not much." For example, British science fiction writer Lisa Tuttle, who wrote the entry on women for the Clute and Nicholls *Encyclopedia,* says "Women's contributions to the genre, while never entirely absent, were not substantial until the late 1960s." On this premise she develops the bulk of her entry, which is devoted to women writers in the 1970s and later. In briefly passing over everything before 1970 she repeats the mantra that even what little women contributed then was usually concealed behind "androgynous bylines, real or assumed."[2]

Of course, if one accepts the standard mythology of a hostile patriarchy that completely dominated pulp science fiction, one has to believe this virtually blank page on early women writers. But, if one believes that early science fiction was "contested terrain," then one is more able to perceive the nature of female accomplishment in pulp science fiction. In fact, some of these early women writers presented views of society and human relations which were daring, experimental, and highly provocative. If we continue to disparage and dismiss such contributions by them, then our knowledge of the genre itself is crippled. And, as Joanna Russ pointed out, "A mode of understanding literature which can ignore . . . half the human race is not 'incomplete'; it is distorted through and through."[3]

I suggest there are two female contributions to pulp science fiction that have been either ignored or not fully explored. The first is a greater empathy with fully conceived aliens. Dr. Tania Singer, a professor at the University College, London, in the rapidly growing field of "social neuroscience," has pointed to social and psychological research which indicates that men are "slightly less empathic in general" than women.[4] I suggest that this tendency of women to be more empathic than men was reflected in much early science fiction by female authors.

Then, with Jane L. Donawerth, I point to a revolutionary and paradigm-shifting early tradition of feminist (even socialist-feminist) utopian speculation.[5] This tradition was unprecedented in American literature. It represented a fundamental departure in theme and type from earlier feminist utopias, such as Charlotte Perkins Gilman's *Herland* (1915). Further, it presaged the type of feminist speculations commonly assumed to have appeared only much later—in the 1970s.

These two elements are exactly what modern critics have long argued were most absent in pulp science fiction. Critic Basil Davenport, for instance, felt that only in the late 1950s did more empathetic and humane values begin to enter the literature. "One of the most striking developments in science fiction since the days of 'The War of the Worlds' and 'The Skylark of Space,'" he said, "has been the realization that men and Martians need not necessarily exterminate or enslave each other."[6]

Similarly, Robert Scholes and Eric Rabkin argued that "Three strands of pulp fiction—adventure, hardware, and weird [as in *Weird Tales*]—dominated American science fiction in the Twenties and Thirties. The only element of the previous century of science fiction not vigorous in the U.S. at this time was the element developed by [Edward] Bellamy, the social concern and commitment that were so important in the European fiction of this period. If Jack London had not died in 1917 at the age of forty, this strand might also have continued to be vigorous in popular American fiction."[7] Likewise, Vonda McIntyre wondered, "Why . . . do so many sf writers leave their female characters back in the twentieth century? Why aren't there more non-sexist futures? One possible explanation was the lack of markets. Few SF editors . . . knew enough about feminism to be open to stories where both women and men were portrayed as fully functioning human beings."[8]

But, in the shadows of the officially recognized male shapers of early science fiction, other writers—unknown and underappreciated women—were already creating a more humane brand of science fiction. In addition, instead of simply writing about The Future As More of the Present, they were engaging in genuine social speculation. So we do not have to yearn for the ghosts of Jack London or Edward Bellamy. A fourth science fiction strand *was* in existence at the time, and there *were* markets and editors who were open to such speculations and portrayals of women as fully functioning human beings.

Hence, I am not advocating a kind of reclamation project for a few forgotten writers in a peripheral arena. Rather, I assert that a type of science fiction which more recent authors have championed as crucial to the field (but was lacking) was, in fact, there from the very beginning. While male writers were, as a group, viewing science fiction as a playground for technological experimentation and development (the strands of hardware and adventure Scholes and Rabkin discern), many female writers were using it to express empathy with "others" and as a laboratory of the kind of social speculation critics say was missing from the literature.[9]

Let me be clear: I am *not* arguing that *all* early women writers offered such social speculations. Nevertheless, I feel enough of them were expressing such ideas to justify claiming an alternative "feminine" tone for many of their stories. In a sense, they were attempting to create a type of fiction that joined technical concerns with social concerns, which melded adventure with empathy. Had these alternate roots of the genre been better nourished, a more mature literature might have flowered much earlier. And had the traditional exclusion narrative not dominated our thinking about this period, we might long since have rediscovered this lost legacy.

Before we look more closely at the two tendencies I have identified, however, let us explore the question of why women may have been more empathetic toward aliens in their stories. Perhaps one component of the answer (I will suggest an additional component in part 2) is that the female image was itself contested terrain. Because of this, the powerful image of the alien-as-female was often presented as a positive alternative to the traditional negative portrayal of women.

It is true that there were many stereotypical images of women in pulp science fiction, both in the stories and on the covers of the magazines. Such images reinforced traditional gender roles of male dominance and female subordination. In most of the stories women were portrayed in patronizing, sexist, and boringly unimaginative ways, which is ironic for a literature that prided itself upon imagination. Thus, Joanna Russ seemed to be correct when she famously asserted in 1974 that, "There are plenty of images of women in science fiction. There are almost no women."[10]

However, this interpretation presents a starkly delineated interpretation of the field that does not tell the whole story. The reality is more complicated. There were also many female images that subverted the stereotypes and presented women as powerful and independent actors in their own right. Thus, one of the most salient validations of the contested terrain thesis is the ambiguous female image presented in pulp science fiction.

First of all, what Russ meant by her statement was that there were no *real* women characters in early science fiction, only cardboard cutouts. However, even the *male* characters in early science fiction, written by *male* authors, were also only cardboard stereotypes. As Ursula K. Le Guin pointed out in 1975, "'Golden Age' writers were not writing a fiction of character or of passion; they were writing in an impersonalized genre of ideas-technology-adventure; and so all their characters were necessarily two-dimensional. Male characters were more frequent than female, but just as wooden, vapid, and stereotyped."[11] When viewed in the larger context, therefore, the stereotypical portrayal of women so often found pulp science fiction does not seem so one-sided. The men were also stereotypes. That was the style of the literature.

It is also true that scantily clad women routinely appeared on the covers of many science fiction pulps, often being menaced by a bizarre alien of some kind. However, as Robin Roberts has perceptively observed, very often it was the *woman* who was the alien doing the menacing. For this reason, she argued, "Science fiction critics and feminist critics should *examine* rather than dismiss the pulps' depiction of women [because] science fiction has a long-standing and well-developed tradition of powerful female aliens. . . . Many of the stories from these years do depict women stereotypically and unattractively. Nevertheless, much pulp science fiction depicts strong, independent women in both text and illustrations. . . . [these] protofeminist portrayals of women in science fiction . . . reveal many strong female characters, with potentially feminist qualities."[12]

These "protofeminist portrayals" of strong women and female aliens—femaliens, if you will—can be found in the literature even before the appearance of pulp science fiction. For example, H. Rider Haggard's famous "She-Who-Must-Be-Obeyed" ("She: A History of Adventure," *The Graphic*, 1886–1887) was an immortal and sensuous incarnation of the goddesses Isis and Aphrodite who ruled the lost world of Kor in the jungle depths of Africa. We also find a powerful female character in C. L. Moore's famous Jirel of Joiry stories in the fantasy magazine *Weird Tales*. But even in pulp science fiction itself we find depictions of powerful women, notably in the stories of Stanley G. Weinbaum. "The Red Peri" ("The Red Peri," *Astounding Stories*, November, 1935), for instance, was a notorious space pirate who raided the interplanetary space lanes.

Weinbaum's most famous such female character, however, was "Margaret of Urbs," also known as "The Black Flame." She burst upon the science fiction world in the debut issue of a new magazine edited by Mort Weisinger, *Startling Stories,* January, 1939. Seven years later, in January 1946, when female fan Jim-E Daugherty launched her feminist fanzine, she entitled it, *Black Flames*. In her editorial, she explained why.

"Once upon a time," she wrote, "there lived an outstanding, wise and beautiful, Amazon-type woman. . . . Black Flame was the title given to her, which stood for authority and power, and also for the raven black hair that crowned her exquisite features and head. She excelled in every field, over man and woman. Margaret of Urbs lived in the first stages of science fiction and has become a legend among fans. . . . The editor dedicates this mag [sic] to Mr. Weinbaum's memory and to *The Black Flame*, being the first SF story that, when she was first introduced to the field, left such an individual and vivid impression among the stories she had read."

However, it wasn't just in the stories that one could find such "Amazon-type" women. One critic, writing at about the same time as Robin Roberts (but less perceptively), incorrectly maintained that, during the Golden Age, women were "present *only* as voluptuous and helpless objects on the lurid pulp covers."[13] But Roberts, in her examination of the medium, found much art depicting powerful female aliens on the covers of these magazines. Hence, "the SF magazines of the late forties and early fifties contain portrayals of women that prepare for the feminist sf heroines of the nineteen-seventies and eighties. . . . [although] In most cases, neither the stories nor their protofeminist illustrations are preserved in the many illustrated histories of science fiction."[14] Had these stories and these illustrations been preserved and presented, we might, in fact, have a more nuanced and accurate understanding of the depiction of women in early science fiction.

Notoriously weak and stereotypical on characterization, early science fiction has also (and more accurately) been criticized for failing to engage in genuine social extrapolation, especially in the realm of gender relations. In 1975 Ursula K. Le Guin noted that, "The women's movement has made most of us conscious of the fact that SF has either totally ignored women, or presented them as squeaking dolls subject to instant rape by monsters—or old-maid scientists desexed by hypertrophy of the intellectual organs—or, at best, loyal little wives or mistresses of accomplished heroes. Male elitism has run rampant in SF."[15] Sociologically, the future was the past: conservative, rigid, and sexually hierarchical. It was the Victorian age writ large on an interstellar canvas.

Thus, one can point to stories, even by women, written as late as the 1950s and early 1960s that reflect stereotypical gender roles and expectations. Because they partook of the same tropes as most male-authored fiction, many such female-written stories didn't stand out as distinctively female contributions. What are we to make of this?

Such mimicry is part of a larger problem. We live, and have lived, in a patriarchal culture. This means that the buried bias of sexism distorts all our views, especially of who "counts." Therefore, as Simone de Beauvoir famously observed half a century ago (and many others have elaborated upon since), women are universally seen as a subsidiary "second sex" because "Humanity is male and man defines woman not in herself but relative to him. . . . He is the Subject, he is the Absolute—she is the Other."[16]

In other words, because of sexism, which privileges males, our (public) culture is seen as "male" culture, to which women are outsiders. What is viewed as a "human" or "universal" experience is described in male terms. It thus becomes a wholly male experience. Therefore, if we wish to explore the "human condition," we are essentially exploring the "male condition." Indeed, this is essentially what the prolific feminist science fiction critic Marleen Barr said while discussing the work of "James Tiptree, Jr." (Alice Sheldon). Women are seen as aliens in our patriarchal culture, Barr said, because, quoting Tiptree (and echoing de Beauvoir), "to be human is to be male."[17]

We should not be surprised, then, when we come across science fiction written by women which reads as if written by men. The authors were merely trying to describe a universal human experience, as they felt our culture defined and accepted it. Nor should they be condescendingly denigrated, as some critics have, for not being a "mutant"—i.e., for not presenting an outsider's (and hence marginalized) view. They were simply attempting to engage in the common discourse of literature. That meant "writing like a man."

Unfortunately, this sometimes meant replicating male stereotypes of women. As an elemental ideology, the very foundation of a patriarchal society, sexism permeated the culture and colored virtually *everyone's* worldview. Hence, with its often cliched portrayals of gender relations, whether written by a man or a woman, early science fiction often reflected the sexism of society at large.

But, such presentations did not represent the sum total of how women were portrayed in pulp science fiction stories and illustrations. Writing in the passion of the initial stages of the Seventies women's movement, Le Guin perhaps overstated the prosecution's case against early science fiction. Again, reality is more ambiguous than usually presented. Eric S. Rabkin, for instance, in his largely-ignored revisionist overview of the treatment of women in science fiction, challenged this depiction, arguing that the sexist stereotype is overdrawn and not entirely justified.[18] And, writing a dozen years after Le Guin's comments, Robin Roberts also examined the treatment of women in early science fiction and was not quite as dismissive. Indeed, some of Roberts's evidence for the defense came from the very examples the prosecution had used against early science fiction. The stories of Leigh Brackett are illustrative.

Critics have pointed to Leigh Brackett's science fiction as male-protagonist, gadget-driven space operas that reflected the same sexist female images found in most male-authored fiction. In fact, however, Roberts argued that "Leigh Brackett wrote a number of fine stories focusing on mysterious and powerful female aliens. As the cover art for her story 'Black Amazon of Mars,' from *Planet Stories*, March 1951, demonstrates, woman sf writers endorsed the portrait of the strong female alien. In F. Anderson's painting, the Amazon dominates the cover, swinging aggressively—at first glance apparently at the reader. In the background, lower left, John Stark [her partner] is engulfed by the predatory fronds. His figure is dwarfed by that of the Amazon, Ciara. . . . Brackett's story differs from those by male sf writers; unlike them, she does not cast her hero and heroine's relationship in terms of a mother-son bond nor even mention Ciara's reproductive capacity. Brackett can envision a union of equals. At the end of the story, Ciara will rule the city she has conquered and Stark agrees to remain with her, at least for a while. At the end, as well as the beginning of the story, Stark is silenced by Ciara's 'strength and splendor.'"[19]

As noted by Roberts, Brackett's stories often centered around "Warrior Princess" heroines and presented visions of powerful women acting as equals to men in a violent and uncertain world. Science fiction author Paul Dellinger recalls Brackett complaining at the 1974 DisCon World SF Convention in Washington, D.C., about an editor who objected to such stories from her. The editor noted that all her women characters tended to "come down from the mountain swinging their swords." Brackett said of course they did! That was the sub-genre of story she chose to write, so "what did he expect them to do, bring their hem-stitching?"[20]

By viewing such stories with an unprejudiced eye, it is easier to discern that the image of women in pulp science fiction was far more "contested" than commonly portrayed. As Robin Roberts reminds us, "science fiction has always been fascinated by the figure of the woman. Male SF writers *did* exclude human women from their texts, but represent the feminine through the female alien. These woman aliens were initially powerful and threatening and thrust their sex aggressively towards the reader and the men in the stories."[21]

The female image itself, then, was "contested terrain," a major battlefield in this particular popular culture arena. This may have contributed to the empathetic treatment of aliens in female science fiction. In many cases, presenting the *alien* as female was the best way to present a powerful female image. It was a subversive reinterpretation of the millennia-old male tradition of presenting the *female* as alien.

When the first humans (presumably male) began creating art, they also began objectifying women as "the Other." Throughout many millennia, humans apparently existed art-free. Then, around 30,000 years ago in the period known as the Upper Paleolithic, art in the form of sculptures, cave paintings, and petroglyps suddenly appeared in Europe. We don't know what this art meant to the artists, although scholars have their theories. Perhaps they were part of magic or religious rituals, perhaps they were shamanistic aids to hunting, perhaps they were calendars or representations of the cosmos.

These artistic representations ranged from tiny sculptures to larger-than-life-size paintings and were mainly of animals and geometric shapes, as well as outlines of hands on cave walls, presumably the hands of the artists. And then there were the ubiquitous nude female figurines, the most famous of which is the Venus of Willendorf. Were they fertility symbols? Representations of a "female" force? Again, we don't know, but we are probably safe in assuming these female-styled objects were created by male artists to represent something "other" than themselves, an alien something which preoccupied their imaginations.

Ancient Greek artists (also presumably male) of the Archaic period (700–480 B.C.) and earlier also saw women as something "other" than themselves and turned them into things explicitly alien: Sirens, sphinxes, and gorgons.[22] Gorgons are first mentioned in Homer's *Iliad*, his account of the Trojan War, which is thought to have occurred c. 1250 B.C. In Homer's story, the shields of both the goddess Athena and the Greek king Agamemnon portray the heads of gorgons. This was because the mere sight of a gorgon—a fearsome and hideous female monster—could turn a man to stone. The word "gorgon" comes from *gorgos,* something that is scary, fearful, and terrifying. And, indeed, the gorgons were portrayed as terrifying and ugly creatures, often with their hair consisting of coiling snakes. During the Archaic period their bodies were often depicted as being those of panthers, lions, birds, or horses. And gorgons were always female.

Perhaps the most famous story about these female aliens was told by the eighth century B.C. poet Hesiod in his *Theogony.* His story concerned the slaying of the gorgon Medusa by the hero Perseus. Using winged sandals, rendered invisible by the cap of Hades, and gazing only upon the reflection of Medusa in his highly polished shield while Athena guided his hand, Perseus slew Medusa by beheading her. (All this help hardly seems fair.) By the first half of the seventh century B.C. this story was appearing frequently in Greek art.

Archaic Greeks also rendered sphinxes as "human-female animals," winged lions with the heads of women. These fearsome female demons delighted in devouring young men. By 650 B.C. images of them chasing down, straddling, carrying off, or eating handsome young men can be found on vases, reliefs, shields, and gems. The most famous of these femaliens was the Theban Sphinx, who began to appear in Greek stories around the sixth century B.C., with the earliest extant graphic representation dating from c. 530 B.C. In the story, this female monster lay in wait outside the walls of Thebes for unwary male travelers. She asked all who came upon her a riddle: What goes on four legs in the morning, two at noon, and three in the evening? If the unfortunate victim could not correctly answer—the sphinx devoured him. Finally, the hero Oedipus solved the riddle. The answer was a man . . . who crawls as a child, walks upright as an adult, and supports himself with a cane in old age.

But perhaps the most alluring of the female aliens portrayed in Archaic Greek art were the sirens, who first appeared in Book 12 of Homer's epic, the *Odyssey.* In the well-known story, the sirens lured the sailors of passing ships to their doom on the shores of their rocky island by singing the most beautiful song imaginable. The hero Odysseus is the only man known to have heard the song the sirens sang and lived to tell the tale. He did this by having his men lash him to the mast of his ship, while they rowed frantically past the island, their own ears stopped up with wax. In his *Argonautica,* the third century B.C. poet Apollonius of Rhodes also told of an encounter with the seductive and deadly sirens as Jason and the Argonauts searched for the Golden Fleece. This time the mythic singer Orpheus, a member of the band, saved the crew by singing and playing upon his heavenly lyre, downing out the sirens' song with his own unworldly music.

The earliest artistic representations of sirens date to the late eighth or early seventh centuries B.C. While Homer and Apollonius never described what the sirens looked like, they were commonly represented in Greek art as half-female, half-bird hybrids, a model perhaps derived from Near Eastern precursors.

There is thus a long tradition, as long as human art itself, of portraying women as something "other" than males, something decidedly alien. As science fiction literally deals with aliens, it should come as no surprise that we find a conflation of females and aliens—of "femaliens"—in the literature, especially in stories authored by men. They are the "Other," the outsiders, humanity's second-class citizens, not quite human.[23] As Robin Roberts pointed out, "Because most science fiction was written by men, the genre reflected the larger culture's treatment of woman as alien, with the significant difference that in sf, women could be depicted as literally alien."[24] Indeed, in James Gunn's famous and much-anthologized story "The Misogynist" (*Galaxy Science Fiction*, November, 1952), this is exactly the case, as women are revealed to be an actual species of alien extra-terrestrials.

Perhaps this "alien" status was one reason why early women science fiction writers, as a group, brought an empathetic and more fully conceived dimension to their descriptions of people, relationships, and, most especially, aliens than did the great bulk of their male colleagues. They felt they, as femaliens themselves, had something in common with aliens and outsiders in general.

Typical of this approach was the work of Wilmar Shiras, whose fiction emphasized character and relationships. Her debut, "In Hiding" (published by John W. Campbell in *Astounding*, November, 1948), was voted by the members of the Science Fiction Writers of America for induction into the Science Fiction Hall of Fame. Combined with two sequels, "Opening Doors" and "New Foundations" (*Astounding*, March, 1949 and March, 1950), it was published along with two new stories as *Children of the Atom* (1953).

The plot concerns an elementary school guidance counselor who is sent a troubled young boy having difficulty fitting in with his peers. As the story unfolds, he is revealed to be one of a number of a mutant geniuses living a secret life among humanity's "normals." Contrary to the approach of male writers treating this theme, such as Olaf Stapledon's *Odd John*, John Wyndham's *The Midwich Cuckoos*, or A. E. van Vogt's *Slan*, the children are not seen as a danger. "This sensitive book does not present the children as frightening threats, but as interesting and concerned individuals and raises ethical questions about how they should lead their lives," notes Pamela Sargent.[25]

But such ethical concerns—and empathy with those who are "different"— were present in women's science fiction from the beginning. Indeed, we can see this empathy with the outcast, with the "Other," in the very first fully-acknowledged science fiction novel, Mary Shelley's *Frankenstein* (1818). In the story, the Frankenstein "monster," when first created, was actually a loving and gentle creature. But from the moment of its creation, its "father," Dr. Victor Frankenstein, rejected it in horror, again and again. It was this constant rejection that turned the creature into a "monster," made so by loneliness, isolation, and friendlessness. And it is this empathetic depiction of the "monster" which gives that novel its enduring power. Indeed, according to feminist literary critics Sandra Gilbert and Susan Gubar, it is this "disguised, buried, or miniaturized, femaleness . . . [which is] the heart of this apparently masculine book."[26]

We find this same manifestation of empathy in the stories of the very earliest female magazine science fiction writers. Take, for example, Clare Winger Harris, the first woman to publish in the science fiction magazines. Richard Lupoff believes her classic story, "The Miracle of the Lily" (*Amazing Stories*, April, 1928), should have gotten the Hugo Award as the best story of 1928, if those awards had existed then. Lupoff edited four anthologies under the series title *What If?* containing stories which he felt should have won the Hugo from 1952–1978. Mike Ashley asked him to extend his analysis back to April, 1926, when Gernsback published the first SF magazine, and choose a winner for each year.[27]

Harris' story has a surprise ending which powerfully poses the question, "What is Human?" If it is not the first, then it is surely *one* of the first stories to ask this now-standard science fiction query. Harris expanded the definition to include sentient Venusian insects because, she later explained, "I hated to think of the inhabitants of the Earth waging war against the well-meaning insect inhabitants of Venus simply because of the latter's unfortunate physical form."[28]

As Jane Donawerth notes, however, such sensibility was not unique to Harris among early women science fiction writers. "[M]any of these women writers romanticize alien life forms," she says. "In [Clare Winger] Harris and Breuer's 'A Baby on Neptune,' the alien that welcomes humans to Neptune resembles a 'multicolored chandelier,' 'scintillating throughout the chromatic scale' (p. 798), and in [L. Taylor] Hansen's 'What the Sodium Lines Revealed,' the aliens from one of Jupiter's moons 'pulsated like the turquoise transplendency of a nebulous aurora' (p. 130). In the decade in which men writing science fiction invented BEMs (Bug-Eyed Monsters), women writers showed great empathy for their imagined aliens. . . . Even in [Louise] Rice and Tonjoroff-Roberts' 'The Astounding Enemy,' which treats insects as bug-eyed monsters, Mildred Sturtevant, the woman scientist captured by the insects, has great empathy for them: 'I have grown fond of these' giant lightning bugs (p. 97); when the evil giant termite leader is killed, 'to our amazement she ran to him and touched his face,' mourning the death of this 'great intelligence' (p. 103)."[29]

Many have seen empathetic, fully conceived aliens as the unique contribution of Stanley G. Weinbaum and Raymond Z. Gallun in the mid-Thirties. Indeed, Weinbaum's famous Science Fiction Hall of Fame story, "A Martian Odyssey" (*Wonder Stories*, July, 1934), is often credited with revolutionizing the presentation of aliens.[30] A close reading of the early genre magazines, however, forces us to re-think this attribution. For instance, let us consider C. L. Moore's famous "Shambleau" (*Weird Tales*, November, 1933).

According to Pamela Sargent, Moore should be praised because she "flouted one of the conventions of the field by centering several of her stories around strong female characters."[31] Here Sargent was thinking primarily of Moore's Jirel of Joiry stories. This very "flouting of conventions" to portray "strong female characters" is a salient sign of the contested nature of early science fiction, but Sargent failed to make the obvious connections. But, in addition to the portrayal of "strong female characters," perhaps we should also praise Moore for other characteristics of her fiction.

Some have seen "Shambleau" as just stereotypical space opera, with the hard-bitten space-cowboy Northwest Smith being seduced by a beautiful Medusa-like female—an alien gorgon—which he rescues from a howling mob. But, let us look more closely at the depiction of the central character, Shambleau. This memorable and sympathetic female alien—there is nothing "evil" about her in the story—was depicted even earlier than Weinbaum's Tweel of "A Martian Odyssey." Further, as Lester del Rey noted, "Here, for the first time in the field, we find mood, feeling, and color. Here is an alien who is truly *alien*—far different from the crude monsters and slightly-altered humans found in other stories. Here are rounded and developed characters. . . . And—certainly for the first time that I can remember in the field—the story presents the sexual drive of humanity in some of its complexity."[32]

Likewise, Moore's "The Bright Illusion," as I noted earlier, is a powerful love story of a man and an almost inconceivable female alien and here again the alien is described in distinctly empathetic terms. And here, again, the story, when it first appeared in *Astounding*, brought universal acclaim from readers for its depiction of a fully realized and sympathetic alien—which also happened to be *female*.

Science fiction has long been criticized for its depiction of cardboard and hostile aliens. It has also been harshly criticized for its stereotypical depiction of women. A close reexamination of the record, however, makes it clear that both these charges must be reconsidered. "Shambleau" was Richard Lupoff's Hugo Award choice for 1933. Hence, by the modern standards of some editors, women (such as Harris and Moore) were already writing positive "award-winning stories" about females and aliens at an early date. There was much other excellent early science fiction which also embodied all the empathetic and fully conceived characterizations of aliens usually depicted as appearing only later in the genre's development. There was also much pulp science fiction which, both in art and in story, presented non-traditional and positive views of females. And sometimes these females and aliens were combined as femaliens. And this pulp science fiction was mostly written by women.

More than just attribution and priority are involved here. Once we fully integrate into our history of science fiction this early empathetic treatment of aliens and positive portrayal of women, then our entire understanding of the field must change. If nothing else, we realize what it lost when this hopeful beginning was ignored.

Notes

1. Sargent, *Women of Wonder: The Classic Years*, p. 2.

2. Lisa Tuttle, "Women Science Fiction Writers," in Clute and Nicholls, *The Encyclopedia of Science Fiction*, p. 1344.

3. Russ, *How To Suppress Women's Writing*, p. 111.

4. Michael Wood, "Study Says Brain is Hard-Wired to Feel Empathy," reporting on a study conducted only on female subjects in *The Pittsburgh Post-Gazette*, February 20, 2004, p. 1.

5. Jane L. Donawerth, "Science Fiction by Women in the Early Pulps, 1926–1930" in Jane L. Donawerth and Carol A. Kolmerten, Eds., *Utopian and Science Fiction by Women: Worlds of Difference*, Syracuse University Press: Syracuse, N.Y., 1994, p. 137.

6. Basil Davenport, Ed., Introduction, *The Science Fiction Novel: Imagination and Social Criticism*, Advent Publishers: Chicago, 1959, 1969, p. 13. Of course, "Skylark of Space" also had friendly aliens, which can also be found in 1930s stories by Weinbaum, Gallun, Moore, et al. Concerning the general thrust of the literature, however, his point is valid.

7. Robert Scholes and Eric S. Rabkin, *Science Fiction: History, Science, Vision*, Oxford University Press: Oxford and N.Y., 1977, p. 36. Jack London actually died in 1916.

8. Susan Janice Anderson and Vonda N. McIntyre, Eds., "Feminism and Science Fiction, Beyond BEMS and Boobs," Introduction, *Aurora: Beyond Equality*, Fawcett Publications, Inc.: N.Y., 1976, p. 11.

9. I say male authors "as a group" were not engaging in such social speculations, although there were exceptions. For example, S. Fowler Wright's *The World Below* depicted a non-sexist future with empathetic aliens as early as 1925.

10. Joanna Russ, "The Image of Women in Science Fiction," *Vertex*, 1, No. 6, (1971), (February) 1974, p. 57.

11. Ursula K. Le Guin, "Symposium: Women in Science Fiction," *Khatru*, Nos. 3 & 4, p. 6.

12. Robin Roberts, "The Female Alien: Pulp Science Fiction's Legacy to Feminists," *Journal of Popular Culture*, Vol. 21, No. 2, fall, 1987, p. 33. Emphasis added.

13. Curtis C. Smith, Ed., *Twentieth-Century Science-Fiction Writers*, p. viii. Emphasis added.

14. Roberts, pp. 38, 33.

15. Ursula K. Le Guin, "American SF and the Other," in Le Guin, *The Language of the Night: Essays on Fantasy and Science Fiction*, Perigee Books & G. P. Putnam's Sons: N.Y., 1980, p. 97. Originally in *Science Fiction Studies*, No. 7, November, 1975.

16. Simone de Beauvoir, translated by H. M. Parshley, *The Second Sex*, Vintage: N.Y., 1952, 1974, pp. xviii–xix.

17. Marleen S. Barr, *Alien to Femininity: Speculative Fiction and Feminist Theory*, Greenwood Press: Westport, Conn., 1987, p. 31.

18. Eric S. Rabkin, "Science Fiction Women Before Liberation," in Marleen S. Barr, Ed., *Future Females: A Critical Anthology*, Bowling Green State University Press: Bowling Green, Ohio, 1981.

19. Roberts, p. 49.

20. Letter, Paul Dellinger to Eric Leif Davin, September 11, 2003.

21. Roberts, p. 51. Emphasis added.

22. C.f., Despoina Tsiafakis, "Mankillers: Sirens & Sphinxes & Gorgons in Greek Art," *Archaeology Odyssey*, November—December, 2003, pp. 31–41, adapted from *The Centaur's Smile: The Human Animal in Early Greek Art*, a catalog accompanying an exhibition of such art at Princeton University Art Museum, October 11, 2003–January 18, 2004.

23. C.f., Le Guin, "American SF and the Other;" Joanna Russ, "Amor, Vincit Foeminam: The Battle of the Sexes in Science Fiction," *Science Fiction Studies*, 7, 1980, pp. 2–15; Beverly Friend, "Virgin Territory: Women and Sex in Science Fiction," *Extrapolation*, 14, 1972–1973, pp. 49–58; Robin Roberts, "The Female Alien: Pulp Science Fiction's Legacy to Feminists," *Journal of Popular Culture*, 21, 1987, pp. 33–52 and *A New Species: Gender and Science in Science Fiction*, U. of Illinois Press: Urbana, 1993; Marleen S. Barr, *Lost in Space: Probing Feminist Science Fiction and Beyond*, U. of N. Carolina Press: Chapel Hill, 1993, pp. 98–100; Charlotte Spivack, *Merlin's Daughters: Contemporary Women Writers of Fantasy*, Contributions to the Study of Science Fiction and Fantasy No. 23, Greenwood Press: N.Y., 1987, p. 14; and Gregory Benford, "Aliens and Knowability," in George E. Slusser, George R. Guffey, and Mark Rose, Eds., *Bridges to Science Fiction*, Southern Illinois U. Press: Carbondale, 1980.

24. Robin Roberts, "The Female Alien: Pulp Science Fiction's Legacy to Feminists," *Journal of Popular Culture*, 21, 1987, p. 34.

25. Sargent, *Women of Wonder: The Classic Years*, p. 5.

26. Sandra Gilbert and Susan Gubar, *The Madwoman in the Attic*, Yale University Press: New Haven, Conn., 1979, p. 232.

27. "Richard A. Lupoff's Alternative Heroes," in Mike Ashley, *The Illustrated Book of Science Fiction Lists*, Cornerstone Library: N.Y., 1982, p. 90.

28. See her letter, *Amazing Stories*, May, 1929, p. 179.

29. Jane Donawerth, "Science Fiction by Women in the Eary Pulps," p. 138. Actually the tradition of "bug-eyed monsters" predates the 1920s, the period she is discussing.

30. See Davin, *Pioneers of Wonder*, chapters on Weinbaum and Gallun, in which several who made this claim are cited.

31. Sargent, *Women of Wonder: The Classic Years*, p. 5.

32. Lester del Rey, "Forty Years of C. L. Moore," in *The Best of C. L. Moore*, Ballantine Books: N.Y., 1974, pp. 1–2. S. Fowler S. Wright had previously dealt with sexuality in his novels *Deluge* and *Dawn*, but perhaps not in the complexity del Rey felt Moore brought to her story. Others who have suggested a reevaluation of Moore along the lines we indicate include E. L. Bleiler, "Fantasy, Horror . . . and Sex—Early Stories of C. L. Moore," *The Scream Factory*, #13, 1994; Susan Gubar, "C. L. Moore and the Conventions of Women's Science Fiction," *Science Fiction Studies*, 7, 1980, pp. 16–27; and Sarah Gamble, "Shambleau . . . and Others': The Role of the Female in the Fiction of C. L. Moore," in Lucie Armitt, Ed., *Where No Man Has Gone Before: Women and Science Fiction*, Routledge: London, 1991, pp. 29–49.

11

Feminist Futures

THERE IS YET ANOTHER important contribution of early women science fiction writers which has been lost because people presumed it did not exist. The loss, however, is not just to science fiction. The loss is also to American literature—indeed, American society as a whole.

What we have lost is a revolutionary vision of gender relations which dramatically broke with both the older American utopian tradition in general and prior "feminist" utopian visions in particular. The tradition of which I speak is that of socialist and feminist utopias, which appeared in the pulps—and nowhere else—between 1920 and 1950. These tentative explorations represent the very first time such serious social and gender explorations had ever been conducted. The existence of this feminist utopian tradition in pulp science fiction is a persuasive argument in support of the contested terrain thesis.

The period from the end of the Civil War to World War I was one of great social and economic turmoil in America. In 1800 corporations were virtually non-existent and there were no large classes of "bosses" and "employees." While America was not Thomas Jefferson's yeoman Eden, an analysis of the 1798 land tax figures reveals that 52 percent of the free white males were farmers who owned their own land. Thus, they were economically independent and participated in political discourse as socio-economic equals at a time when property ownership was a prerequisite for being a voter. This was no doubt the highest percentage of land-owning "citizens" in the world at that time. Not only was there more equality in 1800 among free white males than anywhere else, there was also probably more equality in America for this population than there ever would be again. We had no starving peasants, as did Europe, nor did we endure Europe's rigid class antagonisms.

But by 1900 the face of America had changed. In the Industrial Revolution's wake, traditional lifestyles and economic modes became extinct as the modern corporation came to dominate the increasingly powerful industrial-capitalist economic order. Already by 1870, according to that year's census, 70 percent of Americans were directly or indirectly dependent upon wages, economically dependent, in other words, upon someone else. By the turn of the century, corporations dominated the landscape like giant dinosaurs, class society was a reality, and many people were starving. To many observers it seemed that American civilization was on the brink of chaos and destruction, as the old order died and a newly emerging order seemed inimical to all that people held dear.

American literature reflected these beliefs. It was poised between visions of worldwide revolutionary transformation and fears of a crushingly inhuman dictatorship as competing worldviews vied for mass acceptance. There were many dystopian novels which predicted the coming of death, destruction and totalitarianism. The most famous of these was Ignatius Donnelly's *Caesar's Column: A Story of the Twentieth Century* (1890), which sold 60,000 copies within a year of publication. Almost as popular was Jack London's 1906 novel of cataclysmic class warfare in bloody streets, *The Iron Heel*.

There was also, however, a proliferation of utopian novels envisioning a better world to come, such as Edward Bellamy's socialistic *Looking Backward From the Year 2000* (1888). Indeed, according to Jean Pfaelzer, "Over one hundred twenty works of utopian fiction appeared in America between the Civil War and World War I."[1]

But the end of World War I in 1918 brought Republican ascendancy and the final triumph of the corporations, politically allied to the Republican Party. At long last, after a period of intense class conflict extending back to the Great Railroad Strike of 1877, corporate capitalism established its cultural hegemony. And with this hegemony, the advocacy of vast alternatives to corporate capitalism became beyond the Pale, almost unthinkable, certainly "unrealistic." So, with this "Return to Normalcy" of the 1920s, the utopian tradition died in American literature.[2]

Most shockingly, it died in science fiction, as it seemed that genre accepted the cultural hegemony of "the powers that be" more than any other literature. As far as social speculations are concerned, science fiction writers seemed to have gone to sleep, not to be awakened from their somnolence until the social movements of the Sixties shook them out of their lethargy. Science fiction seemed to become a literature about change without progress, about the future as More Of The Same. As Basil Davenport observed in the late 1950s, "By and large, science fiction has been at its least imaginative in inventing alternative societies, especially alternative good societies. In general, any society which differs widely from our own is set up only to be overthrown. . . . And what [gets] set up instead is always essentially twentieth century American civilization, plus a few added gadgets. Our own society seems to be not only the best, but the only good society that science fiction has been able to conceive. We need to be reminded there are other possibilities. . . . And certainly, we need to be reminded not only that there are other possible good societies, there are conceivably better societies. Science fiction has produced very few Utopias, and those not very imaginative or even tempting; it has done better with Utopias in reverse, but for them, unfortunately, less imagination is needed. *The last of the Utopians was H. G. Wells.*"[3]

At the same time, Robert Bloch detected the very same unimaginative lack of social speculations in science fiction. He observed that there was a formula to the genre's future societies. In all of them, capitalism reigned supreme, a variation of Anglo-Saxon culture ruled the world and this culture colonized and ruled alien worlds and societies. "The future holds little basic change." Furthermore, individualism was dead. "The hero rebels, yes—but not to superimpose his own notions upon society; merely to restore the 'normal' culture and value-standards of the mass-minds of the twentieth century. You won't find him fighting in defense of incest, homosexuality, free love, nihilism, the Single Tax, abolition of individual property rights, euthanasia, or the castration of the tonsils of Elvis Presley. Stripped down to the bare essentials, our hero just wants to kick the rascals out and put in a sound business administration. . . . Our authors, by and large, seem to believe wholly in the profit incentive; in the trend to superimpose obedience and conformity by means of forcible conditioning; in the enduring liaison between the government, the military, and scientists and technologists; in Anglo-Saxon cultural supremacy, if not necessarily outright 'white supremacy'; in the sexual, aesthetic, and religious mores of the day. Their criticism of the totalitarian states they envision is merely a matter of degree. . . . The implication is that once Law and Order are restored, everything will settle down to a general approximation of life as it is lived today—if not in actuality, at least in the pages of *Better Homes and Gardens.*"[4]

Ursula K. Le Guin agreed with this assessment. "From a social point of view," she said in 1975, "most SF has been incredibly regressive and unimaginative. All those Galactic Empires, taken straight from the British Empire of 1880. All those planets—with 80 trillion miles between them!—conceived of as warring nation-states, or as colonies to be exploited, or to be nudged by the benevolent Imperium of Earth toward self-development—the White Man's Burden all over again. The Rotary Club on Alpha Centauri, that's the size of it. . . . The only social change presented by most SF has been toward authoritarianism, the domination of ignorant masses by a powerful elite—sometimes presented as a warning, but often quite complacently. Socialism is never considered as an alternative, and democracy is quite forgotten. Military virtues are taken as ethical ones. Wealth is assumed to be a righteous goal and a personal virtue. Competitive free-enterprise capitalism is the economic destiny of the entire Galaxy. In general, American SF has assumed a permanent hierarchy of superiors and inferiors, with rich, ambitious, aggressive males at the top, then a great gap, and then at the bottom the poor, the uneducated, the faceless masses, and all the women. The whole picture is, if I may say so, curiously 'un-American.' It is a perfect baboon patriarchy, with the Alpha Male on top, being respectfully groomed, from time to time, by his inferiors. Is this speculation? Is this imagination? Is this extrapolation? I call it brainless regressivism."[5]

Pamela Sargent echoed these complaints, particularly about science fiction before the turmoil of the Sixties. "For a literature that was by definition supposed to be open to new possibilities," she observed, "science fiction remained sociologically conservative. . . . What were the male science fiction writers [of the 1950s] doing? For the most part, assuming that the mores of the future would not be notably different from those of the United States during the early and middle twentieth century. It's important to keep in mind that science fiction in the United States from the '20s to the '60s was largely a pulp magazine literature, written for readers who were looking for escape and entertainment and who presumably did not want certain presuppositions challenged, even as they speculated about the technical wonders that the future might hold."[6]

But despite Sargent's depiction of early pulp magazine literature, pulp science fiction had not always been such an arid desert of social speculation. Nor was Wells (or even Bellamy) the last of the utopians. Thoughtful female authors continued their social speculations in the early science fiction magazines. Moreover, the speculations of these women writers were profoundly different from the earlier utopian tradition that had flourished before the triumph of Republican hegemony following World War I. For the very first time they explored explicitly feminist *social* arrangements. The very fact that such utopian and even feminist speculations continued in science fiction illustrates the contested terrain nature of this popular culture arena.

Of the over 120 known utopian novels which appeared between the Civil War and World War I, Jean Pfaelzer tells us that the vast bulk expounded upon the utopian *economic* notions of the predominantly male authors. "Only four posited a future for women which embodied the demands put forward by women active in the labor movement, farmers' movement, suffrage movement, birth control movement, and the Socialist Party. And even the few which promised political equality for women failed to translate that status into portrayals of strong, competent, independent female characters."[7]

The American utopian tradition, then, for the most part ignored gender relations. And even in the four novels identified by Pfaelzer which dealt with them—Bellamy's *Looking Backward from the Year 2000* (1888), Mary H. Lane's *Mizora: A Prophecy* (1889), W. H. Bishop's *The Garden of Eden, USA* (1894), and Charlotte Perkins Gilman's *Herland* (1915)—these novels failed to envision a truly gender liberated future.

"An analysis of these fictional utopias," says Pfaelzer, "reveals that although

these authors may have corrected the political and economic inequities of capitalism within their works, they maintained the social and cultural assumptions
which justified the inferior status of women. . . . [they] ultimately embodied the
ideological structures of patriarchy [and created] female characters who con-
formed to the Cult of True Womanhood: pure, pious, domestic, and submissive.
. . . For modern readers, consequently, the utopian narratives are provocative
yet frustrating, promising yet incomplete."[8]

Perhaps Pfaelzer's survey isn't entirely comprehensive, however. It seems
there *were* a *handful* of utopian tales written by women during this period that
did envision sexual equality. Sometimes these stories even contemplated *male*
inferiority, although as a means of arguing for sexual equality.

Such was the case in 1870 when Annie Denton Cridge published a sex-role
reversal satire entitled, *Man's Rights; or, How Would You Like It?*. Mrs. J. Wood
did the same in 1882 with, *Pantaletta: A Romance of Sheheland*. In 1885 Miss
M. T. Shelhamer, in *Life and Labor in the Spirit World*, hypothesized that spirits
in the afterlife lived a utopian existence that included complete sexual equality.
In 1893 Alice Ilgenfritz Jones and Ella Merchant, writing as "Two Women of
the West," envisioned sexual equality in a parallel dimension in their novel,
Unveiling a Parallel, A Romance. A little later Mrs. Anna Adolph found sexual
equality in an arctic utopia in her self-published 1899 book, *Arqtiq; A Study of
the Marvels at the North Pole*. And then there is Charlotte Perkins Gilman's 1911
Moving the Mountain, her precursor to *Herland*, which also described a feminist
utopia.

But then, following World War I, novels speculating upon gender relations
(like utopian novels in general) ceased to be published altogether in America,
not to reappear until after 1950.[9]

*Except, that is, in the early genre and science fiction magazines. There—and
there alone—feminist speculations survived.*

And, for the first time in American literature, these were genuinely *feminist*
speculations. Stories such as "Friend Island" by "Francis Stevens" (Gertrude
Bennett) in *All-Story Weekly* (September 7, 1918), and those that followed in
the explicitly science fiction magazines, envisioned an ambience of egalitarian
gender relations. They also portrayed strong female characters who broke out
of the Cult of True Womanhood stereotype to become active agents of social
transformation in their own right.

These were unique and literally unprecedented innovations, both in literature
and in political theorizing. Their themes and their treatment of gender relations
show they were not a tardy echo of late nineteenth-century utopian prophecies,
but unacknowledged precursors of the Second Wave feminism which emerged
in the late 1960s and early 1970s.

But this radical feminist tradition in pulp science fiction has been erased from
our collective memory, as the comments by Bloch, Le Guin, and Sargent make

clear. Hence, speaking of science fiction writers throughout the history of the genre, Sam J. Lundwall states unreservedly, "That the woman's position in the society could be discussed and used as a basis for speculative fiction never occurred to the otherwise progressive writers."[10]

Bloch and Davenport made their comments in the 1950s. Le Guin, Sargent, and Lundwall made their observations twenty years later, in the early 1970s. Their interpretations all reflect the mythology of pulp patriarchy which the Second Wave of the women's movement made the dominant interpretation of the literature in the early 1970s. And, while superseded by the more nuanced contested terrain thesis in other areas of cultural studies, these outdated interpretations remain the dominant ones today in discussing science fiction history. These antiquated views are past due for modification, especially in our study of gender relations in early science fiction.

For instance, contrary to Sargent's statement about early science fiction, male science fiction writers often did tackle the question of gender relations. However, it is true that, almost without exception, they failed until very recently to envision sexually *egalitarian* societies. Nothing really changed in their speculations; the concept of gender equality was beyond them. Unable to escape the traditional paradigm of hierarchy, they merely portrayed topsy-turvy worlds in which women ruled men—until brave male rebels reestablished (to the women's great joy) the "normal" gender role of male dominance. Indeed, Sam Moskowitz published a whole book of such male-authored wish fulfillment fantasies in his collection of early pulp stories, aptly entitled *When Women Rule.*[11]

Hence, the salient science fiction images—presumed to be the *only* images—are those which loomed large in people's awareness during the early stages of the Seventies' women's movement. As Ursula K. Le Guin remarked in 1975 about the science fiction with which she was then familiar, what was desperately needed was more "serious consideration of such deeply radical, futuristic concepts as Liberty, Equality, and Fraternity. And remember that about 53 percent of the Brotherhood of Man is the Sisterhood of Women."[12]

However, as Justine Larbalestier has made clear in her recent work on the "battle of the sexes" motif in pulp science fiction, early women writers *were* challenging the dominant paradigm of gender relations. And in the late 1920s and early 1930s women writers *did* provide exactly the serious consideration of equality Le Guin called for. They explored ways in which to actually improve human society, instead of merely replicate the Victorian age on a galactic scale. In many cases these explorations took the form of what we might call "feminist utopias"—but they actually represented much more than that. They were social speculations that offered chances to examine the kind of intimate personal issues that the best of modern science fiction deals with. They represented, therefore, a lost opportunity to use the literature to investigate greatly different social orders, which anyone seriously interested in science fiction must applaud.

Such speculations were an eddy of a larger stream which was agitating American society in the Twenties. While on the surface the Jazz Age was one of Republican complacency, of gin and flappers, of fun, football and fur coats, there was an undercurrent of post-suffrage dissatisfaction among the "Modern Women" of the age. In 1926–1927, *The Nation* published a series of seventeen autobiographical essays by representatives of the "New Woman" in an attempt to understand the ongoing "modern woman's rebellion."[13] *The Nation* saw these young "modern women"—the first generation inheritors of the triumphant suffrage struggle—as in generic rebellion against the stuffy mores of society. Elaine Showalter saw this rebellion as a new style of feminism which placed more emphasis upon individual liberation than had the more collectivist suffrage movement. "The difference between the modern woman and the suffragist or feminist of the nineteenth century," she said, "was her insistence on the right to self-fulfillment in both public life and in relationships with men."[14]

Indeed, believes Harvard historian Nancy Cott, it was exactly these concerns which marked feminists of the 1920s as true forerunners of modern feminism, for they were the first to struggle with the unique complexities of post-suffrage living. At that time, in her interpretation, a new phase of the women's struggle began. "In any recent history of women in the United States," she says, "you are likely to find comment on the demise of feminism in the 1920s rather than recognition that *the name and phenomenon had just recently cropped up.* Although continuity in the suffrage campaign obscured the important transition, the new language of Feminism marked the end of the woman movement [of the suffrage era] and the embarkation on a modern agenda. Women's efforts in the 1910s and 1920s laid the groundwork and exposed the fault lines of modern feminism. . . . Considerations about women's identity and consciousness as a group that became visible in the 1910s when Feminism did are with us still."[15]

The feminist social speculations that appeared in the science fiction magazines in the late 1920s and early 1930s were thus part of a larger feminist ferment that seeded the modern women's movement. The ideas and ideals expressed by these women science fiction writers were the same that the anarchic, radical, free-spirited feminists of Greenwich Village were expressing at the same time.

The very words, "feminism" and "feminist," were coined in Greenwich Village in the 1910s and became widespread among "New Women" in the 1920s. Their use by science fiction writer M. (Margaret) F. Rupert in 1930 when, for example, her heroine refers to "my sisters in feminism," indicates Rupert's explicit awareness of this larger social milieu ("Via the Hewitt Ray," *Science Wonder Quarterly*, spring, 1930). Such stories, then, did not spring *de novo* from the sea foam, like Venus, nor drop like manna from heaven. Such pulp science fiction feminist stories were part of a larger social ferment.

Stories which expressed this new consciousness appeared quite early. It was in 1914 that Inez Haynes Gillmore (a militant suffragist affiliated with Alice

Paul's National Woman's Party) published "Angel Island." This was a radical feminist Swiftian fantasy which editor Mary Gnaedinger reprinted in *Famous Fantastic Mysteries*, February 1949. Francis Stevens later portrayed an egalitarian society in "Friend Island" (*All-Story Weekly*, September 7, 1918). Again, Gnaedinger reprinted this story in *Fantastic Novels Magazine*, September 1950. On Friend Island, women did everything a man would do on a basis of absolute equality. Indeed, as the hard-bitten old female sea captain who tells the story complained, "There's too much preached nowadays that man is fit for nothing but to fetch and carry and do nurse-work in big child-homes. To my mind, a man who hasn't the nerve of a woman ain't fitted to father children, let alone raise them."

With the coming of science fiction magazines in 1926 there was a proliferation of such feminist stories. Typical of these stories was Minna Irving's strongly feminist "The Moon Woman," *Amazing Stories*, November 1929. Irving had a long track record of publication and saw the science fiction magazines as a new venue in which to express her radical ideas.[16]

Also typical was M. F. Rupert's "Via the Hewitt Ray," (Spring, 1930 *Wonder Stories Quarterly*), here synopsized by Susan Wood: "Lucile Harris is a commercial pilot for an airline which employs only women, because their safety record is superior to that of men. With the help of a woman scientist, she uses her scientist-father's ray to enter the fourth dimension. She finds a world ruled by women, whose dignified leader, Mavia, explains how women gained equality, then superiority. The 'Sex War Epoch' was followed by victory for the women, who 'destroyed millions of the despised masculine sex. For untold centuries they had kept women subjugated and we finally got our revenge' (p. 377). Despite such bloodthirsty beginnings, however, this matriarchy (unlike most in science fiction) is not vicious, not static, and not crumbling from within. It has a highly developed medical technology, for example, and other wonders such as color television. Men are kept for breeding purposes, and the majority are content, neither effeminate nor rebellious. Lucile returns to her own world with one rebellious male, whom she names John. He remains cowed until she scolds him: 'Why, don't you know that you are in every way superior to a woman?' Then she adds, in an aside, 'May my sisters in feminism [!] forgive the lies. I had to be drastic' (p. 420). 'Dad,' the scientist who has to be rescued by Lucile and the women rulers, makes various jocularly derogatory remarks about 'a group of pretty ladies playing at politics,' (p. 381), but these are contrasted with the women's real competence, to underscore the fact that women deserve equality" (p. 377).[17]

Although Jane Donawerth seems unaware of Rupert's work, in her pioneering exploration of feminist utopias in the pulps she noted many more such stories by Clare Winger Harris, Sophie Wenzel Ellis, L. Taylor Hansen, Minna Irving, Lilith Lorraine, Kathleen Ludwick, Louise Rice, and Leslie F. Stone.[18] (See table

1 for bibliographic information on these authors.) In her investigations, Donawerth discovered several generalizations which can be made about this early feminist pulp literature. "Although the women writers shared with men the romanticizing of science, they offered one particular application that the male writers rarely offered: the transformation of domestic spaces and duties through technology. . . . All these women . . . imagine that in the future food will be chemically produced."[19] Meanwhile, "Domestic interiors . . . are designed, like food, for efficiency, cleanliness, and psychological well-being."[20]

Because sexism begins at home, men have long disparaged such treatments, perhaps believing domestic spaces and duties too trivial a subject for serious speculation. Throughout history such spaces and duties have been consigned to the women's sphere, even in science fiction. Typical of male-authored stories that were appearing in the magazines alongside these feminist speculations was "A Daring Trip to Mars," by Max Valier, *Wonder Stories*, July 1931. "What, your wife is going with you?" the daring astronaut is asked. "Somebody must do the housekeeping, even in the rocket," the astronaut replies. "That is not work for men." No, even in science fiction, it was women's work—and so women did not consider such duties beneath consideration.

Further, as I discussed earlier, these same duties and lack of domestic spaces to call their own have been a major reason throughout history that women have remained a minority of artists in most fields. Other than, perhaps, the kitchen, they have not had, as Virginia Woolf put it, "A Room of One's Own." They have always had to steal their time and space in order to create.

Harriet Beecher Stowe, the author of *Uncle Tom's Cabin* and many other novels, wrote her books in the bits and scraps of time stolen from domestic responsibilities. She taught an hour a day in the family school and read to her children every evening for two hours. While working on a single page she would be called away a dozen times on household chores: to buy codfish from a fisherman; to store a barrel of apples brought by a deliveryman; to nurse her infant; to make a chowder for dinner. The miracle was that the resulting page was even produced, much less was readable. Nothing but deadly determination kept bringing her back to her writing. It was like rowing against the wind and tide. The liberation of women from such obligations and burdens had to be a major part of any feminist utopia—a point men usually miss.

Jane Donawerth also noted how the domestic sphere was a prime concern of the feminist utopias of the pulp magazines. "Technology also affects the exterior world of women in these stories," she said. "The living spaces that these women imagine . . . are beautiful and healthful, because both wild nature and also urban dangers have been abolished. With a healthful, clean environment, women's domestic duties disappear: in these stories, women are neither cleaning nor nursing, since dirt and disease are banished. Just as these women abolish food and urban dirt, and so change the domestic circumstances of women, so they also contemplate the radical revision, even abolishment of childbirth and its dangers. . . . Their radical alteration or abolishment of birth and child-raising (and in Lorraine's case, of sex) frees women from domestic duties as the later feminists Shulamith Firestone and Marge Piercy also imagined, for further education and for public responsibilities. In this final use of science to alter domestic duties, these women . . . look forward to the writers of feminist utopias in the 1970s, not back to the writers of the earlier utopias [those writers Pfaelzer analyzed], which revolved around child care."[21]

While these women writers romanticized science as much as male writers, it was not science alone which liberated them. They also envisioned social or political revolutions of various kinds. In Lilith Lorraine's case, a socialist revolution brought the needed gender liberation. There is nothing of Sargent's charge here of sociological conservatism. "The utopian transformation of domestic spaces and duties," Donawerth found, "is as much a result of the transformation of gender roles as of science and technology. These women writers of the 1920s introduce into science-fiction visions of women's roles as socially constructed, changeable and, so, potentially utopian."[22]

And, because women's roles are seen as socially constructed, and are thus changeable, changed women abound in these stories. In Harris's "The Ape Cycle," Sylvia, an airplane mechanic and pilot, explained to her male chauvinist friend why women of the past were not mechanically inclined. "It was purely a matter of environment," she said. While women may appear as housemaids on Mars-bound rockets in male fiction, in Leslie F. Stone's "Out of the Void," her first appearance in *Amazing Stories*, the astronaut for the first Mars rocket is Dana Gleason, a "daring and adventurous" woman.

In Stone's "Through the Veil," women are the rulers of an alternate world. L. Taylor Hansen's "The Prince of Liars" pays homage to Thora, an ancient female scholar. In Clare Winger Harris' "A Baby on Neptune," it is a woman, a kindergarten teacher, who decodes the alien signals which have stumped the best scientific minds for 130 years. Meanwhile, in her story, "The Menace of Mars," Vivian Harley is a chemistry major with a minor in astronomy.

Changed women are not so much the exception as the norm in these stories. Gender roles have been revised for *all* women, not just the few. Donawerth found that such stories of revised gender roles could be generally categorized into two groups.

"The first group—Minna Irving, Kathleen Ludwick, and Lilith Lorraine—imagine revised gender roles along the lines of Victorian feminism and the theory of women's work." Hence, in their stories we find women as social reformers, abolishing war and transforming government and society. In Irving's "The Moon Woman," the genetically superior Lunarian women become the rulers of Earth through their greater knowledge, in the process abolishing war and disease. Meanwhile, "Lorraine presents a socialist revision of marriage: in

The Brain of the Planet a socialist revolution removes the economic pressure on women to marry, and so 'the relations between the sexes became perfect, for . . . all marriages were based on real love, on affinity of tastes' (p. 19)."[23] In addition, "new inventions do away with menial work now that capitalists no longer stand against labor saving devices; national boundaries and superstitious religions crumble; and with unlimited leisure, humans begin a golden age of art and science."[24]

However, Donawerth continued, "Leslie F. Stone, Louise Rice and Clare Winger Harris, in contrast, envision revised roles for women along strict lines of equality between men and women." In their stories there is an emphasis upon revised gender roles, and of education and careers for women.[25]

In Louise Rice and Tonjoroff-Roberts's "The Astounding Enemy," Mildred Sturtevant is a career scientist and officer of The Woman's Party. In fighting off an alien insect invasion of Earth, Sturtevant enlists in the army—as do other women—as a fighting soldier. When friends try to talk her into taking a safe rear echelon position, she rejects the idea out of hand. "Fancy trying to put me into my place—in the rear! You'd think we were back in the nineteen hundreds." As luck would have it, she is captured by the insect enemy—and, typically in female-authored stories, comes to have great respect for the alien invaders.

In Leslie F. Stone's "Men With Wings," women also fight side-by-side with their male comrades. In her story, "When the Sun Went Out," "sex made no difference" in who governed politically and the two astronomers, a man and a woman, are peers who eventually fall in love with each other because, "Astronomers both, they spoke the same language, had the same hopes and desires." And in "Out of the Void," Stone tells the story of the first astronaut to Mars, a woman, who is described by her male friend as, "brave, strong, great willed." On the trip to Mars they do all jobs equally—including cooking and competitive dish washing.

This tradition of socialist and feminist utopias, which appeared in the pulps—and nowhere else—between 1920 and 1950 stands in glaring contrast to the reigning mythology of a hostile patriarchy which completely dominated pulp science fiction. Obviously, there were many stories by male authors which validated traditional gender roles and the accepted social order. But that is not the entire story. As the work of Jean Pfaelzer, Jane Donawerth, Justine Larbalestier, as well as Robin Roberts and others have demonstrated, there were explicitly "feminist" challenges to the male paradigm throughout the literature. The proliferation of these "feminist futures," feminist images, and strong female protagonists in pulp science fiction is convincing testimony to the contested terrain reality of the literature. From its very genesis, science fiction was a gender battleground.

But the science fiction world at large—much less mainstream literature—

knows nothing of this exceedingly rich tradition of feminist speculation in the early science fiction magazines. It is a forgotten legacy of sociological and gender extrapolation which most observers believe only appeared in American literature in the wake of the Sixties' women's movement. Since this treasure trove has been lost, our history of the science fiction field itself is incomplete and distorted—and our knowledge of the role of women writers in American literature as a whole is also impoverished.

Why were they forgotten? The answer is quite clear to Joanna Russ. "There they are," she says of the women I have discussed, "and of course it's sexism that made them vanish in the first place!"[26] In other words, the reason these women and their stories did not appear in the largely male-edited anthologies of later years—which kept male pulp authors alive for future generations—was because those later editors reflected the deeply ingrained sexism of the larger culture.

Groff Conklin, for instance, a leading genre anthologist of the late 1940s and 1950s, claimed that between 1946 and 1952, at least fifty-three hardcover science fiction anthologies were published, an average of about eight or nine collections a year. The 1952 anthology in which he tells us this was typical of that era's slighting of women science fiction writers by such later editors as he who, like Conklin, had never actually been a pulp magazine editor. Of the forty-five authors represented in his collection, only three were female: newcomer Katherine MacLean, Ann Griffith, and C. L. Moore (represented as half the "Lewis Padgett" team).[27]

Nor did this trend change over time. In his 1975 anthology of classic stories from the "fantastic" pulps, Peter Haining saw fit to reprint only one female, C. L. Moore, among the twenty-two authors he chose.[28] Likewise, women authors tended to make few appearances in the field's reference works. For example, one important 1982 science fiction study of the seventy-six "*major* authors from the early nineteenth century to the present day" found only seven women worthy of note for that almost 200-year period, one being the obligatory Mary Shelley.[29]

Or one could say these women were forgotten simply because most science fiction historians and critics seem to have an astonishing ability to work in blissful ignorance. Even academics and feminists who write about them simply don't know what was published in the pulps. As A. Langley Searles observed about the state of historical research and criticism in the field a quarter century ago, "So many books and serious magazines seem to have no anchor in the past. . . . All too often, opinions of science-fiction authors, because of close association and facile writing style, become those automatically (and unwisely) chosen."[30]

As we have seen, much of science fiction's accepted history continues to be based on the unsubstantiated opinions and personal anecdotes of genre writers. In other fields of literature, critics and academic historians would not be so uncritically reliant on such a source. But, as Searles also noted, "This is another strange aspect of science fiction. In most disciplines, the production of mere fiction is usually taken as evidence of lack of seriousness, and that opinions in the area of criticism are *not* to be relied on."[31]

Perhaps the personal opinions and self-aggrandizing anecdotes of writers carry so much weight in science fiction history simply because it *is* a young field, and the traditional norms of scholarship—research and verification—have not yet put down roots among the field's practitioners. Maybe only generational change will alter this situation and eventually produce scholars who adhere to scholarly standards.

Perhaps there is also an additional reason these women have been forgotten: The continuing influence of the early Seventies feminist critique of science fiction. As we have seen, the contested terrain thesis is now the commonly accepted interpretation of popular culture. Except in science fiction studies. There, the study of this literature of the future remains mired in the intellectual past. There the 1970s' women's movement worldview continues to dominate the field's concept of its own past. Perhaps this has something to do with the powerful connection in the public imagination between the male-oriented professional field of science and the more contested terrain of that branch of popular culture known as science fiction. But, for whatever reason, the net result of it has been to blind us to the origins, antiquity, and nature of the field's female past.

Ironically, then, it is not only the sexism to which Joanna Russ pointed that must be viewed as the culprit in this story. Perhaps sexism helped make invisible science fiction's female past "in the first place." But Seventies feminism then conspired with sexism to *keep* that female past invisible. It was a past which feminist political theory said *could* not exist—and therefore it *did* not exist. And so the politics of memory erased these women from our consciousness.

But, perhaps times are changing. Perhaps we are becoming more willing to apply the accepted standards of scholarship to the writing of science fiction history. Perhaps we are becoming more willing to move the study of science fiction into the mainstream of cultural studies.

And perhaps, also, we can begin to use more intellectual tools than just a hammer to explore the twentieth century social and cultural phenomenon known as science fiction. Earlier I noted psychologist Abraham Maslow's observation that if the only tool one has is a hammer, then all problems look like nails to be hammered. If the only intellectual tool one has to discuss gender disparities is the concept of "prejudice," then the hammer of gender accusation is all one will be able to use. For too long the sound of hammering has prevented us from discovering the truth about science fiction's female past.

Notes

1. Jean Pfaelzer, "A State of One's Own: Feminism as Ideology in American Utopias, 1880–1915," *Extrapolation*, winter, 1983, V. 24, No. 4, p. 311.

2. Again, I am here discussing American literature. Utopianism continued to thrive in British literature, producing such important works as James Hilton's *Lost Horizon* (1933), Robert Graves's *Seven Days in New Crete* (1949, U. S. title *Watch the North Wind Rise*), and Aldous Huxley's *Island* (1962).

Perhaps the most notable American exception would be Austin Tappan Wright's *Islandia* (1942), but this was written purely for private enjoyment and was published (in highly edited form) as a labor of love by his daughter after his death. Interestingly, the most memorable depictions at this time of triumphant dystopias, Huxley's *Brave New World* (1932), and George Orwell's *Animal Farm* (1945) and *1984* (1949), also came from the hands of British authors.

3. Davenport, *The Science Fiction Novel*, pp. 11–12. Emphasis added. And Wells wasn't even American! Davenport isn't entirely correct here, but I interpret his comment about Wells as hyperbole to make a point.

4. Robert Bloch, "Imagination and Modern Social Criticism," in Davenport, *The Science Fiction Novel*, pp. 109–110.

5. Le Guin, "American SF and the Other," pp. 98–99.

6. Sargent, *Women of Wonder: The Classic Years*, p. 10.

7. Pfaelzer, "A State of One's Own," p. 311.

8. Pfaelzer, pp. 311, 312.

9. See Carol Farley Kessler, Ed., *Daring to Dream: Utopian Stories by United States Women, 1836–1919*, Pandora: Boston, 1984, p. 9. Also see Lyman Tower Sargent, *British and American Utopian Literature, 1516–1975: An Annotated Bibliography*, G. K. Hall & Co.: Boston, 1979. The Lyman Sargent bibliography makes clear there continued to be a fair number of utopian novels written by women between 1920–1950—but they were by British women and published in England.

10. Sam J. Lundwall, *Science Fiction: What It's All About*, Ace Books: N.Y., 1971, p. 146.

11. Sam Moskowitz, Ed., *When Women Rule*, Walker & Co.: N.Y., 1972.

12. Le Guin, "American SF and the Other," p. 100.

13. These essays have been republished in Elaine Showalter, Ed., *These Modern Women: Autobiographical Essays from the Twenties*, The Feminist Press: N.Y., 1979.

14. Showalter, p. 4.

15. Nancy Cott, *The Grounding of Modern Feminism*, Yale University Press: New Haven, 1987, pp. 4, 5. Emphasis added.

16. See her short poem from 1888 published as the frontispiece in Jessica Amanda Salmonson, Ed., *What Did Miss Darrington See?—An Anthology of Feminist Supernatural Fiction*, The Feminist Press: NY, 1989.

17. Wood, "Women and Science Fiction," p. 11.

18. Donawerth, "Science Fiction by Women in the Early Pulps."

19. Donawerth, p. 138.

20. Donawerth, p. 139.

21. Donawerth, p. 140, 142.

22. Donawerth, p. 142.

23. Donawerth, p. 143.

24. Jane Donawerth, "Lilith Lorraine: Feminist Socialist Writer in the Pulps," *Science-Fiction Studies*, V. 17, #51, Part 2, July, 1990, p. 254.

25. Donawerth, "Science Fiction by Women in the Eary Pulps," p. 145.

26. Letter, Joanna Russ to Eric Leif Davin, June 10, 2002.

27. See Groff Conklin, Ed., *The Omnibus of Science Fiction*, Crown Publishers, Inc.: N.Y., 1952, p. ix.

28. See Peter Haining, Ed., *The Fantastic Pulps*, Vintage Books: N.Y., 1975.

29. See E. F. Bleiler, Ed., *Science Fiction Writers: Critical Studies of the Major Authors from the Early Nineteenth Century to the Present Day*, Charles Scribner's Sons: N.Y., 1982. Emphasis added.

30. A. Langley Searles, "A Critical Evaluation of Books on SF," p. 193.

31. Searles, footnote 139, p. 201.

12

History and Mythistory

A s Robert Silverberg once noted, "Men in search of a myth will usually find one, if they work at it."[1] Myth-making, it seems, is so much more fun than mundane history—and so myths easily pass for history all too often. People believe such mythology because it tells them what they already wish to believe. Therein lies the power of myth.

But, despite this great persuasive power, mythology is nevertheless composed of fable and fantasy, not facts. Rather, it is history that is composed of facts. What I have tried to do is to counterpose history to a science fiction mythology which, for far too long, has passed as history—a form of "mythistory." I have tried to introduce the traditional norms of scholarship—research and verification—into the discussion of prejudice against women (as well as Jews and blacks) in the early science fiction magazines. In so doing, I have discovered that the accepted history of the field is false, it is mythistory, and that none of the presumptions of prejudice are supported by evidence. In summation:

1) Critics and commentators have asserted that a hostile patriarchy completely dominated pulp science fiction in this early period. I have argued that the more nuanced theory of "contested terrain" far more accurately depicts science fiction history. Indeed, one could even argue that pulp science fiction offered an "open door" to outsiders, such as women, welcoming their participation.

2) Critics and commentators have asserted that science fiction, due to its emphasis upon science, was male-oriented and sexist. I have argued that they have confused the male-oriented professional field of science with the more ambiguous popular culture field of science *fiction*.

3) They have asserted that a supposed uniformly sexist image of women presented in the literature proved that there was also a prejudice—bigotry—against publishing women writers. I have shown that not only was there no prejudice against publishing women writers—but that the image of women was much more ambiguous than has been presented. There were many positive images of strong females presented in both the literature and in the art of pulp science fiction. Thus, the female image in pulp science fiction was especially contested terrain.

4) They have also asserted that there were either very few or no early female science fiction writers. I have shown there was a significant number—sixty-five female-identified authors publishing 288 stories in the period under discussion.

5) They have pointed to the minority status of women writers during our period as inherent proof of prejudice against women writers. I have found no evidence for that assumption, and have identified other periods in the history of the genre (including the present) that have similar female minorities, yet are not labeled as biased eras. For example, the female 17 percent of all fiction authors in *Weird Tales* and the 16 percent female participation rate at *The Magazine of Fantasy and Science Fiction* in the 1950s compares favorably with the 10–18 percent estimate for female participation in science fiction in the 1970s. Further, I presented an alternate explanation, *viz.*, the existence of patriarchal forces in society at large, which denied women access to formal domains of knowledge, and which more plausibly explains this minority status.

6) Further, I argued that the actual *nature* of gender relations between individuals tells us far more about gender relations than does numbers alone. And, once we look at the nature of gender relations in pulp science fiction, we find an egalitarian acceptance of women as equal partners.

7) Critics and commentators have pointed to the use of male pseudonyms by female authors as a *deliberate subterfuge to escape their gender identity*. I could not find a single instance of this supposedly widespread practice.

8) They have pointed to the presumed widespread use of initials or androgynous names by women as deliberate and conscious attempts to circumvent presumed male prejudice. The single instance I could find of this practice, that of L. Taylor Hansen, was by a woman who did *not* see herself primarily as a writer of science *fiction*, but as a writer of science *fact*. It is for the latter reason that she attempted to conceal her gender identity.

9) Critics and commentators have asserted that there was an editorial bias—bigotry—against women writers based upon publishers' prejudice. I have shown, on the contrary, a wide acceptance of women writers by the entire gamut of magazines over an extended period of time. *Further*,

every magazine editor, without a single exception, published women writers at some point in his or her career.

10) They have cited dubious personal anecdotes from modern writers as proof of earlier prejudice. I have shown why those self-aggrandizing anecdotes cannot be accepted at face value. Further, I cited denials of discrimination by some of the very women the proclaimers of prejudice champion as their path-breaking models.

11) Critics and commentators have used the supposed prejudice of science fiction editors in others areas, such as the alleged anti-Semitism and racism, to bolster their contention that these same editors were, by extension, also prejudiced against women. If one, then most likely the other. I have shown these allegations of anti-Semitism and racism to be baseless and demonstrated that, in fact, the reality was the exact opposite of the mythistory of discrimination. One might be tempted to say, "if one, then the other."

12) I have suggested two areas—the empathetic creation of fully-conceived aliens and the tradition of genuine social speculation—in which a more complete knowledge of the contributions of early women science fiction writers revolutionizes our understanding of the genre's development. In addition, I postulated that these women generated alternate—and in some ways, richer—literary currents from the very beginning of the genre's existence.

13) Finally, I suggested an additional reason—beyond society's sexism and the historical ignorance of most who have written on the genre's past—for why these women were forgotten: The lingering influence of Seventies feminism which insisted, against the facts, that these women did not exist, thus ironically helping to erase these women from our collective memory.

The continuing mythistory resulting from this early feminist (mis)interpretation actually does great harm to women. It hides the early history of women's science fiction and blinds us to what these early women actually accomplished. Women, we have discovered, were not the passive victims and mere objects which the mythistory presents. Rather, they actively helped to create and shape this literature. Women were partners in the very birth of science fiction.

Notes

1. Robert Silverberg, ". . . And the Mound Builders Vanished From the Earth," in *A Sense of History: The Best Writing from the Pages of American Heritage,* American Heritage: N.Y., 1985, p. 46.

Part II

The Crest of the First Wave:

Science Fiction's Female Counter-Culture, 1950–1960

13

Ecce Femina

I HAVE PREVIOUSLY DEMONSTRATED that women writers were present and welcome in the science fiction field from its magazine beginnings. I have also discussed the lost legacy of literary themes—the empathetic creation of fully-conceived aliens and the tradition of genuine social speculation—which women writers introduced in the formative years of the genre, 1926–1949. Both of these phenomena validate the contested terrain thesis. Here I demonstrate how this thesis also best describes the nature of science fiction culture in the crucial decade of the 1950s.

This is the decade that the most generous historians of the field cite as the time when a handful of daring women writers first began testing the genre waters. This is also the decade when these first women writers were supposedly just beginning to be accepted by a reputedly hostile male establishment.

Of course, none of this is true. Rather, it was the decade that witnessed a flowering of the long-maturing female counter-culture within the receptive environment of the science fiction world. It is this flowering of science fiction's female counter-culture which will be my main theme.

My approach has been the same as before. I did not rely upon what others have said about women writers in the Fifties. Of necessity, this is how most modern readers are introduced to earlier science fiction writers. Lacking extensive magazine collections of their own, or access to such, they have relied on retrospective anthologies for their knowledge.

Unfortunately, these give only partial views of the past, seen through the editor's particular filter. Although Pamela Sargent, for instance, has resurrected the work of a respectable number of early women writers in her *Women of Wonder* anthologies, most editors have overlooked their work. They have followed the lead of Damon Knight in his influential *Science Fiction of the Thirties* (1975).[1] Knight chose eighteen stories (by nineteen authors) to represent the 1930s. Not one of them was by a woman. Likewise, Martin Harry Greenberg and Joseph Olander, in their *Science Fiction of the Fifties,* also slighted the role of women.[2] Out of twenty-one stories they picked to represent the 1950s, only two were by women. In their recommended reading list, they named sixty-five books by thirty-seven writers, including such now-obscure authors as Kendall Foster Crossen and "J. T. McIntosh" (James Murdoch MacGregor). Only two of the sixty-five books were by women.

Similarly, in his 1996 unearthing of the "greatest stories of the decade," Robert Silverberg found eighteen stories from the Fifties worth noting. Only one was by a woman.[3] And in *The End of Summer: Science Fiction of the Fifties,* edited by Barry N. Malzberg and Bill Pronzini, we find ten stories they claim to be representative of the decade. Not even one is by a woman.[4]

Had I relied on such works, I would have had as skewed a vision of the past as have most others in the field, and there would have been little to write about. Instead, I depended on the primary sources. I tracked the publication record of women in American science fiction magazines for the inclusive eleven years of 1950–1960. Again, this means the physical examination of *every* issue of *all* the sixty-one science fiction magazines published in the United States during that period. I sought stories written under female names, as well as known initials and pseudonyms of women.

One of the results of this research is the first comprehensive bibliography of female authors in U.S. science fiction magazines of the 1950s, as well as those of unknown gender (see tables 2 and 3). I also present the first complete bibliography of known female authors in the British science fiction magazines of the 1950s, as well as those of unknown gender (tables 4 and 5), although I do not base my argument upon these data.[5]

And what does this new information tell us? It reveals that during these crucial years there was a dramatic increase in the number of stories by women, written by an amazingly large number of authors. *During the 1950s, 154 authors identifiable as women produced a total of 634 stories.* (These numbers will undoubtedly climb after further research.) Thus, the female presence was much larger, both in terms of authors and number of stories, than has usually been asserted.

I want to emphasize, however, that this was not a sudden "coming out of the closet." Rather, it was an organic development, a natural progression of past trends. Unlike other commentators, I do not accept the traditional exclusion narrative. I have not assumed a period of female absence in science fiction. Hence, I have not tried to pinpoint "When It Changed," the date at which women "stormed the barricades" and suddenly appeared in the literature.

The reason there has been so much disagreement over "When It Changed" in science fiction is because *there is no female Bastille Day*. No one has ever documented any feminist "storming of the barricades," because it never happened. It is a fictitious non-event which mythology has enshrined in legend. The fact is women were "partners in wonder" with men from the founding of the genre—and the partnership grew steadily over the decades.

That this evolving partnership was robust can be seen by the exponential growth of women's participation, from its beginning with Clare Winger Harris in 1927, to 1960. During that period, *203 known female authors appeared in the science fiction magazines* (the eventual numbers are possibly even larger). *Each decade witnessed a regular doubling, tripling, or quadrupling of female authors and stories by them.* For example, six female authors appeared in the science fiction magazines during the last three years of the 1920s. In the 1930s, the number quadrupled to twenty-five. In the 1940s, the number again climbed, virtually doubling to forty-seven. (See summary figures for table 1.) And in the 1950s, the number of known female authors again more than tripled, to 154.

We see the same steady and regular increase in the number of stories women contributed over the decades. *Between 1927–1960 there were 922 known female-authored stories in the science fiction magazines.* For the earliest period, the last three years of the Twenties, there were seventeen stories. This figure more than tripled in the Thirties to sixty-two stories. In the Forties the figure again more than tripled to 209 stories. And this pattern was repeated in the Fifties when the number again tripled, with 634 stories by female authors.

This steady upward progression over the decades resulted in almost a thousand science fiction stories by 203 women for the entire period—a significant, but largely unknown, body of literature. (Were we to include the 365 stories that 127 female authors contributed to *Weird Tales* alone between 1923–1954, we would have well over a thousand.) Perhaps the reason some commentators (though, clearly, not all of them) finally discerned a female presence in science fiction by the 1950s is because this trend had, by then, reached some kind of a critical mass, making "the women SF doesn't see" at last clearly visible.

Thus, the 1950s—at least as far as the female presence is concerned—was neither some kind of a coda to the "Golden Age" of Campbell's Forties, nor the "real" beginning of women's activity in the genre (although some, of course, argue the "real" beginning was the 1960s or later). Instead, the 1950s was a way-station, although a crucial and highly-visible one, on the well-travelled path to greater female participation in the shaping of a maturing literary field.

That brings us to my second main point about the Fifties. Peter Haining, admittedly speaking of an earlier period, said that, "Women writers were rarely to be found in the pages of pulp magazines. . . . This is primarily because both Science Fiction and fantasy are predominantly a man's literature."[6] This is clearly false. And, amidst the more familiar "male" form we commonly think of as solely characterizing the "man's literature" of science fiction in the Fifties, a female variant existed.

The increasing female participation during this time resulted in the elaboration of a distinctly female literary viewpoint, essentially a female counter-culture. Many of the male writers of the Fifties were busy creating conformist future hells, dystopian visions of alienated and reactionary individualism. But at the same time, many female writers were engaged in a quest for community and espousing very different values from those expressed by men. In a sense, these "female" values can be seen as a variation on one of the two themes—that of female empathy—which I identified in the stories of the women writers of the Twenties and early Thirties.

The Cold War anti-Communist crusade of the Fifties and the triumph of consumer capitalism made the tradition of utopian social speculation found in the earliest female science fiction a dangerous one to continue—if it could have been continued at all. Those socialist and feminist utopias were now beyond the pale, not to be imagined again until the transformed political conditions of the next two decades once more made genuine social speculation viable.

But there remained the second theme I discerned in the earliest female science fiction: the empathetic creation of fully-conceived aliens. This now took the form of a primary emphasis upon communication, emotional attachments, and the creation of community—motifs more traditionally identified as "female" than as "male."

This is not to say that *all* stories by *all* female writers in the Fifties exhibited these qualities. I am not claiming that. Nor is it to deny that *some* stories by *some* male authors expressed the same values and concerns. Obviously, some did. Nevertheless, there is a thematic unity among enough of the decade's stories by women for us to say that a variant form of "female" science fiction flourished in the Fifties.

Let us now look more closely at the contested terrain of 1950s science fiction and the women writers at the heart of that decade's female counter-culture.

The pulps were dying. *Fantastic Adventures* folded in 1953, while the venerable *Amazing Stories* changed to digest form with its April–May 1953 issue. *Startling Stories* died in 1955. In the fantasy field, *Weird Tales* ceased publication in 1954 after changing to a digest in 1953.

But as the pulps died, other magazines, different types of magazines, took their places. *The Magazine of Fantasy & Science Fiction* was launched at the end of 1949. *Galaxy* appeared a year later. These joined *Astounding* to become the Big Three of the Fifties. *If* came along in 1952 as a second tier runner-up. In addition to these major newcomers, there was a host of lesser lights. By 1953 there were thirty-five science fiction magazines simultaneously on the newsstands. Over the course of the decade, sixty-one different magazines were published.

Thus, although commercial SF books began appearing more frequently from both hardcover publishers such as Doubleday and paperback publishers such as Ace, Ballantine and Pocket Book, science fiction remained primarily a magazine medium throughout the Fifties. And what appeared in the books had, for the most part, been printed in magazines first. Rare was the author such as Andre Norton, who wrote mainly for book publication alone. The magazines were where you found most of the stories and writers.

And in these magazines, among readers and editors alike, there was a new focus on ideas, not just on favorite authors. Satire became more popular, as did more sophisticated and philosophically "adult" stories. While John W. Campbell's *Astounding/Analog* continued to dominate the field with its emphasis on hard science fiction, *The Magazine of Fantasy and Science Fiction* gained a reputation for publishing fiction with a more literary cast. H. L. Gold's *Galaxy* specialized in stories with a sociological or satirical bent—but "safe" sociological stories and "safe" satire. Over-population, consumerism, advertising, even religion were subject matters for speculation—but in the age of McCarthyism, the dominant political mores of the day went, for the most part, unchallenged.

Nevertheless, science fiction was becoming a more mature genre. Book review columns became more prevalent in the magazines, and accepted standards of literary criticism were beginning to be applied. Foremost in this trend was Damon Knight, whose collected reviews were published by Advent in 1956 as the influential *In Search of Wonder*. That same year he was presented with a Hugo for his book reviewing. In 1960 Kingsley Amis published *New Maps of Hell*, a serious critical evaluation of the genre, which had first been presented in 1959 as a series of lectures at Princeton University. Also in 1959 *Extrapolation,* a literary journal devoted entirely to science fiction criticism, was founded.

All of the myriad new magazines needed stories, lots of stories. Inevitably, many new names appeared—and among them we also find the bylines of many new women. In all, 138 new women joined sixteen "old-timers" who had debuted earlier and who continued to publish, for a total of 154 women authors in the Fifties.

Magazine editors could not help but notice the greatly increased number of female writers, even at the very beginning of this crucial decade. Thus, they "discovered" the "sudden appearance" of women in the genre—a perennial discovery and favorite pastime of amnesiac commentators. For example, Sam Merwin, Jr., editor of *Thrilling Wonder Stories,* noted in a December 1950 editorial (pp. 6–7, 140), that there was a "Great Invasion" underway of women writers into science fiction.

The "Great Invasion" of women into the field, he said, actually began in the 1930s. Suddenly, "at some indeterminate point in the nineteen thirties something happened. Just how or why it happened lies beyond our current ken but at any rate the girls got interested and began to move in. This metamorphosis

. . . is too well and too long established to be regarded as any mere passing trend. The girls are in and in to stay. [How similar this sounds to Shawna McCarthy's claim that, suddenly, "no one *really* knows why," women abruptly appeared out of nowhere to invade science fiction in the mid-to-late 1960s. The date of "When It Changed" seems to be a moving target.]

"A number of women writer [sic], ranging from adequate to brilliant, began [in the 1930s] to turn out science fiction stories of such excellence that in magazine after magazine they grabbed their share not only of inside short stories but of lead novelets and novels, hitherto an exclusively masculine prerogative. Certainly the fantasies of C. L. Moore were and are as fine as any work in the field. And right up alongside her work we have today that of E. Mayne Hull, Leigh Brackett [editor Merwin obviously knew Moore, Hull, and Brackett were female], Margaret St. Clair, Judith Merril, Catherine [sic] MacLean, Betsy Curtis, and Miriam Allen deFord, to say nothing of an ambitious platoon of youngsters who are promising to crash into print professionally at almost any moment.

"Naturally, with such a group of talented women writers practicing successfully for more than a dozen years, the entire story-perspective on women in science fiction has changed. It is no longer uncommon to find a female chief protagonist in an stf story—and not a two-dimensional valentine or a cold-fire priestess-empress but a female who acts, talks and thinks like a woman alive. . . . The girls have not yet blossomed into full partnership as yet—but give them time. Certainly they are well on the way. . . . It is our belief that this female uprising, inrush or whatever it may be termed is entirely in line with the world-trend toward woman's emancipation and equality that has endured at least since the fiery pronunciamentos of Mary Wollstonecraft and her companions."

Some of the newcomers Merwin praised and welcomed were destined for fame. Among them were Marion Zimmer Bradley, Joanna Russ, Kate Wilhelm, Anne McCaffrey, Andre Norton, Shirley Jackson, Zenna Henderson, Phyllis Gotlieb, Kit Reed, Miriam Allen deFord, Mildred Clingerman, Rosel George Brown, Julian May, Madeleine L'Engle, and Carol Emshwiller.

Although none of these novices won major SF awards in the Fifties, perhaps some of them *should* have. At least Richard A. Lupoff thought so. He collected the stories he felt should have won the Hugo for each year in a series of anthologies. In them he awarded his "alternate" Hugos to three women debuting in the Fifties.

For 1955, he felt that Shirley Jackson should have gotten the Short Story Hugo for "One Ordinary Day, With Peanuts," from the January *Magazine of Fantasy and Science Fiction.*

Kate Wilhelm should have taken the 1957 Hugo for "The Mile-Long Spaceship," from John W. Campbell's April *Astounding.*

And for 1960, "Pauline Ashwell" (Pauline Whitby) (nominated for "Best

New Author" in 1958 for "Unwillingly to School" in Campbell's January *Astounding)* should have won the Hugo for "The Lost Kafoozalum." Her story appeared in Campbell's October *Astounding/Analog*, and was, in fact, nominated.[7]

Others of these novices almost grabbed the top prize. (Elizabeth M.) "Betsy" Curtis, for instance, was one of those women Anthony Boucher discovered and praised in *The Magazine of Fantasy & Science Fiction*, where her debut, "Divine Right," appeared in the summer, 1950 issue. Until 1973 her work regularly appeared in *Amazing Stories, Galaxy, Planet Stories, Imagination, Marvel Science Stories, Universe Science Fiction, Infinity Science Fiction, Authentic Science Fiction*, and *Worlds of If*.

William L. Hamling published her second story, "The Old Ones," in his new magazine, *Imagination: Stories of Science and Fantasy* (December, 1950). Calling attention to her story in the October debut issue of his magazine, he said, "Elizabeth Curtis . . . has a novelette coming up soon that shows a remarkable talent . . . We predict that Miss Curtis will go far in the science-fantasy field." And she did. But it was "The Stieger Effect," which John W. Campbell published in *Analog* (October, 1968), with which Curtis came closest to the brass ring, it being a 1969 Hugo Award nominee for Best Short Story.

But, there is no need to speculate on what awards the new women writers of the Fifties *ought* to or *might* have received, for many of them *did* go on to win the highest prizes the fans and their peers could bestow. Kate Wilhelm is one of these.

Wilhelm debuted with "The Pint-Size Genie" in the October 1956 issue of *Fantastic*, the first issue of that magazine edited by Cele Goldsmith. She published only 15 more short stories over the remainder of the Fifties. However, her peers nominated her *The Clone* for the Best Novel Nebula in 1965 (the first year it was presented) and she won the Best Novel Hugo in 1977 for *Where Late the Sweet Birds Sang*. Her peers also thrice awarded her Nebulas for her short fiction, first in 1968 for "The Planners," in 1986 for "The Girl Who Fell Into the Sky," and in 1987 for "Forever Yours, Anna." She was also a Worldcon Guest of Honor (along with her husband, Damon Knight) at the 1980 Boston World Science Fiction Convention and in 2003 she was inducted into the Science Fiction and Fantasy Hall of Fame.

Joanna Russ, who debuted in the September, 1959, issue of *The Magazine of Fantasy and Science Fiction* with "Nor Custom Stale," was awarded the Nebula by her peers in 1972 for her short story, "When It Changed." In 1983 she won the Best Novella Hugo for "Souls." And in 1988 Russ won the Pilgrim Award for best SF criticism, given for her body of work. She was also honored for her body of work in 1995 with a Special Retrospective James Tiptree, Jr. Memorial Award.

In October 1953, *Science Fiction Plus* editor Sam Moskowitz discovered Anne

McCaffrey and published "Freedom For the Race," her first story, in Hugo Gernsback's last venture into the field. She would go on to win the Hugo, the Nebula, the Balrog, the Gandalf, and the Ditmar International award, while also becoming one of the most popular writers in the field with her Dragonrider series.

Nor are the careers of some of these Fifties newcomers over, even half a century later. Wilhelm and McCaffrey, for instance, are still busily productive. And in 2002, Carol Emshwiller (who debuted in 1955) won the Philip K. Dick Award for her novel *The Mount,* presented by the Philadelphia Science Fiction Society for the year's most distinguished original paperback. But that wasn't all. Also in 2002 her peers awarded her the Nebula for "Creature," which they deemed the best short story of the year.

While not winning science fiction laurels, in 1961 Miriam Allen deFord was awarded the highest prize in the mystery field, the Edgar Allen Poe Award. Others became nominees for the highest awards in science fiction. The year 1958 witnessed three women nominated for the best Short Story Hugo: Pauline Ashwell, Zenna Henderson, and Katherine MacLean—the latter going on to be awarded the Best Novella Nebula in 1971. Ashwell was again Hugo-nominated for the Best Short Story of 1960.

Andre Norton's *Witch World* would be a Hugo contender for Best Novel in 1963. In 1983 her peers presented her with the Grand Master Nebula Award for career achievements, the first woman to be so honored. Meanwhile, Marion Zimmer Bradley not only published a long list of short stories and novels, but also the 1982 crossover Arthurian novel, *The Mists of Avalon* (made into a 2001 TV mini-series), making her wealthy enough to subsidize her own fantasy magazine. It was a distinguished cohort of writers.

And, as we shall see, these newer women writers of the Fifties, as well as veterans from earlier days, found a receptive home in the science fiction magazines of the day. And why should they not have? The editors of all the leading magazines welcomed them and solicited their stories.

Previously, I recounted the great lengths to which John W. Campbell went to nurture Katherine MacLean and shepherd her first stories into print in *Astounding,* her debut being "Defense Mechanism" in 1949. Over the course of the Fifties he published six more of her stories. Campbell also published the 1940 debut of Leigh Brackett, the 1948 debut of Judith Merril, the 1951 debut of Julian May, and the 1958 debut of Pauline Ashwell, "Unwillingly to School," which was Hugo-nominated. He also published her Hugo-nominated "The Lost Kafoozalum" in 1960 and Kate Wilhelm's "The Mile-Long Spaceship" in 1957, which perhaps *should* have been a Hugo-winner.

I also discussed Anthony Boucher's stated commitment to discovering and publishing women writers for *The Magazine of Fantasy and Science Fiction.* Indicative of this support was the dedication of his seventh annual collection of the "best" from that magazine in 1959 to "Mildred Clingerman, most serendipitous of discoveries."[8] Clingerman, of course, debuted in his magazine. Over the course of the 1950s, *The Magazine of Fantasy and Science Fiction* published *183 stories by 64 different women*, including debut stories by Miriam Allen deFord (1950), Zenna Henderson (1951), Kit Reed (1958), and Joanna Russ (1959). These 64 women writers represented 16.12 percent of the authors published in *The Magazine of Fantasy and Science Fiction* between 1949–1960. This figure is comparable with the 17 percent in *Weird Tales* during its 1923–1954 life span and to the overall percentage, c.16–18 percent, of women science fiction writers in the 1970s.[9]

The editors of the other front rank magazines were likewise supportive. Just as she'd criticized John W. Campbell earlier for rejecting one of her stories, Leslie F. Stone described Horace L. Gold, editor of *Galaxy* (where Vera Cerutti was editor-in-chief), as "a male chauvinist" who was violently opposed to women writing science fiction. "On one of his rejection slips to me," she said, "he had scribbled, 'Why not face up to it? Women do not belong in science-fiction!' "[10] This allegation seems extremely dubious because in the very first issue of *Galaxy*, October 1950, Gold published the novice Katherine MacLean's outstanding "Contagion." That story appeared in the magazine, MacLean said, because Gold called her up and (in her words) "begged" her to send him a story.[11]

Thereafter, Gold published forty-one more stories by twenty women over the course of his editorial tenure, which ended in October 1961. These stories included the 1952 debut of Evelyn E. Smith and the 1958 debut of Rosel George Brown. Indeed, Robert Sheckley described Evelyn Smith as being part of "Horace's circle" of authors whom he regularly published (others being Sheckley, Fred Pohl, Cyril Kornbluth, Algis Budrys, Damon Knight, Jerome Bixby, and "William Tenn" (Philip Klass)).[12] All told, these twenty women writers accounted for 10–15 percent of the authors published in *Galaxy* between 1950–1960.[13]

Gold made a point of publishing the work of female authors because, he said, "In every issue I always made sure that I had at least one story that appealed to women."[14] An example of this policy was MacLean's, "The Carnivore" (*Galaxy SF*, October, 1953), which she wrote specifically for Gold because he again called her (as he often did) and asked her to write a story with a female character. The story appeared under the pseudonym "G. A. Morris" because, explained MacLean, "it was not an original concept and I was ashamed of it."[15]

In fact, according to Damon Knight, Gold wanted to increase the female presence in *Galaxy* desperately, and would have published even more female authors if he could have found them. He even proposed hiring Knight as a "utility writer" to write stories to order, "maybe even under women's names," Knight quotes him as saying. Knight balked and this idea seems never to have been implemented.[16] But it wasn't just female bylines and story lines that Gold encouraged. He also used female artists, such as Jean Fawcette.[17]

The situation was similar at *If*, launched in April, 1952 by James L. Quinn. He was an upstate New York publisher of crossword puzzle magazines who wanted to get into the then-booming science fiction market. Lawrence "Larry" T. Shaw came aboard as the magazine's associate editor with the May 1953 issue, although Quinn continued as editor and involved himself in most editorial decisions. And, as with the top three magazines, *If* was receptive to female authors. This was because, Shaw said, Quinn "had a thing about female writers. . . . He *liked* women writers." Indeed, agent Forrest Ackerman was so aware of this pro-female bias at *If* that he targeted Quinn for his female clients.[18]

But Larry Shaw was also favorable toward women writers and his editorial tenure came to an end because of his protectiveness of one. Damon Knight tells us that, "when Larry returned a story of Judith Merril's because he thought she could sell it elsewhere for more money, Quinn took this as disloyalty and fired him."[19]

Evidently Quinn also liked female *editors*, as well as writers, since Eve P. Wulff replaced Shaw immediately after he left in 1954. Eve Wulff retained this editorial position until 1958, when Knight replaced her. Wulff thus joined the company of the many other female magazine editors who blossomed in the Fifties, such as Cele Goldsmith.

A 1955 graduate of Vassar College, Cele Goldsmith's first job that fall, at age twenty-two, was at Ziff-Davis publications, where she began uncredited editorial work simultaneously on *Amazing* and *Fantastic*. Within a year, September 1956, she was being credited as the assistant editor at *Amazing*. There she discovered and published the first stories of Keith Laumer in 1959 and Roger Zelazny in 1962. It was also under her stewardship that *Amazing* received its first Hugo nomination.

However, it was as editor of *Fantastic* that Goldsmith discovered Kate Wilhelm in 1956 and Phyllis Gotlieb in 1959, as well as Ursula K. Le Guin and Thomas M. Disch, both in 1962. She lured Fritz Leiber back to active writing (most notably his popular Fafhrd and Grey Mouser series) with an entire issue of *Fantastic* (November, 1959) devoted to him and his stories. This innovation made popular the idea of single-author issues. Her work on both magazines was honored in 1962 with a Worldcon Special Convention Award. She went on to become one of the most prolific science fiction editors of all time, male or female, with 193 issues to her credit.[20]

Goldsmith, however, was not the first female editor at *Fantastic*. That was Lila E. Shaffer, who, as managing editor, helped launch the magazine in 1952 with editor Howard Browne. They were also the editorial team which was already producing *Amazing Stories* at this time. In their very first issue (summer, 1952) they proudly presented Louise Lee Outlaw's "The Runaway" amongst stories by a host of stellar contributors. It was Lila Shaffer and Howard Browne who also published Shirley Jackson's genre magazine debut, "Root of Evil," in their January-February 1953 issue. (Jackson's famous horror tale, "The Lottery," appeared in *The New Yorker* in 1948.) And, besides making a point of publishing female writers, they also published female artists, such as Greisha Dotzenko.[21]

Such was the situation, then, at the top science fiction magazines of the Fifties. All essentially had a female affirmative action program in place, as all of their editors, both male and female, made deliberate efforts to find and publish female authors.

Editors at lesser-ranked magazines also welcomed female talent. *Fantastic Universe,* for example, published eighty-four stories by women in the Fifties, including the 1953 professional magazine debut of Andre Norton and the 1956 genre debut of Madeleine L'Engle. Long-time *Weird Tales* author Mary Elizabeth Counselman made her science fiction debut in *Planet Stories* in 1951, Marion Zimmer Bradley debuted in *Vortex Science Fiction, #2* in 1953, Carol Emshwiller debuted in *Future Science Fiction* in 1955, and Sam Moskowitz (as noted) discovered Anne McCaffrey for *Science-Fiction Plus* in 1953.

Sam Moskowitz was typical of Fifties SF editors in his support of female writers. In her account of her discovery by Moskowitz, McCaffrey says nothing about any hesitancy or fear she might have had in writing and sending her first attempts at science fiction to male editors in the early 1950s. She didn't think there was any bias upon the part of male editors against women. "I never had any trouble about writing SF," she said, "whether I used a woman as the main character or a man. For starters, no one told me a woman shouldn't write SF: that there'd be any other than the problem of telling the story you wanted to tell. For this attitude, I am indebted to Lila Shaffer, ex-editor of *Amazing* and *Fantastic.* (She became my roommate's roommate after I married and she was very encouraging when she discovered I actually enjoyed reading SF and wanted to write.) . . . The writers themselves don't think it's odd for a woman to write SF. I got encouraged from every one. . . . I've never had to mask my name either and it never occurred to me I'd have to to be published in SF."[22]

The first genre editor she met and spoke with (and who rejected her) was a female editor (probably Lila Shaffer) at *Fantastic Adventures,* who "kindly read some of my earliest attempts at short stories. She also kindly told me just how far off telling a good one I was."

Nevertheless, McCaffrey persevered. "There was a lot of excitement over Civil Rights then," she recalled, "and I was trying to get pregnant. So it occurred to me that one of the most basic rights was having a child of your own species. So I sat me down and typed out 'Freedom of the Race'. . . . All enthused with myself, I sent the story to *Science Fiction Plus*, which Sam Moskowitz had just started—on the notion that he wouldn't have enough stories sent in yet. He did kindly pick mine, edited out the worst blunders, and since it was under 1,000 words, whomped up some advertising that I had won a contest for a good story under 1,000 words. . . . And I got a whole $100 for the yarn. . . . and when I got the check, I waved it in all the doubters' faces."[23]

When McCaffrey submitted her story, then titled "The New Freedom," to Moskowitz, her by-line clearly indicated not only her gender, but her marital status as well, as "Mrs." was on the manuscript.[24] Neither the by-line nor the pregnancy subject matter made any difference to Moskowitz, who accepted it as the winner of his monthly short-short story contest. To qualify, a story had to be 1,000 words in length. McCaffrey's story was actually 1,300 words long, but Moskowitz liked the story so much he edited it down to 1,000 words. If purchased at three cents a word, the magazine's top rate, McCaffrey would have received only $39 for the story. As a monthly contest-winner, she received $100. No doubt the $100 for her debut encouraged McCaffrey greatly. It took her five and a half years to publish her next story—but she persevered.

Moskowitz tells us that publisher Hugo Gernsback read the manuscript and also "liked the story and gave it his seal of approval by changing the title to 'Freedom of the Race.'" The story concerned conquering Martians who used human females as living incubators. The Earth women carried to term Martian fetuses which Martian females could not successfully carry due to the higher gravity of Earth. To counter this exploitation, human females deliberately contracted German Measles, resulting in complete fetal death for all the Martian embryos. After the story appeared, McCaffrey, then age twenty-seven, dropped by to visit Moskowitz in his office and Moskowitz found her "warmly congenial" and "instantly likeable."

The only fly in the ointment was McCaffrey's husband. He was one of the "doubters" who (like Kate Wilhelm's first husband) was not as supportive of his wife's writing as editor Moskowitz and the other people at Gernsback's magazine. The publicity man for *Science Fiction Plus* managed to place a story about McCaffrey's debut in her local newspaper. *The Montclair* (New Jersey) *Times* (August 11, 1953) ran it under the headline, "Anne McCaffrey Johnson Writes Prize-Winning Magazine Story." The reporter had interviewed McCaffrey's husband and found that, "Being a Princeton man, Mr. Johnson takes a somewhat dim view of his wife's flights into outer space. . . . He is not quite sure whether to be proud or dismayed at his wife's breaking into print."

Moskowitz, on the other hand, was unreservedly proud and encouraging of the new writer. "I hope you will get to work on something new and let me see it," he wrote McCaffrey. "Nothing would tickle me more than to have each of our short-short sellers turn into a regular contributor."

McCaffrey did get to work. Although *Science Fiction Plus* died that same year and Moskowitz was not able to publish another story by her, Anne McCaffrey went on to a distinguished career, which still flourishes half a century later. But it was also the beginning of a bitter schism between McCaffrey and her husband, which resulted in divorce three children later.

In 1971, when she was a middle-aged woman of forty-five, genre editor Ben Bova wrote of Anne McCaffrey that, unlike the presumed untalented and weak dullards who made up the emerging Women's Movement, she was, ". . . the kind of girl [sic] who doesn't need Women's Lib [sic] because she's obviously talented, fast-thinking, and tough."[25]

The slander against women's liberation and the patronizing attitude toward McCaffrey aside, Bova's comment also slandered the very field in which he made his reputation and his living. It did so because it implied that *only* a talented woman writer who was also exceptionally "fast-thinking and tough" could have been successful in the presumably hostile world of 1950s magazine science fiction. Certainly McCaffrey dealt with a lot of resistance from her husband. But the only toughness really required of women writers to deal with editors and the field itself was the ability to handle the same amount of rejection that any male writer would have faced. And perhaps not even that, as we have story after story of editors like Moskowitz and Gold and Campbell going out of their way to encourage and support women writers.

We also find an open door for women writers in the expanding science fiction *book* market of the 1950s. There was, of course, the proliferation of juvenile books from the typewriter of Andre Norton. But there were also sophisticated treatments of post-nuclear holocaust society by Leigh Brackett in her 1955 novel, *The Long Tomorrow* (perhaps the best story she ever wrote), and by Judith Merril in her impressive 1950 novel, *Shadow on the Hearth*. P. Schuyler Miller, the influential book reviewer for Campbell's *Astounding*, made a point of praising Merril's book for its "warm humanity" and unfavorably compared other novels on the same theme to her work.[26]

Beginning in 1950, only two years after she debuted, Judith Merril also began to exercise a considerable influence on the field with a series of anthologies. That year she edited *Shot in the Dark*, followed in 1952 with *Beyond Human Ken* and then *Beyond the Barriers of Time and Space* and *Human?* (both 1954), followed by *Galaxy of Ghouls* (1955). Her greatest influence, however, came after 1955 when she began her popular and long-running series of annual anthologies of "the year's best SF." These pioneering anthologies were widely supported by the science fiction field with *The Magazine of Fantasy and Science Fiction*, for instance, offering free copies of the first in the series to all new subscribers in 1955. Of Merril, the magazine said she "is famous as one of s-f's top talents."[27] Not bad for someone who only discovered science fiction less than a decade earlier and published her first story only seven years earlier.

For the next dozen years, until her last two collections in 1968 (*SF 12* and *England Swings SF*), Merril's selections and accompanying critical commentary went far in shaping the direction of the evolving field. In those anthologies (and in the book review column she wrote for *The Magazine of Fantasy and Science Fiction*, 1965–1969) Merril campaigned for an eclectic expansion of the genre and became the first important champion of the British "New Wave" in America. And in 2003 her posthumously published autobiography won the Hugo Award for best non-fiction book.

As women SF writers flourished in the Fifties, so too did the number and range of female main characters in the literature. This, however, is usually over-looked. Pamela Sargent, for instance, asserted that, "women characters in science fiction before the '60s were conspicuous chiefly for their absence."[28] Looking at the handful of female characters she found in Fifties science fiction, Sargent termed them dim, dull, and domestic. "Some of these stories," she said, "featured homemaker heroines, who were often depicted as passive or addle-brained and who solved problems inadvertently, through ineptitude, or in the course of fulfilling their assigned roles in society. Often they, unlike the reader, would not really understand what was going on, even by the end of the story."[29]

Perhaps Sargent merely saw what she expected to see. Certainly this is not how Leigh Brackett sought to portray her female characters. Although she debuted earlier, Brackett continued to publish prolifically in the Fifties and in all her stories she felt that, "My women are usually on the bitchy side—warm-blooded, hot-tempered, but gutty and intelligent."[30]

In fact, female protagonists are found throughout women's science fiction in this period and are portrayed as being of all ages, from five-year-olds to grand-mothers, from teenagers to middle-aged women. Further, as well as being daughters, mothers, and grandmothers, they are also presented as assassins, doctors, explorers, scientists, soldiers, spaceship pilots, teachers, time travelers, and telepaths. In Miriam Allen deFord's "The Old Woman" (*Fantastic Universe*, October 1957), for example, a seemingly crazy old woman sits outside a bank daily from dawn to dusk for sixteen years. She is dismissed by all as a harmless nobody. In reality, however, she is the high priestess and ultimate leader of her far-away planet waiting patiently to assassinate the Earth scientist who has dis-covered a secret which will eventually destroy her home planet if he is not stopped.

Portrayals of competent professional women were also increasingly typical in stories written by women in the Fifties. Further, contrary to Jane Donawerth's contention that, "almost no women before 1960 used female point of view," women writers were, in fact, writing more and more from a female point of view.[31] An example is Katherine MacLean's "And Be Merry . . ." (*Astounding Science-Fiction*, February, 1950), one of two stories by her which Campbell pub-lished to encourage her to finish "Incommunicado" (June, 1950). Its protago-nist is thirty-eight-year-old Dr. Helen Berent, expert endocrinologist and wife of an archaeologist, whom she loves. Dedicated to her work, she experiments on herself in an attempt to discover the secret of immortality. She doesn't discover it, but she does rejuvenate herself back to the age of eighteen. At the end of the story she remains devoted to her work, happily married—and with an eighteen-year-old body. Evidently, as early as 1950 MacLean was arguing that a career woman could have it all!

Also increasingly common is a character like Dr. June Walton in MacLean's "Contagion," in the debut issue of *Galaxy* (October, 1950). Dr. Walton, along with her husband, Dr. Max Stark (note the different last name), is a medical doctor to a ship of 100 Earth explorer-colonists, which sets down on the planet Minos. A native contagion, similar to a fast-acting leukemia, fells all the men. It is Dr. Walton who not only figures out the nature of the contagion, but saves their lives. She also unilaterally makes the decision that maroons the entire ship of colonists on the planet as the only way to maintain intact the relationships of all the couples aboard the ship. (I will return to this theme later.)

A similar story, from the same year, is Miriam Allen deFord's debut, "The Last Generation?" (*The Magazine of Fantasy and Science Fiction*, winter-spring, 1950). Because of a nuclear accident, all mammals on Earth have been rendered sterile. As humanity faces the prospect of extinction, all resources are poured into an international research effort headed by four of Earth's most eminent scientists. These four include a Chinese, an American black, a German-Jewish Irishman—and an English-Russian woman.

After years of experimentation, the woman scientist and her Russian husband fellow-scientist succeed in making her fertile once more and she becomes pregnant. But, in the meantime, the world has become a much better place. Faced with extinction, humanity has created a prosperous, democratic, peaceful world government. Racial and gender equality have become a reality, and crime and class distinctions have ceased to exist. The female scientist leads her colleagues in debate over their next steps. Do we want to go back to the way it had been? Can the future be different? Should we reveal to the people that we have solved the problem of infertility? Is humanity fit to survive? The story ends as the question is put to the scientific body.

These scientists and doctors are illustrative of the resourceful and successful female protagonists who appeared more and more in the science fiction of the Fifties. And their efforts to maintain relationships and safeguard the larger community was also becoming a recurring theme. In this, we find a major thematic difference from the stories written by male SF authors of the time.

Both male and female writers, however, were responding, in their differing ways, to the huge and stressful changes which were sweeping over America in the Fifties.

Notes

1. Damon Knight, Ed., *Science Fiction of the Thirties,* The Bobbs-Merrill Co.: N.Y., 1975.

2. Martin Harry Greenberg, and Joseph Olander, Eds., *Science Fiction of the Fifties,* Avon Books: N.Y., 1979.

3. Robert Silverberg, Ed., *A Century of Science Fiction, 1950–59: The Greatest Stories of the Decade,* MJF Books: N.Y., 1996. This is part of a series which looks at twentieth-century science fiction decade by decade.

4. Barry N. Malzberg and Bill Pronzini, Eds., *The End of Summer: Science Fiction of the Fifties,* Ace Books: N.Y., 1979.

5. These tables could not have been completed without the help of Norm Metcalf, for which I am thankful.

6. Peter Haining, Ed., *The Fantastic Pulps,* Vintage Books: N.Y., 1975, p. 315. Haining said this in introducing C. L. Moore's *Weird Tales* story, "The Tree of Life." Moore was the only female among the twenty-two authors Haining reprinted from the pulps. Even in 1975, when Haining made this comment, there were enough female authors active in fantasy and science fiction to make his claim that both genres represented a "man's literature" absurd.

7. See Richard A. Lupoff, Ed., *What If?, Stories That Should Have Won the Hugo, Vols. 1 & 2,* Pocket Books: N.Y., 1980, 1981.

8. Anthony Boucher, *The Best From Fantasy and Science Fiction, Seventh Series,* Doubleday & Co.: N.Y., 1959, dedication page.

9. This is my gender analysis of the complete listing of authors in Ray F. Bowman, *Index to The Magazine of Fantasy and Science Fiction,* Bowman, Carmel: Indiana, 1988. From 1949–1960 *The Magazine of Fantasy and Science Fiction* published 424 poets and fiction authors. Of these, I was unable to identify the gender of 27 due to ambiguous first names or the use of initials. Of the remaining 397 gender-identifiable authors, 64 were female. These 64 represented 15.10 percent of the 424 grand total and 16.12 percent of the 397 gender-identifiable total.

10. Leslie F. Stone, "Day of the Pulps," *Fantasy Commentator,* IX, 1997, p. 101, originally delivered as a speech at Balticon, March, 1974. However, in that speech Stone also stated that, by 1945 "my own well had run dry . . . . But a few years ago [the early 1970s?] there came to me again a strong urge to write, and I found I had to learn how all over again, for a new style had been overtaking science-fiction. This wasn't easy for someone who had arrived in the wake of Edgar Rice Burroughs, when adventure was presented for the sake of adventure on other worlds and our own," p. 102.

Stone began her career in 1929 and the last new science fiction story she ever published was "Gravity Off," *Future Fiction,* July, 1940, a decade before *Galaxy* was launched. As she says, she had run out of ideas by 1945 and, stylistically, was completely out-of-step when she later tried to re-enter the field. Is it conceivable that when Gold rejected her submission, sometime in the 1950s, she was already too old-fashioned and what he had *actually* written to her was along the lines of, "Why not face up to it? *You* do not belong in science-fiction!"? And this Stone later remembered as "*Women* do not belong in science-fiction!"?

11. Letter, Katherine MacLean to Eric Leif Davin, June 21, 2002.

12. Charles Platt, *Dream Makers: The Uncommon People Who Write Science Fiction,* Berkley Books: N.Y., 1980, p. 20.

13. This is my gender analysis of the complete listing of authors in Ray F. Bowman, *An Index to Galaxy Science Fiction,* Bowman, Toledo: Ohio, 1987. From 1950–1960, *Galaxy* published 203 authors, of which I was unable to gender-identify six due to ambiguous first names or the use of initials. Of the remaining 197 gender-identifiable authors, 20 were female. These 20 represented 9.85 percent of the 203 grand total and 10.15 percent of the 197 gender-identifiable total.

14. H. L. Gold, "Gold on *Galaxy,*" in Frederik Pohl, Martin H. Greenberg, and Joseph D. Olander, Eds., *Galaxy: Thirty Years of Innovative Science Fiction,* Playboy Press Books: N.Y., 1980, p. 7.

15. Letter, Katherine MacLean to Eric Leif Davin, May 26, 2002.

16. Damon Knight, "Knight Piece," in Brian W. Aldiss and Harry Harrison, Eds., *Hell's Cartographers*, Futura Publications Ltd.: London, 1976, 1975, p. 133.

17. See Jean Fawcette's interior illustration, e.g., in *Galaxy*, November, 1951.

18. Larry T. Shaw, "As *If* Was in the Beginning," in Frederik Pohl, Martin Harry Greenberg, and Joseph D. Olander, Eds., *Worlds of If*, Bluejay Books, Inc.: N.Y., 1986, p. 7, 16. Emphasis added.

19. Damon Knight, "Knight Piece," in Aldiss and Harrison, *Hell's Cartographers*, p. 137.

20. These included 105 issues of *Amazing Stories* (October 1956-June 1965), 85 issues of *Fantastic*, and three issues of *Dream World*, for which she was either editor, assistant editor, or managing editor. Only three American editors, one of them female, have had more prolific tenures. These were John W. Campbell (451), Catherine Tarrant (309 when listed on the staff of *Astounding/Analog*, or 372 if she was on the staff as Campbell's assistant from December 1943 to February 1949 when she wasn't listed), and Raymond A. Palmer (268).

21. C.f., the interior illustrations of Greisha Dotzenko in *Amazing Stories*, June–July, 1953. The cover of this issue was devoted to Harriet Frank, Jr.'s "The Man From Saturn."

22. Anne McCaffrey interview in Paul Walker, ed., *Speaking of Science Fiction*, pp. 256–257. Originally in *LUNA Monthly 56*, 1974.

23. Anne McCaffrey, Introduction to "Freedom of the Race," in Steven H. Silver and Martin H. Greenberg, Eds., *Wondrous Beginnings*, DAW Books: N.Y., 2003, pp. 79–80.

24. The following account comes from Sam Moskowitz, "The Return of Hugo Gernsback, Part IV," *Fantasy Commentator*, Vol. X, Numbers 3 & 4, spring, 2003, pp. 215–216.

25. Ben Bova, Ed., *The Many Worlds of Science Fiction*, E. P. Dutton & Co.: N.Y., 1971, p. 128.

26. P. Schuyler Miller, book review, *Astounding Science-Fiction*, September, 1954, p. 149.

27. *The Magazine of Fantasy and Science Fiction*, September, 1955, p. 2.

28. Pamela Sargent, Ed., *Women of Wonder, The Classic Years: Science Fiction by Women from the 1940s to the 1970s*, Harcourt, Brace & Co.: N.Y., 1995, p. 13.

29. Sargent, *Women of Wonder, The Classic Years*, p. 9.

30. Leigh Brackett, "The Science-Fiction Field," *Writer's Digest*, July, 1944, p. 26.

31. Jane Donawerth, *Frankenstein's Daughters: Women Writing Science Fiction*, Syracuse University Press: Syracuse, N.Y., 1997, p. 112.

14

Alone Against Tomorrow

A NEW AMERICA came into existence in the Fifties, bringing with it vast social transformations. In the wake of World War II's devastation, America—which, as early as the 1880s, had already become the world's biggest industrial power[1]—stood alone as the only major industrial nation to emerge unscathed. America was also politically stabile in a world roiled by post-war turmoil in Europe and national liberation struggles in the colonial Third World. This combination gave the United States undisputed military, economic, and political hegemony over the entire non-Communist world. America reaped vast economic benefits from this status and entered into a period of unprecedented and widespread affluence and prosperity. The American socioeconomic system seemed to most to be not only the best in the world, but the best in the history of the world. Success was its own vindication. There seemed to be no viable alternative. Even more than in the wake of World War I, American corporate capitalism luxuriated in a seemingly all-powerful cultural hegemony.

This phenomenal economic growth changed the entire culture. Poverty for most had been the norm up until this time. A majority of Americans, for example, could never afford to own their own homes until the late 1950s. Home ownership became the American norm only in 1960, by which time three out of every five families owned their own dwelling.[2] Thus, for the first time in our national history, the years after World War II brought prosperity, not just for the lucky few, but on a mass scale. In real dollar terms (adjusted for inflation), the Gross National Product more than doubled between 1929–1953. Likewise, blue collar wages doubled in real dollar terms in the twenty-year span of 1945–1965. In terms of income, blue collar workers essentially became middle class over the course of the Fifties and early Sixties.[3]

One result of this mass-based prosperity was a car in every garage. Five million cars were sold in 1949, breaking the pre-Depression record year of 1929. Production and sales climbed throughout the 1950s and 1960s. By the early 1970s, there were two cars for every three Americans.[4] There was a subsequent decline in the use of mass transit. Even by 1960 the impact of this transition was evident. According to that year's report of the Committee for Economic Development, "Between 1950 and 1958 transit riding in American cities fell from 17.2 billion to 9.7 billion rides per year, a drop of 43 percent. More and more people are getting to work or shopping by car."[5]

The car, in turn, along with cheap energy supplies and government subsidies, made possible the explosive growth of a new American nation called "Suburbia." "Of 13 million dwelling units erected in non-farm areas from 1946 through 1958," the Committee for Economic Development tells us, "approximately 11 million, or 85 percent, have been located outside of central cities."[6] In the thirty years from 1940–1970 there was an increase of 56 million people living in these suburbs. This figure represents *almost twice* the *total* number of immigrants who flooded into America in the entire century between 1820 and 1920. That immigrant flood had been part of the largest mass movement of people in the history of humanity. The creation of the "nation" of Suburbia in the thirty years after 1940 dwarfed that earlier immigration tide.[7]

A "nation" with 56 million people is larger than most European countries, even large ones such as France. And this new nation was built from scratch, along with all its infrastructure—roads, bridges, hospitals, water filtration plants, homes, schools, sewers—in only thirty years. A daunting task, swiftly accomplished, bringing even greater economic growth in its wake. Not only did blue-collar building trades boom, but Suburbia also needed an entire nation's worth of service workers to keep it functioning smoothly.

Suburbia thus became the heart of American society. The new national culture became that of dispersed automobile-based mass consumption. All that is today identifiably "American" to the rest of the world—vast highway networks, shopping malls, fast food franchises, etc.—came to dominate not only the physical, but also the cultural landscape at this time. Between the mid-1950s and the late 1970s, America built 22,000 suburban shopping malls. Meanwhile, lavish federal highway funding guaranteed there would be new roads to connect the suburbs to the cities, while the lack of investment in public transportation meant that buses and trains were insufficient in themselves to service this new suburban nation. Increasingly, Americans became encased in their mobile isolation chambers, as cars were needed to reach work, the marketplace, and leisure centers.

The unintended consequence of this residential and transportation dispersal and isolation was the destruction of "community" as America knew it. The old urban cultural forms, based on tight-knit, ethnic, urban, blue-collar communities, dissolved in the acid of the new society. For most large cities in America's traditional Northeastern heartland, 1950 marked the peak of their population. The last half-century has brought steady population declines throughout what came to be known as "the Rust Belt." In place of the close "urban villages" of old, America became a nation of strangers, anonymous neighbors, alienated suburbanites, and declining central cities.

This transformation had serious social consequences. One of them was the post-war "Baby Boom" brought about by unprecedented prosperity. The American birth rate had fallen by 50 percent from 1880–1940. After 1945, however, the birth rate leaped by 25 percent and remained high throughout the 1950s. This fueled mushrooming suburban school populations and, by the 1960s, the "youth culture" of the exploding numbers of college students—many of them the first in their families to attend college. Raised in affluence and with drastically different worldviews from their parents, these children of the Fifties would become the young rebels of the Sixties.[8]

Another cloud on the horizon was the status of women. The Fifties decade is now seen through highly gendered filters as either a lost Eden of "Ozzie and Harriet" domesticity or an era of proto-"Stepford Wives" indoctrination and female subordination. Both home sales and family sizes boomed as women married younger and their husbands brought home larger paychecks. For social conservatives, the result was welcomed as a highly gendered utopia in which the sexes knew their proper places—a paradise conservatives have been trying to replicate ever since.

For Fifties' homemakers (and future feminists) like Betty Friedan, however, the resulting "feminine mystique" of suburban female domesticity masked a viciously anti-female national culture based on male supremacy. This sexist national culture resulted in private nightmares for millions of isolated, depressed, and bitter women trapped in a suburban purdah. Indeed, the very ideal of the freestanding single-family suburban house conjures up images of isolation from neighbors and community.[9]

Yet, even as the dominant ideology of the era was one of complacent and happy domesticity, female workforce participation continued to rise, especially for middle-class and married women. The new nation of Suburbia needed workers, lots of them, and its insatiable demand pulled women out of their homes in record numbers. The workforce participation rate for married women tripled and the rate for mothers doubled.

That internal contradiction alone introduced tremendous strains into traditional patriarch-oriented families in which the male was seen as the sole breadwinner—with consequent authority. But this growing female workforce participation also took place in a context of continued occupational sex segregation. These increasing numbers of working women were channeled into low-paying "women's work," such as nursing, secretarial, and clerical jobs. For them, there was rising frustration over society's economic restrictions on their lives.[10] All of these factors contributed to the anger which found expression in the late Sixties explosion known as "the women's movement."

Yet another consequence of the Fifties socioeconomic transformation was racial polarization. As whites fled the cities, "people of color" moved in. The 1960 Report of the Committee for Economic Development recalled that, "An historic function which the central city continues to perform is that of reception center for low-income migrants from outside the region. A steady stream of people from the rural South and Puerto Rico has replaced earlier migrations from abroad as the chief source of unskilled and semiskilled labor in urban centers."[11]

These blacks and Hispanics, who didn't have the money to flee to Suburbia, were left in the cities. But, it wasn't lack of money alone that kept then in urban centers. Federal housing policies also legitimized racially discriminatory lending standards, exclusionary suburban developments, and restrictive covenants, thereby subsidizing "white flight" to the suburbs. This "middle-class welfare" thus also undergirded substantial wealth accumulation in the form of white-owned suburban property. State policy makers, banks, realtors, and the construction industry abetted this creation of affluent white suburban neighborhoods, where credit profiles operated like electric fences, red-lining and zoning Suburbia off from an increasingly ghettoized inner-city black populace.

And, with the white middle class moving out and their populations dropping, the economic base of the cities eroded and tax revenues dried up. Cities became poorer and fell into decay and fiscal crisis, as the needs of their remaining populations rose at the same time that urban revenues fell. "White flight" to the suburbs therefore created two nations: white and wealthy Suburbia and the dark and decaying cities, segregated from each other and mutually hostile. The bill came due in the Sixties, as that decade erupted into urban riots, black revolts, and social rebellion.

The "white" social rebellion took two forms, that of the youth revolt and the women's movement (which would give rise to early-Seventies feminist science fiction). Both of these groups discovered that "the personal is political" and that what they had assumed were private problems actually masked vast social distortions best faced collectively.

But, these revolts were the social movements of *the Sixties*. They were the future consequences of the Fifties transformation. For the most part, Fifties magazine science fiction did not deal with such possible future social movements.

One of the exceptions was a novel by the interloper Kurt Vonnegut, a mainstream writer who sometimes wrote science fiction novels which his publishers made sure were never billed as "science fiction." In his 1952 novel *Player Piano*, Vonnegut imagined an economic future for America eerily like the present. It was an America with superfluous workers who had no hope other than enlisting in the imperial forces fighting in distant corners of the world for oil and other scarce raw materials. The dregs of the skilled working class formed a millenarian resistance movement, the "Ghost Shirts," before their final defeat by the triumphant corporations.

But only this science fiction "outsider" managed to see this future. The professional seers seemed blind to these trends. They accepted the cultural hegemony of corporate capitalism, patriarchy, and the white worldview. Thus, they never imagined such things as the youth revolt or the Women's Movement.

Perhaps they can be excused this oversight. Sociologists who studied social trends professionally also failed to foresee the near future. For example, even as the women's movement swirled around him in the late Sixties, renowned Harvard sociologist David Riesman assured Americans that, in the coming years, "If anything remains more or less unchanged, it will be the role of women."[12]

So, instead of speculating about such social trends, most Fifties science fiction authors dealt with "obvious" issues, such as the mass, middle class, anonymous, consumer society of Suburbia then under formation. According to John Clute, for instance, most of the stories which appeared in the pages of *Galaxy* during this period dealt with the "popular" theme of "an automated suburban America in the near future . . . and the 1950s *Galaxy* can be seen as a kind of extended debate on the nature of Eisenhower-era America."[13]

For some white middle class males, the debate was one-sided. They already knew that the new "ticky-tacky" suburban utopia of the Fifties was fast becoming a bourgeois dystopia, a conformist hell of mass-produced consumption and mind-deadening manipulation. "These have been years of conformity and depression," Norman Mailer said in 1957. "A stench of fear has come out of every pore of American life, and we suffer from a collective failure of nerve."[14]

Indeed, the immediate post-World War II years produced a kind of mass hysteria which decried the supposed decline of individualism in all its myriad manifestations. In its place white middle class male intellectuals discerned the rise of "group-think," of mindless uniformity, while sociologists found "the organization man" in the gray-flannel suit to be the prototypical "modern man." In 1951 University of Chicago (later Harvard) sociologist David Riesman published *The Lonely Crowd*, which characterized mid-century Americans as "other-directed" personality types who sought peer approval "by conforming to group aspirations." Evidently the book struck a chord, as it went on to sell 1.4 million copies, earn the author an appearance on the cover of *Time* magazine, and help usher in a long and intense period of social soul searching.

It was in this context that the first faint discussions of cultural hegemony theory began to be bandied about by intellectuals. Failing to comprehend the full nuances, these intellectuals saw Gramsci and the Frankfurt School as the prophets of the problems they now faced. Mass consumer society was all-powerful, soul-destroying, a cultural hegemony against which nothing could stand.

The avant garde eagerly grasped this simplistic interpretation as the best intellectual description of the transformations going on.

Some responded to this perceived "cultural hegemony" by asserting the worth of their unique individuality and their independence from the cookie-cutter society they saw all around them. Already, in 1943, Ayn Rand had published a best-selling novel, *The Fountainhead,* which glorified the right of the individual of genius to discard society's rules. In the post-war years the Rand cult blossomed in college towns across America.

In some cases, the increasing numbers of white, middle class, male rebels against the unfolding future were called Beatniks. In 1955, Disneyland ("The Happiest Place on Earth") opened in Anaheim, California. That same year Allen Ginsburg howled that, "I saw the best minds of my generation destroyed!" That of his friend Jack Kerouac seemed to be one of them. And maybe it was. It was cirrhosis of the liver that was officially listed on his death certificate, but just living in Eisenhower's America seemed to have burned out Kerouac's mind long before the booze rotted his guts.

With the 1957 publication of *On The Road,* Kerouac became the High Priest of the Dharma Bums, the Chief Spokesman of the Zen Barbarians who extolled sex, drugs, jazz, and Eastern religions as the only way to survive the soul-destroying karma of Fifties America. Something was wrong, they said, with the consumer culture of triumphant American capitalism, with gas hogs and split-levels, the rat race and grey flannel suits. Ginsburg, Kerouac, and the Beats knew in their guts that the Great American Barbecue was rancid. They knew there was something more important than the orgy of materialism.

But what that might be, they never knew for sure. They knew only that it had to be primal and instinctual—of that they were certain. If the increasingly suburbanized American society was rational and ordered and predictable, then salvation must be in all that America was not: irrational, chaotic, unpredictable, wild and crazy. Salvation had to wail and moan, howl and groan, scream and caper.

All this Ginsburg was reputed to have done as a stoned Kerouac sat before him composing *On The Road* on a never-ending roll of butcher paper in a one-draft-only, non-stop writing jag, trying to find it, "*IT*," the elusive purpose to all the madness: "We found the wild, ecstatic Rollo Greb," Kerouac wrote. "He played Verdi operas and pantomimed them in his pajamas with a great rip down the back. He didn't give a damn about anything. . . . He lisped, he writhed, he flopped, he moaned, he howled, he fell back in despair. . . . [Dean] took me into a corner. 'That Rollo Greb is the greatest. . . . He's never hung-up, he goes every direction, he lets it all out . . . he has nothing to do but rock back and forth. . . . You see, if you go like him all the time you'll finally get it.'

"'Get what?'

"'IT! IT! I'll tell you—now no time, we have no time now.'"[15]

Unfortunately, there never was any time to go into detail—but Kerouac got the sacred text in its totality anyway. That was all there was to "IT." Just never be hung-up, go in every direction, let it all hang out and just rock back and forth. That's IT: The Beat generation's critique of mid-century America—aimless, directionless, rocking in stoned nothingness—but at least it was spontaneous, unpredictable, anarchic and uniquely individual, and therefore held to be the only authentic reality in a plastic world of lobotomized conformity. As Marlon Brando's outlaw biker in *The Wild One* (1954) replied, when asked what he was rebelling against: "Whaddya got?" In the end, Jack Kerouac may as well have been the James Dean character in *Rebel Without a Cause* (1955). Any cause, or no cause, was acceptable, so long as the individual rebelled.

Such aimless rebellion was, in the end, no fundamental rebellion at all. It was like the perennial youthful rebellion portrayed by the advertising industry. Advertising romanticizes the cool image of the rebel merely to make the corporate sponsor more acceptable through association, thus reinforcing the status quo. So, too, with the Fifties obsession with the rebellious individual. This was the contradiction at the heart of Beat culture. Despite surface appearances, its rebellious glorification of individualism was, in fact, right in step with mainstream America's long infatuation with "rugged individualism." Indeed, a close textual analysis of articles published during the 1950s in that quintessential American compendium of magazine articles, *The Reader's Digest*, reveals a relentless mainstream magazine emphasis on individualism as a mainstay of the American way of life.[16] In their differing ways, therefore, the Beats and the Squares were both vociferously championing and reinforcing a traditional American ideal, which they perceived to be under siege from the new hegemony of corporate-sponsored mass consumption culture.

As a sophisticated understanding of cultural hegemony theory would predict, the various genres of popular culture reflected this same obsession. The obsession itself—the emphasis upon individualism in opposition to encroaching mass society—was a manifestation of the innate contested terrain of culture.

Cultural critics, for example, have discerned a sea change in hard-boiled detective fiction in the Fifties as the "paperback noirs" of Mickey Spillane and other best-selling authors like him displaced the Raymond Chandler and Dashiell Hammett ethos of an earlier age. Thus, Michael Aaron Rockland, professor of American Studies at Rutgers University, uses Spillane's books to demonstrate the values of vigilantism and individualism that seemed to permeate post-World War II America.[17] Spillane's hero, Mike Hammer, broke free from the enveloping human mass to devise his own, personal, code of ethics and values. All true individuals must do this, Spillane preached, in order to survive. Increasingly, in books like Spillane's first venture into the field *I, The Jury* (1947), Spillane and other new authors reflected the deeply conservative, individualistic cultural norms of the Eisenhower era which were being threatened by massive socioeconomic change. Thus, Spillane's gospel touched a popular nerve and, within a decade of his debut, he had sold an astounding 30 million copies of his novels.[18]

The same deification of the individual in opposition to mass society was also a salient feature of Fifties male-authored science fiction. In this, these writers were brothers to the Beats and the Spillanes. The problem they faced was that society was dramatically changing all around them. The world wouldn't stop turning. The truly revolutionary movement of the 1950s was mass-market capitalism. It was this that was rapidly destroying the old social order in a mad rush to the future. And male science fiction writers reacted fearfully against the growing mass consumption culture of the Fifties. They feared it threatened to transform tomorrow into a homogenized suburban hell. They didn't want to tread the pavement of that particular inferno. This Damon Knight made clear in his 1955 novel, *Hell's Pavement*, a psychological dystopia of universal mind-control.

As white middle-class males, these writers materially benefitted from the changes. However, market forces were simultaneously robbing them of a social attribute they valued highly. This was the cherished individualism that they felt had made America great in days of old. British author Brian Aldiss noted their reaction as manifested in their fiction. He studied the work produced by American male science fiction authors "between the Bomb and the Apollo." He concluded that it "gained its power by having as unspoken topic one of the great issues of the day: the sense that the individual's role in society is eroded as society itself becomes wealthier and more powerful. This is certainly so with novels as unalike as Pohl and Kornbluth's *The Space Merchants*, Silverberg's *The Time Hoppers*, and Knight's *A for Anything*."[19]

While suburbia was a comfortable crabgrass utopia, it was also faceless, anonymous, and unendingly the same. In revulsion male authors produced a flood of stories, such as Cyril Kornbluth's "The Marching Morons" and "William Tenn's" "Null-P" (both 1951), which decried the frightening conformity they saw all around them.

In "Null-P" Tenn (Philip Klass) described a political movement that discovered an absolutely mediocre individual named George Abnego who was completely average in all ways. The movement, promoting Agnegist conformity, swept into political power and enforced abject normality upon all citizens. The result was the collapse of human civilization, replaced by a species of intelligent dogs. The title was suggested by Tenn's editor, Damon Knight (who termed it an "elegant satire"), to denote the negation of Plato's ideal of "philosopher kings"—that is, the best—ruling society.[20]

Thus, as Kingsley Amis observed at the time, "Conformist utopias maintained by deliberate political effort are a cherished nightmare of contemporary science fiction." Male authors were busy drawing "new maps of hell," he said. However, "Whereas twenty years ago [science fiction] would locate its authoritarian society on Venus or in the thirtieth century, it would nowadays, I think, set its sights at Earth within the next hundred years or so."[21] Indeed, the very titles of many fiction and non-fiction books of or about Fifties male-authored science fiction describe their view of mid-century America: *Hell's Pavement, Hell's Cartographers, New Maps of Hell.*

The antidote to such future conformist hells, of course, was the rampant individualism Amis found everywhere in the literature. In many stories, as in any good Western, a future surrogate for Shane would ride into town, single-handedly set things right, and then ride off into the sunset—or blast off into space. What resulted was the creation of a male science fiction literature of paranoid fantasies celebrating atomistic individualism. It was an attitude very much in tune with the mainstream intelligentsia's critique of Fifties America. David Riesman, for instance, declared that, "I am insisting that no ideology, however noble, can justify the sacrifice of an individual to the needs of the group."[22]

Male science fiction authors agreed. In such stories as Damon Knight's "The Country of the Kind" (1955), Amis noted that, "The need to be swimming against the stream is clearly and repeatedly sounded. In particular, the social value of the deviant, the maverick, is canvassed at all levels of sophistication. . . . there is almost no trace of the tendency to rate the interests of the group higher than those of the individual."[23] It was not society or community which these writers saw as threatened and under assault, only their own unique individualism. "A very representative story . . . is Robert Sheckley's 'The Academy.' Here the detection of deviants is achieved by the use of nasty machines called sanity meters. . . . The doctor . . . explains to [the hero] that . . . 'society . . . must be protected against the individual.' "[24]

Perhaps the story which exemplifies this conformist hell motif most in current memory is Jack Finney's classic, *The Invasion of the Body Snatchers.* In it, an alien life form slowly turns the population of an entire California town into literally brain-dead conformists. Finally, only a single heroic individual is left to warn society of its impending doom. Originally serialized in the slick magazine *Collier's* (November 26–December 24, 1954), it tapped into a pervasive fear of conformity in the nation's psyche, even though Finney later denied trying to write a "message" story about the virtues of individuality.[25]

An expanded version was quickly published as a Dell paperback in 1955 and Hollywood just as quickly purchased it for a 1956 film, directed by Don Siegel and starring Kevin McCarthy and Dana Wynter. The film was remade not once, but twice, in 1978 and 1997, while the paperback was finally published as a hardcover with handsome red-gold stamping on the spine by Gregg Press in 1976. Simon & Schuster then published yet another hardcover version in 1998. It remains perhaps the most evocative vision of the conformist paranoia that Fifties male science fiction writers were manifesting.

At the time, however, Amis saw Ray Bradbury's work, in *Fahrenheit 451* and in stories like "Usher II," from *The Martian Chronicles,* as most illustrative of this theme. In the latter, the "Investigator of Moral Climates . . . orders demolition [of the cloned House of Usher], under the ordinances which have prohibited and destroyed all works of fantasy from Poe to *The Wizard of Oz*, while no films are allowed except remakes of Ernest Hemingway. . . . The suppression of fantasy, or of all books, is an aspect of the conformist society often mentioned by other writers, but with Bradbury it is a specialty."[26]

Bradbury has confirmed this interpretation of his work. "The power of any country is the sum total of its individuals," he believes, "each individual rich . . . with his own revolution."[27] In America, he continues, "We have always been revolutionary [and] science fiction . . . is the fiction of revolutions. Revolutions in time, space, medicine, travel, and thought. . . . For ours is a field with no intellectual elite. . . . We are a true field of loners. . . . No one man rules the roost, so no man follows. There are just wild and lovely individuals."[28]

This "wild and lovely" individualism inevitably had a political dimension. Individualism is not a bad thing, per se, nor do I mean to cast it in a pejorative light. Individualism in the service of a great transforming vision is one of the main motive forces in human progress. But in light of the social and political orientations exemplified by their heroes, it might not be right to think of the attitude of Fifties' male science fiction writers as that of "transformative individualism." Setting things right, like Shane did, is a literally "reactionary" exercise in that it restores the presumably better *status quo ante*.

Thus, "reactionary individualism" seems to be a more appropriate description of the attitude of these male writers. They didn't want to change society from what they *imagined* it to be circa 1950. Technologically, they would have liked a few more super-duper gizmos and gadgets to play with, as boys always like their toys, but socially things were OK just the way they were.

The challenge for male science fiction writers, then, was to resist the forces of socioeconomic change, to fight the future in the name of the past, to rebel against tomorrow. I have previously cited Robert Bloch's 1959 critique of Fifties' science fiction for its political conservatism, even when framed as "revolutionary." "The future holds little basic change," he found in his survey of the literature. "The hero rebels, yes—but not to superimpose his own notions upon society; merely to restore the 'normal' culture and value-standards. . . . The implication is that once Law and Order are restored, everything will settle down to a general approximation of life as it is lived today—if not in actuality, at least in the pages of *Better Homes and Gardens*."[29]

Amis also discerned this same rebellion against the future on the part of typical male-created Fifties science fiction heroes. They were always reactionary revolutionaries, he found, in the literal sense of the word. They were champions of the past, "reacting" against changes they didn't like, "reacting" to preserve the social and economic status quo. They were rebelling to enthrone that glorious imaginary past of Eisenhower's America, before the dark side of Suburbanization changed it into something alien and unAmerican.

"One invariable feature of them," Amis noted, "is that however activist they may be, however convinced that the individual can, and will, assert himself, their program is always to resist or undo harmful change, *not to promote useful change*. It is quite typical that the revolutionary party in *The Space Merchants* [Frederik Pohl and Cyril Kornbluth, 1953, serialized as "Gravy Planet" in *Galaxy*, June–Aug., 1952] should be called the Conservationists. Thus, to call the generic political stance of science fiction 'radical,' as I have done, is not quite precise: it is radical in attitude and temper, but strongly conservative in alignment. . . . 'Negative' might be a better description. Such glimpses of the post-totalitarian future as we can glean show a society just like our own, but with more decency and less television. . . . Further, no positive utopias, dramatizing schemes of political or other betterment, can be found in contemporary science fiction. Modern visionaries, in general, seem to have lost interest in any kind of social change."[30]

Of course, the enforced Cold War political consensus of the Fifties—an age of loyalty oaths, blacklists, and informers—mandated such political conservatism. There is little indication, however, that male science fiction writers chafed under this restriction. That, alone, is an indication of their acceptance of political conservatism's cultural hegemony. They wrote about the future to enshrine the past and this sociopolitical conservatism seemed to be exactly what the majority of the science fiction readership wanted. Fred Pohl claimed, for instance, that *The Space Merchants* sold ten million copies in forty languages.[31] Exceptions to this conservatism stand out simply because they are so anomalous. One such would be Eric Frank Russell's ". . . And Then There Were None," (*Astounding Science-Fiction*, June, 1951). But, of course, Russell was not an American, but a *British* writer, which simply reinforces my point about the conservatism of American male writers.

Despite the popularity of such fictions, British literary critic Raymond Williams, writing in 1956, viewed such male "stories of a future secular hell" (as he termed them) as politically reactionary because they were profoundly elitist and anti-democratic. Like Amis, he cited Bradbury's *Fahrenheit 451* as "at once articulate and representative" of such "Putropian" literature, which he believed to be "the characteristic twentieth-century corruption of the Utopian romances."

In Bradbury's work, said Williams, the central "myth" is that of "the defense of culture, by a minority, against the new barbarians. In [George Orwell's] *1984*, the 'myth' is the struggle between clean and unclean intellectuals, who determine the future without reference to the dumb 'proles.' The form of feeling which dominates this putropian thinking is, basically, that of the isolated intellectual, and of the 'masses' who are at best brutish, at worst brutal. . . . I am not disposed to modify this adverse criticism by the fact that the apparent values of such works are liberal and humane. . . . I believe, for my own part, and against this central myth, that to think, feel, or even speak of people in terms of 'masses' is to make the burning of the books and the destroying of the cities just that much more possible."[32]

Looking back from 1975, Ursula K. Le Guin discerned this same elitist and politically reactionary individualism. "Where are the poor, the people who work hard and go to bed hungry?" she asked. "Are they ever *persons*, in SF? No. They appear as vast anonymous masses fleeing from giant slime-globules from the Chicago sewers, or dying off by the billion from pollution or radiation, or as faceless armies being led to battle by generals and statesmen. In sword and sorcery they behave like the walk-on parts in a high-school performance of *The Chocolate Prince*. Now and then there's a busty lass amongst them who is honored by the attentions of the Captain of the Supreme Terran Command, or in a spaceship crew there's a quaint old cook, with a Scots or Swedish accent, representing the Wisdom of the Common Folk. The people, in SF, are not people. They are masses, existing for one purpose: to be led by their superiors. From a social point of view most SF has been incredibly regressive and unimaginative."[33]

In her essay, Le Guin viewed this subordination of "the people" to the superior individual as part and parcel with the subordination of women in most male-authored science fiction. Indeed, living as we are in the wake of the Seventies' women's movement, we can see that perhaps the most obvious aspect of Fifties male writers' conservatism was in the realm of gender relations.

There were notable exceptions. Philip Jose Farmer explored alien sex and love in his explosive 1952 story, "The Lovers" (which was rejected by both Campbell and Gold). Theodore Sturgeon challenged sexual taboos in stories like "The World Well Lost" (1953) which dealt with alien homosexuality. But they *were* exceptions. For the most part, their colleagues could imagine only the sexual *status quo* projected into the furthest regions of space and time.

"Amid the most elaborate technological innovations," observed Amis, "the most *outre* political or economic shifts, involving changes in the general conduct of life as extreme as the gulf dividing us from the Middle Ages, man and woman, husband and wife, lover and mistress go on doing their stuff in the mid-twentieth-century way with a kind of brutish imperturbability. . . . Though it may go against the grain to admit it, [male] science-fiction writers are evidently satisfied with the sexual status quo—the female-emancipation of a Wylie or a Wyndham is too uncommon to be significant. Nor has anything more surprising than a new contraceptive been imagined as a specific pressure operating against that status quo."[34] Male SF authors were so enamored of the sexual status quo, it seems, that they were even unable to notice the tremendously increased numbers of women entering the workforce all around them—a "specific pressure operating against the status quo" which would soon have radical consequences.

This unimaginative sexual conservatism on the part of male science fiction writers was, of course, part of their larger social and political conservatism and their acceptance of a cultural status quo they saw as timelessly valid. Their fiction celebrated heroic atomistic male individuals. These heroes struggled against the transforming forces of mass-market capitalism to preserve what they perceived to be the desirable social, sexual, and political matrix of 1950s America— the very best of all possible worlds. In a sense, this male science fiction was schizophrenic. While, for instance, it championed capitalism as the best economic system it could imagine—it was that same capitalism which was the most revolutionary force in society. It was capitalism that was responsible for the future conformist hells these writers envisioned. They failed to comprehend fully what it was they were rebelling against.

Perhaps for this reason they could conceive of no alternative but a nostalgic yearning for a past that never was, an imaginary and unchanging Fifties Eden before the serpent was introduced. It was a contradictory and a lonely vision. Its hero stood alone against tomorrow. Adam with no Eve.

In this, it was decidedly different from the counter-culture of female science fiction which flourished unnoticed in its midst.

Notes

1. See chart on worldwide distribution of industrial production in Nelson Lichtenstein, Susan Strasser, and Roy Rosenzweig, *Who Built America?: Working People and the Nation's Economy, Politics, Culture, and Society, Vol. 2, Since 1877,* Worth Pub.: N.Y., 2000, p. 321.

2. Lichtenstein, et al., *Who Built America?,* p. 593.

3. See "The Post-War Economic Boom," in Lichtenstein, et al., *Who Built America?,* pp. 570–576.

4. Lichtenstein, et al., p. 570.

5. Report of the Committee for Economic Development, in Charles N. Glaab, Ed., *The American City,* Homewood: Ill., 1963, pp. 461–473.

6. Report of the Committee for Economic Development, pp. 461–473.

7. See "Suburban America," in Lichtenstein, et al., pp. 591–595. The roots of Suburbia, of course, go back much further than the post-World War II era, beginning to grow as early as the 1850s. See, e.g., Sam Bass Warner, Jr., *Streetcar Suburbs: The Process of Growth in Boston, 1870–1900,* 2nd Ed., Harvard University Press: Cambridge, 1978; Jon C. Teaford, *City and Suburb: The Political Fragmentation of Metropolitan America, 1850–1970,* Johns Hopkins University Press: Baltimore, 1979.

The two acknowledged classic histories of the suburbanization process are Kenneth T. Jackson, *Crabgrass Frontier: The Suburbanization of the United States,* Oxford University Press: N.Y., 1985 and Robert Fishman, *Bourgeois Utopias: The Rise and Fall of Suburbia,* Basic Books: N.Y., 1987. Both books pinpointed the political and economic forces and racial tensions driving suburban growth. Two newer books by Yale professor Dolores Hayden reconceptualize the historical development of suburbia and its more recent transformation. They are *Building Suburbia: Green Fields and Urban Growth, 1820–2000,* Pantheon: N.Y., 2004, and *A Field Guide to Sprawl,* Norton: N.Y., 2004.

8. Lichtenstein, et al., p. 572.

9. This is not a caricature. For a recent overview of the women's movement which does, indeed, present this picture of the Fifties, see Ruth Rosen, *The World Split Open: How the Modern Women's Movement Changed America,* Viking: N.Y., 2000.

10. See Alice Kessler-Harris, *In Pursuit of Equity: Women, Men and the Quest for Economic Citizenship in 20th-Century America,* Oxford University Press: N.Y., 2001.

11. Report of the Committee for Economic Development, pp. 461–473.

12. Quoted in *Time,* July 21, 1967.

13. John Clute, in E. F. Bleiler, Ed., *Science Fiction Writers: Critical Studies of the Major Authors from the Early Nineteenth Century to the Present Day,* Charles Scribner's Sons: N.Y., 1982, pp. 491–492.

14. Quoted in Lichtenstein, et al., p. 598.

15. Jack Kerouac, *On The Road,* Viking-Penguin, Inc.: N.Y., 1957, pp. 105–106.

16. C.f., Joanne P. Sharp, *Condensing the Cold War: Reader's Digest and American Identity,* U. of Minnesota Press: Minneapolis, 2000.

17. James M. O'Neill, "TV's Homer Replaces Classical Homer in Pop-Culture Classrooms," Knight Ridder Newspapers syndicated story reprinted in *The Pittsburgh Post-Gazette,* February 11, 2004, p. ED-11.

18. C.f., Sean McCann, *Gumshoe America: Hard-Boiled Crime Fiction and the Rise and Fall of New Deal Liberalism,* Duke University Press: Durham, N.C., 2000.

19. Aldiss and Harrison, *Hell's Cartographers,* pp. 5, 4. Although published in 1967, Silverberg's *The Time Hoppers* was an expansion of a short story he'd written in 1954. See Robert Silverberg, "Sounding Brass, Tinkling Cymbal," in Aldiss and Harrison, *op. cit.,* p. 31. Knight's book was originally published as *The People Maker,* 1959. Before that it appeared as a short story in *The Magazine of Fantasy & Science Fiction.* It concerned a brave rebel leader fighting a future slave society.

20. Damon Knight, "Knight Piece," in Aldiss and Harrison, *Hell's Cartographers,* p. 128.

21. Kingsley Amis, *New Maps of Hell,* , Ballantine Books: N.Y., 1960, p. 84.

22. David Riesman, *Individualism Reconsidered,* Doubleday Anchor: Garden City, N.J., 1954, p. 27.

23. Amis, p. 82.

24. Amis, p. 89.

25. Jack Finney to Stephen King in Kevin McCarthy and Ed Gorman, Eds., *"They're Here . . .": Invasion of the Body Snatchers: A Tribute,* Berkley Boulevard Books: N.Y., 1999, p. 4.

26. Amis, pp. 91, 92.

27. Quoted in Neal T. Jones, Ed., *A Book of Days for the Literary Year,* Thames & Hudson: London, 1984, entry for August 22 (Bradbury's birthday).

28. Ray Bradbury, "Science Fiction: Before Christ and After 2001," Introduction to Edmund J. Farrel, et al., Eds., *Science Fact/Fiction,* Scott, Foresman, & Co.: Glenview, Ill., 1974, pp. xi–xii, xiii, xv.

29. Robert Bloch, "Imagination and Modern Social Criticism," in Basil Davenport, Ed., *The Science Fiction Novel: Imagination and Social Criticism,* Advent Publishers: Chicago, 1959, 1969, pp. 109–110.

30. Amis, pp. 94–95. Emphasis added.

31. Frederik Pohl, "Ragged Claws," in Aldiss and Harrison, *Hell's Cartographers,* p. 158.

32. Raymond Williams, "Science Fiction," *Science-Fiction Studies,* 15, pp. 357, 358 (1988), originally in *The Highway,* journal of the Workers' Educational Association (London, England), 48, pp. 41–45, (December, 1956).

33. Ursula K. Le Guin, "American SF and the Other," in Le Guin, *The Language of the Night: Essays on Fantasy and Science Fiction,* Perigee Books & G. P. Putnam's Sons: N.Y., 1980, p. 98. Originally published in *Science Fiction Studies,* No. 7, November, 1975.

34. Amis, pp. 98, 99.

15

Across the Great Divide

I N THE 1950s, science fiction was responding to the intense and widespread stress of a new society being born out of an older America. However, observers such as Isaac Asimov claimed that this made no difference in the type of fiction male and female science fiction authors wrote. "The stories that were written demonstrated a purely masculine point of view," he said. Female contributions were completely indistinguishable from those of male. Further, illustrating the automatic and never-proven assumption of male reader hostility to a female point-of-view, he claimed that the supposedly few women authors who existed in the Fifties "carefully wrote very much the kind of stories that men did. . . . Nothing else was possible as long as 90 percent or more of the readers were young men."[1]

Asimov's claim is presently the accepted wisdom of both male and female historians of the genre. But again, the accepted wisdom is false. In fact, male and female science fiction writers of the 1950s reacted to the social stresses of the age in very different ways. Hence, science fiction in the 1950s was highly gendered. The solution of male writers to the perceived problem—a conformist and anonymous future—was an alienated and reactionary individualism. However, the solution offered by female writers was often the bridging of solitude and loneliness to establish emotional rapport. We simply *do not* find women writing stories about lone rebels struggling in almost pathological isolation against a conformist future hell. That is strictly a male nightmare.

But we *do* find women writing about the quest for community. Where male writers saw only the soul-deadening uniformity of the group, female writers realized the necessity of human interdependence, recognizing that community is not the same as uniformity. In many of their stories we see an attempt to communicate, to connect with others (even aliens). We see an attempt to transcend the isolation of individualism and create or recreate an emotionally ful-filling community, ranging in size from the family to all sentient beings—themes more traditionally identified as "female" than "male."

The thematic unity of so many of these stories makes it clear that—while not *all* stories by *all* women can be described this way—there was indeed a distinctly female viewpoint discernable in Fifties' science fiction. To borrow a phrase from the next decade, we find a female "counter-culture" in Fifties' science fiction which social commentators and historians have failed to acknowledge. Given the pervasive sexism of the larger American culture, this thriving female counter-culture was an inviting oasis of alternative values and visions. In this sense, female science fiction in the Fifties was subversive fiction, even if uncon-sciously so, because it ran counter to the dominant paradigm.

Further, science fiction culture was itself subversive to the dominant social values of a highly authoritarian and sexually conservative Fifties' America. This was because in the world of science fiction, women could participate on a basis of equality, not only as writers and fans, but also as editors.

Two caveats, however. The first of these deals with "feminism" and the nature of ideology. Some feminist science fiction historians, echoing the decon-structionist literary theories of Jacques Derrida, argue that fiction expressing even the *unconscious* concerns and interests of the author is inherently ideologi-cal—at least when these are "masculine" concerns and interests.

We find this argument, for instance, in an influential work by British aca-demic feminist Sarah Lefanu. Seemingly unaware that women science fiction authors existed before the Sixties, Lefanu studied only more recent female authors, such as Suzy McKee Charnas, Ursula K. Le Guin, Joanna Russ, and "James Tiptree, Jr." Praising such writers, Lefanu said, "Previous to the inter-vention by feminist writers in the late Sixties and early Seventies, science fiction reflected, in its content at least, what could be called masculine concerns, based around the central theme of space exploration and the development of technol-ogy: masculine concerns because access to these areas was effectively denied to women in the real world, and science fiction, like all writing, is written from within a particular ideology."[2]

Lefanu is thus in agreement with Asimov that "masculine" science fiction was the only kind of science fiction before the late Sixties "feminist intervention." But there are several things wrong with this long and convoluted sentence, so typical of opaque academic writing. Its final phrase, of course, is a non-sequitur. But also, before the Soviets launched Sputnik in 1957, women were no more "effectively denied" access to space exploration than were men. This is because space exploration itself did not exist. It was entirely imaginary and few took it seriously in the Twenties, Thirties, Forties, or even early Fifties. If real-world access is the measure, as Lefanu argues, then imaginary space exploration was no more a "masculine" concern than a "female" concern. Men, too, were denied access to space exploration.

But men were involved in experimental rocketry before Sputnik. And so were women. One example is Mari Wolf, who wrote science fiction about space exploration in the 1950s and also edited a column on genre fanzines for *Imagination: Stories of Science and Fantasy*. In the February, 1954 issue of that magazine (p. 147), she tells us about her employment, which is relevant to this discussion. "I work at a rocket testing lab, in the wind tunnel section," she tells us. "Rockets have always been one of my major interests—I've read science fiction for years and years. . . . I belong to the Pacific Rocket Society and have had some of the best times of my life out in the Mojave Desert on PRS field trips, watching the members static test and flight test their small and un-V-2 creations. . . . Several times a day [at the rocket testing lab where she worked] a horn blows, and after a few seconds there's the unmistakable sound of a rocket motor firing. Sometimes it fires smoothly, sometimes it doesn't, sometimes it blows up."

So, it seems this female science fiction writer from the early 1950s had real-world access to rocket testing, not only on a daily basis at work, but even during her leisure moments as a member of an amateur rocket society. And she tells us rockets had "always been one of my major interests." It would seem there was nothing inherently "masculine" about either rocketry or space exploration. Rather, Lefanu is magnifying her own, personal, lack of interest in rockets and space exploration into a generic female trait.

Which brings us to my final and most important point here. Lefanu's sentence reflects an exceedingly narrow view of female concerns, and not just because Mari Wolf worked around and was fascinated with rockets. Lefanu argues that science fiction before the late Sixties or early Seventies was ideologically "masculine" because it expressed, perhaps unconsciously, "masculine" content and concerns.

But she does not allow a similar latitude for women. For her (and many like her), an expression of female concerns exists only if it is what she, personally, is interested in. Stories by women writers are legitimate only if the content is the kind of explicitly politicized fiction written by the self-consciously feminist writers of the late Sixties and early Seventies. This, for example, seems to have been the only kind of science fiction Marleen S. Barr read as a graduate student. Dr. Barr is now a noted English professor at Virginia Polytechnic Institute who has published many books on women and science fiction. But her grad school roommate recalls that, "when we were roomies, she never read any but the most literarily-correct SF."[3] Such narrow concerns, such limited vistas, is why academic feminists claim that "women's science fiction" is purely "feminist" science fiction and, as such, came into existence only in the late Sixties and early Seventies.

But science fiction, like all literature, can be "gendered" by female-identified concerns and content just as much as by male-identified concerns and content. It does not have to be explicitly and blatantly "feminist" to make it so. Thus, the highly-politicized "feminist" science fiction which began to appear in the late Sixties and early Seventies is, in reality, a subset of a much larger female science fiction counter-culture which existed prior to the coming of late Sixties feminism. We should, therefore, think of it, not as the *beginning* of women's science fiction, but as a "Second Wave" of women's science fiction.

And it is that much larger counter-culture of women's science fiction with which I am dealing. Specifically, I am dealing with the forms that were initially manifested in "First Wave" women's science fiction.

Therefore, I am not claiming the female literary viewpoint I have identified in Fifties science fiction was ideologically "feminist," with a conscious and specific political agenda. Rather, these "female" concerns, attitudes, sensibilities, and worldviews were for the most part expressed *unconsciously.*

They were nonetheless significantly different from traditional worldviews found in most male-authored science fiction of the day, which also expressed mostly *unconscious* male concerns.

This is why I say Fifties science fiction was both male- *and* female-gendered, and conclude that a female counter-culture, a First Wave of "women's science fiction," existed at the time.

Now the second caveat: I am not attempting to enforce a rigid distinction between male and female writers—nor do I think it can be done. Instead, I think that differences in gender interpretations exist on a continuum, which may involve more or less of one approach than the other. Thus, for example, Theodore Sturgeon often provides an exception to the pattern I discern. His outstanding novel of a mutant gestalt "individual" composed of six "normals" with wild talents, *More Than Human* (1953), is illustrative of this female sensibility—although written by a man.

"The Lady Who Sailed the *Soul*" (*Galaxy,* April, 1960) by "Cordwainer Smith" (Paul Linebarger) is another example. In this story, the protagonist is Helen America, the daughter of a "feminist" who fought for the "complete identity of the two genders." Helen is also the first woman to pilot (or "sail") a starship and, after sacrificing forty years of her life to be reunited with the man she loves, she becomes the heroine of a love story that rivals that of Romeo and Juliet.

Likewise, David C. Knight's "The Amazing Mrs. Mimms" (*Fantastic Universe,* August, 1958) exhibits many of the traits I discern as more commonly "female." Mrs. Mimms is a time-traveling operative from a future agency which sends people into the past to create and nurture community. Disguised as a mild-mannered, middle-aged babysitter, she is inserted into crisis periods where she encourages life-affirming attitudes, patches up frayed relationships, and turns children from violent games and mindless TV to constructive play and reading. Time travel agents such as she were responsible for the birth of Voltaire, Darwin, and others who fostered human progress.

One can point, therefore, to *some* male authors who wrote *some* stories in the "female" tradition. Thus, we might compare such gendered literary patterns to gendered differences in physical strength. While one can identify *some* women who are physically stronger than *some* men, nevertheless men are generally stronger than women. So, too, with Fifties' science fiction I am speaking not of all-inclusive differences, but of general patterns.

Let us now look at the pattern of the female counter-culture.

"Loneliness," said Thomas Wolfe in his masterpiece, *You Can't Go Home Again*, "is and always has been the central and inevitable experience of every man." Perhaps. But is it the central and inevitable experience of every *woman*? Or was Wolfe writing about a quintessentially *male* experience?

In fact, a wide range of biological and behavioral studies seem to suggest that loneliness and social isolation is more of a male than a female experience. They have also confirmed the reality of gender differences in many other areas, including emotions in particular. Many of these studies have been synopsized by Cambridge University professor of psychology and psychiatry Dr. Simon Baron-Cohen. His book, *The Essential Difference: The Truth About the Male and Female Brain*, provides an overview of the science behind the "Venus and Mars" dichotomy.

Dr. Baron-Cohen states his thesis clearly on page one: "The female brain is predominantly hard-wired for empathy. The male brain is predominantly hard-wired for understanding and building systems." The operative word here is "predominantly," and he makes it clear that he is speaking about statistical majorities, rather than "all women" or "all men." He also makes a point of emphasizing that he is not valuing one trait over another or arguing that one gender is more "intelligent" than another. Rather, they are equally intelligent in different ways.[4]

Baron-Cohen then presents massive amounts of evidence, ranging from the anthropological to the anecdotal, from the neurological to the case study, to establish his thesis. Gender differences in outlook appear within days of birth, and society reinforces these differences thereafter. Most people are on a medium between the extremes, but the basic trends are clear. Women tend to be more empathetic, easily identifying feelings in other people, responding appropriately when sympathy is needed, and readily attempting to bond with others. Meanwhile, he argues, men are less oriented toward such objectives. Rather, they are more likely to try to understand "systems," technology, mechanics, how things work. This leads them away from the intimacy that women more frequently find in others and, in extreme cases, can turn men into "loners."

Extensive psychological studies also reveal that such gender differences tend to be highlighted during periods of stress. One of the most important analyses of such studies was conducted by University of California, Los Angeles (UCLA) psychology professor Shelley E. Taylor, who specifically looked at gendered responses to stress. Her findings are particularly pertinent to our discussion. This is because American society was undergoing great social stress in the Fifties and I argue that male and female science fiction writers reacted to that stress very differently in their stories, in ways typically "male" or "female."

Dr. Taylor led a group of UCLA researchers that discovered that there is a distinct difference between women's and men's responses to stress. She described the former as being one of "tend and befriend," as opposed to the more familiar male "fight-or-flight" response, which has come to be regarded as the prototypical human reaction. Her conclusion was based on re-analyzing every single one of the many hundreds of laboratory studies of stress-response conducted between 1932, the year when psychologist Walter Cannon first described the "fight-or-flight" response, and 1995.

This re-analysis of all studies conducted since 1932 showed that *only 17 percent of the study subjects were female* (with most of those females becoming subjects only between 1985–1995). Conclusions of the studies were thus inevitably "skewed in favor of one sex's life experiences," so that what the scientific community currently "knows" about the "human" response to stress is, therefore, only what it knows about the *male* response to stress. Since males were presumed to be the "norm," psychologists over the last six decades didn't think to ask if female response might be different and so did not study it.[5]

But when Dr. Taylor's researchers *did* isolate and examine only the psychological studies (17 percent of the total) of *women* in stressful situations, they discovered responses that were quite different. The "human female responses to stress," they said, "are . . . more typically characterized by a pattern we term 'tend and befriend.' . . . females respond to stress by nurturing offspring . . . and by befriending, namely, affiliating with social groups. . . . [which they] create, maintain, and utilize . . . to manage stressful conditions." However, they did not suggest that this was a rigidly segregated gender pattern, and did not deny that females can sometimes engage in aggressive physical behavior, especially in defense of their young. Thus, "Biology is not so much destiny as it is a central tendency," a conclusion Baron-Cohen would agree with.[6]

As these researchers emphasized, they did not deny that aggressive tendencies existed among females. However, even when women show aggression it does not *usually* conform to the male pattern of solitary, "lone wolf," physical aggression, although it is no less devastating for all that. Rather, it tends to be psychological or "relational aggression" manifested through the Machiavellian manipulation of relationships to form cliques, enforce conformity, and turn the group against chosen victims. Malicious gossip and subtle shunning played out within these cliques are the weapons of choice, as anyone from an older generation who is familiar with Clare Booth Luce's famous 1936 play, "The Women," is aware. But, the same phenomenon could be seen in the 2004 Lindsay Lohan movie, *Mean Girls*, which was a box office hit, being particularly popular among young teenage girls.[7]

It should surprise no one, then, that taunts hurt girls more than sticks and stones. In fact, a 2003 study of thousands of girls aged eight to seventeen conducted by the Girl Scout Research Institute discovered that the number one fear of such teen and pre-teen girls, noted by 32 percent of all the girls, was being made fun of or teased by their peers. Fears of such "emotional aggression"—name-calling, gossip, teasing—were especially prevalent among middle-school and junior high girls, but even 22 percent of the older teenage girls rated such fears as their primary concern.[8]

Such patterns as these were the basis for the "girl empowerment movement" which roiled American education in the 1990s. Believing that young girls communicated with and related to others differently from boys, that movement argued that these differences should be taken into consideration by educators when designing school curricula.[9] But, such different gender patterns do not appear *only* in response to stress. It seems they are always present. It is perhaps for this reason that they were also found by Deborah Tannen in her now-famous work on language patterns.

Just as Shelley Taylor surveyed all prior research on responses to stress, Dr. Deborah Tannen, a professor of linguistics at Georgetown University, surveyed prior research on communication. Her analysis of this research revealed that men and women tend to use language in greatly differing ways. This is the basis, she argued, for much of the misunderstanding between men and women. Men, she found, tend to use language for "report-talk." For them, language is primarily a tool for reporting information and competitively establishing status in a hierarchical relationship with other men.

Women, however, tend to use language for "rapport-talk." For them, she argues, language is primarily a tool for establishing affiliation and creating community in an essentially egalitarian relationship with other women and, if possible, with men.[10] NASA engineer Donna Shirley had a vivid experience of this phenomenon in action one day at a meeting of engineers working on the Mars Pathfinder spacecraft that landed the rover Sojourner on Mars in 1997. From 1994 to 1998 Shirley was manager of NASA's Mars exploration program and led the team which built the Pathfinder and Sojourner spacecrafts. In that capacity she had helped hire more women engineers until between 10 and 20 percent of the engineers at the NASA's Jet Propulsion Laboratory in Pasadena were women. "I remember one meeting," she recalled. "Everything was going so smoothly and all of a sudden we realized it was all women, and it never happened to any of us before. We'd never been in a meeting where there were no men."[11]

Even when women lie, they tend to lie differently than men and in the same styles that Deborah Tannen discerned. For example, University of Massachusetts social psychologist Robert Feldman studied social interactions involving 121 pairs of students. Dr. Feldman found that male lies tended to be more competitive and tended to create invidious distinctions between people. Men, for instance, lied to puff themselves up and make themselves look better. Men tended to claim they had done things they had never done. Men tended to claim they always knew where they were, even when they were lost. Men tended to claim they always knew how to do something, even when they didn't.

On the other hand, "Women generally tried to smooth out social situations," said Dr. Feldman. "They try to make everyone feel good." Female lies tended to be told in order to ensure harmonious relations, to bond the community more closely together. They would say they'd seen a movie they had not seen, or that a gift had been absolutely wonderful (even if it had not been) in order to make their conversational partner feel more at ease.[12]

Further, men and women not only *speak* differently, researchers are now discovering that they also *write* differently, even in the most highly formal contexts. Using a computer program called "Winnow," a text categorization tool similar to that of Internet search engines, a research team at the Illinois Institute of Technology was able to correctly identify the sex of an anonymous author 80 percent of the time. Looking at books and scientific reports, the team searched for sex-specific grammar, sentence structure, word preference, and other features revealing a distinct gender difference between the writing of men and women. In one study of 264 novels, Winnow correctly identified the gender of 258 authors.

In another study the program analyzed over 600 documents in the British National Corpus, a 100-million word collection of nonfiction covering science, business, politics, art, and similar topics.[13] Even in technical scientific documents, written in an exceedingly formal style, Winnow correctly identified the authors' sex 73 percent of the time. In these studies the researchers found that women tend to write more "personally" than men. Women use more personal pronouns such as "I," "you," "she," "her," "their," "myself," "yourself," and "herself." They are also more likely to use words indicating relationships, such as "for," "and," "in," and "with."

Meanwhile, men tend to use impersonal and generic pronouns, such as "it," "this," "that," "these," "those," and "they." Additionally, men tend to favor words which specify the number or properties of objects, such as "a," "the," "its," "one," "two," "some," and "more." As Dr. Shlomo Argamon, leader of the research team, concluded, "We have shown convincingly that gender differences in [written] language do exist."[14]

Similar research has also demonstrated that, for the most part, women would rather just not compete. Two economics professors, Dr. Muriel Niederle of

Stanford and Dr. Lise Vesterlund of the University of Pittsburgh, recently paid
male and female subjects to add a series of numbers in their heads. On average,
the subjects did equally well, regardless of gender. Next, the subjects were
offered the opportunity to compete in a four-person five-minute tournament
for four times as much money, with the loser getting nothing—or to continue
adding numbers individually for a quarter of the money. Most female subjects
declined to compete, even the ones who had done the best earlier.

Meanwhile, most men chose to compete, even the ones who had shown the
worst mathematical abilities earlier. Further experiments and post-experiment
interviews convinced the researchers that this gender gap wasn't due mainly to
women's insecurities about their ability to compete. They just didn't want to.
"Even in tasks where they do well," Dr. Niederle said, "women seem to shy
away from competition, whereas men seem to enjoy it too much."[15]

This may help explain why, even in the absence of gender barriers, men are
more likely to remain a majority of Wall Street traders and corporate leaders.
Men are more likely to desire highly competitive jobs which require working
sixteen hour days with the high risk of never seeing one's family and friends and
dying young. Meanwhile, women are more likely to realize that there is more to
life than just making lots of money.

It is possible that this greater female emphasis on community, relationships,
and sociability is a survival mechanism rooted deeply in our primate past. Thus,
these gender differences may be a result not only of testosterone levels, but also
of evolution. For example, a recent study of wild baboon groups in Kenya discovered that the most sociable females with the most female friends were a third
more successful in raising their infants successfully to one year than were the
least sociable females. Dr. Joan B. Silk, of UCLA, the study's first author, said
the finding was the first in lower primates to demonstrate that a large time
investment in building social contacts could significantly improve child-rearing
success.

Since the study showed that social networking is a positive for baboons, Dr.
Susan C. Alberts, of Duke University and a co-author of the study, said it
strongly suggested that evolution favored primates that were sociable and able
to work cooperatively. The male pattern of lone wolf individualism, then, might
have major drawbacks, at least when it comes to building a civilized and nurturing society.[16]

Thus, it seems that the main thrust of scientific research has been to confirm
that there are major male-female gender differences in speaking and in writing,
in sociability and in relationships, in thinking and in worldviews, which evolution has nurtured over the millennia. It should come as no surprise, therefore,
if we discover such deeply ingrained tendencies in science fiction women, as
well.

And, indeed we do, as Brian Attebery discovered. Attebery was the lone male judge on the 1994 James Tiptree, Jr. Award jury charged with honoring the best SF stories exploring gender relations. His experience highlights exactly what Dr. Tannen means about "rapport-talk."

"One thing that surprised me," he wrote to Justine Larbalestier, "was the degree of agreement among the committee members. . . . The most frequent way of introducing comments was, 'Susanna is right when she says . . .' or 'I agree with Lucy that . . .' I wonder if one of the reasons it worked as well as it did was that . . . there was always a bit of chitchat in and around the discussion: My dealings with pre-school-age children and travels around the wilds of Idaho, Ellen's radio work, Susanna's horseback rides on the beach, Lucy's new neighborhood, etc. All of this not only made us feel like old friends, but it also gave a groundedness to our readings."[17]

A lot of "surprising" (to the lone male) "rapport-talk" was obviously going on among these feminist science fiction women of the 1990s. And this trait was also what they valued and searched for in the stories they evaluated.

But in this they were not unique because they were post-Seventies feminists. The many female science fiction fans and readers who had come before them also sought such traits in the stories they read. Thus, Patti J. Bowling, of San Antonio, TX, lamented in the April, 1947 *Thrilling Wonder Stories* (p. 105), that, "I've read hundreds and hundreds of stf [science fiction] and fantasy, etc., and the thing that always strikes me as being unsound is the fact that the authors never envision a change in the psychology of human beings. This seems completely haywire to me. . . . Why must all conflict in stf revolve around greed, conquest, jealousy, all the baser human emotions? Why not imagine that a thousand years or more from now every human from birth is conditioned, psychologically, to live ethical, logical lives for the betterment of themselves and each other?"

But, while readers like Patti Bowling may not have been finding such themes in the stories by male science fiction writers—they were often able to find them in stories by women writers.

And this was increasingly true as the decade of the 1950s dawned. In the female science fiction of the Fifties, a lot of "rapport-talk" was going on.

Notes

1. Isaac Asimov, "The Feminization of Science Fiction," in *The Tyrannosaurus Prescription and 100 Other Essays*, Prometheus Books: Buffalo, N.Y., 1989, pp. 294–295.

2. Sarah Lefanu, *Feminism and Science Fiction*, Indiana University Press: Bloomington, 1989, p. 3.

3. Janice Morningstar, *April Showers Bring May . . . Showers*, May, 2005, p. 3. Personal fanzine produced for mailing #271 of the Fantasy Amateur Press Association (FAPA).

4. Simon Baron-Cohen, *The Essential Difference: The Truth About the Male and Female Brains*, Perseus Publishing: N.Y., 2003.

5. Shelley E. Taylor, et al., "Biobehavioral Responses to Stress in Females: Tend-and-Befriend, Not Fight-or-Flight," *Psychological Review,* July, 2000, Vol. 107, No. 3, pp. 412, 424.

6. Taylor, et al., pp. 424, 411, 423.

7. There was an explosion of books on this subject in 2001 and 2002, mostly by female authors, indicating that these ideas had been percolating for some time. See, e.g., Phyllis Chesler, *Woman's Inhumanity to Woman,* Avalon Books: N.Y., 2001; Sharon Lamb, *The Secret Lives of Girls: What Good Girls Really Do—Sex Play, Aggression, and Their Guilt,* Free Press: N.Y., 2001; Michael Thompson, Lawrence J. Cohen, and Catherine O'Neill Grace, *Best Friends, Worst Enemies: Understanding the Social Lives of Children,* Ballantine Publishing Group: N.Y., 2001; Emily White, *Fast Girls: Teenage Tribes and the Myth of the Slut,* Scribner: N.Y., 2002; Rachel Simmons, *Odd Girl Out: The Hidden Culture of Aggression in Girls,* Harcourt: N.Y., 2002; Roni Cohen-Sandler, *Trust Me, Mom—Everyone Else Is Going,* Viking Penguin: N.Y., 2002; Kenneth H. Rubin and Andrea Thompson, *The Friendship Factor: Helping Our Children Navigate Their Social World—And Why It Matters for Their Success and Happiness,* Viking Penguin: N.Y., 2002; and Rosalind Wiseman, *Queen Bees and Wannabes: Helping Your Daughter Survive Cliques, Gossip, Boyfriends, and Other Realities of Adolescence,* Crown Publishing Group: N.Y., 2002. The 2004 movie, *Mean Girls,* starring Lindsay Lohan and with a screenplay by *Saturday Night Live* writer Tina Fey, gave screen credit to Wiseman's *Queen Bees and Wannabes* as its inspiration.

8. Monica L. Haynes, "Taunts Cut Girls More Than Sticks and Stones," *The Pittsburgh Post-Gazette,* November 12, 2003, p. 1.

9. See, e.g., the discussion of these studies in Michael Gurian, *The Wonder of Girls,* Pocket Books: N.Y., 2001.

10. Deborah Tannen, *You Just Don't Understand: Women and Men in Conversation,* Ballantine Books: N.Y., 1990.

11. Kenneth Chang, "Making Science Fact, Now Chronicling Science Fiction," *The New York Times,* June 15, 2004.

12. Associated Press story published in *The Pittsburgh Post-Gazette,* June 24, 2002, and "Why We Lie," *The Week,* June 28, 2002, p. 16.

13. This can be found at www.natcorp.ox.ac.uk.

14. Michael Woods, "Men, Women Not Only Speak But Also Write Uniquely," *The Pittsburgh Post-Gazette,* September 7, 2003, p. A-3.

15. See Muriel Niederle and Lise Vesterlund, "Do Women Shy Away from Competition?," working paper. For more research on gender differences in competition, see Uri Gneezy, Muriel Niederle, and Aldo Rustichini, "Performance in Competitive Environments: Gender Differences," *Quarterly Journal of Economics,* August, 2003, pp. 1049–1074; Linda Babcock and Sara Laschever, *Women Don't Ask: Negotiation and the Gender Divide,* Princeton University Press: Princeton, N.J., 2003; James McBride Dabbs with Mary Godwin Dabbs, *Heroes, Rogues, and Lovers: Testosterone and Behavior,* McGraw-Hill: N.Y., 2000; and Helen Fisher, *The First Sex: The Natural Talents of Women and How They Are Changing the World,* Random House: N.Y., 1999.

16. Paul Recer, "Sociability Among Baboons Key to Raising Young," Associated Press story reprinted in *The Pittsburgh Post-Gazette,* November 14, 2003.

17. Letter, Brian Attebery to Justine Larbalestier, May 17, 1995, quoted in Justine Larbalestier, *The Battle of the Sexes in Science Fiction,* Wesleyan University Press: Middleton, Conn., 2002, pp. 220–221.

Larbalestier's book itself is also a long and personal "rapport-talk" about the extended female science fiction community. As she tells us (p. 16), "My concern . . . is to present science fiction as . . . a *series* of social activities," of which female fandom is a crucial part. I am told she is currently at work on a study of male-female relations among the Futurians of the 1930s. If so, this would also be a presentation of science fiction as a "series of social activities."

This approach is worlds away from the Brian Aldiss-David Wingrove approach, in *Trillion Year Spree,* which sees the history of science fiction merely as a collection of texts totally divorced from any "social activities." One is almost tempted to say it is the difference between female and male worldviews.

16

A Counter-Culture of Tending and Befriending

COMMUNICATION, EMPATHY, friendship—community: It seems these are more typically female than male concerns. Indeed, these gender differences were discerned by Joanna Russ as the unique features of the "new" feminist science fiction which emerged in the early 1970s. Speaking in 1976, Russ believed that new work by women writers differed vastly from earlier science fiction, written predominantly by men. Included among the new work Russ cited were Ursula K. Le Guin's *The Dispossessed*, Suzy McKee Charnas's *Walk to the End of the World*, Marion Zimmer Bradley's *The Shattered Chain*, and Marge Piercy's *Woman on the Edge of Time*. These books all had a "communal characteristic," Russ declared, exhibiting a new "social cohesiveness and closely-knit extended family" ethos which did not exist in science fiction before the coming of feminism to the genre in the early 1970s.[1]

And, in fact, many more recent female science fiction writers have, indeed, emphasized these traits in their work. We find, for instance, science fiction writer Joan Vinge, bestselling author of the Hugo-winning 1981 novel, *The Snow Queen*, telling us, "I suppose my favorite themes are the difficulty of communication between beings—human, alien, and otherwise—and the importance of that communication, of overcoming the misunderstandings that cause most of the problems in our lives."[2]

But this theme was not a recent discovery of Seventies feminist science fiction. A "communal social cohesiveness" might well have been the distinguishing feature of the feminist science fiction of the 1970s, as Joanna Russ claimed. But if this trait was the salient indicator of "feminist science fiction," then women had been writing "feminist science fiction" from the birth of the genre. This theme, for instance, is the principal element of the "femalien empathy"

Chapter 16

I discussed in part 1 as being a primary feature of women's pulp science fiction.

And such elements remained major features of women's science fiction throughout the following years. For example, Madeleine L'Engle's first work of science fiction, "Poor Little Saturday" (*Fantastic Universe*, October, 1956), was also about communication, as a lonely boy discovers the companionship of a strange witch in a deserted house. It is a theme that runs through all of her juvenile SF novels, beginning with *A Wrinkle in Time* (1962).

It can also be discerned in the work of Zenna Henderson in her stories of "The People." Henderson, who debuted in 1951 and was extremely prolific in the 1950s, wrote *only* about the search for community and communication. "The isolation I write about," she said, "and that apparently finds an answering 'me, too!' from my readers, is the isolation of person from person. . . . I don't consider myself 'sentimental.' Maybe I'm 'sympathetic.' *I know I'm empathetic.*"[3]

In fact, we can find this worldview even in Mary Shelley's *Frankenstein* (1818), the first fully recognized science fiction novel. *Frankenstein* is commonly presented as a tale of (male) hubris, of challenging the cosmos for knowledge that "man was not meant to know." However, because a woman wrote it, female commentators have long applied various other interpretations to it. Bonnie Friedman, for example, sees it as "a parable about sacrificing family for the sake of artistic ambition."

Dr. Victor Frankenstein wishes to be "A Modern Prometheus," who brings light to the world. But, "To do his work," Friedman says, "Frankenstein must ignore his family. When he is in touch with them, when he so much as writes them a letter, he cannot go on. Being in touch with them puts him in touch with his own natural sense of horror, and he realizes what in fact his hands have been touching: things meant by all spiritual authority to be let rest underground. So Frankenstein turns a deaf ear to his family, their anxious questions and pleas. 'I knew well therefore what would be my father's feelings,' he says, 'but I could not tear my thoughts from my employment, loathsome in itself, but which had taken an irresistible hold of my imagination. I wished, as it were, to procrastinate all that related to my feelings of affection until the great object, which swallowed up every habit of my nature, should be completed.'"[4]

Throughout history, male adventurers like Dr. Frankenstein have set out to conquer the unknown. But, suggests Mary Shelley, the price has usually been the destruction of family and community. "In Shelley's tale, which ends in such famous catastrophe," argues Friedman, "the artist's decision to ignore his family is not merely part of the problem; it is the problem. The author has Dr. Frankenstein proclaim, 'If this law was always observed; if no man allowed any pursuit whatsoever to interfere with the tranquility of his domestic affections,

Greece had not been enslaved, Caesar would have spared his country . . . and the empires of Mexico and Peru had not been destroyed.' "5

And, if this "law" had been observed in Victor Frankenstein's case, his family and community would not have been destroyed, as well. Once the creature has been created, Dr. Frankenstein is filled with horror at what he has done and rejects the initially loving and gentle being. Transformed into a savage "monster" through rejection and loneliness, the creature pursues his fleeing "father" back to Frankenstein's native town and proceeds to murder the Frankenstein family, most notably Elizabeth, Dr. Frankenstein's idealized young bride.

But first, "the monster slays Frankenstein's angelic youngest brother, and goes on to strangle Frankenstein's highly virtuous best friend. On Frankenstein's wedding night, the 'demoniacal corpse' seizes Elizabeth, the bride, and chokes her to death. Frankenstein's aged father [his mother having already died] perishes of grief," leaving Frankenstein, much like his creation, an orphan. Soon, Dr. Frankenstein, too, will perish, along with his "son," and the destruction of the Frankenstein family will be complete.6

In a sense, Dr. Frankenstein's creation was a "mutation," an abnormal form of life, an alien "Other" which initially sought only love and acceptance. It was the rejection of this "mutant" by the horrified "normal" world, represented primarily by Victor Frankenstein, which turned it into a "monster." Thus, we can see the gender patterns at work in the novel, the female concern to "tend and befriend" when presented by a threat (lest dire consequences result) opposed to the (at least here) destructive male response of "fight or flight."

We can also discern these same gender patterns in the differing attitudes toward mutants in Fifties' science fiction. Kingsley Amis noted in post-war science fiction the development of "a new type of human being, sometimes *outre* in appearance, more often gifted with the 'wild talent' that has become a science-fiction catch-phrase and convention. By an overwhelming vote, the talent is . . . extrasensory perception. . . . Often we are shown the first telepaths being relentlessly hunted down by the non-gifted mass of humanity, and it is hard not to see in this an allegory of intolerant conformism, especially since the authors are given to explaining that it is just that."7

Typical of this approach is Frank M. Robinson's 1956 Lippincott novel *The Power*, which first appeared in *Blue Book* (March, 1956). Now considered by many to be a classic (and republished by Tor in 1999), this story about the terrifying search for a villainous mutant superman in hiding was popular enough to be adapted for television. It must have struck a chord, as it was then turned into a critically acclaimed George Pal movie of the same name in 1968. In the film, a research team discovers that one among them is an evil telepath who—as in Agatha Christie's *Ten Little Indians*—begins killing off the other team members one by one.

Although we have come to see this description of symbolic "wild talents" as the universal interpretation of such mutants in Fifties' science fiction, it is not. This purely male interpretation, which has been accepted as the standard, presents only half the picture. For the other half, we must look at how women writers handled the same theme. When we do, we discover a pattern in which the emphasis tends *not* to be on conformist and faceless mobs hunting down persecuted and fleeing individuals, but rather on communication, empathy, and the creation of community. The pattern is one of "femalien" empathy with the alien.

All writers, of course, write out of their own life experiences and worldviews. Such certainly seems to be the case with Wilmar Shiras, who was already a grandmother before she began to write science fiction. The emphasis on "tend and befriend" can be seen in Shiras's book *Children of the Atom* (1953), based on her Science Fiction Hall of Fame and retrospective Nebula story "In Hiding" (published by John W. Campbell in *Astounding Science-Fiction*, November, 1948).[8]

Shiras's work, which I have already touched upon, tells the story of thirty children born after a nuclear power plant explosion who are mutants of superior intelligence. At first they conceal their existence but, with the aid of a sympathetic school psychiatrist, come to understand that they have nothing to fear from other humans. People, they realize, will willingly accept super-geniuses and welcome them into the fold. Aware that intelligence should be used for the common good, the children come out of hiding to help build a better tomorrow for the entire human race.

Phyllis Gotlieb, now hailed by many as the doyenne of Canadian SF, also emphasized harmony and community in her treatment of mutants. Gotlieb was finishing her first novel in 1960 when she mentioned it to Cele Goldsmith, who had published her first story, "A Grain of Manhood," at *Fantastic* the previous year. The novel, *Sunburst*, told of a group of mutant children maturing into a harmonious gestalt relationship and their coming to an eventual understanding with the larger world of normal humans around them. Goldsmith said she was interested and wanted to see it. She then published it as a serial before it came out as a novel in 1964.[9]

This gendered pattern is also clearly on display in the long series of stories on "The People" by Zenna Henderson, which were published in *The Magazine of Fantasy and Science Fiction* over the course of the Fifties. (See her entry in table 2.) First collected in *Pilgrimage: The Book of the People* (1961), Henderson's stories focus on women and children and idealize the extended family. Education, often at the hands of a woman teacher, is frequently central, as it is in "Pottage," which introduced the series in September 1955.

"The People" are human-appearing aliens who were stranded and scattered on Earth by the destruction of their spacecraft. They possess "wild talents," psionic abilities such as teleportation, which they always use for beneficent purposes. Indeed, they are morally superior to humans, models of what we should aspire to be. The protagonist in "Pottage" is Melodye Amerson. She is a human who comes to teach in the remote village of Bendo, which, she discovers, is inhabited solely by The People.

The People have taught their children to suppress their "wild talents" out of fear of persecution by earthlings. Melodye, however, encourages the children to express them. This eventually leads the aliens to discover that they are not alone—there are other colonies like theirs that survived the long-ago crash. Establishing rapport between the human teacher and the aliens thus not only brings the two species together, but also brings the aliens themselves out of their long isolation. In her story, "The Anything Box" (1956), Henderson most explicitly describes the themes of these (and other) stories: "all the worry and waiting, the apartness and loneliness were over and forgotten, their hugeness dwindled by the comfort of a shoulder, the warmth of clasping hands—and nowhere, nowhere was the fear of parting."

Appearing slightly after our period, but exhibiting the same desire to establish rapport is Henderson's non-People story, "Subcommittee" (*The Magazine of Fantasy and Science Fiction*, July, 1962). Earth is at war with humanoid alien invaders. At a truce conference, the males of the two species exhibit the hostile jockeying for position one would expect. Meanwhile, the wife of the chief Earth delegate manages to befriend the wife and child of one of the alien delegates. She learns a bit of their language and, because of this, discovers that the aliens do not want to invade Earth after all. They are merely searching for salt, necessary for their reproductive process. She takes her discovery to the antagonistic male negotiators and demonstrates that peaceful co-existence is possible.

Critic Farah Mendelsohn thought this story so emblematic of gendered differences toward conflict resolution in pre-feminist science fiction that she made it the subject of an insightful essay on "Gender, Power, and Conflict Resolution." She argued that the actions of the female protagonist, Serena, were part of "a complex social community with its own values and demands." Serena thus represented a highly gendered—and admirable—social milieu and set of values which feminist critics have usually disparaged and trivialized when discussing female science fiction before the 1970s.[10]

Establishing rapport between humans and aliens is also the theme of Mildred Clingerman's earlier and famous debut, "Minister Without Portfolio" (*The Magazine of Fantasy and Science Fiction*, February, 1952). Editors Anthony Boucher and J. Francis McComas hailed this story as "a new approach to the theme of Invasion from Space."[11] Ida Chriswell is a sixty-year-old widowed grandmother living with her son and daughter-in-law. On a trip to the country, she stumbles upon visiting aliens and their ship, although she remains unaware of their extraterrestrial nature. A pleasant conversation ensues and family photographs and other gifts are exchanged before Ida bids farewell to her new-found friends. As it turns out, Ida has saved Earth, as the aliens consider her to be the only "sane" human they have found on the planet. (The protagonist of Jane Roberts's "A Demon At Devotions"—*The Magazine of Fantasy and Science Fiction*, September 1958—also saves Earth from interstellar invasion by a militarily superior species. In this case, a convent's Mother Superior uses the theological arguments of St. Thomas Aquinas to forestall invasion.)

As with Zenna Henderson's work, feminist critics have also disparaged and denigrated Mildred Clingerman's story. Pamela Sargent, for example, saw it as a "notable example" of "a pattern of relying on the ignorance of its main female character to make its point."[12] However, it helps to understand just what a radical departure from the norms this story (as well as Henderson's "Subcommittee") was by contrasting it with the paranoia about "alien" invasions pervasive in Cold War America at that very time. What officials in Pittsburgh were doing was absolutely typical.

In the summer of 1952 (the same year that Clingerman's story appeared) the Chief Observer for Allegheny County (where Pittsburgh is located) said he needed 500 new civilian "skywatcher" volunteers to take two-hour shifts at eleven Civil Defense posts in the county to spot for all aircraft, especially low-flying planes that could slip under radar. The U.S. Air Force, warning that the Soviet Union was capable of sending a large fleet of atomic bombers over the United States at any time, had just ordered an around-the-clock watch on the nation's borders.[13] That same year, Hollywood released a shrill propaganda-saturated feature film entitled *Invasion, U. S. A.*, which used much documentary footage of air battles and bombings to depict a Soviet conquest of America.

In tune with such paranoia is a typical male portrayal of First Contact between humans and aliens written at almost exactly this time. In this case, the author is the usually empathetic Theodore Sturgeon and the story is "Verdict From Space," the August 3, 1951 series premiere for the early television program, *Tales of Tomorrow*. In the story, a million-year-old alien artifact is discovered by an archaeologist. It is a "sentinel" who has recorded and transmitted earth tremors, such as quakes and volcanic eruptions, over the eons. Now, however, it is also recording and transmitting the aftershocks of nuclear test explosions. As the archaeologist watches, it records and transmits the shock of the first hydrogen bomb explosion.

Alerted, an alien armada soon arrives and destroys Earth before Earth can venture into space and destroy the aliens. The story is thus saturated with Cold War paranoia and the certainty that the only way to deal with alien others is to conquer or be conquered. Given the tenor of the times, Sturgeon's story was an unimaginative extrapolation, perhaps all that was acceptable for mass consumption via television.[14]

Clingerman's story of "peaceful co-existence" with "threatening" aliens, therefore, courageously departed from the dominant Cold War paranoia of the nation. It also exhibited a greatly differing worldview from the majority of the science fiction male authors like Ted Sturgeon were writing at the same time on the same theme. It is thus historically ignorant, narrow-minded, and simply unbecoming for contemporary critics to mock such an imaginative and bold challenge to the national hysteria because it was not "radical" in the proper "feminist" mode they deem acceptable.

"Stair Trick," Clingerman's second story (*The Magazine of Fantasy and Science Fiction*, August, 1952), played a variation on the theme of emotional connection. For twenty years a lonely bartender has been searching for a companion. He has access to a better, alternate world, but does not want to go there alone. At last he finds a woman willing to believe in its existence, and they go there together.

This theme can also be found in Ann McCaffrey's "Lady in the Tower" (*The Magazine of Fantasy and Science Fiction*, April, 1959). Here the female protagonist is twenty-three-year-old Rowan, a lonely and isolated telepath and teleporter who has been trained to use her "wild talent" for the common welfare. Along with other "Primes," one to each star system, her job is to be a psi-powered way station facilitating interstellar travel. When the male Prime of another star system comes under attack, Rowan telepathically comes to his aid. She eventually links the minds of all the various Primes into a single powerful unit that drives off the attackers. The story ends with Rowan and the male Prime falling in love and working together in the same star system. Loneliness and isolation are bridged, not only between individual Primes, but among all of them for humanity's mutual benefit.

Although this story emphasized emotional connection, empathy, and community, these themes are most obviously to be found in McCaffrey's long-running and popular (especially among women) Dragonriders of Pern series, which she launched in the Sixties. These stories brought McCaffrey many awards, including a joint Hugo in 1968 for her novella, "Weyr Search" (which was also nominated for the 1968 Nebula); a Nebula in 1969 for "Dragonrider"; the Gandalf in 1979 for *The White Dragon*; and the Balrog for her 1980 *Dragondrums*. The series also made Ann McCaffrey one of the few science fiction writers (and the *only* female SF writer) to make the *Publishers Weekly* annual bestseller list, that being in 1983 for *Moreta: Dragonlady of Pern*.[15]

McCaffrey's Dragonriders series also spawned a vast network of fan clubs. Pittsburgh alone, for instance, has two such clubs, Fort Weyr, founded in 1983, and the younger High Reaches Weyr. The combined membership of the two clubs is over 200, of which about 70 percent is female.

Obviously, something in the series, which she continues to enlarge upon forty years later, deeply touched the psyches of many readers. When asked about its origins she explained, "The true genesis of the Dragon series was a conversation I had with an underground film director . . . [who] wanted to do a film on the 'aloneness' of man. I suggested that that had been done to death, but had he ever considered filming those times when man/woman/child are united in a common emotion? . . . That's why the dragons are telepathic: their riders are never alone. . . . This is the facet of the dragon stories which, I feel, has captured the attention of readers . . . . the great togetherness urge."[16] Again and again we find this "great togetherness urge" (what Joanna Russ termed "social cohesion") in women's science fiction in the Fifties. It is not the "done to death" theme of man's "aloneness" which they utilized, but the less explored ideas of union and rapport, communication and community.

As with the Dragonriders stories, these ideas were often represented by female telepathy, which figures prominently in women's science fiction, even to this day. Jane Donawerth argues that, "In much science fiction by women, telepathy represents the permeable boundaries of women deriving from empathy."[17] Certainly this telepathic empathy is on display in McCaffrey's 1968 novel, *Dragonflight*, as the protagonist, Lessa, telepathically bonded with her dragon for the first time: "A feeling of joy suffused Lessa; a feeling of warmth, tenderness, unalloyed affection, and instant respect and admiration flooded mind and heart and soul. Never again would Lessa lack an advocate, a defender, an intimate, aware instantly of the temper of her mind and heart, of her desires."[18]

A similar emphasis on community and bonding is found in Judith Merril's 1950s stories, such as "Stormy Weather" (*Startling Stories*, summer, 1954), a story somewhat similar to McCaffrey's "Lady in the Tower." Here the protagonist is Cathy Andauer, an "expert psichosomanticist" of the "Traffic Control Service," and the story is a "month in the life" of a working girl of the future. In this future, women are portrayed as more psychologically stable than men and therefore better suited for isolated jobs in space. Stationed on a lonely outpost, Andauer's duty is to use her psi power to sweep space debris from the "busiest space-lanes in the System." On her thirty-day shift the lack of communication from her boyfriend, Mike, eats at her. Nevertheless, she is able to do her job and is joyfully reunited with Mike afterwards, loneliness and isolation at an end.

In Merril's "Survival Ship" (*Worlds Beyond*, January, 1951), we not only find an almost-all female community, but the women also command and run a generation starship, with the four men on board relegated to subsidiary positions. Again, this is because the greater psychological stability of women better qualifies them to command starships than notoriously unstable men.

The creation and preservation of community is also the concern of Merril's powerful 1950 novel of post-nuclear holocaust society, *Shadow on the Hearth*. This story is not like the typical male cliche of isolated bands of ragged survivors scrabbling for existence in the ruined rubble of civilization. Rather, Merril's work focuses on a middle class suburban mother and her two young daughters as they learn self-reliance and mutual support after a nuclear exchange has obliterated Washington, New York City and, presumably, her husband. In 1954 *Shadow on the Hearth* was dramatized as "Atomic Attack," an episode on early television's live anthology series, *Motorola TV Theater*. The missing husband, who turns up at the end, was played by Walter Matthau. Meanwhile, in her 1960 novel, *The Tomorrow People*, a central character, Lisa Trovi, is a sensitive telepath uniquely able to establish contact with native Martians via human babies born on Mars.

An accessible source for seven of Merril's stories from the Fifties is her 1960 Pyramid Books collection, *Out of Bounds*. (See table 2 for original magazine publications.) Each story is an expression of "the great togetherness urge," often expressed through the medium of telepathy. Telepathic aliens in "Whoever You Are" (1952) empathize with all living things and offer their unconditional love to humanity. Two lonely people find soul mates in each other via telepathy in "Connection Completed" (1954). "Dead Center" (1954) is an emotionally powerful story of love and death in an astronaut's family following the first Moon landing. Editor Martha Foley was so moved by the latter that she chose it for her prestigious anthology *The Best American Short Stories: 1955*. "The Lady Was a Tramp" (1957) is about sex, love, and complicated emotional relationships among a space freighter's crew. And so it goes.

Complicated emotional relationships among and beyond humans is also the theme of Merril's excellent "Daughters of Earth," published in the Twayne anthology *The Petrified Planet* (1952). It is the family saga of six generations of mothers and daughters and the conflicts among them as they ride the crest of humanity's expansion into space. The protagonist, Dr. Emma Tarbell, is described as "direct . . . determined . . . intellectual . . . [and] *strong*." Like her grandmother before her and her granddaughter after her, she is absolutely passionate about space. The grandmother was a biophysicist who, with her husband, pioneered the settlement of Pluto. Dr. Tarbell and her husband were among the first to settle a planet beyond the solar system, Ullr. Her granddaughter carries on the tradition by leaving Ullr for a new star system in the first joint stellar expedition with the intelligent natives of Ullr—who Dr. Tarbell was responsible for making contact with, despite the resistance of her fellow humans.

The "great togetherness urge" is also evident in the work of the prolific Miriam Allen deFord in such stories as "The Daughter of the Tree" (*The Magazine of Fantasy and Science Fiction*, August, 1951). It is a surreal allegory of gender conflict set in the Pacific Northwest of 1875. The wife of a settler is left alone in the forest for months at a time while her husband returns to civilization for supplies. Even when he is not physically absent, however, he is emotionally absent. Driven to despair by loneliness, the woman turns to the forest for love and understanding. A mighty tree of the forest responds, becoming her lover.

Her tree lover kills her husband and fathers a feral daughter with the woman—a hybrid family, but yet a family.

In deFord's "Throwback" (*Startling Stories*, October, 1952), the protagonist is an award-winning ceramic artist in an overpopulated future global society. She illegally becomes pregnant by her lover without his knowledge, and plots to have both the baby and him in an unauthorized family. Predictably, he does not share her desires and has her committed to an insane asylum as an atavistic "throwback" with antiquated yearnings for children and family. In "The Children" (*Startling Stories*, December, 1952), a geneticist, having lost his wife and children in an accident, conceives of a way to father more children in the distant future and thus regains his will to live in the present.

An aging couple in a similarly overpopulated future in deFord's "One Way" (*Galaxy Science Fiction*, March, 1955) lose their only son when he is drafted for space exploration. It is a "one way" trip, from which he will never return. But before he leaves, in collusion with his mother, he manages to illegally impregnate his girlfriend. After the fact, the mother and the girlfriend inform his father of what they have done. The aged couple then conspires to keep the illegal baby in a new extended family into which they welcome the parentless girlfriend.

In deFord's "Operation Cassandra" (*Fantastic Universe*, November 1958) we find four volunteers, comprising two white men, a black Harvard philosopher and poet, and a woman, who awake from suspended animation after a nuclear holocaust. Naturally, they confront the necessity of rebuilding civilization. The woman, a graduate of "one of the big colleges for women in the East," is not the passive sex object we have come to expect from so many similar stories written by men. She is intelligent, resourceful, and treated as an equal. Further, when the men avoid considering the possibility, it is she who suggests and insists upon the fact that she will need all three of them as potential mates, as one or more might be sterile due to radiation. There will therefore not be one New Adam for the New Eve. There will be three cooperating Adams, as polyandry is to be the nature of the new extended family.

In all these stories, deFord presents us with strong, intelligent, resourceful, self-aware women who, had they been portrayed by a man, would no doubt have been heroic models of rugged individualism. But they are not. Instead, they face and solve their problems as part of a group. They bridge their individual isolation to become part of a larger community.

The hunger to bridge that isolation is also the struggle at the heart of Marion Zimmer Bradley's much-anthologized story, "The Wind People" (*If*, February, 1959). The main character is Dr. Helen Murray, medical doctor for the exploratory starship *Starholm*. She is impregnated by a shipmate in a one-night tryst during a long stay on "a soft, windy, whispering world." Because the leap into "overdrive" would kill her fetus, she elects to stay behind on the uninhabited planet to bear and rear the child. Sixteen years of loneliness follow as she nurtures her son, Robin. They appear to be alone on the planet. However, Robin insists there are other people there, and tells her of seeing a woman. Dr. Murray insists this is a delusion caused by her son's own loneliness, his aching for companionship.

Eventually, however, she discovers that Robin is right. The planet is inhabited by "wind people," gossamer and nebulous beings. Robin can see them plainly, while his mother cannot, because his father was, in fact, one of them. It seems that a barely remembered apparition, with whom she made love, came to Dr. Murray after the cold and emotionless tryst with her shipmate. But she dismisses her passionate lovemaking with the "wind person" as merely a dream born of loneliness. Despite her longing for companionship, she is unable to fully accept the existence of such beings. It is her half-human son, Robin, who is finally able to bridge the gulf between the species as, following his mother's death, he merges completely with the planet's inhabitants.

These examples hardly exhaust the selection of Fifties' science fiction stories by women featuring their own gender as strong and resourceful main characters. Nor do they exhaust the thematic subject matter. But perhaps they serve to illustrate my point that a perceptible gender difference—the quest for community in its various guises—can be found in many of the stories women authors were writing in the Fifties. Science fiction women were tending and befriending each other in their stories long before the politicized science fiction feminists of the early Seventies said this is what they should do.

Notes

1. Barbara Baumgarten, "Science Fiction Eyes Women," *Boulder Daily Camera*, August 4, 1976. Russ was then a professor of English at the University of Colorado in Boulder.

2. Charles Platt, *Dream Makers, Volume II: The Uncommon Men & Women Who Write Science Fiction*, Berkley Books: N.Y., 1983, p. 216.

3. Zenna Henderson interview in Paul Walker, ed., *Speaking of Science Fiction*, pp. 274–275. Originally in *LUNA Monthly 52*, 1974. Emphasis added.

4. Bonnie Friedman, *Writing Past Dark: Envy, Fear, Distraction, and Other Dilemmas in the Writer's Life*, HarperCollins: N.Y., 1993, pp. 29–30.

5. Friedman, p. 31.

6. Friedman, p. 32.

7. Amis, pp. 83–84.

8. In addition to "In Hiding," her book contains four sequels, including two published by Campbell, "Opening Doors" (*Astounding Science-Fiction*, March, 1949) and "New Foundations" (*Astounding Science-Fiction*, March, 1950). The remaining two stories, "Problems" and "Children of the Atom," are original to the book.

9. See Phyllis Gotlieb's letter describing this meeting and discussion, *Locus*, February, 2002, pp. 87–88.

10. Farah Mendelsohn, "Gender, Power, and Conflict Resolution: 'Subcommittee' by Zenna Henderson," *Extrapolation*, 35, No. 2, summer, 1994, p. 125.

11. Anthony Boucher and J. Francis McComas, Eds., *The Best From Fantasy and Science Fiction, Second Series,* Little, Brown, & Co.: Boston, 1953, p. 225.

12. Sargent, *Women of Wonder, The Classic Years,* p. 9.

13. See *The Pittsburgh Post-Gazette,* June 17, 1952.

14. Interestingly, at virtually the same time Sturgeon wrote his teleplay, British science fiction writer Arthur C. Clarke published his famous story, "Sentinel of Eternity" (*10 Story Fantasy,* Spring, 1951). Clarke's story placed the sentinel on the Moon and its purpose was to alert its alien masters of human presence once humans developed the capacity to travel there and find it. The story leaves open the question of whether or not the aliens will be friendly or hostile when they arrive. Clarke's story later became the basis for Stanley Kubrick's 1968 film, *2001: A Space Odyssey.*

15. See Michael Korda, *Making the List: A Cultural History of the American Bestseller, 1900–1999,* Barnes & Noble Books: N.Y., 2001, p. 180.

16. Anne McCaffrey in R. Reginald, Ed., *Science Fiction and Fantasy Literature: A Checklist, 1700–1974, Vol. 2: with Contemporary Science Fiction Authors II,* Gale Research Co.: Detroit, 1979, p. 994.

17. Donawerth, *Frankenstein's Daughters,* p. 50.

18. Anne McCaffrey, *Dragonflight,* Ballantine Books: N.Y., 1968, 1982, p. 83.

Part Three

Hidden from History

The Ebbing of First Wave Women's Science Fiction, 1961–1965

17

Into Time's Abyss

A T LEAST 154 female-identified authors published at least 634 science fiction stories in the decade of the 1950s. (See summary figures at the end of table 3.) These numbers are minimal and represent only authors whose gender I have been able to verify. Were I to include authors with ambiguous names or initials, the number of female authors for the Fifties alone would climb to well over 200 and the total of their stories would approach 750.

Perhaps a presumption of prejudice by a "male science fiction establishment" toward women has kept critics from noticing just how many women writers there actually were in the 1950s. The popularity of this presumption of prejudice is understandable, for it tells us something we want to believe. The "ugly duckling" myth of a righteous minority disdained by an unenlightened majority—but which eventually comes into its own—is powerful and endlessly appealing.

Indeed, this fairy tale was the "hook" by which the Associated Press reported on the first Worldcon of the twenty-first century. "With a huge number of female authors and publishers on hand, *the genre finally appears to be exploring its feminine side*," wrote the AP about the 2001 Philcon. "Sci-fi has come a long way from its early years, when female authors like Andre Norton took male-sounding pen names so they could get their novels published."[1]

So, we are told, at long last women have "finally" entered science fiction. And we also have the makings of a new myth about "When It Changed." Science fiction, it seems, didn't "finally" begin to "explore its feminine side" with the so-called "feminist intervention" of the 1970s. Even less did it begin to do so even earlier. Rather, science fiction "finally" began accepting women only at the beginning of the twenty-first century.

Unknown to this reporter (and no doubt most of the Worldcon attendees) is the fact that it was a woman, Julian May, who chaired the 1952 Worldcon almost half a century earlier. One wonders if women "finally" entering science fiction will still be the big news that leads the story in another half century, at the 2050 Worldcon! Given the enduring amnesia about female participation in the field, this is very possible.

Nevertheless, this traditional exclusion narrative, however seductive, remains a myth. As such, it is a form of cultural hegemony which has helped to conceal the participation of women in the shaping of science fiction.

However, in addition to such universally-accepted, but unexamined, presumptions about the past (the very hallmarks of cultural hegemony), there were also market forces and technological changes which conspired with this hegemony to hide the history of early women's science fiction.

From its appearance in Hugo Gernsback's *Amazing Stories* in 1926 until the mid- or late-1960s, science fiction was found primarily in magazines, and in the form of short stories. Indeed, the 1950s witnessed a proliferation of science fiction magazines, with sixty-one different SF magazines being published in that decade alone. These were thus the "Glory Days" of magazine science fiction.

And the practitioners of science fiction, male and female, accepted that their output was for this transient magazine market alone. They realized they were producing ephemeral work which would have its short day in the sun and be thereafter consigned to oblivion. There was no alternative. As Fritz Leiber explained, "When I got into writing, in the 1940s, there wasn't much prospect of book publication if you were writing science fiction—it was something you merely dreamed about. My first book, *Night's Black Agents*, was published by a small press, Arkham House, and the idea of making any sizable amount of money that way didn't seem very practical. The only income you could rely on was from selling stories to the magazines, until paperbacks came in at the end of World War II."[2]

As Leiber indicated, things did begin to change in the late 1940s. The "Magazine Era" of science fiction was lurching toward an end, even as it flared briefly in the Fifties. There had always been a certain number of genre books appearing from commercial publishers, such as Grosset & Dunlap, but they had never been a major venue for this type of fiction. Meanwhile, as early as the 1930s Edgar Rice Burroughs, Inc. sold ERB's works in hardcover for $2. This, however, was a price beyond many in the midst of the Depression. In 1948 Burroughs reissued many of his novels, which he then sold for $1 each. However, he died in 1950 and thereafter the caretaker of his estate did nothing to promote his books. Therefore, these cheaper hardcovers did not reach a mass audience.

There was also a trickle of hardcover books from small fan presses like Arkham House (which published Leiber's first book), Shasta, Fantasy Press, and Gnome Press. Martin Greenberg, of Gnome Press, offered his customers a

"Pick-A-Book" service of cheapened first editions and reprints for $1.25, postage paid, and seemed to have some success.

Then, in 1949, Doubleday's Walter Bradbury took note of such fan publishing and spoke with Gnome's Martin Greenberg about the business. Greenberg suggested to him a number of top candidates for book publication from the magazines, should Bradbury wish to enter the field. Shortly thereafter Doubleday launched a program of hardcover science fiction.

This trend was strengthened after 1953 when Nelson Doubleday, Inc. (associated with, but separate from Doubleday) launched the Science Fiction Book Club (SFBC), which still exists. From the beginning SFBC's offerings were $1.00, plus 24-cents postage. And, unlike the small fan presses, SFBC reached a mass audience with these affordable books. Also, perhaps because of its specialization, it succeeded beyond anything Grosset & Dunlap could match. Thus, in the 1950s, book publication began to emerge as a rival to magazine publication for both science fiction writers and readers.

There were also other factors bringing an end to the "Magazine Era of Science Fiction." Robert Silverberg had become a prolific SF magazine writer in the 1950s, but he recalled that towards the end of the decade, "upheavals were happening in the magazine industry, and most of my steady markets were going out of business. First came a collapse of a generations-old distribution system, bringing many of the magazines crashing down with it. Then came the rise of paperback publishing. Some of the veteran magazine publishers, sensing what was going on, abruptly jettisoned their magazines and switched to paperback operation. In 1953 there had been thirty or forty science fiction magazines; ten years later [i.e., in 1963] there were, maybe, seven."[3] The huge 1950s boom in science fiction magazines was over. In 1958–1959 alone a dozen science fiction magazines collapsed and disappeared.

Ted White, later editor of *Amazing,* recalled that, at the 1959 Detroit Worldcon, "the apparently eminent death of magazine science fiction" was the major topic of discussion. Another attendee at the 1959 Worldcon confirmed that, "The most urgent question" of the most popular panel "was what could be done to end today's scarcity of science fiction magazines."[4] Michael Moorcock also remembered that by 1960, "The healthier pulps, *Planet, Super Science, Famous Fantastic Mysteries, Startling* had folded. . . . Most of the short-lived magazines had collapsed—*Fantastic Universe, Infinity,* and so on, were gone."[5]

Damon Knight also noted the collapse and disappearance of the science fiction magazines by the end of the 1950s and, in the last issue of *Infinity* (November, 1958) said, "There is not going to be another wide-open science fiction boom. What I hope to see happening next is more in the nature of a silent revolution: more and more novelists working for the general book public."

In fact, while the details were different, the entrance of book publishers into science fiction publishing around this time seems to have been a British phenomenon as well. The avant garde British SF magazine *New Worlds* felt the pressure. "In 1963 magazine circulations were declining badly," Moorcock said, "and [the publisher] decided to close down *New Worlds* and [sister magazine] *Science Fantasy*. *SF Adventures* . . . was already dead. [Editor "Ted"] Carnell gave up any further attempts to nurse the magazines along."[6] (However, various white knights, including the British government, appeared with funding and *New Worlds* crept along for the remainder of the 1960s.)

The "rise of paperback publishing" in the 1950s, like the entrance of hardcover publishers, was also a factor which helped to bring about a "scarcity of science fiction magazines" by the end of the Fifties. This rise was a further development of an ongoing technological revolution in paperback production. Introduced by at least the 1870s, the cheap mass-produced paperback book proliferated in the late 1930s, 1940s, and, especially, the 1950s. Paperback houses like Ace, Ballantine, and Pocket Book became major publishers in the field. Indeed, the very first Pocket Book was a fantasy, James Hilton's *Lost Horizon*, May, 1939. (The William Morrow hardcover had been published in September, 1933.) However, the roles played by Ace and Ballantine Books were especially crucial to this transformation.

Before World War II, Ian and Betty Ballantine had headed Penguin Books when it began publishing paperbacks. After the war they launched the paperback publisher Bantam Books. Then, in 1952, they founded Ballantine Books with Betty as editor-in-chief. The next year they started one of the first regular lines of science fiction paperback books. This was the prestigious *Star* anthologies of original science fiction stories, edited by Frederik Pohl. Thereafter they produced at least one science fiction title a month, while other publishers were still tentatively putting out perhaps four or five per year.

In her first two years Betty chose and published such soon-to-be classics as *The Space Merchants*, by Frederik Pohl and C. M. Kornbluth, Ray Bradbury's *Fahrenheit 451*, Arthur C. Clarke's *Childhood's End*, and Poul Anderson's *Brainwave*. Later, in 1964, she published the first authorized American edition of J. R. R. Tolkien's *The Lord of the Rings*, followed by the first mass market fantasy publishing program.

Meanwhile, in 1953 Ace Books also began a regular series of paperback science fiction publication. Ace was founded by publisher A. A. Wyn and Donald A. Wollheim, who became editor-in-chief. The latter had been a top editor at the fledgling paperback publisher Avon Books since 1948. Their first science fiction offering was two stories by A. E. van Vogt combined as one of their now-famous Ace Doubles (D-31). On one side was *The World of Null-A* (originally in *Astounding Science-Fiction*, August-October, 1945) and on the other was *The Universe Maker* (originally "The Shadow Men," *Startling Stories*, January, 1950).

Thereafter, throughout the Fifties and into the Sixties, Ace published a large number of cheap paperback science fiction titles, discovering many neophytes who went on to stardom in the field. Then, explained Charles Platt, "A. A. Wyn dies in 1968 and his estate sells Ace to a Wall Street conglomerate. They decide to expand the business; so with shrewd commercial acumen they hire a man whose entire experience has been in manufacturing pumps. Within three years [i.e., 1971], Ace is almost bankrupt."[7]

So, in 1971, Donald A. Wollheim and his wife Elsie launched DAW Books, a paperback house which published nothing but fantasy and science fiction. Wollheim negotiated a partnership with New American Library, a well-established paperback publisher, to use their printing facilities and distribution network in return for a share of the subsequent profits. Meanwhile, he retained full financial and editorial control of his own company. DAW quickly became a major player in science fiction publishing by flooding the paperback racks in the 1970s and 1980s with its novels and anthologies.

Thus, due to such technological changes as the rise of paperback publishing and competitive market forces, the magazine declined as the major vehicle for science fiction after the 1950s. Even so, women remained a presence in the dwindling world of magazine science fiction. Cele Goldsmith, for example, continued to edit two of the field's major magazines—*Amazing* and *Fantastic*—up until mid-1965. And she continued to discover and publish major new female talents during those years, such as Ursula K. Le Guin and Phyllis Gotlieb. But the post-Fifties collapse and contraction of the magazine medium meant that the book was now the cutting edge of the field's evolution.

This transformation was as momentous as the transition from silent film to talkies, and it brought about a subsequent reading revolution. For many new fans, the cheap paperback book or the Science Fiction Book Club not only became their introduction to the field, but mainly what they continued to read. Hence, instead of the short story, the reading revolution emphasized the novel. This became the literary form which dominated and shaped the genre, the one by which reputations were made and maintained.

And the novel also became virtually the only form of science fiction with which most Seventies feminists and subsequent academic commentators were familiar. For them, as with the fans, their knowledge of science fiction thus extended only back to the mid-Sixties. The first forty years of the genre's history was terra incognita to them. And upon this unknown past they projected their own presumptions and prejudices.

Some of the First Wave female writers, such as Andre Norton, had always appeared primarily in book form. Indeed, she published only two stories in the magazines in the 1950s. One can also point to a handful of novels from other First Wave writers, such as Leigh Brackett, Marion Zimmer Bradley, C. L. Moore, and Kate Wilhelm, or to collections of short stories by Zenna Henderson or Margaret St. Clair. But, for the most part, the First Wave of women's science fiction was tied to the short story format. Unlike their male counterparts, who were more successful in making the leap, few of the many female writers who had appeared in the magazines made the transition to the new medium of novels.

Perhaps book-length work in the days when the genre paid very little was simply too much like the kind of commitment the professions have traditionally demanded for success. High-powered employers have usually expected much job time from employees, a continuity of effort and productivity throughout the employee's life cycle, and an overall sacrifice of family life. For the most part, a higher percentage of married men have been willing to live this kind of life than have married women, or even women in general. In a similar manner, was the new book medium too great a poorly rewarded commitment to interest most genre women?

In any case, with the decline of magazine markets and the rise of books as the dominant form of science fiction, most of the First Wave women science fiction writers—as with similar silent film stars who could not adapt to talkies—simply disappeared from the field. We need only look at numbers for early Sixties magazine publication to grasp the drastic decline in female authors and their stories, as the magazine market as a whole contracted. In the first five years of the Sixties, from 1961–1965 inclusive, only fifty-six female authors published in the few remaining science fiction magazines, with thirty of them being new writers who had not previously published. These fifty-six female authors published a total of 133 stories during that half decade. (See table 10 and accompanying synopsis for details.)

In contrast, the decade of the 1950s produced 154 female authors (with 138 of them new to the Fifties) and 634 female-authored stories. The exponential growth of women authors and their stories in the magazines—which had characterized the medium from its birth in 1926 and which crested in the Fifties—came to an end in the early Sixties, as the magazine market itself imploded.

Additionally, female authors of the early Sixties tended to be published in only certain of the remaining magazines, further lowering their profile. Almost half (62) of the stories published by women between 1961–1965 appeared in only one place, *The Magazine of Fantasy and Science Fiction*. Under editors Robert P. Mills, Avram Davidson, and Joseph W. Ferman, this magazine published thirty-one women writers during these five years. Many of these writers, such as Zenna Henderson, Kit Reed, and Evelyn E. Smith, had *always* been closely identified with this magazine and continued their affiliation with it, despite the changing editors.

Female editor Cele Goldsmith accounted for most of the rest, publishing thirty-four stories by eleven different women in *Amazing* and eleven different women in *Fantastic*, both of which she edited simultaneously until June, 1965, when Ziff-Davis sold the magazines. And Fred Pohl published most of the remainder. He published thirteen stories by seven female authors in *Galaxy*, where he took over the editorship from H. L. Gold in December 1961. He published another nine stories by nine women in *If*, which he began formally editing in November, 1961, but where he had been doing most of the editorial work since 1960.

Meanwhile, from 1961–1965 only one story by a woman appeared in the field's premiere magazine, John W. Campbell's *Astounding/Analog*. And that story was a collaboration with a male author, the husband of the female collaborator. Previous female authors who had appeared in *Astounding*—such as Campbell discoveries Katherine MacLean and Leigh Brackett—published nothing in Campbell's magazine in these years. Indeed, MacLean published nothing in *any* magazine during this period. Meanwhile, Brackett published only two new stories (although she *was* co-Guest of Honor with her husband, Edmond Hamilton, at the 1964 Worldcon in Oakland). Even the once-prolific Judith Merril, whom Campbell had also discovered, published only three stories during these five years.

Thus, in addition to the decline of magazine markets for short fiction, there seemed to be an exhaustion of some old stalwarts. For these reasons, in the *immediate* past of the Second Wave feminists, female science fiction authors indeed had a low profile. There *was* a relative paucity of women writers in the field during the first half of the Sixties. And these declining numbers may have been one reason why Second Wave feminists believed few had come before them.

But, feminists were additionally hampered by their allegiance to their mythology about the field. That mythology said that early science fiction was a sexist patriarchy which excluded women from equal participation. And that mythology said this situation remained unchanged until feminists "stormed the barricades" in the late Sixties and early Seventies.

Thus, for political reasons, Second Wave feminists did not believe science fiction *had* a female past. They were not able to see back, *beyond* the early-Sixties contraction, to that female past because their mythology said it had never existed. And one does not seek something one believes does not exist.

First wave female authors and science fiction's female past in general therefore remained mostly unknown to Seventies' feminists—and to later academics who have inherited their allegiance to the traditional exclusion narrative.

Thus, by the early Seventies, a Second Wave of women's science fiction, an explicitly feminist one, began to appear, with new female authors, new stars. And the field responded warmly to these new stars, showering upon them many of the genre's highest awards.

Few awards had actually existed in the field before this time. While the Hugos had been launched earlier, the Nebulas, awarded by the Science Fiction Writers of America, only began in 1966. Meanwhile, the Locus Awards were not started until 1971 and the World Fantasy Awards were not created until 1975.

But, as soon as these awards came into existence, women writers began winning them. Perhaps this, too, was a reason so many felt women "suddenly appeared" in science fiction in the late Sixties and early Seventies. As we have seen, the actual percentage of women writers at this time was no greater than the percentages of female authors at *The Magazine of Fantasy and Science Fiction* in the 1950s or at *Weird Tales* throughout its 1923–1954 existence. But the fact that awards now existed and these new female stars were winning them meant that these writers were highly visible.

However, what few seemed to realize was that many of these "new" stars weren't all that new. Rather, they were veterans of the First Wave of women's science fiction who had just simply continued to write, continued to publish, getting better all the time.

For example, women short story winners during these years included Kate Wilhelm, "The Planners," 1969 Nebula (as well as the 1977 Hugo and Locus Awards for her novel, *Where Late the Sweet Birds Sang*); Joanna Russ, "When It Changed," 1972 Nebula; "James Tiptree, Jr." (Alice Sheldon), "Love Is the Plan, the Plan Is Death," 1974 Nebula; Ursula K. Le Guin, "The Ones Who Walk Away From Omelas," 1974 Hugo. Le Guin's story, "The Day Before the Revolution," also won the 1975 Nebula, Jupiter, and Locus Awards. Of these winners, only Tiptree was new. The rest were actually "First Wave" writers. Le Guin came into the field in 1962, while Wilhelm and Russ debuted in the 1950s.

Likewise, women novelette winners included Vonda McIntyre, who won the 1974 Nebula for "Of Mist, and Grass, and Sand," and Ursula Le Guin, who won the 1976 Locus Award, for "The New Atlantis." Only McIntyre was new.

Novella winners included Anne McCaffrey, who won a joint Hugo Award in 1968 for "Weyr Search" and a Nebula in 1969 for "Dragonrider"; Katherine MacLean, who took the 1972 Nebula for "The Missing Man"; Le Guin, who won the 1973 Hugo for "The Word For The World is Forest"; and James Tiptree, Jr., who took the 1974 Hugo for "The Girl Who Was Plugged In." Again, only Tiptree was new. Again, the rest were "First Wave" writers. McCaffrey and MacLean debuted in the early 1950s and Le Guin in the early Sixties.

And veteran Le Guin was also winning awards for her novels (in fact, she was the only woman who won an award for a science fiction novel before 1975), including the 1970 Hugo and Nebula Awards for *The Left Hand of Darkness*, the 1972 Locus Award for *The Lathe of Heaven*, and the 1975 Hugo, Nebula, Jupiter, and Locus Awards for *The Dispossessed*. She also won the 1976 Locus Award for her short story collection, *The Wind's Twelve Quarters*. Indeed, Ursula K. Le Guin is one of the most award-winning writers in science fiction. Her awards include five Hugos, five Nebulas, three Jupiters, and one Gandalf. She has also won the Locus Award sixteen times, the World Fantasy Award twice, the James Tiptree, Jr. Award three times, and the Ditmar, Prometheus, Endeavour, Rhysling, and Theodore Sturgeon Memorial Awards. She has also received the World Fantasy Award for Lifetime Achievement (1995) and has been inducted into the Science Fiction Hall of Fame. In addition, in 1975 she was chosen as the Guest of Honor at the Melbourne Worldcon.

These "new" female authors were celebrated for storming science fiction's patriarchal barricades in the late Sixties and early Seventies. But, of them all, only *two*—James Tiptree and Vonda McIntyre—were, in fact, new. So, only these two could possibly have "stormed the barricades" at all—and not even Tiptree, as no one knew she was a woman at the time. All the rest of the female science fiction award winners of the late Sixties and early Seventies were already long since inside the sacred precincts!

But, their First Wave origins were largely forgotten. The mythology obscured their histories. Anne McCaffrey, Katherine MacLean, Kate Wilhelm, Joanna Russ, and Ursula K. Le Guin were essentially women without a past, annexed into Second Wave women's science fiction as exemplars of a new phenomenon: Women "finally" entering science fiction.

But, it was not just the First Wave origins of these female award winners of the late Sixties and early Seventies which were forgotten. Almost all of their First Wave contemporaries were also forgotten. And, as this happened, an entire school of women's literature, whose themes and sensibilities could once be found throughout the genre, was also forgotten, even by women themselves. Thus, in her "encyclopedic" 1993 survey of women science fiction writers, Lisa Tuttle would claim that, "Women's contributions to the genre were not substantial until the late 1960s."[8]

Some felt that we lost nothing in the process. Poul Anderson, for example, claimed that, "Women have not been relevant" in science fiction stories, and the presumed lack of female characters and their concerns during the "Glory Days" of magazine SF "has no great significance, perhaps none whatsoever."[9]

Others, including many women who came into the field with a working knowledge of only Second Wave feminist science fiction, denigrated the Fifties female counter-culture for its somehow "inferior" emphasis upon "hearth and home."[10] These feminist critics expressed enormous condescension toward what Lisa Tuttle termed "sentimental stories"—such as those by Mildred Clingerman, Zenna Henderson, and Judith Merril (all cited and denigrated by Tuttle). Such stories portrayed characters and concerns thought to be unworthy of the same respect and consideration given to male fiction or Second Wave feminist science fiction about "important" subjects.[11]

Thus, asserting that only their own overtly-politicized version of women's science fiction really mattered, they disparaged and denigrated the vast bulk of early women's writing. Speaking of Judith Merril, for example, one critic in a major 1982 reference work declared, "Too often, Merril does her sex no service by concentrating ad nauseam on the minutiae of caring for small children. This may be the very first appearance of kitchen-sink science fiction, but it falls short of being entertainment."[12]

To get a feel for how sexist this dismissal is, let us imagine this critic's attitude toward such themes if the gender roles were reversed as, in fact, James Tiptree, Jr. (Alice Sheldon) imagined. "Consider," she observed. "If men alone had always raised infants, how monumental, how privileged a task it would be! We would have tons of conceptual literature on infant-father interaction, technical journals, research establishments devoted to it, a huge esoteric vocabulary. It would be sacred as the Stock Exchange or football, and we would spend hours hearing of it. But, because women do it, it is invisible and embarrassing."[13] Or, as the cited critic above labeled it, trivial and boring.

But this view, no matter which gender espouses it, is a disservice to women. The counter-cultural concerns and worldviews expressed in First Wave women's science fiction are just as valid and important as the themes, concerns, and sensibilities found in male or Second Wave feminist science fiction. We are talking about such concerns as human interdependence and the struggle for emotional connection, we are talking about cooperation, and community.

To trivialize and disparage these concerns, as Poul Anderson, Lisa Tuttle, and many Second Wave critics have done when discussing First Wave fiction, is to trivialize and disparage the most beneficial urges in human history. As Eleanor Arnason, a more recent science fiction writer, observed, "Society requires cooperation. Without altruism and a sense of community, people would do none of the things that don't really pay—such as raising children, creating art, helping other humans."[14]

Surely cooperation, altruism, and community are worth writing about. And First Wave women's science fiction writers did exactly that.

Notes

1. David B. Caruso, "Women Increase Presence at Science Fiction Gathering," Associated Press story, *The Desert Sun* (Palm Springs, Calif.), September 1, 2001, p. A2. Emphasis added.

2. Platt, *Dream Makers, Volume II,* p. 135.

3. Robert Silverberg, "Introduction," in Robert Silverberg, *World of a Thousand Colors,* Arbor House: N.Y., 1982, p. 13.

4. See comments by Ted E. White and John Magnus, "The Detroit Convention," *Fantastic Universe,* January, 1960, pp. 90, 87.

5. Michael Moorcock, Ed., Introduction, *New Worlds: An Anthology,* Thunder's Mouth Press: N.Y., 2004, p. xix.

6. Moorcock, p. xiii. Actually, *Fantastic Universe* survived into 1960, with the March, 1960 issue being the last.

7. Platt, *Dream Makers, Volume II,* p. 230.

8. Lisa Tuttle, "Women SF Writers," in John Clute and Peter Nicholls, *The Encyclopedia of Science Fiction,* St. Martin's Griffin: N.Y., 1993, update 1995, p. 1344.

9. Poul Anderson, "Reply to a Lady," *Vertex* 2, No. 2, (June) 1974, p. 99. The "Lady" Anderson was replying to was Joanna Russ and her seminal article, "The Image of Women in Science Fiction," *Vertex,* February, 1974.

10. Although I am not saying she is one of those who know only Second Wave women's science

fiction, the description of women's science fiction of the Fifties as centering around "hearth and home" comes from Pamela Sargent, *Women of Wonder, The Classic Years*, p. 10.

11. Lisa Tuttle, "Women SF Writers," p. 1344.

12. Chris Morgan, entry on Judith Merril in Bleiler, *Science Fiction Writers*, p. 435.

13. James Tiptree, Jr., "Symposium: Women in Science Fiction," *Khatru*, Nos. 3 & 4, November 1975, 2nd Printing, May, 1993, p. 54.

14. Lyda Morehouse, "SFC Interview: Eleanor Arnason," *Science Fiction Chronicle*, August, 2001, p. 31.

18

The Persistence of Myth

E VERYBODY KNOWS that officials at Ellis Island in the early years of the twentieth century forced poor European immigrants to anglicize their "unpronounceable" names.

Everybody knows that the Eskimos have 50 (or 100 or 200) words for snow.

Everybody knows that ignorant European peasants quivered in panic as the year 1000 rolled around because they feared the world would end.

Everybody knows that contemporary scholars thought Columbus would sail off the edge of the world in 1492 because they believed the earth was flat.

Everybody knows that the Pilgrims landed at Plymouth in 1620 to establish freedom of religion for everyone.

Everybody knows that George Washington had wooden teeth.

Everybody knows that an impoverished Mozart, abandoned by friends and patrons, was buried in a mass grave with no ceremony or mourners.

Everybody knows that the government covered up a 1947 UFO crash at Roswell, New Mexico.

Everybody knows that there are (or were) Vietnam War MIAs still held captive in Vietnam decades after the war ended.

Everybody knows that California will someday sink beneath the waves after "The Big One."

And everybody knows that there were no women in science fiction before the mid-1960s—or 1960—or 1950—or 1940. Or, if there were, everybody knows that these women had to carefully conceal their gender lest the hostile male majority turn on them.

The fact that *none* of these beliefs are true does not change what "everybody knows." Lord Byron famously observed that "Truth is stranger than fiction." But fiction is more popular and more enduring. Fiction fits our perceptions of the past, of what *ought* to be true—which truth often does not. Thus, as Jacques Barzun has noted, "The dissemination of historical knowledge tends to be slow in proportion as the error is dramatic and 'fitting.' "[1] Or, as the error conforms to the cultural hegemony of a particular myth.

Nevertheless, although it may not be as "fitting" and may not conform to the myth, allegiance to the truth demands that we retrieve the hidden history of women's science fiction and give it the place it deserves.

To do so will also transform the genre's usable past. In 1993 science fiction author Karen Joy Fowler (a co-creator of the James Tiptree, Jr. Memorial Award, which annually honors gender-related science fiction) looked back two decades to the 1970s and thanked the writers—Suzy McKee Charnas, Vonda N. McIntyre, Joanna Russ, Kate Wilhelm, Ursula K. Le Guin, "James Tiptree, Jr.," Chelsea Quinn Yarbro, and others perceived to be of the feminist Seventies— who she believed had launched women's science fiction. "I really appreciated the opportunity," she said, "to read the [1975 *Khatru*] round-table [on women in science fiction] and to thank . . . those women whose work and struggle and thought has meant and continues to mean so much to me. My whole writing life I have had the luxury of feeling part of a tradition. The achievements of other women have comforted and inspired me."[2]

One reads her words with sadness, for they are the words of an amnesiac, cut off from her own past, unaware that the truncated tradition she celebrated extended much further back than a mere twenty years. How much more com- forted and inspired might Karen Joy Fowler have felt had she realized that women writers were present at the creation of the genre, welcome "partners in wonder" from the very beginning? That women were there at the very birth of science fiction?

We now know that at least 203 female authors published at least 922 stories in American science fiction magazines in the years 1926–1960. Between 1961–1965 another thirty new women writers (along with twenty-six "old-timers") pub- lished another 133 stories in the magazines, for a total of 1,055 female-authored stories in the science fiction magazines between 1926–1965. (Additionally, at least 127 women writers published 365 stories between 1923–1954 in the fantasy magazine *Weird Tales* alone.)

These stories represent an entire school of literature, with its own themes and concerns. It is an impressive body of work—a thousand and one tales of Scheherazade, existing like some secret female script, unknown to the larger world. Unacknowledged and trivialized they may be, yet the authors and their stories are there. They represent a female counter-culture flourishing in the midst of the larger male body of work which historians of both genders have wrongly assumed characterized the entire genre in those years.

However, as Lloyd Biggle, Jr., pointed out, "Too often history is not what we find out. It is what we want to believe."[3] Such is the case here. The amnesia that surrounds this alternate tradition of First Wave women's science fiction represents the triumph of "mythistory," of a mythology and ideology the field *wants* to believe, no matter the facts of history. So, what I am challenging here is not simply ignorance of the facts. I am attempting something far more difficult. I am challenging the powerful and deeply entrenched cultural hegemony which the dominant mythology supports.

And by "mythology" I do not only mean falsehood, although the accepted mythology does indeed depict the past falsely. Nor have I been using the term merely as a rhetorical device. Instead, I have been using it in its anthropological sense: a collective memory about a group's past meant to sustain a belief system—an ideology—which shapes a worldview. That ideology has come to exercise almost complete cultural hegemony over our interpretation of the field's past, excluding other interpretations as absurd. It claims that the field's past *had* to have been oppressively sexist and bigoted, just like society at large, before the coming of Second Wave feminist science fiction. By believing this mythology we can then congratulate our enlightened selves on how far we've progressed since that benighted past, luxuriating in our moral and temporal superiority.

But social and historical experience is much more complex than the stark simplicities of myth would have us believe. And popular culture—and science fiction culture in this case—is much more ambiguous than the mythistory proclaims. And if our literature's past was, in truth, *not* as benighted and bigoted as the ideology claims, then we have no right to that pleasantly warm glow of moral and temporal superiority over the past in which the myth bathes us. But, faced with this cold alternative, no doubt it is much more comforting to believe the myth and to print the legend.[4]

Challenging the ingrained ideological basis for any group's mythological worldview is always harder than just setting the record straight. Such ideologies—such cultural hegemonies—are highly impervious to evidence. As science fiction writer John Sladek tells us, "people don't really like books which tell them things *aren't* true."[5] For the most part, people believe what they *want* to believe, regardless of the facts.

At least that is what Dr. Drew Westen, a psychology professor at Emory University, discovered. In a study that is still-unpublished as of this writing, Westen tested whether people made decisions based on bias or fact. Bias won, overwhelmingly. Over 80 percent of the respondents in his study simply ignored facts that contradicted what they already believed.[6] The facts simply didn't correspond to the dominant paradigm, so they didn't consciously register.

For that reason, my effort to demythologize our past and uncover the alternate roots of science fiction may not succeed. Nevertheless, the mythology must be challenged—because the accepted wisdom is false. And false history is dangerous. "False history," Philip Gerard reminds us, "does damage. It gives us a distorted view of who we are, where we came from, how well or badly we've honored our founding principles. It creates the wrong stories to live by."[7]

I believe I have produced the documentation to prove my belief that the contested terrain thesis about the nature of popular culture in general also best describes the reality of pulp science fiction in particular. Conversely, I believe the contested terrain nature of pulp science fiction also reinforces and validates the accuracy of that thesis as a description of popular culture as a whole.

Those who support the dominant mythology and claim that women (or Jews or the black presence) were deliberately excluded from early science fiction have never documented anything. They have never presented the evidence. They have merely made assertions which we are expected to accept without proof. As with any cultural hegemony, their mythology precludes any real interrogation of the past, of "the way things were," because we already *know* how they were. There is no need for evidence, as "common sense" tells us what we need to know about the past. The past is "obvious."

But the truth is, the past is *not* "obvious." The truth is, the "common sense" is merely an article of faith. It is now time for the evidence to be presented and the assertions to be proven—or to be abandoned as the self-serving myths they are.

Approximately 15 percent of the respondents in Professor Westen's study actually considered the evidence before reaching a decision. My case now lies with their compatriots among my readers. Those who do consider the evidence will also, I hope, acknowledge and celebrate the 203 women writers who published in the science fiction magazines from 1926 to 1960 and who helped make possible the birth of science fiction.

The presence of these women and their contributions to the genre make it clear that the history of early science fiction is not one of exclusion and prejudice, but one of acceptance and partnership.

And that is the right story by which to live.

Notes

1. Jacques Barzun and Henry F. Graff, *The Modern Researcher*, Harcourt Brace Jovanovich, Inc.: N.Y., 1977, third edition, p. 101.

2. Karen Joy Fowler, "Symposium: Women in Science Fiction," *Khatru*, Nos. 3 & 4, November 1975, 2nd Printing, May, 1993, p. 130.

3. Lloyd Biggle, Jr., untitled column in *The Science Fiction Oral History Association Newsletter*, January, 1994, reprinted in Biggle, *The Loom of History: Essays on the Significance of Oral History*, limited edition booklet published by the SFOHA: Ypsilanti, Mich., 2002, p. 3.

4. I owe this insight to George Governan.

5. Platt, *Dream Makers, Volume II*, p. 67.

6. Leonard Pitts, Jr., "Truth Under Fire: Forget Slanting the News. It's People Who Are Biased," *The Pittsburgh Post-Gazette*, December 30, 2004, p. A-19.

7. Philip Gerard, *Writing a Book That Makes a Difference*, Story Press: Cincinnati, Ohio, 2000, p. 213.

Appendix I: Bibliography of Women Science Fiction Writers 1926–1965

The Tales of Scheherazade

TABLE 1
Known Women Writers in the Science Fiction Magazines 1926–1949

Author Story	Magazine (Editor)	Date
Ainsworth, Lillian M. (w/ *Robert W. Lull*)		
"An Astral Gentleman," (listed on cvr.)	*Famous Fantastic Mysteries* (orig. *All-Story,* Jan. 20, '17)	Jan. 1940
"Alden, Thaedra" (Elizabeth Hansen)		
"Two-Timing Man," (w/ her pic)	*Thrilling Wonder Stories* (Friend)	June 1943
Black, Pansy E.		
The Valley of the Great Ray	SF Series No. 11, Stellar Pub. Corp.	1930
The Men From the Meteor	SF Series No. 13, Stellar Pub. Corp.	1932
Brackett, Leigh		
"Martian Quest,"	*Astounding* (Campbell)	Feb. 1940
"The Treasures of Ptakuth,"	*Astounding*	April 1940
"The Stellar Legion," (on cvr.)	*Planet Stories* (Reiss all issues)	Winter 1940–1941
"Water Pirate,"	*Super Science Stories* (Pohl)	Jan. 1941
"The Demons of Darkside,"	*Startling Stories* (Weisinger)	Jan. 1941
"Interplanetary Reporter,"	*Startling Stories*	May 1941
"The Dragon-Queen of Jupiter," (subj. of cvr.)	*Planet Stories*	Summer 1941
"Lord of the Earthquake,"	*Science Fiction* (Hornig)	June 1941
"No Man's Land in Space," (w/ her pic)	*Amazing Stories* (Palmer to 12/49)	July 1941
"A World Is Born,"	*Comet Stories* (Tremaine)	July 1941
"Retreat to the Stars,"	*Astonishing Stories* (Pohl to 4/43)	Nov. 1941
"Sorcerer of Rhiannon,"	*Astounding*	Feb. 1942
"Child of the Green Light," (on cvr.)	*Super Science Stories* (Pohl)	Feb. 1942
"Child of the Sun," (on cvr.)	*Planet Stories*	Spring 1942
"Out of the Sea," (on cvr.)	*Astonishing Stories*	June 1942
"Cube From Space," (on cvr.)	*Super Science Stories*	August 1942
"Outpost on Io,"	*Planet Stories*	Winter 1942–1943
"The Halfling," (on cvr.)	*Astonishing Stories*	Feb. 1943
"Citadel of Lost Ships," (subj. of cvr.)	*Planet Stories*	March 1943
"The Blue Behemoth," (subj. of cvr.)	*Planet Stories*	May 1943

Author Story	Magazine (Editor)	Date
"Thralls of the Endless Night," (subj. of cvr.)	*Planet Stories*	Fall 1943
"Jewel of Bas," (on cvr.)	*Planet Stories*	Spring 1944
"The Veil of Astellar," (on cvr.)	*Thrilling Wonder Stories* (Friend)	Spring 1944
"Terror Out of Space," (subj. of cvr.)	*Planet Stories*	Summer 1944
"Shadow Over Mars," (subj. of cvr. & pic)	*Startling Stories* (Friend)	Fall 1944
"The Vanishing Venusians," (on cvr.)	*Planet Stories*	Spring 1945
"Lorelei of the Red Mist," (w/ Ray Bradbury) (subj. of cvr.)	*Planet Stories*	Summer 1946
"The Beast-Jewel of Mars," (subj. of cvr.)	*Planet Stories*	Winter 1948
"The Moon That Vanished," (subj. of cvr.)	*Thrilling Wonder Stories*	Oct. 1948
"Quest of the Starhope,"	*Thrilling Wonder Stories*	April 1949
"Queen of the Martian Catacombs," (subj. of cvr.)	*Planet Stories*	Summer 1949
"Sea-Kings of Mars," (subj. of cvr.)	*Thrilling Wonder Stories*	June 1949
"Enchantress of Venus," (subj. of cvr.)	*Planet Stories*	Fall 1949
"The Lake of the Gone Forever,"	*Thrilling Wonder Stories*	Oct. 1949
Calhoun, Dorothy Donnell		
"Afraid of His Shadow,"	*Famous Fantastic Mysteries*	August 1941
Chestnutt, Clara E.		
"Escape From Ceres,"	*Amazing Stories*	Oct. 1935
Claire, Mollie		
"Peril in Dragonia,"	*Fantastic Adventures* (Palmer)	April 1949
"Dane, Clemence" (Winifred Ashton)		
"The Tunnel" (aka "Transatlantic Tunnel")		1935
(screenplay w/ *Kurt Siodmak* & *L. Du Garde Peach*—not counted)		
"Third Person Singular," (on cvr.)	*Famous Fantastic Mysteries* (From *The Babyons*, book, orig. 1927)	Oct. 1946
de Courcy, Dorothy (w/ *John de Courcy*)		
"Don't Mention It,"	*Amazing Stories* (Palmer)	May 1946
"Some Are Not Men,"	*Amazing Stories*	August 1946
"Morton's Fork,"	*Amazing Stories*	Sept. 1946
"The Man Who Went Nowhere,"	*Amazing Stories*	Nov. 1946
"Chess And Double Chess,"	*Amazing Stories*	March 1947
"The Miracle Man,"	*Amazing Stories*	April 1947
"Once To Die,"	*Fantastic Adventures* (Palmer)	Sept. 1947
"Come Into My Garden,"	*Fantastic Adventures*	Nov. 1947
"The Devil To Pay,"	*Fantastic Adventures*	Dec. 1947
"Evensong,"	*Fantastic Adventures*	Jan. 1948
"Goma's Follicles,"	*Planet Stories*	Summer 1948
"The Man From Agharti," (subj. of cvr.)	*Amazing Stories*	July 1948
"Rat Race,"	*Startling Stories*	Sept. 1948
"Traitor To War,"	*Amazing Stories*	August 1949
"The Night Has a Thousand Eyes,"	*Planet Stories*	Winter 1949
Deegan, Frances M.		
"Martian and the Milkmaid,"	*Fantastic Adventures* (Palmer)	Oct. 1944
"The Radiant Rock,"	*Amazing Stories* (Palmer)	June 1945
"Something for Herbert,"	*Amazing Stories*	Sept. 1945
"Gallery of Glacial Doom,"	*Amazing Stories*	Dec. 1945
"Little Drops of Water,"	*Amazing Stories*	Feb. 1946
"The Third Bolt,"	*Amazing Stories*	Oct. 1947
"The Cat-Snake,"	*Fantastic Adventures*	April 1948
Du Bois, Theodora		
"The Devil's Spoon," (subj. of cvr.)	*Famous Fantastic Mysteries* (orig. 1930)	June 1948
Easton, Norma Lazell		
"The Avenger,"	*Amazing Stories* (Palmer)	Nov. 1949
Eberle, Merab		
"The Mordant,"	*Amazing Stories*	March 1930
Ellis, Sophie Wenzel		

Author Story	Magazine (Editor)	Date
"Creatures of the Light,"	*Astounding* (Bates)	Feb. 1930
"Slaves of the Dust,"	*Astounding*	Dec. 1930
"The Shadow World,"	*Amazing Stories*	Dec. 1932
"Farnsworth, Mona" (Muriel Newhall)		
"Who Wants Power?,"	*Unknown* (Campbell)	March 1939
"Whatever,"	*Unknown*	May 1939
"The Joker,"	*Unknown*	July 1939
"All Roads," (subj. of cvr.)	*Unknown*	August 1940
"Are You There?,"	*Unknown*	Nov. 1940
Garby, Lee Hawkins (w/ E. E. "Doc" Smith)		
"The Skylark of Space (Pt. 1)," (subj. of cvr.)	*Amazing Stories*	August 1928
"The Skylark of Space (Pt. 2),"	*Amazing Stories*	Sept. 1928
"The Skylark of Space (Pt. 3),"	*Amazing Stories*	Oct. 1928
(Counted as one sale, as are all serials.)		
Garfield, Frances		
"Gulpers Versus Earthmen,"	*Amazing Stories* (Palmer)	Dec. 1939
Gillmore (Irwin), Inez Haynes		
"Angel Island," (on cvr.)	*Famous Fantastic Mysteries* (orig. 1914)	Feb. 1949
Groner, Augusta		
"City of the Dead," (on cvr.)	*Famous Fantastic Mysteries*	April 1948
Hansen, L. (Lucile) Taylor		
"What the Sodium Lines Revealed,"	*Amazing Stories Quarterly* (Gernsback)	Win. 1929
"The Undersea Tube," (subj. of cvr.)	*Amazing Stories*	Nov. 1929
"The Man From Space,"	*Amazing Stories*	Feb. 1930
"The Prince of Liars," (subj. of cvr.)	*Amazing Stories*	Oct. 1930
"The City on the Cloud,"	*Wonder Stories*	Oct. 1930
"Lords of the Underworld," (subj. of cvr.)	*Amazing Stories* (Palmer)	April 1941
"The Ghost Ship of Aztlan,"	*Startling Stories*	July 1942
"The Fire Trail," (as "Oge-Make")	*Amz. Stories; Fantastic Adv.* (2 sales)	Jan. 1948
57 Articles on Science & History	*Amazing Stories* (Palmer)	1941–1949
Harris, Clare Winger		
"The Fate of the Poseidonia,"	*Amazing Stories*	June 1927
"The Miracle of the Lily,"	*Amazing Stories*	April 1928
(Considered "alternate Hugo winner" by Richard Lupoff)		
"The Menace of Mars," (on cvr.)	*Amazing Stories*	Oct. 1928
"The Fifth Dimension," (on cvr.)	*Amazing Stories*	Dec. 1928
"The Evolutionary Monstrosity," (on cvr.)	*Amazing Stories Quarterly*	Winter 1929
"The Diabolical Drug," (on cvr.)	*Amazing Stories*	May 1929
"The Artificial Man," (w/ her pic)	*Science Wonder Quarterly*	Fall 1929
"A Baby on Neptune," (w/ *Miles J. Breuer*) (subj. of cvr.)	*Amazing Stories*	Dec. 1929
"The Ape Cycle,"	*Science Wonder Quarterly*	Spring 1930
Heald, Hazel		
"The Man of Stone," (w/ her pic)	*Wonder Stories*	Oct. 1932
Holmberg, Millicent		
"To Whom It May Concern,"	*Amazing Stories* (Palmer)	June 1946
Hull, E. (Edna) Mayne		
"The Flight That Failed,"	*Astounding*	Dec. 1942
"The Ultimate Wish," (subj. of cvr.)	*Unknown* (Campbell)	Feb. 1943
"Abdication,"	*Astounding*	April 1943
"Competition,"	*Astounding*	June 1943
"The Wishes We Make," (subj. of cvr.)	*Unknown*	June 1943
"The Patient,"	*Unknown*	Oct. 1943
"The Debt,"	*Astounding*	Dec. 1943
"The Contract,"	*Astounding*	March 1944
"The Winged Man (Pt. 1),"	*Astounding*	May 1944
"The Winged Man (Pt. 2),"	*Astounding*	June 1944
"Enter the Professor,"	*Astounding*	Jan. 1945
"Bankruptcy Proceedings,"	*Astounding*	August 1946

Author Story	Magazine (Editor)	Date
"Irving, Minna," (*Minna Odell*)		
"The Moon Woman,"	*Amazing Stories* (Sloane)	Nov. 1929
Kerruish, Jessie Douglas		
"The Undying Monster," (on cvr.)	*Famous Fantastic Mysteries*	June 1946
	(Orig. book pub. 1922.)	
LesTina, Dorothy		
"When You Think That . . . Smile!"	*Future Fantasy & Science Fiction*	Feb. 1943
Long, Amelia Reynolds		
The Mechanical Man (subj. of cvr.)	SF Series No. 7, Stellar Pub. Corp.	1930
"Omega," (as "Ameilia" on contents p.)	*Amazing Stories* (Sloane)	July 1932
"Scandal in the Fourth Dimension,"	*Astounding* (Street & Smith, pub.)	Feb. 1934
"A Leak in the Fountain of Youth,"	*Astounding* (Tremaine)	August 1936
"Cosmic Fever,"	*Astounding*	Feb. 1937
"Reverse Phylogeny,"	*Astounding*	June 1937
"The Mind Master,"	*Astounding* (Campbell)	Dec. 1937
"Death By Fire,"	*Science Fiction* (Hornig)	March 1939
"When the Half Gods Go,"	*Astounding*	July 1939
"Castaways in Space,"	*Science Fiction*	June 1940
"Lorraine, Lilith," (*Mary Maude Dunn Wright*)		
The Brain of the Planet (subj. of cvr.)	SF Series No. 5, Stellar Pub. Corp.	1929
"Into the 28th Century," (w/ her pic)	*Science Wonder Quarterly*	Winter 1930
"Jovian Jest,"	*Astounding* (Bates)	May 1930
"The Celestial Visitor,"	*Wonder Stories*	March 1935
"Isle of Madness,"	*Wonder Stories*	Nov.–Dec. 1935
Ludwick, Kathleen (listed as "Luckwick" on contents page)		
"Dr. Immortelle,"	*Amazing Stories Quarterly* (Sloane)	Fall 1930
McClintic, Winona,		
"In the Days of Our Fathers," (on cvr.)	*The Magazine of Fantasy*	Fall 1949
	(became *Mag. of F & SF* next issue)	
MacLean, Katherine (Future Nebula Award winner 1971)		
"Defense Mechanism,"	*Astounding*	Oct. 1949
"Merril, Judith," (*Josephine Juliet Grossman*)		
"That Only A Mother," (SF Hall of Fame)	*Astounding*	June 1948
"Death Is the Penalty,"	*Astounding*	Jan. 1949
Moore, C. (Catherine) L. (Lucille)		
(Voted Grand Master by World Fantasy Convention. Considered "alternate Hugo winner" by		
Richard Lupoff for "Shambleau," *Weird Tales,* Nov. 1933.)		
"The Bright Illusion," (on cvr.)	*Astounding*	Oct. 1934
"Greater Glories," (on cvr.)	*Astounding*	Sept. 1935
"Tryst in Time,"	*Astounding*	Dec. 1936
"Greater Than Gods,"	*Astounding*	July 1939
"Fruit of Knowledge," (subj. of cvr.)	*Unknown* (Campbell)	Oct. 1940
(Fantasy Hall of Fame)		
"There Shall Be Darkness," (subj. of cvr.)	*Astounding*	Feb. 1942
"Clash by Night," (as "Lawrence O'Donnell")	*Astounding*	March 1943
(subj. of cvr.)		
"Judgment Night (Pt. 1)," (subj. of cvr.)	*Astounding*	August 1943
"Judgment Night (Pt. 2),"	*Astounding*	Sept. 1943
"Doorway Into Time,"	*Famous Fantastic Mysteries*	Sept. 1943
"Earth's Last Citadel," (w/ *Henry Kuttner*)	*Argosy* (Not counted)	Apr.–Jul. 1943
"The Children's Hour," (as "Lawrence	*Astounding*	March 1944
O'Donnell")		
"No Woman Born,"	*Astounding*	Dec. 1944
"The Code," (as "Lawrence O'Donnell")	*Astounding*	July 1945
"Vintage Season," (as "Lawrence O'Donnell") (SF	*Astounding*	Sept. 1946
Hall of Fame)		
"Daemon,"	*Famous Fantastic Mysteries*	Oct. 1946

Author Story	Magazine (Editor)	Date

The following stories were co-authored by Moore with *Henry Kuttner* under various aliases:

As by "Lawrence O'Donnell"

"Fury, (Pt. 1)"	*Astounding*	May 1947
"Fury, (Pt. 2)"	*Astounding*	June 1947
"Fury, (Pt. 3)"	*Astounding*	July 1947

As by "Keith Hammond"

"Valley of the Flame," (subj. of cvr.)	*Startling Stories*	March 1946
"Call Him Demon," (subj. of cvr.)	*Thrilling Wonder Stories*	Fall 1946
"Dark Dawn,"	*Thrilling Wonder Stories*	August 1947
"Lord of the Storm," (subj. of cvr.)	*Startling Stories*	Sept. 1947

As by "Hudson Hastings"

"The Big Night,"	*Thrilling Wonder Stories*	June 1947
"Noon,"	*Thrilling Wonder Stories*	August 1947

As by "Lewis Padgett"

"Deadlock,"	*Astounding*	August 1942
"The Twonky,"	*Astounding*	Sept. 1942
"Piggy Bank,"	*Astounding*	Dec. 1942
"Time Locker,"	*Astounding*	Jan. 1943
"Mimsy Were the Borogoves," (SF Hall of Fame)	*Astounding*	Feb. 1943
"Shock,"	*Astounding*	March 1943
"Open Secret,"	*Astounding*	April 1943
"The World Is Mine," (subj. of cvr.)	*Astounding*	June 1943
"Endowment Policy,"	*Astounding*	August 1943
"The Proud Robot,"	*Astounding*	Oct. 1943
"Gallegher Plus,"	*Astounding*	Nov. 1943
"The Iron Standard,"	*Astounding*	Dec. 1943
"When The Bough Breaks,"	*Astounding*	Nov. 1944
"The Piper's Son," (subj. of cvr.)	*Astounding*	Feb. 1945
"Three Blind Mice,"	*Astounding*	June 1945
"The Lion and the Unicorn,"	*Astounding*	July 1945
"Camouflage,"	*Astounding*	Sept. 1945
"What You Need,"	*Astounding*	Oct. 1945
"Line to Tomorrow,"	*Astounding*	Nov. 1945
"Beggars in Velvet,"	*Astounding*	Dec. 1945
"The Fairy Chessmen (Pt. 1),"	*Astounding*	Jan. 1946
"The Fairy Chessmen (Pt. 2),"	*Astounding*	Feb. 1946
"We Kill People,"	*Astounding*	March 1946
"The Cure,"	*Astounding*	May 1946
"Rain Check,"	*Astounding*	July 1946
"Time Enough,"	*Astounding*	Dec. 1946
"Tomorrow and Tomorrow (Pt. 1),"	*Astounding*	Jan. 1947
"Tomorrow and Tomorrow (Pt. 2),"	*Astounding*	Feb. 1947
"Project,"	*Astounding*	April 1947
"Jesting Pilot,"	*Astounding*	May 1947
"Margin for Error,"	*Astounding*	Nov. 1947
"Ex Machina,"	*Astounding*	April 1948
"Private Eye," (subj. of cvr.)	*Astounding*	Jan. 1949
"The Prisoner in the Skull,"	*Astounding*	Feb. 1949

Moravsky, Maria

"Calling of the Harp,"	*Startling Stories* (Friend)	July 1941

"O'Hearn, Marian" *(Anita Allen)*

"Soldiers of the Black Goat," (subj. of cvr.)	*Unknown* (Campbell)	Jan. 1940
"The Spark of Allah (Pt. 1)," (subj. of cvr.)	*Unknown*	July 1940
"The Spark of Allah (Pt. 2)," (subj. of cvr.)	*Unknown*	August 1940
"The Spark of Allah (Pt. 3),"	*Unknown*	Sept. 1940

Author *Story*	*Magazine (Editor)*	*Date*
"Perri, Leslie," (Doris Baumgardt)		
"Space Episode,"	*Future combined w/ Science Fiction*	Dec. 1941
Quick, Dorothy		
"Blue and Silver Brocade,"	*Unknown* (Campbell)	Oct. 1939
"Transparent Stuff,"	*Unknown*	June 1940
"Two for a Bargain," (subj. of cvr.)	*Unknown*	Dec. 1940
"A Year from Tonight,"	*Fantastic Adventures* (Palmer)	Jan. 1945
Raymond, Kaye		
"Into the Infinitesimal," (subj. of cvr.)	*Wonder Stories*	June 1934
"The Comet," (as by "K. Raymond")	*Astounding* (Tremaine)	Feb. 1937
"The Great Thought," ("K. Raymond")	*Astounding*	March 1937
"Air Space," ("K. Raymond")	*Astounding*	Sept. 1937
Rea, Margaretta W.		
"Delilah,"	*Amazing Stories*	Jan. 1933
Redman, Amabel		
"Out of the Dark,"	*Famous Fantastic Mysteries*	Oct. 1940
	(Orig. *Argosy-All-Story*, Apr. 12 1924)	
Rice, Jane		
"The Dream,"	*Unknown* (Campbell)	July 1940
"The Forbidden Trail,"	*Unknown*	April 1941
"The Crest of the Wave,"	*Unknown*	June 1941
"The House," (subj. of cvr.)	*Unknown*	Dec. 1941
"Pobby," (subj. of cvr.)	*Unknown*	April 1942
"The Idol of the Flies," (subj. of cvr.)	*Unknown*	June 1942
"Magician's Dinner," (subj. of cvr.)	*Unknown*	Oct. 1942
"The Elixir," (subj. of cvr.)	*Unknown*	Dec. 1942
"The Golden Bridle," (subj. of cvr.)	*Unknown*	April 1943
"The Refugee," (subj. of cvr.)	*Unknown*	Oct. 1943
Rice, Louise (w/ Tonjoroff-Roberts)		
"The Astounding Enemy,"	*Amazing Stories Quarterly* (Sloane)	Win. 1930
Rogers, Margaret		
"I Have Been in the Caves,"	*Amazing Stories* (Palmer)	Jan. 1947
Ronan, Margaret		
"Finger! Finger!,"	*Unknown* (Campbell)	Oct. 1941
Rosmond, Babette		
"Are You Run-Down, Tired—,"	*Unknown*	Oct. 1942
"One Man's Harp," (subj. of cvr.)	*Unknown*	August 1943
Rupert, M. (Margaret) F.		
"Via the Hewitt Ray," (w/ her pic)	*Science Wonder Quarterly*	Spring 1930
St. Clair, Margaret (Voted Member of Fantasy Hall of Fame by SFFWA)		
"Rocket to Limbo," (w/ her pic & autobio)	*Fantastic Adventures* (Palmer)	Nov. 1946
"The Soma Racks,"	*Startling Stories*	March 1947
"Super Whost,"	*Startling Stories*	July 1947
"The Stroller,"	*Thrilling Wonder Stories*	August 1947
"Whenever the Sun Shines,"	*Fantastic Adventures*	Oct. 1947
"Probate,"	*Thrilling Wonder Stories*	Oct. 1947
"Piety,"	*Thrilling Wonder Stories*	Dec. 1947
"Aleph Sub One,"	*Startling Stories*	Jan. 1948
"The Dobridust,"	*Thrilling Wonder Stories*	Feb. 1948
"The Metal Lark,"	*Thrilling Wonder Stories*	June 1948
"Quis Custodiet . . . ?,"	*Startling Stories*	July 1948
"The Rotohouse,"	*Thrilling Wonder Stories*	August 1948
"The Himalaychalet,"	*Thrilling Wonder Stories*	Feb. 1949
"The Hierophants,"	*Thrilling Wonder Stories*	April 1949
"Garden of Evil," (on cvr.)	*Planet Stories*	Summer 1949
"The Sacred Martian Pig,"	*Startling Stories*	July 1949
"The Dreadful Dreamer,"	*Super Science Stories*	July 1949
"The Counter Charm,"	*Famous Fantastic Mysteries*	August 1949
"The Neo-Geoduck,"	*Thrilling Wonder Stories*	August 1949
"Bride of Eternity," (on cvr.)	*Super Science Stories*	Sept. 1949
"The Gardener,"	*Thrilling Wonder Stories*	Oct. 1949
"Child of Void,"	*Super Science Stories*	Nov. 1949
"Jamieson,"	*Famous Fantastic Mysteries*	Dec. 1949

Author Story	Magazine (Editor)	Date
St. John-Loe, G. (Gladys)		
"Where Four Roads Met,"	*Astounding* (Tremaine)	Oct. 1933
Shiras, Wilmar H. (House)		
"In Hiding," (SF Hall of Fame)	*Astounding*	Nov. 1948
"Opening Doors,"	*Astounding*	March 1949
Stephens, I. (Inga) M. (Marie), (w/ Fletcher Pratt)		
"The Pineal Stimulator,"	*Amazing Stories*	Nov. 1930
"A Voice Across the Years," (on cvr.)	*Amazing Stories Quarterly*	Winter 1932
"Stevens, Francis," (Gertrude Barrows Bennett)		
"Behind the Curtain," (on cvr.)	*Famous Fantastic Mysteries*	Jan. 1940
	(Orig. *All-Story*, Sept. 21 1918)	
"Claimed," (subj. of cvr.)	*Famous Fantastic Mysteries*	April 1941
	(Orig. *Argosy Weekly*, Mar. 6–20 1920)	
"The Citadel of Fear," (subj. of cvr.)	*Famous Fantastic Mysteries*	Feb. 1942
	(Orig. *Argosy Weekly*, Sept. 14–Oct. 26 1918)	
"Serapion,"	*Famous Fantastic Mysteries*	July 1942
	(Orig. *Argosy Weekly*, June 19-July 10 1920)	
"The Elf-Trap,"	*Fantastic Novels*	Nov. 1949
	(Orig. *Argosy Weekly*, July 5 1919)	
Stone, Leslie F.		
When the Sun Went Out (on cvr.)	SF Series No. 4, Stellar Pub. Corp.	1929
"Men With Wings,"	*Air Wonder Stories*	July 1929
"Out of the Void (Pt. 1),"	*Amazing Stories* (Sloane)	August 1929
"Out of the Void (Pt. 2),"	*Amazing Stories*	Sept. 1929
"Letter of the 24th Century"	*Amazing Stories*	Dec. 1929
"Through the Veil,"	*Amazing Stories*	May 1930
"Women With Wings," (on cvr., w/ her pic)	*Air Wonder Stories*	May 1930
"The Conquest of Gola," (w/ her pic)	*Wonder Stories*	April 1931
"Across the Void (Pt. 1)," (on cvr.)	*Amazing Stories*	April 1931
"Across the Void (Pt. 2)," (on cvr.)	*Amazing Stories*	May 1931
"Across the Void (Pt. 3)," (on cvr.)	*Amazing Stories*	June 1931
"The Hell Planet," (w/ her pic)	*Wonder Stories*	June 1932
"The Man Who Fought a Fly,"	*Amazing Stories*	Oct. 1932
"Gulliver, 3000 A.D.," (w/ her pic)	*Wonder Stories*	May 1933
"The Rape of the Solar System," (on cvr.)	*Amazing Stories*	Dec. 1934
"Cosmic Joke,"	*Wonder Stories*	Jan. 1935
"The Man With the Four-Dimensional Eyes,"	*Wonder Stories*	August 1935
"The Fall of Mercury," (subj. of cvr.)	*Amazing Stories*	Dec. 1935
"The Human Pets of Mars," (on cvr.)	*Amazing Stories*	Oct. 1936
"The Great Ones,"	*Astounding* (Street & Smith)	July 1937
"Gravity Off,"	*Future Fiction*	July 1940
"Thomas, Doris," (Doris Vancel)		
"The Bracelet,"	*Fantastic Adventures* (Palmer)	April 1943
Vanne, Emma		
"The Moaning Lily,"	*Wonder Stories*	May 1935
Washburn, Ruth		
"Unsung Hero," (w/ her pic)	*Thrilling Wonder Stories*	Spring 1944
Weinbaum (Kasson), Helen (sister of Stanley G. Weinbaum)		
"Tidal Moon," (solo, but pub. as w/ S. G. W.) (on cvr., w/ her pic)	*Thrilling Wonder Stories*	Dec. 1938
"Honeycombed Satellite,"	*Thrilling Wonder Stories*	July 1940
"The Radium Bugs,"	*Super Science Stories*	Sept. 1940
"Bargain With Colossus," (on cvr.)	*Science Fiction*	March 1941
"The Genius Bureau," (on cvr.)	*Future Fiction*	April 1941
"Devil Dogs of Space," (on cvr.)	*Science Fiction*	Sept. 1941
"Double Destiny," (on cvr.)	*Science Fiction Quarterly*	Winter 1941

Author	*Story*	*Magazine (Editor)*	*Date*
Wentz, Elma (w/ "Lyle Monroe," aka Robert A. Heinlein)			
	"Beyond Doubt,"	*Astonishing Stories*	April 1941
"Wilson, Gabriel" (Gabrielle Wilson Cummings and Ray Cummings)			
	"Earth-Venus 12"	*Thrilling Wonder Stories*	Dec. 1936
Withrow, Laura			
	"The Kiss of Death," (on cvr.)	*Famous Fantastic Mysteries* (orig. *All-Story*, Apr. 8 1916)	Feb. 1940
Yerxa (Hamling), Frances			
	"Negative Problem,"	*Amazing Stories* (Palmer)	August 1947
	"One More Spring,"	*Amazing Stories*	Sept. 1947
	"I Wake Up Dreaming,"	*Fantastic Adventures* (Palmer)	June 1948
	"Freddie Funk's Flippant Fairies,"	*Fantastic Adventures*	Sept. 1948

Men Publishing As Women*:

"Eldon, Cleo," (Don Wilcox)			
	"Sapphire Enchantress,"	*Fantastic Adventures* (Palmer)	Dec. 1945
"Grey, Carol," (Robert W. "Doc" Lowndes)			
	"Passage to Sharanee,"	*Future combined w/ Science Fiction*	Apr. 1942
	"The Leapers,"	*Future Fantasy & Science Fiction*	Dec. 1942
"MacGregor, Mary," (Malcolm Jameson)			
	"Transients Only,"	*Unknown* (Campbell)	Dec. 1942
Matheson, "Florence" (or Donald?)			
	"The Molecule Trapper,"	*Amazing Stories*	Sept. 1934

*I have been criticized for not including "Aladra Septama" (Judson W. Reeves) in this list, on the presumption that a name ending in "a" must be female. However, a careful reading of all editorial and readers' references to this author reveals that in all cases the references are to a male. No one, at the time, thought him to be a "female" writer.

SUMMARY FIGURES

Number of "Female" Authors: 65 (of whom four were men writing as women)

Number of Stories Published by "Women": 288 (five by men writing as women)

Number of Magazines Which Published Women: 20 (all of them)

Number of Female Authors With Male Pseudonyms: Three Dubious Cases (Moore, after marriage, Mrs. Raymond K. Cummings in collaboration on one story with her husband, and the reprinted classics of the well-known Francis Stevens.)

Number of Female Authors w/ Initials or Androgynous Names: 12 (inc. Long & Raymond)

Number of Female Authors w/ Clearly Female Names: 52 (inc. Long & Raymond)

Number of Female Authors w/ Bizarre Asexual Names: 1 (Hansen as "Oge-Make")

Number of Female Authors Pub. 1927–1929: 6

Number of Female Authors Pub. 1930–1939: 25

Number of Female Authors Pub. 1940–1949: 47

Number of Stories Pub. 1927–1929: 17

Number of Stories Pub. 1930–1939: 62

Number of Stories Pub. 1940–1949: 209

Number of Female Authors w/ 3 or More Stories (SFFWA Threshold): 19

Number of Stories in SF Hall of Fame (Retrospective Nebulas): 4 (by Merril, Moore, & Shiras)

Number of Future Nebula Award Winners: 1 (MacLean)

Number of Future Hugo Award Winners: 2 (Brackett 1980, for the screenplay of *The Empire Strikes Back,* and Merril, 2003, for her posthumously published autobiography)

Number of Members of Fantasy Hall of Fame: 2 (Moore & St. Clair)

Number of Science & History Articles by Women: 57 by Hansen alone, many more by others.

TABLE 2
Known Women Writers in U.S. Science Fiction Magazines 1950–1960

Author Story	Magazine	Date
Agate, Mrs.		
"Slammy and the Bonneygott,"	*Mag. of F & SF*	June 1960
Anderson, Karen *(w/Poul Anderson)*		
"Innocent at Large" (debut)	*Galaxy*	July 1958
Armock, Mary		
"First Born"	*Fantastic*	Feb. 1960
Armstrong, Charlotte *(Charlotte Armstrong Lewi)*		
"Three Day Magic"	*Mag. of F & SF*	Sept. 1952
"Ashwell, Pauline" *(Pauline Whitby)*		
"Unwillingly to School" (Hugo nom.)	*Astounding*	Jan. 1958
"Big Sword" (as by "Paul Ash")	*Astounding*	Oct. 1958
"The Lost Kafoozalum" (Hugo nom.)	*Astounding/Analog*	Oct. 1960
Benedict, Myrle		
"Sit by the Fire"	*Fantastic Universe*	May 1958
"The Dancing That We Did"	*Fantastic Universe*	Sept. 1959
"The Comanleigh"	*Fantastic Universe*	Oct. 1959
Bennett, Margot		
"An Old-Fashioned Poker for My Uncle's Head"	*Mag. of F & SF*	May 1954
Borgese, Elizabeth Mann		
"For Sale, Reasonable"	*Mag. of F & SF*	July 1959
"True Self"	*Galaxy*	Oct. 1959
Borison, Lila		
"A Candle for Katie"	*Fantastic Universe*	July 1957
"Bowen, Elizabeth" *(Dorothea Cole)*		
"The Cheery Soul"	*Mag. of F & SF*	April 1952
(Orig. in *The Demon Lover and Other Stories*, Cape: London 1945)		
Bower, M. (Female I.D. by ed.)		
"The Signals to Mars"	*Fantastic Universe*	May 1957
Brackett, Leigh *(Debuted pre-1950)*		
"The Dancing Girl of Ganymede"	*Thrilling Wonder Stories*	Feb. 1950
"The Truants"	*Startling Stories*	July 1950
"The Citadel of Lost Ages"	*Thrilling Wonder Stories*	Dec. 1950
"Black Amazon of Mars"	*Planet Stories*	March 1951
"The Starmen of Llyrdis"	*Startling Stories*	March 1951
"Child of the Green Light"	*Super Science Stories*	April 1951
"The Woman from Altair"	*Startling Stories*	July 1951
"The Shadows"	*Startling Stories*	Feb. 1952
"The Last Days of Shandakor"	*Startling Stories*	April 1952
"The Veil of Astellar"	*Fantastic Story Magazine*	Spring 1944
	(Orig. *Thrilling Wonder Stories*)	Summer 1952
"Shannach—the Last"	*Planet Stories*	Nov. 1952
"The Big Jump"	*Space Stories*	Feb. 1953
"Citadel of Lost Ships"	*Tops in Science Fiction*	Spring 1953
	(Orig. *Planet Stories*)	March 1943
"Shadow Over Mars"	*Fantastic Story Magazine*	March 1953
	(Orig. *Startling Stories*)	Fall 1944
"The Ark of Mars"	*Planet Stories*	Sept. 1953
"Lorelei of the Red Mist" (w/ Ray Bradbury)	*Tops in Science Fiction*	Fall 1953
	(Orig. *Planet Stories*)	Summer 1946
"Mars Minus Bisha"	*Planet Stories*	Jan. 1954
"Runaway"	*Startling Stories*	Spring 1954
"The Tweener"	*Mag. of F & SF*	Feb. 1955
"Teleportress of Alpha C"	*Planet Stories*	Win. 1954–1955
"Last Call For/From Sector 9G"	*Planet Stories*	Summer 1955
"The Queer Ones"	*Venture SF*	March 1957
"All the Colors of the Rainbow"	*Venture SF*	Nov. 1957

Author Story	Magazine	Date
Bradley, Marion Zimmer		
"Women Only" (debut)	*Vortex Science Fiction, #2*	(1953)
"Keyhole" (debut)	*Vortex Science Fiction, #2*	(1953)
"Centaurus Changeling"	*Mag. of F & SF*	April 1954
"Year of the Big Thaw"	*Fantastic Universe*	May 1954
"Jackie Sees a Star"	*Fantastic Universe*	Sept. 1954
"The Crime Therapist"	*Future SF*	Oct. 1954
"The Climbing Wave"	*Mag. of F & SF*	Feb. 1955
"Exiles of Tomorrow"	*Fantastic Universe*	March 1955
"Death Between the Stars"	*Fantastic Universe*	March 1956
"Peace in the Wilderness"	*Fantastic Universe*	July 1956
"Falcons of Narabedla"	*Other Worlds*	May 1957
"Bird of Prey"	*Venture SF*	May 1957
"The Stars Are Waiting"	*Saturn*	March 1958
"Collector's Item"	*Satellite SF*	June 1958
"The Planet Savers"	*Amazing Stories*	Nov. 1958
"The Wind People"	*If*	Feb. 1959
"A Dozen of Everything"	*Fantastic*	April 1959
"To Err is Inhuman"	*Science Fiction Stories*	Sept. 1959
"Conquering Hero"	*Fantastic*	Oct. 1959
"Seven From the Stars"	*Amazing Stories*	March 1960
Broughton, Rhoda		
"The Man With the Nose"	*Mag. of F & SF*	Oct. 1954
	(Orig. *Temple Bar*, Oct. 1872)	
Brown, Florence V. (Verbell)		
"Bride of the Dark One"	*Planet Stories*	July 1952
Brown, Rosel George		
"From an Unseen Censor" (debut)	*Galaxy*	Sept. 1958
"Virgin Ground"	*If*	Feb. 1959
"Lost in Translation"	*Mag. of F & SF*	May 1959
"Car Pool"	*If*	July 1959
"Save Your Confederate Money, Boys"	*Fantastic Universe*	Nov. 1959
"Flower Arrangement"	*Galaxy*	Dec. 1959
"Signs of the Times"	*Amazing Stories*	Dec. 1959
"A Little Human Contact"	*Mag. of F & SF*	April 1960
"Step IV"	*Amazing Stories*	June 1960
"David's Daddy"	*Fantastic SF Stories*	June 1960
"There's Always a Way"	*Fantastic SF Stories*	July 1960
"Just A Suggestion"	*Mag. of F & SF*	August 1960
Buck, Doris P. (Pitkin)		
"Aunt Agatha" (debut)	*Mag. of F & SF*	Oct. 1952
"The Appraiser"	*Mag. of F & SF*	Feb. 1954
"Two-Bit Oracle"	*Mag. of F & SF*	August 1954
"Dywyk"	*Mag. of F & SF*	Oct. 1955
"Spanish Spoken"	*Mag. of F & SF*	August 1957
Bullock, Alice		
"Asylum"	*Future Science Fiction*	August 1954
Carlson, Esther		
"Happy Landing"	*Mag. of F & SF*	Dec. 1952
"Heads You Win"	*Mag. of F & SF*	April 1953
"Long Distance"	*Mag. of F & SF*	Oct. 1953
"Night Life"	*Mag. of F & SF*	Dec. 1953
"Somewhere East of Rudyard"	*Mag. of F & SF*	Feb. 1954
Christie, Agatha		
"The Last Seance"	*Mag. of F & SF*	April 1951
	(Orig. *Ghost Stories*, Nov. 1926)	

Author Story	Magazine	Date
"The Call of Wings"	*Mag. of F & SF*	June 1952
(Orig. in *The Hound of Death & Other Stories*, Odhams: London 1933)		
"The Fourth Man"	*Mag. of F & SF*	Sept. 1955
(Orig. in *The Hound of Death & Other Stories*, Odhams: London 1933)		
Clarke, Pauline		
"The Potato Cake"	*Mag. of F & SF*	Jan. 1955
Clarkson (McCloy), Helen (Worrell)		
"The Last Day"	*Satellite SF*	April 1958
Clingerman, Mildred (Also see British Table 4)		
"Minister Without Portfolio" (debut)	*Mag. of F & SF*	Feb. 1952
"Stair Trick"	*Mag. of F & SF*	August 1952
"Winning Recipe"	*Mag. of F & SF*	Nov. 1952
"Stickney and the Critic"	*Mag. of F & SF*	Feb. 1953
"The Word"	*Mag. of F & SF*	Nov. 1953
"Letters From Laura"	*Mag. of F & SF*	Oct. 1954
"Birds Can't Count"	*Mag. of F & SF*	Feb. 1955
"The Last Prophet"	*Mag. of F & SF*	August 1955
"Mr. Sakrison's Halt"	*Mag. of F & SF*	Jan. 1956
"First Lesson"	*Mag. of F & SF*	Dec. 1956
"The Wild Wood"	*Mag. of F & SF*	Jan. 1957
"The Little Witch of Elm Street"	*Mag. of F & SF*	April 1957
"A Day For Waving"	*Mag. of F & SF*	August 1957
"The Day of the Green Velvet Cloak"	*Mag. of F & SF*	July 1958
Coblentz, Adrien		
"The Perverse Erse"	*Fantastic Universe*	March 1960
Constant, Barbara		
"Ugly Duckling"	*Science Fiction*	May 1955
Cores, Lucy		
"Deborah and the Djinn"	*Fantastic Universe*	Sept. 1959
Counselman, Mary Elizabeth		
"The Conquistadors Come"	*Planet Stories*	Nov. 1951
"The Black Stone Statue"	*Avon Science Fiction Reader #3*	(1952)
(Orig. *Weird Tales*, Dec. 1937)		
Cross, Virginia		
"Adversity"	*Other Worlds*	May 1955
Cummings, M. (Monette) A.		
"The Brides of Ool"	*Planet Stories*	Summer 1955
"The Weirdies"	*Fantastic Universe*	March 1957
"No Pets Allowed"	*Fantastic Universe*	August 1957
Curtis, (Elizabeth M.) "Betsy" (Also see British Table 4)		
"Divine Right" (debut)	*Mag. of F & SF*	Summer 1950
"The Old Ones"	*Imagination*	Dec. 1950
"The Protector"	*Galaxy*	Feb. 1951
"The Ones"	*Marvel Science Stories*	May 1951
"A Peculiar People"	*Mag. of F & SF*	August 1951
"Temptress of Planet Delight"	*Planet Stories*	May 1953
"The Trap"	*Galaxy*	August 1953
"Of the Fittest"	*Universe Science Fiction #6*	July 1954
"Rebuttal"	*Infinity Science Fiction*	June 1956
Davis, Dorothy Salisbury,		
"The Muted Horn"	*Fantastic Universe*	May 1957
Davis, Lavinia R.		
"Randall"	*Mag. of F & SF*	August 1953
de Camp, Catherine C. (Mrs. Lyon Sprague de Camp)		
"Windfall"	*Astounding Science Fiction*	July 1951

Author	Story	Magazine	Date
de Courcy, Dorothy (w/ John de Courcy) (Debuted pre-1950)			
	"The Golden Mask of Agharti"	*Fantastic Adventures*	Jan. 1950
	"Captain Ham"	*Other Worlds*	Oct. 1950
	"Alchemy"	*Out of This World Adventures*	Dec. 1950
	"Foundling on Venus"	*Fantastic Universe*	March 1954
Deegan, Frances M. (Debuted pre-1950)			
	"Keep It Simple"	*Amazing Stories*	May 1950
	"The Moon Pirates"	*Amazing Stories*	June 1950
	"Shouldn't Happen to a Dog"	*Fantastic Adventures*	August 1950
	"The Wizard of Blue Gap"	*Fantastic Adventures*	Dec. 1950
	"This Curse For You"	*Amazing Stories*	Jan. 1951
	"Who Sleeps With the Angels . . ."	*Fantastic Adventures*	Jan. 1951
	"Pink Wind"	*Fantastic Adventures*	March 1951
	"The Master Key"	*Fantastic Adventures*	March 1952
	"Murder on Mars"	*Amazing Stories*	April 1952
	"The Green Cat"	*Fantastic Adventures*	April 1952
deFord, Miriam Allen			
	"The Last Generation?" (debut)	*Mag. of F & SF*	Win.–Spg 1950
	"The Daughter of the Tree"	*Mag. of F. & SF*	August 1951
	"Mr. Circe"	*Startling Stories*	July 1952
	"Old Man Morgan's Grave"	*Mag. of F & SF*	Oct. 1952
	"Whatsits"	*Space Stories*	Oct. 1952
	"Throwback"	*Startling Stories*	Oct. 1952
	"The Children"	*Startling Stories*	Dec. 1952
	"Mrs. Hinck"	*Mag. of F & SF*	March 1954
	"Henry Martindale, Great Dane"	*Beyond Fantasy Fiction*	March 1954
	"One Way"	*Galaxy*	March 1955
	"Mary Celestial" (w/ "Anthony Boucher")	*Mag. of F & SF*	May 1955
	"Time Out For Redheads"	*Startling Stories*	Summer 1955
	"Martie and I"	*Mag. of F & SF*	Feb. 1956
	"The Margenes"	*If*	Feb. 1956
	"Time Trammel"	*Mag. of F & SF*	Nov. 1956
	"The Apotheosis of Ki"	*Mag. of F & SF*	Dec. 1956
	"The Old Woman"	*Fantastic Universe*	Oct. 1957
	"Featherbed on Chlyntha"	*Venture*	Nov. 1957
	"Freak Show"	*Fantastic Universe*	Feb. 1958
	"The Eel"	*Galaxy*	April 1958
	"Gathi"	*Mag. of F & SF*	June 1958
	"Operation Cassandra"	*Fantastic Universe*	Nov. 1958
	"Timequake"	*Mag. of F & SF*	Dec. 1958
	"First Dig"	*Mag. of F & SF*	May 1959
	"Prison Break"	*Fantastic Universe*	July 1959
	"Not Snow Nor Rain"	*If*	Nov. 1959
	"The Season of the Babies"	*Fantastic Universe*	Dec. 1959
	"The Monster"	*Mag. of F & SF*	March 1960
	"Do It Yourself"	*Future SF*	April 1960
	"All In Good Time"	*Mag. of F & SF*	July 1960
	"Rope's End"	*Mag. of F & SF*	Dec. 1960
Detzer (de Reyna), Diane			
	"The Tomb"	*Science Fiction*	Nov. 1958
Drake, Leah Bodine			
	"Foxy's Hollow"	*Fantasy Fiction*	August 1953

Author Story	Magazine	Date
Drussai, Garen (Mrs. Kirk Drussai)		
"Extra-Curricular"	*Mag. of F & SF*	August 1952
"The Closet"	*Vortex #2*	1953
"Grim Fairy Tale"	*Vortex #2*	1953
"The Twilight Years" (w/ Kirk Drussai)	*If*	June 1955
"Woman's Work"	*Mag. of F & SF*	August 1956
Economou, Phyllis H.		
"Cycle"	*Infinity*	June 1957
Edgerly, Dorothy H.		
"The Farmer in the Dell"	*Fantastic Universe*	Feb. 1957
"Backward Turn Backward"	*Fantastic Universe*	July 1957
"Elliott, Beth"		
"Cocktails at Eight"	*Fantastic Universe*	March 1959
Emshwiller, Carol		
"This Thing Called Love" (debut)	*Future SF #28*	1955
"Love Me Again"	*Science Fiction Quarterly*	Feb. 1956
"The Piece Thing"	*Science Fiction Quarterly*	May 1956
"Bingo and Bongo"	*Future Science Fiction*	Winter 1956–1957
"Nightmare Call"	*Future Science Fiction*	Spring 1957
"The Coming"	*Mag. of F & SF*	May 1957
"Hunting Machine"	*Science Fiction*	May 1957
"You'll Feel Better . . ."	*Mag. of F & SF*	July 1957
"Two-Step For Six Legs"	*Science Fiction Quarterly*	August 1957
"Idol's Eye"	*Future Science Fiction*	Feb. 1958
"Baby"	*Mag. of F & SF*	Feb. 1958
"Pelt"	*Mag. of F & SF*	Nov. 1958
"Day at the Beach"	*Mag. of F & SF*	August 1959
"Puritan Planet"	*Science Fiction*	Jan. 1960
Frank, Jr., Harriet		
"The Man from Saturn" (bio in ish)	*Amazing Stories*	June–July 1953
Fuller, Betty (w/ Maurice Ogden)		
"Mister Pinschur"	*Astounding SF*	Sept. 1954
Gilbert, Doris		
"The Chocolate Coach"	*Mag. of F & SF*	Jan. 1953
"Arrangement in Green"	*Mag. of F & SF*	Feb. 1954
Glasgow, Ellen		
"The Shadowy Third"	*Fantastic Novels Magazine* (Orig. *Scribner's Magazine* Dec. 1916)	June 1951
Godden, Rumer (Margaret Rumer Godden)		
"Ghost of Mr. Kitcat"	*Worlds Beyond*	Jan. 1951
Goforth, Laura (w/ Avram Davidson)		
"Love Called This Thing"	*Galaxy*	April 1959
Goldsmith, Ruth		
"Yankee Exodus"	*Mag. of F & SF*	July 1953
"Moonshine"	*Mag. of F & SF*	June 1957
Goldstein, Evelyn		
"The Land Beyond the Flame"	*Planet Stories*	May 1954
"Recalcitrant"	*Fantastic Universe*	Sept. 1954
"The Killing Winds of Churgegon"	*Fantastic Universe*	Nov. 1954
"Hour of Surprise"	*Fantastic Universe*	Jan. 1955
"God of the Mist"	*Fantastic Universe*	June 1957
"Man Under Glass"	*Fantastic SF*	August 1959
"Days of Darkness"	*Fantastic SF*	Jan. 1960
"The Vandal"	*Fear*	May 1960

Author Story	Magazine	Date
Gotlieb, Phyllis		
"A Grain of Manhood" (debut)	*Fantastic SF Stories*	Sept. 1959
"Phantom Foot"	*Amazing Stories*	Dec. 1959
"No End of Time"	*Fantastic SF Stories*	June 1960
"A Bone to Pick"	*Fantastic SF Stories*	Oct. 1960
Greenberg, Doris		
"The Unemployed"	*Fantastic SF Stories*	April 1957
"Momma Blew a Fuse"	*Amazing Stories*	June 1957
Griffith, Ann (Warren)		
"Zeritsky's Law"	*Galaxy*	Nov. 1951
"Captive Audience"	*Mag. of F & SF*	August 1953
Griffith, Barbara J.		
"The Little One"	*Fantastic*	March 1959
Gross, Marion		
"The Good Provider"	*Mag. of F & SF*	Sept. 1953
Hall, Joy		
"The Still Waters"	*Fantastic*	April 1955
Hamm, T(helma) D. (Evans) (Also see British Table 4)		
"The Last Supper"	*If*	Sept. 1952
"The Corner"	*Vortex #2*	(1953)
"Native Son"	*Imagination*	July 1953
"Gallie's House"	*Mag. of F & SF*	Sept. 1953
"The Weapon"	*Amazing Stories*	Dec. 1953–Jan. 1954
"Gallie's House" (abridged)	*Science Fiction Digest #1*	(Spring 1954)
"Gallie's Hit"	*Mag. of F & SF*	Nov. 1954
"Ourselves of Yesterday"	*Fantastic*	Feb. 1955
"Place in the Sun"	*Amazing Stories*	Feb. 1959
Haugen, Genevieve		
"Attic for Rent"	*Fantastic*	June 1957
"The Ugly Beauty"	*Fantastic*	Oct. 1957
"Everything's Different Up There"	*Amazing Stories*	Feb. 1958
"The Illegitimate Egg"	*Fantastic*	May 1958
Haynes, Dorothy K.		
"A Story at Bedtime"	*Mag. of F & SF*	June 1951
Henderson, Zenna		
"Come On, Wagon!" (debut)	*Mag. of F & SF*	Dec. 1951
"The Dark Came Out to Play . . ."	*Imagination*	May 1952
"Ararat"	*Mag. of F & SF*	Oct. 1952
"Loo Ree"	*Mag. of F & SF*	Feb. 1953
"The Grunder"	*Imagination*	June 1953
"The Substitute"	*Imagination (w/ bio & pix)*	August 1953
"Hush!"	*Beyond*	Nov. 1953
"Food to All Flesh"	*Mag. of F & SF*	Dec. 1953
"Gilead"	*Mag. of F & SF*	August 1954
"Before the Fact"	*Universe #9*	Jan. 1955
"Walking Aunt Daid"	*Mag. of F & SF*	July 1955
"Pottage"	*Mag. of F & SF*	Sept. 1955
"Anything Box"	*Mag. of F & SF*	Oct. 1956
"Wilderness"	*Mag. of F & SF*	Jan. 1957
"Turn the Page"	*Mag. of F & SF*	May 1957
"The Last Step"	*Mag. of F & SF*	Feb. 1958
"Captivity" (Hugo Nominee, '59)	*Mag. of F & SF*	June 1958
"Jordan"	*Mag. of F & SF*	March 1959
"And a Little Child"	*Mag. of F & SF*	Oct. 1959
"Something Bright"	*Galaxy*	Feb. 1960
"The Closest School"	*Fantastic*	April 1960
"Things"	*Mag. of F & SF*	July 1960

Author Story	Magazine	Date
"Henneberg, Charles" (C. & Nathalie Henneberg)		
"The Blind Pilot"	*Mag. of F & SF*	Jan. 1960
"The Non-Humans"	*Mag. of F & SF*	June 1960
Hill, Alma		
"Norte Americanos, You Are Doomed!"	*Other Worlds*	March 1950
"Pearls of Parida"	*Spaceway*	June 1954
"It's Me, O Lord"	*Future*	April 1959
Hodgson, Louise		
"For Sale—Super Ears"	*Science Fiction*	Nov. 1959
Holding, Elizabeth Sanxay		
"Friday, the Nineteenth"	*Mag. of F & SF*	Summer 1950
"Shadow of Wings"	*Mag. of F & SF*	July 1954
"The Strange Children"	*Mag. of F & SF*	August 1955
Huber, Helen		
"I'll Kill You Tomorrow"	*If*	Nov. 1953
Hunt, Margaret S.		
"Madness in Aezaeliet"	*Fantastic Universe*	Jan. 1958
Irwin, Margaret		
"Monsieur Seeks a Wife"	*Famous Fantastic Mysteries*	Oct. 1951
"The Book"	*Famous Fantastic Mysteries*	Dec. 1951
"The Earlier Service"	*Mag. of F & SF*	Dec. 1951
(Orig. in *Madam Fears the Dark*, A. D. Peters: London 1935)		
Jackson, Shirley		
"Root of Evil" (genre mag debut, w/ bio)	*Fantastic*	March–April 1953
"Bulletin"	*Mag. of F & SF*	March 1954
"One Ordinary Day, With Peanuts"	*Mag. of F & SF*	Jan. 1955
(Lupoff's alt. Hugo choice)		
"The Missing Girl"	*Mag. of F & SF*	Dec. 1957
"The Omen"	*Mag. of F & SF*	March 1958
Jacobs, Sylvia		
"A Stitch in Time"	*Astounding SF*	April 1951
"The Pilot and the Bushman"	*Galaxy*	August 1951
"Old Purply-Puss"	*Vortex #1*	(1953)
"The Sportsmen"	*Vortex #2*	(1953)
"Up the Mountain or Down"	*Universe #2*	Sept. 1953
"Time Payment"	*If*	July 1960
Jamieson, Garda		
"The Next Time"	*Science Fiction*	Jan. 1955
Janis, Jean M.		
"Queen's Mate"	*Beyond #9*	(1954)
"Rough Translation"	*Galaxy*	Dec. 1954
Jesse, F. (Friniwyd) Tennyson		
"The Railway Carriage"	*Mag. of F & SF* (orig. *The Strand Magazine*, Nov. 1931)	Feb. 1951
Jones, Alice Eleanor		
"Life, Incorporated"	*Fantastic Universe*	Apr. 1955
"Miss Quatro"	*Fantastic Universe*	June 1955
"Created He Them"	*Mag. of F & SF*	June 1955
"Recruiting Officer"	*Fantastic*	Oct. 1955
"The Happy Clown"	*If*	Dec. 1955
Jones, Leslie		
"The Devil and Mrs. Ackenbaugh"	*Mag. of F & SF*	August 1958
Kamien, Marcia		
"Alien Invasion"	*Universe #4*	March 1954
"And a Little Child"	*Fantastic Universe*	Sept. 1954
"Holiday"	*Fantastic Universe*	June 1957

Author Story	Magazine	Date
Kaye, D. (Doris) E.		
"I'll Meet You Yesterday"	*Fantastic Adventures*	Oct. 1952
"The Letter"	*Fantastic*	April 1954
"Appointment with Mr. Armstrong"	*Fantastic*	Feb. 1958
Kaye, Phyllis L.		
"They Die on Mars"	*Fantastic SF*	August 1952
"The Murder Machine"	*Fantastic SF*	Dec. 1952
Kessler, Zelda		
"The Foreign Beat"	*Fantastic Universe*	March 1957
"High Style"	*Fantastic Universe*	Nov. 1958
Knarr, Emilie H.		
"Carne Vale"	*Mag. of F & SF*	Feb. 1953
Kuykendall, Karen		
"Sepp of Sixen"	*Fantastic Universe*	Jan. 1958
Leache, Joy		
"The Pity of the Wood"	*Future*	Feb. 1959
"Miss Millie's Rose"	*Fantastic Universe*	May 1959
L'Engle, Madeleine		
"Poor Little Saturday"	*Fantastic Universe*	Oct. 1956
Lewis, Elisabeth R.		
"Know Thy Neighbor,"	*Galaxy*	Feb. 1953
Lewis, Ethel G.		
"Device for Decadence"	*Fantastic Universe*	Nov. 1955
"The Vapor Horn"	*Fantastic Universe*	Feb. 1956
"Lights Out for Rosalie"	*Fantastic Universe*	June 1956
"Daedalus Was Not a Myth"	*Fantastic Universe*	Oct. 1956
Lightner (Hopf), A.(Alice) M. (Martha)		
"A Great Day for the Irish"	*If*	May 1960
Lincoln, Victoria (Endicott)		
"No Evidence"	*Mag. of F & SF*	April 1958
Lord (Loeb), (Mildred) "Mindret"		
"Dr. Jacobus Meliflore's Last Patient"	*Mag. of F & SF*	Nov. 1953
Lyon, (Mabel) Dana		
"Mr. Elsie Smith"	*Mag. of F & SF*	May 1953
McCaffrey, Anne		
"Freedom of the Race" (debut)	*Science-Fiction Plus*	Oct. 1953
"The Lady in the Tower"	*Mag. of F & SF*	April 1959
McClintic, Winona (Debuted pre-1950)		
"There Did Not Remain a Word to Say"	*Mag. of F & SF*	May 1953
"The Ultimate Price"	*Mag. of F & SF*	Feb. 1956
"Tea from Chirop Terra"	*Mag. of F & SF*	Oct. 1956
"The Makers"	*Fantastic Universe*	Feb. 1958
"The Way Out of Town"	*Mag. of F & SF*	Dec 1960
McCloy, Helen		
"The Unexpected"	*Satellite SF*	Dec. 1957
McCune, Mildred		
"Alterations as Usual"	*Fantastic Universe*	April 1957
"The Home Stretch"	*Fantastic Universe*	Oct. 1957
MacLean, Katherine (Debuted pre-1950) (Also see British Table 4)		
"And Be Merry . . . ,"	*Astounding*	Feb. 1950
"Incommunicado"	*Astounding*	June 1950
"Contagion"	*Galaxy* (v. 1, no. 1)	Oct. 1950
"The Fittest"	*Worlds Beyond*	Jan. 1951
"High Flight"	*Super Science Stories*	April 1951
"Syndrome Johnny," (as by Charles Dye)	*Galaxy*	July 1951
"Pictures Don't Lie"	*Galaxy*	August 1951
("Pictures Don't Lie" [as TV broadcast]	*Out of This World* [Britain]	Aug. 11 1962)

Author Story	Magazine	Date
"Feedback"	*Astounding*	July 1951
"Communicado" ("article")	*Science Fiction Quarterly*	Feb. 1952
"The Man Who Staked the Stars" (as by Charles Dye)	*Planet Stories*	July 1952
"The Snowball Effect"	*Galaxy*	Sept. 1952
"The Natives"	*Science Fiction (#1)*	(1953)
"Games"	*Galaxy*	March 1953
"The Diploids"	*Thrilling Wonder Stories*	April 1953
"Where or When?"	*Future*	July 1953
"Gimmick"	*Astounding SF*	Sept. 1953
"The Carnivore" (as by "G. A. Morris")	*Galaxy SF*	Oct. 1953
"Web of the Worlds" (w/ Harry Harrison)	*Fantasy Fiction*	Nov. 1953
"Collision Orbit" (as by "K. MacLean")	*Science Fiction Adventures*	May 1954
"The Second Game" (w/ Chas. v. DeVet)	*Astounding SF*	March 1958
"Unhuman Sacrifice"	*Astounding SF*	Nov. 1958
"Interbalance"	*Mag. of F & SF*	Oct. 1960
Maddux, Rachel		
"Final Clearance"	*Mag. of F & SF*	Feb. 1956
"Overture and Beginners"	*Mag. of F & SF*	Sept. 1957
Madle, Dorothy (Haynes)		
"Crystal of Macaosu"	*Fantastic Universe*	Feb. 1955
"A Rite for Stalek"	*Fantastic Universe*	April 1955
"Magill, Rory," (Dorothea M. Faulkner)		
"The Last Gentleman"	*If*	Jan. 1953
"A Posy for Rosie"	*Spaceway*	April 1955
Martin, Evelyn		
"Narkeeta"	*Other Worlds*	July 1955
"Reluctant Eve" (abridged)	*Other Worlds*	Nov. 1956
"Ghost Planet"	*Other Worlds*	Jan. 1957
"A Woman is a Non-Mechanical Thing"	*Other Worlds*	July 1957
May, Julian		
"Dune Roller" (as by "J. C. May")	*Astounding SF*	Dec. 1951
"Star of Wonder"	*Thrilling Wonder Stories*	Feb. 1953
"Merril, Judith" (Josephine Juliet Grossman) (Debuted pre-1950) (Also see British Table 4)		
"Barrier of Dread"	*Future combined w/ Science Fiction Stories*	July–August 1950
"Survival Ship"	*Worlds Beyond*	Jan. 1951
"Women's Work is NEVER Done!"	*Future*	March 1951
"Hero's Way"	*Space SF*	Nov. 1952
"Whoever You Are"	*Startling Stories*	Dec. 1952
"A Little Knowledge"	*Science Fiction Quarterly*	Feb. 1953
"A Big Man With the Girls" (w/ "James MacCreigh," aka Frederik Pohl)	*Future*	March 1953
"Peeping Tom"	*Startling Stories*	Spring 1954
"Rain Check"	*Science Fiction Adventures*	May 1954
"Stormy Weather"	*Startling Stories*	Summer 1954
"Dead Center" (Martha Foley anth. choice)	*Mag. of F & SF*	Nov. 1954
"Connection Completed"	*Universe Science Fiction #8*	Nov. 1954
"Pioneer Stock"	*Fantastic Universe*	Feb. 1955
"Project Nursemaid"	*Mag. of F & SF*	Oct. 1955
"Exile From Space"	*Fantastic Universe*	Nov. 1956
"Homecalling"	*Science Fiction Stories*	Nov. 1956
"A Woman of the World" (as by "Rose Sharon")	*Venture SF*	Jan. 1957
"The Lady Was a Tramp" (as by "Rose Sharon")	*Venture SF*	March 1957
"Wish Upon a Star"	*Mag. of F & SF*	Dec. 1958
"Death Cannot Wither"	*Mag. of F & SF*	Feb. 1959

Author Story	Magazine	Date
As by "Cyril Judd" w/Cyril Kornbluth		
"Mars Child" (Pt. 1)	*Galaxy*	May 1951
"Mars Child" (Pt. 2)	*Galaxy*	June 1951
"Mars Child" (Pt. 3)	*Galaxy*	July 1951
(Counted as one sale, as are all serials.)		
"Gunner Cade" (Pt. 1)	*Astounding SF*	March 1952
"Gunner Cade" (Pt. 2)	*Astounding SF*	April 1952
"Gunner Cade" (Pt. 3)	*Astounding SF*	May 1952
"Sea-Change"	*Dynamic SF*	March 1953
Moore, C. (Catherine) L. (Lucille) (Debuted pre-1950)		
"Promised Land" (As by "Lawrence O'Donnell")	*Astounding SF*	Feb. 1950
"Heir Apparent" (As by "Lawrence O'Donnell")	*Astounding SF*	July 1950
"Paradise Street" (As by "Lawrence O'Donnell")	*Astounding SF*	Sept. 1950
"Song in a Minor Key"	*Fantastic Universe*	Jan. 1957
	(Orig. in fanzine *Scienti-Snaps*, Feb. 1940)	
Co-authored with Henry Kuttner as by Moore & Kuttner:		
"Earth's Last Citadel"	*Fantastic Novels Magazine*	July 1950
	(Orig. in *Argosy*, Apr.-July 1943)	
"Home is the Hunter"	*Galaxy*	July 1953
"Two-Handed Engine"	*Mag. of F & SF*	August 1955
"Rite of Passage"	*Mag. of F & SF*	May 1956
As by "C. H. Liddell" (Moore & Kuttner)		
"The Sky is Falling"	*Planet Stories*	Fall 1950
"Carry Me Home"	*Planet Stories*	Nov. 1950
"The Odyssey of Yiggar Throlg"	*Startling Stories*	Jan. 1951
"Golden Apple"	*Famous Fantastic Mysteries*	March 1951
"Android"	*Mag. of F & SF*	June 1951
"We Shall Come Back"	*Science Fiction Quarterly*	Nov. 1951
"The Visitors"	*Science Fiction Quarterly*	May 1953
"Where the World is Quiet"	*Fantastic Universe*	May 1954
"Norton, Andre" (Alice Mary Norton)		
"All Cats Are Gray" (as by "Andrew North")	*Fantastic Universe*	Aug.–Sept. 1953
"Mouse Trap"	*Mag. of F & SF*	June 1954
Nuttall, M. (Mary) J. (Jane)		
"Eighth Day"	*Other Worlds*	Sept. 1955
Outlaw, Louise Lee		
"The Runaway"	*Fantastic* (v. 1, no. 1)	Summer 1952
Pabel, Avis		
"Basic Agreement"	*Astounding SF*	Sept. 1958
"Perri, Leslie" (Doris Baumgardt Pohl Wilson) (Debuted pre-1950) (Also see British Table 4)		
"In the Forest"	*If*	Sept. 1953
"Under the Skin"	*Infinity*	June 1956
Peterson, Phyllis Lee		
"Pamela Pays the Piper"	*Mag. of F & SF*	Fall 1950
Pettis, Nina		
"Quintet"	*Mag. of F & SF*	Sept. 1959
"Rand, Ayn" (Alyssa "Alice" Rosenbaum)		
"Anthem"	*Famous Fantastic Mysteries*	June 1953
(Orig. *Anthem*, Cassell: London 1938)		
Reed, "Kit" (Lillian Craig)		
"The Wait" (debut)	*Mag. of F & SF*	April 1958
"Devotion"	*Mag. of F & SF*	June 1958
"The Reign of Tarquin the Tall"	*Mag. of F & SF*	July 1958
"Here, Kitty Kitty"	*Science Fiction*	May 1959
"Empty Nest"	*Mag. of F & SF*	August 1959

Author Story	Magazine	Date
"The Quest"	*Fantastic Universe*	Jan. 1960
"Two in Homage"	*Mag. of F & SF*	Sept. 1960
"Reynolds, L. Major" (Louise Leipiar) (Also see British Table 4)		
"Chrysalis"	*Fantastic Adventures*	Dec. 1950
"The River"	*Avon Fantasy Reader #16*	(1951)
"Blight"	*Famous Fantastic Mysteries*	Feb. 1952
"Flood"	*Mag. of F & SF*	Feb. 1952
"Who's Zoo?"	*Marvel Science Stories*	May 1952
"Holes, Incorporated"	*If*	Sept 1952
"Fair Exchange"	*Vortex #1*	(1953)
"One Man War"	*Vortex #2*	(1953)
"Such Blooming Talk"	*Fantastic Universe*	March 1954
"The River" (reprint)	*Science Fiction Digest #1*	(Spring 1954)
"Then There Was Peace"	*Spaceway*	June 1955
Rhoads, Gerda		
"My Past is Mine"	*Fantastic Universe*	Oct. 1954
"Rice, Craig" (Georgiana Ann Randolph)		
"Pink Fluff"	*Fantastic Universe*	Oct. 1955
"The Golden Flutterby"	*Satellite SF*	Oct. 1956
Rice, Jane (Debuted pre-1950)		
"The Willow Tree"	*Mag. of F & SF*	Feb. 1959
"The Rainbow Gold"	*Mag. of F & SF*	Dec. 1959
"The White Pony"	*Mag. of F & SF*	Feb. 1960
Roberts, Jane		
"The Red Wagon"	*Mag. of F & SF*	Dec. 1956
"First Communion"	*Fantastic Universe*	March 1957
"The Canvas Pyramid"	*Mag. of F & SF*	March 1957
"The Chestnut Beads"	*Mag. of F & SF*	Oct. 1957
"The Bundu"	*Mag. of F & SF*	March 1958
"A Demon at Devotions"	*Mag. of F & SF*	Sept. 1958
"Nightmare"	*Mag. of F & SF*	April 1959
"Impasse"	*Mag. of F & SF*	July 1959
Roberts, Mary-Carter		
"When Jack Smith Fought Old Satan"	*Mag. of F & SF*	July 1957
"One Sent"	*Mag. of F & SF*	Feb. 1958
Rogers, Kay		
"Love Story"	*Mag. of F & SF*	June 1951
"Bitterness of Ghoril"	*Mag. of F & SF*	April 1952
"Experiment"	*Mag. of F & SF*	Feb. 1953
"Letter to a Tiger"	*Mag. of F & SF*	Oct. 1953
"Command Performance"	*Mag. of F & SF*	August 1954
Rupert, M. (Margaret) F. (Debuted pre-1950)		
"Via the Hewitt Ray"	*Fantastic Story Magazine* (Orig. *Science Wonder Quarterly*, Spring 1930)	Summer 1951
Russ, Joanna		
"Nor Custom Stale" (debut)	*Mag. of F & SF*	Sept. 1959
St. Clair, Margaret (Debuted pre-1950)		
"Hathor's Pets"	*Startling Stories*	Jan. 1950
"World of Arlesia"	*Mag. of F & SF*	Win-Spg. 1950
"The Pillows"	*Thrilling Wonder Stories*	June 1950
"Flowering Evil"	*Planet Stories*	Summer 1950
"Meem"	*Planet Stories*	Fall 1950
"The Everlasting Food"	*Thrilling Wonder Stories*	Dec. 1950
"Age of Prophecy"	*Future*	March 1951
"Then Fly Our Greetings"	*Startling Stories*	March 1951
"The Replaced"	*Thrilling Wonder Stories*	April 1951

Author Story	Magazine	Date
"Follow the Weeds"	*Imagination*	June 1951
"The Inhabited Men"	*Planet Stories*	Sept. 1951
"The Way Back"	*Future*	Nov. 1951
"Return Engagement"	*Imagination*	Jan. 1952
"The Vanderlark"	*Planet Stories*	Jan. 1952
"The Dancers" (as by "*Wilton Hazzard,*" house name)	*Planet Stories*	Jan. 1952
"Vulcan's Dolls"	*Startling Stories*	Feb 1952
"The Muralist"	*Startling Stories*	May 1952
"Continued Story"	*Space Stories*	Oct. 1952
"Prott"	*Galaxy*	Jan. 1953
"The Unreliable Perfumist"	*Thrilling Wonder Stories*	Feb. 1953
"The Espadrilles"	*Famous Fantastic Mysteries*	April 1953
"The Goddess on the Street Corner"	*Beyond Fantasy Fiction*	Sept. 1953
"The Monitor"	*Startling Stories*	Jan. 1954
"Rations of Tantalus"	*Fantastic Universe*	July 1954
"Finders Keepers"	*Startling Stories*	Summer 1954
"The Marriage Manual"	*Startling Stories*	Fall 1954
"Fort Iron"	*Science Fiction Quarterly*	Nov. 1955
"Crescendo"	*Thrilling Wonder Stories*	Winter 1955
"Mistress of Viridis"	*Universe Science Fiction #10*	March 1955
"Lazarus"	*Startling Stories*	Fall 1955
"The Death Wish"	*Fantastic Universe*	June 1956
"Horror Howce"	*Galaxy*	July 1956
"Consumership"	*Science Fiction Stories*	Sept. 1956
"The Monitor" (reprint)	*Wonder Stories*	(1957)
"Inauguration"	*Science Fiction Quarterly*	Feb. 1957
"Starobin"	*Future Science Fiction #34*	Fall 1957
"Squee"	*Future Science Fiction #35*	Feb. 1958
"Birthright"	*Fantastic Universe*	April 1958
"To Please the Master"	*Space Travel*	July 1958
"The Invested Libido"	*Satellite Science Fiction*	August 1958
"Vector"	*Future Science Fiction #40*	Dec. 1958
"The Anaheim Disease"	*Science Fiction Stories*	Jan. 1959
"Discipline"	*If*	Feb. 1959
"The Scarlet Hexapod"	*If*	Sept. 1959
"The Autumn After Next"	*If*	Jan. 1960
"The Nuse Man"	*Galaxy*	Feb. 1960
"The Airy Servitor"	*Galaxy*	April 1960
"Parallel Beans"	*If*	Sept. 1960
As by "Idris Seabright"		
"The Listening Child"	*Mag. of F & SF*	Dec. 1950
"?" (vt, "Brightness Falls From the Air")	*Mag. of F & SF*	April 1951
"The Man Who Sold Rope to the Gnoles"	*Mag. of F & SF*	Oct. 1951
"The Hole in the Moon"	*Mag. of F & SF*	Feb. 1952
"The Causes"	*Mag. of F & SF*	June 1952
"An Egg a Month From All Over"	*Mag. of F & SF*	Oct. 1952
"New Ritual"	*Mag. of F & SF*	Jan. 1953
"Thirsty God"	*Mag. of F & SF*	March 1953
"Judgement Planet"	*Mag. of F & SF*	July 1953
"The Altruists"	*Mag. of F & SF*	Nov. 1953
"Short in the Chest"	*Fantastic Universe*	July 1954
"Change the Sky"	*Mag. of F & SF*	March 1955
"Personal Monster"	*Mag. of F & SF*	Sept. 1955
"Asking"	*Mag. of F & SF*	Nov. 1955
"White Goddess"	*Mag. of F & SF*	July 1956
"Stawdust"	*Mag. of F & SF*	Sept. 1956
"The Hero Comes"	*Mag. of F & SF*	Nov. 1956
"Eithne"	*Mag. of F & SF*	July 1957
"The Wines of Earth"	*Mag. of F & SF*	Sept. 1957
"The Death of Each Day"	*Mag. of F & SF*	April 1958
"Graveyard Shift"	*Mag. of F & SF*	Feb. 1959

Author Story	Magazine	Date
Seeley, Mabel		
"The Footprint"	*Mag. of F & SF*	Jan. 1953
Shafer, Elizabeth		
"The Green Bottle"	*Fantastic Universe*	Nov. 1958
Shiras, Wilmar H. (House) (Debuted pre-1950)		
"New Foundations"	*Astounding SF*	March 1950
"A Day's Work"	*Science Fiction Adventures*	Nov. 1952
Shirley, Vivian		
"Out of Tomorrow"	*Other Worlds*	Nov. 1950
Silverberg, Barbara (w/ Robert Silverberg)		
"Deadlock"	*Astounding SF*	Jan. 1959
Sinclare, Anna		
"Murmur of Dawn"	*Vortex #1*	(1953)
Smith, April		
"Settle To One" (w/ Charles Dye)	*Astounding SF*	April 1953
"Birthright"	*If*	August 1955
Smith, Evelyn E.		
"Tea Tray in the Sky" (debut)	*Galaxy*	Sept. 1952
"The Martian and the Magician"	*Mag. of F & SF*	Nov. 1952
"Not Fit for Children"	*Galaxy*	May 1953
"The Last of the Spode"	*Mag. of F & SF*	June 1953
"Nightmare on the Nose"	*Fantastic Universe*	Oct.–Nov. 1953
"Call Me Wizard"	*Beyond*	Jan. 1954
"Gerda"	*Mag. of F & SF*	April 1954
"The Agony of the Leaves"	*Beyond*	July 1954
"At Last I've Found You"	*Mag. of F & SF*	Oct. 1954
"The Laminated Woman"	*Fantastic Universe*	Dec. 1954
"Collector's Items"	*Galaxy*	Dec. 1954
"The Vilbar Party"	*Galaxy*	Jan. 1955
"Helpfully Yours"	*Galaxy*	Feb. 1955
"The Big Jump"	*Fantastic Universe*	March 1955
"Man's Best Friend"	*Galaxy*	April 1955
"The Princess and the Physicist"	*Galaxy*	June 1955
"The Faithful Friend"	*Mag. of F & SF*	June 1955
"Teragram"	*Fantastic Universe*	June 1955
"The Good Husband"	*Fantastic Universe*	August 1955
"The Doorway"	*Fantastic Universe*	Sept. 1955
"Weather Prediction"	*Fantastic Universe*	Oct. 1955
"Jack of No Trades"	*Galaxy*	Oct. 1955
"Dragon Lady"	*Beyond #10*	(1955)
"Floyd and the Eumenides"	*Fantastic Universe*	Dec. 1955
"The Captain's Mate"	*Mag. of F & SF*	March 1956
"The Venus Trap"	*Galaxy*	June 1956
"Baxbr Daxbr"	*Mag. of F & SF*	Sept. 1956
"Mr. Replogle's Dream"	*Fantastic Universe*	Dec. 1956
"Woman's Touch"	*Super Science Fiction*	Feb. 1957
"The Lady From Aldebaran"	*Fantastic Universe*	March 1957
"The Ignoble Savages"	*Galaxy*	March 1957
"Once A Greech"	*Galaxy*	April 1957
"Outcast of Mars"	*Mag. of F & SF*	May 1957
"The 4D Bargain"	*Saturn*	May 1957
"The Hardest Bargain"	*Galaxy*	June 1957
"The Most Sentimental Man"	*Fantastic Universe*	August 1957
"The Man Outside"	*Galaxy*	August 1957
"The Weegil"	*Super Science Fiction*	Dec. 1957
"The Blue Tower"	*Galaxy*	Feb. 1958
"My Fair Planet"	*Galaxy*	March 1958
"Two Suns of Morcali"	*Fantastic Universe*	July 1958
"The People Upstairs"	*Fantastic Universe*	March 1959
"The Alternate Host"	*Fantastic Universe*	Sept. 1959
"Send Her Victorious"	*Mag. of F & SF*	Feb. 1960
"A Day in the Suburbs"	*Mag. of F & SF*	Sept. 1960

Author Story	Magazine	Date
Smith, Phyllis Sterling		
"What is POSAT?"	*Galaxy*	Sept. 1951
"The Best Policy"	*Startling Stories*	July 1952
"The Quaker Lady and the Juelph"	*Thrilling Wonder Stories*	August 1952
"Notice of Intent"	*Startling Stories*	Oct. 1952
"The Toy Tiger"	*Space Stories*	Dec. 1952
Stapleton, Dorothy (w/ Douglas Stapleton)		
"Invasion"	*Thrilling Wonder Stories*	Fall 1954
"Superior Weapons"	*Future*	Dec. 1959
Sterling, Ruth		
"An Apartment for Rent"	*Fantastic Universe*	Oct. 1955
"The Far-Off Stars"	*Fantastic Universe*	August 1956
Stern, G.(Gladys) B.(Bronwyn)		
"Gemini"	*Mag. of F & SF*	July 1955
	(Orig. in book *Slower Judas,* 1929)	
"Stevens, Francis" (Gertrude Barrows Bennett. Debuted pre-1950)		
"Friend Island"	*Fantastic Novels Magazine*	Sept. 1950
	(Orig. *All-Story Weekly,* Sept. 7 1918)	
Stone, Leslie F. (Debuted pre-1950)		
"When the Flame-Flowers Blossomed"	*Avon SF Reader #2*	(1951)
	(Orig. *Weird Tales,* Nov. 1935)	
"Struther, Jan" (Joyce Anstruther Placzek)		
"Ugly Sister"	*Mag. of F & SF*	Feb. 1952
Trevelyan, Judith		
"Case of the Vanishing Yeast"	*Fantastic Universe*	April 1957
Urban, Helen M. (Also see British Table 4)		
"The Finer Breed"	*Mag. of F & SF*	March 1956
"The Cat and the Canaries"	*Fantastic Universe*	Feb. 1957
Vale, Rena M.		
"The Shining City"	*Science Fiction Quarterly*	May 1952
Vatsek, Joan		
"The Duel"	*Mag. of F & SF*	May 1958
Venable, (Marilyn) "Lyn" (Also see British Table 4)		
"Homesick"	*Galaxy*	Dec. 1952
"Time Enough at Last"	*(as "Lynn" Venable) If*	Jan. 1953
(Aired under same name and as by "Lynn" Venable on Rod Serling's *The Twilight Zone,* Nov. 20 1959, starring Burgess Meredith.)		
"Punishment Fit the Crime"	*Other Worlds*	July 1953
"Grove of the Unborn"	*Fantastic Universe*	Jan. 1957
Wainwright, Ruth Laura		
"Green Grow the Lasses"	*Galaxy*	July 1953
"Mint, in d/j"	*Mag. of F & SF*	June 1954
Walker, Anne		
"A Matter of Proportion"	*Astounding SF*	August 1959
Wilber, Elaine		
"The Hero"	*If*	Feb. 1958
Wilhelm, Kate (Meredith),		
"The Pint-Size Genie" (debut)	*Fantastic S-F Stories*	Oct. 1956
"The Mile-Long Spaceship"	*Astounding*	April 1957
(Lupoff's alt. Hugo choice)		
"The Last Threshold"	*Future*	August 1958
"Gift from the Stars"	*Future*	Dec. 1958
"The Trouble with Toys"	*Future*	Feb. 1959
"Project Starlight"	*Science Fiction*	March 1959
"The Ecstasy of It"	*Fantastic*	April 1959
"Android, Kill for Me!"	*Science Fiction*	May 1959
"Love and the Stars—Today!"	*Future #43*	June 1959

Author Story	Magazine	Date
"One for the Road"	*Fantastic Universe*	July 1959
"A is for Automation"	*Future*	Oct. 1959
"Brace Yourself For Mother"	*Fantastic SF*	Dec. 1959
"It's a Good Trick If . . ."	*Amazing Stories*	Feb. 1960
"UFObia"	*Science Fiction*	March 1960
"The Living Urn"	*Science Fiction*	May 1960
"When the Moon was Red"	*Amazing Stories*	Sept. 1960
Williams, Jeanne		
"The Upholstered Chaperone"	*Beyond #9*	(1954)
"The Happy Music"	*Fantastic Universe*	Jan. 1955
"The Hunter and the Cross"	*Fantastic*	August 1958
"What Other Color is There?"	*Fantastic*	June 1959
"Wilson, Gabriel" (Mr. & Mrs. Ray Cummings) (Debuted pre-1950)		
"Earth-Venus 12"	*Wonder Stories Annual*	1952
	(Orig. *Thrilling Wonder Stories*, Dec. 1936)	
Windser, Therese		
"Longevity"	*Amazing Stories*	May 1960
Winslow, Thrya Samter		
"Rudolph"	*Mag. of F & SF*	Sept. 1955
Witt, Ede		
"The Convention"	*Fantastic*	May 1959
Wolcott, Holly		
"Mr. Peavey's Tiger"	*Universe #3*	Dec. 1953
Wolf, Mari		
"The House on the Vacant Lot"	*Fantastic Story Mag.*	Summer 1952
"The First Day of Spring"	*If*	June 1952
"Robots of the World! Arise!"	*If*	July 1952
"An Empty Bottle"	*If*	Sept. 1952
"The Statue"	*If*	Jan. 1953
"Homo Inferior"	*If*	Nov. 1953
"The Very Secret Agent"	*If*	Nov. 1954
Men Publishing As Women:		
"Grey, Carol" (Robert W. Lowndes) (Debuted pre-1950)		
"Passage to Sharanee"	*Future SF*	Feb. 1960
	(Orig. *Future combined w/ SF*, April 1942)	
"McGowan, Inez" ("Rog Phillips"—Roger P. Graham)		
"In This Dark Mind"	*Fantastic*	Sept. 1958
"Rogers, Melva" ("Rog Phillips"—Roger P. Graham)		
"To Give Them Welcome"	*Other Worlds*	Jan. 1950

Initialled authors in table 2 identified as female via editorial or external evidence.

TABLE 3
Writers of Unknown Gender in U.S. Science Fiction Magazines 1950–1960*

Author Story	Magazine	Date
Bigelow, Leslie		
"Sorcerer's Apprentice"	*Mag. of F & SF*	March 1953
"Clockwork"	*Startling Stories*	April 1953
"The Immovable Object"	*Startling Stories*	May 1953
Bonnett, Leslie		
"Game with a Goddess,"	*Mag. of F & SF*	Sept. 1959

Author *Story*	*Magazine*	*Date*
Donnelson, Allyn		
"Welcome to Paradise"	*Imagination SF*	Sept. 1954
Gilman, La Selle		
"The Last Dark"	*Super Science Stories*	April 1951
Grimes, Lee		
"Lease on Life"	*Mag. of F & SF*	Nov. 1954
Hawk, G. K.		
"Lost Art"	*If*	March 1955
Henley, E. (Also see British Table 5)		
"The Temporal Paradox"	*Fantastic Universe*	Feb. 1957
"Strange Menhir"	*New Worlds* (U.S. ed.)	March 1960
Hilary, S.		
"Feud Woman"	*Fantastic*	March 1958
Hornsby, E. C.		
"Overlooked"	*Mag. of F & SF*	March 1955
Hutton, J. F.		
"Justice"	*Fantastic Universe*	March 1956
Johnson, H. W.		
"This is the Way the World Ends"	*Astounding SF*	August 1954
Jourdan, D. A.		
"Change of Color"	*Science Fiction Quarterly*	Nov. 1954
"Live in Amity"	*Science Fiction*	May 1955
"Children of Fortune"	*Science Fiction Quarterly*	Feb. 1957
"Consolation Prize"	*Science Fiction Quarterly*	August 1957
"Little Brother"	*Science Fiction*	August 1958
"Lovers Subversive"	*Future*	April 1959
Kazar, L.		
"Brave Feast"	*Fantastic Universe*	Jan. 1958
Kella, Lu		
"The Dreamers"	*Thrilling Wonder Stories*	Winter 1954
"Image of Splendor"	*Planet Stories*	Summer 1955
Loring, J. M. (w/ Atlantis Hallam)		
"The 7,000 Steps"	*Spaceway*	Dec. 1954
Lucey, J. D.		
"Fair Prey"	*Astounding SF*	Feb. 1951
McKenzie, E. J.		
"The Lost Vegan"	*Astounding SF*	April 1957
MacLennan, J. Munro		
"The Vicar and the Devilkins"	*Fantastic*	June 1954
Major, R. W.		
"Monument"	*If*	March 1960
Martin, W. Bradford		
"Spoilers of the Spaceways"	*Planet Stories*	July 1953
"Mayfield, M. I." (H. I. Hirshfield & G. M. Mateyko)		
"On Handling the Data"	*Astounding SF*	Sept. 1959
Melton, Jan		
"Publicity Stunt"	*Fantastic Universe*	Oct. 1957
Merliss, R. R.		
"The Stutterer"	*Astounding SF*	April 1955
Mittleman, E.		
"The Non-Electronic Bug"	*If*	July 1960
Morton, J. B.		
"On the Way to Her Sister"	*Mag. of F & SF*	April 1955
"Paine, J. Lincoln"		
"The Dreistein Case"	*Mag. of F & SF*	June 1958
Peters, Robin		
"The Last Enemy"	*Imaginative Tales*	Nov. 1956

Author Story	Magazine	Date
Phillips, J. P.		
"'Space' Salesman"	*Science-Fiction Plus*	Dec. 1953
Priestley, Lee		
"Trouble at the Training Table"	*Thrilling Wonder Stories*	April 1953
"The Outlaws"	*Fantastic*	Oct. 1954
"Salvage" (typoed as by "Lee Priestly")	*Science Fiction Quarterly*	Nov. 1955
"Brave New Strain"	*Fantastic Universe*	June 1958
"Golden Age"	*Fantastic Universe*	Sept. 1958
R., N.		
"Terran Menace"	*Cosmos SF #2*	Nov. 1953
Reese, D. C.		
"Gift of Zar"	*Other Worlds*	May 1955
Remington, R. H.		
"Amoeba-Hunt"	*Science Fiction Adventures*	May 1954
Rice, R. J.		
"The Miserly Robot"	*Imagination*	Oct. 1958
Rogers, B. J.		
"The Pure Observers"	*If*	Oct. 1958
Rose, J. W.		
"World of Creeping Terror"	*Super Science Fiction*	August 1959
Sargent, E. N.		
"The Girl in the Mirror"	*Fantastic*	March 1958
Scholtz, C. G.		
"Saucer in the Klondike"	*Fantastic Universe*	Sept. 1958
"Shango, J. R."		
"A Matter of Ethics"	*Mag. of F & SF*	Nov. 1954
Skupeldyckle, W. W.		
"The Romantic Analogue"	*If*	Sept. 1953
Smith, A. E. D.		
"The Coat"	*Famous Fantastic Mysteries*	Dec. 1952
Sones, J. A. (w. Roy Robinson)		
"Incident"	*New Worlds* (U.S. ed.)	June 1960
Stockheker, R. W.		
"The Rogue Waveform"	*Startling Stories*	Summer 1955
"Gadget Baghdad"	*Fantastic Story Mag.*	Sept. 1953
Stucke, H. A.		
"Caravan"	*Universe #8*	Nov. 1954
Sutton, Lee		
"Soul Mate"	*Mag. of F & SF*	June 1959
Sycamore, H. M.		
"Success Story"	*Mag. of F & SF*	July 1959
Taylor, J. A.		
"Far From Home"	*Astounding SF*	Dec. 1955
Thiessen, V. E.		
"Spiders of Saturn"	*Amazing Stories*	Feb. 1950
"Reach for the Stars"	*Fantasy Stories*	Nov. 1950
"They Who Sleep"	*Amazing Stories*	May 1951
"The Beast-Jewel of Mars"	*Planet Stories*	Spring 1955
"There Will Be School Tomorrow"	*Fantastic Universe*	Nov. 1956
Tourneau, Jan		
"Flight to Utopia"	*Science Stories*	Oct. 1953
Veenstra, K. R.		
"The Gift"	*Vortex #1*	(1953)

Author Story	Magazine	Date
von Wald, E. G.		
"Runaway Home"	*Astounding SF*	Feb. 1954
"Fair and Warmer"	*If*	July 1954
"World Without War"	*If*	Sept. 1954
"Easy Does It"	*If*	May 1955
"Shock Absorber"	*Astounding SF*	June 1955
Wallot, Lee		
"Corbow's Theory"	*If*	August 1956
Waltham, Leslie		
"Imperfection"	*Startling Stories*	June 1953
"Sibling"	*Thrilling Wonder Stories*	August 1953
"The Thirteenth Juror"	*Startling Stories*	Summer 1955
"I Like a Happy Ending"	*Startling Stories*	Fall 1955
Watt, T. S.		
"Visitors from Venus"	*Mag. of F & SF*	June 1954
Webster, C. M.		
"The Venus Gipsy"	*Vortex #2*	(1953)
"The Venus Gipsy" (reprint)	*Science Fiction Digest #2*	(Fall 1954)
West, H. H.		
"The Book of the Dead"	*Startling Stories*	Dec. 1952
Wolf, M. B. (Mari? Michael? Both Wolfs active at time.)		
"Hunger"	*Spaceway*	Dec. 1954
Woodley, J. B.		
"With a Vengeance"	*Galaxy*	Oct. 1953
Zimmerman, M. G.		
"Blurble"	*Fantastic*	June 1959

*I have excluded other authors writing under initials or ambiguous names who have been verified as male. In the Fifties many male authors wrote under initials and it cannot be automatically assumed that an initialed author is female.

SUMMARY FIGURES:

Number of Known Female-Identified Authors 1927–1949: 65
Number of Known Female-Identified Authors 1950–1960: 154 (16 debuted before 1950)
Number of Known Female-Identified Authors 1927–1960: 65 + 138 (new '50s authors) = 203
Number of Stories by Known Female-Identified Authors 1927–1949: 288
Number of Stories by Known Female-Identified Authors 1950–1960: 634
Number of Stories by Known Female-Identified Authors 1927–1960: 288 + 634 = 922

Note: All figures for U.S. magazines only.

Selected Percentages:

Planet Stories 1939–1955
    Number of Gender-Identified Authors: 195
    Number of Female Authors: 10
    Percentage of Female Authors: 5.1%

Famous Fantastic Mysteries and *Fantastic Novels*
    Number of Gender-Identified Authors: 164
    Number of Female Authors: 19
    Percentage of Female Authors: 11.58%

Galaxy 1950–1960
    Number of Gender-Identified Authors: 197
    Number of Female Authors: 20
    Percentage of Female Authors: 10.15%

The Magazine of Fantasy and Science Fiction 1949–1960
  Number of Gender-Identified Authors: 397
  Number of Female Authors: 64
  Percentage of Female Authors: 16.12%

Weird Tales 1923–1954 (Not included in science fiction totals)
  Number of Gender-Identified Fiction Authors: 728
  Number of Female Authors: 124
  Percentage of Female Authors: 17.03%

  Number of Gender-Identified Poets: 155
  Number of Female Poets: 62
  Percentage of Female Poets: 40%

Professional Authors Listed in 1999 Science Fiction and Fantasy Writers of America Directory
  Number of Gender-Identified Authors: 940
  Number of Female Authors: 366
  Percentage of Female Authors: 38.9%

TABLE 4
Known Women Writers in British Science Fiction Magazines 1950–1960

Author	Story	Magazine	Date
Bradley, Marion Zimmer			
"The Climbing Wave" (longer version)		*Science Fantasy #19*	August 1956
		(Orig. *Mag. of F & SF*, Feb. 1955)	
Clingerman, Mildred			
"Stair Trick"*Science Fantasy #19*		August 1956	
		(Orig. *Mag. of F & SF*, August 1952)	
Curtis, (Elizabeth M.) "Betsy"			
"Of the Fittest" (longer version)		*Authentic SF #73*	Sept. 1956
		(Orig. *Universe SF #6*, July 1954)	
Hamm (Evans), T. (Thelma) D. (Also see U.S. Table 2)			
"The Servant Problem"		*Authentic SF #48*	August 1954
Hemming, N. (Norma) K.			
"Loser Take All"		*Science Fantasy*	Winter 1951–1952
"Dwellers in Silence"		*New Worlds #51*	Sept. 1956
"Debt of Lassor"		*Nebula SF #33*	August 1958
"Call Them Earthmen"		*SF Adventures #10*	Oct. 1959
Lowe, Margaret			
"The Shimmering Tree"		*Science Fantasy #8*	May 1954
"Blind Chance"		*Science Fantasy #24*	August 1957
MacLean, Katherine			
"The Prize" *(w/ Michael Porjes)*		*Authentic SF #54*	Feb. 1955
"Web of the Norns" *(w/ Harry Harrison)*		*Science Fantasy #28*	April 1958
(Orig. "Web of the Worlds"		*Fantasy Fiction*	Nov. 1953)
("Pictures Don't Lie" [as TV broadcast]		*Out of This World*	Aug. 11 1962)
Marcuse, Katherine			
"Twenty-First Century Mother"		*Authentic SF #41*	Jan. 1954
"The Holiday"		*Authentic SF #55*	March 1955
"Children Should Be Seen"		*Authentic SF #65*	Jan. 1956
"Merril, Judith" (Josephine Juliet Grossman)			
"Survival Ship"		*New Worlds #35*	May 1955
		(Orig. *Worlds Beyond*, Jan. 1951)	
"Connection Completed"		*Science Fantasy #17*	Feb. 1956
		(Orig. *Universe #8*, Nov. 1954)	
"Perri, Leslie" (Doris Baumgardt Pohl Wilson)			

Author Story	Magazine	Date
"The Untouchables"	*New Worlds #49*	July 1956
(Orig. "Under the Skin"	*Infinity*, June 1956)	
Polinda, Nita		
"Prodigy"	*New Worlds #55*	Jan. 1957
"Reynolds, L. Major" (Louise Leipiar)		
"Holes, Incorporated"	*Authentic SF #33*	May 1953
	(Orig. *If*, Sept. 1952)	
"It Will Grow on You"	*Nebula SF #6*	Dec. 1953
"The River"	*Nebula #23*	August 1957
	(Orig. *Avon Fantasy Reader #16* 1951 & *SF Digest #1*, Spring 1954)	
Urban, Helen		
"Pass the Salt"	*Science Fantasy #13*	April 1955
"Heart Ache"	*Authentic SF #65*	Jan. 1956
Venable, (Marilyn) "Lyn"		
"Parry's Paradox"	*Authentic SF #57*	May 1955
Welwood, Veronica		
"Last Journey"	*Authentic SF #48*	August 1954
"The Wilder Talents"	*Authentic SF #70*	June 1956
Wood, Stella Ann		
"You Do Take It With You"	*Authentic SF #71*	July 1956
Men Publishing As Women:		
"Beecham, Alice" (E. C. Tubb)		
"Lover, Where Art Thou?"	*Authentic SF #55*	March 1955
"The Letter"	*Authentic SF #68*	April 1956
"Like A Diamond"	*Authentic SF #70*	June 1956

Note: "Pauline Ashwell" (Pauline Whitby) made her debut as fourteen-year-old "Paul Ashwell" with "Invasion from Venus" in *Yankee Science Fiction*, No. 21, July 1942.

TABLE 5
Writers of Unknown Gender in British Science Fiction Magazines 1950–1960*

Author Story	Magazine	Date
Henley, E.		
"Strange Menhir"	*New Worlds, #84*	June 1959
"Strange Menhir" (reprint)	*New Worlds* (U.S. ed)	March 1960
Hill, S. D.		
"An Affair of Gravity"	*Authentic SF #75*	Dec. 1956
Huegh, J. S.		
"Metamorphosis"	*Authentic SF #80*	May 1957
Lane, S. M.		
"Won't Power"	*Authentic SF #50*	Oct. 1954
Lindsley, F.		
"The Star Virus"	*Authentic SF #44*	April 1954
St. Clair, A. M.		
"Lunar Bridge"	*Authentic SF #70*	June 1956
"No Way Back"	*Authentic SF #73*	Sept. 1956
Schneider, D. M.		
"One Man"	*Nebula #20*	March 1957
Smith, K. E.		
"The Kid"	*Authentic SF #50*	Oct. 1954
"Incident"	*Science Fantasy #22*	April 1957
Sones, J. A. (w. Roy Robinson)		
"Aberration"	*New Worlds #88*	Feb. 1959
"Aberration" (reprint)	*New Worlds* (U.S. ed)	June 1960

Author Story	Magazine	Date
Stanton, Lee		
"Mushroom Men from Mars"	*Authentic SF Series (#1)*	(no date)
"Seven to the Moon"	*Science Fiction Fortnightly #5*	March 1 1951
"Report from Mandazo"	*Authentic SF #15*	Nov. 1951
Thomson, R.		
"Sauce for the Goose"	*Authentic SF #60*	August 1955
Wilcox, D. (David?)		
"The Wall"	*Authentic SF #85*	Oct. 1957
Wingfield, R. C.		
"The Mutilants"	*Authentic SF #47*	July 1954
Woodhouse, M. C.		
"The Higher Mathematics"	*Authentic SF #46*	June 1954
Young, R. Whitfield		
"The Locusts"	*Science Fantasy #28*	May 1958

*I have excluded other authors writing under initials or ambiguous names who have been verified as male.

TABLE 6
Not the Usual Suspects

Twenty-six Early Women
Science Fiction, Fantasy, & Weird Magazine Editors,
1928–1960

1. Daisy Bacon, Editor
   The Shadow, Fall 1948–Summer 1949
   Doc Savage, Winter 1949–Summer 1949
   (Also, Editor, *Detective Story Magazine, Detective Story Annual 1948 1949*)

2. Miriam Bourne, Associate Editor, Managing Editor
   Amazing Stories, October 1928–November 1932
   Amazing Stories Quarterly, October 1928–November 1932

3. Marge Sanders Budwig, Associate Editor
   Other Worlds, May 1950–June 1951

4. Vera Cerutti, Editor-in-Chief (but actually publisher)
   Galaxy Science Fiction, October 1950–September 1951

5. Katherine Daffron, Editor
   Two Complete Science-Adventure Books, Winter 1953–Spring 1954

6. Fanny Ellsworth, Managing Editor, Executive Editor
   Fantastic Story Magazine, September 1952–Winter 1954
   Managing Editor, Executive Editor, *Startling Stories*, September 1952–October 1953
   Managing Editor, Executive Editor,
   Thrilling Wonder Stories, October 1952–November 1953
   Managing Editor, *Space Stories*, October 1952–June 1953

7. Phyllis Farren, Associate Editor
   Cosmos SF & Fantasy, September 1953–July 1954

8. Mary Gnaedinger, Editor
   Famous Fantastic Mysteries, September 1939–June 1953
   Editor, *Fantastic Novels*, March 1948–June 1951
   Editor, *A. Merritt's Fantasy*, December 1949–October 1950

 9. Cele Goldsmith, Assistant Editor, Managing Editor, Editor
    Amazing Stories, March 1957–June 1965
    Fantastic Stories, March 1957–June 1965

10. Frances (Yerxa) Hamling, Managing Editor
    Imagination Science Fiction, January 1953–October 1958

11. Madeline Heath, Editor
    All-Story (combined with *Argosy*) 1929–1930

12. Lee Hoffman, Assistant Editor
    Infinity Science Fiction, November 1955–November 1958

13. Beatrice Jones, Editor
    Fantastic Universe, January–March 1954

14. Cylvia Kleinman, Managing Editor, Editorial Director
    Satellite Science Fiction, October 1956–May 1959

15. Gloria Levitas, Assistant Editor
    The Magazine of Fantasy & Science Fiction, March 1954–May 1956

16. Dorothy McIlwraith, Editor
    Editorial Assistant,*Weird Tales* 1938–1940
    Editor,*Weird Tales,* May 1940–September 1954
    (Also Editor, *Short Story Magazine.*)

17. Beatrice "Bea" Mahaffey, Managing Editor, Editor
    Other Worlds Science Stories, March 1950–July 1953
    Editor, *Science Stories,* October 1953–April 1954
    Editor, *Universe Science Fiction,* December 1953–March 1955
    Editor, *Mystic,* November 1953–October 1955
    Editor (Creator), *Other Worlds,* May–November 1955

18. Marcia Nardi, Associate Editor
    All-Story (combined with *Argosy*) 1929–1930

19. Evelyn Paige, Assistant Editor, Managing Editor
    Galaxy Science Fiction, October 1951–September 1956
    Assistant Editor, Managing Editor, *Beyond,* July 1953–January 1955

20. Marie A. Park, Associate Editor
    Future SF, June 1954–September 1956
    Associate Editor, *Science Fiction Stories,* January 1955–May 1960
    Associate Editor, *Science Fiction Quarterly,* February 1955–November 1956

21. Babette Rosmond, Editor
    Doc Savage, June 1944–June 1948
    The Shadow 1946–1948

22. Dorothy B. Seador, Associate Editor
    Science Fiction Stories, January 1955–May 1960
    Associate Editor, *Science Fiction Quarterly,* February 1955–November 1956
    Associate Editor, *Future SF,* Winter 1955–April 1960

23. Lila E. Shaffer, Associate Editor, Managing Editor
    Amazing Stories, October 1948–March 1953
    Associate Editor, Managing Editor, *Fantastic Adventures,* October 1948–March 1953
    Managing Editor, *Fantastic,* Summer 1952–March 1953

24. Catherine "Kay" Tarrant, Assistant Editor
    Astounding/Analog, January 1942–February 1972

25. Eve P. Wulff, Assistant Editor
    If: Worlds of Science Fiction, May 1954–April 1958

26. Rose Wynn, Editor
    Secret Agent 'X' 1934–1937
    Captain Hazzard 1938

SYNOPSIS—WEIRD SISTERS 1
127 Known Women Fiction Writers in *Weird Tales* Magazine 1923–1954*
(Not Included as Part of the 203 Women Science Fiction Writers)

1. Vida Tyler Adams (1924)
2. Marguerite Lynch Addis (1927) (Article)
3. Edith M. Almedingen (1929)
4. Frances Arthur (1972)
5. Meredith Beyers (1924)
6. Annie M. Bilbro (1928)
7. Zealia B. Bishop (Reed) (1929–1940)
8. Lady Anne Bonny (1925)
9. Edna Goit Brintnall (1932)
10. Mary S. Brown (1923)
11. Dulcie Browne (1940)
12. Loretta G. Burrough (1931–1941)
13. Brooke Byrne (1934)
14. Grace M. Campbell (1930)
15. Lenore E. Chaney (1925)
16. Valma Clark (1923–1924)
17. Martha May Cockrill (1926)
18. Ethel Helene Coen (1935)
19. "Eli" (Elizabeth) Colter (1925–1929 1939)
20. Mary Elizabeth Counselman (1933–1953)
21. Florence Crow (1934)
22. Marjorie Darter (1924)
23. Meredith Davis (1923)
24. Miriam Allen deFord (1954)
25. Edith de Garis (1932)
26. Leah Bodine Drake (1953–1954)
27. Elsie Ellis (1926)
28. Mollie Frank Ellis (1923)
29. Sophie Wenzel Ellis (1929–1933)
30. Betsy Emmons (1942–1946)
31. Mary McEnnery Erhard (1927)
32. Caroline Evans (1940)
33. Alice Drayton Farnham (1952)
34. Effie W. Fifield (1923)
35. Alice T. Fuller (1925)
36. Frances Garfield (1939–1940)
37. Louise Garwood (1925)
38. Elizabeth Cleghorn Gaskell (1927)
39. Myrtle Levy Gaylord (1923)
40. Dorothea Gibbons (1953–1954)
41. Nellie C. Gilmore (1925)
42. Victoria Glad (1951)
43. Gertrude Gordon (1938)
44. Sonia H. Greene (1923)
45. Anne H. Hadley (1924)
46. Allison V. Harding (1943–1951)
47. Clare Wagner Harris (1926–1927)
48. Lyllian Huntley Harris (1924)
49. Margaret M. Hass (1925)
50. Hazel Heald (1933–1937)
51. Helen Rowe Henze (1923)
52. Vennette Herron (1938)
53. Terva Gaston Hubbard (1927)
65. "Mindret Lord" (Mildred Loeb) (1934–1943)
66. Maybelle McCalment (1923)
67. Laurie McClintock (1923)
68. Sylvia Leone Mahler (1943)
69. Isa-Belle Manzer (1924)
70. Rachael Marshall (1928)
71. Kadra Maysi (1930–1938)
72. Violet M. Methley (1930–1932)
73. Frances Bragg Middleton (1935)
74. C. (Catherine) L. (Lucille) Moore (1933–1939)
75. Maria Moravsky (1926–1948)
76. "Bassett Morgan" (Grace Jones) (1926–1936)
77. Sarah Newmeyer (1930)
78. Dorothy Norwich (1931)
79. Alice Olsen (1940)
80. G. (Gladys) G. Pendarves (Trenery) (1926–1939)
81. Stella G. S. Perry (1931)
82. Suzanne Pickett (1952–1954)
83. Mearle Prout (1933–1939)
84. Dorothy Quick (1935–1954)
85. Edith Lyle Ragsdale (1924–1926)
86. Ellen M. Ramsay (1927)
87. Alicia Ramsey (1926)
88. Sybla Ramus (1924)
89. Helen M. Reid (1932)
90. Susan A. Rice (1925)
91. Eudora Ramsay Richardson (1924–1925)
92. "Flavia Richardson" (Christine Campbell Thomson)
93. Jean Richepin (1936)
94. Katherine Metcalf roof (1930)
95. Gretchen Ruediger (1940)
96. Margaret St. Clair (1950–1954)
97. Mrs. Edgar Saltus (1924)
98. Sylvia B. Saltzberg (1924)
99. Jane Scales (1931)
100. Mary Scharon (1926)
101. Alice-Mary Schnirring (1942–1944)
102. Edna Bell Seward (1927)
103. Mary Sharon (1924)
104. Elizabeth Sheldon (1931–1954)
105. Mary Wollstonecraft Shelley (1932)
106. Ann Sloan (1941)
107. Mrs. Chetwood Smith (1924)
108. Lady Eleanor Smith (1931)
109. Mrs. Harry Pugh Smith (1924)
110. Emma-Lindsay Squier (1926)
111. Marjorie Murch Stanley (1953)
112. "Francis Stevens" (Gertrude Bennett) (1923)
113. Edith Lichty Stewart (1924–1934)
114. Leslie F. Stone (1935–1938)
115. Gertrude Macaulay Sutton (1930)
116. Pearl Norton Swet (1932–1936)
117. Tessida Swinges (1925)

54. Fanny Kemble Johnson (1935)
55. Mildred Johnson (1950)
56. Helen W. (Weinbaum) Kasson (1940–1945)
57. Theda Kenyon (1950)
58. Ida M. Kier (1935)
59. Lois Lane (1929)
60. Genevieve Larsson (1928)
61. Greye La Spina (1924–1951)
62. Nadia Lavrova (1923)
63. Helen Liello (1925)
64. Amelia Reynolds Long (1928–1936)

118. Signe Toksvig (1928)
119. Louise van de Verg (1929)
120. (Marilyn) Lyn Venable (1953)
121. Isobel Walker (1923)
122. Evangeline Walton (1950)
123. Elizabeth Adt Wenzler (1926)
124. Phyllis A. Whitney (1935)
125. Everil Worrell (1926–1954)
126. Stella Wynne (1928)
127. Katherine Yates (1925)

*Excludes poetry. *Weird Tales* was founded in 1923 and its first incarnation ceased publication in 1954. Dates after names indicate dates of publication.

These 127 authors represent over 17% of the gender-identifiable authors to appear in the magazine. Note: There are only two initialed authors, C. L. Moore and G. G. Pendarves. It is possible there were other women who published under initials. "Bassett Morgan" is ambiguous, as is "Mindret Lord." "Francis Stevens," though the male version of this name, was well known at the time to be female. "Eli" (Elizabeth) Colter wrote primarily for the Western pulps, where she deemed the male-sounding abbreviation of her name was more appropriate. Once established, she used it for the rest of her fiction in other genres. However, at least 121 used clearly female names.

TABLE 7
127 Known Women Fiction Writers in *Weird Tales* Magazine 1923–1954
(Not Included as Part of the 203 Women Science Fiction Writers)

Author	Story	Date
Adams, Vida Tyler	"Whoso Diggeth a Pit—"	May–June 1924
Addis, Marguerite Lynch	"Sorcery Past and Present" (Article)	June 1927
Almedingen, Edith M.	"An Examination in Diplomacy"	August 1929
Arthur, Frances	"A Problem in the Dark"	October 1927
Beyers, Meredith	"The Last Entry"	May–June–July 1924
Bilbro, Annie M.	"Through the Veil"	May 1928
Bishop (Reed), Zealia B.	"The Curse of Yig" (As by Reed)	November 1929
	(Reprinted as by Bishop	April 1939)
	"Medusa's Coil"	January 1939
	"The Mound" (Abridged)	November 1940
Bonny, Lady Anne	"Wings of Power" (3-part serial)	January 1925 (1st part)
Brintnall, Edna Goit	"Dust"	July 1932
Brown, Mary S.	"The Magic Mirror"	November 1923
Browne, Dulcie	"Ghost Farm"	November 1940
Burrough, Loretta G.	"Creeping Fingers"	August 1931
	"What Waits in Darkness"	March 1935
	"A Visitor from Far Away"	February 1936
	"At the Time Appointed"	February 1937
	"The Will of the Dead"	August 1937
	"The Snowman"	December 1938
	"Person or Persons Unknown"	January 1941
Byrne, Brooke	"The Werewolf's Howl"	December 1934
Campbell, Grace M.	"The Law of the Hills"	August 1930
Chaney, Lenore E.	"White Man's Madness"	January 1925
Clark, Valma	"Two Men Who Murdered Each Other"	July–August 1923
	"Zillah"	March 1924
Cockrill, Martha May	"The Fiend of the Marsh"	November 1926
(w/ Maj. Robert Emmett Lewis)		
Coen, Ethel Helene	"One Chance"	September 1935
Colter, "Eli" (Elizabeth)	"Farthingale's Poppy"	July 1925
	"The Deadly Amanita"	December 1925

Author	Story	Date
	"On the Dead Man's Chest" (4-part serial)	January 1926 (Pt. 1)
	"Corpus Delicti"	October 1926
	"The Last Horror"	January 1927 (Reprinted Feb. 1939)
	"The Greatest Gift"	March 1927
	"The Dark Chrysalis" (3-part serial)	June 1927 (Pt. 1)
	"The Golden Whistle"	January 1928
	"Curse of a Song"	March 1928
	"The Man in the Green Coat"	August 1928
	"Vengeance of the Dead" (2-part serial)	February 1929 (Pt. 1)
	"The Man Who Died Twice"	November 1939
Counselman, Mary Elizabeth	"The House of Shadows"	April 1933
	"The Girl with the Green Eyes"	May 1933
	"The Cat Woman"	October 1933
	"The Accursed Isle"	November 1933
	"The Three Marked Pennies"	August 1934
	"The Black Stone Statue"	December 1937
	"Mommy"	April 1939
	"The Web of Silence"	November 1939
	"Twister"	January 1940
	"Drifting Atoms"	May 1941
	"Parasite Mansion"	January 1942
	"The Seventh Sister"	January 1943
	"The Breeze and I"	July 1947
	"The Lens"	November 1947
	"A Death Crown for Mr. Hapworthy"	May 1948
	"The Devil's Lottery"	September 1948
	"The Bonan of Baladewa,"	January 1949
	"The Shot-Tower Ghost"	September 1949
	"The Green Window"	November 1949
	"The Smiling Face"	January 1950
	"The Tree's Wife"	March 1950
	"The Monkey Spoons"	May 1950
	"Cordona's Skull"	July 1950
	"Something Old"	November 1950
	"The Unwanted"	January 1951
	"Chinook"	July 1951
	"Rapport"	September 1951
	"The Prism"	March 1952
	"Night Court"	March 1953
	"Way Station"	November 1953
Crow, Florence	"The Road Nightmare"	March 1934
Darter, Marjorie	"The God Yuano"	May-June-July 1924
Davis, Meredith	"The Accusing Voice"	March 1923
deFord, Miriam Allen	"Never Stop to Pat a Kitten"	July 1954
de Garis, Edith	"The Dragon Girl"	January 1932
Drake, Leah Bodine	"Whisper Water" (cover illus.)	May 1953
	"Mop-Head"	January 1954
Ellis, Elsie	"McGill's Appointment"	January 1926
Ellis, Mollie Frank	"Case No. 27"	May 1923
Ellis, Sophie Wenzel	"The White Wizard" (cover illus.)	September 1929
	"The Dwellers in the House"	June 1933
Emmons, Betsy	"The Ghost of the Model T"	November 1942
	"Threshold of Endurance"	September 1946

Author	Story	Date
Erhard, Mary McEnnery	"Tangled Skeins"	July 1927
Evans, Caroline	"San Francisco"	May 1940
Farnham, Alice Drayton	"Morne Perdue" (cover illus.)	March 1952
	"Black as the Night"	November 1952
Fifield, Effie W.	"The Amazing Adventure of Joe Scranton"	October 1923
Fuller, Alice T.	"The Tomb-Dweller"	February 1925
Garfield, Frances	"The High Place"	April 1939
	"Not Both!"	May 1939
	"Forbidden Cupboard"	January 1940
Garwood, Louise	"Fayrian"	February 1925
	"Candle-Light"	November 1925
Gaskell, Elizabeth Cleghorn	"The Old Nurse's Story"	October 1927
Gaylord, Myrtle Levy	"The Wish"	April 1923
Gibbons, Dorothea	"The Crying Child"	November 1953
	"The Lily Maid"	March 1954
	"The Green Huntsman"	July 1954
Gilmore, Nellie C.	"The White Scar"	April 1925
Glad, Victoria	"Each Man Kills"	March 1951
Gordon, Gertrude	"The Cavern"	September 1938
(w/ Manly Wade Wellman)		
Greene, Sonia H.	"The Invisible Monster"	November 1923
Hadley, Anne H.	"Exhibit 'A'"	April 1924
Harding, Allison V.	"The Unfriendly World"	July 1943
	"Night Must Not Come"	September 1943
	"Death Went That Way"	November 1943
	"House of Hate"	January 1944
	"The Marmot"	March 1944
	"The Day the World Stood Still"	May 1944
	"Guard in the Dark"	July 1944
	"The Seven Seas Are One"	September 1944
	"Ride the El to Doom"	November 1944
	"Revolt of the Trees"	January 1945
	"Fog Country"	July 1945
	"Night of Impossible Shadows"	September 1945
	"The Murderous Steam Shovel"	November 1945
	"Tunnel Terror"	March 1946
	"The Wings"	July 1946
	"The Machine"	September 1946
	"Shipmate"	November 1946
	"The House Beyond Midnight"	January 1947
	"The Immortal Lancer"	March 1947
	"The Place With Many Windows"	May 1947
	"The Damp Man"	July 1947
	"The Damp Man Returns"	September 1947
	"The Inn by Doomsday Falls"	November 1947
	"The Frightened Engineer"	January 1948
	"The Coming of M. Alkerhaus"	March 1948
	"City of Lost People"	May 1948
	"Isle of Women"	July 1948
	"The Follower"	September 1948
	"The House on Forest Street"	November 1948
	"Four from Jehlam" (cover illus.)	January 1949
	"The Holiday"	March 1949
	"The Damp Man Again" (cover illus.)	May 1949
	"The Deep Drowse"	September 1949
	"The Underbody" (cover illus.)	November 1949

Author	Story	Date
	"Take the Z Train"	March 1950
	"Scope"	January 1951
Harris, Clare Winger	"A Runaway World"	July 1926
	"A Certain Soldier"	November 1927
Harris, Lyllian Huntley	"The Vow on Hallowe'en"	May-June-July 1924
Hass, Margaret M.	"The Weird Green Eyes of Sari"	March 1925
Heald, Hazel	"The Horror in the Museum"	July 1933
	"Winged Death"	March 1934
	"Out of Eons"	April 1935
	"The Horror in the Burying-Ground"	May 1937
Henze, Helen Rowe	"The Escape"	June 1923
Herron, Vennette	"Toean Watjan"	January 1938
Hubbard, Terva Gaston	"The Phantom Photoplay"	August 1927
Johnson, Fanny Kemble	"The Dinner Set"	February 1935
Johnson, Mildred	"The Cactus"	January 1950
	"The Mirror" September 1950	
Kasson, Helen W. (Weinbaum)	"The Valley of the Undead"	September 1940
	"Time and Again"	May 1943
	"Speed the Parting Ghost"	November 1943
	"Please Go 'Way and Let Me Sleep"	March 1945
Kenyon, Theda	"The House of the Golden Eyes"	September 1930
Kier, Ida M.	"Together"	June 1935
Lane, Lois	"The Purple Sedan"	August 1929
Larsson, Genevieve	"The City of Lost Souls"	October 1928
La Spina, Greye	"The Tortoise-Shell Cat"	November 1924
	"The Remorse of Professor Panebianco"	January 1925
	"The Scarf of the Beloved"	February 1925
	"The Last Cigarette"	March 1925
	"Invaders from the Dark" (3 pt. serial)	April 1925 (1st part)
	"The Gargoyle" (3 part serial) (cvr.)	September 1925 (1st part)
	"Fettered" (4 part serial)	July 1926 (1st part)
	"A Suitor from the Shades" (cover)	June 1927
	"The Dead-Wagon"	September 1927
		(Reprinted April 1937)
	"The Portal to Power" (4 pt. serial)	October 1930 (1st part)
	"The Devil's Pool" (cover illus.)	June 1932
	"The Sinister Painting"	September 1934
	"The Rat Master"	March 1942
	"The Deadly Theory"	May 1942
	"Death Has Red Hair"	September 1942
	"Great Pan Is Here"	November 1943
	"The Antimacassar"	May 1949
	"Old Mr. Wiley"	March 1951
Lavrova, Nadia	"The Talisman"	September 1923
Liello, Helen	"For Sale, A Country Seat"	February 1925
Long, Amelia Reynolds	"The Twin Soul"	March 1928
	"The Thought-Monster"	March 1930
	"The Magic-Maker"	June 1930
	"The Undead"	August 1931
	"Flapping Wings of Death"	June 1935
	"The Album"	December 1936
Lord (Loeb), "Mindret" (Mildred)	"Naked Lady"	September 1934
	"First Night"	July 1941
	"The Mystery of Uncle Alfred"	November 1941
	"Lil"	March 1943
	"Lost Vacation"	May 1943

Author	Story	Date
McCalment, Maybelle	"The Closed Room"	November 1923
McClintock, Laurie (w/ Culpeper Chunn)	"The Whispering Thing" (2 parts)	April 1923 (1st part)
Mahler, Sylvia Leone	"Colleagues"	May 1943
Manzer, Isa-Belle	"The Transparent Ghost" (3 parts)	February 1924 (1st part)
Marshall, Rachael (w/ Maverick Terrell)	"The Mystery in Acatlan" (cover)	November 1928
Maysi, Kadra	"The Boat on the Beach"	December 1930
	"Conjure Bag"	April 1932
	"The Isle of Abominations"	October 1938
Methley, Violet M.	"Dread at Darracombe"	April 1930
	"The Milk Carts"	March 1932
Middleton, Frances Bragg	"Once in a Thousand Years"	August 1935
Moore, C. (Catherine) L. (Lucille)	"Shambleau"	November 1933
	"Black Thirst"	April 1934
	"Scarlet Dream"	May 1934
	"Dust of Gods"	August 1934
	"The Black God's Kiss" (cover)	October 1934
	"The Black God's Shadow"	December 1934
	"Julhi"	March 1935
	"Jirel Meets Magic"	July 1935
	"The Cold Gray God"	October 1935
	"The Dark Land"	January 1936
	"Yvala" (w/ Forrest J. Ackerman)	February 1936
	"Lost Paradise"	July 1936
	"The Tree of Life"	October 1936
	"Quest of the Starstone"	November 1937
	"Hellsgarde"	April 1939
	"Nymph of Darkness" (w/ Henry Kuttner)	December 1939
Moravsky, Maria	"The Ode to Pegasus"	November 1926
	"The Castle of Tamara"	April 1927
	"Beyond the Frame"	July 1940
	"Lover of Caladiums"	May 1943
	"The Green Brothers Take Over"	January 1948
"Morgan, Bassett" (Grace Jones)	"Laocoon"	July 1926 (Reprinted December 1937)
	"The Head"	February 1927
	"Gray Ghouls"	July 1927 (Reprinted September 1939)
	"The Wolf Woman" (cover illus.)	September 1927
	"The Devils of Po Sung"	December 1927 (Reprinted March 1939)
	"The Skeleton Under the Lamp"	May 1928
	"Bimini"	January 1929
	"Demon Doom of N'Yeng Sen"	August 1929
	"Island of Doom"	March 1932
	"Tiger Dust"	April 1933 (Reprinted January 1954)
	"The Vengeance of Ti Fong"	December 1934
	"Black Bagheela" (cover illus.)	January 1935
	"Midas"	November 1936
Newmeyer, Sarah	"Gerard 7932"	March 1930
Norwich, Dorothy	"The Game"	January 1931
Olsen, Alice	"Winter Night"	May 1940

Author	Story	Date
Pendarves (Trenery), G. (Gladys) G. (Gordon)		
	"The Devil's Graveyard"	August 1926
	"The Return"	April 1927
	"The Power of the Dog"	August 1927
	"The Lord of the Tarn"	November 1927
	"The Doomed Treveans"	May 1928
	"The Eighth Green Man"	March 1928
		(Reprinted January 1937)
		(Reprinted May 1952)
	"The Laughing Thing"	May 1929
	"The Footprint"	May 1930
	"The Grave at Goonhilly"	October 1930
		(Reprinted March 1954)
	"From the Dark Halls of Hell"	January 1932
	"The Altar of Melek Taos" (cover)	September 1932
	"Abd Dhulma, Lord of Fire"	December 1933
	"Werewolf of the Sahara"	Aug.–Sept. 1936
	"The Dark Star"	March 1937
	"The Whistling Corpse"	July 1937
	"Thing of Darkness" (cover illus.)	August 1937
		(Reprinted November 1953)
	"The Black Monk"	October 1938
	"The Sin-Eater" (cover illus.)	December 1938
		(Reprinted July 1954)
	"The Withered Heart"	November 1939
Perry, Stella G. S.	"Old Roses"	August 1931
Pickett, Suzanne	"A Bit of Moss"	May 1952
	"There Was Soot on the Cat"	July 1952
	"I Can't Wear White"	January 1953
	"Effie's Pets" (cover illus.)	January 1954
	"Nepthae"	March 1954
	"Dorgen"	September 1954
Prout, Mearle	"The House of the Worm"	October 1933
	"Masquerade"	February 1937
	"Guarded"	March 1938
	"Witch's Hair"	May 1939
Quick, Dorothy	"The Horror in the Studio" (cvr. ill.)	June 1935
	"The Lost Door"	October 1936
	"Strange Orchids" (cover illus.)	March 1937
	"The Witch's Mark" (cover illus.)	January 1938
	"Turn Over"	November 1940
	"Edge of the Cliff"	March 1941
	"The Lost Gods"	September 1941
	"The White Lady,"	January 1942
	"The Enchanted River"	May 1942
	"The Gothic Window"	May 1944
	"The Man in Purple"	May 1946
	"The Cracks of Time"	September 1948
	"The Woman on the Balcony"	September 1949
	"The Artist and the Door"	November 1952
	"More Than Shadow"	July 1954
Ragsdale, Edith Lyle	"The Purple Death"	May-June-July 1924
	"The Burning Wrath of Allah"	March 1925
	"Vials of Wrath"	May 1926

Author	Story	Date
Ramsay, Ellen M.	"The Brimstone Cat"	February 1927
Ramsey, Alicia	"The Black Crusader"	January 1926
Ramus, Sybla	"Coils of Darkness" (3 part serial)	February 1924 (1st part)
Reid, Helen M.	"Under the Eaves"	June 1932
Rice, Susan A.	"The Ghost Farm"	May 1925
Richardson, Eudora Ramsay	"The Voice of Euphemia"	March 1924
	"The Haunting Eyes"	April 1925
"Richardson, Flavia" (Christine Campbell Thomson)		
	"Out of the Earth"	April 1927
	"The Gray Lady"	October 1929
Richepin, Jean	"A Masterpiece of Crime"	March 1936
Roof, Katherine Metcalf	"A Million Years Aftr" (cover illus.)	November 1930
Ruediger, Gretchen	"Wind in the Moonlight"	May 1940
St. Clair, Margaret	"The Family"	January 1950
	"The Corn Dance"	March 1950
	"The Last Three Ships"	May 1950
	"Mrs. Hawk"	July 1950
	"The Invisible Reweaver"	November 1950
	"Professor Kate"	January 1951
	"The Little Red Owl"	July 1951
	"The Bird"	November 1951
	"The Island of the Hands"	September 1952
	"Brenda"	March 1954
Saltus, Mrs. Edgar	"Kaivalya"	December 1924
Saltzberg, Sylvia B. (w/ Henry Lieferant)	"A Game of Chance"	January 1924
Scales, Jane	"The Thing in the Bush"	Feb.–March 1931
Scharon, Mary	"The Cat of Chiltern Castle"	September 1926
Schnirring, Alice-Mary	"Child's Play"	March 1942
	"Crystal Vision"	May 1942
	"The Possessed"	November 1942
	"One-Man Boat"	January 1943
	"Lost"	July 1943
	"The Dear Departed"	May 1944
Seward, Edna Bell	"The Land of Creeping Death"	June 1927
Sharon, Mary	"The Door of Doom"	February 1924
Sheldon, Elizabeth	"The Ghost That Never Died"	November 1931 (Reprinted March 1954)
Shelley, Mary Wollstonecraft	"Frankenstein" (8 part serial)	May 1932 (1st part)
Sloan, Ann	"The Cream-Colored Cat"	March 1941
Smith, Mrs. Chetwood	"An Egyptian Lotus"	May-June-July 1924
Smith, Lady Eleanor	"Satan's Circus"	October 1931
Smith, Mrs. Harry Pugh	"The Hook of Death"	January 1924
Squier, Emma-Lindsay	"The Door of Hell"	August 1926
Stanley, Marjorie Murch	"Hand of Death"	January 1953
"Stevens, Francis" (Gertrude Barrows Bennett)		
	"Sunfire" (2-part serial) (cover illus.)	July–August 1923 (1st part)
Stewart, Edith Lichty	"The Sixth Tree"	May-June-July 1924 (Reprinted February 1934)
Stone, Leslie F.	"When the Flame-Flowers Blossomed"	November 1935
	"Death Dallies Awhile"	June 1938
Sutton, Gertrude Macaulay	"Gesture"	September 1930
Swet, Pearl Norton	"The Man Who Never Came Back"	July 1932
	"The Medici Boots"	Aug.–Sept. 1936
Swinges, Tessida	"A Mind in Shadow"	October 1925

Author	Story	Date
Toksvig, Signe	"The Devil's Martyr" (cover illus.)	June 1928
van de Verg, Louise	"The Three"	February 1929
Venable, (Marilyn) Lyn	"The Missing Room"	July 1953
Walker, Isobel	"Black Cunjer"	July–August 1923
Walton, Evangeline	"At the End of the Corridor"	May 1950
Wenzler, Elizabeth Adt	"The Demons of Castle Romnare"	July 1926
Whitney, Phyllis A.	"The Silver Bullet"	February 1935
Worrell, Everil	"The Bird of Space" (cover illus.)	September 1926
	"The Castle of Furos"	October 1926
	"Leonora"	January 1927 (Reprinted Nov. 1938)
	"The Canal"	December 1927 (Reprinted April 1935)
	"From Beyond"	April 1928
	"The Elemental Law"	June 1928
	"Vulture Crag"	August 1928
	"The Rays of the Moon"	September 1928
	"An Adventure in Anaesthesia"	February 1929
	"The Gray Killer" (cover illus.)	November 1929
	"Light-Echoes"	May 1930
	"Deadlock"	September 1931
	"The Hollow Moon" (cover illus.)	May 1939
	"The High Tower"	July 1942
	"Hideaway"	November 1951
	"Once There Was a Little Girl"	January 1953
	"I Love Her with My Soul"	September 1953
	"Call Not Their Names"	March 1954
Wynne, Stella	"Ebony Magic"	March 1928
Yates, Katherine	"Under the Hau Tree"	November 1925

Most Prolific Authors: Allison V. Harding: 36; Mary Elizabeth Counselman: 30; G. G. Pendarves: 19; Everil Worrell: 18; Greye La Spina: 16; C. L. Moore: 16; Dorothy Quick: 15; "Bassett Morgan": 13; Eli Colter: 12; and Margaret St. Clair: 10.

Total number of short stories and serials published in *Weird Tales*: 2712.
Number of short stories and serials by identifiable female authors: 365.
Percentage of total short stories and serials by identifiable female authors: 13.45%.
Note: This percentage is not based upon an elimination of stories by authors of unknown gender. Were we to look at the percentage of stories by known women authors compared to a list only of stories by gender-identifiable authors, this percentage would no doubt be higher.

SYNOPSIS—WEIRD SISTERS 2
63 Known Women Poets in *Weird Tales* Magazine 1923–1954*
(Not Included as Part of the 203 Women Science Fiction Writers)

1. Leona May Ames (1931)
2. Dorothy Agard Ansley (1939)
3. Muriel Cameron Bodkin (1933)
4. Pauline Booker (1942–1953)
5. Harriet A. Bradfield (1946–1953)
6. Katherine Buoy (1935)
7. Hazel Burden (1934)
8. Patricia Burgess (1954)
9. Brooke Byrne (1933)
10. Hanna Baird Campbell (1929–1930)

11. Page Cooper (1942–1951)
12. Mary Elizabeth Counselman (1932–1941)
13. Elma Dean (1935)
14. Leah Bodine Drake (1935–1954)
15. Frances Elliot (1933–1937)
16. Louise Garwood (1926–1931)
17. Yetza Gillespie (1946–1952)
18. Winona Montgomery Gilliland (1937)
19. Dorothy Gold (1943)
20. Julia Boynton Green (1935–1936)

21. Cristel Hastings (1926–1938)
22. Marietta Hawley (1927)
23. Sarah Henderson Hay (1930)
24. Leona Ames Hill (1935)
25. Marjorie Holmes (1931)
26. Edith Hurley (1928–1940)
27. Alice I'Anson (1930–1932)
28. "Minna Irving" (Minnie Odell) (1937)
29. Thelma E. Johnson (1929)
30. Victoria Beaudin Johnson (1935)
31. Donna Kelly (1935)
32. Minnie Faegre Knox (1928)
33. Binny Koras (1926)
34. Jean Lahors (1926)
35. Marie W. Linne (1934)
36. Frances Rogers Lovell (1953)
37. Josie McNamara Lydon (1927)
38. Leslyn MacDonald (1941)
39. Dorothy Haynes Madle (1946)
40. Maria Moravsky (1942)
41. Ethel Morgan-Dunham (1934)
42. Maisie Nelson (1940)

43. Nichol (w/Hannes Bok 1944)
44. Edith Ogutsch (1954)
45. Dorothy Marie Peterkin (1929)
46. Alice Pickard (1930)
47. Lilla Poole Price (Savino) (1926–1928)
48. Dorothy Quick (1934–1954)
49. Janice Hall Quilligan (1943)
50. Elizabeth Virgins Raplee (1937)
51. June Power Reilly (1935)
52. Mary Sharon (1924)
53. Mary C. Shaw (1934)
54. Katherine Simons (1943–1947)
55. Grace Stillman (1934)
56. Vivian Stratton (1939)
57. Jewell Bothwell Tull (1930)
58. Lida Wilson Turner (1930)
59. Maude E. Uschold (1929)
60. Katherine van der Veer (1934–1935)
61. Wilma Dorothy Vermilyea (1936)
62. Irene Wilde (1938)
63. Geraldine M. Wright (1925–1927)

*Dates after names indicate dates of publication. These 63 poets represented 40 percent of all the gender-identifiable poets to appear in the magazine. Note: None of these authors felt any need to hide their gender behind initials. Nor is there a single sexually ambiguous name. Not included is Mary Carolyn Davies, who published in *The Thrill Book*, in 1919.

TABLE 8
63 Known Women Poets in *Weird Tales* Magazine 1923–1954

(Not Included as Part of the 203 Women Science Fiction Writers)

Author	Poem	Date
Ames, Leona May	"Return"	November 1931
Ansley, Dorothy Agard	"And Thus I Knew"	January 1939
Bodkin, Muriel Cameron	"A Witch Passes"	March 1933
Booker, Pauline	"The Eldritch One"	May 1948
	"Ghost Port"	May 1952
	"Requiem for a Sinner"	May 1953
Bradfield, Harriet A.	"The Door"	November 1946
	"Demon Lover"	May 1948
	"Demon Lure"	November 1949
	"Unexpiated"	November 1951
	"Cat-Eyes"	January 1952
	"Suspicion"	November 1953
Buoy, Katherine	"Ghost of the Lava"	November 1935
Burden, Hazel	"The Star-Gazer Climbs"	February 1934
Burgess, Patricia	"Beware of Vampire Women"	July 1954
Byrne, Brooke	"Sic Transit Gloria"	November 1933
Campbell, Hanna Baird	"Ballade of Wandering Ghosts"	March 1929
	"At Eventide"	February 1930
Cooper, Page	"The Curse"	January 1942
	"Hunger"	March 1942
	"A Charm"	July 1944
	"Quest Unhallowed"	March 1945

Author	Poem	Date
	"Remorse"	September 1945
	"Incantation"	September 1950
	"My Timid Soul"	January 1951
Counselman, Mary Elizabeth	"Madman's Song"	April 1932
	"Echidna"	July 1932
	"Voodoo Song"	July 1933
	"Nostalgia"	September 1933
	"Witch-Burning"	October 1936
	"Ring Eclipse"	January 1941
Dean, Elma	"There Is a Might"	July 1935
Drake, Leah Bodine	"In The Shadows"	October 1935
	"The Witch Walks in Her Garden"	April 1937
	"Witches on the Heath"	October 1938
	"They Run Again"	June–July 1939
	"Bad Company"	March 1941
	"Haunted Hour"	November 1941
	"Wood Wife"	March 1942
	"Changeling"	September 1942
	"A Verse From Araby"	March 1943
	"Sea Shell"	September 1943
	"The Path Through the Marsh"	September 1944
	"The Nixie's Pool"	May 1946
	"Heard on the Roof at Midnight"	November 1946
	"The Seal-Woman's Daughter"	January 1947
	"The Stranger"	September 1947
	"The Steps in the Field"	November 1947
	"The Heads on Easter Island"	January 1949
	"The Vision"	January 1950
	"Revenant"	March 1951
	"Swan Maiden"	May 1951
	"The Mermaid"	November 1952
	"Red Ghosts in Kentucky"	January 1953
	"Six Merry Farmers"	September 1953
Elliott, Frances	"The House by theSea"	August 1933
	"The Hill Woman"	October 1934
	"The Beggar"	February 1937
Garwood, Louise	"Ghosts"	July 1926
	"The Living"	September 1929
	"Ghost"	December 1931
Gillespie, Yetza	"Forgetful Hour"	March 1946
	"The Haunted Stairs"	May 1946
	"Hallowe'en Candle"	November 1951
	"Black Candles"	July 1952
	"The Singing Shadow"	September 1952
Gilliland, Winona Montgomery	"The Old House on the Hill"	December 1937
Gold, Dorothy	"On Lake Lagore"	November 1943
Green, Julia Boynton	"The Return"	September 1934
	"Painted Cave"	April 1936
Hastings, Cristel	"Fear"	July 1926
	"Painted Dragons"	May 1927
	"The Swamp"	August 1927
	"An Old House"	November 1927
	"The Jungle"	December 1927
	"The Phantom"	April 1928
	"Neptune's Neighbours"	April 1929
	"The Haunted House"	May 1929

Author	Poem	Date
	"Swamp Symphony"	March 1930
	"The Empty House"	November 1931
	"Fog"	April 1932
	"Mystery"	May 1932
	"The Haunted Room"	August 1932
	"Penalty"	November 1932
	"Ghost Town"	November 1933
	"An Empty House at Night"	April 1935
	"Listening"	February 1935
	"Empty House"	August, 1938
Hawley, Marietta	"The Haunted Mansion"	November 1927
Hay, Sarah Henderson	"Night Terror"	July 1930
Hill, Leona Ames	"Ghost"	August 1935
Holmes, Marjorie	"The Piper of the Pines"	April–May 1931
Hurley, Edith	"The Haunted Forest"	July 1929
	"Sonnet of Death"	June 1930
	"The City of Death"	February 1939
	"The Dream"	October 1939
	"The Great God Death"	November 1940
I'Anson, Alice	"Teotihuacan"	November 1930
	"Phantoms"	June–July 1931
	"Jungle Feud"	November 1931
	"Shadows of Chapultepec"	May 1932
	"Kishi, My Cat"	October 1932
"Irving, Minna" (Minnie Odell)	"Sea Wind"	August 1937
Johnson, Thelma E.	"Fate"	October 1929
Johnson, Victoria Beaudin	"Disillusionment"	December 1935
Kelly, Donna	"Witches"	February 1935
Knox, Minnie Faegre	"Claire de Lune"	May 1928
Koras, Binny	"For Clytie"	November 1926
Lahors, Jean	"The Dance of Death"	May 1926
	"Danse Macabre"	December 1926
Linne, Marie W.	"Mementos"	May 1934
Lovell, Frances Rogers	"Who Are We?"	March 1953
Lydon, Josie McNamara	"White Lilies"	December 1927
MacDonald, Leslyn	"The Ballad of Lalune"	May 1941
Madle, Dorothy Haynes	"Moon Phantoms"	July 1946
Moravsky, Maria	"Into Fantasy"	November 1942
Morgan-Dunham, Ethel	"Magic Carpets"	July 1934
Nelson, Maisie	"Enduring"	September 1940
Nichol (w/ Hannes Bok)	"Weirditties"	July 1944
Ogutsch, Edith	"Reflections of an Egyptian Princess While Being Interred"	January 1954
Peterkin, Dorothy Marie	"The Doomed"	June 1929
Pickard, Alice	"Death"	December 1930
Price (Savino), Lilla Poole	"A Grave"	June 1926
	"The Haunted Castle"	April 1928
Quick, Dorothy	"Candles"	January 1934
	"Ann Boleyn"	November 1934
	"Vampires"	September 1935
	"Unsought Advice"	May 1937
	"After an Air Raid"	January 1943
	"Strange Music"	July 1943
	"Tree Woman"	March 1946
	"Long Watch"	July 1946
	"The River"	September 1948

Author	Poem	Date
	"The Ghostlings"	November 1948
	"Forest God"	November 1949
	"Sea King's Daughter"	January 1950
	"Pattern"	July 1950
	"For a Sea Lover"	January 1951
	"Three Men"	July 1951
	"Sleepers"	September 1951
	"Out of Space"	May 1952
	"House of Life"	July 1953
	"The Dark Things"	September 1953
	"Demon Lover"	November 1953
	"Walpurgis Night"	January 1954
	"Out!"	March 1954
	"Witch's Brew"	March 1954
	"Witch Woman"	May 1954
	"This Night"	September 1954
Quilligan, Janice Hall	"Avalon"	May 1943
Raplee, Elizabeth Virginia	"To a Skull on My Bookshelf"	October 1937
Reilly, June Power	"Why Was My Dream So Real?"	July 1935
Sharon, Mary	"The Ghost"	February 1924
Shaw, Mary C.	"Remembrance"	March 1934
	"Fog"	December 1934
Simons, Katherine	"Because the Moon is Far"	November 1943
	"The Others Said"	September 1947
Stillman, Grace	"The Woods of Averoigne"	June 1934
Stratton, Vivian	"The Dead Speak"	October 1939
	"Weird Things"	December 1939
Tull, Jewell Bothwell	"Ghosts"	August 1930
Turner, Lida Wilson	"The Crow"	June 1930
Uschold, Maud E.	"Old Ghosts"	January 1929
van der Veer, Katherine	"Place Names"	January 1934
	"A Ship Is Sailing"	August 1934
	"Drums of the Congo"	March 1935
Vermilyea, Wilma Dorothy	"Fear: A Fantasy"	February 1936
Wilde, Irene	"Ally of Stars"	February 1938
Wright, Gertrude M.	"The Suicide's Awakening"	May 1925
	"Ghost Lore"	June 1927

Top Three Most Prolific Female Poets: Dorothy Quick: 25; Leah Bodine Drake: 23; Cristel Hastings: 18.

Total number of poems by female poets: 170.
This number represents 29.56% of the total of 575 poems published by all authors.

Note: This percentage is not based upon an elimination of poems by poets of unknown gender. Were we to look at the percentage of poems by known women poets compared to a list only of poems by gender-identifiable poets, this percentage would no doubt be higher.

Omitted from this list is Mary Carolyn Davies and her poem, "Prayer," in *The Thrill Book*, June 15 1919.

SYNOPSIS
Thirty-one Known Women Writers in Six Other Weird Fiction Magazines 1919–1941*
(Not Included as Part of the 203 Women Science Fiction Writers)

1. Bernice T. Banning (1930–1931)
2. Pansy E. Black (1939)
3. Carol Boyd (1939)
4. Leigh Brackett (1940)
5. S. (Susan) Carleton (Jones) (1919)
6. Anna Alice Chapin (1919)

  7. Eli (Elizabeth) Colter (1939–1941)
  8. Marian Stearns Curry (1939)
  9. Mary Caroline Davies (1919)
 10. May Freud Dickenson (1919)
 11. Sophie Wenzel Ellis (1933)
 12. Ada Louvie Evans (1919)
 13. Dorota Flatau (1930–1931)
 14. Phyllis M. Gallagher (1939)
 15. Grace Keon (1932–1933)
 16. Greye La Spina (1919)
 17. Lottie Lesh (1930)
 18. Amelia Reynolds Long (1939)
 19. C. (Catherine) L. (Lucille) Moore (1939)

 20. Maria Moravsky (1939–1940)
 21. "Bassett Morgan" (Grace Jones) (1931–1932)
 22. G. (Gladys) G. (Gordon) Pendarves (Trenery) (1930–1934)
 23. Dorothy Quick (1932 1940)
 24. Olga L. Rosmanith (1940)
 25. "Virginia Stait" (Winfred Brent Russell) (1932)
 26. "Francis Stevens" (Gertrude Barrows Bennett) (1919)
 27. Clare Douglas Stuart (1919)
 28. Pearl Norton Swet (1930)
 29. Lillian Beynon Thomas (1919)
 30. Evangeline Weir (1919)
 31. Sophie Louise Wenzel (Sophie Wenzel Ellis?) (1919)

*Dates after names indicate dates of publication.

TABLE 9
Thirty-one Known Women Writers in Six Other
Weird Fiction Magazines 1919–1941

(Not Included as Part of the 203 Women Science Fiction Writers)

Author	Story	Date	Magazine*
Banning, Bernice T.	"Finger of Kali"	Dec.–Jan. 1930–1931	OS
Black, Pansy E.	"Graah, Foiler of Destiny"	March 1939	GF
Boyd, Carol	"The Man Who Looked Beyond"	December 1939	SS
Brackett, Leigh	"The Tapestry Gate"	August 1940	SS
Carleton (Jones), S. (Susan)	"The Clasp of Rank"	April 1, 1919	TB
Chapin, Anna Alice	"When Dead Lips Speak"	August 1, 1919	TB
Colter, Eli (Elizabeth)	"The Crawling Corpse"	December 1939	SS
	"One Man's Hell"	April 1940	SS
	"Design for Doom"	August 1940	SS
	"The Band of Death"	February 1941	SS
Curry, Marian Stearns	"Kaapi"	October 1939	SS
Davies, Mary Caroline	"Words That Came Alive"	October 1, 1919	TB
Dickenson, May Freud	"The Mate"	July 15, 1919	TB
Ellis, Sophie Wenzel	"White Lady"	January 1933	ST
Evans, Ada Louvie	"Between Two Worlds"	October 1, 1919	TB
Flatau, Dorota	"Golden Rosebud"	Dec.–Jan. 1930–1931	OS
Gallagher, Phyllis M.	"A Despicable Cavalier"	January 1939	GF
Keon, Grace	"The Dance of Yesha"	Winter 1932	OS
	"The Maid of Mir Ammon"	January 1933	MC
	"The Garden of the Nawwab"	April 1933	MC
La Spina, Greye	"Wolf of the Steppes"	March 1, 1919	TB
	"The Broken Idol" (As by "Isra Putnam")	March 15, 1919	TB
	"The Inefficient Ghost" (As by "Isra Putnam")	May 1, 1919	TB
	"From Over the Border"	May 15, 1919	TB
	"The Haunted Landscape"	June 1, 1919	TB
	"The Wax Doll" (As by "Isra Putnam." Reprinted in *Avon Fantasy Reader No. 16* 1951, under her own name.)	August 1, 1919	TB
	"The Ultimate Ingredient"	October 15, 1919	TB
Lesh, Lottie	"The Circle of Illusion"	Oct.–Nov. 1930	OS
Long, Amelia Reynolds	"The Box from the Stars"	April 1939	SS

Author	Story	Date	Magazine*
	"Bride of the Antarctic" (As by "Mordred Weir")	June 1939	SS
Moore, C. (Catherine) L. (Lucille)	"Miracle in Three Dimensions"	April 1939	SS
	With Henry Kuttner & as by "Keith Hammond"		
	"The Invaders"	February 1939	SS
	"Bells of Horror"	April 1939	SS
	"The Body and the Brain"	June 1939	SS
Moravsky, Maria	"The Great Release"	June 1939	SS
	"Let Me Out!"	October 1939	SS
	"Soul of the 'Cello"	December 1939	SS
	"Spider Woman"	April 1940	SS
	"The Hydroponic Monster"	June 1940	SS
	"I Am Going to Cracow!"	August 1940	SS
"Morgan, Bassett" (Grace Jones)	"Rats at the Silver Cheese"	Autumn 1931	OS
	"Tiger"	March 1932	ST
Pendarves (Trenery), G. (Gladys) G. (Gordon)			
	"The Black Camel"	Oct.–Nov. 1930	OS
	"The Veiled Leopard"	Dec.–Jan. 1930–1931	OS
	"The Secret Trail"	Feb.–March 1931	OS
	"Thirty Pieces of Silver"	Summer 1931	OS
	"El Hamel, The Lost One"	Winter 1932	OS
	"The Djinnee of El Sheyb"	Spring 1932	OS
	"Passport to the Desert"	January 1934	MC
Quick, Dorothy	"Scented Gardens"	Spring 1932	OS
	"The Black Adder"	Summer 1932	OS
	"The Bag of Skin"	February 1940	SS
	"The Manci Curse"	December 1940	SS
Rosmanith, Olga L.	"Seance"	April 1940	SS
"Stait, Virginia" (Winfred Brent Russell)			
	"Red Moons"	Spring 1932	OS
"Stevens, Francis" (Gertrude Barrows Bennett)			
	"The Heads of Cerberus" (5 pts.)	August 15, 1919	TB (1st pt.)
Stuart, Clare Douglas	"The Web of Death" (cover)	March 15, 1919	TB
Swet, Pearl Norton	"The Tiger's Eye"	Oct.–Nov. 1930	OS
Thomas, Lillian Beynon	"When Wires Are Down"	September 1, 1919	TB
Weir, Evangeline	"The Kiss of the Silver Flask"	September 1, 1919	TB
Wenzel, Sophie Louise	"The Unseen Seventh"	June 15, 1919	TB

*Magazine Abbreviation Guide:
GF = *Golden Fleece*, published 1938–1939.
MC = *The Magic Carpet Magazine*, published 1933–1934.
OS = *Oriental Stories*, published 1930–1932.
SS = *Strange Stories 1939–1941*.
ST = *Strange Tales of Mystery and Terror*, published 1931–1933.
TB = *The Thrill Book*, published 16 issues only in 1919.

Total Number of Stories by Women Writers: 61
Total Number of Stories in *Thrill Book*: 107
Number of *Thrill Book* Stories by Women: 17
Percentage of *Thrill Book* Stories by Women: 15.8%
Total Number of Stories in *Oriental Stories* by Women: 15
Percentage of Stories in *Oriental Stories* by Women: 16.3%

SYNOPSIS
Fifty-six Known Pre-Second Wave Women Writers
in the Science Fiction Magazines 1961–1965

(Not Included as Part of the 203 Women Science Fiction Writers 1926–1960)

1. Karen Anderson
2. Janet Argo
3. "Jane Beauclerk"
4. Mrs. Virginia Blish (Virginia Kidd)
5. Leigh Brackett
6. Marion Zimmer Bradley
7. Rosel George Brown
8. Doris P. (Pitkin) Buck
9. Susan Chandler
10. Mildred Clingerman
11. Juanita W. Coulson (as "John Jay Wells")
12. Sylvia Dees (Sylvia Dees White Langley)
13. Miriam Allen DeFord
14. Leah Bodine Drake
15. Sylvia Edwards
16. Carol Emshwiller
17. T. (Thelma) D. Hamm (Evans)
18. Gertrude Friedberg
19. Estelle Frye
20. Alice Glaser
21. Phyllis Gotlieb
22. Frances T. Hall
23. L. (Lucile) Taylor Hansen
24. Rosemary Harris
25. Ida Helmer
26. Zenna Henderson
27. Nathalie Henneberg
28. Patricia Highsmith
29. Alma Hill
30. Dorothy B. (Belle) Hughes
31. Sylvia Jacobs
32. Toni Heller Lamb
33. Mary Larson (or Carlson)
34. Ursula K. LeGuin
35. Joy Leache
36. Phyllis MacLennan
37. Suzanne Malaval
38. Francesca Marques
39. Anne McCaffrey
40. Winoa McClintic
41. Beta McGavin
42. Judith Merril
43. Mildred Posselt
44. Florence Engel Randall
45. (Lillian Craig) "Kit" Reed
46. Jane Roberts
47. Joanna Russ
48. Maria Russell
49. Margaret St. Clair
50. Sue Sanford
51. Judith E. Schrier
52. Wilma Shore
53. Evelyn E. Smith
54. Sydney (Joyce) Van Scyoc
55. Anne Walker
56. Kate Wilhelm

Number of Authors 1961–1965: 56
Number of Previously Published Authors 1961–1965: 26
Number of New Authors 1961–1965: 30
Number of Authors 1926–1960: 203
Number of Female Authors 1926–1965: 30 + 203 = 233

TABLE 10
Fifty-six Known Pre-Second Wave Women Writers in the Science Fiction
Magazines 1961–1965

Author Story	Magazine	Date
Anderson, Karen (June Millichamp Kruse)		
"The Piebald Hippogriff"	*Fantastic*	May 1962
"Landscape With Sphinxes"	*Mag. of F & SF*	Nov. 1962
"Treaty In Tartessos"	*Mag. of F & SF*	May 1963
Argo, Janet (with Sam Argo)		
"Hail to the Chief"	*Astounding*	Feb. 1962
"Beauclerk, Jane"		
"We Serve the Star of Freedom"	*Mag. of F & SF*	July 1964
"Lord Moon"	*Mag. of F & SF*	April 1965

Author Story	Magazine	Date
Blish, Mrs. Virginia (Virginia Kidd) (with James Blish)		
"On the Wall of the Lodge"	Galaxy	June 1962
Brackett, Leigh		
"The Road to Sinharat"	Amazing	May 1963
"Purple Priestess of the Mad Moon"	Mag. of F & SF	Oct. 1964
"Quest of the Starhope"	Treasury of Great SF, #1	1964
	(Orig. Thrilling Wonder April 1949)	
"The Woman From Altair"	Treasury of Great SF, #2	1965
	(Orig. Startling Stories July 1951)	
Bradley, Marion Zimmer		
"Black and White"	Amazing	Nov. 1962
"Measureless to Man"	Amazing	Dec. 1962
"Phoenix" (with Ted White)	Amazing	Feb. 1963
"Another Rib" (w/ "John Jay Wells")	AmazingMag. of F & SF	June 1963
Brown, Rosel George		
"Visiting Professor"	Fantastic	Feb. 1961
"The Ultimate Sin"	Mag. of F & SF	Oct. 1961
"And A Tooth"	Fantastic	August 1962
"Fruiting Body"	Mag. of F & SF	August 1962
"The Artist"	Amazing	May 1964
Buck, Doris P. (Pitkin)		
"Birth of a Gardener"	Mag. of F & SF	June 1961
"Green Sunrise"	Mag. of F & SF	Nov. 1961
"Come Where My Love Lies Dreaming"	Mag. of F & SF	Feb. 1964
"Story of a Curse"	Mag. of S & SF	June 1965
Chandler, Susan (with A. Bertram Chandler)		
"The Long Way"	Worlds of Tomorrow	Nov. 1964
Clingerman, Mildred		
"Measure My Love"	Mag. of F & SF	Oct. 1962
"A Red Heart and Blue Roses"	Mag. of F & SF	May 1964
Coulson, Juanita W. (as "John Jay Wells")		
"Another Rib" (w/ Marion Zimmer Bradley)	Mag. of F & SF	June 1963
(counted previously under Bradley)		
DeFord, Miriam Allen		
"The Dreaming Eyes"	Fantastic	Jan. 1961
"The Cage"	Mag. of F & SF	June 1961
"Oh, Rats!"	Galaxy	Dec. 1961
"The Akkra Case"	Amazing	Jan. 1962
"The Transit of Venus"	Mag. of F & SF	June 1962
"The Voyage of the 'Deborah Pratt'"	Mag. of F & SF	April 1963
"Where the Phph Pebbles Go"	Worlds of Tomorrow	April 1963
"Inside Story"	Gamma	1964
"Slips Take Over"	Mag. of F & SF	Sept. 1964
"The 1980 President"	Galaxy	Oct. 1964
"The Absolutely Perfect Murder"	Mag. of F & SF	Feb. 1965
"The Expendables"	Mag. of F & SF	July 1965
"The Smiling Future"	If	Oct. 1965
Dees, Sylvia (Sylvia Dees White) (with Ted White)		
"Policy Conference"	Gamma	Sept. 1965
Drake, Leah Bodine		
"Time and the Spinx"	Mag. of F & SF	Feb. 1965
Edwards, Sylvia		
"The End of Evan Essant . . . ?"	Mag. of F & SF	April 1962
Emshwiller, Carol		
"Adapted"	Mag. of F & SF	May 1961

Author Story	Magazine	Date
Evans, T. (Thelma) D. Hamm (Mrs. E. Everett Evans)		
"Floor of Heaven"	*Amazing*	Jan. 1961
"The Survivors"	*Amazing*	August 1961
"Masters of Space"	*If*	Nov. 1961–
(with E. Everett Evans & E. E. Smith)		Jan. 1962
Friedberg, Gertrude		
"The Short and Happy Death of George Frumkin"	*Mag. of F & SF*	April 1963
Frye, Estelle		
"The Face in the Mask"	*Fantastic*	June 1961
Glaser, Alice		
"The Tunnel Ahead"	*Mag. of F & SF*	Nov. 1961
Gotlieb, Phyllis		
"Gingerbread Boy"	*If*	Jan. 1961
"Sunburst"	*Amazing*	March–May 1964
"Valedictory"	*Amazing*	August 1964
Hall, Frances T.		
"A as in Android"	*If*	August 1964
Hansen, L. (Lucile) Taylor		
"The Undersea Tube"	*Amazing*	May 1961
"The Prince of Liars"	*Amazing*	Oct. 1963
Harris, Rosemary		
"Hamlin"	*Mag of F & SF*	Sept. 1961
Helmer, Ida		
"Temptation"	*Fantastic*	March 1961
Henderson, Zenna		
"Return"	*Mag of F & SF*	March 1961
"Shadow on the Moon"	*Mag of F & SF*	March 1962
"Subcommittee"	*Mag of F & SF*	July 1962
"Deluge"	*Mag of F & SF*	Oct. 1963
"No Different Flesh"	*Mag of F & SF*	May 1965
"The Effectives"	*Worlds of Tomorrow*	May 1965
Henneberg, Nathalie ("Charles Henneberg")		
"Moon Fishers"	*Mag of F & SF*	April 1962
Highsmith, Patricia		
"The Snail Watcher"	*Gamma*	1964
Hill, Alma		
"Answering Service"	*If*	Jan. 1965
Hughes, Dorothy B. (Belle)		
"The Granny Woman"	*Gamma*	Fall 1963
Jacobs, Sylvia		
"Young Man from Elsewhen"	*If*	March 1961
Lamb, Toni Heller		
"The Happy Place"	*Mag of F & SF*	July 1964
Larson, Mary (Carlson)		
"The Time of Cold"	*If*	Sept. 1963
Le Guin, Ursula K.		
"April in Paris" (debut)	*Fantastic*	Sept. 1962
"The Masters"	*Fantastic*	Feb. 1963
"Darkness Box"	*Fantastic*	Nov. 1963
"The Word of Unbinding"	*Fantastic*	Jan. 1964
"The Rule of Names"	*Fantastic*	April 1964
"Selection"	*Amazing*	August 1964
"The Dowry of Angyar"	*Amazing*	Sept. 1964
Leache, Joy		
"Satisfaction Guaranteed"	*Galaxy*	Dec. 1961
MacLennan, Phyllis		
"A Contract in Karasthan"	*Fantastic*	July 1963

Author Story	Magazine	Date
Malaval, Suzanne		
"The Devil's God-Daughter"	Mag of F & SF	Sept. 1962
Marques, Francesca		
"Michael"	Gamma	Fall 1963
McCaffrey, Anne		
"The Ship Who Sang"	Mag of F & SF	April 1961
McClintic, Winona		
"Four Days in the Corner"	Mag of F & SF	August 1961
McGavin, Beta		
"Dear Nan Glanders"	Amazing	August 1962
Merril, Judith		
"The Deep Down Dragon"	Galaxy	August 1961
"The Shrine of Temptation"	Fantastic	April 1962
"The Lonely"	Worlds of Tomorrow	Oct. 1963
Posselt, Mildred		
"The Flower"	Mag of F & SF	May 1961
Randall, Florence Engel		
"One Long Ribbon"	Fantastic	July 1962
"The Boundary Beyond"	Fantastic	July 1964
Reed, (Lillian Craig) "Kit"		
"Judas Bomb"	Mag of F & SF	April 1961
"Piggy"	Mag of F & SF	August 1961
"To Lift a Ship"	Mag of F & SF	April 1962
"The New You"	Mag of F & SF	Sept. 1962
"Tell Me Doctor—Please"	Mag of F & SF	April 1963
"The Automatic Tiger"	Mag of F & SF	March 1964
"Cynosure"	Mag of F & SF	June 1964
"Rescue Mission"	If	Oct. 1964
"On the Orphan's Colony"	Mag of F & SF	Dec. 1964
Roberts, Jane		
"Three Times Around"	Mag of F & SF	May 1964
Russ, Joanna		
"My Dear Emily"	Mag of F & SF	July 1962
"There is Another Shore, You Know, On the Other Side"	Mag of F & SF	Sept. 1963
"I Had Vacantly Crumpled It Into My Pocket . . . But by God, Eliot, *It Was a Photograph from Life!*"	Mag of F & SF	August 1964
"Wilderness Year"	Mag of F & SF	Dec. 1964
Russell, Maria		
"The Deer Park"	Mag of F & SF	Jan. 1962
St. Clair, Margaret		
"The House in Bel Aire"	If	Jan. 1961
"Lochinvar"	Galaxy	August 1961
"An Old Fashioned Bird Christmas"	Galaxy	Dec. 1961
"Roberta"	Galaxy	Oct. 1962
"The Monitor"	Wonder Stories	1963
"The Rotohouse"	Treasury of Great SF Stories	1964
Sanford, Sue		
"Mrs. Pribley's Underdog"	Mag of F & SF	Feb. 1965
Schrier, Judith E.		
"Satyr"	Amazing	June 1965
Shore, Wilma		
"A Bulletin From the Trustees of the Institute for Advanced Research at Marmouth, Mass."	Mag of F & SF	August 1964

Author Story	Magazine	Date
Smith, Evelyn E.		
"Sentry of the Sky"	*Galaxy*	Feb. 1961
"Softly While You're Sleeping"	*Mag of F & SF*	April 1961
"Robert E. Lee at Moscow"	*Mag of F & SF*	Oct. 1961
"They Also Serve"	*Mag of F & SF*	Sept. 1962
"Little Gregory"	*Mag of F & SF*	Feb. 1964
Van Scyoc, Sydney (Joyce)		
"Shatter the Wall"	*Galaxy*	Feb. 1962
"Bimmie Says"	*Galaxy*	Oct. 1962
"Pollony Undiverted"	*Galaxy*	Feb. 1963
"Zack With His Scar"	*Mag of F & SF*	March 1963
"Cornie on the Walls"	*Fantastic*	August 1963
"Soft and Soupy Whispers"	*Galaxy*	April 1964
"One Man's Dream"	*Mag of F & SF*	Nov. 1964
"The Dead Ones"	*Worlds of Tomorrow*	Jan. 1965
Walker, Anne		
"The Oversight of Dirty-Jets Ryan"	*Mag of F & SF*	Dec. 1961
Wilhelm, Kate		
"A Time to Keep"	*Mag of F & SF*	Jan. 1962
"The Man Without a Planet"	*Mag of F & SF*	July 1962
"The Last Days of the Captain"	*Amazing*	Nov. 1962
"The Man Who Painted Tomorrow"	*Fantastic*	March 1965

Number of Stories 1961–1965: 133
Number of Stories 1926–1960: 922
Number of Female-Authored Stories 1926–1965: 133 + 922 = 1,055.

TABLE 11
Twenty Women Screenwriters of Fantasy & Science Fiction Films 1916–1949

Author	Film	Studio	Date
Anderson, Doris	*The Girl from Scotland Yard*	Paramount	1937
Barish, Mildred	*The Phantom Creeps* (co-author) (serial)	Universal	1939
Berenger, Clara S.	*Dr. Jekyll and Mr. Hyde*	Paramount	1920
Dane, Clemence	*The Trans-Atlantic Tunnel* (co-author with Curt Siodmak)	Gaumont-British	1935
Hayward, Lillie	*The Walking Dead* (co-author)	Warner Bros.	1936
	Television Spy (co-author)	Paramount	1939
Kelly, Nancy	*Tarzan's Desert Mystery*	RKO	1943
Kuhn, Irene	*The Mask of Fu Manchu* (co-author)	MGM	1932
Leblanc, Georgette	*L'Inhumaine (The Inhuman One)* (co-author)	France	1923/24
Lucoque, Nellie E.	*She*	Barker-Lucoque (British)	1916
Murillo, Mary	*She*	Fox	1917
Neville, Grace	*Air Hawks* (co-author)	Columbia	1935
O'Neill, Ella	*The Phantom of the Air* (co-author) (serial, based on her story)	Universal	1933
	Flash Gordon (co-author) (serial)	Universal	1936
Perkins, Lynn	*The Purple Monster Strikes* (co-author) (serial, also known as *D-Day on Mars* in feature form 1966)	Republic	1945

Author	Film	Studio	Date
Purcell, Gertrude	*The Invisible Woman* (co-author)	Universal	1941
Ramsay, Alicia	*The Secret Kingdom*	Stoll (British)	1925
Rose, Ruth	*King Kong* (co-author)	RKO	1933
	Son of Kong	RKO	1933
	She	RKO	1935
	Mighty Joe Young	RKO	1949
Ryerson, Florence	*The Return of Dr. Fu Manchu* (co-author)	Paramount	1930
Stadie, Hildegarde	*Maniac*	Roadshow Attractions	1934
	Marihuana (co-author)	Roadshow Attractions	1936
von Harbou, Thea	*Destiny*	UFA	1921
	Dr. Mabuse	Decla-Bioscop/UFA	1922
	Metropolis (based on her novel of same title)	UFA/Paramount	1927
	Woman in the Moon (co-author with Fritz Lang)	GMBH-UFA	1928
	M	UFA	1931
Weisberg, Brenda	*The Mad Ghoul* (co-author)	Universal	1943

Appendix II: The Women That Time Forgot

Brief Biographies of 133 Early Women Science Fiction Writers, 1926–1960*

Karen Anderson (June Millichamp Kruse), (1932–   ): Anderson was born in Erlanger, Kentucky. In 1953 she married Poul Anderson (1926–2001) and is the co-author with him of the "King of Ys" novels, including *Roma Mater* (1986), *Gallicenae* (1987), *Dahut* (1988), and *The Dog and the Wolf* (1988). In 1958 she edited an appreciation of Henry Kuttner, in which well-known authors remembered him, with an extensive bibliography. An avid mystery reader, while living in Washington, D.C., she founded the Red Circle, the local branch of the Baker Street Irregulars, the Sherlock Holmes fan club. For more than twenty years (May, 1956–February, 1978) she was also a member of the legendary science fiction fan group, the Fantasy Amateur Press Association (FAPA).

Charlotte Armstrong (Lewi) (1905–1969): Born and raised in the gritty Upper Peninsula mining town of Vulcan, Michigan, Armstrong attended the University of Wisconsin and graduated from Barnard College, Columbia University, in 1925. She then began working as a fashion writer while writing poetry for magazines such as *The New Yorker*, as well as plays. Two of her plays, *The Happiest Days* (1939) and *The Ring Around Elizabeth* (1941), had short Broadway runs. She then became a prolific mystery novelist, with her first such novel, *Lay On, MacDuff* (1942), centering around a murder in a theatrical setting. This was soon followed by *The Case of the Weird Sisters* (1943).

In the late 1940s she and her family moved to Southern California, where she remained the rest of her life. While there, she became a scriptwriter for the TV series, *Alfred Hitchcock Presents. Trouble in Thor* (1953) takes place in a hardscrabble Michigan mining town similar to her hometown of Vulcan. Her 1956 novel, *A Dram of Poison*, won the Edgar Allen Poe Award for best novel of the year from the Mystery Writers of America. This "Edgar" Award is the mystery equivalent of science fiction's Hugo Award. Her short fiction was twice nominated for Edgars and "The Enemy" won an *Ellery Queen* award for best story in that magazine.

Martin H. Greenberg, Joseph Olander, and Charles Waugh reprinted "Three Day Magic," her story from *The Magazine of Fantasy and Science Fiction,* in their 1979 anthology, *Mysteri-*

ous Visions. In introducing it they said Armstrong, "may have been America's best mystery authoress. . . . Most famous for suspense and style. But 'Three Day Magic,' a powerful and almost forgotten novella, indicates that had she chosen, she could have become equally famous for humor and style."

Armstrong died at age 64 in Glendale, CA, and her final novel, *The Protege,* was published posthumously in 1970.

"Pauline Ashwell" (Pauline Whitby) (1928–   ): As far as America is concerned, British writer "Pauline Ashwell" was discovered by John W. Campbell. He published her first American story ("Unwillingly to School," *Astounding,* January, 1958), which was later Hugo-nominated for best short story of the year. Because of it, she was nominated for "Best New Author," a promising debut for any writer. Campbell also published her second and third stories, the latter ("The Lost Kafoozalum," *Astounding/Analog,* October, 1960) also being Hugo-nominated for best short story.

However, she actually made her debut as "Paul Ashwell" with "Invasion from Venus" in an obscure war-time British SF magazine, *Yankee Science Fiction* (No. 21, July, 1942), which, despite "No. 21," only published three issues. At the time, she was only fourteen years old.

After her American debuts, she published nothing more until two stories appeared in 1966 under the pseudonym "Paul Ash." One of these, "The Wings of a Bat," was a Nebula nominee that year, the first year the Nebulas were awarded. Thereafter she dropped from sight again, not reappearing until 1982 when her story, "Rats in the Moon" appeared, also as by "Paul Ash."

There was nothing more until 1988, when she published a spurt of stories, including "Fatal Statistics," "Interference," "Make Your Own Universe," "Shortage in Time," and "Thingummy Hall." In 1990 she published "The Hornless Ones" and in 1991 "Man Opening a Door," which was a Nebula nominee for that year. In 1993 her novel, "The Man Who Stayed Behind," was serialized in *Analog,* but it never appeared outside that magazine. Her first novel to appear in book form was *Unwillingly to Earth,* published by Tor in 1992. This was followed by Tor's 1995 publication of *Project Farcry.* That same year she published the short stories "Hunted Head" and "Time's Revenge." In 1996 came "Bonehead."

Having twice been nominated for the Hugo and twice for the Nebula, and having been hailed in the Fifties as one of the "Best New Authors," no doubt her talent would have won her a larger reputation had her output not been so sporadic over the decades.

Myrle Benedict, (?–?): *Fantastic Universe* editor Hans Stefan Santesson published three of her stories in the late 1950s. He chose her 1958 story, "Sit by the Fire," for his 1960 "best of" anthology, *The Fantastic Universe Omnibus.* In his introductory note he told us that, "Myrle Benedict's more poetical friends say she looks like Ondine; others say Lilith. Not having met her, I can only report that this unusually sensitive writer, who now lives in Corpus Christi [Texas], is described as tall and green-eyed—and partial to cats. . . ." "Ondine" is a variant of "Undine," the elemental being who inhabits water according to the 1657 theory of Paracelsus. In other words, she looked like a water nymph.

Margot Bennett, (1912–1980): British mystery writer, beginning in 1945. Novels included *The Widow of Bath* (1952), *The Man Who Didn't Fly* (1956) (nominated for the Edgar Allan Poe Award), and *The Furious Masters* (1968). Her first SF novel, *The Long Way Back* (1954), finds Africa colonizing a post-holocaust Great Britain.

Pansy E. Black, (?–?): Hugo Gernsback published two of her stories in his SF Series booklets in 1930 and 1932, but she also published in other genre magazines of the day. For example, her historical-fantasy, "Graah, Foiler of Destiny," appeared in the short-lived late 1930s' magazine, *Golden Fleece Historical Adventure.*

Elizabeth Mann Borgese, (1918–2002): Borgese was the youngest of Nobel Prize-winning novelist Thomas Mann's three daughters and last surviving child. Trained as a classical pianist and cellist, she graduated from the Zurich Conservatory of Music in 1938. In 1939 she married Giuseppe Antonio Borgese, thirty-six years her senior. He was a noted Sicilian-American anti-Fascist exile and scholar of Italian literature who taught at the University of Chicago. She was also the sister-in-law of gay British poet W. H. Auden, who married her actress-writer sister, Erika Mann, in 1935. This was solely to provide her with a British passport so that she could escape from Nazi Germany.

Elizabeth became an American citizen in 1941 and worked as a researcher and editor in Chicago, including two years as executive secretary of the board of the Encyclopedia Britannica in the mid–1960s. After her husband's death in 1952, she continued her studies. She eventually became a senior fellow at the Center for the Study of Democratic Institutions in Santa Barbara, California, where Frank K. Kelly, a well-known early 1930s' science fiction writer, served as vice president. In 1979 she joined the faculty of Dalhousie University in Halifax, Nova Scotia, first as a professor of political science, then as an adjunct law professor. In 1983 she became a Canadian citizen.

An environmentalist much concerned with the oceans, she was a founder of the International Oceans Institute based in Malta and wrote many books on the subject. The best known of these is *The Future of the Oceans* (1986). She helped organize the Peace in the Oceans Conference in 1970, the first of 30 such international meetings. These worldwide gatherings eventually resulted in the 1982 United Nations Law of the Seas treaty.

She died while vacationing in St. Moritz, Switzerland and is survived by a son and two daughters: Marcel Deschamps Borgese, of Halifax, Angelica Borgese, of New York City, and Turkey, and Dr. Domenica Borgese, of Milan, Italy.

In addition to the two 1959 magazine stories on the list, she published another 1959 story, "Twin's Wail," in Frederik Pohl's pioneering original paperback anthology, *Star SF No. 6.*

Elizabeth Bowen (Dorothea Cole), (1899–1973): Bowen was born in Dublin, Ireland, and educated at Downe House School in England. She was a prolific and major Anglo-Irish novelist and short story writer, as well as a critic and a popular touring lecturer. Her first novel, *The Hotel* (1927), was an upper-class romance, but her 1929 short story, "The Cat Jumps," one of her best known, was a haunted house tale wherein the supernatural elements were used to explore the nature of fear.

She moved to London in 1933 and became friends with Virginia Woolf and Iris Murdoch. Her 1938 novel, *The Death of the Heart,* catapulted her to fame as a major novelist. The Blitz during World War II inspired many of her best stories. She published an autobiographical novel, *Seven Winters,* in 1942 while *Bowen's Court* (1942) was a family history. Her perceptive works of literary criticism included *English Novelists* (1942) and *Collected Impressions* (1950). Her 1934 collection, *The Cat Jumps,* displayed her gift for supernatural fiction and *The Demon Lover* (1941), her most famous short story, is considered a major contribution to the form. She died in London at age 73.

Leigh (Douglass) Brackett, (1915–1978): Brackett was born and raised in Los Angeles. She was discovered by John W. Campbell in 1940 and became a major and prolific writer who contributed to many genres, including the fantasy, science fiction, western, and detective fields. She was the recipient of both the Jules Verne Award and, from the Western Writers of America, the Silver Spur Award. In 1946 she married noted SF writer Edmond Hamilton (1904–1977). They were joint Guests of Honor at the 22nd World Science Fiction Convention in 1964.

In the late Forties and early Fifties she was the incontestable "Queen of the Space Opera." Perhaps the best example of her work of this type is *The Sword of Rhiannon* (1953). However, she was quite capable of writing other types of science fiction, such as her 1955 novel, *The Long Tomorrow* (perhaps her best SF story), a sophisticated treatment of post-nuclear holocaust society.

She also wrote many hard-boiled detective short stories and novels. It was the latter which brought her to the attention of Hollywood director Howard Hawks, who recruited her to work for him. She then wrote many Hollywood screenplays, including co-authorship with William Faulkner of Raymond Chandler's classic, *The Big Sleep* (1946), starring Humphrey Bogart and Lauren Bacall. She also wrote John Wayne's *Rio Bravo* (1958). Both of these were directed by Howard Hawks. Her other notable screenplays included Chandler's *The Long Goodbye* (1973) and *The Empire Strikes Back* (1979), the latter for George Lucas. This was the middle film in the original *Star Wars* trilogy. She died before the film was released, but was posthumously awarded a 1980 Hugo for the screenplay.

Marion (Eleanor) Zimmer Bradley, (1930–1999): Bradley was born in Albany, New York, and studied at the N.Y. State College for Teachers before graduating from Hardin-Simmons University in Abilene, Texas, in 1964. She was married to Robert A. Bradley from 1949–1963, with whom she had a son. In 1964 she married Walter Breen, with whom she had a son and a daughter. She claimed to have once been a target in a circus knife-throwing act.

She was a prolific fantasy and science fiction writer who also dabbled in other genres, such as the romance field and lesbian literature. She contributed to the lesbian magazine, *The Ladder,* and wrote several lesbian romances under pseudonyms. One of her significant contributions to science fiction was the Darkover planetary romance series, which she began in 1958. Her most successful novel, however, was *The Mists of Avalon* (1982). This retold the King Arthur story from the viewpoint of Morgan le Fay and other women. Its success made her wealthy enough to briefly subsidize her own fantasy magazine (*Marion Zimmer Bradley's Fantasy Magazine,* 1988–2000) and resulted in a 2001 TV mini-series. Her editorship of the long-running *Sword and Sorceress* series of paperback anthologies also did much to transform the male-dominated sword-and-sorcery sub-genre into an "equal opportunity" literary field.

Rhoda Broughton, (1840–1920): British author Broughton was the niece by marriage of famous English ghost story writer J. Sheridan Le Fanu. She lived for many years with her widowed sister in Oxford. She published her first novel in 1867. By the 1870s she had become well known as the author of many light and witty three-volume novels of Victorian country life featuring outspoken and articulate heroines. Among the most noteworthy are *Belinda* (1884) and *Not Wisely But Too Well* (1904). In her later career she focused on short stories. Some of these were ghost stories, such as "It Was a Dream" (1873), collected in *Tales for Christmas Eve* (1873), enlarged and reprinted as *Twilight Stories* (1879, 1947).

Rosel George Brown, (1926–1967): Brown was born and died in New Orleans, where she was a welfare worker and teacher. She married W. Burlie Brown, a professor at Tulane University. She was the mother of two children and the holder of B.A. from Tulane (1946) and an M.A. in ancient Greek history from the University of Minnesota (1950). She is most well known for her mid–1960s "Sibyl Sue Blue" series of stories. These featured the interstellar adventures of a tough female cop and her teenage daughter. Her early work is collected in *A Handful of Time* (1963). She collaborated with Keith Laumer on the space opera, *Earthblood* (1966), and was just becoming popular when she died at age forty-one.

Doris P. (Pitkin) Buck, (1898–1980): Buck was born in New York City and graduated from Bryn Mawr College in 1920. She earned a Master's from Columbia University in 1925. She said she became "wedded to space" at age seven when she saw a photo of Saturn's rings. She became a semi-professional stage actress before marrying Richard Buck and settling in Alexandria, Virginia and then Washington, D.C. She taught English at Ohio State University and attended the renowned Milford Science Fiction Writers Conference. She was a founding member of the Science Fiction Writers of America (SFWA) and her 1966 short story, "The Little Blue Weeds of Spring," was nominated for that year's Nebula Award.

In addition to science fiction, she wrote numerous articles for newspapers and magazines on travel, remodeling, gardening, and landscaping. She wrote right up to her death at age 82 on December 4, 1980. Her last publication, the SF poem "Travel Tip," appeared in June 1981 issue of *The Magazine of Fantasy and Science Fiction.*

Alice Bullock, (?–?): Like several other women science fiction writers, Bullock seems to have come out of SF fandom. She seemed familiar with the fanzines of the late 1940s and early 1950s, which published her fan fiction. For example, Rog Phillips, in his September, 1951 *Amazing Stories* column reviewing various fanzines, praised the "nice theme" of her story, "Dormitory of the Dead." This story was published by W. Paul Ganley in a 1951 issue of his fanzine, *Fan-Fare.*

"Esther Carlson" (Joanna Collier), (1920–   ): She was born in Marshalltown, Iowa, and attended Grinnell College and the University of Wisconsin. She lived in Rochester, New York and worked as a legal secretary during World War II and as a public school secretary thereafter. *Moon Over the Back Fence,* her 1947 novel, featured an imaginary companion to a little girl. Her mainstream fiction appeared in such magazines as *Atlantic Monthly.* Her stories in *The Magazine of Fantasy and Science Fiction* were a linked fantasy sequence featuring the adventures of Dr. Aesop Abercrombie. Her "Room With a View" was first published in *Fantastic* (May–June, 1953) and later anthologized in Charles Beaumont's *The Fiend in You* (1962). She eventually married the noted British poet, screenwriter, and short story writer John Collier (1901–1980).

Agatha (Miller) Christie (Mallowan), (1890–1976): Christie was born in Torquay, Devon, England, and was one of the most famous detective writers of all time. She was home-schooled by her mother until age 16 and married Colonel Archibald Christie in 1914. During World War I she worked in a hospital dispensary, which gave her an intimate knowledge of poisons. Her first novel, *The Mysterious Affair at Styles* (1920), introduced her famous Belgian detective, Hercule Poirot (her other main detective was Miss Marple). In 1926 she divorced her husband and in 1930 married the noted archaeologist Sir Max Mallowan, whom she accompanied on digs in Iraq and Syria.

She wrote sixty-six detective novels, six novels as "Mary Westmacott," two autobiographies, and several plays, including *The Mousetrap*. This play holds the record for the longest-running British play and is still running in London decades after its premiere. Her excellent collection of supernatural tales, *The Hound of Death* (1933), included the classic, "The Last Seance." She was presented with a Grand Master Edgar Allan Poe Award in 1954 by the Mystery Writers of America.

(Anne) Pauline Clarke, (1921–   ): She is a prolific British writer of children's books, such as *Merlin's Magic* (1953), many under the pseudonym of "Helen Clare." Her Young Adult fantasy novels include *The Twelve and the Genii* (1962), *The Return of the Twelve* (1964), and *The Two Faces of Silenus* (1972).

Helen (Worrell) Clarkson (McCloy), (1904–1994): Primarily a writer of detective fiction under the name of Helen McCloy, Clarkson was born in New York City. Her mother, Helen Worrell McCloy, was also a writer, while her father, William McCloy, was the managing editor of the *New York Evening Sun*. She was educated at Brooklyn's Quaker Friends School and in 1923 attended the Sorbonne, in Paris. She remained in Europe until 1932, working as a correspondent for *Hearst's Universal News Service* (1927–1932), a freelance contributor to *Parnassus* and London's *Morning Post*, as well as an art critic for *International Studio*.

She began writing mysteries in 1930. Her first novel, *Dance of Death*, appeared in 1933. In *The One That Got Away* (1945), she explored the psychology of fascism, which she felt was rooted in the hatred of women. In 1946 she married David Dresser, author of the popular "Mike Shayne" detective novels under the pseudonym "Brett Halliday." Together they founded the Torquil Publishing Co. and the Halliday and McCloy literary agency.

In the Fifties and Sixties she reviewed mysteries for Connecticut newspapers and received the Edgar Allen Poe Award from the Mystery Writers of America in 1953 for her criticism. She also served as the first female president of the Mystery Writers of America. Her 1950 novel, *Through a Glass, Darkly*, was recommended by Anthony Boucher as an excellent treatment of the Doppelganger theme. Her only SF novel was *The Last Day: A Novel of the Day After Tomorrow* (1959), in which a woman on an isolated island witnesses a nuclear holocaust. This was an expansion of her 1958 short story, "The Last Day," which Mike Ashley praised as, "a poignant story of the end of mankind and of the last human and the last songbird alive."

Mildred (McElroy) Clingerman, (1918–1997): Born in Oklahoma not too long after it became a state, Clingerman became a housewife in Arizona. She also collected Victorian travel journals. Most of her fiction appeared in *The Magazine of Fantasy and Science Fiction* in the 1950s, although some work also appeared in mainstream women's magazines, such as "The Little Witch of Elm Street" (*Woman's Home Companion*, October, 1956). Much of her best work was collected in *A Cupful of Space* (1961).

Lucy Cores (Kortchmar), (1912–2003): A writer of historical and romance novels and musical mysteries, such as *Corpse de Ballet*. She was born in Moscow, Russia, where her father was a prosperous attorney. The Cores family fled Russia for Poland and then Paris following the 1917 revolution. In 1921 they emigrated to America, where her father became a violinist with the NBC Philharmonic, under the direction of Arturo Toscanini. Her uncle was also a violinist, who taught Jack Benny how to play poorly.

As a girl she attended Manhattan's Ethical Culture School and graduated from Barnard

College. She then worked as a graphic artist and book illustrator. She met Emil Kortchmar in 1942, quickly married, and their first child, Michael, was born in 1944. Another son, Daniel, came in 1946 and the family moved to Larchmont, New York. She had a good friend who was a dancer and began writing mysteries set in the world of the ballet.

In the 1950s the family began spending summers on Martha's Vineyard and in 1957 they moved to the island permanently. She continued to publish numerous novels, such as *Mermaid Summer,* about the island, *Woman in Love,* about an early love affair, and *The Year of December,* a novel about the Russian adventures of Claire Clairmonte, a mistress of Lord Byron.

In 1988 the couple welcomed the first of four grandchildren. In 1990 Emil died and Lucy left Martha's Vineyard for New York City, although she continued to summer on the island. She was writing a novel about Russian poet Alexander Pushkin when she died in her sleep at her summer home on the island at age 91.

Mary Elizabeth Counselman, (1911–1995): Counselman was born and raised in Alabama, which featured prominently in her fiction. She married in 1941 and spent most of her life in Gadsden, Alabama, where she lived on a houseboat. She attended the University of Alabama and Montevallo University. Her work, which began to appear in 1931, was mostly regional supernaturalism and appeared in such mainstream publications as *Collier's, The Saturday Evening Post, Good Housekeeping,* and *Ladies' Home Journal.*

Counselman began writing poetry as a child, selling her first poem when she was only six. She debuted in Weird *Tales* in 1933, where she quickly became recognized as one of the foremost writers of macabre fiction. She eventually published thirty stories in that magazine. In addition, her poetry appeared often in the magazine between 1932–1941. Her "Three Marked Pennies" (August, 1934) was one of the most popular stories to appear in *Weird Tales.* "Seventh Sister" appeared in *Weird Tales* in 1942 and is one of the handful of voodoo stories (a rare sub-genre in itself) written by a woman. Her fiction was published in several collections, most notably *Half in Shadow* from Arkham House (1964, 1978). Her 1977 collection, *African Yesterdays,* featured her jungle stories from the old pulps. She also published much fantasy poetry and some of her verse was published in August Derleth's *Dark of the Moon* (1947).

M. (Monette) A. Cummings, (1914–?): She was a writer in various pulp genres who began writing SF in 1955. Her fiction was collected in *Exile and Other Tales of Fantasy* (1968).

(Elizabeth M.) "Betsy" Curtis (1918–2002): Curtis was born in Toledo, Ohio, and earned a B.A. (1939) and an M.A. (1941) in English from Oberlin College. She earned a second Master's, in Education, from Allegheny College in 1966. She debuted in *The Magazine of Fantasy and Science Fiction* in 1950 with her story, "Divine Right." When her second story, "The Old Ones," appeared in the December, 1950 issue of *Imagination: Stories of Science and Fantasy,* the editor said she was then living in Canton, New York.

Until 1973 her highly praised work appeared regularly in *Amazing Stories, Galaxy, Planet Stories, Imagination, Marvel Science Stories, Universe Science Fiction, Infinity Science Fiction, Authentic Science Fiction,* and *Worlds of If.* But it was "The Stieger Effect," which John W. Campbell published in *Analog* (October, 1968), with which Curtis came closest to the brass ring, it being a 1969 Hugo Award nominee for Best Short Story.

She was also active in the Society for Creative Anachronism and her costumes won awards at many science fiction conventions, including Worldcons in Philadelphia, Detroit, Pittsburgh and Cleveland.

"Clemence Dane" (Winifred Ashton), (1888–1965): Dane was a teacher, actress, and noted British novelist, dramatist, and screenwriter. She took her pseudonym from the Church of St. Clement Danes in The Strand. She studied art at the Slade School, then began an acting career in 1913 under the stage name of "Diana Cortis." Her first novel, *Regiment of Women* (1917), appeared during World War I. Her third book, *Legend* (1919), was about the supernatural relationship between a dead author and her biographer. It was rewritten as the successful play, *A Bill of Divorcement* (1921). In 1932 it was produced as a successful Hollywood movie of the same name. It was in this production that Katharine Hepburn made her impressive film debut, almost eclipsing her co-star, the great actor John Barrymore.

Dane's 1927 book, *The Babyons,* traced a family curse over four generations. Her 1932 play, *Wild Decembers,* was about the Bronte sisters. In 1935 she co-authored (with Kurt Siodmak) the screenplay for the famous early British SF movie, *The Tunnel* (aka *Transatlantic Tunnel*). That same year she wrote the screenplay for Greta Garbo's starring vehicle in Leo Tolstoy's *Anna Karenina.* She followed these with the screenplays for *Fire Over England* (1937), starring Laurence Olivier and Vivien Leigh, and *The Sidewalks of London* (1938), starring Leigh with Charles Laughton, Rex Harrison, and Tyrone Guthrie.

In her 1939 novel, *The Arrogant History of White Ben,* the hero was an animated scarecrow charged with leading Britain out of the Great Depression. Between 1955–1957 she edited the "Novels of Tomorrow" series for publisher Michael Joseph Ltd., which attempted to establish science fiction in Britain as a "legitimate" literary genre worthy of book publication. For this series she published both British authors, such as John Christopher and John Wyndham, as well as American authors, such as C. M. Kornbluth and Wilson Tucker.

Her last play was *Eighty in the Shade* (1958), written especially for the golden wedding anniversary of actors Lewis Casson and Dame Sybil Thorndike, who created the principal roles. She died in London at age 77.

Dorothy Salisbury Davis (1916–   ): Davis was born and raised in Chicago. She later moved to New York City, the setting for many of her short stories. She was a prolific mystery writer of more than 20 novels who won many awards and received four Edgar Allen Poe Award nominations for best novel. Davis was also voted a Grand Master by the Mystery Writers of America in 1984. She also served as president and executive vice president of that organization.

Her first novel was *The Judas Cat* (1949), which features a small town newspaper fighting powerful corporate interests. Her novel *A Town of Masks* (1952) is set in her home state of Illinois. *The Clay Hand* (1950), however, takes place in the impoverished coal regions of Appalacia. Her most famous and most critically acclaimed novel, *A Gentle Murderer* (1951), is sensitive to the impact of poverty upon character and features an Irish Catholic priest hunting for a murderer for whom he has much compassion. Noted crime writer Sara Paretsky termed it "one of the best crime novels of the post-World War II era." Paretsky also praised her for "an enviable reputation for her ability to write . . . [about] *both* believable rural and urban settings." Her crime story "The Puppet" can be found in the famous 1991 anthology, *A Woman's Eye,* edited by Paretsky.

Only in *A Death in the Life* (1976) did Davis finally create a series character, and such tardiness may have contributed to her neglect by readers. The series heroine is a New York reporter who appeared in three more novels, the last being *The Habit of Fear* (1987). In 1989 she was awarded a lifetime achievement Anthony Award, named after "Anthony Boucher," at that year's Bouchercon. A notable late novel is *The French Collection* (1993).

Lavinia R. (Riker) Davis, (1909–1961): Beyond this information, nothing is known.

Catherine (Adelaide) C. (Crook) de Camp, (1907–2000): She was a 1933 graduate of Barnard College, Columbia University, with a double major in English and economics. She later did post-graduate work in economic history, consumer economics, and psychology. Although she taught as adjunct faculty at Temple University, it was as a teacher at a secondary prep school that her sister introduced her to L. Sprague de Camp (1907–2000), whom she married in 1939. Thereafter she officially collaborated with him on several non-fiction works, including one of the earliest books on how to write science fiction, *The Science Fiction Handbook* (1953, 1975). Other collaborations included *Ancient Ruins and Archaeology* (1964), which surveyed twelve sacred ancient sites; *Spirits, Stars and Spells* (1966), a survey of magic rituals; and *The Day of the Dinosaur* (1968).

With her husband she also co-authored the definitive biography of Conan creator Robert E. Howard, *Dark Valley Destiny: The Life of Robert E. Howard* (1983). She also collaborated with him on his short story collection, *Footprints on Sand* (1981), as well as on the anthologies *3000 Years of Fantasy and Science Fiction* (1972) and *Tales Beyond Time* (1973). She was also the co-author of the novels *The Bones of Zora* (1983), *The Incorporated Knight* (1987), *The Stones of Nomuru* (1988), *The Pixilated Peeress* (1991), and *The Swords of Zinjaban* (1991). She was perhaps the unofficial collaborator on many others. She was also the solo author of *The Money Tree: A New Guide to Successful Personal Finance* (1972) and other books on financial affairs.

Dorothy de Courcy (?–?): A resident of Vista, California, and Seattle, de Courcy published nineteen SF stories between 1946 and 1954, all in collaboration with her husband, John. The team was a favorite of editor Ray Palmer.

Frances M. Deegan, (1901–?): One source claimed that her name was a house pseudonym used by the publisher Street & Smith. And, in fact, Deegan did publish mystery stories in the 1940s in Street & Smith's *Detective Story Magazine,* edited by Daisy Bacon (e.g., "The Want-Ad Murders," *Detective Story Magazine,* March, 1944, reprinted in the Bacon edited *Detective Story Annual, 1948).* However, this claim is not likely, as none of the seventeen fantasy and science fiction stories she published in our period were for a Street & Smith publication. All were for the Ziff-Davis magazines *Amazing Stories* and *Fantastic Adventures.*

The best source of information on her is a short and dramatic memoir in the January, 1946 *Mammoth Detective,* which accompanied one of her detective stories. (Thanks to Monte Herridge for bringing this to my attention.) With it was a photo of an attractive middle-aged woman. In the text she said of herself that she was "5 feet 2 inches tall, have red hair, brown eyes, and weigh 90 pounds. I have never been married because nobody ever asked me to get married." She went on to write that she was born in Iowa and graduated from high school at sixteen, "just in time to be a charter member of the Lost Generation. However, I hadn't heard about that yet, so I got a job with the local office of a large national insurance company."

She soon left to be a singer and actress in Roaring Twenties Chicago. "Bookings were plentiful in the booming cafes and night clubs. . . . I was pretty terrible, but so was the liquor, and nobody seemed to mind. I got acquainted with all the prominent gangsters, their cohorts and connections—political and otherwise. After a while I graduated into vaudeville. Where upon vaudeville gave one last gasp and expired and I wound up in New York.

"The Twenties were roaring and flashing past. Speakeasies, floor shows, elaborate musical shows, more gangsters, butter-and-egg men. . . . Somewhere in the melee I bought a typewriter. 'I must write some of this down while I think of it,' I said. But, of course, I never did. . . . I've been shot at and missed, had knives thrown at me in a waterfront dive. And once I was taken for a ride by a Brooklyn gangster (humorously known as Mike Shots) and beaten to a bloody pulp with his gun butt. I'm still alive, but he isn't.

"When New York began to pall I went to St. Louis with a theatrical organization. Came the Depression. I applied for and got the job of press agent with a feminine political organization devoted to repeal of the 18th Amendment [Prohibition]. Although I didn't know from nothing, the newspaper men were very kind. . . .

"I had been reading Ziff-Davis fiction mags for some time. I suddenly remembered that I had always intended to write, so I went down to see Mr. [Ray] Palmer [editor of both detective magazines as well as *Amazing Stories* and *Fantastic Adventures* for Ziff-Davis]. The reception room was elegant, but it was very informal inside. I simply walked in and said, 'Do you mind if I write something for you?' And Mr. Palmer said, 'No, go right ahead.' I went home and wrote a story, and he bought it." Although he began by buying Deegan's detective stories, Palmer also published "Martian and the Milkmaid," her first science fiction story, in *Fantastic Adventures*, October 1944. In addition to her numerous detective stories, she went on to publish sixteen more SF stories, the last appearing in 1952.

Miriam Allen deFord, (1888–1975): She was born in Philadelphia, the daughter of two physicians. She published her first story at age twelve. Speaking in 1942 she said, "I was born a feminist [sic], and have been a freethinker since I was thirteen." She was educated at Wellesley College and Temple University, from which she received her Bachelor's in 1911. She received a scholarship to the University of Pennsylvania, where she did graduate work in English and Latin, 1911–1912.

She lived in Boston from 1912–1915, where she worked as a journalist. She then moved to San Diego, where she married Armistead Collier in 1915 and worked as a stenographer and freelance journalist. In 1917 they moved to Baltimore, where she became the editor of a house newsletter for the Pompeiian Oil Company. In 1918 she became an insurance claims adjuster, and served in that capacity in Baltimore, Chicago, and San Francisco until 1923, having been divorced in 1920. In every city she was active in the woman suffrage and radical movements and was jailed for her suffrage activities. She once noted that, when she worked in Chicago, she knew half the "Wobblies" (members of the radical IWW, the Industrial Workers of the World, headquartered in Chicago) imprisoned and tried there for opposition to America's participation in World War I.

In 1921 she married Maynard Shipley, a writer and lecturer on natural science. Shipley was the founder and president of the Science League of America (1924–1932), which championed the theory of evolution in numerous states which had passed laws banning the teaching of evolution. It was the Science League which provided most of the expert defense witnesses at the so-called "Scopes Monkey Trial" in which Clarence Darrow defended a Tennessee high school biology teacher for teaching the theory of evolution. Shipley was, "The greatest personal influence in my life," wrote deFord, "the profoundest mind, the most lovable nature, and the noblest spirit I have ever known."

Shipley was also a prominent Leftist and both he and deFord were members of the Socialist Party from 1919–1922. They left the Party in 1922 because, said deFord, "they were going too far to the right—they were practically a branch of the Democratic party. . . . I've always been for complete revolution, not reform. I suppose you'd say we were good Marxists."

Until Shipley's death of a stroke at age 61 in 1934, their home was in Sausalito, near San

Francisco. After his death she lived in Honolulu, the Far East, and Berkeley, before settling in San Francisco. Her 1956 biography of Shipley was published by Antioch University Press.

From 1921–1956 she was the San Francisco correspondent for the Federated Press, a newspaper syndication service for over 300 labor newspapers. In this way became a well-known reporter in labor and leftist circles. She covered all the radical crusades of the time, such as the trial and execution of anarchists Sacco and Vanzetti, and numbered Jack London and other famous socialists of the day among her friends. She wrote the authorized biography of well-known labor activist and political prisoner Tom Mooney in 1935 while he was still in San Quentin Prison. From 1956–1958 she was the staff correspondent for *Labor's Daily.*

Like her husband, deFord wrote for the series of inexpensive paperback Little Blue Books published by Haldeman-Julius of Girard, Kansas. She authored fifteen biographies and Latin translations in this series, as well as *The Facts about Fascism,* and *The Truth about Mussolini,* both 1926. From 1936–1939 she was an editor on the Federal Writers Project writing histories of California cities for the WPA guide to that state. She was fired from the project for spending too much time covering the deportation hearings of radical longshoreman union leader Harry Bridges. That Great Depression job was the last salaried position she held. By then, however, she was already earning "a sufficient living as a freelance writer," so she threw herself into that. "I wrote stories, I wrote articles, and as I developed new interests I got better acquainted with the periodicals that dealt with them. Whatever I was doing, I wrote about."

Her 1930 story, "The Silver Knight," was chosen for inclusion in that year's anthology of O. Henry Award Prize Stories, edited by Blanche Cotton Williams, who described her as a poet who had translated Lucretius, Juvenal, and Catullus from the Latin. Indeed, deFord's poetry appeared in many of the magazines of the day and was reprinted in approximately thirty-five anthologies and collected in her 1939 book, *Children of the Sun.* Another of her stories was chosen for inclusion in the 1934 O. Henry anthology. Her novel, *Shaken with the Wind,* appeared in 1942.

She also published many biographical books, a sampling of which include *Love Children: A Book of Illustrious Illegitimates* (1931); *Who Was When? A Dictionary of Contemporaries* (1940); *They Were San Franciscans* (1941); *Thomas More* (1967); *The Real Bonnie and Clyde* (1968); and *The Real Ma Barker* (1970).

She published thirty-one SF stories 1950–1960 in *Galaxy, If, Fantastic Universe, Startling Stories, Space Stories, Beyond Fantasy Fiction, Future SF, Venture,* and Anthony Boucher's *The Magazine of Fantasy and Science Fiction,* where she debuted. Her story, "Mary Celestial," was a collaboration with Boucher. Another story, "The Malley System," appeared in Harlan Ellison's famous path-breaking anthology, *Dangerous Visions* (1967). She also published fantasy in *Weird Tales.*

And deFord also became well known in the mystery field. In 1961 she was awarded the Edgar Allen Poe Award for her non-fiction book, *The Overbury Affair: The Murder That Rocked the Court of James I.* In 1960 and 1963 she served on the Board of Directors of the Mystery Writers of America. She edited a genre anthology *Space, Time and Crime* (1964), which successfully merged the genres of mystery and science fiction. Her story, "The Kookhouse Murderer," is a spy-mystery for *The Girl From U.N.C.L.E. Magazine* (December, 1966). Many of her science fiction stories were collected in *Xenogenesis* (1969) (which deals entirely with gender relations) and *Elsewhere, Elsewhen, Elsehow* (1971).

She continued to publish into the 1970s and was a familiar sight at both mystery and science fiction conventions until her death. When arthritis crippled her fingers, making it impossible for her to type, she dictated her stories and articles and books and carried on. The best information about her can be found in her long memoir, from which the quotes in this profile are taken, in Sherna Gluck, Ed., *From Parlor to Prison: Five American Suffragists Talk About Their Lives,* Vintage Books: NY, 1976.

Diane Detzer (de Reyna), (1930–   ): Detzer produced a series of space operas in the late 1950s and early 1960s as "Adam Lukens," beginning with *The Sea People* (1959). The most interesting of these was *Conquest of Life* (1960) about a future Earth where women vastly outnumber men, who the women buy and sell. She published *The Return of the Starships* (1968) as by "Jorge de Reyna," but *Planet of Fear* (1968) was published under her own name.

Leah Bodine Drake (1914–1964): Born in Kansas, Drake was primarily a poet, with much verse appearing in *Weird Tales* between 1935–1954. Some of her fantasy poetry can be found in the August Derleth anthology, *Dark of the Moon* (1947). Derleth's specialty press, Arkham House, also published her collection of supernatural verse, *Hornbook for Witches* (1950). A second poetry collection, *This Tilting Dust,* appeared in 1955 from the small specialty press, Golden Quill. Her poetry also appeared in such glossies as *The Atlantic* (for which she was also a poetry reviewer) and *The Saturday Evening Post.*

She also published fantasy fiction in *Weird Tales* and *The Magazine of Fantasy and Science Fiction.* "The Woods Grow Darker" was reprinted in *The Best from Fantasy and Science Fiction: Sixth Series* (1957), while "They Run Again" was chosen for Peter Haining's *Weird Tales, Vol. I* (1978).

Garen Drussai (Mrs. Kirk Drussai), (?–?): Her science fiction stories appeared in the mid-Fifties, but she also wrote short mystery fiction, such as "Why Don't You Answer, Theodore?" (*Mike Shayne Mystery Magazine,* May, 1970).

Theodora (McCormick) Du Bois (1890–1986): Du Bois was an American novelist, primarily of detective and children's literature. She published thirty mystery novels between 1930–1966. Some of these, such as *The Emerald Crown* (1955), appeared under the name of Theodora McCormick. She was important to the mystery field for pioneering the medical murder mystery. Her series characters, Dr. Jeffrey McNeill and his wife, appeared in a number of novels, most notably *Death Dines Out* (1939). From 1932–1966 she also published ten novels for juveniles.

In her fantasy novel, *The Devil's Spoon* (1930), a young devil takes possession of a man's body to stop the Satan from dominating the world. In one of her mysteries, *Murder Strikes an Atomic Unit* (1946), she combined the murder and SF genres. Her 1951 SF novel, *Solution T-25,* portrayed a nuclear attack on America, followed by Soviet conquest. An American underground resistance eventually overthrows the Communist domination.

Merab Eberle (?–1959): Eberle attended Oxford College, in Oxford, Ohio, and served as art editor of the *Dayton (Ohio) Journal Herald.* She was associated with the Red Cross during World War I. She authored many children's plays, including The *Spirit of Democracy* (1917), *Bobby in Belgium* (1918), and *Anne of the Red Cross* (1918). A collection of her poetry, *Many Doors,* was published posthumously in 1961. It is unclear if she was married to Joseph Eberle, a cover artist for science fiction magazines in the 1950s, such as Lester del Rey's *Rocket Stories* and Ray Palmer's *Universe.*

Phyllis H. Economou, (c.1920s–?): She was a resident of Milwaukee, Wisconsin, and active in Midwest SF fandom in the 1950s. As a member of the well-known Fantasy Amateur Press Association (FAPA) from May, 1954 to February, 1964, she produced a regular fanzine, *Phlotsam,* for the membership. She also contributed regularly to the fanzines of other fans, such as Ted White, later editor of *Amazing.* She was described as being friendly, attractive, and the life of the party at conventions, such as the 1960 Pittsburgh Worldcon. Ted White believes she was born in the 1920s and is under the impression that she is now deceased.

Sophie Wenzel Ellis (1893–1984): A long-time resident of Little Rock, Arkansas, Ellis contributed to many pulps, including *Amazing Stories, Astounding Stories, Ghost Stories, Love Stories, Strange Tales,* and *Weird Tales.* She wrote for *Thrill Book* in 1919 under her maiden name of Sophie Louise Wenzel.

Carol (Fries) Emshwiller (1921–   ): Emshwiller was born and raised in Ann Arbor, Michigan, where she also attended college, receiving a B.A. in music from the University of Michigan, and, later, a B.A. in design in 1949. That same year she wed noted SF artist Edmund Emshwiller ("Ed Emsh") (1925–1990), with whom she had three children. They moved to Paris where she was a Fulbright Fellow and her husband studied art at the Ecole des Beaux Arts. Afterward they motorcycled around Europe for a while before returning to Long Island, NY, where she has lived most of her life.

   She published her first science fiction story in 1955 and much of her early fiction appeared in *The Magazine of Fantasy and Science Fiction* or Damon Knight's *Orbit* anthology series. The cover of the February 1958, issue of *The Magazine of Fantasy and Science Fiction* was devoted to her story, "Baby," and was painted by her husband. She also wrote mystery fiction, such as "Hands" (*Double-Action Detective and Mystery Stories,* Summer, 1957).

   Her story, "Sex and/or Mr. Morrison," appeared in Harlan Ellison's legendary anthology, *Dangerous Visions* (1967). Her early fiction was collected in *Joy in Our Cause* (1974). Other collections include *Verging on the Pertinent* (1989), *The Start of the End of It All* (1990) and *Report to the Men's Club* (2001).

   Her first novel, *Carmen Dog* (1988), was a feminist allegory in which women were transformed into dogs and dogs into women. In 1991 she won the World Fantasy Award for best short story collection for *The Start of the End of It All and Other Stories.* In 2002 Emshwiller won the Philip K. Dick Award, presented by the Philadelphia Science Fiction Society for the year's most distinguished original paperback, for her novel *The Mount.* Also in 2002 her peers awarded her the Best Short Story Nebula for "Creature." She has also written Western novels, such as *Ledoyt* (1995) and the sequel, *Leaping Man Hill* (1999).

"Mona Farnsworth" (Muriel Newhall) (c.1904–1981): In addition to her work in science fiction, Farnsworth wrote dozens of stories for the romance pulps. She was also the author of ten-to-fifteen Gothic romance paperbacks in the 1970s.

Harriet Frank, Jr. (1918–   ): Frank was born and raised in Portland, Oregon. She attended the University of California at Los Angeles (UCLA) while her mother worked as a Hollywood script editor. She followed in her mother's footsteps, becoming an apprentice writer in MGM's stable after World War II. There she met Irving Ravetch, another young writer, whom she married in 1946. She remained an obscure and relatively unknown screenwriter for the next decade. Her first production credit was as co-writer of *Steel River* (1948), a "B" picture for Warner Brothers. This was followed the same year by *Whiplash,* another minor film she co-authored.

In 1955 she began collaborating with her husband, producing a storyline (which was adapted by another writer) for the conventional Western, *Ten Wanted Men,* starring Randolph Scott. In 1958 they adapted three William Faulkner stories into *The Long Hot Summer.* Directed by Martin Ritt and starring Orson Welles, Paul Newman, and Joanne Woodward, it was the film on which Newman and Woodward met. The film was also the first of eight film collaborations the husband and wife writing team conducted with Ritt, many of them starring Newman.

Their next collaboration with Ritt, *The Sound and the Fury* (1959), was also an adaptation of Faulkner. That same year they wrote *Home From the Hill* (1959) for Vincente Minnelli. The next year (1960) they adapted William Inge's Pulitzer Prize-winning play, *The Dark at the Top of the Stairs.* They next began producing films with Martin Ritt, who continued directing stories written by the duo. Their first effort of this nature was an adaptation of Larry McMurtry's first novel into the film *Hud* (1963), starring Paul Newman. *Hud* earned Frank and Ravetch their first Oscar writing nomination and earned Patricia Neal the Oscar for Best Actress, with Melvyn Douglas winning the Oscar for Best Supporting Actor. This same team of writers, director, and star Paul Newman returned for *Hombre* (1967).

Frank and Ravetch then returned to Faulkner for their next film, *The Reivers* (1969), starring Steve McQueen. Next they adapted Pat Conroy's memoir about teaching black children in the South for *Conrack* (1974), directed by Ritt and starring Jon Voight. They teamed with Ritt again for *Norma Rae* (1979), which earned a Best Actress Oscar for star Sally Field and a second Academy Award writing nomination for Frank and Ravetch. Writers, director, and star Sally Field returned for *Murphy's Romance* (1985), a romantic comedy co-starring James Garner. The last film Harriet Frank and her husband wrote was *Stanley and Iris* (1990), in which Jane Fonda taught Robert De Niro to read.

Lee Hawkins Garby (1892–1953): Between 1915–1920 Garby collaborated with E. E. "Doc" Smith on *The Skylark of Space (Amazing Stories,* 1928), the first great space opera. She was the wife of Dr. Carl Garby, a chemist who was one of Smith's college friends. It seems they began collaborating on the story when all lived in Washington, D.C., where Smith worked at the Bureau of Agriculture.

After Smith's work took him to Michigan, the collaboration continued via the mails. Smith said that he asked Garby's help as he did not feel competent to deal with the romance aspect of the story, as well as some of the dialog. Her son, Dr. Rodes Garby, said much the same. Perhaps she was also responsible for the baroque descriptions of alien weddings and costumes in the novel. In any case, her contribution to the creation of this important sub-genre is usually ignored.

Frances Garfield, (?–?): In addition to her science fiction, Garfield also published fantasy in *Weird Tales* between 1939–1940.

Doris Gilbert, (?–?): Gilbert was a 1940s Hollywood script writer who also wrote for early television in the Fifties. In the single year of 1944 she wrote the movies *Atlantic City, Ladies Courageous* (about World War II Women's Air Force pilots), *Lake Placid Serenade,* and *Storm Over Lisbon.* In 1951 she wrote the movie *Little Egypt,* about the famous nineteenth-century belly dancer. After that she concentrated on television. Among the many shows for which she wrote stories were *The Adventures of Superman* and *Mr. & Mrs. North*, both in 1952, and *Science Fiction Theater* in 1955.

Inez Haynes Gillmore (Irwin) (1873–1970): Born in Rio de Janeiro, but raised in Boston, Gillmore spent most of her life in New York City. She graduated from Radcliffe in 1900 and had become active in the woman suffrage movement while there, co-founding the National Collegiate Equal Suffrage League. Attracted to Alice Paul's more radical National Women's Party, she eventually became a member of the party's Advisory Council. She also headed the World Center for Women's Archives. Her first husband, Rufus Gillmore, was a journalist who supported her suffrage activities.

She published her first novel, *June Jeopardy,* in 1908 and shortly thereafter became the fiction editor of *The Masses,* the most influential Leftist magazine of the age. An official in many early writers' societies, most of her own work was either mainstream or in the fields of mysteries or children's literature. Her second novel, *Maida's Little Shop* (1910), launched her long sequence of children's books about that heroine. The last in the series was *Maida's Little Treasure Hunt* (1955). Her primary genre novel, *Angel Island* (1914), concerned a war between men and winged women.

In 1916 she married William Henry Irwin and the two of them lived in Europe during World War I, reporting on the war. Her 1917 feminist novel, *The Lady of Kingdoms,* featured a working class heroine. In 1924 her short story, "The Spring Flight," won the O. Henry Prize for that year's best short story.

She also published nonfiction books, such as *The Story of the Women's Party* (1921) and *Angels and Amazons: A Hundred Years of American Women* (1933). She became the first female president of the Author's League of America. After the death of her second husband in 1948, she retired to Scituate, Massachusetts. She died at age 97 in Norwell, Mass. In 1988 *Angel Island* was reprinted as a classic of early feminist literature.

Ellen Glasgow (Ellen Anderson Gholson) (1874–1945): Pulitzer Prize-winning novelist Ellen Glasgow was born in Richmond, Virginia, where she lived all her life, and was educated at home. She became deaf in 1893 following the death of her mother. Her novels dominated American bestseller lists between 1900–1930.

Primarily a mainstream novelist, Glasgow began writing (unknown to her family and against her family's wishes) in the 1890s and her first novel was *The Descendant* (1897), which was published anonymously. The next year, to rave reviews, she published *Phases of an Inferior Planet* under her own name. Rejecting the romantic image of the antebellum South and its code of male superiority, she determined to write the true story of social change which empowered women in Virginia from 1850 to her present. The first of this five-book project was *The Voice of the People* (1900). The series concluded with *Virginia* in 1913. Many of her heroines were strong women who chose to remain single. Her most feminist novel was *Life and Gabriella: The Story of a Woman's Courage* (1916). In 1942 she won the Pulitzer Prize for her novel, *In This Our Life.*

Her main work of genre interest was *The Shadowy Third and Other Stories* (1923). Her autobiography, *The Woman Within,* was published posthumously in 1954. Her last novel was *Beyond Defeat* (1966), also published posthumously and a sequel to *In This Our Life.*

(Margaret) Rumer Godden, (1907–1998): Godden was born at Lydd House, Aldington, Kent, England. She is best known as a children's author and for such adult works as *Black Narcissus* (1939), about a group of nuns attempting to establish a mission in the Himalaya region.

India, where she long resided, was the background for much of her fiction, although she later settled in Scotland. Her first children's book was *The Dolls' House* (1947). One of her last was *Great Grandfather's House* (1992), set in ancient Japan. Her romance novel, *Coromandel Sea Change* (1991), was set in southern India.

Her three memoirs are *Two Under the Indian Sun* and *A Time to Dance, No Time to Weep* (1987) and *A House with Four Rooms* (1989). She was inducted as a member of the Order of the British Empire (OBE) in 1993. Her twenty-first novel, *Cromartie vs. the God Shiva*, was published in 1997, the year before her death.

Laura Goforth, (?-?): Goforth was a music teacher and the daughter of an attorney in Chattanooga, Tennessee. She married Futurian Chester Cohen in the early Fifties. They had three children, one of whom they named "Damon" after fellow Futurian and good friend Damon Knight. However, after his marriage to Kate Wilhelm in 1963, Knight broke off his friendship with the Cohens, as he wanted nothing to do with people he'd known while married to his previous wife.

Ruth M. Goldsmith (1919-?): Goldsmith made her genre debut in *The Magazine of Fantasy and Science Fiction* in 1953, but she also had a mainstream literary career. Much of her mainstream fiction appeared in *The Atlantic Monthly.*

Phyllis (Fay) Gotlieb (Bloom) (1926–   ): Gotlieb was born in Toronto, Canada, and obtained a B.A. (1948) and an M.A. in English (1950) from the University of Toronto. She married Calvin Gotlieb in 1949, with whom she had one son and two daughters.

Her first novel, *Sunburst*, appeared in 1964 and treated the SF trope of mutant children quite sympathetically. Many other novels followed, including *O Master Caliban!* (1976), *A Judgment of Dragons* (1980), *Emperor, Swords, Pentacles* (1982), *The Kingdom of Cats* (1985), and *Heart of Red Iron* (1989), a sequel to *O Master Caliban*. She co-edited a 1987 anthology, *Tesseracts 2*, which showcased Canadian SF. In 1998 she published *Flesh and Gold*, a science fiction mystery that featured a female judge. Her 1972 short story, "Son of the Morning," was nominated for the Nebula Award by her peers. It and other early works were collected in *Son of the Morning and Other Stories* (1983).

Gotlieb is also well known in Canada for her poetry and has published at least five collections of verse. She has said that, "I like to work in as broad a range of genres as possible, and in all of them I am primarily interested in people, their emotions, actions, dynamics." She also loves cats, which have figured prominently in much of her work.

Ann (Warren) Griffith (?-?): In addition to her genre work, her fiction also appeared in mainstream magazines such as *The Atlantic Monthly, Reader's Digest,* and *The Woman.*

Augusta Groner (?-?): She was a prolific Austrian mystery novelist active at the start of the twentieth century. Prominent among her works translated into English by Grace Isabel Colbron (usually credited as co-author) are *The Case of the Pocket Diary Found in the Snow, The Case of the Pool of Blood in the Pastor's Study, The Case of the Golden Bullet, The Case of the Registered Letter,* and *The Case of the Lamp That Went Out.* All of these feature the adventures of detective Joe Muller, a secret service officer in the imperial Austro-Hungarian police force in Vienna before World War I.

T. (Thelma) D. Hamm (Evans) (1905–1994): Wife of SF author E. Everett Evans (1893–1958).

L. (Lucile) Taylor Hansen, (1897–1976): Hansen was the only pre-Fifties author who deliberately attempted to conceal her gender identity. A California author for most of her life, she attended UCLA in the 1920s, although without graduating. She may have been the sister of chemist Louis Ingvald Hansen. Although she wrote a handful of stories, she is primarily important for her fifty-seven popular science articles in *Amazing Stories* from 1941–1949. She died in Phoenix, Arizona. Everett and Richard Bleiler have definitively established that her first name was Lucile and not "Louise," as long believed.

Clare Winger Harris (1891–1969): A long-time resident of Freeport, Illinois, Harris was living in Lakewood, Ohio, when she became the first woman to publish in a science fiction magazine. This first story was "The Fate of the Poseidonia," *Amazing Stories,* June 1927. It had won third prize in Hugo Gernsback's first story contest. Thereafter Harris became a regular contributor to Gernsback's magazine and one of his most popular writers.

She had previously appeared in *Weird Tales* with "A Runaway World" (July 1926), which was an early (perhaps the earliest) portrayal of the Earth as an electron in a larger universe. She is best remembered for "The Miracle of the Lily," *Amazing Stories,* April 1928. A Frank R. Paul portrait of her depicting an attractive young woman appeared with her story, "The Artificial Man," *Science Wonder Quarterly,* fall 1929. Most of her stories were reprinted in *Away From the Here and Now* (1947), one of the first story collections of a science fiction writer.

In 1930, as a favor to a fan who greatly admired her stories, she contributed an original tale to *Cosmic Stories,* the first amateur science fiction magazine. It was edited and published by a Cleveland fan named Jerome ("Jerry") Siegel—who went on to become the co-creator of Superman with fellow Cleveland fan Joseph Schuster. When Siegel and Schuster launched *Science Fiction,* the second amateur science fiction magazine, in 1932, Harris continued to help out by contributing stories.

While there is a James Tiptree, Jr. Award honoring a woman who began publishing science fiction *as a male* in 1968, there is no Clare Winger Harris Award honoring the first woman to publish in the science fiction magazines *as a woman*—forty years earlier. This is illustrative of the amnesia even women in the field suffer when it comes to the history of women in science fiction.

Dorothy K. (Kate Gray) Haynes (1918–1987): Haynes was a British writer born in Scotland. She is of genre interest for her story collection, *Thou Shalt Not Suffer a Witch* (1949), with illustrations by Mervyn Peake, better known as the author of *Titus Groan* and its sequels. A regular contributor to the British Fontana horror series, she sold her first story at age sixteen.

Hazel Heald (1895–1961): A Massachusetts writer who was friends with H. P. Lovecraft. The latter revised some of her stories, which were published in *Weird Tales,* 1933–37. It is possible Lovecraft may also have made some revisions to her "The Man of Stone," *Wonder Stories,* October 1932, which featured a portrait of her by Frank R. Paul.

Zenna (Charlson) Henderson (1917–1983): A Tucson, Arizona teacher, Henderson came from a family of Mormon pioneers to the Southwest. She was oldest girl in a family of five children and graduated from Phoenix Union High School, the first high school in Phoenix,

Arizona. She then earned a B.A. (1940) and an M.A. (1955) in literature and languages from Arizona State University (then Arizona Teachers College), the first and only one in her family to graduate from college. Despite the Master's, and graduate study beyond it, she spent the rest of her life teaching the first grade. She married in 1944, but was soon divorced. No children.

During World War II, all Pacific Coast Japanese-Americans were arrested and removed from the coast due to their Japanese ancestry, which brought their loyalty into question. Many such families, including children, were imprisoned in Arizona internment camps. Henderson taught the children in one of these camps at Sacaton for the duration of the war.

Except for a two-year stint teaching on a U.S. Air Force base in France (1956–1958) and a brief tenure teaching at the Seaside Children's Hospital in Waterford, Connecticut, she spent the rest of her career in Tucson, Arizona. There her classes were composed mostly of Mexican-American children. Unsurprisingly, teachers and their students figure prominently in her stories. Her 1960 story, "The Closest School," was a satirical look at school integration. Because the law allowed children to attend the school closest to them, regardless of color, a school board is faced with a new family of extraterrestrial aliens in town. The family is purple and fuzzy and want to send their daughter to the local school.

Henderson is principally remembered for her stories about "The People," humanoid aliens stranded on Earth. All of these stories appeared in *The Magazine of Fantasy and Science Fiction,* beginning in 1952. They were collected in *Pilgrimage: The Book of the People* (1961), *The People: No Different Flesh* (1966), and *Ingathering: The Complete People Stories of Zenna Henderson* (1995). The best of her other stories were collected in *The Anything Box* (1965) and *Holding Wonder* (1971).

Henderson remembered that, "When I was about 12 I began reading science fiction—Jules Verne, Haggard, and Edgar Rice Burroughs, and all the current magazines I could get hold of, but it wasn't until I had graduated from college that I began writing fantasy and science fiction. . . . Mottos I try to observe when I write: stories consist of unusual people in ordinary circumstances or ordinary people in unusual circumstances; write about what you know; don't let your subtleties become obscurities."

"Charles Henneberg" (Nathalie Henneberg) (1907–1978): Stories under this byline were co-authored by French writers Nathalie Henneberg and her husband, Charles Henneberg zu Irmelshausen Wasungen (1899–1959). She was a Russian journalist who met her future husband in Syria, where he was a German serving in the French Foreign Legion. After marriage they lived for years in the Arabian desert. During World War II Charles was an officer with General Charles de Gaulle's Free French forces.

The couple collaborated on a number of French-language science-fantasy novels and, after Charles' death in 1959, Nathalie continued to write genre stories and novels as "Nathalie-Charles Henneberg" in honor of her husband. Damon Knight described her as the most popular science fiction writer in France during the 1960s and translated and published three of her stories in his anthology, *13 French SF Stories* (1965). Her story, "Ysolde," appeared in Donald A. Wollheim's *The Best from the Rest of the World* (1976). Her classic "The Blind Pilot" (translated by Knight) appeared in David G. Hartwell's *The World Treasury of Science Fiction* (1989). *The Green Gods* (1961) was an early exploration of the greenhouse effect and was translated by C. J. Cherryh in 1980.

Alma Hill (?–?): Hill was active in fandom during the 1950s and was especially active in organizing and running the 1960 Worldcon in Pittsburgh. Dirce Archer, the Pittcon Chair, made a point of thanking her for her work in the first paragraph on the first page of the Pittcon program. Ted White, later editor of *Amazing,* knew her in the late Fifties and early Sixties and recalled her as being "grandmotherly" at that time. He also believed she lived in Boston. She published three stories from 1950–1959 in *Other Worlds, Spaceway,* and *Future.* She published a fourth story in the January, 1965 issue of *If.*

Elizabeth Sanxay Holding (1889–1955): Holding was born in Brooklyn, New York. She was the wife of novelist George E. Holding (*The Unlit Lamp,* 1922; *The Silk Purse,* 1928; *The Death-Wish,* 1934, etc.) and a prolific writer herself of romance and mystery novels for over 30 years. She began with romances, such as *Invincible Minnie* (1920) and *Angelica* (1921).

Her psychological suspense mysteries then became the prototype for the modern murder mystery. Among her better-known mysteries are *Miasma* (1929), *Dark Power* (1930), *The Unfinished Crime* (1935), *The Obstinate Murderer* (1938), *Who's Afraid?* (1940), *The Girl Who Had to Die* (1940), *Speak of the Devil* (1941), *Lady Killer* (1942), *Kill Joy* (1942), *Net of Cobwebs* (1945), *The Innocent Mrs. Duff* (1946), *The Virgin Huntress* (1951), *Too Many Bottles* (1951), and *Widow's Mite* (1953).

Many of her books have been turned into movies beginning in the silent film era. Such novels include *The Price of Pleasure* (1925), followed by *The Bride Comes Home* (1935) and *The Blank Wall* (1947). The latter was turned into the movie, *The Reckless Moment* (1949), directed by Max Ophuls, and starring Joan Bennett as a murderer pursued by blackmailer James Mason. It was remade once again in 2001 as the film, *The Deep End,* starring Tilda Swinton and Peter Donat.

Holding was productive to the end, with her last genre short story ("The Strange Children," August, 1955) appearing in *The Magazine of Fantasy and Science Fiction* the year she died, at age sixty-five, in New York City. Martin H. Greenberg, Joseph Olander, and Charles Waugh reprinted it in their 1979 anthology, *Mysterious Visions.* In the introduction they termed Holding "A pioneer of the psychological suspense novel . . . [and] also one of its most skillful practitioners." She was "Noted for her characterization and style" and this story was one of her best.

E. (Edna) Mayne Hull (1905–1975): Born in Brandon, Manitoba, Canada, Hull was the daughter of a Canadian journalist. In 1939 she married fellow Canadian and noted SF writer A. E. van Vogt (1912–2000), with whom she remained the rest of her life, pre-deceasing him. In 1944 they immigrated to the United States. Along with him she was Guest of Honor at the Fourth World Science Fiction Convention in 1946.

She began writing for John W. Campbell in 1942, for whom her husband was already writing. Much of her fiction was co-authored with her husband. About this she said, "The great problem was my almost total lack of scientific knowledge. To overcome this handicap, my husband and I figured out a story pattern which would bypass the need to show a science explanation." Thus, most of her stories centered around an unscrupulous interstellar businessman in a hyper-capitalist society and were collected in *Planets for Sale* (1954).

She stopped writing after 1950. That same year she and her husband converted to L. Ron Hubbard's Dianetics (later the Church of Scientology). Because of this, van Vogt, also, ceased writing, although he began writing again in the early 1960s.

"Minna Irving" (Minna Odell) (c.1857–1940): Born in Tarrytown, NY, Irving was primarily a poet who contributed much verse to mainstream magazines around the turn of the twentieth century. Her poetry also appeared in *Weird Tales,* 1937. She died in Wycoff, NY.

Margaret Irwin (1889–1967): A British fantasy and historical novelist, Irwin was educated at Oxford University and was the wife of artist John Robert Monsell. Her first novel, *Still She Wished for Company* (1924), was first narrated by a girl who sees ghosts from 1779, then by the people in 1779 who see the girl as a "ghost" from the future. Her second novel, *These Mortals* (1925), centered around a young girl raised in isolation at her father's magical palace. Together these two novels contributed to the rebirth of fantasy in Britain following the Great War. Some of her short fantasy fiction (including the excellent 1930 short story, "The Book") was collected in *Madame Fears the Dark* (1935) and *Bloodstock and Other Stories* (1953).

Irwin later became a noted historical novelist. The first of her historical novels was *The Gay Galliard* (1941). The first of her popular Queen Elizabeth I trilogy was *Young Bess,* (1941). She also published popular historical non-fiction, such as *That Great Lucifer: A Portrait of Sir Walter Raleigh* (1960).

Shirley Jackson (1919–1965): Born in San Francisco, Jackson began publishing fiction with her 1937 short story, "Janice." However, she began writing as a child, winning a poetry prize at age twelve.

Her family moved from California to Rochester, NY, in 1933 when Jackson was fourteen. She later attended the University of Rochester for one year. She left college due to depression and her novel about schizophrenia, *The Bird's Nest* (1954), dealt with the gradual mental breakdown of a teenage girl in her first year of college and away from home for the first time. She re-entered college life in 1937 when she enrolled at Syracuse University. There she published in the student literary magazine. There she also met Stanley Edgar Hyman (1919–1970), who became a literary critic and *New Yorker* staff writer. They married in 1940 and had four children. With him she wrote two acclaimed and popular memoirs of family life with their children, *Life Among the Savages* (1953) and *Raising Demons* (1957).

Her most famous short story is "The Lottery," a horror tale which appeared in *The New Yorker* in 1948 and which was made into a TV movie several times. Her first novel, *The Road Through the Wall*, also published in 1948, was a mainstream novel set in Burlingame, California, where she grew up. Her 1951 novel, *Hangsaman,* was a Gothic thriller.

Her 1958 novel, *The Sundial*, is a story about the end of the world. More well known is *The Haunting of Hill House* (1959), a classic ghost story. It was filmed by director Robert Wise in 1963 as *The Haunting*, starring Julie Harris and Claire Bloom. While the 1963 film is a masterpiece of psychological suspense, the 1999 remake of the same name, starring Liam Neeson, Catherine Zeta-Jones, Bruce Dern, and Owen Wilson, is plodding and dull. Jackson's other well-known work is the suspenseful novel of dark powers and modern witches, *We Have Always Lived in the Castle* (1962). It was named by *Time* as one of the year's ten best novels and was turned into a Broadway play.

Jackson considered herself to be a practicing witch and in 1956 published the non-fiction children's book, *The Witchcraft of Salem Village*. She died at age forty-five in North Bennington, VT. She was working on a novel at the time, the existing parts of which were included in the posthumous story collection, *Come Along with Me* (1968).

F. (Friniwyd) Tennyson Jesse (1889–1958): A British poet, mystery novelist, playwright, journalist, and criminologist, Jesse was the grand-niece of the poet Alfred Lord Tennyson. During the Great War she was a war correspondent. Much of her short fiction was collected as *The Solange Stories* (1931), about Solange Fontaine, a female detective with psychic powers. "The Railway Carriage," *The Magazine of Fantasy and Science Fiction*, February 1951, was one such Solange story.

In 1918 she married dramatist and theater manager Harold Marsh Harwood (1874–1959) and the two of them wrote and produced many well-received London plays, such as *How to be Healthy Though Married*. They also collaborated on the famous World War II collections of letters, *London Front* (1940) and *While London Burns* (1942). Most of her novels were set in Cornwall and include *The White Riband* (1921), *Tom Fool* (1926), and *Moonraker* (1927). *The Lacquer Lady* (1929) is set in Burma and is regarded as her best novel. She edited several volumes of the *Notable British Trials* series and died in London.

Alice Eleanor Jones (?–?): Jones was a supernova who exploded suddenly in 1955, publishing five science fiction stories that year in four magazines. And then no more. However, she also published in mainstream magazines that very same year and continued to do so for a while thereafter. See, e.g., her stories in *Redbook,* "The Honeymoon" (June, 1957), "Morning Watch" (November, 1958), and "One Shattering Weekend" (July, 1960).

Jessie Douglas Kerruish, (1884–1949): Kerruish was a British novelist specializing in romance and historical novels, as well as Arabian Nights pastiches. She gained popularity with her first two novels, *Miss Haroun-al-Raschid* (1917) and *The Girl from Kurdistan* (1918). The first was written for a book contest, with Kerruish winning a large monetary prize.

Her third novel, *The Undying Monster: A Tale of the Fifth Dimension* (1922), was rejected almost everywhere. It eventually found a publisher and is considered her best work. It is an oft-reprinted werewolf tale that notably features a female occult detective who uncovers the horrid family curse. It was made into an atmospheric 1942 movie from Twentieth Century Fox, although Hollywood relegated the female detective to sidekick status. Kerruish was also known for *Babylonian Nights' Entertainment* (1934), a collection of Arabian fantasies. Soon after she became blind and failing health brought an end to her career.

Karen Kuykendall, (?–?): Kuykendall, now deceased, was an Arizona fantasy artist and writer who loved cats. She created an elaborate parallel world called "The Outer Regions" comprising six kingdoms in which cats were the favorite pet in all the lands. She co-authored two novels with Andre Norton—*Mark of the Cat* and *Year of the Rat*—situated in The Outer Regions. Her two solo books were *Cat People and Other Inhabitants of the Outer Regions: The Fantasy Art of Karen Kuykendall* (1979) and *Karen's Cats* (1980).

Madeleine L'Engle (Camp Franklin) (1918–   ): L'Engle was born in New York City, the only child of a pianist (her mother) and a foreign correspondent, playwright, and critic (her father). Her family moved to Europe when Madeleine was twelve, where she was placed in a Swiss boarding school.

She graduated from Smith College with honors (1941) and studied at the New School for Social Research (1941–1942). She published magazine articles and worked in the theater, where she met and then married TV actor Hugh Franklin in 1946, with whom she had three children. She taught at the private St. Hilda's and St. Hugh's School, NY, from 1960–1966. Beginning in 1966 she became the long-time librarian of the Cathedral of St. John the Divine in New York. She was a member of the summer school faculty of the University of Indiana, Bloomington, 1965–1966 and 1971. She was also Writer-in-Residence at Ohio State University, Columbus, in 1970 and the University of Rochester, NY, in 1972. She won the prestigious American Book Award in 1980. In 1997 she was presented with a Life Achievement Award at the World Fantasy Convention.

Her first play was *18 Washington Square South* (1940) and her first novel was *The Small*

Rain (1945). Beginning with *And Both Were Young* (1949), most of her work has been juveniles. Her first work of science fiction, the short story "Poor Little Saturday" (*Fantastic Universe,* October, 1956), was about a lonely boy discovering companionship.

Likewise, her first and best-known SF novel, *A Wrinkle in Time* (1962), featured a child
heroine who rescues her scientist father from abduction to a distant planet. It won the 1963
Newberry Medal as best children's novel of the year. It also launched a series of successful
juvenile fantasies featuring the same girl and her family and friends, including *The Moon by
Night* (1963), *The Arm of the Starfish* (1965), *A Wind in the Door* (1973), *A Swiftly Tilting
Planet* (1978), *Many Waters* (1986), and *An Acceptable Time* (1989). *The Young Unicorns*
(1968) is a non-series fantasy and *The Sphinx at Dawn* (1982) is a collection of her short
fiction.

In 2004 the Science Fiction Book Club offered an omnibus volume of *A Wrinkle in Time,
A Wind in the Door, A Swiftly Tilting Planet,* and *Many Waters.* This acknowledged the fact
that these books continue to sell extremely well. According to data released in 2003 on the
all-time bestselling children's paperback books, *A Swiftly Tilting Planet* ranked 127; *A Wind
in the Door* ranked 110; and *A Wrinkle in Time* ranked number 11. There is perennial Hollywood talk of *A Wrinkle in Time* being made into a movie.

Dorothy LesTina (?–   ): LesTina was from Florida and was the second wife of Frederik Pohl
(1919–   ), after his marriage to "Leslie Perri." Pohl became interested in her while still married to "Perri," from whom he separated in 1942. From its founding in February, 1940, until
September, 1941, Pohl edited the short-lived SF magazine, *Astonishing Stories.* This is perhaps
where he met LesTina, an artist whose work appeared in the magazine.

Pohl and LesTina became engaged in 1943, the same year LesTina became a published
science fiction author. Then both went into the Army, with LesTina quickly becoming a first
lieutenant in the Women's Army Corps (WACs). They married in Paris in August 1945,
shortly after Pohl was promoted to sergeant in the Army Air Force.

Upon their demobilization and return to the States she studied drama at New York's New
School and wrote "endless scripts," according to Pohl. In 1949 William Morrow published
her novel, *Occupation: Housewife.* According to Pohl's memoir, *The Way the Future Was*
(1978) (p.153), "She subsequently published half a dozen good books, but the theater never
opened its doors to her."

Pohl said she was "much more career-minded" than he was willing to accept in a wife.
Also, "She was deathly opposed to having children, and . . . I didn't like having the option
foreclosed. . . . we got along quite well most of the time, but somewhat to my surprise she
went to California in 1948 and I got a letter from her saying, 'The weather is very nice here
and my mother is fine, and by the way, I've filed suit for divorce.'"

Specialty SF dealer Robert A. Madle told me she contacted him in the late 1990s searching
for a copy of the magazine with her 1943 story, "When You Think That . . . Smile!"

Ethel G. Lewis (?–?): Lewis seems to have had a small literary magazine career in the 1950s.
At least that is what one gleans from editor Leo Margulies's introduction to her story, "Lights
Out for Rosalie," in the June, 1956 *Fantastic Universe.* "Ethel G. Lewis," he said, "has been a
quite successful contributor to the little reviews and to be successful in that highly discrimi-
nating field is never easy." She published three other SF stories in 1955–1956, all in *Fantastic
Universe.*

A. (Alice) M. (Martha) Lightner (Hopf), (1904–1988): Lightner was born in Detroit and graduated from Vassar College with a degree in music and English. After graduation she moved to New York City to work on an engineering magazine. She was also a respected entomologist and member of the Lepidopterists' Society who published several well-received books on natural science. She began her SF career in *Boy's Life* ("A New Game," 1959) before making her genre magazine debut.

She was also known for her SF juvenile novels, including *The Rock of Three Planets* (1963), *The Planet Poachers* (1965), *Doctor to the Galaxy* (1965), *The Galactic Troubadours* (1965), *The Space Plague* (1966), *The Space Olympics* (1967), and *The Space Ark* (1968). Her post-holocaust novel, *The Day of the Drones* (1969), found Africa surviving the nuclear destruction and sending an exploration party to the remains of the British Isles, where they find the white remnants have evolved into a hive society. This was followed by *Star Dog* (1973), *Gods or Demons?* (1973), *The Space Gypsies* (1974), and *Star Circus* (1977).

Victoria (Endicott) Lincoln, (1904–1981): Lincoln was a historical novelist and biographer of Teresa of Avila, with many books and short stories in her decades-long career. Born in Fall River, Massachusetts, as a child she knew the famous Fall River axe murderer Lizzie Borden, about whom she wrote, *A Private Disgrace: Lizzie Borden by Daylight* (1967). This won her the 1968 Edgar Allan Poe Award for Best Fact Crime Book from the Mystery Writers of America.

One of her more important historical novels is *February Hill* (1934). Her stories appeared in *The Atlantic Monthly, Collier's, Glamour, Good Housekeeping, Redbook, Vogue,* and, of course, *The Magazine of Fantasy and Science Fiction.* These were collected in her book, *The Wild Honey.*

Amelia Reynolds Long (1904–1978): A resident of Harrisburg, PA, Long wrote detective stories (as "Peter Reynolds"), fantasy, and science fiction. She was a regular in *Weird Tales* between 1928–1936. Her story, "The Thought-Monster" *(Weird Tales,* March, 1930), became the 1957 British film, *Fiend Without a Face.* Similar in theme to *Forbidden Planet* (1956), a scientist perfected the ability to physically project his thoughts, which then carried out dirty deeds. It was unusually graphic for the period.

On a joint car trip Charles D. Hornig and Julius Schwartz visited her in 1935 (when she was in her early thirties) and found her wearing high-buttoned shoes and old-fashioned clothing from Civil War days. In 1963 Forrest J. Ackerman visited her and found her still living alone in Harrisburg. "I guess she died a spinster," he recalled. "I have only the vaguest memory of her as being a kind of 50ish librarian type." (Ackerman, *Gosh! Wow! (Sense of Wonder) Science Fiction,* p. 531.) She stopped writing SF because it began appearing in comic strips and she felt it was undignified to compete with comics.

(Mildred) "Mindret" Lord (Loeb) (1903–1955): Lord was born in Chicago and was a respected Hollywood and TV screenwriter from the end of World War II until her suicide in 1955 at age fifty-two. In addition, she published much fantasy fiction in *Weird Tales* from 1934–1943.

Her film credits include *Strange Impersonation* (1946), *The Glass Alibi* (1946), *Yankee Fakir* (1947), *The Sainted Sisters* (1948), *Alias Nick Beal* (1949), and *The Big Bluff* (1955). Lord also wrote the original story for *Alias Nick Beal,* a contemporary Faustian morality play directed by John Farrow, the father of actress Mia Farrow. In it, Ray Milland is an effective modern-dress Beelzebub (alias "Nick Beal") to whom a crusading judge sells his soul in exchange for the governorship of a state.

Lord's most well known film credit was perhaps as the screenwriter for the 1955 Bette Davis vehicle, *The Virgin Queen*, which also starred a young Joan Collins. Bette Davis had already portrayed England's Queen Elizabeth I in the 1939 classic, *The Private Lives of Elizabeth and Essex*. Here she reprised the role in Lord's story, which suggested an ultimately tragic romance between Elizabeth and the adventurer Sir Walter Raleigh. However, in the story, Sir Walter had designs upon lady-in-waiting Joan Collins.

Lord had just entered the field of television script writing with the short-lived 1955 TV series, *The Lone Wolf*, when she killed herself in Los Angeles three days before Christmas, 1955.

"Lilith Lorraine" (Mary Maude Dunn Wright) (1894–1967): Lorraine was born in Corpus Christi, Texas, and educated at the University of Texas in Austin and the University of Arizona in Tucson. She was discovered by Hugo Gernsback, who published her stories "The Brain of the Planet" (1929) and "Into the 28th Century" (1930), both feminist socialist utopias.

She was also a sometime journalist and a well-known poet who published many volumes of poetry, several of them genre-oriented. She also founded the Avalon World's Arts Academy and edited its journal, *Different*, as well as other poetry magazines, such as *Challenge*. Her magazines published much fan poetry, as well as the work of professionals. In 1953 she discovered a new writer named Robert Silverberg and published his first story in *Different*.

She was a champion of SF verse over many decades and edited a genre poetry column in the original *Fantasy Book*. Her 1951 collection, *Wine of Wonder*, is thought to be the first ever book of science fiction poetry. Despite this, her pioneering work in the field of science fiction poetry has been forgotten. Thus, the science fiction poetry award is not named in her honor. Instead, it is named the Rhysling Award, after a completely fictional Robert A. Heinlein character.

Kathleen Ludwick, (1892–1970?): A resident of Oakland, California, Ludwick contributed to several pulp magazines in various genres, notably *Western Story*. She may have later moved to New York and died in Maryland.

(Mabel) Dana Lyon (1897–1982): Primarily a mystery novelist, her novels included *Retaliation* (1934), *It's My Own Funeral* (1944), *The Tentacles* (1950), and *The Trusting Victim* (1964). Her 1948 novel, *The Frightened Child*, was turned into the 1951 movie, *The House on Telegraph Hill*, directed by Robert Wise and starring Richard Basehart.

Anne (Inez) McCaffrey (1926–   ): McCaffrey was born in Cambridge, Massachusetts, and graduated from Radcliffe College, Harvard University, in 1947 with a B.A. (cum laude) in Slavonic languages and literature. She studied voice and drama and directed opera before turning to writing. She eventually produced and directed the American premiere of Carl Orff's *Ludus de Nato Infante Mirificus*. She was married to E. Wright Johnson, "a Princeton man," for 20 years (1950–1970), and with whom she had two sons and a daughter. She now lives on a horse farm in Ireland.

She was a copywriter for Helena Rubinstein from 1950–1952. However, she always wanted to write fiction and, in 1953, Sam Moskowitz and Hugo Gernsback published her first science fiction story, "Freedom of the Race," in *Science-Fiction Plus*. Her husband did not approve. Even so, she continued writing.

Perhaps her most popular work comprises the multi-novel Dragonriders of Pern series.

These are stories about a long-lost colony of humans telepathically linked to dragons. Together they periodically save the planet Pern from invaders from a nearby planet. Despite the use of dragons, they are scientifically rationalized, having been genetically engineered into existence. These stories won her a joint Hugo in 1968 for the novella, "Weyr Search" (which was also nominated for the 1968 Nebula); a Nebula in 1969 for "Dragonrider"; the Gandalf in 1979 for *The White Dragon*; and the Balrog for her 1980 *Dragondrums*. The series also made her one of the few science fiction writers (and the *only* female SF writer) to make the *Publishers Weekly* annual bestseller list, that being in 1983 for *Moreta: Dragonlady of Pern*. Her Dragonrider stories also spawned a vast network of fan clubs.

Despite this popularity, McCaffrey once said her favorite story was 1961's "The Ship Who Sang." This was the story of a deformed girl grafted into a spaceship, essentially becoming the ship. It was expanded into a 1969 novel of the same name and has generated several popular sequels. She also served as the Secretary-Treasurer of the Science Fiction Writers of America, 1968–1970.

Winona McClintic, (?–?): McClintic published science fiction into the early 1960s, but seems to have ceased thereafter. However, she also wrote excellent genre poetry. In fact, her poetry published in *The Magazine of Fantasy and Science Fiction* more than tripled the number of her stories that appeared in that magazine. Three of the best are "The Doctrine of Original Design" (1955), "I Want My Name in the Title" (1956), and "Ye Phantasie Writer and His Catte" (1958).

Helen (Worrell Clarkson) McCloy (1904–1994): It is likely that Helen McCloy was the same person as "Helen Clarkson" (see her entry). Helen McCloy was known to use "Helen Clarkson" as a pseudonym and both published in the same magazine, *Satellite SF,* within four months of each other in December 1957 and April 1958.

Katherine (Anne) MacLean (1925–   ): Born in Glen Ridge, NJ, MacLean received a B.A. in Economics from Barnard College, Columbia University, in 1950. She was discovered in 1949 by John W. Campbell. Her career as a short story writer quickly blossomed in the 1950s. In 1971 she won the Nebula Award for her short story, "The Missing Man," later expanded into a 1975 novel. Her first novel, *Cosmic Checkmate* (1962), co-authored with Charles de Vet, was also an expansion of a prior short story ("Second Game," 1958).

She worked as a laboratory assistant (1944–1945), a food manufacturing technician (1945–1946), and a technician in New York's Memorial and Knickerbocker Hospitals (1954–1956). Not surprisingly, therefore, medical backgrounds figure prominently in many of her stories, from "Contagion" (1950), in the debut issue of *Galaxy*, to her novel *Dark Wing* (1979). The latter, co-authored with Carl West, her third husband, portrays a society in which medicine has been outlawed. Much of her work also centers around ethical questions involving medical experimentation and scientific "progress."

She helped organize the Free University of Portland (Maine) and taught writing in the English Departments of the University of Connecticut and the University of Maine. From 1951–1953 she was married to fellow science fiction writer Charles Dye (1927–1955). From 1956–1962 she was married to sword and sorcery author David Mason (1924–1974), with whom she had a son. She presently resides in Maine, where she continues to write.

Rachel Maddux (Baker) (1912–1983): Maddux was born in Wichita, Kansas, and graduated from the University of Kansas. She began writing in the 1930s, debuting with "Turnip's

Blood" in *Story Magazine*, December 1936. Her 1957 lost world novel, *The Green Kingdom* (reprinted 1993), centered on the interrelations of five strangers trapped in an unknown landscape.

Dorothy (Haynes) Madle (?–?): In addition to her science fiction, she also published fantasy poetry in *Weird Tales*, 1946.

"Rory Magill" (Dorothea M. Faulkner) (1889–?): "Dottie," as she was known to her friends, became active in the Los Angeles Science Fantasy Society (LASFS) and the affiliated Outlander Society in the late 1940s. She often co-edited the club's famous fanzine, *Shangri-La,* as it was known at the time. She was described by fellow LASFS and Outlander member Len Moffatt as, "a little old grey-haired lady from Covina [an L.A. suburb] and the type of person we used to call a 'pistol.'" She wrote letters to the professional SF magazines under the name "Grandma the Demon" and published both serious and humorous fiction and poetry.

Moffatt went on to say of her, "Intelligent, well-read, opinionated, and articulate, she was fun to be with, to talk with, even if you might not agree with her right-wing politics. She carried on a correspondence with John W. Campbell, Jr., Eric Frank Russell, and Robert A. Heinlein. She was the widow of a Naval officer and had at least one daughter whom I only met once or twice. She was as independent as a hog on ice . . . and an outstanding story teller and limerick reciter." She most likely had more than one child, as she said she wrote the letter which appeared in the September, 1951 *Planet Stories* (p. 110) while babysitting three of her thirteen grandchildren. She would have been about sixty-two at that time.

In a letter to the fall 1955 issue of *Startling Stories* under the name "Rory Magill Faulkner," she complained about the demise of *Thrilling Wonder Stories* and *Fantastic Story* and the fact that *Startling* had fallen to quarterly publication. "Is this a sign of the decline and fall of science fiction? I hope not, for what am I going to read then? I don't like slick magazines, love stories, and am fed to the teeth with murder mysteries. In sheer self defense I have gone back to the beginning of my SF collection and have been reading the old ones over again." She objected to "The Snows of Ganymede," by Poul Anderson, because there was, "Too much sociological stuff in this story for me. I like 'em more human—and I don't mean love stories, either."

She then told us a little about herself: "I had a good going over by my doctor last month, the first one in 20 years, and he gave me at least 40 years more to live. Since I am now 66 [which would put her birth date at 1889], it seems likely I'll get my wish to see the space station launched, and the first moon flight. I hope I can last out till they hit Mars, too! Also, I'd like to see Halley's comet again. I remember it well from 1910."

A photograph of her taken in the late Forties or early Fifties, showing a grandmotherly figure in glasses at a meeting with Anthony Boucher, can be found online at www.smithway .org/fanpix/album/15–04.html.

J. (Julian) C. May (1931–   ): May was married to SF anthologist T. E. Dikty from 1953 until his death in 1991. After her impressive debut story, "Dune Roller," in John W. Campbell's *Astounding Science Fiction*, December 1951, and one other in the 1950s, there was a long genre silence from her. Instead, she concentrated on writing over 290 science fact books, many of them juveniles under the name of Ian Thorne.

However, her fan interests continued during this time and in 1952 she chaired ChiCon II, the World Science Fiction Convention in Chicago, becoming the first woman to chair a Worldcon. In 1957, with Dikty, she established the influential small specialty press, Publication Associates. Also, under the pseudonym of Lee N. Falconer, in 1977 she authored *A Gazetteer of the Hyborian World of Conan.*

In the 1980s she returned to the field as a fiction writer, launching a successful new career with her well-received science fantasy Pliocene Exile series. These included *The Many-Colored Land* (1981), *The Golden Torc* (1982), *The Nonborn King* (1983), and *The Adversary* (1984). She launched a second connected series, the Galactic Milieu, with *Intervention* (1987), *Jack the Bodiless* (1992), *Diamond Mask* (1994), and *Magnificat* (1996).

Meanwhile, she collaborated with Marion Zimmer Bradley and Andre Norton on a fantasy sequence that began with *Black Trillium* (1990) by all three authors. May then wrote *Blood Trillium* (1992) alone, followed by Norton, who wrote *Golden Trillium* (1993) alone. Bradley followed with *Lady of the Trillium* (1995) alone. Then May finished the sequence with *Sky Trillium* (1997). She continues to publish.

"Judith Merril" (Josephine Juliet Grossman) (1923–1997): Born in New York City, Merril was the daughter of two Zionist socialists and attended City College of New York, 1939–1940. A member of the Futurians during and after World War II, she was discovered and first published by John W. Campbell in 1948. Throughout the 1950s she prolifically published short fiction. Her story, "Dead Center" (1954), is an emotionally powerful story of love and death in an astronaut's family following the first Moon landing. Editor Martha Foley was so moved by the story that she chose it for her prestigious anthology *The Best American Short Stories: 1955.*

Merril published her first novel, *Shadow on the Hearth*, in 1950. In 1954 it was dramatized on television as "Atomic Attack." This was an episode on early television's live anthology series, *Motorola TV Theater,* and starred Walter Matthau. She also collaborated with fellow Futurian C. M. Kornbluth on three novels (*Gunner Cade* and *Outpost Mars,* 1952, and *Sin in Space,* 1961) under the joint pseudonym of "Cyril Judd."

She was hired as an editor at Bantam Books in 1947 and began editing her influential series of SF anthologies in 1950 with *Shot in the Dark.* With Damon Knight she organized and from 1956–1961 she was the Director of the Milford Science Fiction Writers Conference. From 1965–1969 she was the book reviewer for *The Magazine of Fantasy and Science Fiction.* After 1960 she concentrated more on editing and reviewing and less on writing. From 1956 to 1968 she helped shape the literature with her annual "year's best" collections. In these and in her book review column in *The Magazine of Fantasy and Science Fiction* (from May, 1965, to May, 1969) she attempted to broaden the field by looking at similar literature published outside genre magazines.

In her anthologies and columns she also campaigned to replace the term "science fiction" with "speculative fiction," which she felt more accurately reflected the nature of the literature. She was an important American champion of British "New Wave" SF, which she spotlighted in her noted 1968 anthology, *England Swings SF.*

Appalled by the police riot at the 1968 Democratic Party convention in Chicago, which she attended, Merril self-exiled herself to Toronto, Canada, for the rest of her life. There she worked as a radio and television documentary scriptwriter for the Canadian Broadcasting Corporation. She was affiliated with Rochedale, an experimental counter-cultural school in Toronto, and was involved in the American community of draft exiles in Canada. She also performed in the long-running British television SF series, *Dr. Who.*

She was married to Daniel Zissman from 1940–1947, with whom she had a daughter, Merril (after whom Judith Merril's last name is taken). She was Frederik Pohl's third wife (after "Leslie Perri" and Dorothy LesTina), with whom she also had a daughter. She and Pohl met in 1948 and were married from 1950–1953. From 1960–1975 she was married to Daniel W. P. Sugrue, a merchant mariner and union organizer, although they were separated for the great bulk of that time.

Her and Pohl's daughter completed Merril's autobiography, which won the non-fiction Hugo Award in 2003. The entry on her in Curtis C. Smith's *Twentieth-Century Science-Fiction Writers* (St. Martin's Press, 1981) is written by Elizabeth Anne Hull, Frederik Pohl's current wife, and contains misleading information about Pohl's marriage to Merril.

C. (Catherine) L. (Lucille) Moore, (1911–1987): Before there was Xena, the Warrior Princess, there was Jirel of Joiry, Catherine Lucille Moore's 1934 creation in the *Weird Tales* story, "Black God's Kiss." Thus, Moore launched the first series of sword-and-sorcery stories to feature a female protagonist. Other immensely popular tales of the warrior queen soon followed in *Weird Tales*, including "Black God's Shadow" (1934), "Jirel Meets Magic" (1935), "The Dark Land" (1936), "Quest of the Starstone" (1937), and "Hellsgarde" (1939).

Born in Indianapolis, Moore was the daughter of a tool and machine designer and manufacturer. Because of ill health, she was home educated until the fifth grade by her mother and tutors. After high school she studied for a year and a half at Indiana University before the financial pressures of the Great Depression forced her to leave.

She was working in an Indianapolis bank as a typist when she made her impressive genre debut with "Shambleu" for *Weird Tales* in 1933. She published it using only her initials in order to conceal her involvement in pulp magazines from her employer. "Shambleu" is perhaps her most famous story. It is a tale of a seductive Medusa-like alien and was extremely erotic for the field at that time. She quickly became one of the foremost writers in *Weird Tales* and proved just as popular in science fiction when she debuted in *Astounding* in 1934. Despite her flourishing genre career, she continued working at the bank until she married fellow fantasy and science fiction author Henry Kuttner (1915–1958) in 1940. By the time of their marriage, Moore had worked her way up to secretary to the bank's president.

Although prolific as a solo artist throughout the Thirties, publication under her own name decreased greatly after her marriage to Kuttner. Thereafter, much of the work of both was of a collaborative nature, with it being extremely difficult to discern who wrote what. Moore once said that, "I felt my contribution was in terms of characterization. I brought a certain texture of sensory detail to our characters, which didn't particularly interest Hank. He had a rather terse style [and] dealt with visual externals more than I did. I dealt more with inner feelings."

They were so prolific as a team that they wrote under seventeen joint pseudonyms, such as "Lawrence O'Donnell," "Keith Hammond," and "Hudson Hastings." But the most famous of their pen names, by far, was "Lewis Padgett," who became a mainstay at *Astounding* during World War II and famous and popular in "his" own right. Indeed, one 1943 Padgett story, "Mimsy Were the Borogroves," is included in the Science Fiction Hall of Fame. Another story by O'Donnell, "Vintage Season" (1946), is now credited to Moore alone and is also in the Science Fiction Hall of Fame. It was filmed in 1992 as *Grand Tour: Disaster in Time,* an excellent made-for-cable movie starring Jeff Daniels.

After their marriage and a brief stint by Kuttner in the Army during World War II, they lived in New York. In the late Forties they moved to Los Angeles. In 1950 they jointly enrolled at the University of Southern California, where they eventually graduated (Moore in 1956) with high honors and as members of the scholastic honor society, Phi Beta Kappa. The next year, 1957, Moore published her last solo SF novel, *Doomsday Morning*. Both she and Kuttner taught creative writing at USC, with Moore continuing to do so after Kuttner's sudden death of a heart attack in 1958 at age forty-three.

In the late Fifties they moved into the mystery field and published several joint mystery-suspense novels, becoming joint vice-presidents of the West Coast chapter of the Mystery Writers of America. This led to them being hired as screenwriters by Warner Brothers. There they conceived the idea for a new Warner Brothers TV Western called "Sugarfoot." It was a traditional Western with plenty of action, but with a light humorous touch that distinguished it from the crowd. It aired from 1957–1961 and centered around a correspondence school law student who was so inept as a cowboy he was one step below a tenderfoot. After Kuttner's death, Moore continued writing for "Sugarfoot," as well as "Maverick," "77 Sunset Strip," and other popular TV shows.

In 1963 she married businessman Thomas Reggie and in 1964 earned her M.A. from USC. In 1975 Lester del Rey edited much of her best work into the appropriately titled collection, *The Best of C. L. Moore*. She announced at the Second World Fantasy Convention in 1976 that she would begin writing fantasy once more, although she published nothing. The World Fantasy Convention also named her a Grand Master in 1981 for her lifetime achievement in the field. She began an autobiography, but never finished it. She suffered from Alzheimer's for many years before her death in 1987.

Maria Moravsky (?–?): Moravsky was a noted Russian Jewish poet and writer in a variety of genres. In January of 1917 woman suffrage leader Alice Paul and her followers began picketing the White House demanding the right to vote. Many, including Paul, were imprisoned and subjected to brutal treatment. Moravsky was visiting America on a speaking tour at that time. In October she testified before Congress in support of the incarcerated women. She told the Congressmen that she had been imprisoned in Siberia twice by the Czar's government for her writings. Neither time, however, was her treatment as harsh as what the jailed suffragists were then suffering.

After the Bolshevik coup d'etat she went into permanent exile in England and, like Joseph Conrad before her, made the difficult transition to writing and publishing in English. In addition to her science fiction, her byline was a familiar sight to fantasy fans, as she also published much fiction and poetry in *Strange Stories* between 1939–1941 and in *Weird Tales* between 1926–1948.

"Andre Norton" (Alice Mary Norton) (1912–2005): Norton published more than 130 novels and almost 100 short stories. She was born in Cleveland, Ohio, the younger of two daughters of a rug salesman. In high school she edited a fiction page for the student newspaper and, while still a student, wrote a novel, *Ralestone Luck*, which became her second published novel in 1938.

She enrolled at Cleveland's Case Western Reserve University hoping to become a history teacher, but dropped out in her freshman year due to the financial pressures of the Great Depression. She published her first book, a juvenile adventure entitled *The Prince Commands*, in 1934 at age twenty-two. Because she envisioned a career writing juvenile historical adventures, that same year she legally changed her name to "Andre Norton." She would not make her professional science fiction debut for another twenty years.

Norton worked as a children's librarian at the Cleveland Public Library from 1932–1950, interrupted in the early 1940s when she worked at the Library of Congress and briefly owned a bookstore in Maryland. From 1950–1958 she worked as a reader for the pioneering small specialty science fiction publisher Gnome Press. When she left Gnome Press to become a full-time writer, she had already published twenty-three novels and several short stories. Thereafter she concentrated on a highly successful writing career.

During the 1950s and early 1960s Norton wrote many juvenile space operas, the most notable of which are *The Time Traders* series. However, her novel, *Witch World*, was a Hugo contender for Best Novel in 1963 and she is perhaps best known for the Witch World series of more than 30 novels, which that book launched. That first novel in the series had an ostensible science fiction beginning, but quickly veered into fantasy. The subsequent novels became outright fantasy.

She was honored for her many juvenile adventure novels by the Boys Clubs of America in 1965. She was also honored by the World Fantasy Convention in 1977 as a Grand Master of Fantasy and in 1978 she became the first woman to be presented with the Gandalf Award. In 1983 her peers awarded her the Grand Master Nebula Award for career achievements, also the first woman to be so honored. That same year she also won the Fritz Leiber Award. In 1998 the World Fantasy Convention presented her with a Life Achievement Award.

She retired to Murfreesboro, Tennessee. In 2004 she divested herself of her vast library and moved into her caregiver's home due to her failing health. She died of congestive heart failure March 17, 2005, at age ninety-three. In her memory the Science Fiction and Fantasy Writers of America established the Andre Norton Award for young adult novels, with the first award being presented in 2006.

"Marian O'Hearn" (Anita Allen) (?–?): She was married to James Perley Hughes, a prolific writer for pulp magazines of various genres. Likewise, O'Hearn wrote in various pulp genres, such as the detective story, but primarily Western romances for *Ranch Romances*. Her short story, "Soldiers of the Black Goat," for John W. Campbell's *Unknown* (January, 1940), was later expanded into a novel the same year.

"Leslie Perri" (Doris Baumgardt), (c.1920–1970): "Leslie Perri" was the fan name of Doris Baumgardt. She and Brooklynite Rosalind Cohen (later long-time editor of puzzle magazines for Dell) joined the Futurian science fiction club in December, 1938. They are thus thought to be the earliest female members of this famous New York club. (Others of the earliest female Futurians were Elsie Balter, who married Futurian Donald Wollheim, and Jessica Gould, who married Futurian Richard Wilson.)

Perri wrote prolifically for the Futurian fanzines. She was also a founding member of the Fantasy Amateur Press Association (FAPA), created by Donald Wollheim for fans to exchange fanzines. Because the Futurians threatened to disrupt the proceedings, Perri was one of only five Futurians Sam Moskowitz allowed inside the hall at the First World Science Fiction Convention in 1939. Isaac Asimov, Richard Wilson, David Kyle, and Jack Rubinson were the others.

Fellow Futurian Damon Knight described her as, "a tall, cool brunette who looked a little like the Dragon Lady in 'Terry and the Pirates'." She had been the high school sweetheart of Futurian Frederik Pohl, who introduced her to the Futurians. Pohl said she was "strikingly beautiful, and strikingly intelligent, too, in a sulky, humorous, deprecatory way." Although he first courted her friend, Rosalind Cohen (who married Futurian "Dirk Wylie"), Pohl married her in 1940.

In the early 1940s she edited (and mostly wrote) a short-lived romance pulp entitled *Movie Love Stories*. According to Richard Wilson, "What she would do would be to get stills from the studios, and then she'd get a copy of the script and fictionalize it—turn it into a short story or a novelette."

As an artist, she also contributed work to *Astonishing Stories,* a short-lived SF magazine Pohl edited from its founding in February, 1940, until September, 1941. Another female science fiction artist and author, Dorothy LesTina, was also contributing artwork to this magazine. Pohl became interested in LesTina and he and Perri separated in 1942.

After Perri divorced Pohl she married Tom Owens, an artist and writer. They had one daughter, Margot. When that marriage ended, she married another science fiction writer. This was fellow Futurian Richard Wilson, who had previously married Perri's good friend and fellow Futurian, Jessica Gould. Perri divorced Wilson in 1965. She died of cancer in 1970.

Phyllis Lee Peterson (1909–?): She was a Canadian writer who debuted in *The Canadian Home Journal.* Her book, *The Log Cabin in the Forest,* was published in 1954. She became a prolific television scriptwriter in the 1960s, adapting many works for serialization.

Dorothy Quick, (1896–1962): Quick was born in New York City and educated at Plainfield Seminary, New Jersey. In 1907, when she was almost eleven, she met Mark Twain, then seventy-two, on a trip aboard the SS. *Minnetonka.* The two of them remained friends until Twain's death in 1910. She visited him many times at both his home at Tuxedo Park in New York and at his Connecticut home. He encouraged her to write and seems to have had a profound influence on her. Quick's well-received memoir of their friendship, *Enchanted: A Little Girl's Friendship With Mark Twain,* was published in 1961, just before her death. It is still in print from the University of Oklahoma Press as *Mark Twain and Me.*

Quick did go on to become an author. She supported herself as a "working girl" in stores and offices before she became popular writing for magazines such as *Weird Tales* and John W. Campbell's *Unknown.* She published her first book of poetry, *Threads,* in 1927. She made her genre debut in *Oriental Stories* (Spring, 1932) with her story "Scented Gardens." It had the honor of being illustrated on the cover by Margaret Brundage, in her own debut as a cover artist. Brundage would go on to paint more covers for *Weird Tales* than any other artist in the 1930s and become the artist most closely identified with that magazine.

Between 1934–1954 Quick published over two dozen stories, as well as much poetry, for these fantasy magazines. Indeed, she was the most prolific female poet to appear in *Weird Tales* and she was one of the most prolific female fiction writers for that magazine.

She also published fifteen books of poetry (for which she became well-known), romances and mysteries, in addition to her Mark Twain memoir. Beginning with *Threads,* these included *Changing Winds* (1935), *Spears Into Life* (1938), *Strange Awakening* (1938), *To What Strange Altar* (1940), *Laugh While You Can* (1940), *Variations On a Theme* (1947), *The Fifth Dagger* (1947), *One Night in Holyrood* (1949), *Interludes* (1953), *Cry in the Night* (1959), *Too Strange a Hand* (1959), *The Doctor Looks at Murder* (1959), and *Bold Heart and Other Poems* (1960).

Mark Twain would have been proud of her.

Ayn Rand (Alyssa "Alice" Rosenbaum), (1905–1982): Rand was born in St. Petersburg, Russia. She graduated from the University of Petrograd (formerly St. Petersburg, then Leningrad, now St. Petersburg again) in 1924.

In 1926 she emigrated to the United States from what was then a Soviet Union in the midst of revolution and civil war. She settled in California and worked hard to learn English in order to be a writer. She became an American citizen in 1931. In 1932 she sold her first screenplay, *Red Pawn*, to Universal Studios. Her first play, *The Night of January 16th*, had a substantial 1935–1936 run on Broadway. It was revived in 1973 as *Penthouse Legend* and continues to be a staple of little theater. Taking place entirely in a courtroom, a jury is selected from the audience each night to decide the fate of the heroine. In 1940 a second play, *The Unconquered*, had a short Broadway run.

She published her first novel, *We, the Living*, in 1936. This was followed in 1938 by the dystopian *Anthem*. This novel is about the protagonist's search for identity in a conformist future society in which even the word "I" is forbidden. When the protagonist realizes he is an individual, he names himself "Prometheus." These first two novels were mostly ignored. But in 1943 she published the best-selling mainstream novel, *The Fountainhead*. It was made into a 1949 movie starring Gary Cooper, directed by King Vidor, and scripted by Rand herself. This established her reputation as a novelist of ideas.

Her next best-seller was the science fictional *Atlas Shrugged*, in 1957. It, too, is a dystopian novel of a near-future socialist America in which things are falling apart because individual excellence is discouraged in favor of mass mediocrity. Worth and performance are devalued, as laws and rewards are established to help only those in need. A small band of brave rebels try to set things "right," rebuilding society along the individualistic "Objectivist" philosophical lines Rand espoused. The theme struck a resonant chord in many readers. A 1991 survey by the Library of Congress and the Book of the Month Club found *Atlas Shrugged* to be second only to the Bible as a book that most influenced readers' lives.

She wrote no more fiction after *Atlas Shrugged*, turning instead to a series of non-fiction books. These included *The Virtue of Selfishness* (1964), *Capitalism: The Unknown Ideal* (1966), and *The New Left: The Anti-Industrial Revolution* (1971). These books expressed her deeply conservative belief in free market capitalism and unapologetic self-interest as the greatest social virtue. She scorned altruism and self-sacrifice for the common good as liberal delusions and social vices. Her views found a wide following on college campuses in the 1950s, where Ayn Rand Clubs proliferated.

In 1971 historian William O'Neill published a biography of her aptly titled, *With Charity Toward None*. In 1991 Mary Gaitskell caricatured Rand and her philosophy in *Two Girls, Fat and Thin*. She was working on an adaptation of *Atlas Shrugged* for a TV miniseries when she died in New York City.

Kaye Raymond (?–?): According to Everett Bleiler, Raymond was living in Chicago in the 1930s at the time her stories appeared in *Astounding* and *Wonder Stories*. He was not impressed with "Into the Infinitesimal," which appeared in *Wonder Stories*, June 1934. He termed it, "Badly written, with a romance on a shopgirl level."

Margaretta W. Rea (?–?): Everett Bleiler searched the Social Security Death Index and discovered a Margaretta Rea (1916–1986) living in New Jersey and a Margaretta Rea (1876–1967) living in Pennsylvania, both of whom fit the age range for this author. Otherwise, nothing is known of her. Bleiler thought her "Delilah," *Amazing Stories*, January 1933, a story about somnambulism, was a bit risqué. "Hardly suitable for a SF magazine," he said, "even if it had been better written."

"Kit" (Lillian Craig) Reed (1932–   ): Catholic writer "Kit" Reed was born in San Diego and earned a B.A. from the College of Notre Dame of Maryland, Baltimore, in 1954. She worked for many years as a newspaper journalist, beginning with the *St. Petersburg Times* (Florida) from 1954–1955. In 1955 she married Joseph Reed, Jr., who became a professor of English at

Wesleyan University in Middletown, CT. They had two sons and a daughter. In Connecticut she worked on the *Hamden Chronicle* (1956) and the *New Haven Register* (1956–1959). She was voted New England Newspaperwoman of the Year in 1958 and 1959 and in 1964–1965 was awarded a Guggenheim Fellowship. She was also the first woman to be awarded the Abraham Woursell Foundation's literary grant.

It was in 1958, while working as a reporter, that she began publishing fantasy and science fiction. She has also published mystery stories, such as "The Perfect Portrait," *Ellery Queen's Mystery Magazine,* July, 1968, and the suspense thriller, *Tiger Rag,* 1973. In addition to her genre fiction she has published at least ten mainstream novels, the first being *Mother Isn't Dead, She's Only Sleeping* (1961). Her second, *At War As Children* (1964), was about the World War II generation. *The Better Part* (1967), dealt with juvenile delinquency. Her non-genre short stories have appeared in both European as well as American magazines, such as *Seventeen.* In 1969 she won the award for Best Catholic Short Story of the Year and in 1976 was awarded an Aspen Institute Rockefeller Fellowship. She has also been a Visiting Professor of English at Wesleyan University, beginning in 1974. In 1982 she published a guide to writing entitled *Story First: The Writer as Insider.*

The focus of much of her work has been the impact of technology on people's lives. The science fiction tropes, however, are not the central concerns. They are mere devices to explore people's relations to each other and society at large. Her first science fiction novel, *Armed Camps* (1969), was very much a reaction to the turbulent Sixties. It featured endemic war as a daily experience, with the female protagonist retreating to a pacifist commune.

In *Magic Time* (1980), America has become a ghoulish theme park run by a Walt Disney-type manager in cryogenic suspension. In *Fort Privilege* (1985), the residents of a privileged high-rise condo are under siege from New York's homeless hordes. *Blood Fever* (1986) was a horror novel written under the name of "Shelley Hyde." Some of her short stories have been collected in *The Killer Mice* (1978), *Other Stories And . . . the Attack of the Giant Baby* (1981) and *Revenge of the Senior Citizens* (1986). She continues to write in many genres.

"L. Major Reynolds" (Louise Leipiar) (?–?): She was a long-time active member of the famous Los Angeles Science Fantasy Society (LASFS). She published a dozen science fiction stories between 1950–1955. She also published mysteries, e.g., "Second Chance," in *Malcolm's Magazine* (January, 1954), reprinted in the single-issue 1960 British magazine, *A Book of Weird Tales.* Editor Donald A. Wollheim lavishly praised her second published story, "The River," when he ran it in *Avon Fantasy Reader No. 16* in 1951. He said the "unknown author" had not submitted it to him, but to "another Avon publication." Even so, it "piqued our imagination" when he saw it in the slush pile, as "this is no pulp story, and fits no magazine's formula." So, he snatched the "unknown author's" manuscript for his own publication.

"Craig Rice" (Georgiana Ann Randolph), (1908–1957): Rice was a California mystery novelist, short story writer, and screenwriter. Her specialty was humorous crime capers reminiscent of Hollywood's screwball comedies of the Thirties and Forties, such as the Thin Man series. She began writing mysteries with her first novel, *Eight Faces at Three* (1939). Her last completed novel was *My Kingdom For a Hearse* (1956). *The April Robin Murders* (1958) was left uncompleted at her death and finished by noted mystery and sometime SF writer Evan Hunter ("Ed McBain"). Under the name "Daphne Sanders" she published *To Catch a Thief* (1943), which some consider her best novel. She also published three mysteries as "Michael Venning."

As a screenwriter she co-wrote two of the well-known series of detective films featuring

"The Falcon," these being *The Falcon's Brother* (1942) and *The Falcon in Danger* (1943). She also wrote the original story for the 1950 film, *The Underworld Story,* about a small town newspaper reporter fighting powerful business interests to unravel a murder cover-up.

She ghosted both of the mysteries attributed to stripper Gypsy Rose Lee, *The G-String Murders* (1941) and *Mother Finds a Body* (1942). *The G-String Murders* was turned into the 1943 movie, *Lady of Burlesque.* For the actor George Sanders (who starred as the Falcon in *The Falcon's Brother*) she ghosted *Crime on My Hands* (1944). It is possible well-known SF author Cleve Cartmill collaborated with her on the latter novel.

At the peak of her prodigious output she was one of the most famous mystery writers in America. Anthony Boucher arranged to have her *Trial by Fury* (1941) reprinted in a series of classic detective novels and in 1946 her photo graced the cover of *Time* magazine. She died in Los Angeles at age forty-nine. Today her work is mostly forgotten.

Jane Rice (?–?): In addition to fantasy and science fiction, she also published short stories in such glossy magazines as *Charm, Cosmopolitan,* and *Ladies' Home Journal.* She also published in *The Magazine of Fantasy and Science Fiction* under the pseudonym, "Mary Austin." Her 1943 werewolf story, "The Refugee," which first appeared in John W. Campbell's *Unknown,* was reprinted in the 1990 collection, *Rivals of Weird Tales.* She collaborated with Ruth Allison under the joint name of "Allison Rice" for "The Loolies Are Here" in Damon Knight's *Orbit 1* anthology (1966). Her horror novelette, *The Sixth Dog,* was published as a chapbook in 1995 by Necronomicon Press, thus becoming her first book.

Louise Rice (1880–?): Everett Bleiler believes this author was Louise Guest Rice, "born in Indiana, writer of cookbooks and mystery stories, and an occasional contributor to the pulp magazines, including a graphology column to *Mystery Magazine.* She is possibly the Louise Rice of Navesink, New Jersey, who contributed a letter to the August [1930] issue of *Amazing Detective Tales."*

Jane Roberts (Butts), (1929–1984): She was born in Albany, New York, and attended Skidmore College, 1947–1950. She married Robert F. Butts in 1954 and lived in Erie and Sayre, Pennsylvania. She was the author of both science fiction and witchcraft fantasy, appearing mainly in *The Magazine of Fantasy and Science Fiction.* Damon Knight was introduced to her in 1956, the same year she began publishing SF, by fellow Futurian Cyril Kornbluth. He described her as "slender and dark, thin to the point of emaciation; she had enormous dark eyes." That year Kornbluth, who was interested in witchcraft, brought her to the first Milford (Pennsylvania) Science Fiction Writers' Conference.

At that Milford Conference, Roberts conducted an emotional seance with Kornbluth, Knight, James Blish, and Algis Budrys, where she went into a trance and prophesied. At one point, Knight remembered, "we were grouped in a tight circle with our arms around each other; all the lights had been turned out except one dim one; it may have been a candle. Cyril was expressing his misery, and I began to sob, feeling as I did so that I was crying as his surrogate. We left the meeting with a feeling of closeness that went beyond friendship . . . the affection the rest of us felt for each other remained undiminished for years."

Agent Virginia Kidd, who was married to Blish, recalled to Knight that, "None of the Five would discuss it, it was a closed subject. I think Jane was a focus. . . . I got the feeling that everybody thought Cyril was the leader, and Jane was the witch—that he was using Jane's potential to bind you all into something that had never happened before. It was maybe something on the order of *More Than Human* (Theodore Sturgeon's novel about a group personality)." (*The Futurians*, pp. 148–49, 154.)

From the sketchy descriptions, this sounds like a pre-Synanon and small-group version of their "game." Synanon was a late-Sixties Santa Monica drug rehabilitation center that evolved into a social movement and then a dictatorial cult before finally dissolving. It perfected a group process for breaking through the normal barriers people place around themselves and using emotion to bond a diverse collection of people into a unified Gestalt.

Harlan Ellison became intrigued by the process and participated in Synanon "games" for some years. In 1969 and 1971 he was a guest instructor at the renowned Clarion Writers' Workshop. The 1969 Workshop was held at Clarion University, in Clarion, Pennsylvania, and the 1971 Workshop was held at Tulane University, in New Orleans. At both Workshops, Ellison became the catalyst for a playing of the Synanon "game." Ellison and the participants described experiences very similar to the smaller "seance" Jane Roberts led at Milford in 1956. For those interested in a detailed description of the "games" at these two Workshops, see Ellison's essay about them, "You Are What You Write," in Robin Scott Wilson, Ed., *Clarion II: An Anthology of Speculative Fiction and Criticism*, Signet Books, 1972.

In Jane Roberts's first novel, *The Rebellers* (Ace Books, 1963), a rebel underground battles a dictatorial government in an overpopulated and ecologically devastated future in which successive plagues have almost exterminated humanity. More typical is *The Education of Oversoul Seven* (1973), in which a student inhabits the bodies and souls of humans living from 35,000 B.C. to A.D. 2300, learning thereby the unity of all time, humanity and reality. Two sequels followed in 1979 and 1984. She also wrote a juvenile novel, *Emir's Education in the Proper Use of Magical Powers* (1979).

In the 1960s Roberts began channeling a ghost named Seth and her most famous book, *Seth Speaks* (1972), is a collection of spiritualist dialogs with him, spoken in a trance by Roberts. Her first such book, however, was *How to Develop Your ESP Powers* (1966). Other books in the same vein were *Seth Material* (1970), *The Nature of Personal Reality* (1974), *The Unknown Reality* (1977), and *Dreams, Evolution and Value Fulfillment* (1986). Another well-known work, a series of connected poems, is *Dialogues of the Soul & Mortal Self in Time* (1975). Roberts is now considered to have been one of the most important psychics of the twentieth century.

Mary-Carter Roberts, (?–?): She was the State Travel Writer for Maryland in 1955, a position she held until her retirement in 1969. She also published in *Collier's*.

Kay Rogers, (?–?): The editorial blurb introducing her debut in the June, 1951 issue of *The Magazine of Fantasy and Science Fiction* described her as a single "a green-eyed redhead" who "lives with 34 cats" in Russell, Pennsylvania. Her story, "Flirtation Walk," appeared in Alice Laurance's 1978 anthology, *Cassandra Rising*.

Babette Rosmond, (1921–1997): Born in New York City, Rosmond was primarily a mainstream novelist, editor, and biographer. She was first married to Leonard M. Lake, with whom she published short fiction in the early 1940s. Then, in 1944, she married Henry J. Stone, a prominent New York City lawyer, with whom she had two sons.

She published her first short story in *The New Yorker* at age seventeen. She also had many non-fiction books to her credit, including *Shut Up, He Explained: A Ring Lardner Selection* (1962), edited by her and actor Henry Morgan. As a teenager she had met Robert Benchley, the famed humorist and drama critic. After his death she gathered his personal files, scrapbooks, and reminiscences of friends and family members to write an appreciative biography. This became the well-received, *Robert Benchley: His Life and Good Times* (1970).

John W. Campbell, who published her, said she "wrote some nice stuff" for him. Like Campbell, she was also an editor for the giant Street & Smith magazine publisher, in her case from 1941–1948. Indeed, while still in her twenties, Rosmond simultaneously edited two of the most legendary of pulp magazines. These were Street & Smith's *Doc Savage*, which she edited from 1944–1948, and Street & Smith's *The Shadow*, which she edited from 1946–1948.

Then, from 1952–1953, she was the fiction editor of *Today's Family*, followed by editorial positions at *Better Living* (1953–1956) and the popular girls' teen magazine, *Seventeen* (1957–1975), where she was also the fiction editor. In the latter position she edited a number of anthologies of fiction drawn from *Seventeen*. These included *Seventeen's Stories* (1958), *Seventeen from Seventeen* (1967), *Seventeen Book of Prize Stories* (1968), and *Today's Stories from Seventeen* (1971).

In the meantime, she was publishing novels, including *The Dewy Dewy Eyes* (1946), *A Party for Grown-Ups* (1948), *Lucy: or, The Delaware Dialogues* (1952), *The Children* (1956), *The Lawyers* (1962), and, as "Francis M. Arroway," *Diary of a Candid Lady* (1964).

In the early 1970s she also became a celebrated pioneer of the breast cancer survivors' movement. In February of 1971, the fifty-year-old Rosmond discovered a lump in her left breast. The reigning surgical wisdom of the day routinely called for a radical mastectomy to remove a cancerous breast in its entirety, along with the underlying arm and chest wall muscles and adjacent lymph nodes. Two of her friends had already undergone such radical mastectomies and Rosmond was horrified by what had been done to them by the medical establishment. Rosmond publicly challenged the medical profession's unwillingness to inform patients about alternatives to radical mastectomy and the unilateral power of doctors to do as they thought best concerning breast cancer—without consulting patients.

When her own physician told her he would anesthetize her and perform a biopsy and, if necessary, a radical mastectomy during the same operation, Rosmond refused permission. She wanted a biopsy first, followed by a discussion of options. She later said that the doctors told her that, "You must sign this paper, you don't have to know what it's all about," telling her that she was the first woman who, in their experience, had refused to approve the one-step procedure. Nevertheless, her original surgeon agreed to only do the biopsy. The biopsy revealed a small eight-millimeter cancer, localized in the outer portion of her breast. He then wanted to immediately perform a radical mastectomy, telling her the diagnosis mandated the procedure and there were no other options.

Rosmond declined, saying she wanted three weeks to decide. Her surgeon, she said, then told her she was "a very silly and stubborn woman" and that, "In three weeks, you may be dead." Even so, she used the next three weeks to do extensive research and finally opted for a lumpectomy with another surgeon, declining follow-up radiation therapy on the rest of the breast. It turned out to be the right decision for her, as she lived without a recurrence for another quarter of a century. She always emphasized, however, that what she fought for was not necessarily a lumpectomy rather than radical mastectomy, but for a personal choice in her treatment.

In "The Right to Choose," a famous February 1972, article in *McCall's* (written under the pseudonym of "Rosamond Campion"), Rosmond described her experience as a breast cancer patient and noted that three-quarters of the women who underwent radical mastectomies died anyway. She decried the medical rush to cut, discussed her decision to have a minimal lumpectomy, and argued that women deserved information about their treatment so that they could give "informed consent." She believed that surgeons who refused to discuss options with their patients and made decisions for them, even under the guise of benevolence, were "arrogant, prejudiced [and] disinterested in human beings."

Her essay resulted in more mail to *McCall's* than any other essay in the history of the magazine. Later that year she published a pathbreaking account of her encounter with breast cancer in the book, *The Invisible Worm* (also as by "Rosamond Campion"). The essay and subsequent book unleashed a tidal wave of subsequent articles in newspapers and magazines, essentially launching the revolt of breast cancer patients against the paternalism of the medical profession.

Rosmond also appeared on a series of television programs in the early Seventies, confronting doctors about their attitudes toward patients. A notable appearance was a January 21, 1973 appearance on the *David Susskind Show*. On the program, Rosmond held her own against three surgeons and two women who were satisfied with their radical mastectomies. One surgeon challenged Rosmond, "Would you rather keep your breast or die of the cancer?" She responded, "There is no such choice. No one knows what the choice is." There were more possible options than this stark choice, she insisted, but the medical profession refused to consider that possibility.

Such activism had an effect. A 1973 Gallup Poll revealed that 48 percent of respondents had come to reject the standard one-step biopsy-and-radical mastectomy procedure in favor of a review of various treatment options, should the biopsy turn out to be positive. Because of the struggles of Babette Rosmond and others like her for a patient's "right to choose," the relationship between doctors and breast cancer patients changed markedly in the 1970s.

In 1979 the National Cancer Institute passed a landmark recommendation (which became standard practice) that breast biopsies be done as part of a two-step procedure in most cases. That is, a diagnostic specimen should first be studied with pertinent histologic sections. Then, a woman should discuss her treatment options (including non-surgical approaches) with her doctor in order to make an informed decision about her health care. By the early 1980s conclusive evidence existed that radical mastectomy was never indicated (automatically mandated) in the treatment of breast cancer.

For more information on this aspect of women's health history, and Babette Rosmond's part in it, see Barron H. Lerner, *The Breast Cancer Wars: Hope, Fear, and the Pursuit of a Cure in Twentieth-Century America*, Oxford University Press, 2001. And for an excellent photo of Babette Rosmond, log on to www.nature.com/nrc/journal/v2/n3/slideshow/nrc744_F2.html.

Rosmond herself went on to a productive career of many more years. She published the books *Error Hurled* (1976) and *Monarch* (1978). In 1985 her classic 1943 short story, "One Man's Harp," originally published by Campbell, was reprinted in *A Treasury of American Horror Stories*, edited by Frank D. McSherry, Jr., Charles G. Waugh, and Martin H. Greenberg. She also authored radio scripts and contributed articles to *The New Yorker, Mademoiselle, McCall's, The New York Times, Punch,* and other popular publications.

Babette Rosmond died in New York in 1997, a week short of her 76th birthday, surrounded by her husband, her children, and her grandchildren. The most likely cause of death was a new breast cancer that she refused to have diagnosed or treated.

M. (Margaret) F. Rupert (?–?): Rupert was a Chicago author. A portrait (based on a photo) of her by noted early science fiction artist Frank Paul was published with her story, "Via the Hewitt Ray," *Science Wonder Quarterly,* Spring, 1930. It showed a middle-aged woman, suggesting she may have been born around the turn of the twentieth century.

The story entails travel to a parallel dimension, wherein we discover a feminist utopia. This utopia came into existence after a sex war in which men were virtually exterminated. "For untold centuries [men] had kept women subjugated," the heroine is told, "and we finally got our revenge." A small number of brainwashed and docile males are kept on hand for breeding or purposes of pleasure. Sam Moskowitz mentioned this story in the introduction to *When Women Rule* (1972), his anthology of female-dominant science fiction stories, but for some unnamed reason did not include it among the stories he reprinted.

Joanna Russ (1937–): Russ comes from a family of Russian Jews who fled Russia around the time of the 1905 Revolution. She was born and raised in New York City's Bronx borough, where her mother was an elementary school teacher and her father a high school carpentry shop teacher. From a young age she was interested in science and in 1953 she was one of the top ten high school finalists in the national Westinghouse Science Talent Search.

She earned a Bachelor's in English from Cornell University in 1957, where she also won both the Browning and the Shakespeare Essay Prizes. She then earned a Master of Fine Arts in playwriting from the Yale University Drama School in 1960. Several of the plays she wrote at Yale have been produced. In 1974 she also won a Fellowship from the National Endowment for the Humanities and in 1975 won the O. Henry Award for "The Autobiography of My Mother."

While a student at Yale she debuted in the September, 1959, issue of *The Magazine of Fantasy and Science Fiction* with "Nor Custom Stale." Her 1970 story, "The Second Inquisition," was nominated for the Nebula. She was Nebula-nominated again in 1971 for the novelette, "Poor Man, Beggar Man." She was finally awarded the short story Nebula by her peers in 1972 for "When It Changed", her savage feminist tale of the all-female planet Whileaway. In 1982 her novelette, "The Mystery of the Young Gentleman," was again Nebula-nominated. In 1983 she won the Best Novella Hugo, Nebula, and Locus Awards for "Souls." Much of her short fiction is collected in *The Zanzibar Cat* (1983), *Extra(ordinary) People* (1984), and *The Hidden Side of the Moon* (1987).

Her first novel, *Picnic on Paradise*, a 1968 Ace paperback, was about the female adventurer Alyx and was also nominated for the Nebula. Its use of a tough and competent female protagonist was pioneering and liberating for subsequent women writers. Her 1970 novel, *And Chaos Died*, was Nebula-nominated, but her third novel is her most important. This is the Nebula-nominated *The Female Man* (1975), a trail-blazing feminist work. It postulates four alternate lives for its female protagonist before bringing these alternate selves together on the utopian female planet of Whileaway. It was followed by five more novels.

Russ was also a long-time book reviewer for *The Magazine of Fantasy and Science Fiction*, in 1988 she won the Pilgrim Award for best SF criticism, given for her body of work. Meanwhile, she became well-known as a close critic of gender and social power relations from a lesbian-feminist perspective. Her *On Strike Against God* (1982), *How To Suppress Women's Writing* (1983), and *Magic Mommas, Trembling Sisters, Puritans and Perverts: Feminist Essays* (1985) are now considered classics in feminist literary criticism. She was honored for this work in 1995 with a Special Retrospective James Tiptree, Jr. Memorial Award.

For many years Russ taught as an English professor at Cornell (1970–1972), the State University of New York at Binghamton (1972–75), the University of Colorado at Boulder (1975–1977), and at the University of Washington at Seattle from 1977 until her retirement in the 1990s. She now lives in Tucson, Arizona.

Margaret St. Clair (Neeley), (1911–1995): St. Clair was born in Hutchinson, Kansas. She moved to California and earned an M.A. (Phi Beta Kappa) from the University of California,

Berkeley, in 1933. In 1932 she married horticulturist "Eric St. Clair" (George A. Pflaum), who was a laboratory assistant in the Physics Department at the University of California. With him she operated the St. Clair Rare Bulb Gardens in El Sobrante, California, from 1938–1941.

With the end of the war in 1945 she turned to full-time detective writing. Her mystery debut, "Letter from the Deceased," appeared in *Detective Story Magazine* in March, 1945, even before the war ended. She also published fiction in *Dime Mystery Magazine* and the men's magazine, *Gent*. Under the pseudonym "Wilton Hazzard" she published an article in the magazine *Indian Stories* on "Geronimo—Red Scourge of the Southwest."

She also began writing science fiction, with her debut being the 1946 story, "Rocket to Limbo," in *Fantastic Adventures*. To introduce this exciting discovery to his readers, editor Ray Palmer published her photo and an autobiographical mini-essay by her on the inside of the cover. In addition to her extensive resume of science fiction short stories, she published at least eight science fiction novels. The first of these was the extraordinary *Agent of the Unknown* (1952) (with its android protagonist), as well as *Mistress of Viridis* (1956), *The Games of Neith* (1960), *Sign of the Labrys* (1963), *Message from the Eocene* (1964), and *The Dolphins of Altair* (1967). The latter is centered on ecological issues and is considered among her best. *The Dancers of Noyo* (1973) is a heady mix of political oppression, androids, Native Americans, and post-holocaust California.

From 1946–1960 (the period under discussion) she published 91 science fiction stories, 70 under her own name and another 21 under the name of "Idris Seabright." She continued to publish many more into the 1980s. The "Idris Seabright" stories appeared mostly in *The Magazine of Fantasy and Science Fiction*, where this "new" author quickly established her own reputation and following. The first story under the Seabright pseudonym, "The Listening Child" (December, 1950), was chosen by Martha Foley of the prestigious *Short Story* magazine as one of the distinguished short stories of the year. She also published fantasy fiction in *Weird Tales* between 1950–1954. Many of her short stories can be found in the collections *Three Worlds of Futurity* (1964), *Change the Sky and Other Stories* (1974), and *The Best of Margaret St. Clair* (1985).

She was voted a member of the Fantasy Hall of Fame by the Science Fiction and Fantasy Writers of America. As "Eric St. Clair" her husband was also an author of science fiction short stories, as well as children's books.

G. (Gladys) St. John-Loe, (1895–?): She was a British author of supernatural and mainstream novels, such as *The Door of Beyond* (1926), *Spilled Wine* (1932) and *Smoking Altars* (1936). Her story, "Where Four Roads Met," *Astounding Stories,* October 1933, is a science fiction mystery story.

Mabel (Hodnefield) Seeley, (1903–1991): Seeley was born in Hermanville, Minnesota, but her family moved to St. Paul while she was young. Her father, Jacob Hodnefield, was the newspaper curator of the Minnesota Historical Society in St. Paul. She graduated summa cum laude from the University of Minnesota in 1926 and married Ken Seeley. They moved to Chicago where she wrote advertising copy while her husband worked on a master's degree. After her husband contracted tuberculosis, they returned to the Twin Cities area to seek medical treatment for him. They later divorced and Mabel turned to writing mystery novels to support herself and her young son, Gregory. By the late 1940s she and her son had settled in California. Her many crime novels were immensely popular from the late 1930s into the 1950s, with many books to her credit.

Some of her more popular novels included *The Listening House* (1938), *The Crying Sisters* (1939), *The Whispering Cup* (1940), *The Chuckling Fingers* (1941), *Eleven Came Back* (1943), *The Beckoning Door* (1950), and *The Whistling Shadow* (1954). While on an East Coast tour to promote *The Whistling Shadow,* she met attorney Henry Ross, whom she married in 1956. After this marriage, Seeley stopped writing.

Wilmar H. (House) Shiras, (1908–1990): Shiras was born and raised in Boston. In 1927, at age 18, she married Russell Shiras, with whom she had three daughters and a son. They moved to Oakland, California, where she attended Holy Names College. Her first book, the 1946 mainstream novel *Slow Dawning,* was published as by "Jane Howes." She also published several non-fiction books under this name. She earned an M.A. from the University of California, Berkeley, in 1956.

Her debut science fiction story, "In Hiding," was published in John W. Campbell's *Astounding,* November 1948. It was judged one of the best stories of the year and is now included in the Science Fiction Hall of Fame. Her expansion of "In Hiding" into the novel, *Children of the Atom* (1953, 1954, 1978), is now considered a classic. She continued to write and publish into the 1970s.

Barbara Silverberg, (c.1940?–): During the period under consideration, she was the first wife of prolific SF author Robert Silverberg. (Since 1987 Robert has been married to SF writer Karen Haber.) Barbara was an electronics engineer with a Bachelor of Science in physics. She was also extremely active in SF fandom. She now lives in Berkeley, California, and produces a fanzine for a small amateur press association.

April Smith, (?–?): The 1953 story she published in *Astounding* was co-authored with Charles Dye, who was then married to SF author Katherine MacLean. It is possible she was therefore part of the same New York SF community as Dye and MacLean and who were then selling to *Astounding* editor John W. Campbell.

Evelyn E. Smith (1927–2000): A native resident of New York City, Smith wrote over 40 SF stories and appeared in almost all the SF magazines of the Fifties, primarily *Galaxy.* Her production of articles was even more prolific. She was also a professional compiler of crossword puzzles for publications ranging from *Curtain and Drapery Magazine* to *The New York Times.* Introducing her crossword themed story in the September, 1955 issue of *The Magazine of Fantasy and Science Fiction,* editor Anthony Boucher said, "As a crossword addict myself, I am astonished to learn that these intricacies can be composed by a delightful and witty brunette in her twenties."

Her popular 1962 satirical novel, *The Perfect Planet,* concerned a planet which had originally been established as a "fat farm" and developed that concept to an extreme after being isolated by an interstellar war. She also wrote SF and fantasy novels as "Delphine C. Lyons" (e.g., *Valley of Shadows,* 1968, and *Unpopular Planet,* 1975). As Lyons she also wrote the nonfiction 1972 book, *Everyday Witchcraft.* Her 1985 satirical novel, *The Copy Shop,* situated space aliens in New York City—where they were unnoticed.

Smith was also a mystery writer and created a unique character in the gently bred art teacher/painter female assassin "Miss Susan Melville." The first in the series of novels featuring this heroine, *Miss Melville Regrets* (1986), finds Miss Melville fallen on hard times after the genteel art school at which she taught closes. As a political protest, she decides to kill herself at a high society social event. However, she changes her mind and kills the hateful and morally corrupt guest of honor instead. She is then recruited by a secret group that specializes in assassinations, which had also targeted the victim. In the following novels, her victims are always rich, pretentious, morally dubious individuals who "deserve to die," for one reason or another.

I. (Inga) M. (Marie) Stephens, (?–?): She was the wife of noted fantasy and science fiction author (as well as historian and biographer) Fletcher Pratt (1897–1956). She was also an artist who illustrated some of Pratt's books. In the Thirties their Hudson River home was a favorite gathering place of New York City science fiction writers.

Fletcher Pratt frequently collaborated with other authors and both of Stephens's early Thirties stories were collaborations with her husband. However, in a 1986 letter to me, legendary SF historian Sam Moskowitz, who knew the couple, commented that Pratt "was never a good story teller" and that "his wife, Inga M. Stephens, collaborated with him for years on his early science fiction." If so, none of this was credited to her. But, the two stories we have from Stephens might be two in which her contributions were so extensive that Pratt felt *obligated* to finally credit her.

Both Pratt and Stephens were Christian Scientists, which may explain why Stephens was referred to as "a scientist" in the blurb for "A Voice Across the Years," *Amazing Stories Quarterly,* winter 1932.

G. (Gladys) B. (Bronwyn) Stern, (1890–1973): Stern was a British mainstream novelist who published over fifty books in a half-century career. Born in London, she married Geoffrey Lisle Holdsworth. Her more notable novels include *Pantomime* (1914), *The Black Seat* (1923), *Tents of Israel* (1924, published in America as *The Matriarch,* later dramatized), *Thunderstorm* (1925), *Debonair* (1928, later dramatized), *Mosaic* (1930), *Monogram* (1936), *The Woman in the Hall* (1939), *Another Part of the Forest* (1941), and *The Young Matriarch* (1942). She died in Wallingford, England.

"Francis Stevens" (Gertrude Barrows Bennett), (1883–1948?): Sam Moskowitz described Gertrude Bennett as "the greatest woman writer of science fantasy in the period between Mary Wollstonecraft Shelley and C. L. Moore." Gary Hoppenstand, an academic who wrote the introduction to a 2004 collection of her fiction, termed her, "The woman who invented dark fantasy." This is a type of horror story in which humanity is threatened by forces beyond human understanding.

Born in Minneapolis, she obtained only an elementary school education. However, she acquired stenographic and secretarial skills and worked as such before marrying an English newspaper reporter named Stewart Bennett. They moved to Philadelphia and in 1910, eight months after the birth of their daughter, Josephine, her husband drowned in a storm while seeking sunken treasure. She then became a secretary for a University of Pennsylvania professor, while typing student papers at night. Toward the end of World War I her father died and she took in her invalid mother.

As a full-time caregiver, work outside the home was no longer practical, so she turned to writing as a means to support her family. She had some realistic hopes for this, as she had already written her first story at age seventeen while working as a secretary in a Minneapolis department store. This was a science fiction story entitled, "The Curious Experience of Thomas Dunbar," as by G. M. Barrows. She sent it to one of the top pulps of the day, *Argosy,* which immediately accepted it and published it in March 1904. Within a week another magazine, *Youth's Companion*, had accepted her first poems. She therefore had reason she would be able to sell stories once more.

Her first such story, "The Nightmare," appeared in the April 14, 1917 of Frank Munsey's *All-Story Weekly*. She had sent the story to the editor, Bob Davis, under her own name. However, she requested that it appear under the pen-name of "Jean Vail." But, Davis seems to have decided otherwise, as it appeared under the pseudonym of "Francis Stevens." Reader response was positive and Davis encouraged her to write more. Having been established under the "Francis Stevens" name, she thereafter continued to publish under that name, even though it was not of her choosing.

Readers praised her stories, with noted fantasy authors A. Merritt and H. P. Lovecraft being among of her most ardent fans. Indeed, according to Hoppenstand, both of these authors, credited as the progenitors of dark fantasy, emulated Bennett's earlier style and themes. "The Citadel of Fear," which appeared in the companion Munsey magazine, *Argosy Weekly*, Sept. 14–Oct. 26, 1918, was a lost race story. In a letter to the magazine of November 15, 1919 (and written under the pseudonym of "Augustus T. Swift"), Lovecraft said of it that, "if written by Sir Walter Scott or Ibanez, that wonderful and tragic allegory would have been praised to the skies," as it offered "masterful evidence of huge mystery, gigantic tragedy, and original and extraordinary situations . . . Stevens, to my mind, is the highest grade of your writers."

Her story, "Friend Island" (*All-Story Weekly*, September 7, 1918), is a mature work of feminist alternative history which rejects traditional gender stereotypes. *The Heads of Cerberus* (*Thrill Book*, 1919) is an early parallel universe dystopia of a totalitarian future. Long-time *Astounding* book reviewer P. Schulyer Miller thought it was the first of this kind. In *Claimed* (*Argosy Weekly*, March 6–20, 1920), a dark sea god reclaimed an ancient artifact taken by humans. Her last original story was the 1923 "Sunfire," a lost race novella serialized in *Weird Tales*.

She moved to California in 1936 and her daughter received a last letter from her in 1939. After that they lost contact and nothing is known of her subsequently, although it is believed she may have died in 1948. From 1940–1950 editor Mary Gnaedinger reprinted six of her stories in *Famous Fantastic Mysteries* and *Fantastic Novels*, including "The Elf-Trap" (*Argosy Weekly*, July 5, 1919), a modern fairy tale and one of her best works. These helped keep her reputation alive. Most of her short fiction was published in 2004 by the University of Nebraska Press in *The Nightmare and Other Tales of Dark Fantasy*.

Leslie F. Stone, (1905–1991): Born in Philadelphia, Stone's family moved to Virginia when she was eight. She began selling fairy tales to newspapers at age fifteen. Perhaps for this reason she studied journalism in school. She was married to William Silberberg from 1927 until his death in 1957. They had two sons. In the late 1940s they moved to Kensington, Maryland, where she became a prize-winning ceramicist and gardener. In the 1960s she worked at the National Institute of Health in Bethesda.

Along with Clare Winger Harris, Stone was one of the first women writers to appear in the science fiction magazines, debuting in 1929. Her science fiction was most popular in the Thirties. She also published two SF novels. In addition to her science fiction, she published fantasy fiction in *Weird Tales* between 1935–1938. Her last story appeared in 1951.

"Jan Struther" (Joyce Anstruther Placzek), (1901–1953): Born in London, she became a well-known English author of poems, sketches, short stories, and novels. She married Adolf Kurt Placzek in 1948. Damon Knight recalled an early 1940s Pocket Books party honoring her in the penthouse of the RCA Building, to which Futurian Donald Wollheim had given him and fellow Futurian Johnny Michel tickets. Michel was an alcoholic and became "an ugly drunk" when drinking. He drank at the party and insulted Struther before tipping over the party cake.

Her most successful creation was "Mrs. Miniver," a typical middle-class English housewife whose activities were first told in stories published in *The Times* (of London), before appearing in book form as *Mrs. Miniver* (1939). Director William Wyler's 1942 film of the same title is considered a classic depiction of British homefront fortitude during the World War II Blitz. It won the Best Actress Oscar for star Greer Garson. The 1950 sequel, *The Miniver Story*, told of Mrs. Miniver's brave struggle against cancer. The author herself died of cancer in New York at age fifty-two not long after the publication of her story, "The Ugly Sister" (1952) in *The Magazine of Fantasy and Science Fiction*.

Helen M. Urban, (?–?): Urban lived in North Hollywood, CA, and was active in the influential Los Angeles Science Fantasy Society (LASFS) during the 1950s. She published only two stories in American SF magazines in the Fifties, and another two in British SF magazines. However, as late as 1980 she published an exquisite little horror story in the original anthology, *Microcosmic Tales: 100 Wondrous Science Fiction Short-Short Stories,* edited by Isaac Asimov, Martin H. Greenberg, and Joseph Olander. Entitled "Tag," it comprised only a single sentence—272 words long!

In a letter she wrote to the March, 1957 *Imaginative Tales,* she praised "The Cosmic Kings," by Alexander Blade, in the November, 1956 issue, and said it "was a fast-paced, interesting space opera and I loved every minute of it. I'm a sucker for a good space opera."

Rena M. (Marie) Vale, (1898–1983): American novelist and short story writer. She began writing SF in 1952 with "The Shining City" in *Science Fiction Quarterly.* Her 1950s novel, *Beyond the Sealed World,* was purchased by Shasta Publishers, the legendary specialty genre press. However, Shasta went bankrupt before they could publish it. Paperback Library finally brought it out in 1965.

It is the story of a man who is expelled into the liberating wilderness from an encapsulated and stagnant far future society. There he finds several different civilizations at various levels of advancement. "At first he struggled only for his own life amidst conditions for which his test-tube life had ill-equipped him," the cover blurb on the paperback edition tells us. "But soon he realized that not only his future was at stake, but the future of all the worlds of Earth—and that he was the one man who could save the Universe!"

Other works included *The Red Court: Last Seat of National Government of the United States of America* (1952), *Beyond These Walls* (1960), *Taurus Four* (1970), and *The Day After Doomsday: A Fantasy of Time Travel* (1970), a polemic on the horrors of nuclear war. *Taurus Four* was a space opera satire that mixed an alien invasion with hippies lost on another planet. *The House on Rainbow Leap* (1973) was her last novel.

Emma Vanne, (?–?): A journalist who, in the mid-Thirties, lived in Westfield, New Jersey. Her fiction indicated a familiarity with gardening. She seems to have been a regular reader of the SF magazines, as she also wrote at least one letter to *Wonder Stories* in July 1935. Nothing else is known about her.

"Lyn" (Marilyn) Venable, (?–?): A resident of Dallas, Texas, Venable was reputed to have been active in Midwestern SF fandom in the Fifties. During that time she published four stories in American SF magazines and a fifth in the British *Authentic SF.*

Her story, "Time Enough at Last" (*If,* January, 1953, as by "Lynn" Venable), was chosen by Rod Serling to be aired November 20, 1959 under the same title (and by-line) on his CBS television series, *The Twilight Zone.* It was the eighth episode of that legendary TV show's first season and the first time main writer Serling turned to another writer for a story. It starred Burgess Meredith as a beleaguered bookworm who finds "time enough at last" to read all he wants after a nuclear holocaust. The story is one of the most memorable, if not the most famous, of TZ episodes and won the director that season's Director's Guild award.

She also published fantasy fiction in *Weird Tales* (1953). A letter of hers in the January, 1952 *Planet Stories* praised Ray Bradbury (whose work she seemed familiar with) as ". . . a great writer, one of the greatest of our generation."

Helen Weinbaum (Kasson) (?–?): She was the sister of Stanley G. Weinbaum, perhaps the best of the early science fiction writers. Her famous brother's incipient career was cut short by cancer in 1935.

Helen debuted with "Tidal Moon," in *Thrilling Wonder Stories,* December 1938. It was supposedly the completion of a story begun by her brother. The story was accompanied by her photo, which portrayed a middle-aged woman, and the editorial note that she "contributes mystery fiction for our companion magazines."

However, Margaret Weinbaum, Stanley Weinbaum's widow, told me that this "collaboration" was a complete fabrication. Margaret typed all of her husband's hand-written stories and possessed the original manuscripts and said there is nothing about this story that came from Stanley Weinbaum. The claim thus embittered the rest of the family toward Helen, as they felt she was exploiting her brother's fame and popularity.

Be that as it may, Helen went on to publish six more solo science fiction stories between 1938–1941, all of which were as good as the norm for genre fare at that time. She also published fantasy stories in *Weird Tales* between 1940–1945 under her married name of Helen W. Kasson.

Elma Wentz (?–?): In 1934 Robert A. Heinlein was a campaign worker for ex-Socialist Upton Sinclair in his run for the governorship of California. Sinclair had formed an organization known as EPIC (End Poverty in California), which drew in many idealistic dissidents like Heinlein. Surprisingly, Sinclair won the Democratic primary to become the Democratic Party's candidate for governor. The Republicans and the corporations stopped at nothing to beat Sinclair. This included voter fraud, as, although officially defeated, Sinclair probably won the election.

Subsequently, EPIC continued for a short time as a "party within the party," putting up candidates for various offices in Democratic primaries. In 1936 Heinlein was one such EPIC candidate for Congress. While working for EPIC, Heinlein became acquainted with Elma Wentz, the wife of a fellow EPIC worker. They shared an interest in science fiction and the eventual result of that interest was a collaboration on the story, "Beyond Doubt," published in *Astonishing Stories* in 1941. By this time Heinlein was an ascendant star in the science fiction firmament and he chose to hide his collaboration with Wentz behind the pseudonym, "Lyle Monroe." Heinlein worked hard (and for the most part successfully) at concealing his EPIC past and any associations with it, and so nothing more is known of Elma Wentz.

Kate (Katie Gertrude Meredith) Wilhelm (Knight), (1928–   ): Wilhelm was born in Toledo, Ohio, and has won many SF awards, including the Short Story Nebula in 1968 for *The Planners*, the Short Story Nebula in 1986 for "The Girl Who Fell Into the Sky," and the Short Story Nebula again in 1987 for "Forever Yours, Anna." She also won the Hugo and Locus Awards for Best Novel in 1977 for *Where Late the Sweet Birds Sang.*

She was married to Joseph B. Wilhelm from 1947–1962, with whom she had two sons. She married Damon Knight (1922–2002) in 1963, with whom she had three children. She was co-director of the famous Milford Science Fiction Writers Conference from 1963–1972 and was a lecturer at the Clarion Science Fiction Writers' Workshop from 1968–1970. She also edited an anthology of stories from the Clarion Workshop, *Clarion SF* (1977). In addition, she was the editor of *Nebula Award Stories 9* (1974).

Her first novel in 1963 was actually a mystery, *More Better Than Death,* followed in 1965 with her first SF novel, *The Clone,* co-authored with Theodore L. Thomas. It was nominated for that year's Nebula, the first year that award was presented.

Also in 1965 her Stepford-Wives-Gone-Awry story, "Andover and the Android," was aired on the prestigious British television SF anthology series, *Out of the Unknown.* Her 1971 story, "The Infinity Box," was Nebula-nominated and became the lead in her 1975 short story collection, *The Infinity Box.* Her 1979 novel, *Juniper Time,* is an effective treatment of ecological themes. In 1980 she and Damon Knight were Worldcon Guests of Honor and in 2003 she was inducted into the Science Fiction and Fantasy Hall of Fame. Her 1993 story, "Naming the Flowers," was nominated for a host of SF awards, including the Hugo and the Nebula. In 1997, "Forget Luck" was also Hugo-nominated.

In recent years she has primarily written mysteries, after writing novels such as 1977's *Fault Lines,* which is actually an intersection of SF and the mainstream. Other early mysteries include *The Killing Thing* (1967) and *Let the Fire Fall* (1969). Her husband-and-wife detectives, Charlie Meiklejohn and Constance Leidel, first appeared in short stories before being featured in a novel, *The Hamlet Trap,* 1987. Another Meiklejohn and Leidel novel, *The Dark Door* (1988), blended science fiction and mystery, as did *Smart House* (1989) and *Sweet, Sweet Poison* (1990). Her legal mysteries began with *Death Qualified: A Mystery of Chaos* (1991), a *New York Times* Notable Book of the Year. It incorporated a science fictional element in an investigation into chaos theory and the perception of reality. She lives in Eugene, Oregon and continues to write and publish prolifically.

Jeanne Williams (1930–?): As with her SF, Williams began writing Western short stories in the early Fifties, selling mostly to *Ranch Romances.* When introducing her second SF story in the January 1955 *Fantastic Universe,* editor Leo Margulies wrote that Williams, "started writing seriously two years ago while studying at Ohio University. She is 24 and has a five-year-old son and an Air Force husband. She has sold thirteen Western stories." Williams went on to publish a number of Western novels, which seems to have been her primary interest.

"Gabriel Wilson" (Gabrielle Wilson Cummings), (?–?): This pseudonym was probably used by Gabrielle Cummings in collaboration with her husband, noted early SF writer Ray Cummings (1887–1957), who published over 750 stories. However, neither Mike Ashley nor Everett Bleiler, who have written on this possibility, are sure. Although only one SF story appeared under this pen name, the couple seem to have used it frequently in writing mystery stories.

Thrya Samter Winslow, (1893–1961): Winslow was an American Jewish journalist, mainstream novelist, and short story writer. Her 1926 novel, *Show Business,* concerning chorus girls on Broadway, was a bestseller. Perhaps for this reason she was featured in a 1927 edition of "Who's Who in American Jewry." Other notable novels included *Blueberry Pie* (1932) and *My Own Native Land* (1935). *Picture Frames* was a 1923 collection of her short work. In 1955 she published the non-fiction book, *Be Slim, Stay Slim.* She died in New York.

Laura Withrow, (?–?): In 1916 Bob Davis, the editor of Frank Munsey's *All-Story Weekly,* announced a policy of publishing what he termed "different" stories, for lack of a better label. These, he said, would be "the queer, *outre,* unusual, bizarre, exotic, misfit manuscripts that . . . are mighty good, but so 'different' that they would ordinarily never be accepted."

Laura Withrow's "The Kiss of Death" was the third such "different" story published under this policy, appearing in the issue of April 8, 1916. However, the only thing really "different" about the story was that it reveled in the happy triumph of a woman who got away with poisoning her hated husband and who felt no remorse.

But it shared with the other stories being published under the "different" policy what Sam Moskowitz termed, in *Under the Moons of Mars,* his study of the Munsey magazines, "direct or implied elements of sex." Moskowitz speculated that Davis published these stories as part of his attempt to, "quite deliberately and calculatingly," build circulation by widening his female readership. Indeed, the August 19th issue of that year would be an almost all-female issue, as all the stories, except two serials carried over from the previous issue, were by women. These included eight of the ten stories and all of the seven poems. In any case, the story must have impressed Mary Gnaedinger, editor of *Famous Fantastic Mysteries,* as she chose to reprint it in 1940 and advertise it on the cover.

Mari Wolf, (1927–?): Unusually for a woman in the Thirties and Forties, Wolf studied mathematics in school. This led to an interest in rockets and a professional science career in rocket testing, which she described in the column on genre fanzines she edited for *Imagination: Stories of Science and Fantasy.* In the February 1954 issue of that magazine (p. 147), she said, "I work at a rocket testing lab, in the wind tunnel section. Rockets have always been one of my major interests—I've read science fiction for years and years. . . . I belong to the Pacific Rocket Society and have had some of the best times of my life out in the Mojave Desert on PRS field trips, watching the members static test and flight test their small and un-V-2 creations. . . . Several times a day [at the rocket testing lab where she worked] a horn blows, and after a few seconds there's the unmistakable sound of a rocket motor firing. Sometimes it fires smoothly, sometimes it doesn't, sometimes it blows up."

She lived in Los Angeles and was also an active member of the Los Angeles Science Fantasy Society, as well as the affiliated Outlander Society. She published seven stories (including the short novel "Homo Inferior") in the Fifties in the magazines *If* and *Fantastic Story Magazine.* She may also have published a 1954 story in *Spaceway* under the name, M. B. Wolf.

Beginning in April 1951, Wolf wrote a popular fandom column entitled "Fandora's Box" in the SF magazine *Imagination,* which she continued until April 1956. Its extensive news of fan activities and reviews of fanzines provided the most comprehensive fan information at the time and is an invaluable source for historians of the genre. Because of this, active fan Earl Kemp anointed her the "First Lady of Fandom" in his own fanzine, *Destiny 7.*

In October 1950, with SF magazine editor Raymond Palmer as the best man, she married prolific SF writer "Rog Phillips," the working name of Roger Phillips Graham (1909–1965). They were divorced in 1955. Soon thereafter, Wolf disappeared from both professional science fiction and from fandom.

Frances Yerxa (Hamling), (?–?): Wife of SF author Leroy Yerxa (1915–1946), who was prolific and popular in the late Thirties and early Forties. After his death she began writing stories herself to support her two sons, with her debut being "Negative Problem" in Ray Palmer's *Amazing Stories,* August, 1947. She also continued her late husband's humorous Freddie Funk series with "Freddie Funk's Flippant Fairies," *Fantastic Adventures,* September, 1948. She later married magazine editor and publisher William L. Hamling. He had been best friends with Leroy Yerxa and after the marriage Hamling raised the two Yerxa boys as his own. He and Frances lived in the Chicago suburb of Evanston and had two more children, a daughter and a son.

Hamling had been an editor at *Amazing Stories* and *Fantastic Adventures,* 1947–1951. From 1950–1958 he was the editor-publisher (and Frances was the assistant editor) of *Imagination,* which featured Mari Wolf's popular "Fandora's Box" column. He had been early friends with a co-worker and *Weird Tales* Club member named Hugh Hefner. When Hefner later launched *Playboy,* Hamling was inspired to produce *Rogue,* a men's magazine which rivaled *Playboy* for a short time from its founding in 1955 to the early 1960s.

Observations: These women writers seem to quickly fall into three categories. For a minority of the women, mostly those who contributed only one or two stories, I could find no information at all. They did not build writing careers, it seems, in either the mundane world or in the science fiction or mystery fields.

The majority—those on this biographical list—can be easily separated into two further groups.

One group is composed of women (e.g., Agatha Christie) who had substantial mainstream or mystery writing careers with which they are primarily associated. They appeared in the science fiction magazines for one of two reasons:

First, a number of their stories were reprinted from mainstream sources. This suggests that the editors were seeking out female authors.

Or, second, these mainstream writers seem to have written an applicable genre story and, as professional authors seeking an appropriate venue, sent it off to a science fiction magazine for publication.

The other group is composed of women who were primarily dedicated to the science fiction field and contributed a number of such stories to the genre magazines. Most of them did not have substantial writing careers outside the field.

These groupings suggest three things about the science fictions magazines between 1926–1960:

First, the editors themselves sometimes sought these women writers or their stories for republication.

Second, if a woman (known or unknown, associated with the field or not) wrote a good genre story and submitted it, it was likely to be accepted.

And third, the field was receptive to women authors who wanted to build long and durable genre careers in the magazines.

Some Online Resources

Isaac Asimov: www.asimovonline.com
www.libraries.wvu.edu/exhibits/asimov

British National Corpus: www.natcorp.ox.ac.uk

ConJose Worldcon—Bjo Trimble: www.conjose.org/Guests/fans.html

Fanzines: www.efanzines.com

Hugo Gernsback: www.hugogernsback.com

Hugo Awards: http://worldcon.org/hugos.html

Implicit Association Test: www.i-a-t.com

Looking Forward, Looking Back—The New York Times:
www.nytimes.com/specials/magazine3

Metrocon, 1954—Men and Women as Fan Equals:
http://fanac.org/Other_Cons/Metrocon/m54–001.html

NASA Space Exploration Projects: www.space.com

Pulps For Sale: www.booksfromthecrypt.com

Pulp Stories On-Line: http://pulpgen.com/pulp/downloads/

Robots: www.robothalloffame.org
www.the-robotman.com/nv_fs.html

Science Fiction Museum and Hall of Fame: www.sfhomeworld.org

Weird Tales Magazine: www.early.com/weirdtales

World's Fair Time Capsules:
www.nytimes.com/specials/magazine3/looking-back.html

Yesterday's Tomorrows: www.yesterdaystomorrows.org

Index

About the Author

Eric Leif Davin has a PhD and teaches American history and popular culture at the University of Pittsburgh. He is the author of *Pioneers of Wonder: Conversations with the Founders of Science Fiction*. He is also the Literary Executor of the Stanley G. Weinbaum Estate.